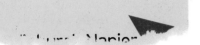

The Encyclopedia
of Operations Management

The Encyclopedia
of Operations Management

A Field Manual and Glossary
of Operations Management Terms
and Concepts

Arthur V. Hill

Vice President, Publisher: Tim Moore
Associate Publisher and Director of Marketing: Amy Neidlinger
Executive Editor: Jeanne Glasser
Editorial Assistant: Pamela Boland
Senior Marketing Manager: Julie Phifer
Assistant Marketing Manager: Megan Colvin
Cover Designer: Chuti Prasertsith
Managing Editor: Kristy Hart
Project Editor: Betsy Harris
Manufacturing Buyer: Dan Uhrig

Published by Pearson Education, Inc.
Publishing as FT Press
Upper Saddle River, New Jersey 07458

FT Press offers excellent discounts on this book when ordered in quantity for bulk purchases or special sales. For more information, please contact U.S. Corporate and Government Sales, 1-800-382-3419, corpsales@pearsontechgroup.com. For sales outside the U.S., please contact International Sales at international@pearson.com.

First Printing July 2011

ISBN-10: 0-13-288370-8
ISBN-13: 978-0-13-288370-2

Pearson Education LTD.
Pearson Education Australia PTY, Limited.
Pearson Education Singapore, Pte. Ltd.
Pearson Education Asia, Ltd.
Pearson Education Canada, Ltd.
Pearson Educación de Mexico, S.A. de C.V.
Pearson Education—Japan
Pearson Education Malaysia, Pte. Ltd.

The Library of Congress Cataloging-in-Publication data is on file.

To the author of all truth.

PREFACE

Purpose – The *Encyclopedia of Operations Management (EOM)* is an ideal "field manual" for students, instructors, and practicing managers. For students, the *EOM* is a useful guide for developing an integrated mental map for the entire field of supply chain and operations management. It has also proven useful as a reference for students preparing for case discussions, exams, and job interviews. It is particularly helpful for students new to supply chain and operations management and for international students who need precise definitions of specialized terms. For instructors, the *EOM* is an invaluable desk reference and teaching aid that goes far beyond the typical dictionaries. Many instructors and doctoral students find the numerous figures, graphs, equations, Excel formulas, VBA code, and references helpful for their lectures and research. For practicing managers, the *EOM* is a valuable tool for black belt and green belt training programs and a powerful tool for helping organizations build a precise standard language.

This encyclopedia has proven to be a useful text for core undergraduate and graduate courses in both business and engineering schools. It is also useful for second-level courses in supply chain management, quality management, lean manufacturing, project management, service management, operations strategy, manufacturing management, industrial engineering, and manufacturing engineering.

Coverage – The *EOM* covers a wide range of operations and supply chain management disciplines, including:

- Accounting
- Customer service
- Distribution
- e-business
- Economics/finance
- Forecasting
- Healthcare management
- Human resources management
- Industrial engineering
- Industrial relations
- Inventory management
- Lean sigma (six sigma)

- Lean thinking
- Logistics
- Maintenance/reliability engineering
- Management information systems
- Manufacturing management
- Marketing/sales
- New product development
- Operations research
- Operations strategy
- Organizational behavior/management
- Personal time management
- Production planning and control

- Purchasing/supply management
- Quality management
- Reliability engineering
- Service management
- Simulation
- Sourcing
- Statistics
- Supply chain management
- Systems engineering
- Theory of Constraints
- Transportation
- Warehousing

Format – This book is designed to be an easily carried "field manual." Each entry begins with a short formal definition followed by a longer description and ends with references to additional resources and cross-references (links) to related terms. The links (cross-references between terms) help the reader develop a complete mental map of the field. Essential terms are marked with a star (✪) at the end of the short definition.

History – As a faculty member at IMD International in Lausanne, Switzerland, I gave my MBA students a one-page list of about 50 essential operations management terms. Several students requested help defining those terms. This encyclopedia grew out of my response to those requests. As shown in the table below, the *EOM* has grown in size over the years. This 2012 edition has 540 new entries and nearly twice the number of links. More importantly, the *EOM* has grown in clarity and precision. About 30% of the entries were completely rewritten and many photos, figures, graphs, tables, examples, references, and footnotes were added and improved. We compressed the 2012 edition by about 50 pages so it is still a handy "field manual." We did this by removing white space, shrinking figures, shortening longer entries, and combining entries to reduce redundancies.

Edition	Terms	Links	References	Pages
2001	291	0	~20	32
2005	533	~500	~50	97
2007	1,089	2,917	~100	288
2010	1,250	3,500	170	360
2012	1,790	6,992	281	400

Comments, additions, and edits are welcomed and should be sent to the author at ahill@umn.edu. Substantive contributions will be acknowledged in the next edition.

Arthur V. Hill, Associate Dean for MBA Programs, John & Nancy Lindahl Professor, Operations & Management Science Department, Curtis L. Carlson School of Management, University of Minnesota

HOW READERS CAN USE THIS ENCYCLOPEDIA

Most students, instructors, and managers struggle to build a simple framework for the supply chain and operations management discipline. Although most standard texts offer some type of framework, none of these frameworks has been widely accepted. The SCOR framework has gained wide acceptance for supply chain management, but less so for operations management. (See the *SCOR* entry.) This author helped create an award-winning framework published in Hays, Bouzdine-Chameeva, Meyer Goldstein, Hill, and Scavarda (2007). (See the *operations management* entry.) More recently, this author developed the much simpler "Better-Faster-Cheaper-Stronger" framework that is based on the following four fundamental premises:

Premise 1: All work is a process.
Premise 2: All processes can be improved.
Premise 3: Processes are improved by making them better, faster, cheaper, and stronger.
Premise 4: Improved processes add more value to customers, shareholders, employees, and society.

Better processes create products and services that more reliably meet customer requirements for both tangible and intangible product attributes. **Faster** processes require less time and provide more customization. **Cheaper** processes reduce cost by achieving a better balance between supply and demand and by improving the product and service design. **Stronger** processes are better aligned with higher-level strategies, are more sustainable, and better mitigate risks. This framework has a logical order. We start with customer requirements for performance and reliability (**better**); then we reduce cycle time for both standard and customized products by reducing non-value added activities (**faster**); then we reduce cost by balancing supply and demand and improving product design (**cheaper**); and finally we make sure that our processes are aligned with our strategic intent, sustainability goals, and safety requirements (**stronger**). It is important to select a limited set of **balanced metrics** to support organizational efforts to make processes better, faster, cheaper, and stronger. Note that this framework is consistent with the sand cone model developed by Ferdows and De Meyer (1990).

In this author's experience, students and managers enthusiastically embrace the four premises and quickly become passionate about making their processes (and lives) better, faster, cheaper, and stronger. This framework is simple, compelling, easy to remember, and easy to apply to any process in any business function (e.g., marketing, sales, finance, MIS, HR, accounting, operations, logistics) in any organizational context (e.g., healthcare, government, education, not-for-profits, distribution, retailing, transportation, and manufacturing).

This ***Encyclopedia of Operations Management*** can help you quickly develop a complete mental map of the entire supply chain and operations management discipline – and help you learn how to make your processes better, faster, cheaper, and stronger. Start by studying the bulleted topics in the framework below. Then follow the links at the end of each entry to the related entries to master the entire subject. Also, make sure you have a clear understanding of the performance metrics needed to support each of the four dimensions. Pay particular attention to the essential terms marked with a star (✪) at the end of the short definition and listed in this preface.

	Better ➡	**Faster** ➡	**Cheaper** ➡	**Stronger**
Topics	• Voice of the customer • New product development • Quality management • Service quality • Process design • Process improvement programs	• Project management • Theory of Constraints • Mass customization • Time based competition • Learning & job design • Lean thinking • Setup reduction (SMED)	• Sourcing/purchasing • Supply Chain Management • Logistics & transportation • Inventory management • Demand management • Capacity management • Design for Manufacturing	• Operations strategy • Hoshin planning/X-Matrix • Risk management • Failure Mode and Effects Analysis (FMEA) • Safety • Green supply chain
Metrics	• Product performance • Customer satisfaction and loyalty metrics • Process capability and performance metrics • Service related metrics	• Time metrics (e.g., cycle time, customer leadtime) • Learning rate metrics • Theory of Constraints metrics • Lean metrics	• Cost metrics • Inventory metrics • Forecast error metrics • Equipment metrics • Warehousing metrics • Transportation metrics	• Income statement • Balanced scorecard metrics • Environmental metrics • Triple bottom line metrics Risk assessment metrics • Safety metrics

HOW INSTRUCTORS CAN USE THIS ENCYCLOPEDIA

Instructors have found the ***Encyclopedia of Operations Management (EOM)*** to be a valuable "field manual" for a variety of courses and training programs. These include:

- **Case courses without textbooks** – The ***EOM*** is an authoritative supplement for a case course. The ***EOM*** provides a precise "language" for supply chain and operations management to help students learn key terms in the context of a teaching case.
- **Case or lecture courses with textbooks** – Even if your course uses a textbook, the ***EOM*** is a valuable supplement to provide precise definitions for important terms that are not always defined in standard textbooks. No textbook can provide the depth and breadth found in the ***EOM***. The extensive linked lists help the reader develop a complete mental map of the field.
- **Lean sigma training courses** – The ***EOM*** defines nearly all terms used in lean sigma, lean six sigma, and lean training programs. Many ***EOM*** entries include examples and references that go well beyond what is offered in any other lean sigma book available on the market today. The ***EOM*** is an indispensable reference for lean sigma training programs and is the only reference that pulls together all major tools and concepts in a precise and easy-to-use "field manual."

Instructors have found practical ways to use the ***Encyclopedia of Operations Management***, including:

- Use the terms in the context of class discussions and refer students to the ***EOM*** for precise definitions.
- Assign key terms to be studied as a part of the syllabus, case studies, and homework assignments.
- Hold students accountable for mastering the key terms used in classroom discussions, exams, and homework assignments. Use homework assignments and exams to test student understanding of the terms and concepts and their ability to apply concepts and tools to solve practical problems.

ABOUT THE AUTHOR

Arthur V. Hill is the Associate Dean for MBA Programs in the Carlson School of Management and the John and Nancy Lindahl Professor for Excellence in Business Education in the Operations and Management Science Department at the University of Minnesota. He holds a B.A. in Mathematics from Indiana University, an M.S. in Industrial Administration, and a Ph.D. in Management from the Krannert School of Management at Purdue University. Professor Hill was the Co-Editor-in-Chief of the ***Journal of Operations Management***, a leading academic research journal in the field. He is a Fellow of the American Production Inventory Control Society and wrote the APICS CPIM and CIRM certification exams for many years. He served two terms on the board of POMS (VP Education and VP Finance), the world's leading society for operations management professors. Dr. Hill has been a professor at the Carlson School of Management for more than 30 years and currently teaches supply chain and operations management for courses for full-time MBA, executive MBA, and doctoral students. He has held visiting faculty positions on four continents – Visiting Associate Professor at Indiana University, Professor at IMD International in Lausanne, Switzerland, Guest Professor at Wits Business School in Johannesburg, South Africa, and a Distinguished Visiting Professor at the National University of Singapore. He also helped found a management institute in Moscow. He has won numerous teaching awards, authored more than 90 research articles, and consulted for over 100 firms including 3M, Allianz, Bank of America, Best Buy, Boston Scientific, Cargill, CentraCare, Ceridian, Delta Air Lines, Deutsche Bank, Easter Seals/Goodwill, Ecolab, FMC, General Mills, GMAC, Goodrich, Home Depot, Honeywell, Honeywell Bull (Switzerland), Imation, JPMorgan Chase, Land O'Lakes, Mayo Clinic, Medtronic, Methodist Hospital, Nestlé, Park Nicollet Health Services, Prime Therapeutics, Radisson, SPX, St. Jude Medical, Staples, Target, Toro, Tyco/ADC, United Healthcare, U.S. Bank, and Wells Fargo. His current research focuses on process improvement and supply chain management.

QUOTES FROM EXECUTIVES

Phillip Brooks, CEO and owner of H. Brooks and Company
"Art Hill has played a key role in the development of our continuous improvement teams. Art is a master teacher and mentor and his *Encyclopedia of Operations Management* serves as a cornerstone reference and tool kit for our company."

Dr. Richard Chua, Executive Vice President, Juran Institute, Inc.
"An excellent, quick but thorough reference for anyone involved in managing or improving operations in any organization. The only book of its kind!"

Lee Cockerell, Executive Vice President, Walt Disney World Resort (Retired)
"The *Encyclopedia of Operations Management* is very well done and I am enjoying reading it."

Joe Dehler, Vice President, Business Process Improvement, Carlson Companies (Retired)
"The *Encyclopedia* will take a place on my office bookshelf next to the quality handbook by Dr. Juran as one of my go-to references. This book has packed so much into one reference. Nicely done!"

Connie Fuhrman, Senior Vice President, Operations Transformation, Best Buy (retired)
"With the pace of change in the business world today, crystal clear communication has become an important management tool. Lack of clarity leads to more waste and errors than any other single factor. This definitive encyclopedia of terms and frameworks should become THE industry standard."

Doug Glade, Vice President, Operations, NestléHealthScience, N.A.
"An excellent resource for both operations professionals and business leaders that provides a common language and definitions to use in improving value chain processes."

James Green, President and CEO, Kemps, LLC
"We have experienced Art Hill's effective training first-hand in our lean sigma program at Kemps, where his program has had an immediate and sustainable impact. Art's new book will be a great resource for all participants in our lean sigma program going forward."

Rick Heupel, Vice-President, Asia Operations, Seagate (retired)
"An invaluable tool for effectively navigating and understanding the rapidly developing technologies in today's modern age of operations."

Adam Hjerpe, Senior Vice President – Distribution Operations, United Health Group
"In today's fast-paced and complex environment, Art's encyclopedia is a must-have reference for any operations manager, new or experienced."

Michael Hoffman, Chairman and CEO, The Toro Company
"Art Hill's new encyclopedia is an excellent source of information for all who are involved in operations management – from business professionals to students. Having both worked and studied under Professor Hill, I know the quality of his work and teaching."

Charlie Honke, Partner, Product Lifecycle Management, IBM Global Business Services
"An excellent, comprehensive, and complete reference that students, consultants, supply chain practitioners, and professionals can use to quickly and easily obtain value to support their educational and professional endeavors."

Paul Husby, Vice President, 3M Supply Chain and Logistic Operations (retired)
"A valuable resource for supply chain professionals, executives, and managers from all business functions."

Tim Larson, Chief Procurement Officer, Michael Foods, Inc.
"Finally, a definitive and comprehensive source of supply chain terminology. This book should be within reach of everyone involved with leading, managing, or learning about supply chain management."

Sandy Meurlot, Vice President of Operations, The Toro Company
"Finally, a comprehensive tool that will aid both the new and experienced operations practitioner in understanding the evolving technological landscape of manufacturing."

Tom Platner, Vice President, Global Product Engineering, HID Global
"We've all heard the terms and like to think we can keep them straight, but in this increasingly complex world, having this ready reference is absolutely essential for practitioners and managers alike."

Mike St. Martin, VP of Express Operations, FedEx Express
"It's a great resource to quickly reference specific operations management terms and acronyms for anyone in business or academics. I will use it!"

QUOTES FROM PROFESSORS AND STUDENTS

Professor Tatiana Bouzdine-Chameeva, Head of the Department of Information, Decision and Management, Bordeaux Business School, France
"This is a GREAT book – fascinating, rich in contents, covering a wide range of disciplines. It will become one of the most precious books in my professional library and will become THE REFERENCE for my students."

Professor Rodney A. Erickson, Executive Vice President and Provost, The Pennsylvania State University
"I'm thoroughly impressed with everything about it, the scope, the attention to detail, the clarity of explanations, and the references for further reading. I can certainly understand why students have reacted so positively to it."

Professor Nancy Hyer, Owen Graduate School of Management, Vanderbilt University
"What an amazing reference! I'm preparing a new reading for my MBA students and the *Encyclopedia* provided the perfect place for me to check definitions. This was really, really helpful."

Professor Amitabh Raturi, Professor and Director of Industrial Management, University of Cincinnati
"A fantastic effort … the first major effort in our field to systematize the knowledge domains in a concise and lucid style."

Professor Kalyan Singhal, McCurdy Professor of Operations Management, Editor-in-Chief, Production and Operations Management, Merrick School of Business, University of Baltimore
"It is an excellent resource for students and operations managers."

Professor Sum Chee Chuong, Associate Professor, National University of Singapore Business School
"An essential, authoritative resource for students, professors, and practitioners. This is a timely effort and Art has done an excellent job in putting together a much-needed reference. Given the pervasiveness of operations, this reference will be extremely useful to managers and executives from all functional areas."

Professor D. Clay Whybark, Macon G. Patton Distinguished Professor of Operations, Technology and Innovation Management (OTIM), University of North Carolina – Chapel Hill
"Art has done us a great service with this comprehensive, completely cross-referenced, and clearly communicated collection. It is required reading for all operations professionals."

Peter Anderson, CSOM BSB Marketing & Entrepreneurial Management 2011
"The well-thought-out definitions and detailed summaries of the various terms and concepts in this encyclopedia made operations a much easier subject to learn and understand."

Nathan Breuer, CSOM BSB 2012
"I really enjoyed the *Encyclopedia*. It was helpful to have the terms in one convenient book. I liked how the explanations and examples helped me comprehend the terms. I will definitely keep this to use in the future."

Ceci Marn, CSOM MBA 2011
"The *Encyclopedia* is my go-to-source for starting research, looking up business terminology, and finding ideas. I used it throughout my summer internship and it's the one book that will find a permanent place in my office."

Brent Miller, CSOM BSB 2011
"I really liked the *Encyclopedia of Operations Management*. It helped me get through my operations class quite easily! I highly recommend this book. It offers excellent, in-depth insight into modern operations issues."

Kathryn Pahl, CSOM BSB 2013
"I loved using this encyclopedia. It was very descriptive and I found it more helpful than our class textbook."

ACKNOWLEDGMENTS

First, I thank my wife Julie and our children (Christopher & Katie, Jonathan & Lindsay, Stephen, and Michael) for their love and support. Second, I thank the countless students, professors, managers, friends, and family members who have added value, especially Lindsay Conner, Paul Haverstock, Jonathan Hill, Lindsay Hill, Stephen Hill, Sheryl Holt, Paul Husby, Brian Jacobson, Matthew Larson, Richard Lemons, Vicki Lund, Brent Moritz, and Heather Wilcox. Third, I thank my mentor Professor Clay Whybark (University of North Carolina) for getting me started on this journey. Last, but certainly not least, I thank John and Nancy Lindahl for their enthusiastic and generous support of the Carlson School of Management, the University of Minnesota, and the John & Nancy Lindahl Professorship.

The author thanks the following professors, students, and friends for their contributions to this encyclopedia.

Luis Acosta, CEMBA 2006
Aaron Anderson, CEMBA 2009
Chas Anderson, CEMBA 2010
Lorri Anderson, CEMBA 2010
Mark Anderson, CEMBA 2009
Steve Arsenault, CEMBA 2009
Pam Aylward, CEMBA 2006
Abigal Bailey, CEMBA 2011
Susan Bartelt, CEMBA 2011
Bill Beam, CEMBA 2012
Tomme Beevas, CEMBA 2011
Cynthia Benson, CEMBA 2009
Heren Berry, Carlson MBA 2007
Claudiomir Berte, CEMBA 2006
Paul Beswetherick, CEMBA 2009
Grant Bistram, CEMBA 2010
Tonja Bivins, CEMBA 2010
Rudolph Blythe, CEMBA 2011
Benjamin Bowman, Carlson MBA
Leslie Bronk, CEMBA 2009
Nina Brooks, H. Brooks and Company
Brian Bruce, Carlson MBA 2009
Tom Buckner, Senior Lecturer, Carlson
    School of Management
Christopher Carlton, CEMBA 2011
Don Chen, Carlson MBA
Hen (Robert) Chen, Carlson MBA 2010
Rick Christensen, MOT 2001
Jian-Ye Chua, Carlson MBA
Richard Chua, Executive Vice President,
    Juran Institute, CSOM Ph.D. 1988
Won Chung, CEMBA 2011
Brian Clark, CEMBA 2009
Keita Cline, CEMBA 2011
Terry Collier, CEMBA 2009
David Collins, CEMBA 2009
Randolph Cooper, Carlson MBA 2009
Ida Darmawan, Carlson MBA
Judy Djugash, CEMBA 2009
Gretch Donahue, Senior Lecturer,
    Carlson School of Management
Karen Donohue, Associate Professor,
    Carlson School of Management
Robert Doty, CEMBA 2010
Randy Doyle, Vice President,
    Manufacturing, Guidant Corporation
Hillary Drake, Carlson MBA 2008
Davor Dujak, University of Osijek,
    Croatia
Brian Dye, MOT 2004
Ami Ebel, CEMBA 2010
Nick Ehrman, CEMBA 2009
Jason Einertson, Carlson MBA
Sam Ellis, CEMBA 2010
Chad Erickson, Carlson MBA 2009
Gary Etheridge, Staff Engineer, Seagate
Nancy Fenocketti, CEMBA 2009
Scott Feyereisen, Carlson MBA 2009
Aaron Forbort, CEMBA 2009
Ryan Foss, CEMBA 2010
Marc Friedman, Carlson MBA

Amit Ganguly, CEMBA 2009
Cullen Glass, CEMBA 2009
Shankar Godavarti, CEMBA 2010
Susan Meyer Goldstein, Associate
    Professor, Carlson School of
    Management
Steven Gort, MOT 2004
Jeremy Green, Carlson MBA
Jim Green, President/CEO, Kemps LLC
Mike Green, CEMBA 2011
Tiffany Grunewald, CEMBA 2009
Puneet Gupta, Carlson MBA 2009
Douglas Hales, Professor, Clemson
    University
Jerome Hamilton, Director, Lean Six
    Sigma & Initiatives, 3M
Andrea Hannan, Carlson MBA
Joel Hanson, CEMBA 2009
Chad Harding, CEMBA 2011
Rob Harveland, CEMBA 2009
Oscar Hernandez, CEMBA 2010
Brent Herzog, Carlson MBA
Gene Heupel, President, GMHeupel
    Associates
Rick Heupel, Vice President, Seagate
    (retire)
Jayson Hicks, CEMBA 2011
Hoffmann, Mike, Chairman & COO,
    The Toro Company
Tanja Horan, CEMBA 2011
Kaaren Howe, CEMBA 2009
Steve Huchendorf, Senior Lecturer,
    Carlson School of Management
Cheryl Huuki, CEMBA 2009
Paul Husby, VP, 3M Supply Chain and
    Logistic Operations (retired)
Ben Irby, CEMBA 2010
Darwin Isdahl, CEMBA 2011
Brian Jacobson, Carlson BSB 2005
Cyrus Jamnejad, Carlson MBA
Yevette Jaszczak, CEMBA 2010
Craig Johnson, CEMBA 2011
Mark Johnson, CEMBA 2011
Michael Kargel, CEMBA 2006
Daniel Kaskubar, Carlson MBA 2009
William Kellogg, CEMBA 2006
Beth Ann Kennedy, CEMBA 2011
Thomas Kennett, Carlson MBA 2009
Chaouki Khamis, Carlson MBA
Ashfaq Khan, CEMBA 2009
Eishi Kimijima, Carlson MBA 2002
Ravi Kiran, Carlson MBA 2009
Rob Klingberg, CEMBA 2009
Chris Knapp, CEMBA 2009
Susan Knox, CEMBA 2009
Aleksandar Kolekeski, ISPPI Institute,
    Skopje, Macedonia
Tushar Kshirsagar, CEMBA 2009
Gagan Kumar, CEMBA 2006
Matthew Larson, Carlson BSB 2008
David Learner, MOT 2004

Richard Lemons, VP of Manufacturing,
    Entegris
William Li, Professor, Carlson School of
    Management
James Lim, United HealthGroup,
    Carlson MBA 2005
Kevin Linderman, Associate Professor,
    Carlson School of Management
Connie Lindor, CEMBA 2009
Molly Litechy, CEMBA 2010
Meifeng Liu, Carlson MBA 2010
Jennifer Lute, CEMBA 2009
Elda Macias, CEMBA 2006
Timothy Macphail, Carlson MBA 2009
Brian Madden, CEMBA 2011
Mohammed Mahmood, CEMBA 2006
Richard Mann, President, Crown
    College, CEMBA 2009
Wael Mohammed, Carlson MBA
Phil Miller, Professional Director,
    Carlson Consulting Enterprise,
    Carlson MBA, 1997
Brent Moritz, Assistant Professor, Penn
    State University, CSOM Ph.D., 2010
Michael Manders, Carlson MBA
Rick Mann, CEMBA 2009
Perry McGahan, CEMBA 2009
Katherine McIntosh, Carlson MBA 2006
Helen McIntyre, CEMBA 2009
Keith McLaughlin, MOT 2004
James Meier, CEMBA 2006
Tom Meline, Plant Manager, Phillips
    Temro, CEMBA 2004
David Mitchell, MOT 2004
David Moe, CEMBA 2009
Aderonke Mordi, CEMBA 2006
Julie Morman, CEMBA 2006
Jessie Morsching, CEMBA 2011
Drew Motylinski, Carlson MBA
Vasanti Mudkanna, CEMBA 2010
John Mullin, Carlson MBA 2007
Chris Nachtsheim, Frank A. Donaldson
    Chair, Carlson School of Management
Ravi Nagapurkar, CEMBA 2010
Suzanne Naimon, CEMBA 2006
Vijay Nangia, Carlson MBA
Eitan Naveh, Professor, Technion
Russ Needham, Honeywell, Carlson
    MBA 2007
Douglas Neimann, CEMBA 2006
Brent Niccum, CEMBA 2009
Tom Novitzki, Lecturer, Carlson School
    of Management
Joseph Novotny, CEMBA 2006
Sonja O'Brien, CEMBA 2009
Nate O'Connor, CEMBA 2009
Kristi Olson, CEMBA 2009
Shyam Pakala, CEMBA 2010
John Parrish, CEMBA 2011
Sanjay Patel, CEMBA 2010
Tushar Patel, CEMBA 2009

Ron Pergande, CEMBA 2001
Chris Perry, CEMBA 2010
Lee Petersen, CEMBA 2010
Celena Plesha, CEMBA 2010
Adam Podbelski, CEMBA 2009
Dwight Porter, Carlson MBA
Reddy Purushotham, Carlson MBA 2009
Michael Pynch, CEMBA 2009
Adam Quinn, Carlson MBA
Didier Rabino, Plant Manager, Andersen Corporation
Tanya Raso, Carlson MBA
Amit Raturi, Professor University of Cincinnati, CSOM Ph.D.
Mahesh Rege, Carlson MBA
Charles Roadfeldt, Carlson MBA
Carol Rodgers, CEMBA 2009
Angel Luis Rodriguez, CEMBA 2011
Caitlyn Rosendahl, CEMBA 2009
Sara Rottunda, CEMBA 2009
Sharon Rozzi, CEMBA 2006
Johnny Rungtusanatham, Associate Professor, Carlson School of Management
Scott Russell, CEMBA 2010
Javier Sanchez, CEMBA 2011
Rebecca Savoie, CEMBA 2009

Connie Scheer, CEMBA 2009
Amy Schmidt, Carlson MBA
Jeff Schmitz, CEMBA 2010
Brenda Schramm, CEMBA 2009
Michael Schroeder, Carlson MBA 2010
Todd Schroeder, CEMBA 2012
Roger Schroeder, Frank A. Donaldson Chair, Carlson School of Management
Neal Schumacher, Vice President, Engineering, Banner Engineering Corporation, CEMBA 2009
Paul Seel, CEMBA 2006
Lynn Sellman, CEMBA 2009
Rachna Shah, Associate Professor, Carlson School
Mrinal Shaw, Carlson MBA
Kingshuk Sinha, Mosaic Company Professor of Corporate Responsibility, Carlson School of Management
Steven Siegel, MOT 2004
Enno Siemson, Assistant Professor, Carlson School of Management
Steven Smith, MOT 2004
Donald Smithmier, CEMBA 2006
James Sonterre, Carlson MBA
Lee Sparks, VP Operations, ev3
Marcellus Spears, CEMBA 2009

Ravi Sripada, CEMBA 2011
Brett Struwe, CEMBA 2011
Kulasekhar Subramaniam, CEMBA 2011
Chee Chuong Sum, Associate Professor, National University of Singapore
Sommer Swanke, CEMBA 2006
Travis Swenson, CEMBA 2009
Dr. Wayne Taylor, Taylor Enterprises
Matthew Tempelis, CEMBA 2006
Jeff Thaler, CEMBA 2010
Kevin Thayer, CEMBA 2006
Mark Thompson, CEMBA 2009
Randall Thorson, Carlson MBA
Raju Thotakura, CEMBA 2010
Mark Thurbush, CEMBA 2010
John Tiedeman, Carlson MBA
Geir Tonnesen, Norwegian Consul, CEMBA 2009
Myra Urness, MOT 2004
Kate Walker, CEMBA 2009
Annie Walsh, Carlson MBA 2010
Kurt Waltenbaugh, CEMBA 2011
Wes Whalberg, Carlson MBA 2010
Julie Woessner, CEMBA 2010
Yarden Wolfe, CEMBA 2009

ESSENTIAL SUPPLY CHAIN AND OPERATIONS TERMS

Every supply chain and operations student and manager should have a good understanding of these essential terms. These are marked with the symbol ✪ at the end of the short definitions in this encyclopedia.

5S
8 wastes
A3 Report
ABC classification
acceptance sampling
Activity Based Costing (ABC)
affinity diagram
appraisal cost
assemble to order (ATO)
automation
balanced scorecard
bathtub curve
benchmarking
bill of material (BOM)
bottleneck
break-even analysis
bullwhip effect
capacity
carrying charge
carrying cost
causal map
cellular manufacturing
commodity
commonality
control chart
control plan
core competence
cost of quality
critical path

Critical Path Method
customer leadtime
cycle counting
cycle stock
cycle time
decision tree
Delphi forecasting
demand
demand management
Design for Manufacturing (DFM)
direct labor cost
diseconomy of scale
distribution
distribution channel
Drum-Buffer-Rope (DBR)
Economic Order Quantity
economy of scale
economy of scope
effectiveness
efficiency
employee turnover
engineer to order (ETO)
Enterprise Resources Planning (ERP)
ergonomics
error proofing
exponential smoothing
facility layout
facility location

Failure Mode and Effects Analysis (FMEA)
financial performance metrics
finished goods inventory
flexibility
focused factory
forecast error metrics
forecasting
Gantt Chart
half-life curve
industrial engineering
inspection
inventory management
inventory position
inventory turnover
Ishikawa Diagram
jidoka
job design
job enlargement
job shop
Just-in-Time (JIT)
kaizen
kanban
leadtime
lean sigma
lean thinking
learning curve
learning organization
linear regression

Little's Law
logistics
lotsizing methods
make to order (MTO)
make to stock (MTS)
make versus buy decision
Malcolm Baldrige National Quality
    Award (MBNQA)
manufacturing order
manufacturing processes
mass customization
Master Production Schedule
Materials Requirements Planning (MRP)
Mean Absolute Deviation (MAD)
Mean Absolute Percent Error (MAPE)
median
min/max inventory system
modular design (modularity)
moment of truth
moving average
muda
Murphy's Law
Net Present Value (NPV)
New Product Development (NPD)
newsvendor model
Nominal Group Technique (NGT)
normal distribution
normal time
offshoring
on-hand inventory
on-order inventory
open order
operations management
operations performance metrics
operations research (OR)
operations strategy
opportunity cost
outsourcing
overhead
Pareto Chart
Pareto's Law
Parkinson's Laws
part number
PDCA
periodic review system

periods supply
picking
postponement
preventive maintenance
probability density function
probability distribution
process
process capability and performance
process design
process improvement program
process map
product design quality
production planning
productivity
product-process matrix
program management office
project charter
project management
pull system
purchase order (PO)
purchasing
push-pull boundary
Quality Function Deployment (QFD)
quality management
queuing theory
Radio Frequency Identification (RFID)
reorder point
respond to order (RTO)
Root Cause Analysis (RCA)
safety stock
Sales & Operations Planning (S&OP)
SCOR Model
service failure
service guarantee
service level
service management
service quality
service recovery
setup cost
setup time reduction methods
setup time
shop floor control
simulation
slack time
sourcing

standard cost
standard deviation
standard time
standardized work
starving
Statistical Process Control
stockout
Strategic Business Unit
strategy map
sunk cost
supplier
supply chain management
sustainability
switching cost
system
takt time
tampering
Theory of Constraints
time series forecasting
time study
time-based competition
Total Productive Maintenance (TPM)
Total Quality Management (TQM)
Transportation Management System
    (TMS)
trend
utilization
value added ratio
value chain
value stream map
variance
vendor managed inventory
vertical integration
voice of the customer
wait time
warehouse
Warehouse Management System (WMS)
work breakdown structure
work measurement
Work-in-Process (WIP) inventory
x-bar chart
yield
yield management

NEW ENTRIES IN THIS EDITION

The list below the 540 new entries in this edition. Revised entries are not listed here.

1-10-100 rule
3Gs
6Ps
7S Model
8 wastes
80-20 rule
acquisition
ad hoc committee
ADKAR Model for Change
aftermarket
allocated inventory
allocation
Analysis of Variance (ANOVA)
Analytic Hierarchy Process (AHP)

ANOVA
anticipation inventory
antitrust laws
Application Service Provider (ASP)
assembly
asset turnover
autocorrelation
Automated Data Collection (ADC)
Automated Identification and Data
    Capture (AIDC)
Automatic Call Distributor (ACD)
autonomous workgroup
back office
back scheduling

backward pass
balance sheet
Baldrige Award
bar chart
barter
batch
Bayes' Theorem
Bernoulli distribution
beta function
bid rigging
big box store
bill of material implosion
bimodal distribution
bin

blind count
blow through
box and whisker diagram
box plot
Box-Muller method
bribery
broker
business capability
business process mapping
buy-back contract
cap and trade
capacity cushion
capacity management
carbon footprint
cargo
carousel
carrier
cash cow
casting
catchball
category captain
category validator
causal forecasting
caveat emptor
CEMS (Contract Electronics Manufacturing Services)
CGS (Cost of Goods Sold)
chain of custody
change management
changeover
channel
chargeback
Chebyshev's inequality
checklist
checksheet
child item
chi-square distribution
cloud computing
coefficient of determination
combinations
committee
competitive analysis
consignee
consolidation
constraints management
continuous probability distribution
Contract Electronics Manufacturing Services (CEMS)
contract warehouse
control limit
coordinate the supply chain
cost center
covariance
crashing
cross-functional team
cross-selling
Croston's Method
CRP (Capacity Requirements Planning)
cube utilization
cumsum control chart
cumulative distribution function
cumulative sum control chart
current reality tree
Customer Effort Score (CES)

customer service
customization flexibility
dampened trend
days on hand
days supply
Decision Support System (DSS)
decomposition
defect
Defective Parts Per Million (DPPM)
deliverables
demonstrated capacity
design quality
devil's advocate
die
die cutting
digital supply chain
dimensional weight
direct cost
directed RF picking
discounted cash flow
discrete order picking
discrete probability distribution
dispatch list
distribution network
distributor
diversion
dock
dollar unit sampling
downtime
DPPM
dual source
due diligence
dunnage
DuPont STOP
durability
Durbin-Watson Statistic
earliness
early detection
earned hours
effective capacity
Efficient Consumer Response (ECR)
eighty-twenty rule
e-kanban
Electronic Product Code (EPC)
Electronics Manufacturing Services (EMS)
empathy
empowerment
EMS (Electronics Manufacturing Services)
energy audit
engineering change review board
Erlang C formula
error function
error proofing
ethnographic research
Everyday Low Pricing (EDLP)
executive sponsor
expatriate
expedite
expert system
extrinsic forecasting model
extrusion
fabrication

factorial
family
Fast Moving Consumer Goods (FMCG)
fast tracking
FED-up model
field service
firm order
firm planned order
first article inspection
five forces analysis
fixed price contract
float time
floor stock
flow rack
FMCG
focus group
force field analysis
force field diagram
forecast consumption
forging
forklift truck
forming-storming-norming-performing model
formulation
forward pass
forward pick area
foundry
fractile
front office
frozen schedule
fulfillment
full truck load
future reality tree
futures contract
gap model
gateway workcenter
GATT
gauge
gemba walk
General Agreement on Tariffs and Trade (GATT)
genetic algorithm
geometric progression
geometric series
Global Data Synchronization Network (GDSN)
Good Manufacturing Practices (GMP)
goodwill
gravity flow rack
gray market
gray market reseller
green supply chain
gross weight
Growth-Share Matrix
help desk
hoshin planning
human resources
implementation
implied shortage cost
inbound logistics
income statement
incoming inspection
Incoterms
incremental cost

indented bill of material
indirect cost
indirect labor
indirect materials
industry analysis
infinite capacity planning
infrastructure
input/output control
in-stock
intellectual property (IP)
interchangeable parts
intermittent demand
intermodal shipments
internal setup
interoperability
interplant order
interpolated median
interquartile range
interval notation
interval scale
in-transit inventory
intrinsic forecasting model
inventory valuation
investment center
invoice
islands of automation
ISO
ISO 26000
ISO 9001:2008
issue
issue log
item master
job
job design
job enrichment
jobber
Joint Commission (JCAHO)
joint venture
just do it
kaizen workshop
kickback
KISS principle
kitting
KJ method
knowledge work
knowledge worker
kurtosis
labor grade
lagging indicator
landed cost
late configuration
late customization
lateness
legacy system
level
level loading
level of service
level strategy
Lewin/Schein Theory of Change
life cycle cost
life cycle planning
linearity
load
load report

locator system
lockbox
logistics network
Lorenz Curve
lot
lot traceability
lot tracking
low level code
Maintenance-Repair-Operations (MRO)
Management By Objectives (MBO)
management by walking around
manifest
Manufacturing and Service Operations
    Management Society (MSOM)
manufacturing order
manufacturing processes
manufacturing strategy
marginal cost
market pull
master scheduler
materials handling
matrix organization
mean
Measurement System Analysis (MSA)
Mergers and Acquisitions (M&A)
Metcalfe's Law
milestone
min-max inventory system
mix flexibility
mode
mold
MRO
multiple source
multiplication principle
NAFTA
nanotechnology
nearshoring
necessary waste
negative binomial distribution
negative exponential distribution
net change MRP
net weight
neural network
new product flexibility
newsvendor problem
Newton's method
nominal scale
normalization
North American Free Trade Agreement
    (NAFTA)
np-chart
objective function
obsolete inventory
Occam's Razor
Occupational Safety and Health
    Administration (OSHA)
Ockham's Razor
OCR
ODM (Original Design Manufacturer)
one-minute manager
on-hand inventory
on-order inventory
on-the-job training (OJT)
on-time and complete

on-time delivery (OTD)
open order
operation
operation overlapping
Optical Character Recognition (OCR)
optimization
order cycle
order entry
order fulfillment
order quantity modifier
order-up-to level
ordinal scale
organizational design
organizational structure
Original Design Manufacturer (ODM)
OSHA
outbound logistics
outlier
Over/Short/Damaged Report
overlapping
pacing process
packing slip
pallet
parent item
Pareto efficiency
Pareto optimality
parking lot
part period balancing
Parts Per Million (PPM)
pay for performance
pay for skill
percentage bill of material
performance-based contracting
period cost
periods supply
permutations
phantom
physical inventory
piece work
pilot test
planned obsolescence
planning bill of material
planning horizon
point of use
Porter's Five Forces
post-project review
predatory pricing
premium freight
prevention
price fixing
primary location
Principal Components Analysis (PCA)
private label
probability density function
probability distribution
probability mass function
process flowchart
product family
product life cycle management
product mix
product proliferation
product rationalization
production activity control
production line

production linearity
production order
production plan
production smoothing
profit center
project management triangle
project network
project team
promotion
prototype
pseudo bill of material
public warehouse
pull system
purchase order (PO)
pushback
put away
Pythagorean Theorem
qualitative forecasting methods
quantitative forecasting methods
quantity flexible contracts
queue
quick hit
RACI Chart
rack jobber
random variable
RASCI
rated capacity
ratio scale
reality tree
real-time
receiving
reconciliation
regeneration
reintermediation
Reliability-Centered Maintenance
  (RCM)
repatriate
repetitive manufacturing
replenishment order
repositioning
request date
Request for Information (RFI)
Request for Quotation (RFQ)
requisition
reserve storage area
resilience
restocking charge
Return Goods Authorization (RGA)
Return Material Authorization (RMA)
return to vendor
revenue center
revenue sharing contract
revision control
revision level
rework
right of first refusal
risk management
risk sharing contract
root cause tree
R-squared

run chart
runs test
SaaS
safety
Sales Inventory & Operations Planning
  (SI&OP)
sampling distribution
sand cone model
satisfaction
scale count
scales of measurement
scheduled receipt
scope
scree plot
scrum
self-check
self-directed work team
serial number traceability
service management
service marketing
service operations
serviceability
setup time reduction methods
shop calendar
shop packet
shortage cost
shortage report
single-piece flow
skewness
skid
slotting
slotting fee
slow moving inventory
SMART goals
Software as a Service (SaaS)
Spearman's Rank Correlation
spend analysis
sponsor
sprint burndown chart
square root law for safety stock
stabilizing the schedule
staging
stakeholder
stamping
standard hours
Standard Operating Procedure (SOP)
standard parts
standard products
statement of work (SoW)
steering committee
stock
stock position
stratified sampling
Student's t distribution
subassembly
subcontracting
Subject Matter Expert (SME)
subtraction principle
successive check
super bill of material

supplier
SWOT analysis
systems engineering
tare weight
target market
tariff
task interleaving
technology push
technology transfer
telematics
theoretical capacity
tier 1 supplier
time bucket
time burglar
time management
Time Phased Order Point (TPOP)
time series forecasting
tolerance
tooling
TPOP
trade barrier
trade promotion allowance
traffic management
trailer
transfer price
transportation
traveler
trimmed mean
truck load
true north
turnaround time
turnkey
two-minute rule
two-second rule
u-chart
unfair labor practice
unnecessary waste
value stream
VBA
Vehicle Scheduling Problem (VSP)
version control
Visual Basic for Applications (VBA)
Voice of the Process (VOP)
volume flexibility
waiting line
warehouse
waste walk
weeks supply
weighted average
what-if analysis
where-used report
white goods
wholesale price
wholesaler
work design
work order
workflow software
X-Matrix

0-9

1-10-100 rule – See *cost of quality*.

3Ds – The idea that an evaluation of a potential automation project should consider automating tasks that are dirty, dangerous, or dull.

The picture at the right is the PackBot EOD robot from the iRobot Corporation designed to assist bomb squads with explosive ordinance disposal. This is a good example of the second "D."

See *automation*.

3Gs – A lean management practice based on the three Japanese words gemba, genbutsu, and genjitsu, which translate into "actual place," "actual thing," and "actual situation" or "real data."

- Gemba (or genba) – The actual place where work takes place and value is created.
- Gembutsu (or genbutsu) – The actual things (physical items) in the gemba, such as tools, machines, materials, and defects.
- Genjitsu (or jujitsu) – The real data and facts that describe the situation.

In Japanese, Genchi Gembutsu (現地現物) means to "go and see" and suggests that the only way to understand a situation is to go to the gemba, which is the place where work is done.

See *gemba, lean thinking, management by walking around, waste walk*.

3PL – See *Third Party Logistics (3PL) provider*.

5 Whys – The practice of asking "why" many times to get beyond the symptoms and uncover the root cause (or causes) of a problem.

Here is a simple example:
- Why did the ink-jet label system stop printing? *The head clogged with ink.*
- Why did the head clog with ink? *The compressed air supply had moisture in it.*
- Why did the compressed air supply have moisture in it? *The desiccant media was saturated.*
- Why was the desiccant media saturated? *The desiccant was not changed prior to expiration.*
- Why was the desiccant not changed prior to expiration? *A change procedure does not exist for the compressed air desiccant.*

Galley (2008) and Gano (2007) argue persuasively that problems rarely have only one cause and that assuming a problem has only single root cause can prevent investigators from finding the best solution.

The focus of any type of root cause analysis should be on finding and fixing the system of causes for the problem rather than finding someone to blame. In other words, use the 5 Whys rather than the 5 Who's.

See *Business Process Re-engineering (BPR), causal map, error proofing, impact wheel, kaizen workshop, Root Cause Analysis (RCA)*.

5S – A lean methodology that helps organizations simplify, clean, and sustain a productive work environment. ✪

The 5S methodology originated in Japan and is based on the simple idea that the foundation of a good production system is a clean and safe work environment. Translated from Japanese words that begin with the letter "S," the closest English equivalents normally used are Sort, Set in order, Shine, Standardize, and Sustain. The following list is a combination of many variants of the 5S list found in various publications:

- **Sort** (separate, scrap, sift) – Separate the necessary from the unnecessary and get rid of the unnecessary.
- **Set in order** (straighten, store, simplify) – Organize the work area (red tag, shadow boards, etc.) and put everything in its place.
- **Shine** (scrub, sweep) – Sweep, wash, clean, and shine everything around the work area.
- **Standardize** – Use standard methods to maintain the work area at a high level so it is easy to keep everything clean for a constant state of readiness.
- **Sustain** (systematize, self-discipline) – Ensure that all 5S policies are followed through the entire organization by means of empowerment, commitment, and accountability.

Some lean practitioners add a sixth "S" for Safety. They use this "S" to establish safety procedures in and around the process. However, most organizations include safety as a normal part of the *set in order* step.

The benefits of a 5S program include reduced waste and improved visibility of problems, safety, morale, productivity, quality, maintenance, leadtimes, impression on customers, and sense of ownership of the workspace. More fundamentally, a 5S program can help the firm develop a new sense of discipline and order that carries over to all activities.

Five stages of understanding the benefits of a 5S program   Source: Professor Arthur V. Hill

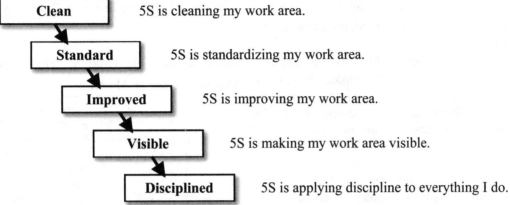

Clean	5S is cleaning my work area.
Standard	5S is standardizing my work area.
Improved	5S is improving my work area.
Visible	5S is making my work area visible.
Disciplined	5S is applying discipline to everything I do.

Awareness of the benefits of a 5S program goes through five stages, as depicted in the figure below.
- **Stage 1: Clean** – People tend to assume initially that 5S is just cleaning up the work area. Cleaning a work area is a good practice, but this is only the beginning of 5S. (Some students joke that 5S is just "Mom telling me to clean up my room.")
- **Stage 2: Standard** – People understand that 5S is about making this clean work process more standard. This makes it easy to find things because everything is always in the same place.
- **Stage 3: Improved** – People begin to understand that 5S is about continually improving how work is done. 5S challenges people to always be looking for better ways to organize their work areas, to make the work simple, visible, error-proof, and wasteless.
- **Stage 4: Visible** – People understand that 5S is about making work more visible so workers can focus on their work and so anything out of place "screams" for immediate attention. A visual work area provides cues that help workers and supervisors know the current status of the system and quickly identify if anything needs immediate attention.
- **Stage 5: Disciplined** – People wholeheartedly embrace the 5S disciplined mindset for how work is done and apply the discipline to everything they do.
  Some practical implementation guidelines for a 5S program include:
- Take pictures before and after to document and encourage improvement.
- Practice the old slogan, "A place for everything and everything in its place."
- Place tools and instruction manuals close to the point of use.
- Design storage areas with a wide entrance and a shallow depth.
- Lay out the storage area along the wall to save space.
- Place items where they are easy to see and access.
- Store similar items together and different items in separate rows.
- Do not stack items together. Use racks or shelves when possible.
- Use small bins to organize small items.
- Use color for quickly identifying items.
- Clearly label items and storage areas to improve visibility.
- Use see-through/transparent covers and doors for visibility.
- Remove unnecessary doors, walls, and other barriers to visibility, movement, and travel.
- Use carts to organize, move, and store tools, jigs, and measuring devices.

The Japanese characters for 5S are on the right (source: http://net1.ist.psu.edu/chu/wcm/5s/5s.htm, November 7, 2004).　整理・整頓・清掃・清潔・躾

See *8 wastes*, *facility layout*, *kaizen workshop*, *lean thinking*, *multiplication principle*, *point of use*, *red tag*, *shadow board*, *standardized work*, *Total Productive Maintenance (TPM)*, *visual control*.

6Ps – The acronym for "Prior Planning Prevents Painfully Poor Performance," which emphasizes the need for planning ahead.

Wikipedia's 7Ps entry includes several other variants. Apparently, the phase originated in the British Army, but is also popular in the U.S. Army[1]. The U.S. Army replaces the word "painfully" with a coarse word.

One somewhat humorous way to write this expression is as Prior Planning Prevents Painfully Poor Performance.

See *personal operations management*, *project management*.

7 wastes – See *8 wastes*.

7S Model – A framework developed by McKinsey to help organizations evaluate and improve performance.

The McKinsey 7S Model (Waterman, Peters, & Phillips 1980) can be used to help organizations evaluate and improve their performance. The elements of the 7S Model (with simplified explanations) are as follows:

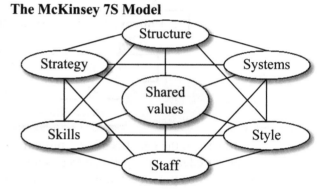

The McKinsey 7S Model

- **Strategy** – How to gain competitive advantage.
- **Structure** – How the organization's units are interrelated. Options include centralized, functional (top-down), de-centralized, matrix, network, or holding.
- **Systems** – The procedures and processes that define how the work is done.
- **Staff** – The employees and their attributes.
- **Style** – The type of leadership practiced.
- **Skills** – The employee capabilities.
- **Shared values** – The organization's beliefs and attitudes. This is the center of McKinsey's model and is often presented first in the list.

These seven elements need to be aligned for an organization to perform well. The model can be used to help identify which elements need to be realigned to improve performance. The hard elements (strategy, structure, and systems) are easy to define and can be influenced directly by management. The soft elements (skills, style, staff, and shared values) are less tangible and harder to define, but are just as important as the hard elements.

See *operations strategy*.

8 wastes – Seven original forms of waste identified by Taiichi Ohno, plus one widely used in North America. ✪

Taiichi Ohno, the father of the Toyota Production System, defined seven categories of waste (Ohno 1978). Waste ("muda") includes any activity that does not add value to the customer. More recently, Bodek (2009) defined the eighth waste and called it "underutilized talents of workers." Liker (2004) used the similar phrase "unused employee creativity." Most sources now label this "waste of human potential." The 8 wastes include:

1. **Overproduction** – Producing more than what is needed or before it is needed.
2. **Waiting** – Any time spent waiting for tools, parts, raw material, packaging, inspection, repair, etc.
3. **Transportation** – Any transportation of parts, finished goods, raw materials, packaging, etc. Waste is particularly apparent here when materials are moved into and out of storage or are handled more than once.
4. **Excess processing** – Doing more work than necessary (e.g., providing higher quality than needed, performing unneeded operations, or watching a machine run).
5. **Inventory** – Maintaining excess inventory of raw materials, in-process parts, or finished goods.
6. **Excessive motion** – Any wasted motion or poor ergonomics, especially when picking up or stacking parts, walking to look for items, or walking to look for people.

---

[1] *This statement is based on this author's experience as a cadet in the U.S. Army at West Point in the early 1970's.*

7. **Defects (correction)** – Repair, rework, recounts, re-packing, and any other situation where the work is not done right the first time.
8. **Unused human potential** – Unused employee minds and creativity.

One of the best approaches for eliminating these wastes is to implement a 5S program. The *lean thinking* entry also suggests many specific approaches for eliminating each of these wastes.

Macomber and Howell (2004) identified several additional wastes, including too much information, complexity, design of goods and services that do not meet users' needs, providing something the customer does not value, not listening, not speaking, assigning people to roles that they are not suited for, not supporting people in their roles, and high turnover.

Many experts distinguish between **necessary waste** and **unnecessary waste** (also known as pure waste). Unnecessary waste is any activity that adds no direct value to the customer, to the team making the product, or to other activities that add direct value to the customer. In contrast, necessary waste is any activity that does not add value directly to the customer, but is still necessary for the team or for another step that does add value. Necessary waste supports the best process known at the current time, but will ideally be eliminated sometime in the future. Examples of necessary waste might include planning meetings and preventive maintenance.

See *5S, efficiency, Lean Enterprise Institute (LEI), lean thinking, muda, overproduction, rework, subtraction principle, waste walk.*

80-20 rule – See *ABC classification, Pareto's Law.*

A

A3 Report – A lean term for a concise document that combines a project charter and progress report on a single large sheet of paper. ✪

The A3 Report is named after the A3 paper size used everywhere in the world except for the U.S. The A3 is equivalent to two side-by-side A4 pages and is 297 x 420 mm (about 11 x 17 inches). In the U.S., most organizations use two side-by-side 8.5 x 11 inch pages, which is about the same size as an A3.

Although many types of A3 Reports are used in practice, the A3 is most often used as a combination of a parsimonious project charter, project status report, and project archive. A3 Reports are often organized so it tells a "story," where the left side is a description and analysis of the current problem and the right side presents countermeasures (solutions) and an implementation plan for the solutions. The A3 Report defines the problem, root causes, and corrective actions and often includes sketches, graphics, simple value stream maps, and other visual descriptions of the current condition and future state. The logical flow from left to right, the short two-page format, and the practice of posting A3s on the wall help develop process thinking and process discipline.

Some lean consultants insist that A3 Reports be done by hand to avoid wasted time in making "pretty" graphs and figures. Although many lean experts in North America insist that A3 problem solving is essential to lean thinking, other lean experts in North America do not use it at all.

See *kaizen workshop, lean thinking, project charter, value stream map.*

ABAP (Advanced Business Application Programming) – The name of the proprietary object-oriented programming language used by SAP, which is the world's largest ERP software firm.

See *SAP.*

ABC – See *Activity-Based Costing (ABC).*

ABC classification – A method for prioritizing items in an inventory system, where A-items are considered the most important; also called ABC analysis, ABC stratification, distribution by value, 80-20 rule, and Pareto analysis. ✪

The ABC classification is usually implemented based on the annual dollar volume, which is the product of the annual unit sales and unit cost (the annual cost of goods sold). High annual volume items are classified as A-items and low annual dollar volume items are classified as C-items. Based on Pareto's Law, the ABC classification system demands more careful management of A-items where these items are ordered more often, counted more often, located closer to the door, and forecasted more carefully.

In contrast, C-items are not as important from an investment point of view and therefore should be ordered and counted less frequently. Some firms classify obsolete or non-moving items as D-items.

One justification for this approach is based on the economic order quantity model. Higher dollar volume items are ordered more often and therefore have a higher transaction volume, which means that they are more likely to have data accuracy problems.

The first step in the ABC analysis is to create a ranked list of items by cost of goods sold (annual dollar volume). The top 20% of the items are labeled A-items. The next 30% of the items in the list are labeled B-items and the remaining 50% are labeled C-items. Of course, these percentages can vary depending upon the needs of the firm. A-items will likely make up roughly 80% of the total annual dollar volume, B-items will likely make up about 15%, and C-items will likely make up about 5%.

A **Lorenz Curve** is used to graph the ABC distribution, where the *x*-axis is the percentage of items and the *y*-axis is the percentage of total annual dollar usage. The graph on the right shows that the first 20% of the items represent about 80% of the annual dollar usage. Items must be first sorted by annual dollar volume to create this graph. See the *Lorenz Curve* entry for information on how to create this graph.

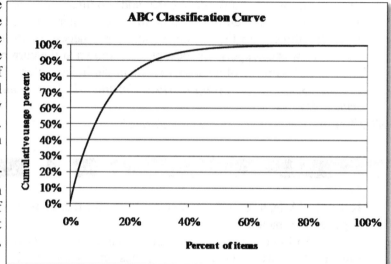

Some firms use other variables for prioritizing items in the ABC classification such as unit sales, annual sales (instead of cost of goods sold), profit margin, stockout cost (such as medical criticality), shelf life, and cubes (space requirements).

Note that the ABC inventory classification has nothing to do with Activity Based Costing.

See *bill of material (BOM), cost of goods sold, cycle counting, Economic Order Quantity (EOQ), inventory management, Lorenz Curve, obsolete inventory, Pareto Chart, Pareto's Law, warehouse, Warehouse Management System (WMS)*.

absorption costing – An accounting practice for allocating overhead to measure product and job costs.

With absorption costing, product costs include the direct cost (i.e., labor and materials) and indirect (fixed) costs (e.g., administrative overhead). Overhead costs from each workcenter are assigned to products as they pass through the workcenter. Traditionally, the overhead (indirect) cost is assigned to the product based on the number of direct labor hours. With Activity Based Costing systems, overhead is assigned to products based on cost-drivers, such machine hours, number of orders per year, number of inspections, and product complexity.

Absorption costing is often criticized because it tends to drive operations managers to produce more inventory in order to absorb more overhead. This is contrary to the lean thinking and is only in the best interests of shareholders when capacity is costly and inventory is cheap. Throughput accounting, developed by Goldratt (Noreen, Smith, and Mackey 1995), is a form of variable costing that ignores overhead.

See *Activity Based Costing (ABC), cost center, lean thinking, overhead, standard cost, Theory of Constraints (TOC), throughput accounting, variable costing*.

absorptive capacity – The ability of an organization to recognize the value of new external information, integrate and assimilate that information, and apply the information to make money.

Absorptive capacity can be examined on multiple levels (an individual, group, firm, and national level), but it is usually studied in the context of a firm. Absorptive capacity can also refer to any type of external information, but is usually applied in the context of research and development (R&D) activities. The theory involves organizational learning, industrial economics, the resource-based view of the firm, and dynamic capabilities. Organizations can build absorptive capacity by conducting R&D projects internally rather than outsourcing them.

The term "absorptive capacity" was first introduced in an article by Cohen and Levinthal (1990). According to the ISI Web of Science, this article has been cited more than 1500 times. This entire article can be found at http://findarticles.com/p/articles/mi_m4035/is_n1_v35/ai_8306388 (May 10, 2010).

Adapted from http://en.wikipedia.org/wiki/Absorptive_capacity and http://economics.about.com/cs/economics glossary/g/absorptive_cap.htm, May 10, 2010.

See *capacity, empowerment, human resources, New Product Development (NPD), organizational design, outsourcing, workforce agility.*

Acceptable Quality Level (AQL) – The maximum percentage defective that can be considered satisfactory as a process average.

When deciding whether to accept a batch, a sample of *n* parts is taken from the batch and a decision is made to accept the batch if the percentage of defects is less than the AQL. The AQL is the highest proportion defective that is considered acceptable as a long-run average for the process.

For example, if 4% nonconforming product is acceptable to both the producer and consumer (i.e., $AQL = 4.0$), the producer agrees to produce an average of no more than 4% nonconforming product.

See *acceptance sampling, consumer's risk, incoming inspection, Lot Tolerance Percent Defective (LTPD), producer's risk, quality management, Statistical Process Control (SPC), Statistical Quality Control (SQC), zero defects.*

acceptance sampling – Methods used to make accept/reject decisions for each lot (batch) based on inspecting a limited number of units. ✪

With attribute sampling plans, accept/reject decisions are based on a count of the number of units in the sample that are defective or the number of defects per unit. In contrast, with variable sampling plans, accept/reject decisions are based on measurements. Plans requiring only a single sample set are known as single sampling plans; double, multiple, and sequential sampling plans may require additional samples.

For example, an attribute single sampling plan with a sample size $n = 50$ and an accept number $a = 1$ requires that a sample of 50 units be inspected. If the number of defectives in that sample is one or zero, the lot is accepted. Otherwise, it is rejected. Ideally, when a sampling plan is used, all bad lots will be rejected and all good lots will be accepted. However, because accept/reject decisions are based on a sample of the lot, the probability of making an incorrect decision is greater than zero. The behavior of a sampling plan can be described by its operating characteristic curve, which plots the percentage defective against the corresponding probabilities of acceptance.

See *Acceptable Quality Level (AQL), attribute, consumer's risk, incoming inspection, inspection, Lot Tolerance Percent Defective (LTPD), operating characteristic curve, producer's risk, quality management, sampling, Statistical Process Control (SPC), Statistical Quality Control (SQC).*

Accounts Payable (A/P) – The money owed to suppliers for goods and services purchased on credit; a current liability; also used as the name of the department that pays suppliers.

Analysts look at the relationship between accounts payable and purchases for indications of sound financial management. Working capital is controlled by managing accounts payable, accounts receivable, and inventory.

See *Accounts Receivable (A/R), invoice, purchase order (PO), purchasing, supplier, terms.*

Accounts Receivable (A/R) – The money customers owe an organization for products and services provided on credit; a current asset on the balance sheet; also used as the name of the department that applies cash received from customers against open invoices.

A sale is treated as an account receivable after the customer is sent an invoice. Accounts receivable may also include an allowance for bad debts. Working capital is controlled by managing accounts payable, accounts receivable, and inventory.

See *Accounts Payable (A/P), invoice, purchase order (PO), purchasing, supplier, terms.*

acquisition – A contracting term used when an organization takes possession of a product, technology, equipment, or another organization.

In a mergers and acquisitions context, acquisition refers to one firm buying another firm. In a learning context, learning is often called acquisition of new knowledge, skills, or behaviors. In a marketing context, the customer acquisition cost is the cost of finding and winning new customers and is sometimes measured as the advertising cost plus other marketing costs targeted toward new customers divided by the number of new customers added during the time period.

See *due diligence, e-procurement, forward buy, mergers and acquisitions (M&A), purchasing, service recovery.*

active item – Any inventory item that has been used or sold in the recent past (e.g., the last year).

It is common for a retailer to have 100,000 items in their item master, but only 20,000 active items.

See *inventory management, part number.*

Activity Based Costing (ABC) – An accounting practice that identifies the cost drivers (variables) that have the most influence on the product (or service) cost and then allocates overhead cost to products and services based on these cost drivers. ✪

Allocating overhead (particularly manufacturing overhead) is an important activity for many firms. Allocating overhead is needed to estimate product costs in product profitability analysis and important decisions with respect to pricing, product rationalization, and marketing and sales efforts.

Traditional standard costing systems usually allocate overhead cost based on direct labor. For example, consider a product that requires one hour of labor and $30 of materials. If the direct labor wage rate (without overhead) is $20 and the overhead burden rate is $200 per direct labor hour, the standard cost for the product is then direct materials ($20), direct labor ($30), and allocated overhead ($200), for a total cost of $250.

One common criticism of traditional standard costing systems is that it does not make sense to allocate the largest cost (the overhead) based on the smallest cost (the direct labor cost). (Overhead is often the largest component of the standard cost and direct labor cost is often the smallest component.) Traditional standard costing systems assume that the only resource related to overhead is direct labor and that all other resources and activities required to create the product or service cannot be related to overhead.

In contrast, Activity Based Costing begins by identifying the major activities and resources required in the process of creating a product or service. ABC then identifies the "cost pools" (overhead cost) for each activity or resource. Finally, ABC defines an equitable way of allocating (assigning) the overhead cost from the cost pools to the products and services based on a variable called a "cost driver."

A cost driver should reflect the amount of the cost pool (resource) consumed in the process of creating the product or service. Cost drivers might include the number of setups (for a shared setup team), direct materials cost (for allocating purchasing overhead), direct labor time (for allocating labor-related overhead), total throughput time (for allocating manufacturing overhead), inspection time (for allocating quality control overhead), and space used (for allocating building related overhead).

Activity Based Management (ABM) is the use of the Activity Based Costing tools by process owners to control and improve their operations. Building an Activity Based Costing model requires a process analysis, which requires management to have a deep understanding of the business and evaluate value-added and non-value-added activities. The cost analysis and the process understanding that is derived from an ABC system can provide strong support for important managerial decisions, such as outsourcing, insourcing, capacity expansion, and other important "what-if" issues.

Some argue that all manufacturing overhead cost should be allocated based on direct labor (or some other arbitrary cost driver), even if the cost is not traceable to any production activity. However, most experts agree that the sole purpose of an ABC system is to provide management with information that is helpful for decision making. Arbitrary allocation of overhead cost does not support decision making in any way. Even with Activity Based Costing, certain costs related to a business are included in overhead without being allocated to the product.

See *absorption costing, burden rate, cost center, customer profitability, hidden factory, outsourcing, overhead, product proliferation, standard cost, throughput accounting, variable costing, what-if analysis.*

Activity Based Management (ABM) – See *Activity Based Costing (ABC).*

ad hoc committee – See *committee.*

addition principle – Combining two tasks and assigning them to one resource (person, machine, etc.).

Love (1979) defines the addition principle for improving a process as combining two or more process steps so one resource (person, machine, contractor, etc.) does all of them. This strategy has many potential advantages, including reducing cost, reducing cycle time, reducing the number of queues, reducing the number of handoffs, reducing lost customer information, reducing customer waiting time, improving customer satisfaction, improving quality, improving job design, accelerating learning, developing people, and improving accountability.

The addition principle is an application of **job enlargement** where a worker takes on some of a co-worker's job and **job enrichment**, where a worker takes on part of the boss's job. This is closely related to the queuing theory concept of **pooling**.

The application of the addition principle is particularly effective in the service context, where it can impact customer waiting time and put more of a "face" on the service process. For example, many years ago, Citibank reduced the number of handoffs in its international letter of credit operation from about 14 to 1. Instead of 14 different people handling 14 small steps, one person handled all 14 steps. This change dramatically reduced customer leadtime, improved quality, and improved process visibility. Citibank required workers to be bilingual, which also improved service quality. The visibility of the new process allowed them to further improve the process and prepared the way for automating parts of the process. However, implementing this new process was not without problems. Many of the people in the old process had to be replaced by people with broader skill sets and the new process increased risk because it eliminated some of the checks and balances in the old process.

See *customer leadtime, handoff, human resources, job design, job enlargement, multiplication principle, pooling, subtraction principle.*

ADKAR Model for Change – A five-step model designed to help organizations affect change.

ADKAR, developed by Prosci (Hiatt 2006), is similar to the Lewin/Schein Theory of Change. ADKAR defines five stages that must be realized for an organization or an individual to successfully change:

- **Awareness** – An individual or organization must know why the change is needed.
- **Desire** – Either the individual or organizational members must have the motivation and desire to participate in the proposed change or changes.
- **Knowledge** – Knowing why one must change is not enough; an individual or organization must know how to change.
- **Ability** – Every individual and organization that truly wants to change must implement new skills and behaviors to implement the necessary changes.
- **Reinforcement** – Individuals and organizations must be reinforced to sustain the changes and the new behaviors. Otherwise, the individuals and organization will likely revert to their old behaviors.

See *change management, control plan, Lewin/Schein Theory of Change.*

adoption curve – The major phases in the product life cycle that reflect the market's acceptance of a new product or technology.

According to the Product Development and Management Association (www.pdma.org), consumers move from (a) a cognitive state (becoming aware of and knowledgeable about a product) to (b) an emotional state (liking and then preferring the product) and finally into (c) a behavioral state (deciding on and then purchasing the product). At the market level, the new product is first purchased by market innovators (roughly 2.5% of the market), followed by early adopters (roughly 13.5% of the market), early majority (34%), late majority (34%), and finally, laggards (16%).

See *Bass Model, New Product Development (NPD), product life cycle management.*

Advanced Planning and Scheduling (APS) – An information system used by manufacturers, distributors, and retailers to assist in supply chain planning and scheduling.

Most APS systems augment ERP system functionality by providing forecasting, inventory planning, scheduling, and optimization tools not historically found in ERP systems. For example, APS systems can calculate optimal safety stocks, create detailed schedules that do not exceed available capacity (finite scheduling), and find the near-optimal assignments of products to plants. In contrast, traditional ERP systems were fundamentally transaction processing systems that implemented user-defined safety stocks, created plans that regularly exceeded available capacity (infinite loading), and did not optimize anything.

The best-known dedicated APS software vendors were i2 Technologies and Manugistics, but they are both now owned by JDA Software. SAP has an APS module called APO, which stands for Advanced Planning and Optimization. According to SAP's website, "SAP APO is a software solution that enables dynamic supply chain management. It includes applications for detailed planning, optimization, and scheduling, allowing the supply chain to be accurately and globally monitored even beyond enterprise boundaries. SAP APO is a component of mySAP Supply Chain Management."

The sales script for these APS systems in the past (exaggerated here for sake of emphasis) has been that the big ERP systems (SAP, Oracle, etc.) were "brain dead" and had little intelligence built into them. These big ERP systems were only transaction processing systems and did little in the way of creating detailed schedules, forecasting, or optimization. The promise of the APS systems was that they were "smart" and could make the ERP systems a lot smarter. In recent years, the lines have blurred and nearly all ERP systems offer add-on products that do much of what only APS systems could do in the past.

Many APS users have found that several APS features were hard to implement and maintain, which has led to some negative assessments of APS systems. The three main complaints that this author has heard are (1) massive data requirements (capacity information on almost every workcenter for every hour in the day), (2) complexity (few managers understand the mathematical algorithms used in APS applications), and (3) lack of systems integration (the APS must work alongside the ERP system and must share a common database). The *finite scheduling* entry discusses some of the needs that motivated the development of APS systems.

See *algorithm, back scheduling, closed-loop MRP, Enterprise Resources Planning (ERP), finite scheduling, I2, infinite loading, job shop scheduling, load, load leveling, Manugistics, Materials Requirements Planning (MRP), optimization, SAP.*

Advanced Shipping Notification (ASN) – An electronic file sent from a supplier to inform a customer when incoming goods are expected to arrive.

An ASN may be a document, a fax, or electronic communication. However, electronic communication is preferred. ASNs usually include PO numbers, SKU numbers, lot numbers, quantity, pallet or container number, carton number, and other information related to the shipment and to each item in the shipment.

ASN files are typically sent electronically immediately when a trailer (destined for a given receiving facility) leaves a DC. The ASN file should be received by the receiving facility well in advance of the time the trailer arrives. When the trailer (or other shipping container) arrives, the contents of the trailer can be electronically compared to the contents of the ASN file as the trailer is unloaded. Any missing items or unexpected items would be highlighted on the OS&D report. The ASN is typically received and processed by the **Transportation Management System (TMS)** or **Warehouse Management System (WMS)** at the receiving facility.

The ASN file serves three important purposes:

- The receiving facility uses the ASN to plan inventory or load movement (interline hauls or ground-route distribution) based on the expected inbound mix of goods. Such planning may include scheduling of other resources (drivers, warehouse personnel) or even advance calls to customers to inform them of their expected delivery time windows.
- The TMS or WMS systems at the receiving facility may use the expected inbound mix of goods to prepare warehouse employees to receive the goods by downloading the information to wireless barcode scanners or alerting warehouse planning staff to the expected incoming volume of goods.
- The TMS or WMS system may ultimately use the expected inbound goods to form the basis of an Over/Short/Damaged (OS&D) report upon actual scanning of the inbound goods.

Although commonly used in over-the-road trucking, an ASN can be sent in relation to any shipment, including air, rail, road, and sea shipments. An ASN file is often sent in the agreed-upon EDI 210 ("Advanced Shipping Notification") format. However, technically, an ASN could be any file format agreed upon by the originating and receiving facilities.

See *consignee, cross-docking, distribution center (DC), Electronic Data Interchange (EDI), incoming inspection, manifest, Over/Short/Damaged Report, packing slip, receiving, trailer, Transportation Management System (TMS), Warehouse Management System (WMS).*

adverse event – A healthcare term used to describe any unintended and undesirable medical occurrence experienced by a patient due to medical therapy or other intervention, regardless of the cause or degree of severity.

The term "adverse event" is often used in the context of drug therapy and clinical trials. In the drug therapy context, it is also called an adverse reaction or an adverse drug reaction.

Very serious adverse events are usually called **sentinel events** or **never events**. However, a few sources treat the terms "adverse event" and "sentinel event" as synonyms. The term "near miss" is used to describe an event that could have harmed the patient, but was avoided through planned or unplanned actions.

Barach and Small (2000) report lessons for healthcare organizations from non-medical **near miss** reporting systems. This interesting report begins by emphasizing that most near misses and preventable adverse events are not reported and that healthcare systems could be improved significantly if more of these events were reported. The report further argues that healthcare could benefit from what has been learned in other industries. The authors studied reporting systems in aviation, nuclear power technology, petrochemical processing, steel production, military operations, and air transportation as well as in healthcare. They argue that reporting near misses is better than reporting only adverse events, because the greater frequency enables better quantitative analysis and provides more information to process improvement programs. Many of the non-medical industries have developed incident reporting systems that focus on near misses, provide incentives for voluntary reporting (e.g., limited liability, anonymous reporting, and confidentiality), bolster accountability, and implement systems for data collection, analysis, and improvement.

The key to encouraging reporting of near misses and adverse events is to lower the disincentives (costs) of reporting for workers. When people self-report an error or an event, they should not be "rewarded" with disciplinary action or dismissal (at least not the first time). Many organizations allow for anonymous reporting via a website, which makes it possible for the person reporting the event to keep his or her identity confidential. It is also important to make the process easy to use.

See *error proofing, Joint Commission, sentinel event*.

advertising allowance (ad allowance) – See *trade promotion allowance*.

affinity diagram – A "bottoms-up" group brainstorming methodology designed to help groups generate and organize a large number of ideas into related groups; also known as the KJ Method and KJ Analysis. ✪

Affinity diagrams are a simple yet powerful way to extract qualitative data from a group, help the group cluster similar ideas, and develop a consensus view on a subject. For example, an affinity diagram might be used to clarify the question, "What are the root causes of our quality problems?"

Despite the name, affinity diagrams are not really diagrams. Occasionally, circles are drawn around clusters of similar concepts and lines or trees are drawn to connect similar clusters, but these drawings are not central to the affinity diagramming methodology.

For example, affinity diagrams are often used with Quality Function Development (QFD) to sort and organize ideas on customer needs. To do this, the facilitator instructs each individual in a group to identify all known customer needs and write them down on 3M Post-it Notes, with each need on an individual piece of paper. The group then shares their ideas one idea at a time, organizes the notes into clusters, develops a heading for each cluster, and then votes to assign importance to each group.

The steps for creating an affinity diagram are essentially the same as the used in the nominal group technique and the KJ Method. See the *Nominal Group Technique (NGT)* entry for the specific steps. An affinity diagram example can be found at http://syque.com/quality_tools/tools/TOOLS04.htm (April 7, 2011).

See *brainstorming, causal map, cluster analysis, Kepner-Tregoe Model, KJ Method, Nominal Group Technique (NGT), parking lot, Quality Function Deployment (QFD), Root Cause Analysis (RCA)*.

aftermarket – An adjective used to describe parts or products that are purchased to repair or enhance a product.

For example, many people buy cases for their cell phones as an aftermarket accessory.

See *service parts*.

aggregate inventory management – The analysis of a large set of items in an inventory system with a focus on lotsizing and safety stock policies to study the trade-offs between carrying cost and service levels.

Inventories with thousands of items are difficult to manage because of the amount of data involved. Aggregate inventory management tools allow managers to group items and explore opportunities to reduce inventory and improve service levels by controlling the target service level, carrying charge, and setup cost parameters for each group of items. Aggregate inventory analysis typically applies **economic order quantity logic** and **safety stock** equations in light of warehouse space limitations, market requirements, and company strategies. Aggregate inventory analysis often results in a simultaneous reduction in overall inventory and improvement in overall service levels. This is accomplished by reducing the safety stock inventory for those items that have unnecessarily high safety stocks and by increasing the safety stock inventory for those items that have poor service levels.

The **Sales and Operations Plan (S&OP)**, sometimes called the **Sales, Inventory, and Operations Plan (Si&OP)**, is similar to the aggregate inventory plan. However, unlike aggregate inventory management, S&OP rarely uses mathematical models and focuses on building consensus in the organization.

See *Economic Order Quantity (EOQ), inventory management, inventory turnover, lotsizing methods, production planning, safety stock, Sales & Operations Planning (S&OP), service level, unit of measure, warehouse.*

aggregate plan – See *production planning.*

aggregate production planning – See *production planning.*

agile manufacturing – A business strategy for developing the processes, tools, training, and culture for increasing flexibility to respond to customer needs and market changes while still controlling quality and cost.

The terms agile manufacturing, **time-based competition**, **mass customization**, and **lean** are closely related. Some key strategies for agile manufacturing include commonality, lean thinking, modular design, postponement, setup time reduction, and virtual organizations.

See Goldman, Nagel, and Preiss (1995) and Metes, Gundry, and Bradish (1997) for books on the subject.

See *commonality, lean thinking, mass customization, modular design (modularity), operations strategy, postponement, Quick Response Manufacturing, resilience, scalability, setup time reduction methods, time-based competition, virtual organization.*

agile software development – A software development methodology that promotes quick development of small parts of a project to ensure that the developers meet user requirements; also known as agile modeling.

Agile software development promotes iterative software development with high stakeholder involvement and open collaboration throughout the life of a software development project. It uses small increments with minimal planning. Agile attempts to find the smallest workable piece of functionality, deliver it quickly, and then continue to improve it throughout the life of the project as directed by the user community. This helps reduce the risk that the project will fail to meet user requirements.

In contrast, the **waterfall scheduling** requires "gates" (approvals) for each step of the development process: requirements, analysis, design, coding, and testing. Progress is measured by adherence to the schedule. The waterfall approach, therefore, is not nearly as iterative as the agile process.

See *beta test, catchball, cross-functional team, Fagan Defect-Free Process, lean thinking, prototype, scrum, sprint burndown chart, stakeholder, waterfall scheduling.*

AGV – See *Automated Guided Vehicle.*

AHP – See *Analytic Hierarchy Process.*

AI – See *artificial intelligence.*

alpha test – See *prototype.*

alignment – The degree to which people and organizational units share the same goals.

Two or more people or organizational units are said to be "aligned" when they are working together toward the same goals. They are said to be "misaligned" when they are working toward conflicting goals. Alignment is usually driven by recognition and reward systems.

For example, sales organizations often forecast demand higher than the actual demand because sales people tend to be much more concerned about running out of stock (and losing sales) than having too much inventory. In other words, they are prone to "add safety stock to the forecast." Given that sales organizations are typically rewarded only based on sales, this bias is completely logical. However, this behavior is generally not aligned with the overall objectives of the firm.

See *balanced scorecard, forecast bias, hoshin planning.*

algorithm – A formal procedure for solving a problem.

An algorithm is usually expressed as a series of steps and implemented in a computer program. For example, some algorithms for solving the Traveling Salesperson Problem can require thousands of lines of computer code. Some algorithms are designed to guarantee an optimal (mathematically best) solution and are said to be **exact** or

optimal algorithms. Other algorithms, known as **heuristics** or heuristic algorithms, seek to find the optimal solution, but do not guarantee that the optimal solution will be found.

See *Advanced Planning and Scheduling (APS), Artificial Intelligence (AI), assignment problem, check digit, cluster analysis, Economic Lot Scheduling Problem (ELSP), gamma function, heuristic, job shop scheduling, knapsack problem, linear programming (LP), lotsizing methods, network optimization, operations research (OR), optimization, transportation problem, Traveling Salesperson Problem (TSP), Wagner-Whitin lotsizing algorithm.*

alliance – A formal cooperative arrangement with another firm, which could be for almost any purpose, such as new product development, sharing information, entering a new market, etc. Alliances usually involve sharing both risks and rewards.

allocated inventory – A term used by manufacturing and distribution firms to describe the quantity of an item reserved but not yet withdrawn or issued from stock; also called allocated stock, allocated, allocations, committed inventory, committed quantity, quantity allocated, or reserved stock.

The inventory position does not count allocated inventory as available for sale. Allocations do not normally specify which units will go to an order. However, firm allocations will assign specific units to specific orders.

See *allocation, backorder, inventory position, issue, Materials Requirements Planning (MRP), on-hand inventory.*

allocation – (1) Inventory reserved for a customer. See *allocated inventory.* (2) A set of rules used to determine what portion of available stock to provide to each customer when demand exceeds supply.

See *allocated inventory.*

all-time demand – The total of all future requirements (demand) for an item; also called all-time requirement, lifetime requirement, and all-time demand.

All-time demand is the sum of the demand until the product termination date or until the end of time. Organizations need to forecast the all-time demand for a product or component in the following situations:

- **Determine the lotsize for a final purchase ("final buy")** – When an item is near the end of its useful life and the organization needs to make one last purchase, it needs to forecast the all-time demand. Future purchases will be expensive due to the supplier's cost of finding tooling, skills, and components.
- **Determine the lotsize for a final manufacturing lot** – When an item is near the end of its useful life and the manufacturer needs to make one last run of the item, it needs to forecast the lifetime demand. Future manufacturing will likely be very expensive.
- **Identify the amount of inventory to scrap** – When an item is near the end of its useful life, a forecast of the all-time demand can be used to help determine how many units should be scrapped and how many should be kept (the **keep stock**).
- **Identify when to discontinue an item** – A forecast of the lifetime demand can help determine the date when an item will be discontinued.

Several empirical studies, such as Hill, Giard, and Mabert (1989), have found that the demand during the end-of-life phase of the product life cycle often **decays geometrically**. The geometric progression suggests that the demand in any period is a constant times the demand in the previous period (i.e., $d_t = \beta d_{t-1}$), where $0 < \beta < 1$. The beta parameter is called the **common ratio**, because $\beta = d_1 / d_0 = ... = d_{t+1} / d_t$. Given that period 0 had demand of d_0 units, the forecasted demand for period 1 is $f_1 = \beta d_0$ and for period 2 is $f_2 = \beta f_1 = \beta^2 d_0$. In general, given that period 0 demand is d_0 units, the forecasted demand t periods into the future is $f_T = \beta^T d_0$.

The cumulative forecasted demand through the next T periods after period 0 is the sum of the finite geometric progression $F_T = f_1 + f_2 + ... + f_T = \beta d_0 + \beta^2 d_0 + ... + \beta^T d_0$. Multiplying both sides of this equation by β yields $\beta F_T = \beta^2 d_0 + \beta^3 d_0 + ... + \beta^{T+1} d_0$ and then subtracting this new equation from the first one yields $F_T - \beta F_T = \beta d_0 - \beta^{T+1} d_0$, which simplifies to $F_T \cdot (1 - \beta) = d_0 \beta (1 - \beta^T)$. Given that $\beta < 1$, it is clear that

$1-\beta \neq 0$, which means that it is possible to divide both sides by $1-\beta$, which yields $F_T = d_0\beta(1-\beta^T)/(1-\beta)$. At the limit, as $T \to \infty$, $\beta^T \to 0$, and the sum of the all-time demand after period 0 is $F_\infty = d_0\beta/(1-\beta)$. In summary, given that the actual demand for the most recent period (period 0) was d_0, the forecast of the cumulative demand over the next T time periods is $F_T = d_0\beta(1-\beta^T)/(1-\beta)$. The cumulative demand from now until the end of time is then $F_\infty = d_0\beta/(1-\beta)$.

The graph on the right shows the geometric decay for four historical data points (100, 80, 64, and 32). With $\beta = 0.737$, the all-time demand forecast is $F_\infty = d_0\beta/(1-\beta) = 100 \cdot 0.737/(1-0.737) = 116$ units, and a forecast over a $T = 16$ period horizon is 113 units.

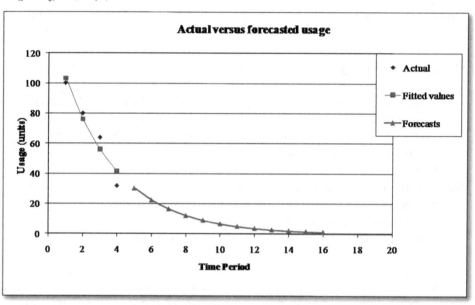

See *all-time order, autocorrelation, Bass Model, demand, forecast horizon, forecasting, geometric progression, obsolete inventory, product life cycle management, slow moving inventory, termination date.*

all-time order – The last order for a particular product in the last phase of its life cycle.

The all-time order is sometimes called the "lifetime buy" or "last buy." The all-time order should be large enough so the inventory provided will satisfy nearly all expected future demand and balance the cost of a stockout with the cost of carrying inventory.

See *all-time demand, product life cycle management.*

alternate routing – See *routing.*

American Society for Quality (ASQ) – A professional association that advances learning, quality improvement, and knowledge exchange to improve business results and create better workplaces and communities worldwide.

ASQ has more than 100,000 individual and organizational members. Founded in 1946, and headquartered in Milwaukee, Wisconsin, the ASQ was formerly known as the American Society for Quality Control (ASQC). Since 1991, ASQ has administered the Malcolm Baldrige National Quality Award, which annually recognizes companies and organizations that have achieved performance excellence. ASQ publishes many practitioner and academic journals, including **Quality Progress, Journal for Quality and Participation, Journal of Quality Technology, Quality Engineering, Quality Management Journal, Six Sigma Forum Magazine, Software Quality Professional**, and **Technometrics**. The ASQ website is www.asq.org.

See *Malcolm Baldrige National Quality Award (MBNQA), operations management (OM), quality management.*

Analysis of Variance (ANOVA) – A statistical procedure used to test if samples from two or more groups come from populations with equal means.

ANOVA is closely related to multiple regression in that both are linear models and both use the F test to test for significance. In fact, a regression with dummy variables can be used to conduct an ANOVA, including exploring multiple-way interaction terms. The test statistic for analysis of variance is the F-ratio.

ANOVA is applicable when the populations of interest are normally distributed, populations have equal standard deviations, and samples are randomly and independently selected from each population.

Multivariate Analysis of Variance (MANOVA), an extension of ANOVA, can be used to accommodate more than one dependent variable. MANOVA measures the group differences between two or more metric dependent variables simultaneously, using a set of categorical non-metric independent variables.

See *confidence interval, covariance, Design of Experiments (DOE), Gauge R&R, linear regression, sampling, Taguchi methods, t-test, variance*.

Analytic Hierarchy Process (AHP) – A structured methodology used to help groups make decisions in a complex environment; also known as Analytical Hierarchy Process.

The AHP methodology, developed by Saaty (2001), can be summarized as follows:[2]

- Model the problem as a hierarchy containing the decision goal, the alternatives for reaching it, and the criteria for evaluating the alternatives.
- Establish priorities among the elements of the hierarchy by making a series of judgments based on pairwise comparisons of the elements.
- Synthesize these judgments to yield a set of overall priorities for the hierarchy.
- Check the consistency of the judgments.
- Come to a final decision based on the results of this process.

For example, a student has three job offers and needs to select one of them. The student cares about four criteria: salary, location, fun, and impact. The offers include (1) a job setting the price for the Ford Mustang in Detroit, (2) a job as a website developer at Google in San Francisco, and (3) a job teaching English in a remote part of China. The goal, criteria, and alternatives are shown in the figure on the right.

Analytic Hierarchy Process example

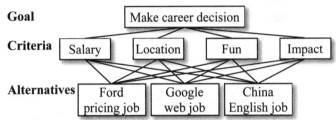

The student scores the relative importance of the objectives by comparing each pair of objectives in a table and scoring them on the scale:

1 = Objectives *i* and *j* are of equal importance.
3 = Objective *i* is moderately more important than *j*.
5 = Objective *i* is strongly more important than *j*.
7 = Objective *i* is very strongly more important than *j*.
9 = Objective *i* is absolutely more important than *j*.

	Salary	Location	Fun	Impact	Vector
Salary	1	3	7	9	57.39%
Location	1/3	1	5	7	29.13%
Fun	1/7	1/5	1	3	9.03%
Impact	1/9	1/7	1/3	1	4.45%

Scores 2, 4, 6, 8 are intermediate values. The respondent only puts a score in a cell where the row is more important than the column. The remainder of the matrix is then filled out by setting all main diagonal values to 1 (i.e., $a_{ii} = 1$) and setting the cell on the other side of the main diagonal to the inverse value (i.e., $a_{ji} = a_{ij}$). In general, participants must score $n(n - 1)/2$ pairs, where n is the number of criteria to be evaluated.

The next step is to compute the eigenvalues and the normalized eigenvector[3] of this matrix. The set of n values will add to one. The consistency index can then be computed. The eigenvalue for this problem is $\lambda = 4.2692$ and the normalized eigenvector is shown in the table above. The consistency ratio is 9.97%, which is considered acceptable. The next step is to evaluate all pairs of the three alternatives on each of the four dimensions using the same 1 to 9 scale. As a result, each alternative now has a weight for each dimension. These are then weighted by the vector, which suggests a final decision to the user.

An AHP tutorial can be found at http://people.revoledu.com/kardi/tutorial/AHP/index.html (April 10, 2011). See the *Kepner-Tregoe Model* and *Pugh Matrix* entries for other methods for multiple-criteria decision making.

See *causal map, conjoint analysis, decision tree, force field analysis, Kano Analysis, Kepner-Tregoe Model, New Product Development (NPD), Pugh Matrix, TRIZ, voice of the customer (VOC)*.

anchoring – Allowing estimates or thinking to be influenced by some starting information or current conditions; also used to describe the difficulty of changing behavior that is heavily influenced by old habits.

According to the *Forecasting Dictionary* (Armstrong 2001), the initial value (or anchor) can be based on tradition, previous history, or available data. Anchoring is a significant problem in many operations contexts,

---

[2] *Adapted from http://en.wikipedia.org/wiki/Analytic_Hierarchy_Process, March 5, 2011.*
[3] *Given a square matrix A, the scalar λ and non-zero vector v are said to be the eigenvalue and the eigenvector of A if $Av = \lambda v$.*

including forecasting and subjective estimation of probabilities. For example, when making a subjective forecast, people often anchor on the previous period's demand.

In one interesting study, Tversky and Kahneman (1974) asked subjects to predict the percentage of nations that were African in the United Nations. They selected an initial value by spinning a wheel in the subject's presence. The subjects were then asked to revise this number upward or downward to obtain an answer. This information-free initial value had a strong influence on the estimate. Those starting with 10% made predictions averaging 25%. In contrast, those starting with 65% made predictions averaging 45%.

See *forecasting, newsvendor model.*

andon board – See *andon light.*

andon light – A lean term (pronounced "Ann-Don") that refers to a warning light, warning board, or signal on (or near) a machine or assembly line that calls attention to defects or equipment problems; also called an andon board; the Japanese word for andon (行灯) means "lamp."

An andon is any visual indicator signaling that a team member has found an abnormal situation, such as poor quality, lack of parts, improper paperwork, missing information, or missing tools. When a worker pulls an andon cord (or pushes a button), the red light goes on, the line is stopped, and a supervisor or technician responds immediately to help diagnose and correct the problem. It is important for management to define exactly who is responsible as the support person. The idea here is to have a simple visual system that immediately calls for the right kind of help from the right people at the right time. This is a good example of Rule 5 in the Spear and Bowen (1999) framework.

The number of lights and their possible colors can vary even by workcenter within a plant. Most implementations have three colors: red, yellow, and green (like a stoplight). Red usually means the line is down, yellow means the line is having problems, and green means normal operations. Some firms use other colors to signal other types of issues, such as material shortages or defective components. Some firms use a blinking light to signal that someone is working on the problem.

See *assembly line, error proofing, jidoka, lean thinking, visual control.*

ANOVA – See *Analysis of Variance.*

anticipation inventory – Inventory held to (1) satisfy seasonal demand, (2) cope with expected reduced capacity due to maintenance or an anticipated strike, or (3) store seasonal supply for a level demand throughout the year (for example, a crop that is harvested only once per year).

See *production planning, seasonality.*

antitrust laws – Government regulations intended to protect and promote competition.

Competition is beneficial because it causes firms to add more value to society. Firms that add value to the market (and society) survive, but those that do not add value go out of business.

The four main antitrust laws in U.S. Federal law are:

The Sherman Antitrust Act – Passed in 1890, this act outlaws "every contract, combination in the form of trust or otherwise, or conspiracy, in restraint of trade or commerce among the several States, or with foreign nations." This law makes it illegal to create a monopoly or engage in practices that hurt competition.

The Clayton Act – Passed in 1914 and revised in 1950, this act keeps prices from skyrocketing due to mergers, acquisitions, or other business practices. By giving the government the authority to challenge large-scale moves made by corporations, this act provides a barrier against monopolistic practices.

Robinson-Patman Act – Passed in 1936 to supplement the Clayton Act, this act forbids firms from engaging in interstate commerce to discriminate in price for different purchasers of the same commodity if the effect would be to lessen competition or create a monopoly. This act protects independent retailers from chain-store competition, but it was also strongly supported by wholesalers who were eager to prevent large chain stores from buying directly from the manufacturers at lower prices.

The Federal Trade Commission Act of 1914 – Like the Clayton Act, this act is a civil statute. This act established the Federal Trade Commission (FTC), which seeks to maintain competition in interstate commerce.

In addition to these acts, antitrust violators may be found guilty of criminal activity or civil wrongdoing through other laws. Some of the other possible charges include perjury, obstruction of justice, making false statements to the government, mail fraud, and conspiracy.

See *bid rigging, bribery, category captain, General Agreement on Tariffs and Trade (GATT), mergers and acquisitions (M&A), predatory pricing, price fixing, purchasing*.

APICS (The Association for Operations Management) – A professional society for operations managers, including production, inventory, supply chain, materials management, purchasing, and logistics.

APICS stands for American Production and Inventory Control Society. However, APICS has adopted the name "The Association for Operations Management," even though the name no longer matches the acronym.

The APICS website (www.apics.org) states, "The Association for Operations Management is the global leader and premier source of the body of knowledge in operations management, including production, inventory, supply chain, materials management, purchasing, and logistics." Since 1957, individuals and companies have relied on APICS for training, certifications, comprehensive resources, and a worldwide network of accomplished industry professionals. APICS confers the CIRM, CPIM, and CSCP certifications. APICS produces a number of trade publications and a practitioner/research journal, the ***Production & Inventory Management Journal***.

See *operations management (OM)*.

A-plant – See *VAT analysis*.

Application Service Provider (ASP) – An organization that provides (hosts) remote access to a software application over the Internet.

The ASP owns a license to the software and customers rent the use of the software and access it over the Internet. The ASP may be the software manufacturer or a third-party business. An ASP operates the software at its data center, which customers access online under a service contract. A common example is a website that other websites use for accepting payment by credit card as part of their online ordering systems. The benefits of an ASP are lower upfront costs, quicker implementation, scalability, and lower operating costs. The term "Software as a Service (SaaS)" seems to have diminished the importance of this term.

The unrelated term Active Server Pages (ASP) describes HTML pages that contain embedded scripts.

See *cloud computing, service management, Software as a Service (SaaS)*.

appraisal cost – An expense of measuring quality through inspection and testing. ✪

Many popular quality consultants argue that appraisal costs should be eliminated and that firms should not try to "inspect quality into the product," but should instead "design quality into the product and process."

See *cost of quality*.

APS – See *Advanced Planning and Scheduling (APS)*.

AQL – See *Acceptable Quality Level*.

arbitrage – Buying something in one market and reselling it at a higher price in another market.

Arbitrage involves a combination of matching deals to exploit the imbalance in prices between two or more markets and profiting from the difference between the market prices. A person who engages in arbitrage is called an arbitrageur.

Arbitrage is a combination of transactions designed to profit from an existing discrepancy among prices, exchange rates, or interest rates in different markets, often without risk of these changing. The simplest form of arbitrage is the simultaneous purchase and sale of something in different markets. More complex forms include triangular arbitrage. To arbitrage is to make a combination of bets such that if one bet loses, another one wins, with the implication of having an edge, at no risk or at least low risk. The term "hedge" has a similar meaning, but does not carry the implication of having an edge.

See *hedging*.

ARIMA – Autoregressive Integrated Moving Average. See *Box-Jenkins forecasting*.

ARMA – Autoregressive Moving Average. See *Box-Jenkins forecasting*.

Artificial Intelligence (AI) – Computer software that uses algorithms that emulate human intelligence.

Many applications of AI have been made in operations management, including decision support systems, scheduling, forecasting, computer-aided design, character recognition, pattern recognition, and speech/voice recognition. One challenge for computer scientists is differentiating AI software from other types of software.

See *algorithm, expert system, neural network, robotics*.

ASN – See *Advanced Shipping Notification (ASN)*.

AS/RS – See *Automated Storage & Retrieval System (AS/RS)*.

ASQ – See *American Society for Quality*.

assemble to order (ATO) – A customer interface strategy that stocks standard components and modules that can quickly be assembled products to meet a wide variety of customer requirements. ✪

ATO allows an organization to produce a large variety of final products with a relatively short customer leadtime. Well-known examples of ATO processes include Burger King, which assembles hamburgers with many options while the customer waits, and Dell Computer, which assembles and ships a wide variety of computers on short notice. ATO systems almost never have any finished goods inventory, but usually stock major components. Pack to order and configure to order systems are special cases of ATO.

See *assembly, build to order (BTO), customer leadtime, Final Assembly Schedule (FAS), make to stock (MTS), mass customization, Master Production Schedule (MPS), respond to order (RTO)*.

assembly – A manufacturing process that brings together two or more parts to create a product or a subassembly that will eventually become part of a product; the result of an assembly process.

A **subassembly** is an intermediate assembly used in the production of higher-level subassemblies, assemblies, and products.

See *assemble to order (ATO), assembly line, manufacturing processes*.

assembly line – The organization of a series of workers or machines so discrete units can be moved easily from one station to the next to build a product; also called a production line.

On an assembly line, each worker (or machine) performs one relatively simple task and then moves the product to the next worker (or machine). Assembly lines are best suited for assembling large batches of standard products and therefore require a highly standardized process. Unlike **continuous processes** for liquids or powders, which can move through pipes, assembly lines are for discrete products and often use conveyer belts to move products between workers. Assembly lines use a **product layout**, which means the sequence is determined by the product requirements. Some automated assembly lines require substantial capital investment, which makes them hard to change.

One issue with an assembly line is assigning work to workers to **balance the line** to minimize wasted time. See the *line balancing* entry.

The term "production line" is more general than the term "assembly line." A production line may include fabrication operations, such as molding and machining, whereas an assembly line only does assembly.

See *andon light, assembly, cycle time, discrete manufacturing, fabrication, facility layout, line balancing, manufacturing processes, mixed model assembly, production line, standard products*.

asset turnover – A financial ratio that measures the ability of the firm to use its assets to generate sales revenue.

Asset turnover is measured as the ratio of a company's net sales to its total assets. The assets are often based on an average. Asset turnover is similar to inventory turnover.

See *financial performance metrics, inventory turnover*.

assignable cause – See *special cause variation*.

assignment problem – A mathematical programming problem of matching one group of items (jobs, trucks, etc.) with another group of locations (machines, cities, etc.) to minimize the sum of the costs.

The assignment problem is usually shown as a table or a matrix and requires that exactly one match is found in each row and each column. For example, matching students to seats has N students and N seats and results in an N x N table of possible assignments. Each student must be assigned to exactly one seat and each seat must be assigned to exactly one student. The "cost" of assigning student i to seat j is c_{ij}, which may be some measure of the student's disutility (dislike) for that seat. This problem can be solved efficiently on a computer with special-purpose assignment algorithms, network optimization algorithms, and general-purpose linear programming algorithms. Even though it is an integer programming problem, it can be solved with any general linear programming package and be guaranteed to produce integer solutions, because the problem is unimodular.

The assignment problem is formulated as the following linear program:

Assignment problem: Minimize $\sum_{i=1}^{N}\sum_{j=1}^{N} c_{ij} x_{ij}$ Subject to $\sum_{i=1}^{N} x_{ij} = 1$ for all j and $\sum_{j=1}^{N} x_{ij} = 1$ for all i

where the decision variables are $x_{ij} \in \{0,1\}$ and c_{ij} is the cost of assigning item i to location j.

See *algorithm, integer programming (IP), linear programming (LP), network optimization, operations research (OR), transportation problem, Traveling Salesperson Problem (TSP).*

Association for Manufacturing Excellence (AME) – A practitioner-based professional society dedicated to cultivating understanding, analysis, and exchange of productivity methods and their successful application in the pursuit of excellence.

Founded in 1985, AME was the first major professional society in North America to promote lean manufacturing principles. AME sponsors events and workshops that focus on hands-on learning. AME publishes the *Target* magazine and puts on several regional and national events each year.

The AME website is www.ame.org.

See *operations management (OM).*

assortment – A retailer's selection of merchandise to display; also known as "merchandise assortment" and "product assortment."

The target customer base and physical product characteristics determine the depth and breadth of an assortment and the length of time it is carried.

See *category captain, category management, planogram, product proliferation.*

ATO – See *assemble to order.*

ATP – See *Available-to-Promise (ATP).*

attribute – A quality management term used to describe a zero-one (binary) property of a product by which its quality will be judged by some stakeholder.

Inspection can be performed by attributes or by variables. Inspection by attributes is usually for lot control (acceptance sampling) and is performed with a p-chart (to control the percent defective) or a c-chart (to control the number of defects). Inspection by variables is usually done for process control and is performed with an x-bar chart (to control the mean) or an r-chart (to control the range or variance).

See *acceptance sampling, c-chart, inspection, p-chart, quality management, Statistical Process Control (SPC), Statistical Quality Control (SQC).*

autocorrelation – A measure of the strength of the relationship between a time series variable in periods t and $t - k$; also called serial correlation.

Autocorrelation measures the correlation between a variable in period t and period $t - k$ (i.e., correlation between x_t and x_{t-k}). The autocorrelation at lag k is then defined as $\rho_k = \dfrac{Cov(x_t, x_{t-k})}{\sqrt{Var(x_t)Var(x_{t-k})}} = \dfrac{Cov(x_t, x_{t-k})}{Var(x_t)}$,

where $Var(x_t) = Var(x_{t-k})$ for a weakly stationary process.

Testing for autocorrelation is one way to check for randomness in time series data. The Durbin-Watson test can be used to test for first-order (i.e., $k = 1$) autocorrelation. The runs test can also be used to test for serial independence.

The Box-Jenkins forecasting method uses the autocorrelation structure in the time series to create forecasts.

Excel can be used to estimate the autocorrelation at lag k using CORREL(*range1, range2*), where *range1* includes the first $T - 1$ values and *range2* includes the last $T - 1$ values of a time series with T values.

See *all-time demand, Box-Jenkins forecasting, correlation, Durbin-Watson statistic, learning curve, runs test, safety stock, time series forecasting.*

Automated Data Collection (ADC) – Information systems used to collect and process data with little or no human interaction; also called data capture, Automated Identification and Data Capture (AIDC), and Auto-ID.

Automated Data Collection is based on technologies, such as barcodes, Radio Frequency Identification (RFID), biometrics, magnetic stripes, Optical Character Recognition (OCR), smart cards, and voice recognition. Most Warehouse Management Systems and Manufacturing Execution Systems are integrated with ADC systems.

See *barcode, Manufacturing Execution System (MES), Optical Character Recognition (OCR), part number, quality at the source, Radio Frequency Identification (RFID), Warehouse Management System (WMS).*

Automated Guided Vehicle (AGV) – Unmanned, computer-controlled vehicle equipped with a guidance and collision-avoidance system; sometimes known as an Automated Guided Vehicle System (AGVS).

AGVs typically follow a path defined by wires embedded in the floor to transport materials and tools between workstations. Many firms have found AGVs to be inefficient and unreliable.

See *automation, robotics*.

Automated Identification and Data Capture (AIDC) – See *Automated Data Collection (ADC)*.

Automated Storage & Retrieval System (AS/RS) – A computer-controlled robotic device used for storing and retrieving items from storage locations; also called ASRS.

Automated Storage and Retrieval Systems are a combination of equipment, controls, and information systems that automatically handle, store, and retrieve materials, components, tools, raw material, subassemblies, or products with great speed and accuracy. Consequently, they are used in many manufacturing and warehousing applications. An AS/RS includes one or more of the following technologies: horizontal carousels, vertical carousels, vertical lift modules (VLM), and the traditional crane-in-aisle storage and retrieval systems that use storage retrieval (SR) cranes.

See *automation, batch picking, carousel, warehouse, zone picking*.

Automatic Call Distributor (ACD) – A computerized phone system that responds to the caller with a voice menu and then routes the caller to an appropriate agent; also known as Automated Call Distribution.

ACDs are the core technology in call centers and are used for order entry, direct sales, technical support, and customer service. All ACDs provide some sort of routing function for calls. Some ACDs use sophisticated systems that distribute calls equally to agents or identify and prioritize a high-value customer based on the calling number. Some ACDs recognize the calling number via ANI or Caller ID, consult a database, and then route the call accordingly. ACDs can also incorporate "skills-based routing" that routes callers along with appropriate data files to the agent who has the appropriate knowledge and language skills to handle the call. Some ACDs can also route e-mail, faxes, Web-initiated calls, and callback requests.

The business benefits of an ACD include both customer benefits (less average waiting time and higher customer satisfaction) and service provider benefits (more efficient service, better use of resources, and less need for training). However, some customers intensely dislike ACDs because they can be impersonal and confusing.

See *automation, call center, customer service*.

automation – The practice of developing machines to do work that was formerly done manually. ✪

Automation is often a good approach for reducing variable cost, improving conformance quality of a process, and manufacturing run time per unit. However, automation requires capital expense, managerial and technical expertise to install, and technical expertise to maintain. Additionally, automation often reduces the product mix flexibility (highly automated equipment is usually dedicated to a narrow range of products), decreases volume flexibility (the firm must have enough volume to justify the capital cost), and increases risk (the automation becomes worthless when the process or product technology becomes obsolete or when the market demand for products requiring the automation declines).

Automation is best used in situations where the work is dangerous, dirty, or dull ("the 3Ds"). For example, welding is dangerous, cleaning a long underground sewer line is dirty, and inserting transistors on a printed circuit board is dull. All three of these tasks can and should be automated when possible. Repetitive (dull) work often results in poor quality work, so automated equipment is more likely to produce defect-free results.

See *3Ds, Automated Guided Vehicle (AGV), Automated Storage & Retrieval System (AS/RS), Automatic Call Distributor (ACD), cellular manufacturing, Flexible Manufacturing System (FMS), flexibility, islands of automation, jidoka, labor intensive, multiplication principle, robotics*.

autonomation – See *error proofing, jidoka, Toyota Production System (TPS)*.

autonomous maintenance – A Total Productive Maintenance (TPM) principle that has maintenance performed by machine operators rather than maintenance people.

Maintenance activities include cleaning, lubricating, adjusting, inspecting, and repairing machines. Advantages of autonomous maintenance include increased "ownership" of the equipment, increased uptime, and decreased maintenance costs. It can also free up maintenance workers to focus more time on critical activities.

See *maintenance, Total Productive Maintenance (TPM)*.

autonomous team – A group of people who work toward specific goals with very little guidance from a manager or supervisor; also called an autonomous workgroup.

The members of the team are empowered to establish their own goals and practices. Autonomous teams are sometimes used to manage production workcells and develop new products.

See *New Product Development (NPD)*.

autonomous workgroup – See *autonomous team*.

availability – A measure used in the reliability and maintenance literature for the percentage of time that a product can be operated.

According to Schroeder (2007), availability is $MTBF/(MTBF + MTTR)$, where $MTBF$ is the mean time between failure and $MTTR$ is the Mean Time to Repair.

See *maintenance, Mean Time Between Failure (MTBF), Mean Time to Repair (MTTR), reliability*.

Available-to-Promise (ATP) – A manufacturing planning and control term used to describe the number of units that can be promised to a customer at any point in time based on projected demand and supply.

In SAP, ATP is the quantity available to MRP for new sales orders and is calculated as stock + planned receipts – planned issues (http://help.sap.com).

See *Master Production Schedule (MPS), Materials Requirements Planning (MRP)*.

average – See *mean*.

B

B2B – Business-to-business transactions between manufacturers, distributors, wholesalers, jobbers, retailers, government organizations, and other industrial organizations.

See *B2C, dot-com, e-business, wholesaler*.

B2C – Business-to-consumer transactions between a business and consumers.

See *B2B, dot-com, e-business*.

back loading – See *backward loading*.

back office – The operations of an organization that are not normally seen by customers; most often used in the financial services business context.

Back office operations handle administrative duties that are not **customer facing** and therefore often focus on **efficiency**. In the financial services industry, back office operations involve systems for processing checks, credit cards, and other types of financial transactions. In contrast, **front office** activities include customer-facing activities, such as sales, marketing, and customer service. Some sources consider general management, finance, human resources, and accounting as front office activates because they guide and control back office activities.

See *e-business, human resources, line of visibility, service management*.

back scheduling – A scheduling method that plans backward from the due date (or time) to determine the start date (or time); in project scheduling, called a backward pass; also called backward scheduling.

Back scheduling creates a detailed schedule for each operation or activity based on the planned available capacity. In project scheduling, the **critical path method** uses back scheduling (called a "backward pass") to determine the late finish and late start dates for each activity in the project network. In contrast, **backward loading** plan backward from the due date but does not create a detailed schedule.

See *Advanced Planning and Scheduling (APS), backward loading, Critical Path Method (CPM), forward scheduling, Master Production Schedule (MPS)*.

backflushing – A means of reducing the number of inventory transactions (and the related cost) by reducing the inventory count for an item when the order is started, completed, or shipped; also called explode-to-deduct and post deduct.

For example, a computer keyboard manufacturer has two alternatives for keeping track of the number of letter A's stored in inventory. With the traditional approach, the firm counts the number of keys that are issued (moved) to the assembly area in the plant. This can be quite costly. In fact, it is possible that the cost of counting the inventory could exceed the value of the inventory. With backflushing, the firm reduces the letter A inventory count when a keyboard is shipped to a customer. The bill of material for the keyboard calls for one letter A for each keyboard; therefore, if the firm ships 100 keyboards, it should also ship exactly 100 letter A's.

Backflushing gives an imprecise inventory count because of the delay between the time the items are issued to the shop floor and the time that the balance is updated. However, it can significantly reduce the shop floor data transaction cost. It is also possible to "backflush" labor cost.

The alternative to backflushing is **direct issue**, where material is pulled from stock according to the **pick list** for an order, deducted from on-hand inventory, and transferred to work in process until the order is complete.

The *floor stock* entry covers this topic in more detail.

See *bill of material (BOM)*, *cycle counting*, *floor stock*, *issue*, *job order costing*, *pick list*, *shop floor control*.

backhaul – A transportation term for a load taken on the return trip of a transportation asset, especially a truck, to its origin or base of operations.

An empty return trip is called **deadheading**. A backhaul will pick up, transport, and deliver either a full or a partial load on a return trip from delivering another load. The first trip is sometimes known as a fronthaul.

See *deadhead*, *logistics*, *repositioning*.

backlog – The total amount of unfilled sales orders, usually expressed in terms of sales revenue or hours of work.

The backlog includes all orders (not just past due orders) accepted from customers that have not yet been shipped to customers. The backlog is often measured in terms of the number of periods (hours, days, weeks, or months) that would be required to work off the orders if no new work were received. The order backlog can disappear when economic conditions change and customers cancel their orders.

See *backorder*, *stockout*.

backorder – A customer order that has to wait because no inventory is available; if the customer is not willing to wait, it is a lost sale.

If a firm cannot immediately satisfy a customer's order, the customer is asked to wait. If the customer is willing to wait, the order is called a backorder and is usually filled as soon as inventory becomes available.

When a product is not available but has been ordered from the supplier, it is said to be **on backorder**. The **order backlog** is the set of backorders at any point in time. The order backlog, therefore, is a waiting line (queue) of orders waiting to be filled. In a sense, an order backlog is an "inventory" of demand.

See *allocated inventory*, *backlog*, *inventory position*, *on-hand inventory*, *stockout*.

backward integration – See *vertical integration*.

backward loading – A planning method that plan backward from the due date to determine the start date; sometimes called back loading.

The word "loading" means that the plan is created in time buckets and is not a detailed schedule. For example, an executive needs to prepare for a trip in one month and "loads" each of the next four weeks with ten hours of work. Backward loading might fill up a time "bucket" (e.g., a half-day) until the capacity is fully committed. Backward loading is not the same as back scheduling because it does not create a detailed schedule.

See *back scheduling*, *finite scheduling*, *load*.

backward pass – See *back scheduling*.

backward scheduling – See *back scheduling*.

bait and switch – See *loss leader*.

balance sheet – A statement that summarizes the financial position for an organization as of a specific date, such as the end of the organization's financial (fiscal) year; this statement includes assets (what it owns), liabilities (what it owes), and owners' equity (shareholders' equity).

The three essential financial documents are the balance sheet, income statement, and cash flow statement.

See *financial performance metrics*, *income statement*.

balanced scorecard – A strategy execution and reporting tool that presents managers with a limited number of "balanced" key performance metrics so they can assess how well the firm is achieving the strategy. ✪

A balanced scorecard is a popular framework that translates a company's vision and strategy into a coherent set of performance measures that was first proposed by Kaplan and Norton in a famous article in the *Harvard Business Review* (Kaplan & Norton 1992). Kaplan and Norton also wrote a number of other articles and books expanding the idea to strategic management (Kaplan & Norton 1996, 2000, 2004), strategic alignment (Kaplan & Norton 2006), and execution of strategy (Kaplan & Norton 2008).

A balanced business scorecard helps businesses evaluate how well they are meeting their strategic objectives. Kaplan and Norton (1992) propose four perspectives: financial, customer, internal, and learning and growth, each with a number of measures. They argue that the scorecard should be "balanced" between financial and non-financial measures and balanced between the four perspectives. This author has broadened the view of the balanced scorecard to five types of balance. These are shown in the table below.

Five types of balance between metrics

Financial metrics – Too much focus on financial metrics without understanding the metrics that drive the financials.		**Non-financial metrics** – Too much focus on quality, time, and satisfaction metrics without regard for financial consequences.
Short-term metrics – Too much focus on metrics from last week or last month at the expense of longer-term performance.		**Long-term metrics** – Too much focus on long-term metrics, which results in lack of action on immediate needs.
Leading metrics – Too much focus on metrics that we believe predict the future, which may not be reliable.		**Lagging metrics** – Too much focus on historical metrics, which may not be relevant to the current situation.
Internal metrics – Too much focus on metrics from internal data, such as financial statements and company reports.	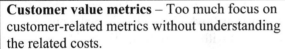	**External metrics** – Too much focus on metrics from external sources, such as market trends and industry cost trends.
Customer value metrics – Too much focus on customer-related metrics without understanding the related costs.		**Cost metrics** – Too much focus on cost-related metrics without understanding the impact on customers.

Source: Professor Arthur V. Hill

The balanced scorecard includes measures of performance that are lagging indicators (return on capital, profit), current indicators (cycle time), and leading indicators (customer satisfaction, new product adoption rates). The following figure illustrates the balanced scorecard as developed by Kaplan and Norton.

See *alignment, benchmarking, causal map, corporate portal, cycle time, dashboard, DuPont Analysis, financial performance metrics, gainsharing, hoshin planning, inventory turnover, Key Performance Indicator (KPI), leading indicator, learning curve, learning organization, Management by Objectives (MBO), mission statement, operations performance metrics, operations strategy, strategy map, suboptimization, supplier scorecard, Y-tree.*

Baldrige Award – See *Malcolm Baldrige National Quality Award.*

balking – The refusal of an arriving customer to join a queue and wait in line.

When customers arrive to a system and find a long line, they will often exit the system. Customers are said to balk when they leave the system. A **queuing system** with an average arrival rate that is dependent upon the length of the queue is called a state-dependent arrival process.

See *queuing theory.*

bar chart – A graph with parallel thick lines with lengths proportional to quantities; also called a bar graph and histogram.

Bar charts can be displayed either horizontally or vertically. A Gantt Chart is an example of a horizontal bar chart. Vertical bar charts (also known as histograms) are particularly helpful for frequency data. A bar chart can only be created for discrete data (e.g., age as an integer) or categorical data (e.g., country of origin). Continuous data can be converted into discrete "buckets" or "bins" so a bar chart can be created.

See *binomial distribution, Gantt Chart, histogram, Pareto Chart.*

barcode – Information encoded on parallel bars and spaces that can be read by a scanner and then translated into an alphanumeric identification code.

Barcodes always identify the product but sometimes also include additional information, such as the quantity, price, and weight. Barcodes are particularly well suited for tracking products through a process, such as retail transactions. A popular example is the UPC code used on retail packaging. Radio Frequency Identification (RFID) is a newer technology that is replacing barcodes in many applications.

Barcodes provide many business benefits, including reducing transaction cost and providing information that can be used to improve service levels, reduce stockouts, and reduce unnecessary inventory.

Barcodes come in many varieties. The 2D (two-dimensional) barcode is in the form of bars and spaces, normally in a rectangular pattern. In contrast, a 3D (three-dimensional) barcode looks like a group of random black boxes scattered across a white background. 3D barcodes are often used in environments where labels cannot be easily attached to items.

A barcode reader (scanner, wand) is a device that scans a barcode to record the information.

The Wikipedia article on barcodes provides detailed information on types of barcodes and barcode standards.

See *Automated Data Collection (ADC), Electronic Product Code (EPC), part number, Radio Frequency Identification (RFID), Universal Product Code (UPC).*

barter – The exchange of goods without using cash or any other financial medium.

For example, oil is sometimes bartered for military equipment in the Persian Gulf.

barriers-to-entry – See *core competence, switching cost.*

base stock system – See *order-up-to level.*

Bass Model – A well-known approach for modeling the sales pattern for the life cycle of a new product introduction developed by Professor Frank Bass.

The demand for a new music title or any other type of new product follows a similar demand pattern through its product life cycle, with early growth, maturity, and finally decline. The Bass Model (and its many extensions) has inspired many academic research papers and has been used in many applications. The basic idea is that some products take off right away due to the early adopters (the "innovators") who immediately make purchases. The "imitators" do not buy right away, but buy soon after they see others with the product. The model requires three parameters:

m Total market potential, which is the total number of unit sales that we expect to sell over the life of the product. This is the sum of the demand during the product life and is also the area under the curve.

p Innovation coefficient, which primarily affects the shape of the curve during the beginning of the life cycle. This parameter is also called the external influence, or the advertising effect.

q Imitation coefficient, which primarily affects the shape of the curve after the peak of the product life cycle. This parameter is also called the internal influence, or word-of-mouth effect.

In summary, m is the scale parameter and p and q are the shape parameters. With these three parameters, the Bass Model can predict almost any realistic new product introduction demand pattern. The challenge is to estimate m, p, and q for a new product introduction. The best approach for handling this problem is to predict m based on marketing research and to select the p and q parameters based on experience with similar products.

The basic idea of the Bass Model (Bass 1969) is that the probability of an initial purchase made at time t is a linear function of the proportion of the population that has already purchased the product. Define $F(t)$ as the fraction of the installed base through time t and $f(t) = dF(t)/dt$ as the rate of change in the installed base fraction at time t. The fundamental model is given by $f(t)/(1-F(t)) = p + qF(t)$. Assuming that $F(0) = 0$ gives $F(t) = \left(1 - e^{-(p+qt)}\right)\left(1 + (q/p)e^{-(p+q)t}\right)^{-1}$ and $f(t) = ((p+q)^2/p)e^{-p(p+q)t}\left(1 + (q/p)e^{-(p+q)t}\right)^{-2}$. From this, the cumulative sales through period t can be estimated as $S(t) = mF(t)$ and the rate of change in the installed base at time t is $dS(t)/dt = mf(t)$. The time of peak sales is $t^* = \ln(q/p)/(p+q)$. The Bass Model has been extended in many ways, but those extensions are outside the scope of this encyclopedia. Mahajan, Muller, Eitan, and Bass (1995) provided a summary of many of the extensions of the Bass Model.

Historical data can be used to estimate the parameters p and q. Define $N(t)$ as the cumulative historical sales through time t. Simple linear regression can now be run using the model $y(t) = a + bN(t) - cN(t)^2$ and then m, p, and q can be estimated with these equations solved in this order $m = b + \sqrt{b^2 + 4ac}/(-2a)$, $p = a/m$, and $q = cm$. The average value of p is around 0.03, but it is often less than 0.01. The value of q is typically in the range (0.3, 0.5) with an average around 0.38.

The example below starts with the empirical data in the table and finds the optimal parameters $m = 87$, $p = 0.100$, and $q = 0.380$. The graph for this curve is shown on the right.

Time period	Predicted sales	Predicted cumulative sales
1	9	9
2	11	20
3	12	32
4	13	45
5	12	58
6	10	68
7	8	76
8	5	80
9	3	83
10	2	85
11	1	86
12	0	86

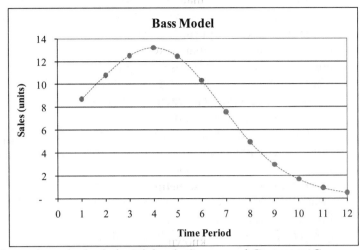

The *logistic curve* entry presents simpler models, such as the logistic, Richards Curve, and Gompertz Curve.

See *adoption curve, all-time demand, forecasting, linear regression, logistic curve, network effect, product life cycle management.*

batch – See *lotsize.*

batch flow – See *batch process.*

batch picking – A warehousing term for an order picking method where multiple orders are picked by one picker in one pass and then later separated by order.

See *Automated Storage & Retrieval System (AS/RS), carousel, picking, wave picking, zone picking.*

batch process – A system that produces a variety of products but produces them in groups of identical items.

Unlike a continuous process, a batch process is characterized by (1) a system that can make more than one product or product type, (2) setups that are used to change the process to make a different product, and (3) work-in-process inventory between steps in the process due to batchsizes and contention for capacity.

A batch process is often associated with a job-shop that has general purpose equipment arranged in a **process layout**. In a process layout, the location of the equipment is not dictated by the product design but rather by groups of similar general purpose equipment that share a common process technology or required skill.

Most batch processes require significant setup time and cost with each batch. In the lean perspective, setup time is waste and reducing setup time and cost is often considered a strategic priority. If a system is dedicated to producing only a single product, it has no setups or changeovers and is a continuous process.

Examples of batch processes include (1) apparel manufacturing, where each batch might be a different style or size of shirt, (2) paint manufacturing, where different colors of paint are mixed in different batches, and (3) bottle filling operations, where each batch is a different liquid (e.g., soft drink).

See *batch-and-queue, continuous process, discrete manufacturing, job shop, sequence-dependent setup time, setup, setup cost, setup time.*

batch-and-queue – A negative term often used by promoters of lean manufacturing to criticize manufacturing operations that have large lotsizes, large queues, long queue times, long cycle times, and high work-in-process.

One-piece flow is a better method because it eliminates batches, which reduces the average time in queue and the average number in queue (assuming that no additional setup time is required).

See *batch process, continuous flow, lean thinking, one-piece flow, overproduction, value added ratio.*

batchsize – See *lotsize.*

bathtub curve – A U-shaped curve used in reliability theory and reliability engineering that shows a typical hazard function with products more likely to fail either early or late in their useful lives. ✪

Reliability engineers have observed population failure rates as units age over time and have developed what is known as the "bathtub curve." As shown in the graph below[4], the bathtub curve has three phases:

Infant failure period – The initial region begins at time zero, when a customer first begins to use the product. This region is characterized by a high but rapidly decreasing failure rate and is known as the early failure, or infant mortality period. Immediate failures are sometimes called "dead on arrival," or DOA.

Intrinsic failure period – After the infant mortality period has passed, the failure rate levels off and remains roughly constant for the majority of the useful life of the product. This long period with a fairly level failure rate is also known as the intrinsic failure period, stable failure period, or random failure period. The constant failure rate level is called the intrinsic failure rate.

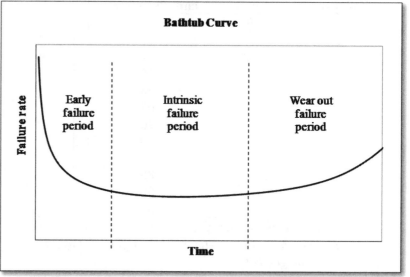

End of life wear out period – Finally, if units from the population remain in use long enough, the failure rate begins to increase again as materials wear out and degradation failures occur at an increasing rate. This is also known as the wear out failure period.

For example, a newly purchased light bulb will sometimes fail when you first install it (or very shortly thereafter). However, if it survives the first few hours, it is likely to last for many months until it fails. Another example is human life. The death rate of infants is relatively high, but if an infant makes it through the first couple of weeks, the mortality rate does not increase very much until old age.

The Weibull distribution is a flexible life distribution model that can be used to characterize failure distributions in all three phases of the bathtub curve. The basic Weibull distribution has two parameters, the shape and scale parameters. The shape parameter enables it to be applied to any phase of the bathtub curve. A shape parameter less than one models a failure rate that decreases with time, as in the infant mortality period. A shape parameter equal to one models a constant failure rate, as in the normal life period. A shape parameter greater than one models an increasing failure rate, as during wear-out. This distribution can be viewed in different ways, including probability plots, survival plots, and failure rate versus time plots (the bathtub curve).

The bathtub curve can inform decisions regarding service parts. However, the need for service parts at the end of the product life cycle is affected by retirement (removal) of the equipment in the field. Although the bathtub curve suggests that the demand for service parts at the end of life might increase, this effect is mitigated by the retirement of machines from the field, making it difficult to predict the demand for service parts at the end of the product life cycle.

See *maintenance, Mean Time Between Failure (MTBF), newsvendor model, Poisson distribution, product life cycle management, reliability, service parts, Total Productive Maintenance (TPM), Weibull distribution.*

Bayes' Theorem – An important probability theory concept that expresses the conditional probability of event A in terms of the conditional and marginal probabilities of events A and B.

Bayes' Theorem stated mathematically is $P(A\,|\,B) = \dfrac{P(B\,|\,A)P(A)}{P(B)}$, where $P(A\,|\,B)$ is the probability of event A given event B, $P(B\,|\,A)$ is the probability of event B given event A, and $P(A)$ and $P(B)$ are the unconditional (marginal) probabilities of events A and B.

---

[4] *This bathtub curve is the sum of four Weibull curves* $f(t) = \alpha\beta^{-\alpha}t^{\alpha-1}\exp(-(t\,/\,\beta)^{\alpha})$ *with* α = 0.5, 1, 3, *and* 10, β = 135, *for t in the range* (1, 250).

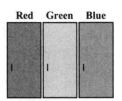
Red   Green   Blue

A popular example is the North American TV game show "Let's Make a Deal," which gave contestants the option of selecting one of three doors (red, green, and blue), where only one door had a prize hidden behind it. After the contestant selected a door, the game show host opened another door where the prize was not hidden. The host then asked the contestant if he or she wanted to select a different door. In this game context, many people incorrectly conclude that the chances are 50-50 between the two unopened doors and that the contestant has no reason to select a different door.

To better understand the probabilities involved in this game, define events R (the prize is behind the red door), G (the prize is behind the green door), and B (the prize is behind the blue door). When the prize is randomly assigned to a door, then $P(R) = P(G) = P(B) = 1/3$. To simplify exposition, assume that the contestant has selected the red door and that the host has opened the blue door to show that the prize is not behind it (event S_B). Without any prior knowledge, the probability that the host will show the blue door is $P(S_B) = 1/2$. If the prize is actually behind the red door, the host is free to pick between the green and blue doors at random (i.e., $P(S_B|R) = 1/2$). If the prize is actually behind the green door, the host must pick the blue door (i.e., $P(S_B|G) = 1$). If the prize is behind the blue door, the host must pick the green door (i.e., $P(S_B|B) = 0$). Given that the host showed the blue door, Bayes' Theorem shows:

Probability of the prize behind the red door: $P(R \mid S_B) = \dfrac{P(S_B \mid R)P(R)}{P(S_B)} = \dfrac{(1/2)\cdot(1/3)}{(1/2)} = 1/3$

Probability of the prize behind the green door: $P(G \mid S_B) = \dfrac{P(S_B \mid G)P(G)}{P(S_B)} = \dfrac{1\cdot(1/3)}{(1/2)} = 2/3$

Probability of the prize behind the blue door: $P(B \mid S_B) = \dfrac{P(S_B \mid A_b)P(A_b)}{P(S_B)} = \dfrac{0\cdot(1/3)}{(1/2)} = 0$

Therefore, in this situation, the contestant should always choose the green door. More generally, the contestant should always change to the other door. Another way of looking at this problem is to understand that the contestant had a 1/3 chance of being right in selecting the red door. When the blue door was shown to not have the prize, the conditional probability of the red door having the prize is still 1/3, but the probability of the green door having the prize is now 2/3. See http://en.wikipedia.org/wiki/Monty_Hall_problem for more details.

See *decision tree*.

beer game – A popular simulation game to help people understand the bullwhip problem in supply chains and learn how to deal with the problem in practical ways.

The beer game was designed by Professor John Sterman (1992) at MIT to demonstrate the bullwhip in supply chains. It emphasizes the importance of information flow along the supply chain and shows how humans tend to overreact and overcompensate for small changes in demand, which results in magnified fluctuations in demand that are passed down the supply chain.

The class is divided into teams of four players at each table. The four players include a retailer, warehouse, distributor, and factory. The "products" are pennies, which represent cases of beer. Each player maintains an inventory and keeps track of backorders. Players receive orders from suppliers after a one-week delay. The instructor privately communicates the demand to the retailer, with a demand for four cases per week for the first four weeks and eight cases per week for the remainder of the game.

The results of the game are fairly predictable, with nearly all teams falling into the trap of wild oscillations. At the end of the game, the instructor asks the factory players to estimate the actual demand history. They usually guess that demand varied widely throughout the game. Students are often surprised to learn that demand was steady except for the initial jump. The teaching points of the game revolve around how the internal factors drive the demand variations and about how this "bullwhip" can be managed.

See *bullwhip effect*.

benchmarking – Comparing products or processes to a standard to evaluate and improve performance. ✪

Finding comparable **numerical comparisons** between two or more firms is very difficult because no two organizations, processes, or products are truly comparable. Although knowing that two processes (or products) have different performance might help an organization prioritize its improvement efforts, it does not help the organization know how to improve. Real improvement only comes when a better process or product is understood and that information is used by the organization to improve its processes and products.

Many consulting firms have moved away from the term "benchmarking" because it focused more on comparing numbers (benchmarks) than on understanding and improving processes. Many of these consulting firms then started to use the term "**best practices**" instead of benchmarking. However, due to the difficulty of knowing if a process or product is truly the best, most consulting firms now use the term "**leading practices**."

Product benchmarking compares product attributes and performance (e.g., speed and style) and **process benchmarking** compares process metrics, such as cycle time and defect rates. **Internal benchmarking** sets the standard by comparing products and processes in the same firm (e.g., another department, region, machine, worker, etc.). In contrast, **external benchmarking** sets the standard based on products and processes from another firm. **Competitive benchmarking** is a type of external benchmarking that sets the standard based on a competitor's products or processes. Of course, no competitor should be willing to share process information. **Informal benchmarking** is done by finding a convenient benchmarking partner (often in a warm climate) who is willing to share information. In contrast, **formal benchmarking** involves mapping processes, sharing process maps, comparing numbers, etc.

Many professional trade organizations provide benchmarking services. For example, several quality awards, such as the Deming Award in Japan, the European Quality Award in Europe, and the Malcolm Baldrige Award in the U.S., serve as benchmarks for quality performance. The PRTM consulting firm and other firms provide benchmarking consulting using the SCOR framework.

See *balanced scorecard, best practices, entitlement, lean sigma, Malcolm Baldrige National Quality Award (MBNQA), operations performance metrics, process improvement program, process map, SCOR Model, supplier scorecard, Y-tree.*

Bernoulli distribution – A discrete probability distribution that takes on a value of $x = 1$ (success) with probability p and value of $x = 0$ (failure) with probability $q = 1 - p$.

Parameter: The probability of success, p.

Probability mass function: If X is a random variable with the Bernoulli distribution, then $P(X = 1) = 1 - P(X = 0) = p = 1 - q$.

Statistics: The Bernoulli has range $(0, 1)$, mean p, and variance $p(1 - p)$.

Excel simulation: The inverse transform method can be used. If RAND() $< p$ then $X = 1$; otherwise, $X = 0$. In Excel, this is IF(RAND()<p,1,0).

Other distributions: The sum of n independent identically distributed Bernoulli random variables with probability p has the binomial distribution with parameters n and p.

History: The Bernoulli distribution was named after Swiss mathematician Jacob Bernoulli (1654-1705).

See *binomial distribution, negative binomial distribution, p-chart, probability distribution, probability mass function.*

best practices – A set of activities that has been demonstrated to produce very good results; the best-known performing process, methodology, or technique.

The term "best practices" is often used in the context of a multi-divisional or multi-location firm that has similar processes in many locations. A best practice is developed by some consensus process (such as the nominal group technique) and then shared across the organizational boundaries.

For example, Wells Fargo (a large bank in North America) has similar processes in many locations. As a result, Wells Fargo is always looking to identify, document, and implement the "best practice" for each process throughout the system.

The challenge, of course, is to identify what is truly the best performing process in light of imperfect information caused by differences in performance measures, process environments, process implementations, and local organizational cultures. To be more accurate, many consulting firms now use the term "leading practice" instead of best practice.

The concept of best practices is closely related to benchmarking and is also closely related to Frederick Taylor's (1911) notion of "one best method" for each process.

See *benchmarking, scientific management.*

beta distribution – A continuous probability distribution used for task times in the absence of data or for a random proportion, such as the proportion of defective items.

Historically, the PERT literature recommended that task times be modeled with the beta distribution with mean $(a + 4m + b)/6$ and variance $(b - a)^2/36$, where the range is (a, b) and m is the mode. The *PERT* entry critically reviews this model.

Parameters: Shape parameters $\alpha > 0$ and $\beta > 0$.

Density and distribution functions: The beta density function for $x > 0$ is $f(x) = x^{\alpha-1}(1-x)^{\beta-1} / B(\alpha,\beta)$, where $B(\alpha,\beta) = \Gamma(\alpha)\Gamma(\beta) / \Gamma(\alpha+\beta)$ is the beta function and $\Gamma(\alpha)$ is the gamma function (not to be confused with the gamma distribution). The beta distribution function has no closed form.

Statistics: The statistics for the beta include range $[0,1]$, mean $\alpha / (\alpha + \beta)$, variance $\alpha\beta / ((\alpha + \beta)^2 (\alpha + \beta + 1))$, and mode $(\alpha-1) / (\alpha + \beta - 2)$ if $\alpha > 1$ and $\beta > 1$; 0 and 1 if $\alpha < 1$ and $\beta < 1$; 0 if $\alpha < 1$ and $\beta \geq 1$ or $\alpha = 1$ and $\beta > 1$; 1 if $\alpha \geq 1$ and $\beta < 1$; $\beta > 1$ or $\alpha > 1$ and $\beta = 1$; the mode does not uniquely exist if $\alpha = \beta = 1$.

Graph: The graph on the right is the beta probability density function (pdf) with parameters $(\alpha, \beta) = (1.5, 5.0)$.

Parameter estimation: Law and Kelton (2000) noted that finding the Maximum Likelihood Estimates for the two parameters requires solving equations involving the digamma function with numeric methods (a non-trivial task) or referencing a table, which may lack accuracy. The method of moments estimates the two parameters based on the sample mean $\overline{x}$ and sample variance s^2 using $\alpha = \overline{x}^2 (1-\overline{x}) / s^2 - \overline{x}$ and $\beta = \overline{x}(1-\overline{x})^2 / s^2 + \overline{x} - 1$.

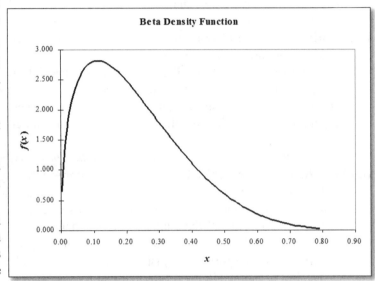

Excel: Excel provides the distribution function BETADIST(x, α, β) and the inverse function BETAINV(p, α, β), but does not provide a beta density function. The beta density function in Excel is x^(α-1)*(1- x)^(β-1)/EXP(GAMMALN(α)+GAMMALN(β)-GAMMALN(α+β)). For the beta distribution transformed to range $[A, B]$, use BETADIST(x, α, β, A, B). The gamma function is EXP(GAMMALN(α)). In Excel 2010, the beta distribution related functions are renamed BETA.DIST and BETA.INV, but still use the same parameters.

Excel simulation: In an Excel simulation, beta random variates can be generated with the inverse transform method using x = BETAINV(1-RAND(), α, β).

See *beta function, gamma distribution, gamma function, probability density function, probability distribution, Project Evaluation and Review Technique (PERT), Weibull distribution.*

beta function – An important function used in statistics; also known as the Euler integral.

The beta function is defined as $B(x,y) = \int_{t=0}^{1} t^{x-1}(1-t)^{y-1} dt$ for $x > 0$ and $y > 0$. The incomplete beta function is $B(x;a,b) = \int_{t=0}^{x} t^{a-1}(1-t)^{b-1} dt$ and the regularized incomplete beta function is $I_x(a,b) = B(x;a,b) / B(a,b)$. The beta and gamma functions are related by $B(x,y) = \Gamma(x)\Gamma(y) / \Gamma(x+y)$. In Excel, $B(x, y)$ can be computed using EXP(GAMMALN(x) + GAMMALN(y) – GAMMALN(x+y)).

See *beta distribution, gamma function, negative binomial distribution.*

beta test – An external test of a pre-production product, typically used in the software development context.

A beta test is an evaluation of new software by a user under actual work conditions and is the final test before release to the public. The purpose of a beta test is to verify that the product functions properly in actual customer use. The term is often used in the context of software released to a limited population of users for evaluation before the final release to customers. In contrast, the alpha test is the first test conducted by the developer in test conditions.

See *agile software development, pilot test, prototype.*

bias – (1) In a statistics context: The difference between the expected value and the true value of a parameter. (2) In a forecasting context: An average forecast error different from zero. (3) In an electrical engineering context: A systematic deviation of a value from a reference value. (4) In a behavioral context: A point of view that prevents impartial judgment on an issue.

See *forecast bias, forecast error metrics.*

bid rigging – A form of fraud where a contract is promised to one party even though for the sake of appearance several other parties also present a bid.

This form of collusion is illegal in most countries. It is a form of price fixing often practiced where contracts are determined by a request for bids, a common practice for government construction contracts. Bid rigging almost always results in economic harm to the organization seeking the bids. In the U.S., price fixing, bid rigging, and other forms of collusion are illegal and subject to criminal prosecution by the Antitrust Division of the U.S. Department of Justice.

See *antitrust laws, bribery, predatory pricing, price fixing.*

big box store – A retailer that competes through stores with large footprints, high volumes, and economies of scale.

Examples of big box stores in North America include Home Depot, Walmart, OfficeMax, and Costco. Carrefour is an example in western Europe. Historically, these big box stores have been built in the suburbs of large metropolitan areas where land was less expensive.

See *category killer, distribution channel, economy of scale.*

bill of lading – A transportation/logistics term for a contract between the shipper and the carrier.

The bill of lading (BOL) serves many purposes, such as (1) providing a receipt for the goods delivered to the carrier for shipment, (2) describing the goods, including the quantity and weight, (3) providing evidence of title, (4) instructing the carrier on how the goods should be shipped, and (5) providing a receiving document for the customer; sometimes abbreviated B/L.

See *consignee, manifest, packing slip, purchasing, receiving, waybill.*

bill of material (BOM) – Information about the assemblies, subassemblies, parts, components, ingredients, and raw materials needed to make one unit of a product; also called bill of materials, bill, product structure, formula, formulation, recipe, or ingredients list. ✪

The **item master** (part master or product master) is a database that provides information for each part (item number, stock keeping unit, material, or product code). A record in the item master may include the item description, unit of measure, classification codes (e.g., ABC classification), make or buy code, accounting method (LIFO or FIFO), leadtime, storage dimensions, on-hand inventory, on-order inventory, and supplier.

The BOM provides the following information for the relationships between items in the item master.

- **BOM structure** – The hierarchical structure for how the product is fabricated or assembled through multiple levels. In a database, this is a double-linked list that shows the "children" and the "parents" for each item.
- **Quantity per** – The quantity of each component required to make one unit of the parent item.
- **Yield** – Yield information is used to inflate production quantities to account for yield losses.
- **Effectivity date** – This indicates when an item is to be used or removed from a BOM.

A simple multi-level BOM product structure for a toy car is shown below. The final product (Item 1, the car assembly) is at level 0 of the BOM. Level 1 in this example has the body and the axle subassembly. Note that plastic is used for both items 2 and 4, but is planned at level 3 rather than at level 2. If plastic were planned at level 2, it would have to be planned again at level 3 when the gross requirements for item 4 were created. Each item should be planned at its "low level code."

Simple bill of material (product structure) for a toy car

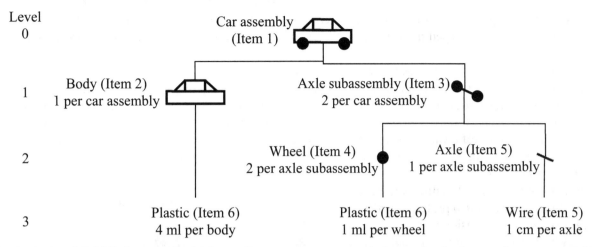

A **single-level BOM** shows only the immediate components needed to make the item, whereas a **multi-level BOM** shows all items. An **indented BOM** is a listing of items where "child" items are intended (moved to the right). The table below is a simple example of the indented bill of material for the above product structure.

Indented bill of material

Level	Item	Item number	Unit of measure	Make/buy
0	Car assembly	1	Each	Make
..1	Body	2	Each	Make
..1	Axle subassembly	3	Each	Make
....2	Wheel	4	Each	Make
....2	Axle	5	Each	Make
......3	Plastic	6	ml	Buy
......3	Wire	5	cm	Buy

A BOM **explosion** shows all components in the BOM, whereas a **where-used report** (sometimes called a BOM implosion) shows a list of the items that use an item. A **single-level where-used report** lists the parent items and quantity per for an item. An **indented where-used report** lists the lowest-level items on the far left side and indents the parent items one place to the right. Each higher-level parent is indented one additional place to the right until the highest-level item (level 0) is reached. **Single-level pegging** is like a single-level where-used report but it only points to higher-level items that have requirements. If a BOM has high **commonality**, items are used by many parent items.

A **planning bill of material**, sometimes called a percentage BOM, super BOM, or pseudo BOM, can be used to plan a family of products using percentages for each option. For example, in the example below, a car manufacturer has historically sold 20% of its cars with radio A, 30% with radio B, and 50% with radio C. The firm forecasts overall sales for cars and uses a planning BOM to drive **Materials Requirements Planning (MRP)** to plan to have about the right number of radios of each type in inventory when needed. A **Final Assembly Schedule (FAS)** is then used to build cars to customer order.

Planning bill of material

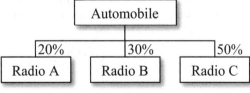

A BOM can define a product as it is designed (**engineering BOM**), as it is built (**manufacturing BOM**), or as it is ordered by customers (**sales BOM**).

The *Master Production Scheduling (MPS)* entry discusses several types of BOM structures and the *Materials Requirement Planning (MRP)* entry explains how the BOM is used in the planning process.

See *ABC classification, backflushing, bill of material implosion, Business Requirements Planning (BRP), commonality, dependent demand, effectivity date, Engineering Change Order (ECO), Enterprise Resources Planning (ERP), Final Assembly Schedule (FAS), formulation, low level code, Master Production Schedule*

(MPS), Materials Requirements Planning (MRP), part number, pegging, phantom bill of material, product family, routing, shop packet, VAT analysis, Warehouse Management System (WMS), where-used report, yield.

bill of material implosion – A manufacturing term used to describe the process of indentifying the "parent" item (or items) for an item in the bill of material; the opposite of a bill of material explosion; also called a where-used report.

See *bill of material (BOM), pegging, where-used report.*

bill of resources – A list of the machine time and labor time required to make one unit of a product.

The bill of resources should only include a few key resources (i.e., those resources that normally have the tightest capacity constraints). Rough Cut Capacity Planning (RCCP) uses the bill of resources to convert the Master Production Schedule (MPS) into a rough cut capacity plan.

See *capacity, Master Production Schedule (MPS), Rough Cut Capacity Planning (RCCP), Theory of Constraints (TOC).*

bimodal distribution – A statistics term for a probability distribution with two identifiable peaks (modes).

A bimodal distribution is usually caused a mixture of two different unimodal distributions. The example on the right shows a histogram for the mixture of two normally distributed random variables with means 14 and 24. (This is a probability mass function because the graph shows frequencies for integer values.)

See *probability distribution, probability mass function.*

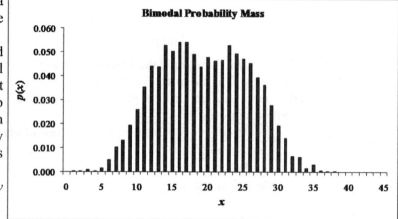

bin – See *warehouse.*

binary logistic regression – See *logistic regression.*

binomial distribution – A discrete probability distribution used for the number of successes (or failures) in n independent trials with probability p for success in each trial.

The binomial is a useful tool for quality control purposes.

Probability mass and cumulative distribution functions: The binomial probability mass function is

$$p(x) = \binom{n}{x} p^x (1-p)^{n-x},$$ where

$$\binom{n}{x} = \frac{n!}{x!(n-x)!}$$ is the binomial coefficient, which is the number of combinations of n things taken x at a time. The cumulative distribution function (CDF) is then

$$F(x) = \Pr(X \le x) = \sum_{i=0}^{\lfloor x \rfloor} \binom{n}{i} p^i (1-p)^{n-i},$$

where $\lfloor x \rfloor$ is the greatest integer less than or equal to x.

Graph: The graph on the right is the binomial probability mass function with $n = 20$ trials of a fair coin ($p = 0.5$).

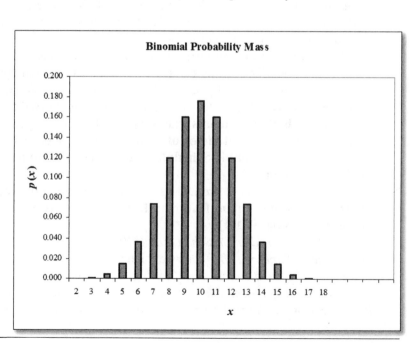

Statistics: Range $\{0, 1, \ldots, n\}$, mean np, variance $np(1-p)$, and mode $\lfloor p(n+1) \rfloor$ or $\lfloor p(n+1) \rfloor - 1$.

Excel: In Excel, the probability mass function is BINOMDIST(x, n, p, FALSE) and the probability distribution function is BINOMDIST(x, n, p, TRUE). Excel does not have an inverse function for the binomial distribution.

Excel simulation: An Excel simulation might use the inverse transform method to generate binomial random variates using a direct search.

Relationships with other distributions: The Bernoulli distribution is Binomial$(1, p)$. The binomial is the sum of n Bernoulli random variables (i.e., if X_1, X_2, $\ldots$, X_n are n independent identically distributed Bernoulli random variables with success probability p, the sum $Y = \sum_{i=1}^{n} X_i$ is binomial). The normal distribution can be used to approximate the binomial when $np \geq 10$ and $np(1-p) \geq 10$. However, a continuity correction factor of 0.5 should be used, which means that $P(X = x)$ for the binomial is estimated using $F(X + 0.5) - F(X - 0.5)$ for the normal. The normal approximation is particularly important for large values of n. The Poisson distribution can be used to approximate the binomial with large n and small p (i.e., $n \geq 20$ and $p \leq 0.05$ or $n \geq 100$ and $np \leq 10$). The binomial is a good approximation for the hypergeometric distribution when the size of the population is much larger than the sample size.

See *bar chart, Bernoulli distribution, combinations, hypergeometric distribution, normal distribution, p-chart, Poisson distribution, probability distribution, probability mass function.*

Black belt – See *lean sigma.*

blanket order – See *blanket purchase order, purchase order (PO).*

blanket purchase order – A contract with a supplier that specifies the price, minimum quantity, and maximum quantity to be purchased over a time period (e.g., one year); sometimes called a blanket or standing order.

Blanket orders usually do not state specific quantities or dates for shipments. Instead, purchase orders (releases) are placed "against" the blanket order to define the quantity and due date for a specific delivery. The advantage of a blanket purchase order for both the customer and the supplier is that it locks in the price so it does not need to be renegotiated very often. The supplier usually gives the customer a quantity discount for the blanket order and may also be able to provide the customer with a reduced leadtime and better on-time performance. Any company representative who knows the purchase order number can purchase items until the value of the blanket order has been exceeded. Providing a blanket order to a supplier may reduce the leadtime and improve on-time delivery.

See *on-time delivery (OTD), purchase order (PO), purchasing, quantity discount.*

blending problem – See *linear programming (LP).*

blind count – An inventory counting practice of not giving counters the current on-hand inventory balance.

With a blind count, the counter is given the item number and location but no information about the count currently in the database. This approach avoids giving counters a reference point that might bias their counts.

See *cycle counting.*

blocking – The lean practice of not allowing a process to produce when an output storage area is full.

Examples of output storage areas include a container, cart, bin, or kanban square. A **kanban square** is rectangular area on a table or floor marked with tape. Blocking is good for **non-bottleneck processes** because it keeps them from overproducing (i.e., producing before the output is needed). Blocking avoids **overproduction** and keeps the total **work-in-process inventory** down to a reasonable level. Blocking for a bottleneck process is bad because it causes the system to lose valuable capacity. Remember that an hour lost on the bottleneck is an hour lost for the entire system. **Starving** and blocking are often discussed in the same context.

See *CONWIP, kanban, lean thinking, starving, Theory of Constraints (TOC), Work-in-Process (WIP) inventory.*

blow through – See *phantom bill of material.*

blue ocean strategy – A business strategy that finds new business opportunities in markets that are not already crowded with competitors.

Kim and Mauborgne (2005), both professors at INSEAD in France, communicated their concept by first describing the traditional "red ocean strategy," where the ocean is blood red with competitors. In contrast, the blue ocean strategy seeks to avoid competing in an existing market space and instead seeks to create an uncontested market space. This approach does not attempt to "beat the competition," but to make the competition irrelevant and create and capture new demand. Those who have been successful with this strategy have found that they can command good margins, high customer loyalty, and highly differentiated products.

Examples of strategic moves that created blue oceans of new, untapped demand:

- Nintendo Wii
- NetJets (fractional Jet ownership)
- Cirque du Soleil (circus reinvented for the entertainment market)
- Starbucks (coffee as low-cost luxury for high-end consumers)

- eBay (online auctioning)
- Sony Walkman (personal portable stereos)
- Hybrid and electric automobiles
- Chrysler minivan
- Apple iPad
- Dell's built-to-order computers

See *operations strategy*.

BOL – See *bill of lading*.

BOM – See *bill of material (BOM)*.

bonded warehouse – See *warehouse*.

booking curve – A graph used to show the expected cumulative demand for a scheduled (booked) service (such as an airline) over time and compare it to the actual cumulative bookings (demand); sometimes called the sales booking curve.

A booking curve is an important yield management tool that guides decision makers with respect to pricing and capacity allocation as the service date (e.g., date of departure) draws near. The graph on the right shows a typical booking curve for an airline. Note that the *x*-axis counts down the number of days until departure. (Some organizations draw the curve with the *x*-axes counting up from a negative value.) The middle dotted line is the expected cumulative demand. In

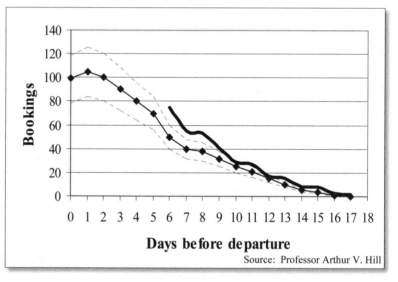

Source: Professor Arthur V. Hill

this example, the expected cumulative demand declines slightly on the day of departure. This could be caused by "no-shows" and last-minute cancellations. The heavy line is the actual cumulative demand from 17 days before departure to 6 days before departure.

People involved in yield management track the actual cumulative demand and compare it to the expected cumulative demand on the booking curve. When the actual cumulative demand is outside the upper or lower control policy limits (shown in the example with dashed lines), decision makers might intervene to either change prices or reallocate capacity. For instance, in the example above, the actual cumulative demand is above the expected cumulative demand and above the control limits. This suggests that decision makers should raise the price or open up more capacity to try to "capture" more revenue.

See *bookings*, *elasticity*, *yield management*.

bookings – The sum of the value of all orders received (but not necessarily shipped) after subtracting all discounts, coupons, allowances, and rebates.

Bookings are recorded in the period the order is received, which is often different from the period the product is shipped and also different from the period the sales are recorded.

See *booking curve*, *demand*.

BOR – See *bill of resources*.

bottleneck – Any system constraint that holds the organization back from greater achievement of its goals. ✪

In a system, a bottleneck is any resource that has **capacity** less than the demand placed on it. Goldratt (1992), who developed the **theory of constraints**, expanded this definition to include any philosophies, assumptions, and mindsets that limit a system from performing better. When the bottleneck is the market, the organization can achieve higher profits by growing the market by offering better products and services.

See *capacity, Herbie, Theory of Constraints (TOC), transfer batch, utilization.*

bounded rationality – The concept that human and firm behavior is limited by partial information and is unable to thoroughly evaluate all alternatives.

Many models in the social sciences and in economics assume that people and firms are completely rational and will always make choices that they believe will achieve their goals. However, Herbert Simon (1957) pointed out that people are only partly rational and often behave irrationally in many ways. Simon noted that people have limits in formulating and solving complex problems and in processing (receiving, storing, retrieving, transmitting) information. As a result, people and firms often use simple rules (heuristics) to make decisions because of the complexity of evaluating all alternatives.

See *paradigm, satisficing.*

box and whisker diagram – See *box plot.*

box plot – A simple descriptive statistics tool for graphing information to show the central tendency and dispersion of a random variable; also known as a boxplot, box-and-whisker diagram, and Tukey box plot.

As shown in the simple example below, a box plot shows five values: the smallest value (the sample minimum), lower quartile, median, upper quartile, and largest observation (sample maximum). A box plot may also indicate outliers. The endpoints of the line are usually defined as the smallest and largest values not considered to be outliers; however, these endpoints could be defined as the lowest and highest values within 1.5 *IQR*, where *IQR* is the interquartile range. Some box plots have an additional dot or line through the box to show the mean.

See *interquartile range, mean, median, range.*

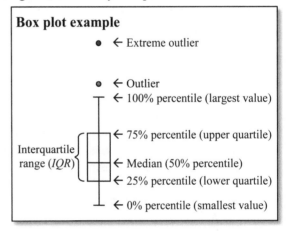

Box plot example

- ● ← Extreme outlier
- ◉ ← Outlier
- ← 100% percentile (largest value)
- ← 75% percentile (upper quartile)
- Interquartile range (*IQR*)
- ← Median (50% percentile)
- ← 25% percentile (lower quartile)
- ← 0% percentile (smallest value)

boxcar – An enclosed railcar, typically 40 to 50 feet long used for packaged freight and bulk commodities.

See *logistics.*

Box-Jenkins forecasting – A sophisticated statistical time series forecasting technique.

Box-Jenkins methods develop forecasts as a function of the actual demands and the forecast errors at lagged time intervals using both moving average (MA) and autoregressive (AR) terms. The autoregressive model is a weighted sum of the past actual data. The AR model of order p is $x_t = \delta + \sum_{k=1}^{p} \phi_k x_{t-k} + \varepsilon_t$, where x_t is the actual value in period t and $\delta = \left(1 - \sum_{k=1}^{p} \phi_k\right)\mu$ (with process mean μ). The constants ϕ_k are estimated using a least squares direct search where ε_t is the error in period t. The AR model can be written as a regression model using past values of a variable to predict future values.

The moving average is a weighted sum of the past forecast errors. The MA model of order q is $x_t = \mu + \sum_{k=1}^{q} \theta_k \varepsilon_{t-k}$, where μ is the process mean. The parameters θ_k are estimated using a least squares direct search where ε_{t-k} is the error in period $t - k$. The MA model can be written as a regression model using past errors to predict future values. The autoregressive-moving average model ARMA(p, q) combines these with

$x_t = \sum_{k=1}^{p} \phi_k x_{t-k} + \sum_{k=1}^{q} \theta_k \varepsilon_{t-k}$. Trend is handled with regular differencing $x_t' = x_t - x_{t-1}$ and seasonality is handled with seasonal differencing $x_t' = x_t - x_{t-L}$, where the time series has an L period season.

The Autoregressive Integrated Moving Average (ARIMA) model combines the AR and MA models with differencing. A forecasting model with p AR terms, d differencing terms, and q MA terms is shown as ARIMA(p, d, q). Simple exponential smoothing can be shown to be equivalent to the ARIMA(0,1,1) model.

The Box-Jenkins methodology has three main steps:

1. **Specification** – Select which lagged terms should be included in the model.

2. **Estimation** – Estimate the least squares parameters ϕ_k and θ_k for the model specified in the first step. A direct search method, such as the Marquardt search, is applied to accomplish this.

3. **Diagnostic checking** – Check the sample autocorrelations and sample partial autocorrelations[5] for opportunities to improve the model by adding (or deleting) terms. A chi-square test is performed to determine if the partial correlations are significant. A correlogram graph is an important part of this process.

The table to the right shows typical rules for interpreting the correlogram and adding new terms to a model.

Automatic Box-Jenkins model fitting software requires less human intervention. Multivariate Box-Jenkins models create forecasts based on multiple time series.

Some empirical studies have shown that Box-Jenkins forecasting models do not consistently perform better than much simpler exponential smoothing methods. Recommended references include Box, Jenkins, Reinsel, and Jenkins (1994) and Armstrong (2000).

Box-Jenkins forecasting model identification

Shape	Model
Decaying to zero	AR
Alternating, decaying to zero	AR
One or more spikes; otherwise zero	MA
Decay starting after a few lags	ARMA
All close to zero	Random
High values at fixed intervals	Seasonality
Not decaying to zero	Take first differences

See the Institute of Business Forecasting & Planning website (www.ibf.org) for more information.

See *autocorrelation, chi-square goodness of fit test, Durbin-Watson statistic, econometric forecasting, exponential smoothing, forecast error metrics, forecasting, linear regression, moving average, seasonality, time series forecasting*.

Box-Muller method – See *normal distribution*.

BPR – See *Business Process Re-engineering (BPR)*.

brainstorming – Using a group of people to generate creative ideas to solve a problem.

Nearly all brainstorming approaches do not allow for debate during the brainstorming session. This is because it is important to allow a free flow of many ideas before evaluating any of them. The **Nominal Group Technique (NGT)** is one of the more popular structured approaches to brainstorming. In contrast, the **devil's advocate** approach assigns the role of challenging ideas to a person or group of people. These challenges should not be allowed until after the brainstorming process has generated many creative ideas.

See *affinity diagram, causal map, Delphi forecasting, devil's advocate, focus group, force field analysis, forming-storming-norming-performing model, ideation, impact wheel, lean sigma, Nominal Group Technique (NGT), parking lot, process map, quality circles*.

brand – A set of associations linked to a name, mark, or symbol associated with a product or service.

A brand is much like a reputation. It is a surrogate measure of quality built over many years and many contacts with the products, services, and people associated with the brand. However, a brand can be damaged quickly. For

Schwinn Panther II from 1959

---

[5] *The partial autocorrelation at lag k is the autocorrelation between x_t and x_{t-k} that is not accounted for by lags 1 through $k - 1$.*

example, when Firestone tires were implicated in many SUV rollovers and deaths in the 1990s, the Firestone brand was damaged significantly.

Brands can be purchased and used for competitive advantage. For example, the Schwinn bike brand, founded in Chicago in 1891, ran into financial difficulty and was bought by Dorel Industries in 2004. Similarly, when Nordic Track faced financial problems, the brand was purchased by another firm. The Schwinn and Nordic Track brands continue to live on long after the firms that developed them went out of business.

See *brand equity, category management, service guarantee*.

brand equity – The value assigned to an organization's product or service.

See *brand*.

breadboard – A proof-of-concept modeling technique that represents how a product will work, but not how a product will look.

See *New Product Development (NPD), prototype*.

break-even analysis – A financial calculation for determining the unit sales required to cover costs. ✪

If the demand is below the break-even point, the costs will exceed the revenues. Break-even analysis focuses on the relationships between fixed cost, variable cost, and profit.

Break-even analysis is a rather crude approach to financial analysis. Most finance professors recommend using a better approach, such as net present value or Economic Value Added (EVA).

See *financial performance metrics, payback period*.

break-even point – See *break-even analysis*.

bribery – The practice of an individual or corporation offering, giving, soliciting, or taking anything of value in exchange for favors or influence; both the giver and receiver are said to be participating in bribery.

A bribe can take the form of money, gift, property, privilege, vote, discount, donation, job, promotion, sexual favor, or promise thereof. Bribes are usually made in secret and are usually considered dishonest. In most business and government contexts around the world, bribes are illegal. Examples of bribery include:

• A contractor kicks back part of a payment to the government official who selected the company for the job.
• A sales representative pays money "under the table" to a customer's purchasing agent for selecting a product.
• A pharmaceutical or medical device company offers free trips to doctors who prescribe its drug or device.
• A sporting officiator or athlete influences the outcome of a sporting event in exchange for money.

Some people humorously assert that "the difference between a bribe and a payment is a receipt." However, that is not necessarily true because a receipt does not make an illegal or dishonest transaction into a proper one.

What is considered a bribe varies by culture, legal system, and context. The word "bribe" is sometimes used more generally to mean any type of incentive used to change or support behavior. For example, political campaign contributions in the form of cash are considered criminal acts of bribery in some countries, while in the U.S. they are legal. Tipping is considered bribery in some societies, while in others it is expected. In some countries, bribes are necessary for citizens to procure basic medical care, security, transportation, and customs clearance. Bribery is particularly common in countries with under-developed legal systems.

In the purchasing context, bribes are sometimes used by agents of suppliers to influence buying authorities to select their supplier for a contract. These bribes are sometimes called **kickbacks**. In 1977, the U.S. Congress passed the **Foreign Corrupt Practices Act**, which made it illegal for an American corporation to bribe a foreign government official with money or gifts in hopes of landing or maintaining important business contacts. According to the act, all publicly traded companies must keep records of all business transactions even if the companies do not trade internationally to ensure that this act is not being violated. However, this act has exceptions, which are used by many U.S. corporations. For example, the act permits "grease payments," which are incentives paid to foreign officials to expedite paperwork and ensure the receipt of licenses or permits.

The book of Proverbs in the Bible, written hundreds of years before Christ, condemns bribes: "A wicked man accepts a bribe in secret to pervert the course of justice" (Proverbs 17:23), and "By justice a king gives a country stability, but one who is greedy for bribes tears it down" (Proverbs 29:4).

See *antitrust laws, bid rigging, predatory pricing, price fixing, purchasing*.

broker – An individual or firm that acts as an intermediary (an agent) between a buyer and seller to negotiate contracts, purchases, or sales in exchange for a commission.

Brokers almost never take possession of the goods. A broker can represent either the buyer or the seller, and in some cases both. The broker's compensation is commonly called a **brokerage fee**.

See *distributor, gray market reseller, supply chain management, wholesaler.*

Brooke's Law – See *project management.*

brownfield – See *greenfield.*

BRP – See *Business Requirements Planning.*

buffer management – A Theory of Constraints (TOC) concept of strategically placing "extra" inventory or a time cushion in front of constrained resources to protect the system from disruption.

See *Theory of Constraints (TOC).*

buffer stock – See *safety stock.*

build to order (BTO) – A process that produces products in response to a customer order.

Some authors equate BTO to assemble to order (ATO), while others equate it to make to order (MTO). Gunasekaran and Ngai (2005, page 424) noted "some confusion in these writings between MTO and BTO. The leadtimes are longer in MTO than in BTO. In MTO, components and parts are made and then assembled. In the case of BTO, the components and parts are ready for assembly." This quote suggests that these authors equate BTO and ATO.

See *assemble to order (ATO), make to order (MTO), respond to order (RTO).*

bullwhip effect – A pattern of increasing variability in the demand from the customer back to the retailer, back to the distributor, back to the manufacturer, back to the supplier, etc. ✪

The four causes of the bullwhip effect include (1) forecast updating, (2) periodic ordering/order batching, (3) price fluctuations, and (4) shortage gaming. Even if customer demand is constant, the raw materials supplier will often see high variability in demand as fluctuations are amplified along the supply chain.

The primary solution to this problem is for the retailer to regularly share actual and projected demand information. Other solutions include vendor-managed inventories (VMI), reducing order sizes by reducing ordering costs, using everyday low prices (instead of promotional prices), avoiding allocation based on orders placed, and reducing cycle time.

The following is a more complete explanation of the subject excerpted from "The Bullwhip Effect in Supply Chains," by Lee, Padmanabhan, and Whang (1997), with some extensions.

The demand forecast updating problem – Ordinarily, every company in a supply chain forecasts its demand myopically by looking at the orders it has recently received from its customers. Each organization in the supply chain sees fluctuations in customer demand and acts rationally to create even greater fluctuations for the upstream suppliers. This occurs even when the ultimate demand is relatively stable.

Mitigation – Share sales information. Use demand data coming from the furthest downstream points (e.g., point-of-sale data) throughout the supply chain. Reduce the number of stocking points and make aggregate forecasts to improve forecast accuracy. Apply lean principles to reduce cycle times, reduce the forecast horizon, and improve forecast accuracy. Use technologies, such as point-of-sale (POS) data collection, Electronic Data Interchange (EDI), and vendor-managed inventories (VMI), to improve data accuracy, data availability, and data timeliness. Dampen trends in forecasts.

The order batching problem – Companies sending orders to upstream suppliers usually do so periodically, ordering batches that last several days or weeks, which reduces transportation costs, transaction costs, or both. These tactics contribute to larger demand fluctuations further up the chain.

Mitigation – Reduce transaction costs through various forms of electronic ordering, reduce setup costs by applying SMED, offer discounts for mixed-load ordering (to reduce the demand for solid loads of one product), use third party logistics providers (3PLs) to economically combine many small replenishments for/to many suppliers/customers, and do not offer quantity discounts to encourage customers to place large orders.

The price fluctuation problem – Frequent price changes (both up and down) can lead buyers to purchase large quantities when prices are low and defer buying when prices are high. This forward buying practice is common in the grocery industry and creates havoc upstream in the supply chain.

Mitigation – Encourage sellers to stabilize their prices (e.g., use everyday low prices). Activity-based costing systems can highlight excessive costs in the supply chain caused by price fluctuations and forward buying. This helps provide incentives for the entire chain to operate with relatively stable prices.

The rationing and shortage gaming problem – Cyclical industries face alternating periods of oversupply and undersupply. When buyers know that a shortage is imminent and rationing will occur, they will often increase the size of their orders to ensure that they get the amounts they need.

Mitigation – Allocate inventory among customers based on past usage, not on present orders, and share information on sales, capacity, and inventory so buyers are not surprised by shortages.

The underweighting open orders problem – Buyers sometimes seem to forget about orders that have already been placed and focus on the on-hand physical inventory rather than the inventory position (on-hand plus on-order). The following teaching question illustrates this point, "I have a headache and take two aspirin. Five minutes later, I still have a headache. Should I take two more?"

Mitigation – Use a system that gives good visibility to open orders and the inventory position. Train suppliers to avoid foolishly applying "lean systems" that place orders based only on the on-hand inventory without regard for the on-order quantities.

More recently, Geary, Disney, and Towill (2006) identified ten causes of the bullwhip effect.

See *beer game, buyer/planner, Everyday Low Pricing (EDLP), forward buy, leadtime syndrome, open order, Parkinson's Laws, quantity discount, SCOR Model, supply chain management, Third Party Logistics (3PL) provider, upstream, value chain.*

burden rate – Overhead allocated to production based on labor or machine hours; also called overhead rate.

For example, a firm might allocate $200 of plant overhead per direct labor hour for an order going through the plant. The burden rate is then $200 per hour. Managers should be careful to avoid the "death spiral," which is the practice of outsourcing based on full cost only to find increased overhead for the remaining products.

See *Activity Based Costing (ABC), make versus buy decision, outsourcing, overhead, setup cost, standard cost.*

business capability – A business function that an organization performs or can perform.

A description of a business capability should separate the function from the process. In other words, the description of a capability should describe what can be done without describing the details of how it is done, what technology is used, or who performs it. The details of the people, process, and technology are prone to change fairly often, but the capability will not change very often.

A business capability framework is a collection of an organization's business capabilities organized in a hierarchy. For example, at the highest level, a firm might have six business capabilities: plan, buy, move, sell, enable, and analyze. Each of these can then be broken down at the next level into many more capabilities.

See *process capability and performance.*

business case – The economic justification for a proposed project or product that often includes estimates of both the economic and non-economic benefits; also called a business case analysis.

A business case is intended to answer two fundamental business questions: Why this project? Why now? Answering these two questions helps the decision maker(s) prioritize the project vis-à-vis other projects. The best way to collect the data to answer these two questions is to follow these four steps:

1. **Gather baseline data** – For example, the cycle time for order entry for the time period X to Y has increased from A to B.
2. **Quantify the problem or opportunity** – For example, what is the cost of excessive order entry cycle time?
3. **Analyze stakeholders' needs (especially customers)** – For example, analyze raw comments from surveys and focus groups.
4. **Define "best-in-class" performance** – For example, our benchmark partner has a cycle time for a process that is half of ours.

   In some cases, a business case analysis will analyze two or more competing business alternatives.

   See *focus group, project charter, stakeholder.*

Business Continuity Management (BCM) – A management process for identifying potential events that might threaten an organization and building safeguards that protect the interests of the stakeholders from those risks; also known as Business Continuity Planning (BCP).

BCM integrates the disciplines of emergency management, crisis management, business continuity, and IT disaster recovery with the goal of creating organizational resilience, which is the ability to withstand and reduce the impact of a crisis event. BCM provides the contingency planning process for sustaining operations during a disaster, such as labor unrest, natural disaster, and war.

The BCM process entails (1) proactively identifying and managing risks to critical operations, (2) developing continuity strategies and contingency plans that ensure an effective recovery of critical operations within a predefined time period after a crisis event, (3) periodically exercising and reviewing BCM arrangements, and (4) creating a risk management culture by embedding BCM into day-to-day operations and business decisions.

The Council of Supply Chain Management Professionals provides suggestions for helping companies do continuity planning in its document *Securing the Supply Chain Research*. A copy of this research is available on www.cscmp.org.

See *error proofing, Failure Mode and Effects Analysis (FMEA), resilience, stakeholder.*

Business Continuity Planning (BCP) – See *Business Continuity Management (BCM).*

business intelligence – A computer-based decision support system used to gather, store, retrieve, and analyze data to help managers make better business decisions; sometimes known as BI.

A good business intelligence system should provide decision makers with good quality and timely information on:
- Sales (e.g., historical sales by product, region, etc.)
- Customers (e.g., demographics of current customers)
- Markets (e.g., market position)
- Industry (e.g., changes in the economy, expected regulatory changes)
- Operations (e.g., historical performance, capabilities)
- Competitors (e.g., capabilities, products, prices)
- Business partners (e.g., capabilities)

Ideally, BI technologies provide historical, current, and predictive views for all of the above. Although BI focuses more on internal activities rather than competitive intelligence, it can include both. Most BI applications are built on a data warehouse.

See *data mining, Decision Support System (DSS), knowledge management, learning organization.*

Business Process Management (BPM) – An information systems approach for improving business processes through the application of software tools, ideally resulting in a robust, efficient, and adaptable information system to support the business.

BPM generally includes tools for process design, process execution, and process monitoring. Information system tools for process design include tools for documenting processes (process maps and data models) and computer simulation. These tools often have graphical and visual interfaces. Information system tools for process execution often start with a graphical model of the process and use business rules to quickly develop an information system that supports the process. Information system tools for process monitoring capture real-time information so the process can be controlled. For example, a factory manager might want to track an order as it passes through the plant.

See *Business Process Re-engineering (BPR), process improvement program, process map, real-time, robust.*

business process mapping – See *process mapping.*

business process outsourcing – The practice of outsourcing non-core internal services to third parties; sometimes abbreviated BPO.

Typical outsourced functions include logistics, accounts payable, accounts receivable, payroll, information systems, and human resources. For example, Best Buy outsourced much of its information systems development to Accenture. In North America, Accenture and IBM are two of the larger BPO service providers.

See *contract manufacturer, human resources, Maintenance-Repair-Operations (MRO), make versus buy decision, outsourcing, purchasing, Service Level Agreement (SLA), service management, sourcing, supply chain management.*

Business Process Re-engineering (BPR) – A radical change in the way that an organization operates.

Business Process Re-engineering (BPR) involves a fundamental rethinking of a business system. BPR typically includes eliminating non-value-added steps, automating some steps, changing organization charts, and restructuring reward systems. It often includes **job enlargement**, which reduces the number of queues and gives the customer a single point of contact. In many firms, BPR has a bad reputation because it is associated with downsizing (firing people). Hammer and Champy (1993) are credited with popularizing BPR and their website www.hammerandco.com offers books and maturity models.

See *5 Whys, Business Process Management (BPM), error proofing, job enlargement, kaikaku, process improvement program, stakeholder analysis, standardized work, work simplification.*

Business Requirements Planning (BRP) – BRP is a conceptual model showing how business planning, master planning, materials planning, and capacity planning processes should work together.

The BRP model starts the business plan (profits), sales plan (revenues), and production plan (sales dollars, cost, or aggregate units). Once the production plan has been checked by Resource Requirements Planning (RRP) to ensure that the resources are available and that the top-level plans are consistent, it is used as input to the Master Production Schedule (MPS), which is a plan (in units) for the firm's end items (or major subassemblies). The diagram below shows the BRP model (Schultz 1989).

Materials Requirements Planning (MRP) translates the MPS into a materials plan (orders defined by quantities and due dates). Capacity Requirements Planning (CRP) translates the materials plan into a capacity plan (load report) for each workcenter, which is defined in terms of planned shop hours per day. Almost no systems have a computer-based "closed-loop" back to the MPS or the materials plan. The feedback is managed by manual intervention in the schedule to adjust the materials plan or add, remove, or move capacity as needed.

Ultimately, the system creates both purchase orders for suppliers and shop orders for the firm's own factories. Buyer/planners convert planned orders in the action bucket (the first period) into open orders (scheduled receipts). This planning process is supported by the ERP database, which provides information on items (the item master), the bill of material (the linked list of items required for each item), and the routings (the sequence of steps required to make an item).

The term "Business Requirements Planning" is not widely used. The concept is closely related to Sales and Operations Planning, which has become a standard term in North America. The *Master Production Schedule (MPS)* and *Sales & Operations Planning* consider very similar issues.

Business Requirements Planning framework

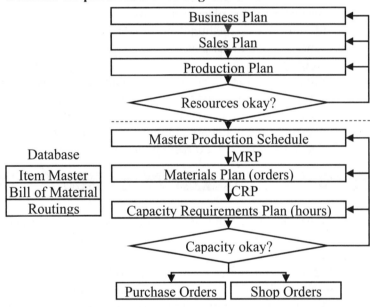

See *bill of material (BOM), Capacity Requirements Planning (CRP), closed-loop MRP, Enterprise Resources Planning (ERP), Master Production Schedule (MPS), Materials Requirements Planning (MRP), open order, production planning, Resource Requirements Planning (RRP), Rough Cut Capacity Planning (RCCP), Sales & Operations Planning (S&OP).*

buy-back contract – An agreement between a buyer and seller that allows the buyer to return unsold inventory up to a specified amount at an agreed-upon price.

The most common buy-back contract is in the retail supply chain, where manufacturers or distributors allow retailers to return products, such as music CDs, with a **restocking charge**. Buy-back contracts increase the optimal order quantity for the seller, which results in the higher product availability for customers and lower lost sales for the seller. These contracts can result in higher profits for both the buyer and the seller. On the negative side, a buy-back contract can result in excess inventory for the supplier. In addition, the supply chain might overreact to the larger orders from sellers and assume that the larger orders represent true demand, when in fact the sellers are just buying for inventory. The most effective products for buy-back contracts are those with low variable cost, such as music, software, books, and magazines, so the supplier can keep the surplus.

A **revenue sharing contract** is similar to a buy-back contract in that it shares the risks between the buyer and the seller and encourages the seller to carry more inventory, which can reduce the probability of a lost sale. As with buy-back contracts, larger orders from buyers can be misinterpreted as indications of increased demand.

Quantity flexible contracts allow the buyer to modify orders after they have been placed within limits. These contracts help match supply and demand and do a better job of communicating the true demand. However, these contracts often require the supplier to have flexible capacity.

According to Cachon (2001, p. 2), "a contract is said to **coordinate the supply chain** if the set of supply chain optimal actions is a Nash equilibrium, i.e., no firm has a profitable unilateral deviation from the set of supply chain optimal actions." Cachon and Lariviere (2005) showed that a continuum of revenue-sharing contracts can coordinate a supply chain with a supplier selling to multiple competing retailers, when the retailers' sole decision is the quantity to purchase from the supplier. In addition, they show that coordinating revenue-sharing contracts can be implemented as profit-sharing contracts.

See *fixed price contract, purchasing, Return Material Authorization (RMA), return to vendor, risk sharing contract, supply chain management.*

buyer/planner – A person who has the dual responsibility of a buyer (selecting suppliers, negotiating agreements, and placing purchase orders with suppliers) and a planner (planning materials for the factory).

In many firms, the buying responsibility is separated from the planning responsibility. The buyer is responsible only for placing **purchase orders** with suppliers and the planner handles releasing (starting) and expediting (or de-expediting) **manufacturing orders** (factory orders). The advantages of combining the two roles into a single buyer/planner role include:

- Both roles require essentially the same skills – The ability to plan ahead, use systems, know part numbers, product structures, and suppliers, understand capacity constraints, know how to expedite (and de-expedite) orders, and understand true customer requirements and priorities.
- Firms can find synergy between the two roles – The planning function in the factory is affected by the availability of materials and the buying function is affected by factory priorities.

See *bullwhip effect, expediting, firm planned order, purchase order (PO), purchasing, supplier scorecard.*

C

C&E diagram – A causal map using the Ishikawa (fishbone) diagram.

See *C&E matrix, causal map, lean sigma, Root Cause Analysis (RCA), Root Cause Tree, seven tools of quality.*

C&E Matrix – An analysis tool used to collect subjective data to make quantitative estimates of the impact of the Key Process Input Variables (KPIVs) on Key Process Output Variables (KPOVs) to identify the most important KPIVs for a process improvement program; also known as a cause and effect matrix.

In any process improvement program, it is important to determine which **Key Process Input Variables (KPIVs)** have the most impact on the **Key Process Output Variables (KPOVs)**. The C&E Matrix is a practical way to collect subjective estimates of the importance of the KPIVs on the KPOVs.

Building the C&E Matrix begins by defining the KPOVs along the columns on the top of the matrix (table) and the KPIVs along the rows on the left side. (See the example below.) Experts then estimate the importance of each KPOV to the customer. This is typically done on a 1-10 scale, where 1 is unimportant and 10 is critically important. Each pair of input and output variables is then scored on a 0-10 scale, where the score is the degree to which the input variable impacts (causes) the output variable. The sum of the weighted scores is then used to rank the input variables to determine which input variables deserve the most attention and analysis.

The example below illustrates the matrix for three KPOVs and seven KPIVs. KPOV 1 to KPOV 3 are the names of the output variables with customer importance weights (w_1, w_2, w_3). The $s_{i,j}$ values are the impact scores for input (KPIV) variable i on output (KPOV) variable j. The weighted score for each KPIV is then calculated as the sum of the weights and the impact scores. Stated mathematically, the weighted score for the *i*-th KPIV is defined as $ws_i = \sum_{j=1}^{J} w_j s_{i,j}$, where J is the number of KPOVs. These scores are then ranked in the far right column.

C&E Matrix example

			Key Process Output Variables				
		KPOV importance to customers	w_1	w_2	w_3	Weighted	
		KPOV name	KPOV 1	KPOV 2	KPOV 3	score	Rank
Key Process Input Variables	Process step 1	KPIV 1	$s_{1,1}$	$s_{1,2}$	$s_{1,3}$	ws_1	r_1
		KPIV 2	$s_{2,1}$	$s_{2,2}$	$s_{2,3}$	ws_2	r_2
	Process step 2	KPIV 3	$s_{3,1}$	$s_{3,2}$	$s_{3,3}$	ws_3	r_3
		KPIV 4	$s_{4,1}$	$s_{4,2}$	$s_{4,3}$	ws_4	r_4
	Process step 3	KPIV 5	$s_{5,1}$	$s_{5,2}$	$s_{5,3}$	ws_5	r_5
		KPIV 6	$s_{6,1}$	$s_{6,2}$	$s_{6,3}$	ws_6	r_6
		KPIV 7	$s_{7,1}$	$s_{7,2}$	$s_{7,3}$	ws_7	r_7

The C&E Matrix is closely related to the C&E Diagram and the causal map. The C&E Matrix is a special type of causal map represented in matrix form that has only one set of input variables (the KPIVs) and one set of output variables (the KPOVs). This can be generalized by including all variables on both rows and columns. This generalized matrix, called the adjacency matrix in the academic literature, allows for input variables to cause other input variables. This matrix can also be represented as a causal map. The "reachability" matrix is an extension of the adjacency matrix and represents how many steps it takes to get from one node to another in the network. Scavarda, Bouzdine-Chameeva, Goldstein, Hays, and Hill (2006) discussed many of these issues.

Some firms and consultants confuse a C&E Matrix with the Kepner-Tregoe Model (KT). KT is a simple scoring system for alternative courses of action, where each alternative is scored on a number of different dimensions, and each dimension has an assigned weight. The idea is that the alternative with the highest weighted sum is likely to be the best one. In contrast, the C&E Matrix scores input variables that *cause* output variables. In the KT Model, the dimensions do not cause the alternatives; they simply evaluate them.

See *C&E Diagram, causal map, Kepner-Tregoe Model, Key Process Output Variable (KPOV), lean sigma.*

CAD – See *Computer Aided Design.*

CAD/CAM – See *Computer Aided Design/Computer Aided Manufacturing.*

CAGR – See *Compounded Annual Growth Rate (CAGR).*

CAI – See *Computer Aided Inspection.*

call center – An organization that provides remote customer contact via telephone and may conduct outgoing marketing and telemarketing activities.

A **call center** can provide customer service such as (1) a **help desk** operation that provides technical support for software or hardware, (2) a **reservations center** for a hotel, airline, or other service, (3) a **dispatch operation** that sends technicians or other servers on service calls, (4) an **order entry** center that accepts orders for products from customers, and (5) a **customer service center** that provides other types of customer help.

A well-managed call center can have a major impact on customer relationships and on firm profitability. Call center management software monitors system status (number in queue, average talk time, etc.) and measures customer representative productivity. Advanced systems also provide forecasting and scheduling assistance. Well-managed call centers receive customer requests for help through phone calls, faxes, e-mails, regular mail, and information coming in through the Internet. Representatives respond via interpersonal conversations on the phone, phone messages sent automatically, fax-on-demand, interactive voice responses, and e-mails. Web-based information can provide help by dealing with a large percentage of common problems that customers might have and can provide downloadable files for customers. By taking advantage of integrated voice, video, and data, information can be delivered in a variety of compelling ways that enhance the user experience, encourage customer self-service, and dramatically reduce the cost of providing customer support.

The **Erlang C formula** is commonly used to determine staffing levels in any time period. (See the *queuing theory* entry for more information.)

See *Automatic Call Distributor (ACD)*, *cross-selling*, *customer service*, *help desk*, *knowledge management*, *order entry*, *pooling*, *queuing theory*, *service management*, *shrinkage*.

CAM – See *Computer Aided Manufacturing*.

cannibalization – The sales of a new product that will be taken from the firm's other products.

For example, a new computer model might take sales from an existing model and therefore add nothing to the firm's overall market share or bottom line.

See *market share*.

cap and trade – A system of financial incentives put in place by the government to encourage corporations to reduce pollution.

The government issues emission permits that set limits (caps) for the pollution that can be emitted. Companies that produce fewer emissions can sell their excess pollution credits to those that produce more.

See *carbon footprint*, *green manufacturing*, *sustainability*.

capability – See *Design for Six Sigma (DFSS)*, *process capability and performance*.

Capability Maturity Model (CMM) – A five-level methodology for measuring and improving processes.

CMM began as an approach for evaluating the "maturity" of software development organizations, but has since been extended to other organizations. Many capability maturity models have been developed for software acquisition, project management, new product development, and supply chain management. This discussion focuses on the Capability Maturity Model for Software (SW-CMM), which is one of the best-known products of the Carnegie Mellon University Software Engineering Institute (SEI). CMM is based heavily on the book *Managing the Software Process* (Humphries 1989). The actual development of the SW-CMM was done by the SEI at Carnegie Mellon University and the Mitre Corporation in response to a request to provide the federal government with a method for assessing the capability of its software contractors.

The SW-CMM model is used to score an organization on five maturity levels. Each maturity level includes a set of process goals. The five CMM levels follow:

Level 1: Initial – The software process is characterized as ad hoc and occasionally even chaotic. Few processes are defined and success depends on individual effort and heroics. Maturity level 1 success depends on having quality people. In spite of this ad hoc, chaotic environment, maturity level 1 organizations often produce products and services that work; however, they frequently exceed project budgets and schedules. Maturity level 1 organizations are characterized by a tendency to over-commit, abandon processes in the time of crisis, repeat past failures, and fail to repeat past successes.

Level 2: Repeatable – Basic project management processes are established to track cost and schedule activities. The minimum process discipline is in place to repeat earlier successes on projects with similar applications and scope. There is still a significant risk of exceeding cost and time estimates. Process discipline helps ensure that existing practices are retained during times of stress. When these practices are in place, projects are performed and managed according to their documented plans. Project status and the delivery of services are visible to management at defined points (for example, at major milestones and at the completion of major tasks).

Level 3: Defined – The software process for both management and engineering activities is documented, standardized, and integrated into a standard software process for the organization. All projects use an approved, tailored version of the organization's standard software process for developing and maintaining software. A critical distinction between maturity levels 2 and 3 is the scope of standards, process descriptions, and procedures. At level 2, the standards, process descriptions, and procedures may be quite different in each specific instance of the process (for example, on a particular project). At maturity level 3, the standards, process descriptions, and procedures for a project are tailored from the organization's set of standard processes to suit a particular project or organizational unit.

Level 4: Managed – Detailed measures of the software process and product quality are collected. Both the software process and products are quantitatively understood and controlled. Using precise measurements, management can effectively control the software development effort. In particular, management can identify ways to adjust and adapt the process to particular projects without measurable losses of quality or deviations from specifications. At this level, the organization sets a quantitative quality goal for both the software process and software maintenance. A critical distinction between maturity level 3 and maturity level 4 is the predictability of process performance. At maturity level 4, the process performance is controlled using statistical and other quantitative techniques and is quantitatively predictable.

Level 5: Optimizing – Maturity level 5 focuses on continually improving process performance through both incremental and innovative technological improvements. Quantitative process-improvement objectives for the organization are established, continually revised to reflect changing business objectives, and used as criteria in managing process improvement. The effects of deployed process improvements are measured and evaluated against the quantitative process-improvement objectives. Both the defined processes and the organization's set of standard processes are targets of measurable improvement activities. Process improvements to address common causes of process variation and measurably improve the organization's processes are identified, evaluated, and deployed. The organization's ability to rapidly respond to changes and opportunities is enhanced by finding ways to accelerate and share learning. A critical distinction between maturity level 4 and maturity level 5 is the type of process variation addressed. At level 4, processes are concerned with addressing special causes of process variation and providing statistical predictability of the results. At level 5, processes are concerned with addressing common causes of process variation and changing the process to improve process performance (while maintaining statistical probability) and achieve the established quantitative process-improvement objectives.

Although these models have proven useful to many organizations, the use of multiple models has been problematic. Further, applying multiple models that are not integrated within and across an organization is costly in terms of training, appraisals, and improvement activities. The CMM Integration project (CMMI) was formed to sort out the problem of using multiple CMMs. The CMMI Product Team's mission was to combine the following:

- The Capability Maturity Model for Software (SW-CMM) v2.0 draft C
- The Systems Engineering Capability Model (SECM)
- The Integrated Product Development Capability Maturity Model (IPD-CMM) v0.98
- Supplier sourcing

CMMI is the designated successor of the three source models. The SEI has released a policy to sunset the Software CMM and previous versions of the CMMI.

Many of the above concepts are from http://en.wikipedia.org/wiki/Capability_Maturity_Model #Level_1_-_Initial (November 4, 2006).

Interestingly, maturity level 5 is similar to the ideals defined in the lean sigma and lean philosophies.

See *common cause variation, lean sigma, lean thinking, operations performance metrics*.

capacity – (a) Process context: The maximum rate of output for a process, measured in units of output per unit of time; (b) Space/time/weight context: The maximum space or time available or the maximum weight that can be tolerated. ✪

This entry focuses on definition (a). The unit of time may be of any length (a day, a shift, a minute, etc.). Note that it is redundant (and ignorant) to use the phrase "maximum capacity" because a capacity is a maximum.

Some sources make a distinction between several types of capacities:

Rated capacity, also known as **effective capacity**, **nominal capacity**, or **calculated** capacity, is the expected output rate for a process based on planned hours of operation, efficiency, and utilization. Rated capacity is the product of three variables, hours available, efficiency, and utilization.

Demonstrated capacity, also known as **proven capacity**, is the output rate that the process has actually been able to sustain over a period of time. However, demonstrated capacity is affected by starving (the process is stopped due to no input), blocking (the process is stopped because it has no room for output), and lack of market demand (we do not use capacity without demand).

Theoretical capacity is the maximum production rate based on mathematical or engineering calculations, which sometimes do not consider all relevant variables; therefore, it is quite possible that the capacity can be greater than or less than the theoretical value. It is fairly common for factories to work at 110% of their theoretical capacity.

Capacity should not be confused with **load**. If an elevator has three people on it, what is its capacity? This is a trick question. The capacity might be 2, 3, 20, or 99. If it has three people on it, the elevator has a current load of three and probably has a capacity of at least three. For many years, this author wrote APICS certification exam questions related to this concept. It was amazing how many people answered this question incorrectly.

The best capacity will minimize the **total relevant cost**, which is the sum of the capacity and waiting costs. All systems have a trade-off between capacity utilization and waiting time. These two variables have a non-linear relationship. As utilization goes to 100%, the waiting time tends to go to infinity. Maximizing utilization is not the goal of the organization. The goal of capacity management is to minimize the sum of two relevant costs: the cost of the capacity and the cost of waiting.

For example, the optimal utilization for a fire engine is not 100%, but much closer to 1%. Utilization for an office copy machine should be relatively low because the cost of people waiting is usually higher than the cost of the machine waiting. One humorous question to ask students is: "Should you go make copies to keep the machine utilized?" The answer, of course, is "no" because utilization is not the goal. The goal, therefore, is to find the optimal balance between the cost of the machine and the cost of people waiting.

In contrast, some expensive machines, such as a bottling system, will run three shifts per day 365 days per year. The cost of downtime is the lost profit from the system and can be quite expensive.

In a manufacturing context, capacity management is executed at four levels: **Resource Requirements Planning (RRP)**, **Rough Cut Capacity Planning (RCCP)**, **Capacity Requirements Planning (CRP)**, and **input/output control**. See those entries in this encyclopedia to learn more.

The **newsvendor model** can be used to find the optimal capacity. The model requires that the analyst define a time horizon, estimate the distribution of demand, and estimate the cost of having one unit of capacity too much and the cost of having one unit of capacity too little.

In some markets, customers can **buy capacity** rather than products. For example, a customer might buy the capacity of a supplier's factory for one day per week. This can often help the customer reduce the procurement leadtime. Of course, if the customer does not use the capacity, the supplier will still be paid.

See *absorptive capacity, bill of resources, bottleneck, capacity management, Capacity Requirements Planning (CRP), closed-loop MRP, downtime, input/output control, Little's Law, load, newsvendor model, Overall Equipment Effectiveness (OEE), process design, queuing theory, Resource Requirements Planning (RRP), Rough Cut Capacity Planning (RCCP), safety capacity, utilization, yield management.*

capacity cushion – See *safety capacity.*

capacity management – Planning, building, measuring, and controlling the output rate for a process.
　　See *capacity.*

Capacity Requirements Planning (CRP) – The planning process used in conjunction with Materials Requirements Planning (MRP) to convert open and planned shop orders into a load report in planned shop hours for each workcenter.

The CRP process is executed after the **MRP** planning process has produced the materials plan, which includes the set of all planned and open orders. CRP uses the order start date, order quantity, routing, standard setup times, and standard run times to estimate the number of shop hours required for each workcenter. It is possible for CRP to indicate that a capacity problem exists during specific time periods even when **Resource Requirements Planning (RRP)** and **Rough Cut Capacity Planning (RCCP)** have indicated that sufficient capacity is available. This is because RRP and RCCP are not as detailed as CRP with respect to timing the load. The output of the CRP process is the **capacity plan**, which is a schedule showing the planned load (capacity required) and planned capacity (capacity available) for each workcenter over several days or weeks. This is also called a **load profile**.

See *Business Requirements Planning (BRP), capacity, closed-loop MRP, input/output control, Master Production Schedule (MPS), Materials Requirements Planning (MRP), planned order, Resource Requirements Planning (RRP), Rough Cut Capacity Planning (RCCP), routing, Sales & Operations Planning (S&OP).*

capacity utilization – See *utilization.*

CAPEX – An abbreviation for the CAPital EXpenditure used as the initial investment in new machines, equipment, and facilities.
　　See *capital.*

capital – Money available for investing in assets that produce output.
　　See *CAPEX, capital intensive.*

capital intensive – Requiring a large expenditure of capital in comparison to labor.

A capital intensive industry requires large investments to produce a particular good. Good examples include power generation and oil refining.

See *capital, labor intensive.*

carbon footprint – A measure of the carbon dioxide (CO_2) and other greenhouse gas emissions released into the environment by a person, plant, organization, or state; often expressed as tons of carbon dioxide per year.

The carbon footprint takes into account energy use (heat, cooling, light, power, and refrigeration), transportation, and other means of emitting carbon.

See *cap and trade, energy audit, green manufacturing, triple bottom line.*

cargo – Goods transported by a vehicle; also called freight.

See *logistics, shipping container.*

carousel – A rotating materials handling device used to store and retrieve smaller parts for use in a factory or warehouse.

Carousels are often automated and used for picking small parts in a high-volume business. The carousel brings the part location to the picker so the picker does not have to travel to the bin location to store or retrieve a part. Both **horizontal** and **vertical** carousels are used in practice. The photo on the right is a vertical carousel.

See *Automated Storage & Retrieval System (AS/RS), batch picking, picking, warehouse.*

carrier – (1) In a logistics context: An organization that transports goods or people in its own vehicles. (2) In a telecommunications context: An organization that offers communication services. (3) In an insurance context: An organization that provides risk management services.

Carriers may specialize in small packages, less than truck load (LTL), full truck loads (TL), air, rail, or sea. In the U.S., a carrier involved in interstate moves must be licensed by the U.S. Department of Transportation. The shipper is the party that initiates the shipment.

See *common carrier, for-hire carrier, less than truck load (LTL), logistics.*

carrying charge – The cost of holding inventory per time period, expressed as a percentage of the unit cost. ✪

This parameter is used to help inventory managers make economic trade-offs between inventory levels, order sizes, and other inventory control variables. The carrying charge is usually expressed as the cost of carrying one monetary unit (e.g., dollar) of inventory for one year and therefore has a unit of measure of $/$/year. Reasonable values are in the range of 15-40%.

The carrying charge is the sum of four factors: (1) the marginal cost of capital or the weighted average cost of capital (WACC), (2) a risk premium for obsolete inventory, (3) the storage and administration cost, and (4) a policy adjustment factor. This rate should only reflect costs that vary with the size of the inventory and should not include costs that vary with the number of inventory transactions (orders, receipts, etc.). A good approach for determining if a particular cost driver should be included in the carrying charge is to ask the question, "How will this cost be affected if the inventory is doubled (or halved)?" If the answer is "not at all," that cost driver is probably not relevant (at least not in the short-term). It is difficult to make a precise estimate for the carrying charge. Many firms erroneously set it to the WACC and therefore underestimate the cost of carrying inventory.

See *carrying cost, Economic Order Quantity (EOQ), hockey stick effect, inventory turnover, marginal cost, obsolete inventory, production planning, setup cost, shrinkage, weighted average.*

carrying cost – The marginal cost per period for holding one unit of inventory (typically a year). ✪

The carrying cost is usually calculated as the average inventory investment times the carrying charge. For example, if the annual carrying charge is 25% and the average inventory is $100,000, the carrying cost is $25,000 per year. Many firms incorrectly use the end-of-year inventory in this calculation, which is fine if the end-of-year inventory is close to the average inventory during the year. However, it is quite common for firms to have a "hockey stick" sales and shipment pattern where the end-of-year inventory is significantly less than the average inventory during the year. Technically, this type of average is called a "time-integrated average" and can be estimated fairly accurately by averaging the inventory at a number of points during the year.

Manufacturing and inventory managers must carefully apply managerial accounting principles in decision making. A critical element in many decisions is the estimation of the inventory carrying cost, sometimes called the "holding cost." Typical decisions include the following:

- **Service level trade-off decisions** – Many make to stock manufacturers, distributors, and retailers sell standard products from inventory to customers who arrive randomly. In these situations, the firm's service level improves with a larger finished goods inventory. Therefore, trade-offs have to be made between inventory carrying cost and service.
- **Lot size decisions** – A small order size requires a firm to place many orders, which results in a small "cycle" inventory. Assuming instantaneous delivery with order quantity Q, the average cycle inventory is approximately $Q/2$. Even though small manufacturing order sizes provide low average cycle inventory, they require more setups, which, in turn, may require significant capacity leading to a large queue inventory and a large overall carrying cost.
- **Hedging and quantity discount decisions** – Inventory carrying cost is also an important issue when evaluating opportunities to buy in large quantities or buy early to get a lower price. These decisions a total cost model to make evaluate the economic trade-offs between the carrying cost and the purchase price.
- **In-sourcing versus outsourcing decisions** – When trying to decide if a component or a product should be manufactured in-house or purchased from a supplier, the inventory carrying cost is often a significant factor. Due to longer leadtimes, firms generally increase inventory levels to support an outsourcing decision. It is important that the proper carrying cost be used to support this analysis.

The above decisions require a "managerial economics" approach to decision making, which means that the only costs that should be considered are those costs that vary directly with the amount of inventory. All other costs are irrelevant to the decision.

The carrying charge is a function of the following four variables:

- **Cost of capital** – Firms have alternative uses for money. The cost of capital reflects the opportunity cost of the money tied up in the inventory.
- **Storage cost** – The firm should consider only those storage costs that vary with the inventory level. These costs include warehousing, handling, insurance and taxes, depreciation, and shrinkage.
- **Obsolescence risk** – The risk of obsolescence tends to increase with inventory, particularly for firms that deal with high technology products, such as computers, or perishable products, such as food.
- **Policy adjustment** – This component of the carrying cost reflects management's desire to pursue this policy and is based on management intuition rather than hard data.

When estimating the unit cost for the carrying cost calculation, most authors argue for ignoring allocated overhead. However, given that it is difficult for most organizations to know their unit cost without overhead, it is reasonable for them to use the fully burdened cost and use the appropriate carrying charge that does not double count handling, storage, or other overhead costs.

See *carrying charge, Economic Order Quantity (EOQ), hockey stick effect, Inventory Dollar Days (IDD), inventory management, inventory turnover, marginal cost, materials management, opportunity cost, outsourcing, overhead, production planning, quantity discount, service level, setup cost, shrinkage, weighted average.*

cash cow – The firm or business unit that holds a strong position in a mature industry and is being "milked" to provide cash for other business units; the cash cow is often in a mature industry and therefore not a good place for significant new investment.

The Boston Consulting Group (BCG) Growth-Share Matrix can help managers set investment priorities for the product portfolio in a business unit or for business units in a multi-divisional firm. Stars are high growth/high

The BCG Growth-Share Matrix[6]

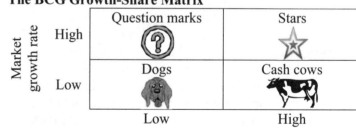

		Question marks	Stars
Market growth rate	High	(?)	☆
	Low	Dogs	Cash cows
		Low	High

Relative position (market share)

Adapted by Professor Arthur V. Hill

---

[6] *The figure above is different from the original because it puts high market share on the right rather than the left.*

market share products or business units. Cash cows have low growth but high market share and can be used to supply cash to the firm. Dogs have low growth and low market share and should be either fixed or liquidated. Question marks have high growth, but low market share; a few of these should be targeted for investment while the others should be divested. Stern and Deimler (2006) and Porter (1985) provide more detail.

See *operations strategy*.

Cash on Delivery (COD) – Contract terms that require payment for goods and transportation at time of delivery.

See *FOB*, *terms*, *waybill*.

casting – See *foundry*.

catchball – A lean term used to describe an iterative top-down/bottom-up process in which plans are "thrown" back and forth between two levels in an organization until the participants at the different levels come to a shared understanding.

The term "catchball" is a metaphor used in the hoshin planning process for participative give-and-take discussions between two levels of an organization when creating a strategic plan. Catchball can help an organization achieve buy-in, find agreement, build a shared understanding, and create detailed execution plans for both the development and execution of a strategy. Catchball is "played" between multiple levels of the organization to ensure that the strategic plan is embraced and executable at every level.

The strategic planning process in many organizations has two common issues: (1) the plan is difficult to implement because the higher-level management is out of touch with the details, and (2) the lower-level managers do not understand the rationale behind the plan and therefore either passively resist or actively oppose the new strategy. With catchball, higher-level management develops a high-level plan and then communicates with the next layer of management to gain understanding and buy-in. Compared to other types of strategic planning, catchball usually results in strategic plans that are embraced by a wider group of managers and are more realistic (e.g., easier to implement).

Catchball essentially has two steps: (1) conduct an interactive session early in the planning process to give the next level of management the opportunity to ask questions, provide feedback, and challenge specific items, and (2) have the next level managers develop an execution plan for the higher-level initiatives and toss it back to the higher-level managers for feedback and challenges.

Catchball is comparable to agile software development where software ideas are tested early and often, which leads to better software. The same is true for strategy development with catchball where strategic plans are tested early and often. Both concepts are similar to the idea of small lotsizes and early detection of defects.

See *agile software development*, *early detection*, *hoshin planning*, *lean thinking*, *operations strategy*, *prototype*.

category captain – A role given by a retailer to a representative from a supplier to help the retailer manage a category of products.

It is a common practice for retailers in North America to select one supplier in a category as the category captain. A retailer usually (but not always) selects the category captain as the supplier with the highest sales in the category. The supplier then selects an individual among its employees to serve in the category captain's role. Traditionally, the category captain is a branded supplier; however, the role is sometimes also given to private label suppliers. Category captains often have their offices at the customer's sites.

The category captain is expected to work closely with the retailer to provide three types of services:

Analyze data:
- Analyze category and channel data to develop consumer and business insights across the entire category.
- Perform competitive analyses by category, brand, and package to identify trends.
- Analyze consumer purchasing behavior by demographic profile to understand consumer trends by channel.
- Audit stores.

Develop and present plans:
- Develop business plans and strategies for achieving category volume, margin, share, space, and profit targets.
- Help the retailer build the planogram for the category.
- Prepare and present category performance reviews for the retailer.
- Participate in presentations as a credible expert in the category.

Support the retailer:
- Respond quickly to the retailer's requests for information.
- Provide the retailer with information on shelf allocation in a rapidly changing environment.
- Educate the retailer's sales teams.
- Advise the retailer on shelving standards and associated software tools.

Craig Johnson, a Kimberly-Clark category captain at Target, adds, "Most category captains also have responsibilities within their own company as well and have to balance the needs of their retailer with internal company needs. It can get hairy sometimes."[7]

The category captain must focus on growing the category, even if requires promoting competing products and brands. This practice will lead to the growth of the entire category and therefore be in the best interests of the supplier. In return for this special relationship, the supplier will have an influential voice with the retailer. However, the supplier must be careful never to abuse this relationship or violate any antitrust laws.

The category captain is usually given access to the retailer's proprietary information, such as point-of-sale (POS) data. This information includes sales data for all suppliers that compete in the category. The retailer and category captain will usually have an explicit agreement that requires the captain to use this data only for category management and not share it with anyone in the supplier's company.

Retailers will sometimes assign a second competing supplier as a category adviser called the "category validator." In theory, the validator role was created as a way for the retailer to compare and evaluate the category captain's recommendations. In practice, however, the adviser is usually used by the retailer as another category management resource. The adviser conducts ad hoc category analyses at the request of the retailer, but does not usually duplicate the services provided by the captain.

See *antitrust laws, assortment, category killer, category management, consumable goods, consumer packaged goods, Fast Moving Consumer Goods (FMCG), planogram, Point-of-Sale (POS), private label.*

category killer – A term used in marketing and strategic management to describe a dominant product or service that tends to have a natural monopoly in a market.

One example of a category killer is eBay, an on-line auction website that attracts large numbers of buyers and sellers simply because it is the largest on-line auction. Other examples include "big box" retailers, such as Home Depot, that tend to drive smaller "mom and pop" retailers out of business.

See *big box store, category captain, category management.*

category management – The retail practice of segmenting items (SKUs) into groups called categories to make it easier to manage assortments, inventories, shelf-space allocation, promotions, and purchases.

Benefits claimed for a good category management system include increased sales due to better space allocation and better stocking levels, lower cost due to lower inventories, and increased customer retention due to better matching of supply and demand. Category management in retailing is analogous to the commodity management function in purchasing.

See *assortment, brand, category captain, category killer, commodity, consumable goods, consumer packaged goods, Fast Moving Consumer Goods (FMCG), private label.*

category validator – See *category captain.*

causal forecasting – See *econometric forecasting, forecasting.*

causal map – A graphical tool often used for identifying the root causes of a problem; also known as a cause and effect diagram (C&E Diagram), Ishikawa Diagram, fishbone diagram, cause map, impact wheel, root cause tree, fault tree analysis, and current reality trees. ✪

A causal map is a diagram that shows the cause and effect relationships in a system. Causal maps can add value to organizations in many ways:
- **Process improvement and problem solving** – Causal maps are a powerful tool for gaining a deep understanding of any problem. As the old adage goes, "A problem well-defined is a problem half-solved." The causal map is a great way to help organizations understand the system of causes that result in blocked goals and then find solutions to the real problems rather than just the symptoms of the problems. People

---

[7] *Email communication with the author in the fall of 2010.*

think in "visual" ways. A good causal map is worth 1000 words and can significantly reduce meeting time and the time to achieve the benefit from a process improvement project.

• **Supporting risk mitigation efforts** – Causal maps are a powerful tool for helping firms identify possible causes of problems and develop risk mitigation strategies for these possible causes.

• **Gaining consensus** – The brainstorming process of creating a causal map is also a powerful tool for "gaining a shared understanding" of how a system works. The discussion, debate, and deliberation process in building a causal map is often more important than the map itself.

• **Training and teaching** – A good causal map can dramatically reduce the time required to communicate complex relationships for training, teaching, and documentation purposes.

• **Identifying the critical metrics** – Many organizations have too many metrics, which causes managers to lose sight of the critical variables in the system. A good causal map can help managers identify the critical variables that drive performance and require high-level attention. Focusing on these few critical metrics leads to strategic alignment, which in turn leads to organizational success.

Many types of causal maps are used in practice, including **Ishikawa Diagrams** (also known as fishbone diagrams, cause and effect diagram, and C&E Diagrams), **impact wheels** (from one cause to many effects), **root cause trees** (from one effect to many causes), and **strategy maps**. The Ishikawa Diagram was developed by Dr. Kaoru Ishikawa (1943-1969) and is by far the most popular form of a causal map. The Ishikawa Diagram is a special type of a causal map that shows the relationships between the problem (at the "head" of the fishbone on the right) and the potential causes of a problem. The figure below is a simple example of an Ishikawa Diagram for analyzing long waiting lines for tellers in a bank.

The Ishikawa Diagram is usually developed in a brainstorming context. The process begins by placing the name of a basic problem of interest at the far right of the diagram at the "head" of the main "backbone" of the fish. The main causes of the problem are drawn as bones off the main backbone.

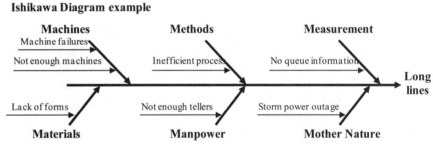

Ishikawa Diagram example

Source: Arthur V. Hill

Many firms prescribe six causes: machines (equipment), methods, measurement, materials, manpower (labor), and Mother Nature (environment). However, many argue that this list is overly confining and a bit sexist. Brainstorming is typically done to add possible causes to the main bones and more specific causes to the bones on the main bones. This subdivision into ever-increasing specificity continues as long as the problem areas can be further subdivided. The practical maximum depth of this tree is usually about four or five levels.

The Ishikawa Diagram is limited in many ways:
• It can only analyze one output variable at a time.
• Some people have trouble working backward from the problem on the far right side of the page.
• It is hard to read and even harder to draw, especially when the problem requires many levels of causation.
• The diagram is also hard to create on a computer.
• The alliteration of Ms is sexist with the terms "manpower" and "Mother Nature."
• The six Ms rarely include all possible causes of a problem.
Causal maps do not have any of these limitations.

The Ishikawa Diagram starts with the result on the right. With root cause trees, current reality trees (Goldratt 1994), and strategy maps (Kaplan & Norton 2004), the result is usually written at the top of the page. With an FMEA analysis and issues trees, the result is written on the left and then broken into its root causes on the right.

The causal map diagram below summarizes the 304-page book *Competing Against Time* (Stalk & Hout 2003) in less than a half-page. This is a **strategy map** using a causal map format rather than the Kaplan and Norton (1992) four-perspective strategy map format. This **time-based competition strategy** reduces cycle times, cost, and customer leadtimes. Reducing customer leadtimes segments the market, leaving the price-sensitive customers to the competition. This strategy map could be taken a step further to show how the firm could achieve lower cycle time through setup time reduction, vendor relationships, 5S, and plant re-layout.

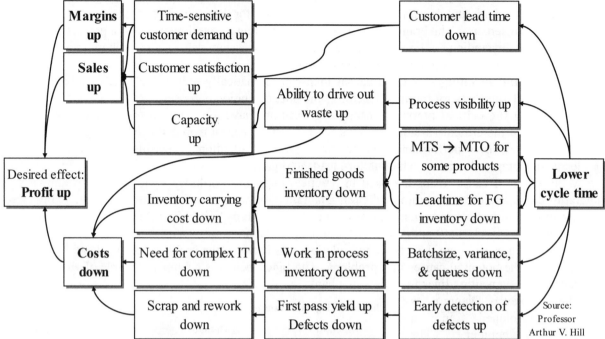

Source: Professor Arthur V. Hill

Regardless of the format used, these diagrams are usually created through a brainstorming process, often with the help of 3M Post-it Notes. The team brainstorms to identify the root causes of each node. The process continues until all causes (nodes) and relationships (arcs) have been identified. It is possible that "loops" will occur in the diagram. A loop can occur for a vicious cycle or virtuous cycle. For example, a vicious cycle occurs when an alcoholic person drinks and is criticized by family members, which may, in turn, cause him or her to drink even more, be criticized further, etc. A virtuous cycle is similar, except that the result is positive instead of negative.

Scavarda, Bouzdine-Chameeva, Goldstein, Hays, and Hill (2006) developed a method for building collective causal maps with a group of experts. This method assigns weights to each causal relationship and results in a meaningful graphical causal map, with the more important causal relationships shown with darker arrows.

Many software tools are available to help brainstorm and document the cause and effect diagrams. However, Galley (2008) insists that Excel is the best tool.

The **C&E Matrix** provides a means for experts to assign weights to certain causal input variables. The same can be done with a causal map. All that needs to be done is to score each input variable on several dimensions that are important to customers and then create a weighted score for each input variable. Priority is then given to those variables that are believed to have the most impact on customers. Alternatively, experts can "vote" (using multi-voting) for the causes that they believe should be the focus for further analysis.

Causal maps should not be confused with **concept maps**, **knowledge maps**, and **mindmaps** that nearly always show similarities (but not causality) between objects. For example, monkeys and apes are very similar, but monkeys do not cause apes. Therefore, a knowledge map would show a strong connection between monkeys and apes, but a causal map would not.

Hill (2011b, 2011c) provides more detail on this subject.

See *5 Whys*, *affinity diagram*, *Analytic Hierarchy Process (AHP)*, *balanced scorecard*, *brainstorming*, *C&E Diagram*, *C&E Matrix*, *current reality tree*, *decision tree*, *Failure Mode and Effects Analysis (FMEA)*, *fault tree analysis*, *future reality tree*, *hoshin planning*, *ideation*, *impact wheel*, *issue tree*, *lean sigma*, *MECE*, *mindmap*, *Nominal Group Technique (NGT)*, *Pareto Chart*, *Pareto's Law*, *parking lot*, *process map*, *quality management*, *Root Cause Analysis (RCA)*, *root cause tree*, *sentinel event*, *seven tools of quality*, *strategy map*, *Total Quality Management (TQM)*, *value stream map*, *Y-tree*.

cause and effect diagram – See *causal map*.

cause map – A trademarked term for a causal map coined by Mark Galley of ThinkReliability.

Cause mapping is a registered trademark of Novem, Inc., doing business as ThinkReliability (www.thinkreliability.com).

See *causal map*.

caveat emptor – A Latin phrase that means "buyer beware" or "let the buyer beware."

This phrase means that the buyer (not the seller) is at risk with a purchase decision. The phrase "caveat venditor" is Latin for "let the seller beware."

See *service guarantee, warranty*.

CBT – See *Computer Based Training (CBT)*.

c-chart – A quality control chart used to display and monitor the number of defects per sample (or per batch, per day, etc.) in a production process.

Whereas a p-chart controls the percentage of units that are defective, a c-chart controls the number of defects per unit. Note that one unit can have multiple defects. The Poisson distribution is typically used for c-charts, which suggests that defects are rare.

See *attribute, control chart, Poisson distribution, Statistical Process Control (SPC), Statistical Quality Control (SQC), u-chart*.

CDF – See *probability density function*.

cell – See *cellular manufacturing*.

cellular manufacturing – The use of a group of machines dedicated to processing parts, part families, or product families that require a similar sequence of operations. ✪

Concept – In a traditional functional (process) layout, machines and workers are arranged in workcenters by function (e.g., drills or lathes), large batches of parts are moved between workcenters, and workers receive limited cross-training on the one type of machine in their workcenter. With cellular manufacturing, machines and workers are dedicated to making a particular type of product or part family. The machines in the cell, therefore, are laid out in the sequence required to make that product. With cells, materials are moved in small batches and workers are cross-trained on multiple machines and process steps. Cells are often organized in a U-shaped layout so workers inside the "U" can communicate and help each other as needed. The figure below contrasts functional and cellular layouts showing that cells can have a much higher value added ratio.

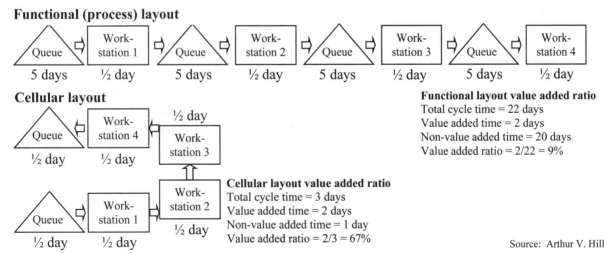

Source: Arthur V. Hill

Advantages of a cell over a product layout – The advantages of a cell over a product layout include reduced cycle time, travel time, setup time, queue time, work-in-process inventory, space, and materials handling cost. Reduced cycle time allows for quicker detection of defects and simpler scheduling. When firms create cells, they often cross-train workers in a cell, which leads to better engagement, morale, and labor productivity. Some firms also implement self-managed work teams to develop workers, reduce overhead, and accelerate process improvement.

Disadvantages of a cell over a product layout – The main disadvantage of a cell is that the machines dedicated to a cell may not have sufficient utilization to justify the capital expense. Consequently, cellular manufacturing is often difficult to implement in a facility that uses large expensive machines. When a firm has one very large expensive machine, it might still use cells for all other steps.

Professors Nancy Hyer and Urban Wemmerlov wrote a book and an article on on using cells for administrative work (Hyer & Wemmerlov 2002a, 2002b).

See *automation, Chaku-Chaku, cross-training, facility layout, Flexible Manufacturing System (FMS), focused factory, group technology, handoff, job design, lean thinking, product family, utilization, value added ratio, workcenter, Work-in-Process (WIP) inventory.*

CEMS (Contract Electronics Manufacturing Services) – See *contract manufacturer.*

censored data – Data that is incomplete because it does not include a subpopulation of the data.

A good example of censored data is demand data that does not include data for lost sales. A retailer reports that the sales were 100 for a particular date. However, the firm ran out of stock during the day and does not have information on how many units were demanded but not sold due to lack of inventory. The demand data for this firm is said to be "censored."

See *demand, forecasting.*

centered moving average – See *exponential smoothing, moving average.*

center-of-gravity model for facility location – A method for locating a single facility on an x-y coordinate system to attempt to minimize the weighted travel distances; also called the center of mass or centroid model.

This is called the "infinite set" facility location problem because the "depot" can be located at any point on the x-y coordinate axis. The model treats the x and y dimensions independently and finds the first moment in each dimension. The one depot serves N markets with locations at coordinates (x_i, y_i) and demands D_i units.

The center-of-gravity location for the depot is then $x_0 = \sum_{i=1}^{N} D_i x_i / \sum_{i=1}^{N} x_i$ and $y_0 = \sum_{i=1}^{N} D_i y_i / \sum_{i=1}^{N} y_i$.

This model does not guarantee optimality and can only locate a single depot. Center-of-gravity locations can be far from optimal. In contrast, the numeric-analytic location model guarantees optimality for a single depot location, can be extended (heuristically) to multiple depots, and can also be extended (heuristically) to multiple depots with latitude and longitude data.

See *facility location, gravity model for competitive retail store location, numeric-analytic location model.*

central limit theorem – An important probability theory concept that can be stated informally as "The sum or average of many independent random variables will be approximately normally distributed."

For example, the first panel in the figure below shows a probability distribution (density function) that is clearly non-normal. (This is the triangular density function.) The second figure shows the distribution of a random variable that is the average of two independent random variates drawn from the first distribution.

The third and fourth figures show the probability distributions when the number of random variates in the average increases to four and eight. In each successive figure, the distribution for the average of the random variates is closer to normal. This example shows that as the number of random variates in the average increases, the distribution of the average (and the sum) converges to the normal distribution.

Central limit theorem example

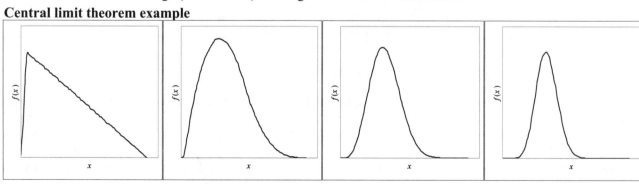

Source: Professor Arthur V. Hill

See *confidence interval, Law of Large Numbers, normal distribution, sample size calculation, sampling, sampling distribution*.

certification – See *supplier qualification and certification*.

CGS (Cost of Goods Sold) – See *cost of goods sold*.

chain of custody – See *traceability*.

Chaku-Chaku – The Japanese phrase "Load, Load" used to describe the practice of facilitating one-piece flow in a manufacturing cell, where equipment automatically unloads parts so the operator can move parts between machines with minimal wasted motion.

With Chaku-Chaku, the operator is responsible for moving parts from machine to machine around an oval or circular-shaped cell and also for monitoring machine performance. When arriving at a machine in the cell, the operator will find a completed part already removed from the machine and the machine ready for a new part. The operator then starts a new part (from the previous machine), picks up the completed part from the machine, and then carries the part to the next machine in the cell to repeat the process.

See *cellular manufacturing, multiple-machine handling*.

champion – A senior manager who sponsors a program or project; also called an executive sponsor or sponsor.

The champion's role is to define the strategic direction, ensure that resources are available, provide accountability, and deal with political resistance. This term is often used in the context of a process improvement program at both the program level (the program champion) and the project level (the project sponsor). Although the role can be either formal or informal, in many contexts, making it formal has significant benefits.

See *deployment leader, lean sigma, lean thinking, program management office, project charter, sponsor*.

change management – A structured approach for helping individuals, teams, and organizations transition from a current state to a desired future state.

Change management is an important discipline in a wide variety of project management contexts, including information systems, process improvement programs (e.g., lean sigma), new product development, quality management, and systems engineering. Organizational change requires (1) helping stakeholders overcome resistance to change, (2) developing new consensus, values, attitudes, norms, and behaviors to support the future state, and finally (3) reinforcing the new behaviors through new organizational structures, reward systems, performance management systems, and standard operating procedures. The benefits of good change management include better engagement of workers, reduced risk of project failure, reduced time and cost to affect the change, and longer lasting results.

The *ADKAR Model for Change* and the *Lewin/Schein Theory of Change* entries in this encyclopedia present specific change management methodologies.

See *ADKAR Model for Change, co-opt, Lewin/Schein Theory of Change, project charter, project management, RACI Matrix, stakeholder analysis*.

changeover – See *setup*.

changeover cost – See *setup cost*.

changeover time – See *setup time*.

channel – See *distribution channel*.

channel conflict – Competition between players trying to sell to the same customers.

For example, a personal computer company might try to compete with its own distributors (such as Sears) for customers by selling directly to customers. This is often an issue when a retail channel is in competition with a Web-based channel set up by the company. Channel conflict is not a new phenomenon with the Internet, but has become more obvious with the disruptions caused by the Internet.

See *disintermediation, distribution channel, distributor, supply chain management*.

channel integration – The practice of extending strategic alliances to the suppliers (and their suppliers) and to customers (and to their customers).

See *distribution channel, supply chain management*.

channel partner – A firm that works with another firm to provide products and services to customers.

Channel partners for a manufacturing firm generally include distributors, sales representatives, logistics firms, transportation firms, and retailers. Note that the term "partner" is imprecise because relationships with distributors and other "channel partners" are rarely legal partnerships.

See *distribution channel, supply chain management.*

chargeback – See *incoming inspection.*

chase strategy – A production planning approach that changes the workforce level to match seasonal demand to keep finished goods inventory relatively low.

With the chase strategy, the workforce level is changed to meet (or chase) demand. In contrast, the **level strategy** maintains a constant workforce level and meets demand with inventory (built in the off-season), overtime production, or both.

Many firms are able to economically implement a chase strategy for each product and a level employment overall strategy by offering counter-seasonal products. For example, a company that makes snow skis might also make water skis to maintain a constant workforce without building large inventories in the off-season. Other examples of counter-seasonal products include snow blowers and lawn mowers (Toro Company) and snowmobiles and all terrain vehicles (Polaris).

See *heijunka, level strategy, Master Production Schedule (MPS), production planning, Sales & Operations Planning (S&OP), seasonality.*

Chebyshev distance – See *Minkowski distance.*

Chebyshev's inequality – A probability theory concept stating that no more than $1/k^2$ of a distribution can be more than k standard deviations away from the mean.

This theorem is named for the Russian mathematician Pafnuty Lvovich Chebyshev (Пафну́тий Льво́вич Чебышёв). The theorem can be stated mathematically as $P(|X - \mu_x| \geq k\sigma) \leq 1/k^2$ and can be applied to all probability distributions. The one-sided Chebyshev inequality is $P(X - \mu \geq k\sigma) \leq 1/(1 + k^2)$.

See *confidence interval.*

check digit – A single number (a digit) between 0 and 9 that is usually placed at the end of an identifying number (such as a part number, bank account, credit card number, or employee ID) and is used to perform a quick test to see if the identifying number is clearly invalid.

The check digit is usually the last digit in the identifying number and is computed from the base number, which is the identifying number without the check digit. By comparing the check digit computed from the base number with the check digit that is part of the identifying number, it is possible to quickly check if an identifying number is clearly invalid without accessing a database of valid identifying numbers. This is particularly powerful for remote data entry of credit card numbers and part numbers. These applications typically have large databases that make number validation relatively expensive. However, it is important to understand that identifying numbers with valid check digits are not necessarily valid identifying numbers; the check digit only determines if the identifying number is clearly invalid.

A simple approach for checking the validity of a number is to use the following method: Multiply the last digit (the check digit) by one, the second-to-last digit by two, the third-to-last digit by one, the fourth-to-last digit by two, etc. Then sum all *digits* in these products (including the check digit), divide by ten, and find the remainder. The number is proven invalid if the remainder is not zero.

For example, the account number 5249 has the check digit 9. The products are 1 x 9 = 9, 2 x 4 = 8, 1 x 2 = 2, and 2 x 5 = 10. The sum of the digits is 9 + 8 + 2 + 1 + 0 = 20, which is divisible by 10 and therefore is a valid check digit. Note that the procedure adds the digits, which means that 10 is treated as 1 + 0 = 1 rather than a 10. The above procedure works with most credit card and bank account numbers.

The check digit for all books registered with an International Standard Book Number is the last digit of the ISBN. The ISBN method for the 10-digit ISBN weights the digits from 10 down to 1, sums the products, and then returns the check digit as modulus 11 of this sum. An upper case X is used in lieu of 10.

For example, *Operations Management for Competitive Advantage*, Eleventh Edition by Chase, Jacobs, and Aquilano (2006) has ISBN 0-07-312151-7, which is 0073121517 without the dashes. The ending "7" is the check digit so the base number is 007312151. Multiplying 10 x 0 = 0, 9 x 0 = 0, 8 x 7 = 56, 7 x 3 = 21, 6 x 1 = 6,

5 x 2 = 10, 4 x 1 = 4, 3 x 5 = 15, and 2 x 1 = 2 and adding the products 0 + 0 + 56 + 21 + 6 + 10 + 4 + 15 + 2 = 114. Dividing 114 by 11 has a remainder of 7, which is the correct check digit. The new 13-digit ISBN uses a slightly different algorithm.

See *algorithm*, *part number*.

checklist – A record of tasks that need to be done for error proofing a process.

A checklist is a tool that can be used to ensure that all important steps in a process are done. For example, pilots often use maintenance checklists for items that need to be done before takeoff. The 5S discipline for a crash cart in a hospital uses a checklist that needs to be checked each morning to ensure that the required items are on the cart. Checklists are often confused with checksheets, which are tally sheets for collecting data.

See *checksheet*, *error proofing*, *multiplication principle*.

checksheet – A simple approach for collecting defect data; also called a tally sheet.

A checksheet is a simple form that can be used to collect and count defects or other data for a Pareto analysis. It is considered one of the seven tools of quality. The user makes a check mark (✓) every time a defect of a particular type occurs in that time period. The table below provides a simple example of a checksheet that records the causes for machine downtime.

Checksheet example

	Mon	Tue	Wed	Thu	Fri	Totals
Machine jam	✓✓✓✓✓	✓✓✓✓✓	✓✓✓✓✓	✓✓✓✓✓	✓✓✓✓	25
Machine failure	✓✓	✓			✓	4
Materials shortage	✓✓	✓✓✓✓	✓	✓	✓✓	10
Power outage				✓		1
Totals	10	10	6	7	7	40

A different format for a checksheet shows a drawing (schematic) of a product (such as a shirt) and counts the problems with a checkmark on the drawing in the appropriate location. For example, if a defect is found on the collar, a checkmark is put on a drawing of a shirt by the shirt collar.

Checksheets should be used in the gemba (the place where work is done), so workers and supervisors can see them and update them on a regular basis. Checksheets are often custom-designed by users for their particular needs. Checksheets are often confused with checklists, which are used for error proofing.

See *checklist*, *downtime*, *gemba*, *Pareto Chart*, *seven tools of quality*.

child item – See *bill of material (BOM)*.

chi-square distribution – A continuous probability distribution often used for goodness of fit testing; also known as the chi-squared and χ^2 distribution; named after the Greek letter "chi" (χ).

The chi-square distribution is the sum of squares of k independent standard normal distributed random variables. If $X_1, X_1, ..., X_k$ are k independent standard normal random variables, the sum of these random variables has the chi-square distribution with k degrees of freedom. The best-known use of the chi-square distribution is for goodness of fit tests.

Parameters: Degrees of freedom, k.

Density function and distribution functions: $f(x,k) = \dfrac{x^{k/2-1}e^{-x/2}}{2^{k/2}\Gamma(k/2)}$, where $k \in I$ and $\Gamma(k/2)$ is the gamma function, which has closed-form values for half-integers (i.e., $\Gamma(k/2) = \sqrt{\pi}(k-2)!!/2^{(k-1)/2}$, where !! is the double factorial function). $F(x,k) = \dfrac{\gamma(k/2, x/2)}{\Gamma(k/2)}$, where $\Gamma(k/2)$ is the gamma function and $\gamma(k/2, x/2)$ is the lower incomplete gamma function $\gamma(s,x) = \int_0^x t^{s-1}e^{-t}dt$, which does not have a closed form.

Statistics: Mean k, median $\approx k(1-2/(9k))^3$, mode max$(k-2, 0)$, variance $2k$.

Graph: The graph below shows the chi-square density function for a range of k values.

Excel: Excel 2003/2007 uses CHIDIST(x, k) to return the one-tailed (right tail) probability of the chi-square distribution with k degrees of freedom, CHIINV(p, k) returns the inverse of the one-tailed (right tail) probability of the chi-square distribution, and CHITEST(actual_range, expected_range) can be used for the chi-square test. The chi-square density is not available in Excel, but the equivalent Excel function GAMMADIST($k/2$, 2) can be used. Excel 2010 has the CHISQ.DIST(x, degrees_of_freedom, cumulative) and several other related functions.

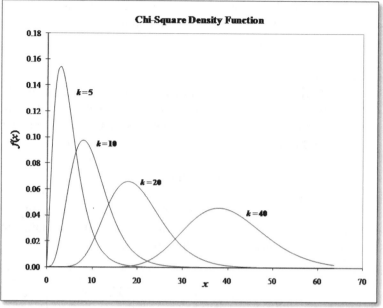

Chi-Square Density Function

Relationships to other distributions: The chi-square is a special case of the gamma distribution where $\chi^2(k) = \Gamma(k/2, 2)$. The chi-square is the sum of k independent random variables; therefore, by the central limit theorem, it converges to the normal as k approaches infinity. The chi-square will be close to normal for $k > 50$ and $(X-k)/\sqrt{2k}$ will approach the standard normal.

See *chi-square goodness of fit test, gamma distribution, gamma function, probability density function, probability distribution.*

chi-square goodness of fit test – A statistical test used to determine if a set of data fits a hypothesized discrete probability distribution.

The chi-square test statistic is $\chi^2 = \sum_{i=1}^{k} \frac{(O_i - E_i)^2}{E_i}$, where O_i is the observed frequency in the i-th bin and E_i is the expected frequency. E_i is $n(F(x_{it}) - F(x_{ib}))$, where $n = \sum_{i=1}^{k} O_i$ is the total number of observations, $F(x)$ is the distribution function for the hypothesized distribution, and (x_{ib}, x_{it}) are the limits for bin i. It is important that every bin has at least five observations.

The hypothesis that the data follow the hypothesized distribution is rejected if the calculated χ^2 test statistic is greater than $\chi^2_{1-\alpha, k-1}$, the chi-square distribution value with $k-1$ degrees of freedom and significance level of α. The formula for this in Excel is CHIINV($1-\alpha$, $k-1$). The Excel function CHITEST(actual_range, expected_range) can also be used.

Failure to reject the null hypothesis of no difference should not be interpreted as "accepting the null hypothesis." For smaller sample sizes, goodness-of-fit tests are not very powerful and will only detect major differences. On the other hand, for a larger sample size, these tests will almost always reject the null hypothesis because it is almost never exactly true. As Law and Kelton (2002) stated, "This is an unfortunate property of these tests, since it is usually sufficient to have a distribution that is 'nearly' correct."

The Kolmogorov-Smirnov (KS) test is generally believed to be a better test for continuous distributions.

See *Box-Jenkins forecasting, chi-square distribution, Kolmogorov-Smirnov test (KS test)*.

CIM – See *Computer Integrated Manufacturing*.

clean room – A work area where air quality, flow, flow direction, temperature, and humidity are carefully regulated to protect sensitive equipment and materials.

Clean rooms are frequently found in electronics, pharmaceutical, biopharmaceutical, medical device, and other manufacturing environments. Clean rooms are important features in the production of integrated circuits, hard drives, medical devices, and other high-tech and sterile products. The air in a clean room is repeatedly filtered to remove dust particles and other impurities.

The air in a typical office building contains from 500,000 to 1,000,000 particles (0.5 micron or larger) per cubic foot of air. A human hair is about 75-100 microns in diameter, but a particle that is 200 times smaller (0.5 micron) than a human hair can cause a major disaster in a clean room. Contamination can lead to expensive downtime and increased production cost. The billion-dollar NASA Hubble Space Telescope was damaged because of a particle smaller than 0.5 micron.

People are a major source of contamination. A motionless person produces about 100,000 particles of 0.3 micron and larger per minute. A person walking produces about 10 million particles per minute.

The measure of the air quality in a clean room is defined in Federal Standard 209E. A Class 10,000 clean room can have no more than 10,000 particles larger than 0.5 micron in any given cubic foot of air. A Class 1000 clean room can have no more than 1000 particles and a Class 100 clean room can have no more than 100 particles. Hard disk drive manufacturing, for example, requires a Class 100 clean room.

People who work in clean rooms must wear special protective clothing called bunny suits that do not give off lint particles and prevent human skin and hair particles from entering the room's atmosphere.

click-and-mortar – A hybrid between a dot-com and a "brick-and-mortar" operation.

See *dot-com*.

clockspeed – The rate of new product introduction in an industry or firm.

High clockspeed industries, such as consumer electronics, often have product lifecycles of less than a year. In contrast, low clockspeed industries, such as industrial chemicals, may have product life cycles measured in decades. High clockspeed industries can be used to understand the dynamics of change that will, in the long run, affect all industries. The term was popularized in the book *Clockspeed* by Professor Charles Fine from the Sloan School at MIT (Fine 1995).

See *New Product Development (NPD)*, *time to market*.

closed-loop MRP – An imprecise concept of a capacity feedback loop in a Materials Requirements Planning (MRP) system; sometimes called closed-loop planning.

Some consultants and MRP/ERP software vendors used to claim that their systems were "closed-loop" planning systems. Although they were never very precise in what this meant, they implied that their systems provided rapid feedback to managers on capacity/load imbalance problems. They also implied that their closed-loop systems could somehow automatically fix the problems when the load exceeded the capacity. The reality is that almost no MRP systems automatically fix capacity/load imbalance problems. Advanced Planning and Scheduling (APS) Systems are designed to create schedules that do not violate capacity, but unfortunately, they are hard to implement and maintain.

See *Advanced Planning and Scheduling (APS)*, *Business Requirements Planning (BRP)*, *capacity*, *Capacity Requirements Planning (CRP)*, *finite scheduling*, *Materials Requirements Planning (MRP)*, *Sales & Operations Planning (S&OP)*.

cloud computing – Internet-based computing that provides shared resources, such as servers, software, and data to users.

Cloud computing offers many advantages compared to a traditional approach where users have their own hardware and software. These advantages include (1) reduced cost, due to less investment in hardware and software and shared expense for maintaining hardware, software, and databases, (2) greater scalability, (3) ease of implementation, and (4) ease of maintainence.

Potential drawbacks of cloud computing include (1) greater security risk and (2) less ability to customize the application for specific business needs. Cloud computing includes three components: Cloud Infrastructure, Cloud Platforms, and Cloud Applications. Cloud computing is usually a subscription or pay-per-use service. Examples include Gmail for Business and salesforce.com.

See *Application Service Provider (ASP)*, *Software as a Service (SaaS)*.

cluster analysis – A method for creating groups of similar items.

Cluster analysis is an **exploratory data analysis** tool that sorts items (objects, cases) into groups (sets, clusters) so the similarity between the objects in a group is high and the similarity between groups is low. Each item is described by a set of measures (also called attributes, variables, or dimensions). The dissimilarity between two items is a function of these measures. Cluster analysis, therefore, can be used to discover structures in data without explaining why they exist.

For example, biologists have organized different species of living beings into clusters. In this taxonomy, man belongs to the primates, the mammals, the amniotes, the vertebrates, and the animals. The higher the level of aggregation, the less similar are the members in the respective class. For example, man has more in common with all other primates than with more "distant" members of the mammal family (e.g., dogs).

Unlike most exploratory data analysis tools, cluster analysis is not a statistical technique, but rather a collection of algorithms that put objects into clusters according to well-defined rules. Therefore, statistical testing is not possible with cluster analysis. The final number of clusters can be a user-input to the algorithm or can be based on a stopping rule. The final result is a set of clusters (groups) of relatively homogeneous items.

Cluster analysis has been applied to a wide variety of research problems and is a powerful tool whenever a large amount of information is available and the researcher has little prior knowledge of how to make sense out of it. Examples of cluster analysis include:

- Marketing research: Cluster consumers into market segments to better understand the relationships between different groups of consumers/potential customers. It is also widely used to group similar products to define product position.
- Location analysis: Cluster customers based on their locations.
- Quality management: Cluster problem causes based on their attributes.
- Cellular manufacturing: Cluster parts based on their routings.

A **dendrogram** is a graphical representation of the step-by-step clustering process. In the dendrogram on the right, the first step divides the entire group of items (set A) into four sets (B, C, D, E). The second step divides B into sets F and G, divides C into sets H and I, and divides E into sets J and K. In the last step, set G is divided into sets L and M, and set J is divided into sets N, O, and P. Therefore, the final clusters are on the bottom row (sets F, L, M, H, I, D, N, O, P, and K). Note that each of these final sets may include only one item or many items.

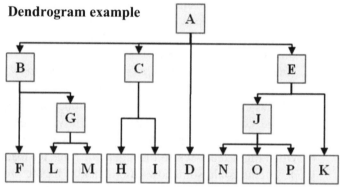

Dendrogram example

Source: Professor Arthur V. Hill

The distance between any two objects is a measure of the dissimilarity between them. Distance measures can be computed from the variables (attributes, dimensions) that describe each item. The simplest way to measure the distance between two items is with the Pythagorean distance. When we have just two variables (x_i, y_i) to describe each item i, the Pythagorean distance between points i and j is $d_{ij} = \sqrt{(x_i - x_j)^2 + (y_i - y_j)^2}$. With three variables (x_i, y_i, z_i) to describe each item, the Pythagorean distance is $d_{ij} = \sqrt{(x_i - x_j)^2 + (y_i - y_j)^2 + (z_i - z_j)^2}$. With K variables, x_{ik} is defined as the measurement on the k-th variable for item i, and the Pythagorean distance between items i and j is defined as

$$d_{ij} = \sqrt{(x_{i1} - x_{j1})^2 + (x_{i2} - x_{j2})^2 + ... + (x_{iK} - x_{jK})^2} = \sqrt{\sum_{k=1}^{K}(x_{ik} - x_{jk})^2}.$$

The Minkowski metric is a more generalized distance metric. If item i has K attributes $(x_{i1}, x_{i2}, ... , x_{iK})$, the distance between item i and item j is given by $d_{ij} = \left(\sum_{k=1}^{K} | x_{ik} - x_{jk} |^r \right)^{1/r}$. The Minkowski metric is equal to the Euclidean distance when $r = 2$ and the Manhattan square distance when $r = 1$.

When two or more variables are used to define distance, the one with the larger magnitude tends to dominate. Therefore, it is common to first standardize all variables, i.e., $x'_{ki} = (x_{ki} - \overline{x}_k) / s_k$, where $\overline{x}_k$ is the sample mean for the k-th variable and s_k is the sample standard deviation. However, even with standardization, not all variables should have the same weight in the summation. Unfortunately, it is usually not clear how to determine how much weight should be given to each variable.

Many clustering algorithms are available. The objective functions include the complete-linkage (or farthest-neighbor), single-linkage (or nearest-neighbor), group-average, and Ward's method. Ward's method is one of the more commonly used methods and measures the distance (dissimilarity) between any two sets (S_I, S_J) as the sum of the squared distances between all pairs of items in the two sets, i.e., $D(S_I, S_J) = \sum_{i \in S_I} \sum_{j \in S_J} d_{ij}^2$. Divisive methods start with all items in one cluster and then split (partition) the cases into smaller and smaller clusters. Agglomerative methods begin with each item treated as a separate cluster and then combine them into larger and larger clusters until all observations belong to one final cluster.

A **scree plot** is a graph used in cluster analysis (and also factor analysis) that plots the objective function value against the number of clusters to help determine the best number of clusters. The scree test involves finding the place on the graph where the objective function value appears to level off as the number of clusters (factors) increases. To the right of this point is only "scree." Scree is a geological term referring to the loose rock and debris that collects on the lower part of a rocky slope.

SPSS offers three general approaches to cluster analysis:

- **Hierarchical clustering** – Users select the distance measure, select the linking method for forming clusters, and then determine how many clusters best suit the data.
- **K-means clustering** – Users specify the number of clusters in advance and the algorithm assigns items to the K clusters. K-means clustering is much less computer-intensive than hierarchical clustering and is therefore preferred when datasets are large (i.e., $N > 1000$).
- **Two-step clustering** – The algorithm creates pre-clusters, and then clusters the pre-clusters.

Exploratory data analysis often starts with a data matrix, where each row in an item (case, object) and each column is a variable that describes that item. Cluster analysis is a means of grouping the rows (items) that are similar. In contrast, factor analysis and principal component analysis are statistical techniques for grouping similar (highly correlated) variables to reduce the number of variables. In other words, cluster analysis groups items, whereas factor analysis and principal component analysis group variables.

See *affinity diagram, algorithm, data mining, data warehouse, factor analysis, logistic regression, Manhattan square distance, Minkowski distance metric, Principal Component Analysis (PCA), Pythagorean Theorem.*

CMM – See *Capability Maturity Model*

CNC – See *Computer Numerical Control.*

co-competition – See *co-opetition.*

COD – See *Cash on Delivery (COD).*

coefficient of determination – See *correlation.*

coefficient of variation – A measure of the variability relative to the mean, measured as the standard deviation divided by the mean.

The coefficient of variation is used as a measure of the variability relative to the mean. For a sample of data, with a sample standard deviation s and sample mean $\overline{x}$, the coefficient of variation is $c = s / \overline{x}$. The coefficient of variation has no unit of measure (i.e., it is a "unitless" quantity).

The coefficient of variation is often a good indicator of the distribution of the random variable. For example, $c = 1$ suggests an exponential distribution. More generally, the k parameter of a k-Erlang (or gamma) distribution is $k = \overline{x}^2 / s^2 = 1 / c^2$.

In forecasting, a good rule of thumb is that any item with a coefficient of variation of demand less than 1 has "lumpy" demand and therefore should not be forecasted with exponential smoothing methods.

See *Croston's Method, Erlang distribution, exponential distribution, exponential smoothing, forecasting, lumpy demand, standard deviation.*

Collaborative Planning Forecasting and Replenishment (CPFR) – A business practice that combines the intelligence of multiple trading partners in the planning and fulfillment of customer demand (source: www.vics.org/committees/cpfr, April 16, 2011).

CPFR is designed to improve the flow of goods from the raw material suppliers to the manufacturer and ultimately to the retailers' shelves. It is also designed to quickly identify any discrepancies in the forecasts, inventory, and ordering data so the problems can be corrected before they impact sales or profits.

With CPRF, customers share their sales history, sales projections, and other important information with their business partners, who, in turn, share their raw material availability, leadtimes, and other important information with the customers. The information is then integrated, synchronized, and used to eliminate excess inventory and improve in-stock positions, making the supply chain more profitable.

CPFR has data and process model standards developed for collaboration between suppliers and an enterprise with methods for planning (agreement between the trading partners to conduct business in a certain way), forecasting (agreed-to methods, technology and timing for sales, promotions, and order forecasting), and replenishment (order generation and order fulfillment). The Voluntary Inter-Industry Commerce Standards (VICS) committee, a group dedicated to the adoption of barcoding and EDI in the department store/mass merchandise industries, has established CPFR standards for the consumer goods industry that are published by the Uniform Code Council (UCC). See www.vics.org for information on the VICS committee.

See *continuous replenishment planning, Efficient Consumer Response (ECR), forecasting.*

Collaborative Product Development – See *Early Supplier Involvement, New Product Development (NPD).*

co-location – The practice of locating people from different functions or different organizations next to each other to improve communications.

Co-location has proven to be very helpful for both customers and suppliers when suppliers have representatives working at their customers' sites. For example, many manufacturers have representatives working in Bentonville, Arkansas, at Walmart's world headquarters.

Co-location makes sense for many large and complex organizations to co-locate workers from different functions to improve communications. For example, Tom Ensign, formerly the business unit manager for 3M Post-it Products, reported that one of his keys to success was the co-location of his office next to his marketing and manufacturing directors. Co-location also makes sense for project teams working on larger projects.

See *JIT II, learning organization, project management, vendor managed inventory (VMI).*

combinations – The number of ways that n items can be grouped in sets of r items without regard to order; also called the binomial coefficient.

In probability and statistics, analysts often need to know the number of ways that it is possible to arrange n things into groups of r items. The number of unique **combinations** of n things taken r at a time is $C(n,r) = \binom{n}{r} = \dfrac{n!}{r!(n-r)!}$. Note that the number of combinations is symmetric, i.e., $C(n, r) = C(n, n - r)$. See the *factorial* entry for the definition of $n!$ For example, a deck of playing cards has 52 cards. In the game of Bridge, each player has a hand of 13 cards. The number of possible combinations (hands) for a Bridge player, therefore, is "52 taken 13 at a time," which is $C(52,13) = \binom{52}{13} = \dfrac{52!}{13!(52-13)!} = 635,013,559,600$. Order does not matter with combinations. The Excel function for combinations is COMBIN(n, r).

In constrast, a unique ordering (sequence) of a set of items is called a **permutation**. The number of unique ways that a set of n items can be ordered is called the number of **permutations** and is written mathematically as $n!$ and read as "n-factorial." For example, the set {1,2,3} has 3! = 3·2·1 = 6 permutations: {1,2,3}, {1,3,2}, {2,1,3}, {2,3,1}, {3,1,2}, and {3,2,1}. A 13-card Bridge hand can be arranged in 13! = 6,227,020,800 different ways. The Excel function for $n!$ is FACT(n).

For both combinations and permulations, most computers will have overflow issues when $n \geq 171$. See the *gamma function* entry for suggestions for handling these issues.

See *binomial distribution, factorial, gamma function.*

commercialization – The process of managing a new product through pilot production, production ramp-up, and product launch into the channels of distribution.

See *New Product Development (NPD)*.

committee – A group of people who work to provide a service for a larger organization.

Committees consist of people who volunteer or are appointed. Although many sources use the terms committee and **project team** interchangeably, the project management literature considers a committee to be an on-going organizational structure and a project team to be a temporary organizational structure that disbands when the task is complete. A **standing committee** serves an on-going function, whereas an **ad hoc committee** is a project team with a limited duration. The Latin phrase "ad hoc" means "for this purpose" and indicates an improvised or impromptu team assigned to fill a particular need.

See *project management*.

commodity – (1) Inventory management: A standard product that is homogenous and cannot be easily differentiated by suppliers (e.g., salt). (2) Purchasing management: A group of similar products often managed by a single buyer (e.g., electronic components). ✪

In the inventory management context, all suppliers offer essentially the same good or product, which means that commodity products from two or more suppliers are essentially interchangeable and uniform. As a result, the main differentiator for commodities is the supplier's price. Common examples of commodities include basic resources (e.g., oil and coal) and agricultural products (e.g., wheat and corn). Many commodities are traded on an exchange and many well-established commodities have actively traded spot and derivative markets. In some cases, minimum commodity quality standards (known as a basis grade) are set by the exchange.

Suppliers often try to differentiate commodity products with packaging, quality, information, service, and delivery. However, in many cases, customers only care about the price. It is often important for sellers to ensure that their products continue to be differentiated so their products are not treated like a commodity and purchased only on the basis of price.

Many industries have found that highly differentiated products can become less differentiated and even commoditized over time. For example, simple handheld calculators were once a highly differentiated luxury item costing hundreds of dollars[8]. Today, they are fairly undifferentiated, sell for under $20, and are essentially a commodity product.

In the purchasing context, the word "commodity" is used to mean any group of purchased materials or components, also known as a commodity class. In this context, a commodity can be any group of purchased items, including highly engineered items. For example, Boston Scientific might have a manager for a commodity group that includes all machined products.

See *category management, futures contract, purchasing, single source, sourcing, standard parts*.

common carrier – An organization that transports people or goods and offers its services to the public, typically on regular routes and regular schedules. ✪

In contrast, **private carriers** do not provide service to the public and provide transport on an irregular or ad hoc basis. Examples of common carriers include airlines, railroads, bus lines, cruise ships, and many trucking companies. Although common carriers generally transport people or goods, the term may also refer to telecommunications providers and public utilities in the U.S.

A common carrier must obtain a certificate of public convenience and necessity from the Federal Trade Commission for interstate traffic. A common carrier is generally liable for all losses that may occur to property entrusted to its charge in the course of business, with four exceptions: (1) an act of God, (2) an act of public enemies, (3) fault or fraud by the shipper, or (4) an inherent defect in the goods. Carriers typically incorporate further exceptions into a contract of carriage, often specifically claiming not to be a common carrier.

See *carrier, for-hire carrier, logistics, private carrier*.

common cause variation – A statistical process control term for natural or random variation that is inherent in a process over time and affects the process at all times.

---

[8] *This author purchased an HP 35 scientific calculator for over $300 in 1973; calculators with the same functions can be purchases today for under $25.*

Common cause variation includes the normal, everyday influences on a process. If a process is in control, it only has common cause variation. This type of variation is hard to reduce because it requires change to the fundamental process. Pande et al. (2000) referred to problems from common causes as "chronic pain." **Special cause variation** is the alternative to common cause variation.

See *Capability Maturity Model (CMM), control chart, process capability and performance, quality management, special cause variation, Statistical Process Control (SPC), Statistical Quality Control (SQC), tampering, tolerance.*

commonality – The degree to which the same parts are used in different products. ✪

In the photo below, the "universal" box in the front middle replaces all the other boxes in the back. The change to this common box dramatically reduced inventory and manufacturing cost. (This photo is used with permission from Honeywell.) Honeywell calls this a "universal" box. These types of components are also called **robust components**. In general, robust components have higher direct labor cost because they have better product design quality. However, increasing commonality can lead to economies of scope in many ways:

- **Reduced setup (ordering) cost** – Because the robust component has a higher demand rate, its economic order quantity is larger and it does not have to be ordered as many times as the current components. This saves on ordering cost.

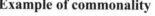
Example of commonality

- **Potential quantity discounts for materials** – However, robust components have higher demand and therefore can qualify for a quantity discount on the price.

- **Reduced cycle (lotsize) inventory** – The economic order quantity logic suggests that robust components have a larger order size than any of the current components. However, the total cycle stock for the robust component will be less than the sum of the cycle stock for the two current components. This will result in lower carrying cost.

- **Reduced safety stock inventory and improved service levels** – The variance of the demand during leadtime for a robust component is likely about equal to the sum of the variance of the demand for the two current components. When this is true, the robust component requires less safety stock inventory. Conversely, the firm can keep the same safety stock level and improve the service level or make improvements in both. This can result in lower carrying cost, lower stockout cost, or both.

- **Reduced forecasting error** – Based on the same logic as above, the robust component has lower forecast error variance than the sum of the variances of the two current components. Again, this can reduce safety stock inventory, improve service levels, or both.

- **Reduced product design cost** – If the firm is using truly robust components, it can use these components in different products and not have to "reinvent the wheel" with each new product design.

- **Reduced purchasing and manufacturing overhead** – As the number of components are reduced, the overhead needed to maintain the engineering drawings, tooling, etc. can also be reduced.

- **Increased reliability** – In some cases, a more robust part is also more reliable and easier to maintain. Commonality is closely related to the concepts of standard parts and interchangeable parts.

See *agile manufacturing, bill of material (BOM), cycle stock, economy of scale, economy of scope, engineer to order (ETO), interchangeable parts, interoperability, mass customization, modular design (modularity), overhead, quantity discount, reliability, robust, service level, standard parts, standard products, value engineering.*

competitive analysis – A methodology used to help an organization identify its most important current and future competitors, analyze how these competitors have positioned their products and services in the market, evaluate these competitors' strengths and weaknesses, and then develop strategies to gain competitive advantage in the market.

See *five forces analysis, industry analysis, operations strategy, SWOT analysis.*

Compounded Annual Growth Rate (CAGR) – The rate of growth for an investment that assumes that the compounded growth rate per period is constant between the first and last values; also called the internal rate of return (IRR) and smoothed rate of return.

The CAGR (pronounced "keg-er") is also called a **smoothed rate of return** because it measures the growth of an investment as if it had grown at a steady rate on an annually compounded basis. Mathematically, the CAGR is the geometric mean growth rate and is computed as $CAGR = \left(\dfrac{\text{ending value}}{\text{starting value}} \right)^{1/n} - 1$, where n is the number of periods (usually years). For example, if someone made an initial investment worth $10,000 at the end of 2007, $11,000 at the end of 2008, $12,000 at the end of 2009, and $19,500 at the end of 2010, the Compounded Annual Growth Rate (CAGR) over this $n = 3$ year period is $(19,500/10,000)^{1/3} - 1 = 24.9\%$. In other words, if the growth rate over the three years was constant each year, it would be an annual growth rate of 24.9%. To prove this, we can see that $10,000 \times 1.249 \times 1.249 \times 1.249 = \$19,500$. Note that this example has balances for four years (2007, 2008, 2009, and 2010), but only three years for computing growth. In summary, the CAGR is not the average (arithmetic mean) annual return but rather the geometric mean annual return.

The Excel functions IRR(*values_range*) and XIRR(*values_range, dates_range*) can be used to calculate the CAGR. IRR is for periodic returns and XIRR allows the user to define a schedule of cash flows. Both functions require at least one positive and one negative value. If this function is not available in Excel and returns the #NAME? error, install and load the Analysis ToolPak add-in.

See *financial performance metrics, geometric mean, Internal Rate of Return (IRR)*.

Computer Aided Design (CAD) – A combination of hardware and software that enables engineers and architects to design everything from furniture to airplanes.

In addition to the software, CAD systems usually require a high-quality graphics monitor, mouse, light pen, or digitizing tablet for drawing, and a special printer or plotter for printing design specifications. CAD systems allow an engineer to view a design from any angle and to zoom in or out for close-ups and long-distance views. In addition, the computer keeps track of design dependencies so that when the engineer changes one value, all other values that depend on it are automatically changed. Until the mid-1980s, CAD systems were specially constructed computers. Today, CAD software runs on general-purpose workstations and personal computers.

See *Computer Aided Design/Computer Aided Manufacturing (CAD/CAM), Computer Numerical Control (CNC), group technology, New Product Development (NPD)*.

Computer Aided Design/Computer Aided Manufacturing (CAD/CAM) – Computer systems used to design and manufacture products.

An engineer can use the system to design a product and generate the instructions that can be used to control a manufacturing process.

See *Computer Aided Design (CAD)*.

Computer Aided Inspection (CAI) – A system for performing inspection through the use of computer hardware and software technologies.

CAI tools are categorized as either contact or non-contact methods:

Contact methods – Coordinate Measuring Machines (CMMs) use a Computer Numerically Controlled (CNC) mechanical probe to inspect parts to an accuracy of as little as 0.0002 inch. However, the CMM probe may damage or deform a product's surface and are not appropriate when contamination is a concern. With many sample points or complex product contours, CMMs may be too slow to support the desired product inspection rate. Contact methods are slower but cost less than non-contact methods.

Non-contact methods/Vision systems – A camera is used to take a video image of a part. The image is processed by software and electronic hardware to compare it against a reference template. The vision system determines the placement, size, and shape of holes and the presence of part features.

Non-contact methods/Laser-scan micrometers – These systems use reflected laser light to measure part dimensions and are used to inspect single dimensions on highly repetitive work, such as intervals, diameters, widths, heights, and linearity.

See *inspection, Statistical Process Control (SPC)*.

Computer Aided Manufacturing (CAM) – See *Computer Aided Design (CAD), Computer Aided Design/Computer Aided Manufacturing (CAD/CAM), Computer Numerical Control (CNC)*.

Computer Based Training (CBT) – Self-paced instruction via interactive software; sometimes called Computer Based Instruction (CBI), e-learning, and distance education.

CBT provides an opportunity for individuals to learn a subject with little or no involvement of an instructor. Content can include videos, quizzes, tests, simulations, and "hands-on" **learning by doing** in a "virtual world."

See *cross-training*.

Computer Integrated Manufacturing (CIM) – See *Computer Aided Design (CAD), Computer Aided Design/Computer Aided Manufacturing (CAD/CAM), Computer Numerical Control (CNC)*.

Computer Numerical Control (CNC) – A type of controller that is typically found on machining centers and other machine tools.

CNC machines typically cut and form metal. A CNC includes a machine tool used to turn, drill, or grind different types of parts and a computer that controls the sequence of processes performed by the machine. Not all computer-controlled machines are CNC. For example, robots are not considered to be CNC machines.

See *Computer Aided Design (CAD), manufacturing processes*.

computer simulation – See *simulation*.

concurrent engineering – A systematic approach to the integrated, simultaneous design of products and their related processes, including manufacturing and support; also called simultaneous engineering and Integrated Product Development (IPD).

The goal of current engineering is to reduce time to market and quality problems. It can accomplish these goals by engaging appropriate cross-functional teams from engineering, operations, accounting, procurement, quality, marketing, and other functions. Suppliers are also involved in some cases.

See *cross-functional team, Early Supplier Involvement (ESI), Integrated Product Development (IPD), New Product Development (NPD), Quality Function Deployment (QFD), simultaneous engineering, waterfall scheduling*.

conference room pilot – See *pilot test*.

confidence interval – A range of values that will contain the true mean for a random variable with a user-specified level of confidence based on a given sample of data.

Given a set of $n > 30$ random observations on a random variable, the confidence interval on the true mean is given by $\bar{x} \pm z_{\alpha/2} s / \sqrt{n}$, where $\bar{x}$ is the sample mean, s is the sample standard deviation, and $z_{\alpha/2} = F^{-1}(1 - \alpha / 2)$ is the z value associated with probability $\alpha/2$. If n random samples are taken many times, this interval will "capture" the true mean about $100 \cdot \alpha/2$ percent of the time. The procedure is as follows:

Step 0. **Define the parameters** – Specify the number of observations (n) that have been collected, the estimated size of the population (N), and the confidence level parameter (α). If the size of N is large but unknown, use an extremely large number (e.g., $N = 10^{10}$).

Step 1. **Compute the sample mean and standard deviation** – Compute the sample mean $\bar{x}$ and sample standard deviation s from the n observations.

Step 2. **Find the z or t value** – When $n < 30$, use the $t_{\alpha/2,n-1}$ value from a Student's t table or the Excel statement TINV(α, $n - 1$). Note: The arguments in this Excel function are correct. The Excel functions TINV and NORMSINV are inconsistent in how they handle the probability parameter (α). TINV returns the probability associated with the two-tailed Student's t-distribution. When $n \geq 30$, use the $z_{\alpha/2}$ value from a normal table or the Excel statement NORMSINV($1 - \alpha/2$).

Step 3. **Compute the half-width** – Compute the half-width of the confidence interval using $h = z_{\alpha/2} s / \sqrt{n}$ (replace $z_{\alpha/2}$ with $t_{\alpha/2,n-1}$ when $n < 30$). If the sample size n is large relative to the total population N (i.e., $n / N > 0.05$), use $h = z_{\alpha/2} s \sqrt{1/n - 1/N}$ instead. The term $\sqrt{1/n - 1/N}$ is called the finite population correction factor. For $n \geq 30$, the half-width can also be found using the Excel function CONFIDENCE(α, s, n). This Excel function should not be used when $n < 30$.

Step 4.   Write the confidence interval – Write the $100(1-\alpha)\%$ confidence interval as ($\overline{x} \pm h$).

Confidence intervals are a useful concept based on the central limit theorem and do not require any assumptions about the distribution of x. The *sample size calculation* entry has more detail on this subject.

See *Analysis of Variance (ANOVA)*, *central limit theorem*, *Chebyshev's inequality*, *dollar unit sampling*, *normal distribution*, *sample size calculation*, *sampling*, *sampling distribution*, *simulation*, *standard deviation*, *Student's t distribution*, *t-test*.

configuration control – See *configuration management*.

configuration management – The process of defining and controlling the information that defines a system.

Configuration control includes all activities needed to control the changes to a configuration after it has been formally documented. Configuration control includes the evaluation, coordination, approval, or rejection of changes.

The best configuration management process is one that can (1) accommodate change, (2) accommodate reuse of proven standards and best practices, (3) assure that all requirements remain clear, concise, and valid, (4) communicate promptly and precisely, and (5) assure that the results conform in each case. CM includes several elements: requirements management, change management, release management, data management, records management, document control, and library management. CM provides the infrastructure that enables an organization to "change faster and document better." CM also accommodates change and keeps requirements clear, concise, valid, and synchronized. A strong CM process is the foundation of a sound business process infrastructure. Adapted from the home page of the Institute of Configuration Management (www.icmhq.com).

See *New Product Development (NPD)*.

configurator – A software tool (usually with an Internet interface) that allows customers, order entry people, or sales people to create customized products by selecting various product features from menus.

Ideally, a configurator will (1) encourage customers to select standard, high-margin combinations of features, (2) prevent customers from selecting prohibitive combinations of features, (3) discourage customers from selecting low margin (or negative margin) combinations, and (4) create manufacturing orders that can be sent electronically to manufacturing. In some cases, the configurator creates instructions for automated equipment. Configurators might contain many expert rules and might draw heavily on science, engineering, and manufacturing expertise. In conclusion, the ideal configurator is easy for the customer to use, creates product configurations that customers want, and guides customers to product configurations that the firm can make and sell profitably.

For example, mycereal.com[9], General Mills' custom-blended breakfast cereal, had a configurator that included tremendous amounts of food science so customers would get healthy food and tasty portions. Lifetouch provides software to high schools so they can configure their own student ID cards, populate a database with student photos, and then send a file to the firm's ID card manufacturing facility.

See *configure to order (CTO)*, *engineer to order (ETO)*, *mass customization*, *order entry*.

configure to order (CTO) – A customer interface strategy that adjusts parameters or adds modules to a product in response to a customer's order.

In a configure to order (CTO) system, a firm sells standard products that require parameter adjustments or modules to be added in response to a customer order. Examples include setting the height of a seat for a riding mower, selecting the language option for a software package, or setting some customer-specific parameters for a medical device. Some people call this reconfigure to order. The *respond to order (RTO)* entry discusses a number of similar customer interface strategies.

See *configurator*, *respond to order (RTO)*, *standard products*.

conformance quality – The degree to which the product or service meets the design specifications or standards; sometimes also called quality of the process or process quality.

---

[9] *This website is no longer active.*

Conformance quality is generally measured by the yield rate (the percentage of units started that are not defective) or the scrap rate (the percentage of units started that have to be discarded because they are defective). In contrast, design quality (also called performance quality) is the degree to which the design meets customer requirements.

For example, the new product development organization has set a performance standard (a specification limit) that a new wristwatch should be able to survive in 100 meters of water. However, the manufacturing process sometimes fails to properly assemble the watch, which results in 10% of all watches failing to meet the standard. In this example, the yield rate is 90% and the percent defective is 10%.

See *product design quality*, *quality at the source*, *quality management*, *scrap*, *yield*.

congestion pricing – The practice of charging a higher price for a service during peak demand periods to discourage arrivals to the system.

For example, the city of Singapore assesses a very high charge to drivers who enter the downtown areas during the workday. This practice is now being used in many large metropolitan areas worldwide. Similar examples can be found in telephone rates, electricity (power) usage, computer usage, restaurants, and other service businesses.

See *yield management*.

conjoint analysis – An analytical marketing research technique that measures the trade-offs made by respondents among product attributes.

Conjoint analysis is a useful tool for both product concept generation and evaluation by rating product attributes in terms of their importance in the market. The method involves the measurement of the collective effects of two or more independent variables (e.g., color, size, ease of use, cost, etc.) on the classification of a dependent variable (overall liking, purchase intention, best buy, or any other evaluative measurement). The stimulus is a product-attribute combination. Various mixed and matched product attributes are put together and rated by the respondent. For example, does the respondent prefer a large, powerful, spacious car that is relatively expensive in its operation or one that is smaller, less powerful, but more economic to operate?

Once the unique product combinations are established, conjoint studies typically collect data via the use of one of the following:

- A paired-comparison methodology, where each of the hypothetical products is directly compared to another product and one of the products is selected over the other. For example, with 16 unique products, a total of 120 binary choices are required.
- A ranking methodology, where product configurations are rank-ordered relative to preferences of the respondent. This is probably the most common method for collecting conjoint data.

For the paired-comparisons model, a telephone survey is often difficult because of the amount of time required to go through each of the possible comparisons.

Adapted from http://mrainc.com/trad_conj.html (April 16, 2011).

See *Analytic Hierarchy Process (AHP)*.

consignee – A transportation term for the party (agent) that accepts a delivery.

The consignee is named on the bill of lading as the party authorized to take delivery of a shipment.

See *Advanced Shipping Notification (ASN)*, *bill of lading*, *consignment inventory*.

consignment inventory – Items in the possession of a retailer or distributor and offered for sale to customers but still owned by the supplier.

Consignment inventory is often used as a marketing tool to entice a retailer or distributor to carry a supplier's inventory. Payment on consignment inventory is usually made when stock is sold or used by a customer. The supplier (the consignor) ships to the agent (the consignee) under an agreement to sell the goods for the consignor. The consignor retains title to the goods until the consignee has sold them. The consignee sells the goods and then pays a commission to the consignor.

Some examples of consignment inventory include: (1) Many retailers of Christmas craft items only pay their suppliers when the craft items are sold. (2) Medical device firms often own the devices in hospital inventories until they are sold to patients. (3) Some manufacturers of fasteners make their products available to assemblers and do not require their customers to pay until the fasteners are used.

See *consignee*, *inventory management*, *vendor managed inventory (VMI)*.

consolidation – (1) In a general context: The combination of separate parts into a single unified whole. (2) In a logistics context: The combination of two or more shipments going to the same destination in a single shipment; related terms include consolidate, consolidation service, freight consolidation, consolidated shipment, consolidated cargo, consolidated load, and consolidated container.

A consolidated shipment can reduce the number of individual shipments and take advantage of lower cost transportation (i.e., full truck or full container load shipments). At the destination, the consolidated shipment is separated (de-consolidated or de-grouped) back into the original individual shipments for delivery to consignees. A consolidation service will combine smaller shipments and then ship them together to achieve better freight rates and cargo security.

Consolidation is also used in the context of reducing the number of stocking locations (e.g., warehouses) and consolidating the "spend" on just a few suppliers for each commodity group (e.g., MRO supplies).

See *cross-docking, hub-and-spoke system, less than truck load (LTL), leverage the spend, Maintenance-Repair-Operations (MRO), pooling, square root law for warehouses, Third Party Logistics (3PL) provider.*

consortium – An association or coalition of two or more individuals, companies, firms, or not-for-profit organizations (or any combination thereof) that pool resources, such as buying power, research capability, manufacturing capability, libraries, or information, to achieve a common goal.

Constant WIP – See *CONWIP.*

constraints management – See *Theory of Constraints.*

consumable goods – An item or product that is used up (consumed) in a relatively short period of time; sometimes called non-durable goods, soft goods, or consumables.

In the economics literature, consumable goods are defined as products that are used up fairly quickly and therefore have to be replaced frequently. In contrast, **durable goods** (also called **hard goods** or **capital goods**), such as refrigerators, cars, furniture, and houses, have long useful lives.

In the **Maintenance, Repair, and Operations (MRO)** context, consumables are items purchased by a firm that do not become part of the product sold to customers. For example, 3M sandpaper might be used for final surface conditioning of a product. Other examples of consumables include printer ink and machine oil.

In a marketing context, many firms make more money selling consumable products than they do selling capital goods or other products. For example, Gillette almost gives away its razors to sell razor blades and HP sells printers with lower margins than it has on its ink cartridges.

See *category captain, category management, consumer packaged goods, durable goods, Maintenance-Repair-Operations (MRO).*

consumer packaged goods – Consumable goods, such as food and beverages, footwear and apparel, tobacco, and cleaning products; sometimes abbreviated CPG.

Some examples of consumer packaged goods include breakfast cereal (such as General Mill's Cheerios) and soap (such as Proctor and Gamble's Ivory soap).

See *category captain, category management, consumable goods, Fast Moving Consumer Goods (FMCG), private label, trade promotion allowance.*

consumer's risk – The probability of accepting a lot that should have been rejected.

More formally, consumer's risk is the probability of accepting a lot with a defect level equal to the Lot Tolerance Percent Defective (LTPD) for a given sampling plan. The consumer suffers when this occurs because a lot with unacceptable quality was accepted. This is called a Type II error. The symbol β is commonly used for the Type II risk.

See *Acceptable Quality Level (AQL), acceptance sampling, Lot Tolerance Percent Defective (LTPD), operating characteristic curve, producer's risk, quality management, sampling, Type I and II errors.*

container – See *shipping container.*

continuous demand – See *demand.*

continuous flow – Producing and moving small batches (ideally with a lotsize of one unit) through a series of processing steps with almost no inventory and almost no waiting between steps.

See *batch-and-queue, discrete manufacturing, facility layout, lean thinking, one-piece flow, repetitive manufacturing.*

continuous improvement – See *kaizen, lean sigma, lean thinking, Total Quality Management (TQM)*.

continuous probability distribution – See *probability density function*.

continuous process – A process that makes only one product with dedicated equipment and never needs to handle changeovers (setups).

> Examples of a continuous process include oil refining, paper making, and chemical processing.
> See *batch process, discrete manufacturing, setup cost, setup time*.

continuous replenishment planning – The practice of working with distribution channel members to change from distributor-generated purchase orders to replenishment based on actual sales and forecast data.

> The principal goal of continuous replenishment planning is to reduce the cost of producing and moving product through the vendor-retailer supply chain. The object is for all stages of the supply chain to operate with greater knowledge of downstream inventory conditions, thereby allowing for a synchronized flow of product from the manufacturer through point-of-sale (Vergin and Barr 1999).
> See *Collaborative Planning Forecasting and Replenishment (CPFR), Efficient Consumer Response (ECR), inventory management*.

continuous review system – A system for managing an inventory that compares the inventory position (on-hand plus on-order less allocated) with the reorder point for every transaction and places a replenishment order when the position is less than the reorder point.

> See *inventory management, inventory position, periodic review system, reorder point, replenishment order*.

Contract Electronics Manufacturing Services (CEMS) – See *contract manufacturer*.

contract manufacturer – An organization that makes products under a legal agreement with the customer.

> Contract manufacturers generally serve the Original Equipment Manufacturing (OEM) market. Contract manufacturers make a large percentage of the products in the computer and electronics fields. These products are usually designed and branded with the OEM's name, built by the contract manufacturer, and then shipped directly to distributors or customers.
>
> A good example is the Microsoft Xbox game console, which is made by Flextronics and other contract manufacturers around the world. Flextronics also makes cell phones for Ericsson, routers for Cisco, and printers for HP. Other major contract electronics manufacturers include Sanmina-SCI Corporation and Celestica.
>
> An "original design manufacturer" (ODM) is a type of contract manufacturer that uses its own designs and intellectual property (IP). The ODM typically owns the IP for the product itself, while the regular contract manufacturer uses its customer's designs and IP. Whereas, contract manufacturers can make hundreds or thousands of different products, ODMs usually specialize in only a handful of categories. Contract manufacturers in the electronics field that not only make products but also offer assistance with the design and supply chain generally call themselves Electronics Manufacturing Services (EMS) or Contract Electronics Manufacturing Services (CEMS).
>
> Porter (2000) listed the most prevalent sources of friction in a contract manufacturing relationship as:
> - Traditional financial metrics.
> - Difficulty defining core competencies.
> - Fear of losing intellectual capital and expertise.
> - Difficulty finding qualified manufacturing-services companies.
> - Difficulty attracting good contract manufacturers for less-desirable programs.
> - Difficulty understanding and documenting capabilities of contract manufacturers.
> - Difficulty earning most-favored-customer status.
> - Necessity of managing risk exposure.
> - Trouble with technology and knowledge transfer.
> - Unforeseeable problems (such as parts shortages).
>
> See *business process outsourcing, co-packer, intellectual property (IP), Original Equipment Manufacturer (OEM), outsourcing, supply chain management*.

contract warehouse – See *warehouse*.

control chart – A graphical tool used to plot the statistics from samples of a process over time and keep the system in control. ✪

If all points are within the upper and lower statistical control limits, variation may be ascribed to "common causes" and the process is said to be "in control." If points fall outside the limits, it is an indication that "special causes" of variation are occurring and the process is said to be "out of control." Eliminating the special causes first and then reducing common causes can improve quality. Control charts are based on the work of Shewhart (1939). The most commonly used control charts are the run chart, x-bar chart, r-chart, c-chart, and p-chart. Less commonly used control charts include the s-chart, s^2-chart, u-chart, and np-chart.

See *c-chart, common cause variation, cumulative sum control chart, lean sigma, np-chart, outlier, p-chart, process capability and performance, quality management, r-chart, run chart, seven tools of quality, special cause variation, specification limits, Statistical Process Control (SPC), Statistical Quality Control (SQC), tampering, u-chart, x-bar chart.*

control limit – See *Statistical Process Control.*

control plan – A formal document that defines how an organization will continue to benefit from an organizational intervention, such as a lean sigma project. ✪

When a process improvement project has been completed, it is important that the organization "sustain the gains." This is often difficult given the normal organizational "entropy," where the system tends to fall back into the old state of disorder. A good control plan includes the following elements:
- **Procedure** – What solutions were implemented to attain the project goals? What control device is in place?
- **Responsible party** – Who is responsible for this? See the *RACI Matrix* entry for a methodology.
- **Nature of control** – How does the control measure sustain the gain? What is the control measure for early detection?
- **What to check** – What does the responsible party inspect/observe? What are the failure modes?
- **Action/Reaction** – What does the responsible party do if the situation is out of control?

If statistical process control is appropriate, the following data items should be specified for each Key Process Output Variable (KPOV): Target value, lower specification limit, upper specification limit, C_{pk}, and the measurement system used to collect the data.

Good control plans go beyond statistical process control and include clear job descriptions, aligned reward systems, standard operating procedures, visual signals and instructions, and error proofing.

See *ADKAR Model for Change, lean sigma, Lewin/Schein Theory of Change, RACI Matrix.*

CONWIP – An approach for manufacturing planning and control that maintains a constant work-in-process inventory in the system.

With CONWIP (Spearman, Hopp, & Woodruff 1989), every time the last step in the process completes one unit, the first step in the process is given permission to start one unit. As a result, CONWIP maintains a constant WIP inventory. This is similar to the Theory of Constraints "drum buffer rope" (DBR) concept, except that CONWIP does not send a signal from the bottleneck, but rather sends the signal from the final step in the process. This concept is similar to a JIT pull system, except that CONWIP does not need to have buffers (kanbans) between each pair of workcenters. Given that CONWIP does not require the firm to identify the bottleneck and does not need to implement any type of kanban system between workcenters, it is clearly easier to operate than many other systems. CONWIP can be implemented with a simple visual control system that has the final operation signal the first operation every time a unit is completed. CONWIP can be applied at almost any level: at a machine, a workcenter, a plant, or even an entire supply chain. Some research suggests that CONWIP is superior to both DBR and JIT in terms of system performance (inventory, capacity, etc.).

See *blocking, Drum-Buffer-Rope (DBR), gateway workcenter, kanban, pacemaker, POLCA (Paired-cell Overlapping Loops of Cards with Authorization), pull system, Theory of Constraints (TOC), Work-in-Process (WIP) inventory.*

co-opetition – A blending of the words "cooperation" and "competition" to suggest that competing firms can sometimes work together for mutual benefit; also called co-competition and coopetition.

Cooperation with suppliers, customers, and firms producing complementary or related products can lead to expansion of the market and the formation of new business relationships, perhaps even the creation of new forms of business. An example can be found in group buying, where multiple, normally competitive, buying group members (such as hospitals) leverage the buying power of the group to gain reduced prices. All members of the buying group benefit from this relationship.

This concept was developed in the book **Co-opetition** (Brandenburger & Nalebuff 1996). Apparently, Ray Noorda, the founder of Novell, coined the term. The concept and term have been widely used in the computer industry, where strategic alliances are commonly used to develop new products and markets, particularly between software and hardware firms. Some industry observers have suggested that Apple and Microsoft need each other and, in fact, are involved in co-opetition.

Do not confuse this term with the term "co-opt," which means to select a potential adversary to join a team. See *game theory*.

co-opt – To appoint, select, or elect someone to become a member of a group, team, or committee, often for the purpose of neutralizing or winning over potential critics or opponents; also spelled coopt, co-option, and co-optation.

According to the **Merriam-Webster Dictionary**, co-opt comes from the Latin word "*cooptare*," which means to choose. When selecting members for a project team, it is often wise to co-opt potential opponents. Ideally, this potential opponent becomes an advocate and recruits support from other like-minded potential opponents.

This term should not be confused with the term "co-opetition," which is a cooperative relationship between competing firms.

See *change management, project management, stakeholder analysis*.

coordinate the supply chain – See *buy-back contract*.

co-packer – A supplier that produces goods under the customer's brand; also copacker.

A co-packer is a contract manufacturer that produces and packs items for another company. The term "co-packer" is frequently used in a consumer packaged goods context, but is also used in other industries. For example, Ecolab, a manufacturer of industrial cleaning products, uses co-packers to manufacture some cleaning agents that require specialized chemical processes and Schwan's Foods uses co-packers when it does not have enough capacity, particularly for seasonal products.

See *contract manufacturer, outsourcing*.

core capabilities – See *core competence*.

core competence – Skills that enable an organization to differentiate its products and services from its competitors; nearly synonymous with distinctive competence. ✪

Coyne, Hall, and Clifford (1997) defined a core competence as "a combination of complementary skills and knowledge bases embedded in a group or team that results in the ability to execute one or more critical processes to a world-class standard." This definition is similar but not identical to the above definition. Nearly all definitions of core competence include the point that a core competence is an attribute of the organization and not just an attribute of a single individual in that organization.

A core competence is unique and hard to copy, which means that it can lead the firm into new products and markets. Some authors make a distinction between core competencies and distinctive competence. They define core competence as the basic product and process technologies and skills that all firms need to compete in an industry and distinctive competence as the set of technologies and skills that a firm uses to differentiate itself in the market. However, it appears that many authors now use the terms almost synonymously. Knowledge of a firm's core competence can lead its management team to find new products and guide its thinking about outsourcing.

Many marketing experts and students tend to define a core competence as a differentiated product. However, a core competence is not a product or service, but rather the processes, abilities, and unique attributes (differentiated processes) that allow the organization to develop and deliver differentiated "core products."

Three requirements for a valid distinctive competence are:

- It must be unique and present a barrier to entry for new competitors.
- The unique competence must offer real value to the marketplace. Something being merely unique without offering value is not a distinctive competence.
- The unique competence must be credible in the marketplace. Its existence and value have to be accepted and believed.

A popular phrase in many MBA classrooms is "An organization should never outsource its core competence." With that said, it is interesting to see how many firms find that they are outsourcing today what they defined as their core competences less than five years ago. It may just be that core competences, like strategies, tend to change and adapt over time as the markets, products, and technologies change. Clearly, an organization's set of core competences should not remain stagnant in a rapidly changing environment.

In this author's experience, most executives cannot clearly identify their core competences when asked. However, one insightful way to help an organization identify its core competence is to ask, "What would keep a competitor from capturing 100% of your market share tomorrow?" This "barriers-to-entry" question usually identifies the organization's core competence. Barriers to entry can include:

- Proprietary product or process technology
- Product differentiation (often based on process differentiation)
- Economies of scale (that lead to a lower cost structure)
- Brand equity

- Switching cost
- Government protection, subsidies, and patents
- Access to raw materials (special relationship or location)
- Access to customers (good location)

Another good question used to identify a core competence is, "Why do customers buy your product instead of another product?" This is the customer's view of core competence.

Zook (2004) emphasizes the need for firms to stay close to their core products and core competence. His book offers a systematic approach for choosing among a range of possible "adjacency moves," while always staying close to the core products and core competencies.

See *economy of scale*, *focused factory*, *market share*, *operations strategy*, *outsourcing*, *resource based view*, *switching cost*.

corporate portal – A Web-based system that allows businesses to make internal (IS/IT) systems or information available in a single location and format.

A portal is a Web site intended to be the first place people see when using the Web. Most portals have a catalog of web sites, a search engine, or both. Portals may also offer e-mail and other services to entice people to use that site as their main point of entry (hence "portal"). Portals are often used to allow access to internal information by providing a secure connection (dashboard) for employees, vendors, or customers.

See *balanced scorecard*, *dashboard*, *extranet*, *intranet*.

correlation – A dimensionless measure of the strength of the linear association between two variables; also known as the Pearson product-moment correlation coefficient or Pearson's correlation coefficient.

If two variables are correlated, they tend to vary together. In other words, when one is higher (lower) than its mean, the other one is too. Correlation is always in the range $[-1, 1]$, where a negative sign shows an inverse relationship. The **coefficient of determination** (also known as **R-squared**) is the square of the correlation coefficient. For example, if the correlation is $r = -0.7$, the coefficient of determination is $R^2 = 0.49$. The R-squared value is often described as the **percent of the variation explained**.

Correlation is a necessary but not sufficient condition for **causation**. Although correlation may sometimes infer causation, correlation does not mean causation. For example, shoe size and reading skill are correlated. This does not mean that large feet cause better reading. It simply means that young children do not read as well as adults. Similarly, roosters might make noise at sunrise, but the rooster's noise does not cause the sun to rise. Causation is also inferred by a time (temporal) ordering, where the cause should precede the effect. Correlation and temporal ordering are both necessary but not sufficient conditions for causation.

The mathematical definition of the sample correlation between random variables x and y is $r = \dfrac{\text{cov}(x, y)}{s_x s_y}$,

where the sample covariance between x and y is $\text{cov}(x, y) = \dfrac{1}{n-1} \sum_{i=1}^{n} (x_i - \overline{x})(y_i - \overline{y})$, the sample standard

deviation of x is $s_x = \sqrt{\dfrac{1}{n-1} \sum_{i=1}^{n} (x_i - \overline{x})^2}$, and the sample standard deviation of y is $s_y = \sqrt{\dfrac{1}{n-1} \sum_{i=1}^{n} (y_i - \overline{y})^2}$.

A mathematically equivalent expression defines the sample correlation as the sum of the products of the

standardized values $r = \sum_{i=1}^{n} z_{xi} z_{yi}$, where $z_{xi} = (x_i - \overline{x}) / s_x$ and $z_{yi} = (y_i - \overline{y}) / s_x$. The variable

$t = r\sqrt{(n-2)/(1-r^2)}$ has a Student's t-distribution (approximately) with $n - 2$ degrees of freedom and can be used to test if an r value is different from zero.

In Excel use CORREL(x_range, y_range), where x_range and y_range are ranges. CORREL will have an error if the variance of x or y is zero. The equivalent formula $(n/(n-1))$*COVAR(x_range, y_range)/STDEV(x_range)/STDEV(y_range) can also be used. The term $n/(n-1)$ is needed because the Excel COVAR function is for the population rather than the sample.

The correlation between two sets of ranked values (x_i, y_i) can be found with the Spearman's rank correlation coefficient, which is $\rho = 1 - 6\sum_{i=1}^{n}(x_i - y_i)^2 / (n(n^2 - 1))$. However, if two or more ranks are tied for either set of numbers, the correlation coefficient (Pearson's) should be used.

See *autocorrelation, covariance, forecast error metrics, linear regression, variance.*

cost center – An accounting term for an area of responsibility that is only held accountable for its cost.

Cost centers are often service and support organizations, such as manufacturing, human resources, and information technology, that do not have any easily assignable revenue.

See *absorption costing, Activity Based Costing (ABC), human resources, investment center, profit center, revenue center.*

cost driver – See *Activity Based Costing (ABC).*

cost of goods sold – An accounting term for all direct costs incurred in producing a product or service during a period of time; also called cost of goods, cost of sales, cost of products sold, and cost of production.

Cost of goods sold usually includes direct materials, incoming transportation, direct labor cost, production facilities, and other overhead (indirect) labor and expenses that are part of the manufacturing process. It does not include indirect costs, such as administration, marketing, and selling costs, that cannot be directly attributed to producing the product.

Inventory is an asset, which means it is not expensed when purchased or produced, but rather goes into an inventory asset account. When a unit is sold, the cost is moved from the inventory asset account to the cost of goods sold expense account. Cost of goods sold is on the income statement and used in the inventory turnover calculation.

See *ABC classification, direct cost, direct labor cost, financial performance metrics, gross profit margin, inventory turnover, Last-In-First-Out (LIFO), overhead, transfer price.*

cost of quality – A framework coined by quality leader Phillip Crosby and used to measure quality-related costs; now called the "price of non-conformance." ✪

The cost of quality concept was popularized by Phillip Crosby, a well-known author and consultant (Crosby 1979). Crosby focused on the following principles:
- Quality is defined as conformance to requirements.
- The system for causing quality is prevention, not appraisal.
- The performance standard is zero defects.
- The measurement of quality is the cost of quality (sometimes called the price of nonconformance).

More recently, Crosby has replaced "the cost of quality" with the "price of nonconformance" in response to quality professionals who did not like the older term. The price of nonconformance assigns an economic value to all waste caused by poor quality. Examples of the price of nonconformance include wasted materials, wasted capacity, wasted labor time, expediting, inventory, customer complaints, service recovery, downtime, reconciliation, and warranty.

According to Feigenbaum (1983), the cost of quality framework includes these four elements:

Prevention costs – Cost of designing quality into the product and process. This includes product design, process design, work selection, and worker training. Some authors also add the cost of assessing and improving process capability. Many firms find that this cost is hardest to measure.

Appraisal costs – Cost of inspection, testing, auditing, and design reviews for both products and procedures.

Internal failure costs – Cost of rework, scrap, wasted labor cost, wasted lost machine capacity, and poor morale. Lost capacity for a bottleneck process can also result in lost gross margin.

External failure costs – Costs incurred after the customer has taken possession of the product and include warranty, repair (both field repair and depot repair), lost gross margin/refunds, customer support, lost customer good will, damage to the brand, damage to channel partnerships, and lawsuits.

An important teaching point with this framework is that most organizations need to move the costs up the list. In other words, it is usually better to have internal failures than external failures. It is usually better to have appraisal than internal failure and usually better to have prevention than appraisal. A couple of metaphors are helpful here. It is better to avoid smoking (prevention) than to try to heal cancer. It is better to avoid toxic waste than to try to clean it up.

The "1-10-100 rule" suggests that $1 on prevention will save $10 in appraisal, $10 on appraisal will save $100 in internal failure, and $100 in internal failure will save $1000 in external failure. Of course, the numbers are not precise, but the concept is an important one.

The old saying "An ounce of prevention is worth a pound of cure" communicates the same concept. A similar old phrase "A stitch in time saves nine" suggests that timely preventive maintenance will save time later. In other words, sewing up a small hole in a piece of clothing will save time later.

See *appraisal cost, early detection, inspection, prevention, process capability and performance, quality management, scrap.*

Council of Logistics Management (CLM) – See *Council of Supply Chain Management Professionals (CSCMP).*

Council of Supply Chain Management Professionals (CSCMP) – A professional society with the mission "to lead the evolving Supply Chain Management profession by developing, advancing, and disseminating supply chain knowledge and research."

Founded in 1963, the Council of Supply Chain Management Professionals (CSCMP) is an association for individuals involved in supply chain management. CSCMP provides educational, career development, and networking opportunities to its members. The National Council of Physical Distribution Management (NCPDM) was founded in 1963 by a group of educators, consultants, and managers who envisioned the integration of transportation, warehousing, and inventory as the future of the discipline. In 1985, the association changed its name to the Council of Logistics Management (CLM) and in 2005 changed its name to CSCMP.

CSCMP publishes a number of trade journals and the academic journal *The Journal of Business Logistics*. The CSCMP website is www.cscmp.org.

See *operations management (OM).*

counting tolerance – The margin for error used when counting items in an inventory.

An item count is considered wrong only when the count is off by more than the "counting tolerance," which is usually a percentage defined for each category of items. High-value items will usually have a counting tolerance of zero; very low-value items might have a counting tolerance of 10% or more.

See *cycle counting, tolerance.*

covariance – A measure of the strength of association between two variables.

If two variables have high covariance, they tend to vary together. In other words, when one is higher (lower) than its mean, the other one is too. The mathematical definition of the sample covariance between random variables X and Y is $\mathrm{Cov}(X,Y) = \left(\dfrac{1}{n-1}\right)\sum_{i=1}^{n}(x_i - \overline{x})(y_i - \overline{y}) = \left(\dfrac{1}{n-1}\right)\left(\sum_{i=1}^{n}x_i y_i - \dfrac{1}{n}\left(\sum_{i=1}^{n}x_i\right)\left(\sum_{i=1}^{n}y_i\right)\right)$, where $\overline{x}$

and $\overline{y}$ are the sample means. The first term is called the definitional form and the last term is called the computational form because it only requires a single pass for the summations. Covariance is related to correlation by the equation $r_{x,y} = \mathrm{Cov}(x,y)/\sqrt{\mathrm{Var}(x)\mathrm{Var}(y)}$, which shows that correlation is the covariance "normalized" by the standard deviations of the two variables. Some basic facts about covariance for random variables X and Y and constants a and b: $\mathrm{Cov}(a,X) = 0$, $\mathrm{Cov}(X,Y) = \mathrm{Cov}(Y,X)$, $\mathrm{Cov}(X,X) = \mathrm{Var}(X)$, $\mathrm{Cov}(aX, bY) = ab\mathrm{Cov}(X,Y)$, $\mathrm{Cov}(X + a, Y + b) = \mathrm{Cov}(X,Y)$.

The Excel population covariance is COVAR(x_range, y_range), where x_range and y_range are the x and y ranges. For the sample covariance, use $(n/(n-1))$COVAR. Note that this issue is not documented in Excel.

See *Analysis of Variance (ANOVA), correlation, variance.*

C_p – See *process capability and performance.*

CPFR – See *Collaborative Planning Forecasting and Replenishment.*

C_{pk} – See *process capability and performance.*

CPM – See *Critical Path Method (CPM).*

CRAFT – See *facility layout.*

crashing – See *critical path.*

critical chain – The set of tasks that determines the overall duration of a project, taking into account both precedence and resource dependencies.

The critical chain is similar to the **critical path** except that it goes one major step further and factors in resource constraints. The steps in the critical chain approach are as follows:

Step 1. Compute the early start, early finish, late start, late finish, and slack times as is normally done with the critical path method – The path through the network with the longest total time is called the critical path, which is the path (or paths) with the shortest slack. The estimated task times for this process should be set at the median rather than the 90-99% point of the task time distribution.

Step 2. Create a detailed schedule, starting from the current date and moving forward in time – When a task is complete, begin the next task in the precedence network if the required resources are available. When a resource becomes available, assign it to the task that has the least amount of slack time as computed in Step 1. Continue this process until the schedule is complete for all activities. This new schedule is called the critical chain and will be longer than the critical path, which only considers the precedence constraints. The critical chain will still follow the precedence constraints, but will never have any resource used more than its capacity.

Step 3. Strategically add time buffers to protect activities on the critical chain from starting late – Non-critical chain activities that precede the critical chain should be planned to be completed early so the critical chain is protected from disruption.

The consulting/software firm Realization markets software called Concerto that implements critical chain concepts in Microsoft Project.

See *critical path, Critical Path Method (CPM), Earned Value Management (EVM), Project Evaluation and Review Technique (PERT), project management, safety leadtime, slack time, Theory of Constraints (TOC).*

critical incidents method – An approach for identifying the underlying dimensions of customer satisfaction.

The critical incidents method involves collecting a large number of customer (or worker) complaints and compliments and then analyzing them to identify the underlying quality dimension (timeliness, friendliness, etc.). It is important to note that in analyzing a complaint or a complement, it does not matter if it is a negative (complaint) or a positive (compliment); the goal is to simply identify the underlying dimensions of quality, regardless if they are satisfiers or dissatisfiers.

This technique is useful for identifying the key dimensions of service quality for a customer satisfaction survey. This technique can also be used in other contexts, such as job analysis to identify the critical dimensions of worker satisfaction.

See *service quality, voice of the customer (VOC).*

critical path – The longest path through a project-planning network; the path that has the least slack (float) time. ✪

The only way to reduce the project completion time is to reduce the **task times** along the critical path. Task times on the critical path are usually reduced by applying more resources (people, money, equipment, etc.) or by overlapping activities that were originally planned to be done sequentially. Reducing times along the critical path is called **crashing**, **schedule compression**, and **fast tracking**. Crashing non-critical activities will not improve the project completion time. Crashing should focus on the critical path tasks that have the lowest cost per unit time saved.

The *Critical Path Method* entry explains the methodology for finding the critical path. Activities not on the critical path can become critical if they are delayed. Therefore, project managers need to monitor schedules and practice risk management. It is possible for a network to have two or more critical paths.

A *critical chain* is similar to a critical path, but the two concepts are not synonymous. The critical chain considers resource constraints, whereas the critical path does not.

See *critical chain, Critical Path Method (CPM), Failure Mode and Effects Analysis (FMEA), project management, slack time.*

Critical Path Method (CPM) – An approach for project planning and scheduling that focuses on the longest path through the project planning network. ✪

Project scheduling begins with the work breakdown structure that defines the "tree" of activities that make up the project. Each task at the bottom of the tree is then defined in terms of a task name, task time, resources (people, machines, money, etc.), and a set of precedence relationships, which is the set of tasks that need to be completed before the task can be started.

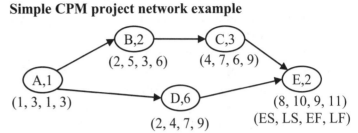

Simple CPM project network example

The simple example to the right shows the scheduling process with a project network with five tasks (A-E) with the times (in days) noted by each task. The process has two passes: a forward pass to create the early start and early finish times, and a backward pass to create the last finish and late start times for each task.

The forward pass begins with task A, which has an early start at the beginning of day 1 (ES = 1) and an early finish at the end of day 1 (EF = 1). Task B cannot start until task A is completed and therefore has an early start at the beginning of day 2 (ES = 2). Task B requires 2 days and has an early finish at the end of day 3 (EF = 3). The forward pass continues until every node is assigned an early start (ES) and early finish (EF).

The backward pass (back scheduling) begins with the desired completion date for the project, which is the late finish for the last task (task E). The required completion date for this project is the end of day 11 (i.e., LF = 11). Planning backward from this completion date, task E has a late start date at the beginning of day 10 (LS = 10). Continuing this backward pass creates the late finish and late start for all nodes. The notation in parentheses beside each task node is (Early Start, Late Start, Early Finish, Late Finish) = (ES, LS, EF, LF).

The slack time (float) for any task is the difference between the early start and the late start (i.e., LS – ES), which is always the same as the difference between the early finish and late finish (i.e., LF – EF). The critical path is the path through the network that has the smallest slack. In this example, the critical path is A→D→E. The slack time for a task may be zero or negative.

Management should prioritize tasks along the critical path for both resource allocation and crashing. When a resource (e.g., person, tool, or machine) becomes free, a good rule for re-allocating this resource is to use the minimum slack rule, which simply assigns the resource to the open task that has the least slack. This is essentially the same process used to identify the critical chain.

If it is necessary to reduce the total project time, the project manager should find the task on the critical path that can be reduced (crashed) at the lowest cost per unit time, make the change, and then repeat the crashing process until the desired project completion time is achieved or until the cost exceeds the benefit. Crashing non-critical activities will not improve the project completion date.

Activities not on the critical path can become critical if they are delayed. This suggests that project managers need to constantly monitor project schedules and practice good risk management to prepare for contingencies. Note that it is possible for a project network to have two or more critical paths.

The above figure uses the "activity-on-node" approach. The alternative "activity-on-arc" approach is presented in some textbooks, but is far more difficult to understand and is rarely used in practice.

Two of the better-known project scheduling packages are Microsoft Project and Primavera sold by Oracle. Microsoft Project is said to be better for smaller projects and Primavera better for larger projects. Many other commercial packages are available.

See *back scheduling, critical chain, critical path, forward scheduling, Gantt Chart, load leveling, Project Evaluation and Review Technique (PERT), project management, project network, slack time, work breakdown structure (WBS).*

critical ratio – See *dispatching rule, newsvendor model.*

Critical to Quality (CTQ) – Key measurable characteristics of a product or process that require performance standards or specification limits to satisfy the customer (internal or external) requirements; also called Key Process Output Variable (KPOV).

CTQ may include the **upper and lower specification limits** or any other factors related to the product or service. A CTQ usually must be interpreted from a qualitative customer statement to an actionable, quantitative business specification. CTQs are what the customer expects of a product. The customer's requirements must be expressed in measurable terms using tools, such as DFMEA.

See *Key Process Output Variable (KPOV), lean sigma, quality management, voice of the customer (VOC)*.

CRM – See *Customer Relationship Management (CRM)*.

cross-functional team – A group of employees from different parts of an organization who come together and use their different viewpoints and skills to address a problem.

Many organizational problems cannot be solved by a single business function. For example, a new product development project might require expertise from marketing, sales, manufacturing, and engineering. Cross-functional teams are often the best approach for addressing these problems. A cross-functional team may be **self-directed** or directed by a sponsor (or sponsors) within the organization. Cross-functional teams are a common component of concurrent engineering, agile software development, and lean sigma projects.

See *agile software development, concurrent engineering, lean sigma, organizational design, project management, Quality Function Deployment (QFD), red tag, sponsor*.

cross-docking – A warehousing term for the practice of moving products directly from incoming trucks or rail cars to outgoing trucks without placing inventory on shelves in the warehouse or distribution center; also called crossdocking and cross docking.

Products that are good candidates for cross-docking have high demand, standardized packaging, and no special handling needs (e.g., security or refrigeration). This is a common strategy for retail distribution where trucks carry large shipments from factories to the cross-dock facility, which loads other trucks with mixed assortments to send to retail stores.

Cross-docking has many advantages over traditional warehouse facilities:

- **Reduced inventory and carrying cost** – The firm replaces inventory with information and coordination.
- **Reduced transportation cost** – For less than truck load (LTL) and small package carriers, cross-docking is a way to reduce transportation costs by consolidating shipments to achieve truck load quantities.
- **Reduced labor cost** – Cross-docking avoids costly moves to and from shelves in the warehouse.
- **Improved customer service** – Cross-docked shipments typically spend less than 24 hours in a cross-dock.

The figure on the right shows a cross-docking process with a top-down view of eight trucks. Four trucks bring products in from suppliers and four take products out to the retail stores.

Napolitano (2000) proposed the following classification scheme for cross-docking:

Trucks coming in from suppliers

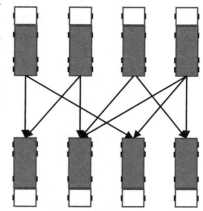

Trucks going out to retailers

Manufacturing cross-docking for receiving and consolidating inbound supplies to support Just-in-Time manufacturing. For example, a manufacturer might lease a warehouse close to its plant and use it to prep subassemblies or consolidate kits of parts. Because demand for the parts is known, say from the output of an MRP system, there is no need to maintain stock.

Distributor cross-docking for consolidating inbound products from different vendors into a multi-SKU pallet, which is delivered as soon as the last product is received. For example, computer distributors often source components from different manufacturers and consolidate them into one shipment in merge-in-transit centers before delivering them to the customer.

Transportation cross-docking for consolidating shipments from different shippers in the LTL and small package industries to gain economies of scale. For small package carriers, material movement in the cross-dock is by a network of conveyors and sorters; for LTL carriers it is mostly by manual handling and forklifts.

Retail cross-docking for receiving product from multiple vendors and sorting onto outbound trucks for different stores. Cross-docking is one reason Walmart surpassed Kmart in retail sales in the 1980s.

Opportunistic cross-docking is transferring an item directly from the receiving dock to the shipping dock to meet a known demand in any type of warehouse.

All of the cross-docking practices involve consolidation and short cycle times, usually less than a day. Short cycle time is possible because the destination for an item is known before or upon receipt.

See *Advanced Shipping Notification (ASN), consolidation, distribution center (DC), distributor, dock, economy of scale, forklift truck, less than truck load (LTL), logistics, Over/Short/Damaged Report, receiving, supply chain management, Transportation Management System (TMS), warehouse, Warehouse Management System (WMS).*

cross-selling – A sales and marketing term for the practice of suggesting related products to a customer during a sales transaction or a customer service encounter.

In contrast to cross-selling, **up-selling** is a sales technique where a salesperson attempts to persuade the customer to purchase better or more expensive items. Cross-selling and up-selling can sometimes be combined to increase the value added for the customer and also increase the sales and margin for the selling organization.

See *call center, Customer Relationship Management (CRM), customer service, order entry.*

cross-training – Training workers in several different areas or functions outside their normal job responsibilities.

Having workers learn a wide variety of tasks has many advantages:

Increased flexibility – Workers can provide backup when the primary worker is unavailable or when the demand exceeds the capacity. This makes it easy to improve flow and reduce inventory. This increased flexibility allows the line workers to dynamically balance the line without any help from an industrial engineer.

Process improvement – When workers have a broader understanding of the organization, they can be more knowledgeable about how to improve it.

Develops human capital – Cross-trained workers are more valuable to the company and often find more satisfaction in their jobs. Cross-training is often an investment in the future for a firm.

See *cellular manufacturing, facility layout, human resources, job design, job enlargement, job rotation, lean thinking, learning organization, line balancing, on-the-job training (OJT), workforce agility.*

Croston's Method – A time series forecasting method that is used for lumpy (intermittent) demand.

When the demand (sales) history for an item has many periods with zero demand, it is said to have **intermittent** or **lumpy demand**. **Exponential smoothing** does a poor job of forecasting lumpy demand because the exponentially smoothed average will approach zero after several zero demand periods and the forecast for the period with the next "demand lump" will therefore be close to zero. Exponential smoothing, therefore, should not be used for lumpy demand. A demand time series is often judged to be lumpy when the coefficient of variation of the demand is greater than one.

Croston (1972) suggests a method for forecasting lumpy demand by decomposing the time series into (1) the average size of the demand lumps and (2) the average time between the demand lumps. Croston's Method uses simple exponential smoothing (SES) for the average size of the demand lumps and also for the average number of periods between the demand lumps. As shown in the table below, it implements three recursive equations.

Croston's Method rules

Average size of a non-zero demand (z_t)	Average number of periods since the last non-zero demand (p_t)	Number of periods since the last demand (q_t)
$z_t = \begin{cases} z_{t-1} & \text{if } d_t = 0 \\ \alpha d_t + (1-\alpha)z_{t-1} & \text{if } d_t > 0 \end{cases}$	$p_t = \begin{cases} p_{t-1} & \text{if } d_t = 0 \\ \alpha q_t + (1-\alpha)p_t & \text{if } d_t > 0 \end{cases}$	$q_t = \begin{cases} q_{t-1} + 1 & \text{if } d_t = 0 \\ 1 & \text{if } d_t > 0 \end{cases}$

The first equation updates the smoothed average size of the non-zero demand z_t. If the demand in period t is zero (i.e., $d_t = 0$), the average size of the demand remains unchanged; otherwise, the average size of a non-zero demand (z_t) is updated with simple exponential smoothing. The second equation updates the average number of periods since the last non-zero demand (p_t) based on q_t, which is the number of periods since the last demand. When the demand is zero, p_t remains unchanged; otherwise, p_t is updated with simple exponential smoothing based on q_t. The third equation updates q_t, which counts the number of periods between non-zero demand. If d_t is zero, the number of periods since the last demand is incremented by 1; otherwise, the number of periods since the last demand is reset to 1.

The forecast for the demand in period $t + n$ is then $f_{t+n} = z_t / p_t$. If every period has a non-zero demand (i.e., $p_t = 1$), Croston's Method is equivalent to simple exponential smoothing with smoothing constant α.

The SAP Library (http://help.sap.com/saphelp_scm50/helpdata/en/ac/216b89337b11d398290000e8a49608/content.htm) recommends initializing $\{z_0, p_0\} = \{0, 2\}$ if $d_1 = 0$ and $\{d_1, 1\}$ if $d_1 > 0$. However, this will create forecasts $f_t = 1$ for all periods when no non-zero demand is encountered. Therefore, the values $z_0 = 0$ if $d_1 = 0$ and $z_0 = d_1$ if $d_1 > 0$ are more logical. The q_0 parameter should be initialized at 1.

An alternative approach is to increase the size of the time buckets so that zero demands are rare or use the average demand over several periods. It is important to avoid using exponential smoothing for intermittent demand because it will forecast relatively high demand right after a "lump" in demand and forecast nearly zero demand about the time the next "lump" in demand occurs.

See *coefficient of variation, exponential smoothing, forecasting, lumpy demand, time bucket, time series forecasting.*

CRP (Capacity Requirements Planning) – See *Capacity Requirements Planning (CRP).*

CTO – See *configure to order (CTO).*

CTQ – See *Critical to Quality (CTQ).*

cube utilization – A warehousing term for the percent of the usable three-dimensional space (volume) used in a trailer, container, or warehouse.

Volume is calculated as the product of the three dimensions – width x height x depth.

See *operations performance metrics, shipping container, slotting, trailer, warehouse.*

cumsum chart – See *cumulative sum control chart.*

Cumulative Distribution Function (CDF) – See *probability density function.*

cumulative leadtime – The critical path leadtime (longest) required to purchase material and create a product to offer to the market; also known as the stacked leadtime.

The cumulative leadtime usually is the time required to purchase materials, fabricate (cut, mold, weld, finish, etc.), assemble, test, package, and ship a product assuming that no inventory is on hand and no materials have been ordered. The customer leadtime might be much less than the cumulative leadtime if intermediate products (e.g., subassemblies) are inventoried.

See *customer leadtime, leadtime, planning horizon, push-pull boundary, time fence.*

cumulative sum control chart – A quality and industrial engineering term for a graphical tool (chart) that plots the cumulative sum of deviations over time; also known as a cumsum control chart or cumsum chart.

A cumulative sum control chart plots the cumulative sum of deviations of successive samples from a target value (i.e., $S_m = \sum_{i=1}^{m}(x_i - \mu)$), where S_m is the cumulative sum, x_i is the observed value (or sample mean), and μ is the target value. This can also be defined recursively as $S_m = S_{m-1} + x_i - \mu$. This concept is very similar to a tracking signal used for forecasting.

See *control chart, Statistical Process Control (SPC), Statistical Quality Control (SQC), tracking signal.*

current reality tree – A Theory of Constraints term for a causal map that describes the current state of a problem.

See *causal map, future reality tree, Theory of Constraints (TOC).*

Customer Effort Score (CES) – A measure of service quality using the single question "How much effort did you personally have to put forth to handle your request?"

Dixon, Freeman, and Toman (2010) developed this simple scale for call centers, service centers, and self-service operations. They argue that customers do not want to be delighted; they just want their needs met without annoying phone calls, transfers, and confusion. They claim that the CES is more predictive of customer loyalty than the Net Promoter Score (NPS) and direct measures of customer satisfaction. They recommend using a CES scale from 1 (very low effort) to 5 (very high effort) and suggest that service providers intervene when customers report a high CES. Note that CES is a measure of dissatisfaction and NPS is a measure of satisfaction.

See *Net Promoter Score (NPS), operations performance metrics, service management, service quality.*

customer leadtime – The planned or actual time in system for a customer (or customer order); planned or actual turnaround time. ✪

Customer leadtime is the difference between the time the customer (or order) enters the system and the time that the customer (or order) is complete. The term "leadtime" suggests that this term should refer to a planning factor rather than the actual time or the historical average leadtime.

In a manufacturing context, the customer leadtime begins after the **push-pull boundary**, which is the location in the process where the firm no longer stocks inventory. Customer leadtime can be nearly zero if the manufacturer has the push-pull boundary at finished goods inventory. In a retail context, customer leadtime is the difference between the time the customer selected and received an item.

See *addition principle, assemble to order (ATO), cumulative leadtime, leadtime, postponement, push-pull boundary, respond to order (RTO), time in system, turnaround time.*

customer profitability – The revenue a customer generates minus the costs needed to acquire and retain that customer.

Customer profitability is closely related to the concepts of customer equity and **lifetime value**. Without a method for estimating customer profitability, a firm may spend scarce marketing dollars to retain its unprofitable (or low profit) customers and may mistreat its most profitable customers.

See *Activity Based Costing (ABC), Customer Relationship Management (CRM).*

Customer Relationship Management (CRM) – An information system that collects data from a number of customer-facing activities to help an organization better understand its customers so that it can better match its products and services to customer needs and thereby increase sales.

Although CRM involves information technology, it is fundamentally a strategic process (and not just an IT project) for helping organizations better understand their customers' needs, better meet those needs, and increase sales and profits. CRM processes and systems combine information from marketing, sales, contact management, and customer service activities. CRM also provides tools to analyze customer/product sales history and profitability, campaign tracking and management, contact and call center management, order status information, and returns and service tracking. A good CRM system provides many benefits:

- Provide exactly the services and products that customers want.
- Offer better customer service.
- Allow for more effective cross-seling (selling complementary products).
- Help sales staff close deals faster.
- Help the firm retain current customers and discover new ones.
- Collect timely complete information on customers through multiple customer interfaces, including call centers, e-mail, point-of-sale operations, and direct contact with the sales force.
- Reduce the transaction cost for buying products and services.
- Provide immediate access to order status.
- Provide support that will reduce the costs of using products and services.
- Help management develop a deeper understanding of customer buying behavior "sliced and diced" in a number of ways, such as geography, demographics, channel, etc.

See *cross-selling, customer profitability, customer service, target price, voice of the customer (VOC).*

customer satisfaction – See *service quality.*

customer service – (1) The organization charged with dealing with customer complaints and other customer needs. (2) A metric used to evaluate how well an organization or an inventory is meeting customer requirements.

See *Automatic Call Distributor (ACD), call center, cross-selling, Customer Relationship Management (CRM), empowerment, fulfillment, order entry, service level, service quality, SERVQUAL, supplier scorecard, Third Party Logistics (3PL) provider.*

customization flexibility – See *flexibility.*

customization point – See *push-pull boundary.*

cycle counting – A methodology for counting items in storage that counts more important items more often and systematically improves the record-keeping process. ✪

Instead of counting all items with a year-end **physical inventory** count, cycle counting counts items throughout the year, with the "important" items counted much more often than other items. Cycle counting is an application of Pareto's Law, where the "important few" items are counted often and the "trivial many" items are counted infrequently.

The benefits of a good cycle counting program over a physical inventory are summarized in the table below. The main benefits of cycle counting are (1) it is better at finding and fixing the problems that cause inaccurate inventory balances and (2) it maintains record accuracy throughout the year.

Year-end inventory versus cycle counting

	Year-end physical inventory	Cycle counting
Frequency	Once per year	Daily or weekly for very important items; less frequently for less important items
Correct balance	Once per year	Almost always throughout the year
Fix root problems	No, only fixes the symptoms	Yes
Improve improvement culture	Very limited	Very strong
Accountability for accuracy	Weak	Strong
Prioritizes counting effort	No	Yes
Disruption of production	Major at year-end	Minimal

Source: Professor Arthur V. Hill

Some factors to consider when determining how often to count an item include:
- Criteria set by accounting and external auditors for the elimination of the annual physical inventory count.
- External regulations that require specific count frequencies.
- Annual dollar volume of an item (also known as the annual cost of goods sold).
- Annual unit volume of an item (number of units sold).
- Unit cost of an item.
- Pilferage risk associated with the item.
- Current inventory accuracy level for that particular item.

Some rules for determining how often to count an item include (1) count items with higher annual dollar volume more often (the **ABC system**), (2) count just before an order is placed, (3) count just before a new order is placed on the shelf, (4) count when the physical inventory balance is zero, (5) count when the physical inventory balance is negative, and (6) count after a specified number of transactions. Rules 2 and 3 are ways to implement rule 1 because "A" items will be ordered more often. Rule 3 minimizes the number of units that need to be counted because the shelf is nearly empty when an order arrives. Rules 2 and 3 can be implemented so that every *n*-th order is counted. Rule 5 is a good rule to use along with any other rule.

An item count is considered wrong only when the count is off by more than the **counting tolerance**, which is usually a percentage defined for each category of items. High-value items will usually have a counting tolerance of zero; low-value items might have a counting tolerance of 10% or more.

With a **blind count** the counter is given the item number and location but no information about the count currently in the database. This approach avoids giving counters reference points that might bias their counts.

Tompkins Associates provides more information on this topic at tompkinsinc.com/publications/monograph/ monographList/WP-19_Cycle_Counting.pdf?monographID=WP-19.

See *ABC classification, backflushing, learning organization, on-hand inventory, Pareto's Law, physical inventory, scale count, shrinkage.*

cycle service level – See *safety stock*.

cycle stock – The inventory due to lotsize quantities greater than one; also called the lotsize inventory. ✪

Cycle stock follows a "saw tooth" pattern (see the *reorder point* entry for an example). For **instantaneous replenishment** and constant average demand, the average cycle stock is $Q/2$, where Q is the fixed order quantity. Organizations can reduce cycle stock by reducing lotsizes and lotsizes can be reduced economically by reducing the order (setup) cost. The *setup time reduction methods* entry provides a methodology for reducing setup cost.

See *commonality, Economic Order Quantity (EOQ), instantaneous replenishment, lotsize, safety stock, setup time reduction methods.*

cycle time – (1) The time between completions (or starts) of a unit of work. (2) The time from beginning to end for a unit of work (also known as throughput time, flow time, and turnaround time). ✪

These two definitions are quite different, but both are used in practice.

Definition 1: For decades, industrial engineers defined cycle time as the time between completions (or starts) of a process step. For example, this could be measured as the time between units "falling off" the end of a manufacturing process or the maximum work time allowed for each worker on an assembly line. In lean terminology, the target cycle time (time between completions) aligned to the market demand rate is called the **takt time** (see the entry for *takt time*). This is the definition for cycle time used in LEI's *Lean Lexicon* (Marchwinski & Shook 2006).

Definition 2: Cycle time can also be defined as the cumulative time (also called total **throughput time**, total **flow time**, and **production leadtime**) required for a unit from start to end and can be measured as the completion time minus the start time for the same unit.

The first definition is the time between completions and the second definition is the time to complete one unit. The second definition (throughput time) has become the more widely used term in practice in North America, and it is now common to use the terms throughput time (or flow time) and cycle time synonymously.

To compare the two definitions of cycle time, imagine an assembly line in an appliance factory that has one dishwasher coming off the end of the line every two minutes. Each of the 20 steps in the assembly process requires exactly two minutes. Using the first definition, this is a cycle time (time between completions) of two minutes. However, using the second definition, a dishwasher that started at 8:00 am will not be complete until 8:40 am (20 steps times two minutes each), which means that the assembly line has a cycle time (throughput or flow time) of 40 minutes. The first definition focuses on the time between units being completed for each step in the process, whereas definition two focuses on the time to complete one unit from beginning to end for the entire process.

Although it is fairly easy to measure the average cycle time (throughput time) for a manufacturing order in a factory, it is often difficult to estimate the average cycle time (throughput time) for a complex product because it is not clear when the product is started. Given that each required component might have a different starting time, it is hard to determine the total cycle time for the completed product. A simple approach for estimating the cycle time (and also the periods supply) is to use the inverse of the inventory turnover ratio for the work-in-process (WIP) inventory. Therefore, if the WIP inventory turnover for a product is four turns per year, the "dollar weighted cycle time" is three months.

In **queuing theory** terms, the average completion rate will be the same as the average production rate (assuming that no units are lost and that sufficient capacity is available). With a production rate λ (lambda), the average time between starts and average time between completions is $1/\lambda$. According to **Little's Law** (Little 1961), the average work-in-process inventory is $L_s = \lambda W_s$, where W_s is the average time in the system. Building on the previous example, the average time between completions was two minutes, which means that the production rate is $\lambda = 1/2$ units/minute. Given that the throughput time was $W_s = 40$ minutes, the average number of units in process is $L_s = \lambda W_s = \frac{1}{2} \cdot 40 = 20$ units. See the *queuing theory* and *Little's Law* entries for more details on these issues.

Many practitioners use the terms "cycle time" (as in throughput time) and "leadtime" synonymously. However, in this author's opinion, it is better to use the term "leadtime" as a planning factor (as in planned leadtime) rather than as the actual throughput time for an order. The *leadtime* entry discusses these issues.

See *assembly line, balanced scorecard, inventory turnover, leadtime, Little's Law, operations performance metrics, order-to-cash, periods supply, pitch, purchasing leadtime, station time, takt time, time in system, touch time, turnaround time, value added ratio, wait time.*

cycle time efficiency – See *value added ratio*.

D

dampened trend – The process of reducing the trend (slope) in a forecast over time.

Gardner (2005) and others suggest that the trend in a forecasting model should be "dampened" (reduced) for multiple period-ahead forecasts because trends tend to die out over time. Almost no trends continue forever.

See *exponential smoothing, linear regression.*

dashboard – A performance measurement and reporting tool that provides a quick summary for the business unit or project status.

Ideally, a dashboard has a limited number of metrics (key performance indicators) to make it easy to comprehend and manage. The term "dashboard" is a metaphor for an automobile's instrument panel, with a speedometer, tachometer, fuel gauge, and oil warning light. Many firms use simple "red, yellow, green" indicators to signal when the organization is not meeting its targets. Ideally, a dashboard should include both financial and non-financial measures and should be reviewed regularly. When the dashboard approach is applied to external supply chain partners, it is usually called a supplier scorecard.

See *Balanced Scorecard, corporate portal, Key Performance Indicator (KPI), operations performance metrics, supplier scorecard.*

Data Envelopment Analysis (DEA) – A performance measurement technique that can be used to measure the efficiency of an organization relative to other organizations with multiple inputs and outputs.

DEA has been used to measure and improve efficiency in many industry contexts, such as banks, police stations, hospitals, tax offices, prisons, defense bases, schools, and university departments. For example, consider a bank that operates many branch banks, each having different numbers of transactions and different teller staffing levels. The table below displays the hypothetical data for this example. (This example is adapted from http://people.brunel.ac.uk/~mastjjb/jeb/or/dea.html, January 6, 2007.)

Branch bank	Number of tellers	Personal transactions per day	Personal transactions per teller	Relative efficiency
St. Paul	18	125	6.94	100%
Edina	16	44	2.75	40%
Bloomington	17	80	4.71	68%
Minneapolis	11	23	2.09	30%

The simplest approach for measuring efficiency for a branch is to calculate the ratio of an output measure (transactions) to an input measure (tellers). In DEA terminology, the branches are viewed as taking inputs (tellers) and converting them with varying degrees of efficiency into outputs (transactions). The St. Paul branch has the highest efficiency ratio in terms of the number of transactions per teller. The efficiency ratio for the St. Paul branch could be used as a target for the other branches and the relative efficiency of the other branches can be measured in comparison to that target.

This simple example has only one input (tellers) and one output (transactions). To take the example one step further, consider how the bank might measure efficiency when it includes both personal and business transactions. The bank will likely find that one branch is more efficient at personal transactions and another is more efficient at business transactions. See the data in the table below.

Branch bank	Number of tellers	Personal transactions per day	Business transactions per day	Personal transactions per teller	Business transactions per teller
St. Paul	18	125	50	6.94	2.78
Edina	16	44	20	2.75	1.25
Bloomington	17	80	55	4.71	3.24
Minneapolis	11	23	10	2.09	0.91

With this data, the St. Paul branch is still the most efficient for personal transactions per teller, but the Bloomington branch is the most efficient for business transactions. One simple way to handle this problem for two ratios is to graph the data. The graph on the right shows that the "efficient frontier" is the convex hull (region) defined by the Bloomington and St. Paul branches and that the Edina and Minneapolis branches are relatively inefficient. From this graph, it is easy to see why it is called Data Envelopment Analysis.

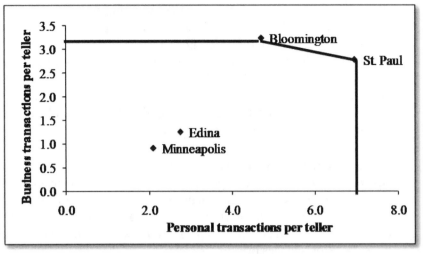

The measurement becomes much more difficult with multiple inputs or with multiple outputs. DEA uses linear programming to measure the efficiency of multiple Decision Maker Units (DMUs) when the production process presents a structure of multiple inputs and outputs.

The benefits of DEA over other similar approaches are that (1) it does not require an explicit mathematical form for the production function, (2) it is useful for uncovering relationships, (3) it is capable of handling multiple inputs and outputs, (4) it can be used with any input-output measurement, and (5) it allows sources of inefficiency to be analyzed and quantified for every evaluated unit.

In the DEA methodology developed by Charnes, Cooper, and Rhodes (1978), efficiency is defined as a weighted sum of outputs to a weighted sum of inputs, where the weights are calculated by means of mathematical programming and constant returns to scale is assumed.

Source: Professor Arthur V. Hill

See *operations performance metrics*, *production function*, *productivity*.

data mining – The process of analyzing a database (often in a data warehouse) to identify previously unknown patterns and relationships in the data and predict behavior of customers, prospective customers, etc.

Data mining tools make use of both statistical and software engineering tools and are often used in conjunction with very large databases. Ideally, data mining allows the user to visualize the data by providing graphical outputs. Standard data mining tools include cluster analysis, tree analysis, binary logistic regression, and neural nets (neural networks).

For example, data mining software can help retail companies find customers with common interests, screen potential donors for a college, and identify the key characteristics that should be considered in granting credit to a new customer.

Data mining is also known as knowledge-discovery in databases (KDD).

The major software vendors in the market are SAS Enterprise Miner, SPSS Clementine, and XLMiner.

See *business intelligence*, *cluster analysis*, *data warehouse*, *logistic regression*, *neural network*.

data warehouse – A database designed to support business analysis and decision making.

The data warehouse loads data from various systems at regular intervals. Data warehouse software usually includes sophisticated compression and hashing techniques for fast searches, advanced filtering, *ad hoc* inquiries, and user-designed reports.

See *cluster analysis*, *data mining*, *logistic regression*, *normalization*.

days of inventory – See *periods supply*.

days on hand – See *periods supply*.

days supply – See *periods supply*.

DBR – See *Drum-Buffer-Rope (DBR)*.

DC – See *Distribution Center (DC)*.

DEA – See *Data Envelopment Analysis*.

deadhead – (1) The move of an empty transportation asset, especially a truck, to a new location to pick up freight or return home. (2) The unloaded, unpaid distance a truck must cover between where it emptied and where it will reload; verb form: moving a transportation asset in this manner.

Backhaul loads are normally taken at lower rates than headhaul loads. For example, long haul trucks often get high rates to move loads from the West Coast to the Northeast. Once they have made delivery in the Northeast, they may have substantial deadhead distance to another location where they can pick up backhauls to the West Coast. Backhaul rates are normally less than headhaul rates.

See *backhaul, logistics, repositioning.*

death spiral – See *make versus buy decision.*

Decision Sciences Institute (DSI) – A multidisciplinary international professional society that is dedicated to advancing knowledge and improving instruction in all business and related disciplines.

DSI facilitates the development and dissemination of knowledge in the diverse disciplines of the decision sciences through publications, conferences, and other services. DSI publishes the ***Decision Sciences Journal (DSJ)*** and the ***Decision Sciences Journal of Innovative Education (DSJIE).*** The DSI website is www.decisionsciences.org.

See *operations management (OM).*

decision theory – See *decision tree.*

Decision Support System (DSS) – An interactive computer-based information system that supports decision makers by providing data and analysis as needed.

DSS software often runs queries against databases to analyze data and create reports. More sophisticated systems will use (1) simulation models to help managers ask "what-if" questions and (2) optimization models to recommend solutions for managers. Business intelligence and business analytics are examples of DSSs.

See *business intelligence, groupware, optimization, simulation.*

decision tree – A graphical decision tool for drawing and analyzing possible courses of action. ✪

A decision tree is a basic tool in the fields of decision analysis (decision theory), risk management, and operations research. A decision tree is usually drawn in time order from left to right. Decision nodes are usually drawn with squares and chance nodes are drawn with circles. When probabilities are assigned to each chance node, the decision nodes can be evaluated in terms of the expected monetary value.

The figure on the right is a verysimple decision tree with one decision node (build or not build) and one chance node (win or not win the contract). (Chery is a Chinese automobile manufacturer.) This example could be taken another step by assigning probabilities to each arc coming out of the chance node and computing the expected monetary value for each decision alternative. Bayes' Theorem is sometimes applied in analyzing such problems in the presence of imperfect information.

Decision tree example

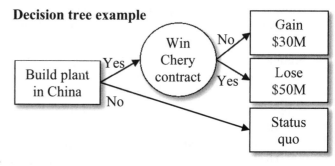

See *Analytic Hierarchy Process (AHP), Bayes' Theorem, causal map, force field analysis, issue tree, Kepner-Tregoe Model, MECE, operations research (OR), Pugh Matrix, risk assessment.*

decomposition – See *forecasting.*

decreasing returns to scale – See *diseconomy of scale.*

decoupling point – See *push-pull boundary.*

deductive reasoning – See *inductive reasoning.*

de-expediting – See *expediting.*

defect – An error in a product or service.

Products and services have specification limits on important characteristics (dimensions). A defect occurs when the characteristic is outside these specification limits. Therefore, a product or service can have as many defects as it has characteristics. A product or service is "defective" if it has one or more defects in the unacceptable range.

See *early detection, lean sigma, lean thinking, quality management, sigma level, Total Quality Management (TQM)*.

Defective Parts per Million (DPPM) – The number of units not meeting standards, expressed as units per million; sometimes also called PPM (Parts per Million).

See *Defects per Million Opportunities (DPMO), sigma level*.

Defects per Million Opportunities (DPMO) – The number of defects (not the number of defective units) per million opportunities, where each unit might have multiple opportunities.

It is possible that a unit (a part) has many defects. For example, a single automobile can have defects in the door, windshield, and muffler. The Defective Parts per Million (DPPM) will be the same as the DPMO only if each unit has only one opportunity for a defect and a unit is judged to be defective if it has this defect. (A part is usually considered defective if it has one defect.) Managers should be careful with this metric because it is easy to make it better by arbitrarily defining more "opportunities" for defects for each unit.

See *Defective Parts per Million (DPPM), lean sigma, process capability and performance, quality management, sigma level*.

delegation – The transfer of responsibility for a job or task from one person or organization to another.

Tasks should be assigned to the most productive resource, which may be outside an organization. Delegation, therefore, can be a powerful tool for managers to increase their productivity. Outsourcing is a form of delegation. Delegation is similar to, but not identical to, the division of labor principle. Whereas division of labor splits a task into two or more pieces and then delegates, delegation does not require that the task be split. Value chain analysis (Porter 1985) is a strategic view of delegation from an organizational point of view.

Good questions to ask to help a manager decide if a task should be delegated: (1) Do you have time to complete the task? (2) Does this task require your personal supervision and attention? (3) Is your personal skill or expertise required for this task? (4) If you do not do the task yourself, will your reputation (or the reputation of your organization) be damaged? (5) Does anyone on your team have the skill to complete the task? (6) Could someone on your team benefit from the experience of performing the task?

In contract law, the term "delegation" is used to describe the act of giving another person the responsibility of carrying out the duty agreed to in a contract. Three parties are concerned with this process: the delegator (the party with the obligation to perform the duty), the delegatee (the party that assumes the responsibility of performing the duty) and the obligee (the party to whom this duty is owed).

See *division of labor, human resources, outsourcing, personal operations management, value chain, vendor managed inventory (VMI)*.

deliverables – The tangible results of a project that are handed over to the project sponsor.

Examples of deliverables include hardware, software, mindmaps, current state and future state analysis (shown in process maps and value stream maps), causal maps, reports, documents, photos, videos, drawings, databases, financial analyses, implementation plan, training, and standard operating procedures (SOPs). In a process improvement context, some projects stop with the proposed plan, whereas others include the actual process improvement. A deliverable can be given to the sponsor in the form of a PowerPoint presentation, report, workshop, Excel workbook, CD, or a training session.

See *DMAIC, milestone, post-project review, project charter, scrum, sponsor, stage-gate process, value stream map*.

delivery time – The time required to move, ship, or mail a product from a supplier to a customer.

See *service level*.

Delphi forecasting – A qualitative method that collects and refines opinions from a panel of anonymous experts to make forecasts; also known as the Delphi Method. ✪

Named after the Greek oracle at Delphi whom the Greeks visited for information about their future, the **Delphi Method** is an iterative procedure for collecting and refining the **opinions of a panel of experts**. The collective judgment of experts is considered more reliable than individual statements and is thus more objective in its outcomes. Delphi forecasting is usually applied to estimate unknown parameters, typically forecasting dates for long-term change in the fields of science and technology.

A survey instrument is used over several iterations. Both statistical and commentary feedback is provided with each iteration. After two or three iterations, opinions converge and a final report is made. The typical steps in a Delphi study are as follows:

Step 1. Define the questions that need to be asked.

Step 2. Identify the experts, who ideally have differing points of view on the questions defined in Step 1.

Step 3. Create the survey instrument. For technological forecasting, the questions are often phrased in the form, "In what year do you believe that event X will occur?"

Step 4. Recruit the experts to respond to this round. Ask them to individually and independently respond to the survey questions with both quantitative responses (e.g., the year that the event will happen) and commentary feedback (assumptions, justifications, explanations). Note that the experts' identities should remain anonymous so feedback from famous or powerful people is not given undue weight.

Step 5. Summarize the results from this round and give statistical and commentary feedback to the expert panel. The statistical feedback is usually presented in the form of a histogram and some basic descriptive statistics.

Step 6. Conduct the next round of the survey if needed.

Delphi overcomes many problems with face-to-face meetings, such as (1) domination by a few strong personalities, (2) anchoring on the first ideas that are presented, (3) pressure on participants to conform, and (4) regularly becoming overburdened with non-essential information.

See *anchoring, brainstorming, forecasting, technological forecasting.*

demand – The quantity the market will buy per period at a particular price. ✪

Whereas **sales** is how many units were actually sold, **demand** is how many units would have been sold if inventory had been available. In other words demand = sales + lost sales. Sales data, therefore, is **censored** because it may not include all demand.

It is often useful to distinguish between **discrete** (integer) and **continuous** demand. When demand is considered to be continuous, the demand variable is not restricted to integer values, which means that a continuous probability distribution (such as the normal, lognormal, or gamma) can be used. Even when demand is an integer, it is often modeled as a continuous variable when the average demand is greater than 10.

See the *forecasting* entry for more discussion on this and related issues.

See *all-time demand, bookings, censored data, dependent demand, economics, elasticity, exponential smoothing, forecasting, independent demand.*

demand chain management – Supply chain management that focuses on the customer end of the supply chain and uses signals (such as point-of-sale data) from the customer to trigger production.

Some North America consulting firms have tried to promote this term. However, at the time of this writing, it has not been widely embraced in industry or academia.

See *supply chain management.*

demand during leadtime – The quantity demanded while waiting for a replenishment order to arrive.

In inventory and purchasing management, the **demand** during the **replenishment leadtime** is a **random variable**. Formulas are available to estimate the mean and standard deviation of the demand during leadtime distribution from estimates of the mean and standard deviation of demand and the mean and standard deviation of the replenishment leadtime. It is important to set the **reorder point** large enough to meet the demand while the firm waits for a replenishment order to arrive.

See *leadtime, reorder point, replenishment order, safety stock.*

demand filter – An exception reporting and control tool for time series forecasting that signals a problem when one forecast value is outside the expected range of forecast values.

When the absolute value of the **forecast error** is very large, the demand filter triggers an exception report to warn the user. The simplest rule is to test if the forecast error is larger than plus or minus three times the standard deviation of the forecast error.

The demand filter at the end of period t is the absolute value of the forecast error divided by an estimate of the standard deviation of the error. One approach for handing this is to define the demand filter at the end of period t as $DF_t = |E_t| / \sqrt{SMSE_{t-1}}$, where $|E_t|$ is the absolute value of the forecast error and $\sqrt{SMSE_{t-1}}$ is the square root of the smoothed mean squared error (an estimate of the recent standard deviation of the forecast error). This uses the smoothed *MSE* because the demand filter is typically implemented in a time series forecasting context. The demand filter exception report is created whenever DF_t exceeds some critical value, DF^*. Assuming that the errors (E_t) are normally distributed, DF_t is a standard normal random variable. Therefore, it can be compared to a *z* value used in basic statistics textbooks. Therefore, a reasonable control limit is $DF^* = 3$. In other words, the system should create an exception report whenever the demand filter exceeds a value of 3. It is important to use the smoothed mean squared error from the *previous* period in the demand filter so an outlier is not included in the estimation of the standard deviation of the forecast error. Alternative forms for the demand filter include $DF_t = |E_t| / \sqrt{SVAR_t}$ and $DF_t = |E_t| / (1.25 SMAD_t)$.

See *exponential smoothing, forecast bias, forecast error metrics, forecasting, Mean Absolute Percent Error (MAPE), mean squared error (MSE), tracking signal.*

demand flow – Another word for Just-in-Time (JIT) manufacturing.
See *lean thinking.*

demand management – (1) The name of an organizational function (i.e., the demand management organization). (2) The name of a set of practices that are designed to influence demand. ✪

The **demand management organization** is a relatively new organizational form in North America. This organization can report to either the manufacturing or sales organization and is charged with creating forecasts, managing the S&OP process, influencing supply policies (manufacturing, purchasing, inventory, logistics), and influencing demand policies (sales, marketing, pricing).

Demand management practices include those activities that collect demand information and affect the demand to better match the capacity. Demand can be influenced through pricing, advertising, promotions, other customer communications, and other mechanisms. Leveling the demand can often reduce capacity change costs.
See *forecasting, heijunka, Sales & Operations Planning (S&OP).*

Deming's 14 points – A summary of the quality improvement philosophy developed and taught by W. Edwards Deming.

Deming (1900-1993) was an American statistician, college professor, author, lecturer, and consultant. He is widely credited with improving production in the U.S. during World War II, although he is perhaps best known for his work in Japan. From 1950, onward he taught top management how to improve design, product quality, testing, and sales. Deming made a significant contribution to Japan's ability to produce innovative high-quality products and is regarded as having had more impact upon Japanese manufacturing and business than any other individual not of Japanese heritage. Adapted from http://en.wikipedia.org/wiki/ W._Edwards_Deming (January 17, 2007).

Deming's work is outlined in two books, ***Out of the Crisis*** (1986, 2000), and ***The New Economics for Industry*** (2000), in which he developed his System of Profound Knowledge. The fourteen points are summarized below. (Author's note: These titles were not in the original 14 points. Many variations for some of Deming's points can be found on the Web. The list below is from Wikipedia with some minor edits, with the exception of point 6.)

1. **Create constancy of purpose** – Create constancy of purpose toward improvement of product and service, with the aim to become competitive, stay in business, and provide jobs.
2. **Adopt the new philosophy** – Adopt a new philosophy of cooperation (win-win) in which everybody wins and put it into practice by teaching it to employees, customers and suppliers.
3. **Cease dependence on inspection to achieve quality** – Cease dependence on mass inspection to achieve quality. Instead, improve the process and build quality into the product in the first place.
4. **End the practice of awarding business on the basis of price alone** – End the practice of awarding business on the basis of price alone. Instead, minimize total cost in the long run. Move toward a single supplier for any one item, based on a long-term relationship of loyalty and trust.
5. **Continuously improve every process** – Improve constantly, and forever, the system of production, service, and planning. This will improve quality and productivity and thus constantly decrease costs.

6. **Institute training on the job** – Institute modern methods of training on the job for all, including management, to make better use of every employee. New skills are required to keep up with changes in materials, methods, product and service design, machinery, techniques, and service.

7. **Improve leadership** – Adopt and institute leadership for the management of people, recognizing their different abilities, capabilities, and aspiration. The aim of leadership should be to help people, machines, and gadgets do a better job. Leadership of management is in need of overhaul.

8. **Drive out fear** – Drive out fear and build trust so that everyone can work more effectively.

9. **Break down functional silos** – Break down barriers between departments. Abolish competition and build a win-win system of cooperation within the organization. People in research, design, sales, and production must work as a team to foresee problems of production and use that might be encountered with the product or service.

10. **Eliminate slogans** – Eliminate slogans, exhortations, and targets asking for zero defects or new levels of productivity. Such exhortations only create adversarial relationships, because most of the causes of low quality and low productivity belong to the system and thus lie beyond the power of the workforce.

11. **Eliminate quotas** – Eliminate numerical goals, numerical quotas, and management by objectives. Substitute leadership.

12. **Encourage pride in work** – Remove barriers that rob people of joy in their work. This will mean abolishing the annual rating or merit system that ranks people and creates competition and conflict.

13. **Institute educational programs** – Institute a vigorous program of education and self-improvement.

14. **Take action** – Put everybody in the company to work to accomplish the transformation. The transformation is everybody's job.

Anderson, Rungtusanatham, and Schroeder (1994) traced the development of the Deming management method, positioned it in the context of theory, and explained the underlying theory of quality management.

See *functional silo, inspection, lean sigma, Management by Objectives (MBO), quality management, Statistical Process Control (SPC), Statistical Quality Control (SQC), Total Quality Management (TQM)*.

demonstrated capacity – See *capacity*.

demurrage – The carrier charges and fees applied when rail freight cars and ships are retained beyond specified loading or unloading times.

See *terms*.

dendrogram – See *cluster analysis*.

dependent demand – Demand that is derived from higher-level plans and therefore should be planned rather than forecasted.

In a manufacturing firm, dependent demand is calculated (not forecasted) from the production plan of higher-level items in the bill of material (BOM). End item demand is usually forecasted. A production plan (aggregate production plan) and a Master Production Schedule (MPS) are created in light of this forecast. These plans are rarely identical to the forecast because of the need to build inventory, draw down inventory, or level the production rate. This dependent demand should almost never be forecasted.

It is common for some items to have both dependent and independent demand. For example, a part may be used in an assembly and has dependent demand. However, this same part might also have independent demand as a service part.

See *bill of material (BOM), demand, independent demand, inventory management, Materials Requirements Planning (MRP)*.

deployment leader – A person who leads the lean sigma program in one part of a business, often a division, strategic business unit, or functional area (operations, new product development, sales, etc.).

In some firms, the deployment leader is not assigned full time to the lean sigma program. Deployment leaders usually report to the overall program champion, at least with a dotted line reporting relationship.

See *champion, lean sigma*.

Design Failure Mode and Effects Analysis (DFMEA) – The application of Failure Modes and Effects Analysis (FMEA) principles to product and service design.

FMEA can be used to anticipate and mitigate risks in both a process improvement context (where a process is already in place) and a design context (where the design does not yet exist). However, a process FMEA and a design FMEA have some significant differences. The term "FMEA" normally refers to a process FMEA.

See *Failure Mode and Effects Analysis (FMEA)*.

Design for Assembly (DFA) – Design for manufacturing concepts applied to assembly.

See *Design for Manufacturing (DFM)*.

Design for Disassembly – A set of principles used to guide designers in designing products that are easy to disassemble for re-manufacturing or repair operations.

Design for Disassembly enables a product and its parts to be easily reused, re-manufactured, refurbished, or recycled at end of life. In the long run, Design for Disassembly could make it possible to eliminate the need for landfills and incineration of mixed waste. Products would be designed so they never become waste, but instead become inputs to new products at the end of their useful lives. Design for Disassembly is a key strategy within the larger area of sustainable product design, which is concerned with a more proactive approach to environmentally responsible design. As environmental concerns grow in the world, re-manufacturing will continue to grow in importance. In Europe, this is already a major issue, with manufacturers, such as Vokswagen, designing products that can be easily disassembled.

See *Design for Manufacturing (DFM)*, *remanufacturing*.

Design for Environment – See *Design for Disassembly (DFD) and remanufacturing*.

Design for Manufacturing (DFM) – A set of methodologies and principles that can be used to guide the design process so that product fabrication and assembly will have low cost, low assembly time, high labor productivity, low manufacturing cycle time, low work-in-process inventory, high conformance quality, low manufacturing ramp-up time, and short time to market. ✪

DFM is the best known of the many DFx ("design-for") acronyms. Boothroyd, Dewhurst, and Knight (2010) wrote what is probably the most popular reference on DFM and DMA.

See *Design for Assembly (DFA)*, *Design for Disassembly*, *Design for Reliability (DFR)*, *value engineering*.

Design for Manufacturing and Assembly (DFMA) – See *Design for Manufacturing (DFM)*.

Design for Quality – See *Design for Manufacturing (DFM)*.

Design for Reliability (DFR) – A concurrent engineering program where the reliability engineer is part of the product development team working with the design engineers to design reliable products with low overall life-cycle costs.

See *Design for Manufacturing (DFM)*, *quality management*, *reliability*.

Design for Six Sigma (DFSS) – An extension of six sigma tools and concepts used for developing new products.

The rationale for DFSS is that it is much easier to design quality into a product than it is to fix problems after the design is complete. Instead of using the lean sigma DMAIC framework, DFSS uses IDOV (Identify, Design, Optimize, and Validate) or DMADV (Define, Measure, Analyze, Design, and Verify). More detail on DMADV follows:

- **Define** the project goals and customer (internal and external) deliverables.
- **Measure** and determine customer needs and specifications.
- **Analyze** the process options to meet the customer needs.
- **Design** the process to meet the customer needs.
- **Verify** the design performance and ability to meet customer needs.

DMAIC and DFSS have the following in common:
- Lean sigma methodologies are used to drive out defects.
- Data intensive solution approaches require cold, hard facts.
- Trained project leaders (black belts and green belts) lead projects with support from master black belts.
- Projects are driven by the need to support the business and produce financial results.
- Champions and process owners oversee and support projects.

The DFSS methodology is used for new product development, whereas the lean sigma (formerly called six sigma) DMAIC methodology is used for process improvement. The DMAIC methodology should be used instead of DMADV when an existing product or process is not meeting customer specification or is not performing adequately. The DMADV methodology should be used instead of the DMAIC methodology when (1) a product or process does not exist and needs to be developed, or (2) the existing product or process exists and has been optimized and still does not meet customer specifications.

Design for Six Sigma does not replace the stage-gate process, but enhances it by providing additional statistical rigor to the gate criteria. Teams are required to bring facts and analytic data to the gate reviews to validate that the tools, tasks, and deliverables are met.

C_{pk} is a measure of how well the product performance meets the customer needs. This is a key DFSS metric throughout the development cycle and is used to ensure that quality is designed into the product.

See *deliverables, DMAIC, lean sigma, New Product Development (NPD), process capability and performance, Pugh Matrix, quality management, stage-gate process.*

Design of Experiments (DOE) – A family of statistical tools designed to build quality into the product and process designs so the need for inspection is reduced.

DOE achieves this by optimizing product and process designs and by making product and process designs robust against manufacturing variability. Experimental designs are used to identify or screen important factors affecting a process, and to develop empirical models of processes. DOE techniques enable teams to learn about process behavior by running a series of experiments. The goal is to obtain the maximum amount of useful information in the minimum number of runs. DOE is an important and complex subject beyond the scope of this book. The reader is referred to a linear models text, such as Kutner, Neter, Nachtsheim, and Wasserman (2004).

See *Analysis of Variance (ANOVA), Gauge R&R, lean sigma, robust, Taguchi methods.*

design quality – See *product design quality.*

Design Structure Matrix (DSM) – A compact matrix representation showing the precedence relationships and information flows in a system/project.

DSM contains a list of all constituent subsystems/activities and the corresponding information exchange and dependency patterns. That is, what information pieces (parameters) are required to start a certain activity and where does the information generated by the activity feed into (i.e., which other tasks within the matrix utilize the output information)? The DSM provides insights about how to manage a complex system/project and highlights issues of information needs and requirements, task sequencing, and iterations.

In the DSM, the tasks for a project are listed on the rows and then repeated for the columns. An X indicates the existence and direction of information flow (or a dependency in a general sense) from one activity in the project to another. Reading across a row reveals the input/dependency flows by an X placed at the intersection of that row with the column that bears the name of the input task. Reading across a column reveals the output information flows from that activity to other activities by placing an X as described above. A green mark below the main diagonal represents a forward flow of information. The red marks above the main diagonal reveal feedback from a later (downstream) activity to an earlier (upstream) one. This means that the earlier activity has to be repeated in light of the late arrival of new information.

See *project management, upstream.*

devil's advocate – The role of providing an opposing and skeptical point of view in a discussion.

The devil's advocate role is taken by a person (or assigned to a person) in a group discussion, debate, or argument. This person's role is to provide a test of the prevailing argument even though the person with this role may not actually believe in the opposing argument. According to Wikipedia, the term "devil's advocate" was a contrarian role that the Catholic Church assigned to a person in the process of evaluating someone for sainthood.

See *brainstorming.*

DFA – See *Design for Assembly (DFA).*

DFD – See *Design for Disassembly.*

DFM – See *Design for Manufacturing.*

DFMA – See *Design for Manufacturing and Assembly.*

DFMEA – See *Design Failure Mode and Effects Analysis (DFMEA).*

DFSS – See *Design for Six Sigma (DFSS).*

die – See *die cutting.*

die cutting – The process of using metal to shape or cut material.

A **die** is a metal plate or block used to make parts by molding, stamping, cutting, shaping, or punching. For example, a die can be used to cut the threads of bolts. Wires are made by drawing metal through a die that is a steel block or plate with small holes. Note the plural of die is "dies."

See *manufacturing processes, stamping.*

digital convergence – A technological trend where a number of technologies, such as entertainment (movies, videos, music, TV), printing (books, newspapers, magazines), news (TV, newspapers, radio), communications (phone, mobile phone, data communications), computing (personal computers, mainframe computers), and other technologies, merge into a single integrated technology.

The term "convergence" implies that these technologies will become more integrated and will tend to radically change each other. For example, cable TV operators are offering bundles of high-speed Internet, digital telephone, and other services. The lines between the technologies that offer entertainment, data transfer, and communications are becoming less clear over time.

digital supply chain – The process of delivering digital media, such as music or video, by electronic means to consumers.

A physical supply chain processes materials through many steps and across many organizations. Similarly, a digital supply chain processes digital media through many stages before it is received by consumers.

See *supply chain management.*

dimensional weight – A method used by shippers to assign a price to a package based on volume and shape rather than just on weight; also called dim weight.

Carriers have found that some low-density and odd-shaped packages are unprofitable when they charge only on weight. The industry's solution to this problem is to calculate the **dimensional weight** for setting prices. Dimensional weight is often based on a volume calculated in terms of the longest dimension. In other words, volume $V = L^3$, where $L = \max(l, w, d)$ for package length l, width w, and depth d. (If the package is a cube, then V is the actual volume. However, if the package is oddly shaped, V is much more than the actual volume.) The dimensional weight is then $DW = V/m$, where m is the minimum density the shipper will use in calculating a price. The weight used to determine the price is the maximum of the dimensional weight and the actual weight.

See *transportation.*

direct cost – Expenses that can be assigned to a specific unit of production.

Direct costs usually include only the material and labor costs that vary with the quantity produced.

See *cost of goods sold, direct labor cost, overhead.*

direct labor cost – The labor cost that is clearly assignable to a part or product. ✪

Direct labor cost is usually computed as the standard (or actual) hours consumed times the pay rate per hour. The pay rate per hour often includes fringe benefits, but does not include materials cost or other overhead.

See *cost of goods sold, direct cost, overhead.*

direct ship – See *drop ship.*

direct store shipment – See *drop ship.*

directed RF picking – See *picking.*

discounted cash flow – See *Net Present Value (NPV).*

discrete demand – See *demand.*

discrete lotsize – See *lot-for-lot.*

discrete order picking – An order picking method where a stock picker will retrieve (pick) all items on one order before starting another.

See *picking, warehouse.*

discrete probability distribution – See *probability mass function.*

discrete manufacturing – A process that creates products that are separate from others and easy to count.

Good examples of discrete manufacturing include building a computer or an automobile. In contrast, a continuous process deals with materials, such as liquids or powders. Examples of continuous processes include oil refining, chemical processing, or paper manufacturing.

See *assembly line, batch process, continuous flow, continuous process, job shop.*

discrete uniform distribution – See *uniform distribution.*

discriminant analysis – A statistical technique that predicts group membership; also called linear discriminant analysis.

See *linear regression, logistic regression.*

diseconomy of scale – The forces that cause organizations to have higher unit costs as volume increases; also called diseconomies of scale. ✪

Most business managers are familiar with the concept of economy of scale, where the unit cost decreases as the volume increases. The less-familiar concept of diseconomy of scale is where the unit cost increases as the volume increases. In many industries, firms will have economies of scale until they grow to be quite large.

For example, it is said that the optimal hospital size is roughly 400 beds[10] and that larger hospitals tend to become less efficient due to the complexity of the operation, which is a function of the number of employees and the distance people have to travel. This is also true for high schools, where the optimal school size is probably between 400 and 600 students[11]. A watch factory in Moscow once had 7,000 people making watches and a U.S. defense factory was so large that workers had to ride bicycles to travel within the plant[12]. These factories were not very competitive due to their size. The reasons why unit cost might increase with volume include:

- **Coordination and communication problems** – As firm size increases, coordination and communication becomes much more difficult and often leads to the creation of a large bureaucracy. The number of unique pairs in an organization with n units or individuals is $n(n-1)/2$, which grows with n^2.
- **Top-heavy management** – As firm size increases, management expense tends to increase.
- **Insulated managers** – As firms increase in size, managers are less accountable to shareholders and markets and are more insulated from reality. Therefore, they tend to seek personal benefits over firm performance.
- **Lack of motivation** – As firms grow, workers tend to be more specialized, have a harder time understanding the organization's strategy and customers, and are more likely to be alienated and less committed to the firm.
- **Duplication of effort** – As firm size increases, it is common for firms to waste money on duplicate efforts and systems. It is reported that General Motors had two in-house CAD/CAM systems and still purchased other CAD/CAM systems from outside firms.
- **Protection from consequences** – In a small firm, most managers immediately see and experience the consequences of their decisions. In many large firms, managers are transferred every few years and rarely have to live with their bad decisions very long. Therefore, they do not learn from their mistakes.
- **Inertia** – It is often very hard for a large organization to change directions. A VP of MIS for a large bank in Seattle reported that it was nearly impossible for his bank to make any significant changes. It was just too hard to understand all the linkages between the more than ten million lines of code.
- **Self-competition** – The managing directors for a large paper products firm in Europe identified their biggest problem as competition with the other operating companies within the same firm.
- **Transportation** – If output for a national or international market is concentrated at a single large plant, transportation costs for raw materials and finished goods to and from distant markets may offset scale economies of production at the large plant.

Canbäck et al. (2006) found empirical support for many of the above statements. Some of the ideas above were adapted from http://en.wikipedia.org/wiki/Diseconomies_of_scale.

See *economy of scale, flexibility, pooling.*

disintermediation – Removing a supplier or distributor from a supply chain; also called "cutting out the middleman."

---

[10] *The website www.ncbi.nlm.nih.gov/pmc/articles/PMC1116851 supports this statement.*
[11] *The website www.wested.org/online_pubs/po-01-03.pdf supports this statement*
[12] *These statements are based on personal experiences of the author.*

A distributor is an intermediary between a manufacturer and its customers. When a firm removes a distributor between it and its customers, it is said to have **disintermediated** the distributor and has practiced **disintermediation**. This is common when a manufacturing firm replaces distributors with a website that sells directly to customers. **Reintermediation** occurs when the distributor finds a way to re-insert itself into the channel, possibly by offering its own website and better service.

See *channel conflict, dot-com, supply chain management.*

dispatch list – See *dispatching rules.*

dispatching rules – Policies used to select which job should be started next on a process; sometimes called job shop dispatching or priority rules.

For example, a manager arrives at work on a Monday morning and has 20 tasks waiting on her desk. Which task should she handle first? She might take the one that is the most urgent (has the earliest due date), the longest one, or the one that has the most economic value. In a very similar way, a shop supervisor might have to select the next job for a machine using the same types of rules.

The best-known dispatching rules include **First-In-First-Out (FIFO), shortest processing time, earliest due date, minimum slack time**, and **critical ratio**, which are factors of the arrival time, processing time, due date, or some combination of those factors. Other factors to consider include value, customer, and changeover cost or time. The FIFO rule may be the "fairest" rule, but does not perform well with respect to average flow time or due date performance. It can be proven that the shortest processing time rule will minimize the mean (average) flow time, but does poorly with respect to on-time delivery. MRP systems backschedule from the due date and therefore are essentially using a minimum slack rule, which has been shown to perform fairly well in a wide variety of contexts. The critical ratio (Berry and Rao 1975) for a job is equal to the time remaining until the due date divided by the work time remaining to complete the job[13]. A critical ratio less than one indicates the job is behind schedule, a ratio greater than one indicates the job is ahead of schedule, and a ratio of one indicates the job is on schedule. (Do not confuse the critical ratio rule with the critical ratio in the newsvendor model.)

Dispatching rules are used to create a daily **dispatch list** for each workcenter. This is a listing of manufacturing orders in priority sequence based on the dispatching rule.

See *expediting, First-In-First-Out (FIFO), heijunka, job shop, job shop scheduling, Last-In-First-Out (LIFO), on-time delivery (OTD), operation, service level, shop floor control, slack time.*

disruptive technology – A term coined by Professor Clayton Christensen (Christensen 1997; Christensen and Raynor 2003) at Harvard Business School to describe a technological innovation, product, or service that eventually overturns the existing dominant technology in the market despite the fact that the disruptive technology is radically different than the leading technology and often has poorer performance (at least initially) than the leading technology.

The disruptive technology often starts by gaining market share in the lower price and less demanding segment of the market and then moves up-market through performance improvements and finally displaces the incumbent's product. By contrast, a sustaining technology provides improved performance and will almost always be incorporated into the incumbent's product.

Examples of displaced and disruptive technologies

Displaced technology	Disruptive technology
Canals	Railways
Railways	Automobile
Photographic film	Digital cameras
Traditional telephone systems	Voice over IP
Vertically integrated steel mills	Mini steel mills
Disk drives	Flash drives

In some markets, the rate at which products improve is faster than the rate at which customers can learn and adopt the new performance. Therefore, at some point the performance of the product overshoots the needs of certain customer segments. At this point, a disruptive technology may enter the market and provide a product

---

[13] *The critical ratio dispatching rule can be implemented in software as: If due > now then CR = (1 + due − now)/(1 + trpt); otherwise CR = (due − now)/(1 + TRPT), where due is the due date (in hours), now is the current date (in hours), and trpt is the total remaining processing time in hours (Rose, 2002). Note that other variants of the critical ratio rule are presented in the literature and used in practice.*

that has lower performance than the incumbent technology, but exceeds the requirements of certain segments, thereby gaining a foothold in the market.

Christensen distinguishes between "low-end disruption" (that targets customers who do not need the full performance valued by customers at the high end of the market) and "new-market disruption" (that targets customers who could previously not be served profitably by the incumbent). The disruptive company will naturally aim to improve its margin and therefore innovate to capture the next level of customers. The incumbent will not want to engage in a price war with a simpler product with lower production costs and will move up-market and focus on its more attractive customers. After a number of iterations, the incumbent has been squeezed into successively smaller markets. When the disruptive technology finally meets the demands of its last segment, the incumbent technology disappears. Some of the above information was adapted from http://en.wikipedia.org/wiki/Disruptive_technology (November 16, 2006).

See *market share, nanotechnology, New Product Development (NPD), technology road map.*

distinctive competence – See *core competence.*

distribution – (1) In the logistics context, management of the movement of materials from the supplier to the customer; also called physical distribution. (2) In the statistics context, a description of the range of values that a random variable can attain and information about the probability of each of these values. ✪

In the logistics context, distribution involves many related disciples, such as transportation, warehousing, inventory control, material handling, and the information and communication systems to support these activities.

For information regarding the statistics context, see the *probability distribution* entry.

See *distribution center (DC), distribution channel, distribution network, DRP, inventory management, logistics, reverse logistics.*

distribution center (DC) – A location used to warehouse and ship products.

See *Advanced Shipping Notification (ASN), cross-docking, distribution, Distribution Requirements Planning (DRP), distributor, logistics, warehouse, Warehouse Management System (WMS), wave picking.*

distribution channel – The way that a product is sold and delivered to customers. ✪

For example, a product, such as 3M sandpaper, might be sold through big box retailers, such as Home Depot, or through national distributers, such as Granger. Other products might be sold through retail grocery stores (e.g., Kroger), national grocery wholesalers (e.g., SuperValu), a company-employed national salesforce (e.g., IBM), or a company-owned Web-based channel (e.g., www.BestBuy.com). Firms in the channel are sometimes called **channel partners**, even though technically the business relationships are rarely partnerships.

See *big box store, channel conflict, channel integration, channel partner, distribution, distribution network, distributor, logistics, supply chain management.*

distribution network – The organizations, facilities, means of transportation, and information systems used to move products from suppliers of suppliers to customers of customers.

See *distribution, distribution channel, logistics.*

Distribution Requirements Planning (DRP) – A planning system for managing inventory in a distribution network; also called Distribution Resource Planning.

DRP is an extension of MRP for planning the key resources in a distribution system. According to Vollmann, Berry, Whybark, and Jacobs (2004), "DRP provides the basis for integrating supply chain inventory information and physical distribution activities with the Manufacturing Planning and Control system."

DRP performs many functions such as:

- Managing the flow of materials between firms, warehouses, and distribution centers.
- Helping manage the material flows like MRP does in manufacturing.
- Linking firms in the supply chain by providing planning records that carry demand information from receiving points to supply points and vice versa.

DRP can use a Time Phased Order Point (TPOP) approach to plan orders at the branch warehouse level. These orders are exploded via MRP logic to become gross requirements on the supplying source enabling the translation of inventory plans into material flows. In the case of multi-level distribution networks, this explosion process continues down through the various levels of regional warehouses, master warehouse, and factory warehouse and finally becomes an input to the master production schedule.

See *distribution center (DC), Enterprise Resources Planning (ERP), logistics, Materials Requirements Planning (MRP), warehouse, Warehouse Management System (WMS)*.

distributor – A wholesaler that buys, stores, transports, and sells goods to customers.

Distributors usually sell products made by others. However, it is common for distributors to conduct some limited "value-adding" operations, such as cutting pipes or packaging potatoes. Although distributors are considered customers for the manufacturer, they are not the end customer or consumer. It is wise for manufacturers to hear the voice of the customer from the consumer's perspective and not just the distributor's.

See *broker, channel conflict, cross-docking, distribution center (DC), distribution channel, inventory management, logistics, supply chain management, wholesaler*.

division of labor – Dividing a job into small, simple, standard steps and assigning one worker to each step.

Frederick Taylor (1911) promoted the concept of dividing work into small pieces so workers could quickly learn jobs without much training. Division of labor and standardization of parts led to rifles made by several people in the 1800s and the Model T Ford in the 1900s. Division of labor is the opposite of **job enlargement**, a practice that has workers take on more tasks rather than fewer.

In the last thirty years or more, many managers have found that taking division of labor too far can lead to boredom, does not develop the whole person, and does not build a learning organization. Division of labor also creates many queues and waits and requires more coordination and supervision. Thus, many process improvement projects enlarge jobs to remove queues and reduce cycle time.

On the other hand, some organizations report situations where processes can be improved by dedicating individuals or teams to certain process steps. For example, Mercy Hospital in Minnesota found that having a team of two people dedicated to the receiving process improved both quality and cost. Both vendor managed inventories and outsourcing can be viewed as examples of division of labor, where the work is divided into pieces that are done internally and other pieces that are done by other organizations. Division of labor is similar to value chain analysis that evaluates outsourcing and insourcing alternatives.

See *delegation, human resources, job design, job enlargement, scientific management, standardized work, value chain*.

diversion – The practice of selling products in unauthorized markets; also called parallel trade.

Gray (or grey) market resellers often acquire unwanted merchandise, overstocked products sold at a discount, obsolete products sold at a discount, and products intended for another market (such as an international market) and "divert" them to another market unintended by the manufacturer. In some cases, the practice is legal, but in other cases resellers engage in theft, counterfeiting, diluting, and misrepresenting the products. This is an issue for a wide variety of consumer products, such as health and beauty (hair products, cosmetics), pharmaceuticals, consumer packaged goods, beverages, music, auto, and electronics. In many cases, service is not available or the product warranty is invalid for gray market goods.

See *gray market reseller*.

DMADV – See *Design for Six Sigma (DFSS), lean sigma*.

DMAIC – A lean sigma problem-solving approach with five steps: Define, Measure, Analyze, Improve, and Control.

Lean sigma projects are usually managed with a five-step problem-solving approach called DMAIC (pronounced "Dee-MAY-ic"). These steps are described in the table below.

Define	Define the problem, scope, metrics, team, and sponsor.
Measure	Collect data and then measure and map the "as-is" state.
Analyze	Identify the system of causes and develop and test hypotheses (solutions, countermeasures). Select the best set of solutions, including just do it, implement now, and implement later solutions.
Improve	Implement the best solutions.
Control	"Sustain the gains" by creating new roles and responsibilities, standard operating procedures (SOPs), job descriptions, metrics, and reviews. Also, share learning and identify potential projects.

Source: Professor Arthur V. Hill

In many firms, the DMAIC process is "gated," which means that the project team is not allowed to progress to the next step until the master black belt or sponsor has signed off on the step. In the new product development literature, this is called a phase review or stage-gate review. This author asserts that many DMAIC projects have too many gates that slow the project down. This author and many consultants now recommend having only two gates for a process improvement project: a midterm report to ensure that the team is on track and a final report when the project is complete (or nearly complete).

Most DMAIC projects find a number of "quick hits" early in the project. These should be implemented immediately and should be documented so the project sponsor and the program champion can capture and compare all project benefits and costs.

See *deliverables, Design for Six Sigma (DFSS), Gauge R&R, kaizen workshop, lean sigma, PDCA (Plan-Do-Check-Act), phase review, quick hit, sigma level, sponsor, stage-gate process.*

dock – A door and platform used to receive and ship materials, usually from trailers; also called a loading dock or receiving dock.

See *cross-docking, dock-to-stock, logistics, trailer, warehouse.*

dock-to-stock – The practice of moving receipts from the receiving dock directly to inventory without inspection.

Dock-to-stock eliminates the customer's incoming inspection cost and reduces handling cost. However, it requires that suppliers assure good quality products.

See *dock, incoming inspection, logistics, point of use, receiving, supplier qualification and certification, Warehouse Management System (WMS).*

DOE – See *Design of Experiments (DOE).*

dollar unit sampling – An auditing technique for stratified sampling transactions that allows the auditor to make statistically reliable statements about the misspecification error.

The auditing profession has considered the problem of how to make statistically reliable statements about an audit when some transactions are more important than others and when the probability of a defect is very small. The best approach is an extension of stratified random sampling called dollar unit sampling. In the auditing literature, dollar unit sampling is also known as probability proportionate to size sampling and monetary unit sampling. Roberts (1978, p. 125) stated, "When the proportion of population units with monetary differences is expected to be small and the audit objective is to test for the possibility of a material overstatement, dollar unit sampling is the best statistical technique." A dollar unit sampling audit enables the auditor to make statistical statements about the results of an audit, such as "Based on this audit, we are 95% confident that the total overstatement amount for this population is no more than $500."

See *confidence interval, Poisson distribution, sample size calculation, sampling.*

dot-com – An adjective used to describe companies that sell products or services over the Internet.

Dot-com companies usually do not sell products or services through "brick-and-mortar" channels. Products are typically ordered over the Internet and shipped from warehouses directly to the customer. Services are typically information services provided through the Internet. Amazon.com and eBay.com are two of the best-known dot-com firms. Dot-com firms can be either business-to-business (B2B) or business-to-consumer (B2C) firms. In some cases, dot-com firms can disintermediate traditional distribution firms.

See *B2B, B2C, click-and-mortar, disintermediation, supply chain management.*

double exponential smoothing – See *exponential smoothing.*

double marginalization – An economics term that describes a situation in which two firms in a supply chain have monopoly power and each producer adds its own monopoly mark-up to the price.

The price of the finished product is higher than it would be if the two producers were vertically integrated.
See *economics.*

double sampling plan – See *acceptance sampling.*

downstream – See *upstream.*

downtime – Time that a resource (system, production line, or machine) is not working; called an outage in the power generation context and a crash in the computer context.

Downtime is often separated into **planned** and **unplanned downtime**. Causes of planned downtime include:
Set-up – Adjustments required to prepare a resource to produce.
Start-up – The time from the end of set-up until the first good units are produced.
Cleaning – All activities required to remove materials and sanitize a process.
Changeover – Time to change from making the last unit of one product to the first good unit of the next.

Operational downtime – Production stoppages imposed by the process for equipment and quality checks.

Maintenance – Scheduled (preventive) maintenance activities.

Personal Time – Line stoppage for meal breaks, shift changes, meetings, and personal time.

Construction – Downtime for re-layout or building construction.

Causes of unplanned downtime include machine failure (followed by emergency maintenance) and quality problems that require the machine or line to stop.

The opposite of downtime is uptime. Service level agreements (SLAs) often specify guaranteed uptimes.

See *capacity, operations performance metrics, Overall Equipment Effectiveness (OEE), reliability, Service Level Agreement (SLA), setup time, Total Productive Maintenance (TPM)*.

DPMO – See *Defects per Million Opportunities (DPMO)*.

DPPM – See *Defective Parts per Million (DPPM)*.

drop ship – A logistics term for a shipment that goes directly from the supplier to the buyer without the seller handling the product; often spelled dropship; sometimes called direct store shipment (DSD) or direct ship.

When a seller (typically a distributor or retailer) has a supplier (often a manufacturer or distributor) send a shipment directly to a buyer (customer), the order is **drop shipped** to the customer. The seller does not handle the product or put it in inventory. The supplier has little or no communication with the buyer. The buyer pays the seller and the seller pays the supplier. Drop shipments reduce the customer's leadtime and the seller's inventory handling cost, but usually increase the distribution cost because a small shipment (less than truck load) must be made to the customer. The term "drop ship" is sometimes also used to describe a shipment to a different location than the customer's normal shipping location. Drop ship can be used as either a noun or a verb.

See *distribution center (DC), logistics*.

DRP – See *Distribution Requirement Planning (DRP)*.

Drum-Buffer-Rope (DBR) – A Theory of Constraints (TOV) concept that sends a signal every time the bottleneck completes one unit, giving upstream operations the authority to produce. ✪

DBR is a production control system based on the TOC philosophy. Like other TOC concepts, DBR focuses on maximizing the utilization of the bottleneck (the constrained resource) and subordinates all non-bottleneck resources so they meet the needs of the bottleneck.

Drum – Completion of one unit at the bottleneck is the drum that signals (authorizes) all upstream workcenters to produce one unit. The unconstrained resources must serve the constrained resource.

Buffer – A time cushion used to protect the bottleneck from running out of work (starving).

Rope – A tool to pull production from the non-bottleneck resources to the bottleneck. The DRB concept is very similar to the "pacemaker workcenter" concept used in lean manufacturing.

See *CONWIP, lean thinking, pacemaker, POLCA (Paired-cell Overlapping Loops of Cards with Authorization), Theory of Constraints (TOC), upstream*.

DSI – See *The Decision Sciences Institute*.

DSD – See *drop ship*.

DSM – See *Design Structure Matrix*.

dual source – The practice of using two suppliers for a single component; also called multiple sourcing.

Multiple sourcing is the use of two or more suppliers for the same component. Some people use the term "dual source" to mean two or more suppliers. This is in contrast to **sole sourcing**, where only one supplier is qualified and only one is used, and **single sourcing**, where multiple suppliers are qualified, but only one is used.

See *single source*.

due diligence – A careful evaluation done before a business transaction.

A common example of due diligence is the process that a potential buyer uses to evaluate a target company for acquisition. Wikipedia offers a very thorough discussion of this subject.

See *acquisition, purchasing*.

dunnage – Fill material used to minimize movement within a container to protect products being shipped.

Dunnage can be any packing material, such as low grade lumber, scrap wood, planks, paper, cardboard, blocks, metal, plastic bracing, airbags, air pillows, bubble wrap, foam, or packing peanuts, used to support, protect, and secure cargo for shipping and handling. Dunnage can also be used to provide ventilation and provide space for the tines of a forklift truck.

See *logistics*.

DuPont Analysis – An economic analysis that can be used to show the return on investment as a function of inventory and other economic variables.

Operations managers can use the DuPont Analysis to analyze the impact of changes in inventory investment on Return on Investment (ROI). The DuPont Analysis can be used to show how much (1) the carrying cost goes down when inventory goes down, (2) profit (return) goes up when the cost goes down, (3) investment goes down when inventory investment goes down, and finally, (4) ROI goes up dramatically as the numerator (return) goes up while the denominator (investment) goes down at the same time. This assumes that revenue is not affected by inventory, which may not be true for a make to stock firm unless the inventory reduction is managed very carefully. From an inventory management point of view, the DuPont Analysis is less important when interest rates and carrying charges are low.

A DuPont Analysis shows the sensitivity of the firm's ROI to changes in input variables (drivers), such as inventory. (Note: Many organizations change ROI to an EVA or economic profit calculation.) This analysis is similar to a strategy map and a Y-tree because it shows the drivers of higher-level performance metrics.

The following is an example of a DuPont Analysis for a hypothetical firm.

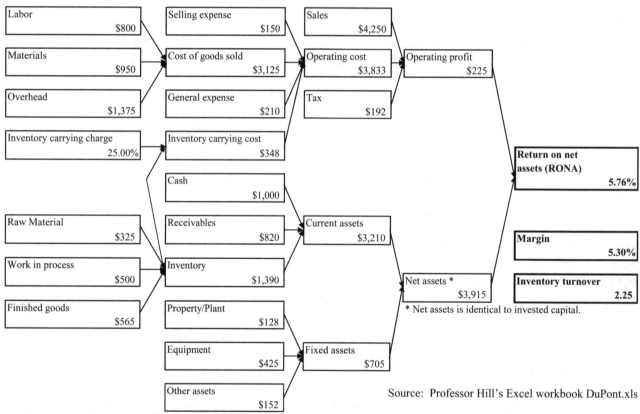

Source: Professor Hill's Excel workbook DuPont.xls

See *balanced scorecard, financial performance metrics, inventory turnover, Return on Net Assets (RONA), strategy map, what-if analysis, Y-tree.*

DuPont STOP – A safety training program developed at DuPont.

The Safety Training Observation Program (STOP) is a widely used safety program that teaches workplace safety auditing skills, with steps to reinforce safe work practices and correct unsafe practices. STOP is based on the following principles:

- All injuries can be prevented.
- Employee involvement is essential.
- Management is responsible for safety.
- All operating exposures can be safeguarded.
- Safety training for workers is essential.

- Working safely is a condition of employment.
- Management audits are a must.
- All deficiencies must be corrected promptly.
- Off-the-job safety will be emphasized.

See *Occupational Safety and Health Administration (OSHA), safety*.

durability – A quality term used to refer to a product's capability to withstand stress, wear, decay, and force without requiring maintenance; also called durable.

See *durable goods, quality management, robust, service guarantee*.

durable goods – Products that people keep for a long time and have useful lives of more than five years; also known as capital goods or hard goods.

Examples of durable products include cars, furniture, and houses. Durable goods can usually be rented as well as purchased. In contrast, non-durable goods are almost never rented.

See *consumable goods, durability, Fast Moving Consumer Goods (FMCG), white goods*.

Durbin-Watson Statistic – A statistical test for first-order autocorrelation (serial correlation) in time series data.

Autocorrelation is the correlation between a variable in one period and the previous period. For example, the weather temperature is highly autocorrelated, which means that the correlation between the weather in one day tends to vary with the weather on the previous day. If today is hot, then so is tomorrow.

The Durbin-Watson Statistic is used to test for first-order autocorrelation in time series data. It is most commonly used to test for autocorrelation in the residuals for regression models that deal with time series data. It is often also used to test for autocorrelation in the forecast error for a time series forecasting model. The term "error" (e_t) is used to mean either the residuals from a regression or the forecast error for a forecasting model.

The Durbin-Watson test compares the error in period t with the error in period $t-1$. The following equation is the Durbin-Watson test statistic $d = \sum_{t=2}^{n} (e_t - e_{t-1})^2 \Big/ \sum_{t=1}^{n} e_t^2$, where t is the time period, e_t is the residual in period t, and n is the total number of observations available. The statistic (d) is constrained to the range (0, 4) with a midpoint of 2. A value of d close to 2 suggests that the time series has no autocorrelation. A low value of d (close to zero) implies positive autocorrelation because the differences between e_t and e_{t-1} are relatively small. A high value of d (close to four) implies negative autocorrelation because the differences between e_t and e_{t-1} are relatively large.

The Durbin-Watson test can be used to test for both positive and negative autocorrelation. However, the null hypothesis is usually no significant autocorrelation and the alterative hypothesis is positive autocorrelation. Tables for the Durbin-Watson test can be found in many standard statistics texts, such as Kutner, Neter, Nachtsheim, and Wasserman (2004).

See *autocorrelation, Box-Jenkins forecasting, linear regression, runs test, time series forecasting*.

Dutch auction – An auction method where the price is lowered until a bidder is prepared to pay; also known as a descending bid auction.

In a Dutch auction, the auctioneer begins with the seller's asking price and then lowers the price until a bidder is willing to accept the price or until a predetermined reserve price (the seller's minimum acceptable price) is reached. The winning bidder pays the last announced price. The Dutch auction is named for the Dutch tulip auctions in the Netherlands.

See *e-auction, e-business, e-procurement, reverse auction, sniping*.

E

EAN (European Article Number) – See *Universal Product Code (UPC)*.
earliness – See *service level*.

early detection – The quality management concept that it is better to find and fix defects early in a process.

See *catchball, cost of quality, defect, Fagan Defect-Free Process, mixed model assembly, quality at the source, scrum, setup time reduction methods.*

Early Supplier Involvement (ESI) – The collaborative product development practice of getting suppliers involved early in the product design process.

Good suppliers have core competences around their product technologies. Therefore, firms that involve their suppliers in product development at an early stage can take advantage of these core competencies and potentially reap financial and competitive rewards.

Companies that involve suppliers early report the following benefits: (a) reduced product development time, (b) improved quality and features, (c) reduced product or service costs, and (d) reduced design changes. Companies do best when they give suppliers the leeway to come up with their own designs rather than simply manufacturing parts to their customers' specifications. Suppliers often have more expertise than their customers in their product technologies.

See *concurrent engineering, JIT II, New Product Development (NPD).*

earned hours – The labor or machine hours calculated by multiplying the actual number of units produced during a period by the standard hourly rate.

Efficiency is calculated as the ratio (earned hours)/(actual hours) during a period. For example, a workcenter has a standard rate of one unit per hour. It worked eight actual hours today, but earned ten hours (i.e., it produced then units). Therefore, the efficiency of this workcenter is (earned hours)/(actual hours) = 10/8 = 125%. Earned hours is similar to the practice of earned value management in project management.

See *Earned Value Management (EVM), efficiency, productivity.*

Earned Value Management (EVM) – A methodology used to measure and communicate the progress of a project by taking into account the work completed to date, the time taken to date, and the costs incurred to date.

Earned Value Management (EVM) helps evaluate and control task/project risk by measuring progress in monetary terms. EVM is sometimes required for commercial and government contracts. Under EVM, work is planned, budgeted, and scheduled in time phased "planned value" increments, constituting a cost and a schedule measurement baseline.

The description below applies EVM to a task; however, the same concept can easily be extended to an entire project. Time and material is spent in completing a task. If managed well, the task will be completed with time to spare and with no wasted materials or cost. If managed poorly, the task will take longer and waste materials. By taking a snap-shot of the task and calculating the Earned Value, it is possible to compare the planned cost and schedule with the actual cost and schedule and assess the progress of the task. When considering an entire project, it is possible to extrapolate the schedule and cost to estimate the probable completion date and total cost.

The basics of EVM can best be shown on an S-curve. In its simplest form, the S-curve is a graph showing how the task budget is planned to be spent over time. The three curves on the graph represent:
- Budgeted cost for work scheduled – The budgets for all activities planned.
- Actual cost of work performed – The actual costs of the work charged so far.
- Budgeted cost of work performed – The planned costs of the work allocated to the completed activities.

Earned Value is defined as the percentage of the project complete times the project budget. The schedule variance is the difference between the Earned Value and the budget. Cost variance is the difference between the Earned Value and the actual costs of the works.

The benefits for project managers of the Earned Value approach come from:
- Disciplined planning using established methods.
- Availability of metrics that show variances from the plan to generate necessary corrective actions.

See *critical chain, earned hours, project management, work breakdown structure (WBS).*

e-auction – A Web-based tool for making a market more efficient.

The best example of an electronic auction is the popular ebay.com. A **reverse auction** is where the buyer calls for bids for something from potential suppliers. For example, General Electric will notify a group of qualified suppliers that they are invited to participate in an electronic auction. The date and product specifications are defined by the buyer. At the time of the auction, the participating bidders assemble at a common Internet site and bid for the contract.

See *Dutch auction, e-business, e-procurement, reverse auction, sniping.*

EBITDA – Earnings Before Interest, Taxes, Depreciation, and Amortization; an indicator of a company's financial performance calculated as revenue minus expenses (excluding tax, interest, depreciation, and amortization); sometimes called EBIDTA (Earnings Before Interest, Depreciation, Taxes, and Amortization).

EBITDA is an approximate measure of a company's operating cash flow based on data from the company's income statement. EBITDA is calculated by looking at earnings before the deduction of interest expenses, taxes, depreciation, and amortization. This measure of earnings is of particular interest in cases where companies have large amounts of fixed assets that are subject to heavy depreciation charges (such as manufacturing companies). Because the accounting and financing effects on company earnings do not factor into EBITDA, it is a good way to compare companies within and across industries. This measure is also of interest to a company's creditors, because EBITDA is essentially the income that a company has free for interest payments. In general, EBITDA is a useful measure only for large companies with significant assets or a significant amount of debt financing. It is rarely a useful measure for evaluating a small company with no significant loans.

EBITDA is a good metric to evaluate profitability, but not cash flow. Unfortunately, however, EBITDA is often used as a measure of cash flow, which is a very dangerous and misleading thing to do because there is a significant difference between the two. Operating cash flow is a better measure of how much cash a company is generating because it adds non-cash charges (depreciation and amortization) back to net income and includes the changes in working capital that also use/provide cash (such as changes in receivables, payables, and inventories). These working capital factors are the key to determining how much cash a company is generating. If investors do not include changes in working capital in their analyses and rely solely on EBITDA, they may miss clues that indicate whether a company is losing money because it cannot sell its products.

See *financial performance metrics, income statement.*

e-business – The conduct of business over the Internet; sometimes used interchangeably with e-commerce.

Bartels (2000) defines **e-commerce** as using electronic network support for customer- and supplier-facing processes and e-business as using electronic network support for the entire business. Based on these definitions, he argues that e-business is more difficult that e-commerce because it involves integration e-commerce activities with back office operations such as production, inventory, and product development.

See *B2B, B2C, back office, Dutch auction, e-auction, e-procurement, extranet, intranet, reverse auction, sniping.*

ECO – See *Engineering Change Order (ECO).*

e-commerce – See *e-business.*

econometric forecasting – A forecasting method that considers a number of different leading economic indicators, such as disposable income and meals away from home, to make forecasts; also known as extrinsic forecasting.

Econometric models use leading indicators to make forecasts. For example, a sharp rise in the cost of gasoline may well be a good indicator (predictor) of an increased demand rate for fuel-efficient cars.

Most econometric studies use multiple regression models. For example, the Onan Division of Cummings Engine developed a regression model and found that fast-food sales and disposable income could be used to forecast the sales of recreational vehicles one quarter ahead.

See *Box-Jenkins forecasting, forecasting, leading indicator, linear regression.*

Economic Lot Scheduling Problem (ELSP) – A class of lotsizing problems that involves finding the optimal (or near optimal) order size (or cycle length) to minimize the sum of the carrying and ordering (setup) costs for multiple items that share the same capacity resource (the "bottleneck").

Even though the problem has the word "scheduling" in its name, it is a lotsizing problem rather than a scheduling problem. This ELSP methodology can be implemented fairly easily for any manufacturing process that builds to stock and has a fairly level demand throughout the year. The procedure finds the optimal order intervals n_i* (periods supply) for each item i. When the demand varies over time, it is better to use the periods supply than the order quantities. It may also be important to find the optimal safety stock for these order quantities, where the leadtime for each item is based on the order interval. The time phased order point system can then be used to determine order timing.

See *algorithm, Economic Order Quantity (EOQ), lotsizing methods, run time, setup time.*

Economic Order Quantity (EOQ) – The optimal order quantity (batch size or lotsize) that minimizes the sum of the carrying and ordering costs. ✪

If the order quantity is too large, the firm incurs too much carrying cost; if the order quantity is too small, the firm incurs too much ordering (setup) cost. The EOQ model can help managers make the trade-off between ordering too much and ordering too little (Harris 1913, 1915; Wilson 1934). The *EOQ* finds the Fixed Order Quantity that minimizes the sum of the ordering and carrying costs.

Define D as the annual demand in units, Q as the order quantity in units, S as the order cost per order, i as the **carrying charge** per dollar per year, and c as the unit cost. A firm with a fixed order quantity of Q units and an annual demand of D units will have D/Q orders per year and a total annual ordering cost of $(D/Q)S$. The average **cycle inventory**[14] is $Q/2$ units and the annual **carrying cost** is $(Q/2)ic$. Therefore, the total incremental annual cost is $TIC = (D/Q)S + (Q/2)ic$.

Taking the first derivative of the total incremental cost function and setting it to zero yields $\dfrac{dTIC}{dQ} = -DQ^{-2}S + ic/2 = 0$, which means that $Q^2 = \dfrac{2DS}{ic} \Rightarrow EOQ = \sqrt{\dfrac{2DS}{ic}}$. The second derivative of the *TIC* is $2DQ^{-3}S$, which is greater than zero for all $Q > 0$. This proves that the Economic Order Quantity $EOQ = \sqrt{2DS/(ic)}$ is the order quantity that has the global minimum total increment cost. Note that the optimal solution (the *EOQ*) will always be where the annual ordering and annual carrying costs are equal.

The graph below shows that the annual carrying cost increases with Q and the annual ordering cost decreases with Q. The optimal Q (the *EOQ*) is where the annual carrying cost and ordering cost are equal. In this example, the parameters are demand $D = 1200$ units, ordering cost $S = \$54$, carrying charge $i = 12\%$, and unit cost $c = \$50$. The *EOQ* is 147 units and total annual carrying cost and total annual ordering cost are both \$440.91, which means that the total incremental cost is \$881.81.

The *EOQ* model is considered to be of limited practical value for three reasons. First, it is very difficult to estimate the four parameters in the model. As a joke, the *EOQ* can be written as $EOQ = \sqrt{2\,??/(??)}$. Second, even with perfect estimates of the four parameters, the total incremental cost function is usually flat near the optimal solution, which means that the total incremental cost is not sensitive to errors in the *EOQ*. Third, managerial intuition is usually good at finding the *EOQ* without the equation. It is fairly obvious to most managers that high-volume, expensive items should be ordered more often than low-volume inexpensive items.

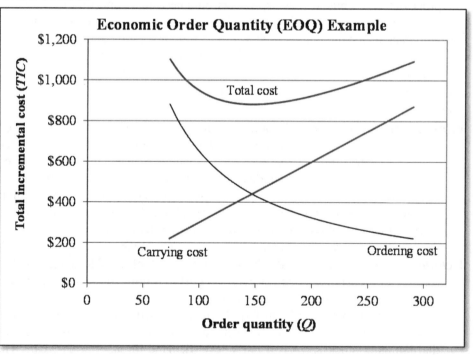

------

[14] *Cycle stock is also called the lotsize inventory. This is inventory in the "saw-toothed" graph that goes up when an order is received and then goes down over time as units are drawn out of inventory. The lotsize inventory does not include the safety stock, which is the inventory below the "saw-toothed" graph.*

On the positive side, the *EOQ* model has several benefits. First, it helps people get a better understanding of lotsizing issues and can help students and managers refine their thinking about the managerial economics of the lotsizing problem. Second, in some cases, the trade-offs can have significant economic impact, especially when accumulated over many items. Third, the *EOQ* model is the foundation for several other models, such as the quantity discount model and the Economic Lot Scheduling Problem (ELSP).

See *ABC classification, aggregate inventory management, carrying charge, carrying cost, cycle stock, Economic Lot Scheduling Problem (ELSP), fixed order quantity, instantaneous replenishment, inventory management, lotsize, lotsizing methods, marginal cost, Period Order Quantity (POQ), quantity discount, safety stock, time-varying demand lotsizing problem.*

Economic Value Added (EVA) – A financial performance metric for the true economic profit of an enterprise from the shareholders' point of view; closely related to economic profit.

EVA is the net operating profit minus an appropriate charge for the opportunity cost of all capital invested in an enterprise. As such, EVA is an estimate of true "economic" profit, or the amount by which earnings exceed or fall short of the required minimum rate of return that shareholders and lenders could get by investing in other securities of comparable risk. The capital charge is the most distinctive and important aspect of EVA. Economic profit is similar to EVA, but is not adjusted in the same way as EVA.

Under conventional accounting, most companies appear profitable. As Drucker (1995) argues, "Until a business returns a profit that is greater than its cost of capital, it operates at a loss. Never mind that it pays taxes as if it had a genuine profit. The enterprise still returns less to the economy than it devours in resources ... Until then it does not create wealth; it destroys it."

EVA corrects this error by explicitly recognizing that when managers employ capital, they must pay for it, just as if it were a wage. By taking all capital costs into account, including the cost of equity, EVA shows the dollar amount of wealth a business has created or destroyed in each reporting period. In other words, EVA is profit the way shareholders define it. If the shareholders expect, say, a 10% return on their investment, they "make money" only to the extent that their share of after-tax operating profits exceeds 10% of equity capital.

Stern Stewart & Company owns a registered trademark for the name EVA for a brand of software and financial consulting/training services. Their proprietary component makes adjustments related to amortization of goodwill, capitalization of brand advertising to convert economic profit to into EVA.

See *financial performance metrics, goodwill.*

economics – The social science that studies how people and groups (families, businesses, organizations, governments, and societies) choose to produce, distribute, consume, and allocate limited goods and services.

Economics deals primarily with supply and demand of scarce goods and services and how people and societies assign prices to these goods and services to allocate them in some rational way.

The word "economics" is from the Greek for house (οίκος = oikos) and custom or law (νόμος = nomos); in other words, economics is about the "rules of the house(hold)." (This definition from the Greek is adapted from http://en.wikipedia.org/wiki/Economics, February 26, 2008).

See *demand, double marginalization, economy of scale, economy of scope, elasticity, opportunity cost, Pareto optimality, production function, sunk cost.*

economy of scale – An economics principle that refers to situations where the cost per unit goes down as the production volume increases; also called economies of scale. ✪

Stated in more precise terms from the field of economics, economies of scale is the decrease in the marginal cost of production as a firm's scale of operations increases. Economies of scale can be accomplished because, as production increases, the cost of producing each additional unit falls. The increase in efficiency often comes by means of allocating the fixed costs over a larger number of units.

See *big box store, commonality, core competence, cross-docking, diseconomy of scale, economics, economy of scope, marginal cost, mergers and acquisitions (M&A), network effect.*

economy of scope – A concept from economics that states that the cost per unit declines as the variety of products increases. ✪

In other words, economies of scope arise from synergies in the production of similar goods. A firm with economics of scope can reduce its cost per unit by having a wide variety of products that share resources. Scope economies exist whenever the same investment can support multiple profitable activities less expensively in combination than separately.

Economies of scope can arise from the ability to eliminate costs by operating two or more businesses under the same corporate umbrella. These economies exist when it is less costly for two or more businesses to operate under centralized management than to function independently. Cost savings opportunities can stem from interrelationships anywhere along a value chain.

See *commonality, economics, economy of scale, mass customization.*

ECR – See *Efficient Consumer Response (ECR).*

EDI – See *Electronic Data Interchange (EDI).*

effective capacity – See *capacity.*

effectiveness – Capability to produce a desired result, without respect to efficiency. ✪

For example, the maintenance engineers in a milk plant found that a particular disinfectant was very effective in killing bacteria in a vat that was used to produce cottage cheese. However, if the disinfectant was very expensive and required significant time to apply, the firm might be able to find another more efficient approach that was equally effective. In summary, effectiveness is about getting the right job done and efficiency is about getting the job done using the minimum resources.

See *efficiency, Overall Equipment Effectiveness (OEE).*

effectivity date – The calendar date that an engineering change order for the bill of material (BOM) will come into effect; sometimes called the effective date.

Nearly ERP systems include software for managing the BOM. In addition to storing the current product structure, these systems are usually also able to store future product structures that will be implemented at some future date (the effectivity date). When the effectivity date is reached, the second structure comes into effect.

The effectivity date may be determined by the effectivity quantity. With an effectivity quantity, the engineering change comes into effect when the current inventory has fallen to zero or to a specified quantity. However, one problem with this approach is that the inventory position usually does not fall to zero instantaneously. When this is the case, the replenishment system may generate a new purchase order for the old item. A second problem is that the small quantity of remnant stock that remains may be uneconomical to use, leading to its scrap.

See *bill of material (BOM), Engineering Change Order (ECO), Materials Requirements Planning (MRP).*

effectivity quantity – See *effectivity date.*

efficiency – (1) Industrial engineering: The ratio of the standard processing time to the average actual processing time; a process that can perform at a very low cost compared to some standard. (2) LEI's **Lean Lexicon** (Marchwinski & Shook 2006): Meeting exact customer requirements with the minimum amount of resources. (3) Economics: The amount of resource products per unit of resource consumed. (4) Finance: An efficient market is one that quickly and accurately incorporates information into prices. ✪

The industrial engineering definition is the most widely accepted definition in the operations field. Efficiency is calculated as the ratio (earned hours)/(actual hours) during a period. For example, a workcenter has a standard time of one hour per unit. It worked eight actual hours today and earned ten hours (i.e., it produced then units). Therefore, the efficiency of this workcenter is (earned hours)/(actual hours) = 10/8 = 125%. Earned hours is similar to the practice of earned value management in project management.

The above economics definition is indistinquishable from the definition of **productivity**.

See *8 wastes, earned hours, effectiveness, operations performance metrics, Overall Equipment Effectiveness (OEE), productivity, standard time, utilization.*

Efficient Consumer Response (ECR) – A consumer goods initiative aimed at reducing inefficient practices and waste in the supply chain.

Efficient Consumer Response (ECR) is an application of lean thinking to retail distribution, primarily in fast moving consumer goods supply chains. ECR is defined by the Joint Industry Project for Efficient Consumer Response (1994) as follows:

A strategy in which the grocery retailer, distributor, and supplier trading partners work closely together to eliminate excess costs from the grocery supply chain. ECR focuses particularly on four major opportunities to improve efficiency:

1. Optimizing store assortments and space allocations to increase category sales per square foot and inventory turnover.
2. Streamlining the distribution of goods from the point of manufacture to the retail shelf.
3. Reducing the cost of trade and consumer promotion.
4. Reducing the cost of developing and introducing new products.

See *Collaborative Planning Forecasting and Replenishment (CPFR), continuous replenishment planning, Fast Moving Consumer Goods (FMCG), lean thinking, Quick Response Manufacturing*.

eight wastes – See *8 wastes*.

eighty-twenty rule – See *Pareto's Law*.

e-kanban – See *faxban*.

elasticity – An economics term used to describe the sensitivity of the demand to a change in price.

For example, Target is a major discount retailer in North America. When the inventory analysts at Target want to clear (dispose) end-of-season inventory, they want to know the elasticity (sensitivity) of the demand to a reduced price. They use a linear model based on percentages that relates the percent increase in demand to a percent decrease in price (e.g., a 5% decrease in price will result in a 10% increase in the average demand).

The three main approaches for modeling the price-elasticity of demand include the linear model, the power model, and the exponential model. The linear model is $D(p) = \alpha - \beta p$, where $D(p)$ is the demand at price p and α and β are the parameters of the model to be estimated from historical data. The power model is $D(p) = \alpha p^{-\beta}$. The exponential model is $D(p) = \alpha e^{-\beta p}$. The β parameter is the elasticity parameter for all three models. All three models show that the demand decreases as the price increases. The linear model is the easiest to use, but the power and exponential models generally make more sense. For the power model, the demand is infinite when price is zero; for the exponential model, the demand is α when the price is zero. Therefore, the exponential model makes the most sense for most operations/inventory/pricing models.

See *booking curve, demand, economics, forecasting*.

Electronic Data Interchange (EDI) – A system and related set of standards that firms can use to communicate routine business transactions between computers without human intervention.

EDI transactions can include information for inquiries, planning, purchasing, acknowledgments, pricing, order status, scheduling, test results, shipping and receiving, invoices, payments, and financial reporting. The simplest form of EDI is to send purchase orders to suppliers. More advanced forms of EDI include sending invoices, electronic payments, and planned orders (requirements). The advantages of EDI include:

- Reduced transaction cost – Electronic transactions are cheaper than manual/paper ones.
- Reduced transaction time – Electronic ordering is nearly simultaneous, versus days or weeks for a manual/paper transaction sent via mail.
- Improved forecast accuracy – Forward visibility of the customer's requirements can dramatically improve forecast accuracy. For many firms, this is the most important benefit.
- Improved data quality – Sending information electronically can improve quality because it eliminates almost all the human data entry from the process.

With the rapid growth of e-commerce, many expect that the phrase "EDI" will soon die. E-commerce will, of course, serve the same purposes as EDI and will have to include the same functionality.

See *Advanced Shipping Notification (ASN), Enterprise Resources Planning (ERP), firm order, forward visibility, invoice, Over/Short/Damaged Report, purchase order (PO), purchasing, Transportation Management System (TMS), XML (eXtensible Markup Language)*.

Electronic Product Code (EPC) – A number used to identify products using RFI technology in a supply chain.

Like the Universal Product Code (UPC), the EPC is used to identify item numbers (SKUs) for products moving through a supply chain. Unlike the UPC, the EPC uses radio frequency (RFID) technology rather than Optical Character Recognition (OCR) technology and provides a serial number that can be referenced in a database. The serial number enables the specific item to be tracked as it moves through the supply chain.

The EPC number can be from 64 to 256 bits and contains at least the (1) EPC version, (2) company identification number assigned by EPCglobal, (3) product number (object class), and (4) unique serial number. A 96-bit EPC is capable of differentiating 68 billion items for each of 16 million products within each of 268 million companies. For example, an EPC can differentiate between the first and the thousandth can in a shipment of cans of soup.

See *barcode, Optical Character Recognition (OCR), part number, Radio Frequency Identification (RFID), traceability, Universal Product Code (UPC).*

Electronics Manufacturing Services (EMS) – See *contract manufacturer.*

emergency maintenance – See *maintenance.*

empathy – A service quality term that refers to the amount of caring and individualized attention shown to customers by the service firm.

According to Parasuraman, Zeithaml, and Berry (1990), empathy involves the provision of caring and individualized attention to customers that includes access, communication, and understanding the customer.

See *service quality, SERVQUAL.*

employee turnover – The average percentage of employees who exit a firm per year. ✪

For example, the turnover for hotel staff is very high, often on the order of 100%. This means that the number of employees exiting a firm in a year (voluntarily or involuntarily) equals the number employed. Employee turnover can be greater than 100% (e.g., 200% employee turnover means an average tenure of six months). Employee turnover is a surrogate measure of employee satisfaction.

See *inventory turnover, turnover.*

empowerment – The practice of granting decision rights to subordinates.

Empowerment often helps people build confidence, develop self-reliance, and derive greater job satisfaction. In a service context, empowerment often results in better customer service because the workers closest to the customer can make better decisions on the customer's behalf. Empowerment can also increase the absorptive capacity of an organization.

See *absorptive capacity, customer service, High Performance Work Systems (HPWS), human resources, jidoka, job design, job enlargement, service quality.*

EMS (Electronics Manufacturing Services) – See *contract manufacturer.*

energy audit – The process of inspecting and analyzing the energy use in a facility with the intention of reducing energy consumption, cost, and pollution while increasing safety and comfort.

An energy audit might consider issues such as repairing or replacing heating and cooling systems, insulation and weatherization, location of heating/cooling losses, safety, and comfort. These audits are often conducted by qualified inspectors who use benchmark data to support engineering analyses. Opportunities are often found with new lighting, better control systems, more efficient systems, and better use of solar and wind energy.

See *carbon footprint, green manufacturing, sustainability.*

engineer to order (ETO) – A customer interface strategy with engineering done in response to a customer order; sometimes called design to order. ✪

Examples of engineer to order (ETO) products include custom-built homes, the space shuttle, plastic molds, and specialized capital equipment. With an ETO customer interface, engineering work usually needs to be done before any specialized components can be purchased or fabrication can begin. This means that ETO customer leadtime is the sum of the engineering, procurement, fabrication, assembly, packing, and shipping time.

Although some assemblies and components may be standard items stored in inventory, some items may be designed specifically to the customer's order. Standard items do not need to be stocked unless their procurement leadtime is longer than the leadtime for the engineering effort. Purchase orders may be pegged (assigned) to specific customer orders. The ERP system may treat the engineering organization as a workcenter in the factory. Actual costing is used because many items are purchased or manufactured just for that one customer order.

In an ETO system, the main challenges are often in (1) making reasonable promise dates and keeping them up to date as the situation changes (ask any owners of a custom-built home if their home was completed on time), (2) managing **Engineering Change Orders (ECOs)** to support design changes, and (3) developing modular designs, where many of the components are standard with standard interfaces with other components that can be "mixed and matched" to meet a wide variety of customer requirements and reduce engineering time and effort.

See *commonality, configurator, Engineering Change Order (ECO), make to order (MTO), mass customization, respond to order (RTO).*

Engineering Change Order (ECO) – A request for a change in a product design; also called an engineering change request.

The Engineering Change Order (ECO) should include the reason for the change, level of urgency, affected items and processes, and an evaluation of the costs and benefits. The engineering change review board, with representatives from engineering, R&D, manufacturing, and procurement, evaluates the cost, benefits, and timing before an ECO is implemented. Improving the ECO process can be a good opportunity for improvement in many firms. ECOs tend to be complicated and error-prone. Most ERP systems allow the system to implement an ECO when the inventory position of the older component goes to zero.

See *bill of material (BOM), effectivity date, engineer to order (ETO), Integrated Product Development (IPD), Materials Requirements Planning (MRP), version control.*

engineering change review board – See *Engineering Change Order (ECO).*

Enterprise Resources Planning (ERP) – Integrated applications software that corporations use to run their businesses. ✪

ERP systems typically handle accounts payable, accounts receivable, general ledger, payroll, Materials Requirements Planning (MRP), purchasing, sales, human resources, and many other interrelated systems. One of the key concepts for an ERP system is that the firm stores data in one and only one location. In other words, the organization has only a single database that all departments share. SAP and Oracle are the two main ERP systems vendors currently on the market.

ERP systems grew out of Materials Requirements Planning (MRP) systems that were developed in the 1970s and 1980s. The Materials Requirements Planning module in an ERP system supports manufacturing organizations by the timely release of production and purchase orders using the production plan for finished goods to determine the materials plan for the components and materials required to make the product. The MRP module is driven by the master production schedule (MPS), which defines the requirements for the end items. The three key inputs to the MRP module are (1) the master production schedule, (2) inventory status records, and (3) product structure records.

See *Advanced Planning and Scheduling (APS), bill of material (BOM), Business Requirements Planning (BRP), Distribution Requirements Planning (DRP), Electronic Data Interchange (EDI), human resources, implementation, legacy system, Materials Requirements Planning (MRP), SAP, turnkey.*

entitlement – A lean sigma term used as a measurement of the best possible performance of a process, usually without significant capital investment.

Entitlement is an important process improvement concept that is particularly useful in project selection. It is usually defined as the best performance possible for a process without significant capital investment. However, some firms define it as the performance of the perfect process. As the term implies, the organization is "entitled" to this level of performance based on the investments already made.

Knowing the entitlement for a process defines the size of opportunity for improvement. If entitlement is 500 units per day and the baseline performance is 250 units per day, the process has significant room for improvement. If higher production rates are needed, a search for a totally new process may be in order (i.e., reengineering or DFSS).

Entitlement should be determined for all key process performance measures (yield, cost of poor quality, capacity, downtime, waste, etc.). Entitlement may be predicted by engineering and scientific models, nameplate capacity provided by the equipment manufacturer, or simply the best prolonged performance observed to date.

Entitlement can also be predicted from empirical relationships. In one instance, it was observed that a process operating at a cost of $0.36/unit had at one time operated at $0.16/unit (correcting for inflation). This suggests that the process entitlement (as determined by best prolonged performance) should be $0.16/unit. On further investigation, it was observed that there was a linear relationship between defects and cost/unit of the form: Cost = $0.12 + 3(defects)/1,000,000. Therefore, if defects could be reduced to very low levels, the true process entitlement may be as low as $0.12/unit.

The following steps should be followed when using entitlement for project selection:
1. Look at the gap between baseline performance (current state) and entitlement (desired state).
2. Identify a project that will close the gap and can be completed in less than four to six months.
3. Assess the bottomline impact of the project and compare it to other potential projects.

The gap between the baseline and entitlement is rarely closed in the course of a single project. It is common for several projects to be required.

Keep in mind that process entitlement can, and often does, change as more is learned about the process. After a few lean sigma projects, processes are sometimes performing beyond the initial entitlement level.

See *benchmarking, lean sigma.*

EOQ – See *Economic Order Quantity (EOQ).*

EPC – See *Electronic Product Code (EPC).*

e-procurement – A Web-based information system that improves corporate purchasing operations by handling the specification, authorization, competitive bidding, and acquisition of products and services through catalogs, auctions, requests for proposals, and requests for quotes.

See *acquisition, Dutch auction, e-auction, e-business, purchasing, reverse auction.*

ergonomics – The scientific discipline concerned with the understanding of interactions among humans and other elements of a system and the profession that applies theory, principles, data, and methods to design to optimize human well-being and overall system performance; ergonomics is also called human factors. ✪

Source: This is the approved definition of the International Ergonomics Association, www.iea.cc, representing 19,000 ergonomists worldwide, and was provided by Jan Dul, Professor of Ergonomics Management, Department of Management of Technology and Innovation, Rotterdam School of Management, Erasmus School of Business, Erasmus University, Rotterdam.

See *error proofing, human resources, job design, process design.*

Erlang C formula – See *queuing theory.*

Erlang distribution – A continuous probability distribution useful for modeling task times.

The Erlang is the distribution of the sum of k independent identically distributed random variables each having an exponential distribution with mean β.

Parameters: The shape parameter (k), which must be an integer, and the scale parameter (β).

Density and distribution functions: The Erlang density and distribution functions for $x > 0$ are:

$$f(x) = e^{-x/\beta} \frac{\beta^{-k} x^{k-1}}{(k-1)!} \quad \text{and} \quad F(x) = 1 - e^{-x/\beta} \sum_{j=0}^{k-1} \frac{(\beta x)^j}{j!}$$

Statistics: Range $[0, \infty)$, mean $k\beta$, variance $k\beta^2$, and mode $(k-1)\beta$.

Graph: The graph below is the Erlang density function with parameters $\beta = 1$ and $k = 1, 2,$ and 3.

Parameter estimation: Given the sample mean ($\overline{x}$) and sample standard deviation (s), the k parameter can be estimated as $k = \overline{x}^2 / s^2 = 1/c^2$, where $c = s/\overline{x}$ is the sample coefficient of variation.

Excel: In Excel, the density and distribution functions are GAMMADIST(x, k, β, FALSE) and GAMMADIST(x, k, β, TRUE).

Excel simulation: In an Excel simulation, Erlang random variates can be generated with the inverse transformation

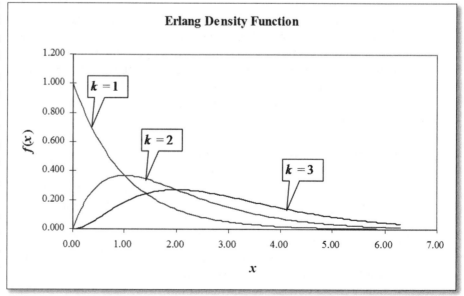

Erlang Density Function

method using x = GAMMAINV(1-RAND(), k, β, TRUE). Alternatively, Erlang random variates can be generated by taking advantage of the fact that the Erlang is the sum of k independent exponential variates, i.e.,

$x = -\sum_{j=1}^{k} \beta \ln(r_j)$, where r_j is a random number.

    Relationships to other distributions: The exponential is a special case of the Erlang with $k = 1$. The Erlang distribution is a special case of the gamma distribution with parameters k and β, where k is an integer.

    History: The Erlang distribution was developed by Danish mathematician A. K. Erlang (1878-1929) to examine the waiting times for telephone calls.

    See *coefficient of variation, exponential distribution, gamma distribution, inverse transform method, probability density function, probability distribution, random number.*

ERP – See *Enterprise Resources Planning (ERP).*

error function – A mathematical function that is useful for dealing with the cumulative distribution function for the normal and lognormal distributions; also called the Gauss error function.

    The error function is defined as $erf(z) = \frac{2}{\sqrt{\pi}} \int_{t=0}^{z} e^{-t^2} dt$ or $erf(z_0, z_1) = \frac{2}{\sqrt{\pi}} \int_{t=z_0}^{z_1} e^{-t^2} dt$ and the complementary error function is defined as $erfc(x) = 1 - erf(x)$. The normal distribution CDF is then

$F(x) = P(X < x) = \frac{1}{\sqrt{2\pi\sigma^2}} \int_{t=-\infty}^{t=x} e^{-(t-\mu)^2/(2\sigma^2)} dt = \frac{1}{2}\left[1 + erf\left(\frac{x-\mu}{\sqrt{2\sigma^2}}\right)\right]$ and the lognormal distribution CDF is

$F(x) = \int_{t=-\infty}^{t=x} \frac{1}{t\sqrt{2\pi}\sigma} e^{\frac{-(\ln t - \mu)^2}{2\sigma^2}} dt = \frac{1}{2}\left[1 + erf\left(\frac{\ln x - \mu}{\sqrt{2}\sigma}\right)\right]$. Excel offers the functions ERF(z), ERF(z0,z1), and

ERFC(z). The error function has no closed form, but numerical methods are available with as much precision as allowed by the computer. Winitzki (2003) developed useful closed-form approximations for both erf(x) and its inverse. The error function can also be computed from the gamma function.

    See *gamma function, lognormal distribution, normal distribution.*

error proofing – The process of identifying likely causes of a failure and preventing the failure or at least mitigating the impact of the failure; also known as mistake proofing, fool proofing, idiot proofing, and fail safing, making fault tolerant and robust; the Japanese phrase "poka yoke" (ポカヨケ) means to avoid mistakes.

✪

    Error proofing principles can improve both product and process design in all types of organizations. Ideally, error proofing devices are (1) simple and cheap, (2) deployed close to where the work is being done, and (3) result in what Shingo calls "100%" inspection and zero errors.

    Product design – An error-proof product design can reduce errors to improve quality, efficiency, and safety in the manufacturing process and in the use of the product by the customer. For example, the gas fueling system in a typical automobile integrates different error proofing devices (see the photo below). The plastic tether keeps the gas cap from getting lost, the gas cap has a ratchet to signal proper tightness and prevent over-tightening, the filler hole is too small for the leaded-fuel nozzle, the gas cap has warning messages on it, and the fuel pump will shut off when the tank is full[15].

    Process design – An error-proof process design prevents errors in the process that produces goods or services. Error proofing can be applied to all types of processes to improve safety, which is a major issue in nearly all industries in all countries. In 2006, in the U.S., OSHA recorded 4,085,400 non-fatal workplace

Source: Professor Arthur V. Hill

injuries and 5,703 fatal workplace injuries (source: www.bls.gov/iif/home.htm#News, December 7, 2007).

---

[15] *This example was motivated by a similar one from Professor John Grout. Professor Grout has many other interesting examples of error proofing on his website at http://facultyweb.berry.edu/jgrout/everyday.html (April 17, 2011).*

Application of error proofing principles is the key to improving these sad statistics. Error proofing can also be applied to assembly operations to improve efficiency.

Error proofing methods can also be classified as either **prevention** or **detection/warning**. Whereas, prevention makes it impossible (or nearly impossible) for the error to occur, detection/warning only signals that an error is about to occur or has already occurred. For example, a microwave will not work if the door is open (a prevention device) and many cars will sound an alarm if the key is left in the ignition (a detection/warning device). Prevention methods can be further broken into three types:

1. **Control** – An action that self-corrects the problem, such as an automatic spell-checker that automatically corrects a misspelled word.
2. **Shutdown** – A device that shuts down the process when the error condition occurs, such as a home iron that shuts off after ten minutes of non-use.
3. **Human factors** – Use of colors, shapes, symbols, sizes, sounds, and checklists to simplify a process to make it less error-prone for human operators. An example is a **shadow board** for a tool, which is an outline of the tool painted on a pegboard to signal to the worker where the tool belongs. Another example is the use of symbols for hazardous materials. For example, the symbol on the right is for radioactive materials.

Detection/warning methods detect a problem and warn the operator when an error is about to occur or has already occurred. Unlike prevention methods, detection/warning methods do not control or shut down the system. A car's oil light is a good example. Prevention is almost always better than detection/warning because detection/warning relies on human intervention and warnings can be ignored, whereas prevention is automatic without any human intervention.

Failure Mode and Effects Analysis (FMEA) is a more formal approach to error proofing and risk management. FMEA is a process used to identify possible causes of failures (failure modes) and score them, helping establish which failure modes should be addressed first. Business continuity planning applies error proofing concepts at a more strategic level.

See *5 Whys, adverse event, andon light, autonomation, Business Continuity Management (BCM), Business Process Re-engineering (BPR), checklist, ergonomics, fail-safe, Failure Mode and Effects Analysis (FMEA), fault tree analysis, Hazard Analysis & Critical Point Control (HACCP), inspection, jidoka, muda, multiple-machine handling, Murphy's Law, Occupational Safety and Health Administration (OSHA), Pareto's Law, prevention, process, process design, process improvement program, quality management, risk mitigation, robust, Root Cause Analysis (RCA), safety, sentinel event, service recovery, shadow board, stamping, work simplification.*

ESI – See *Early Supplier Involvement (ESI)*.

ethnographic research – An approach for gathering qualitative cultural and behavioral information about a group of people.

Ethnography is based almost entirely on fieldwork where the **ethnographer** goes to the people who are the subjects of the study. Ethnography studies what people actually say and do, which avoids many of the pitfalls that come from relying on self-reported, focus group, and survey data. Ethnographers sometimes live among the people for a year or more, learning the local language and participating in everyday life while striving to maintain objective detachment. Ethnographers usually cultivate close relationships with **informants** who can provide specific information on aspects of cultural life. Although detailed written notes are the mainstay of fieldwork, ethnographers may also use tape recorders, cameras, or video recorders. Ethnography is closely related to anthropology.

Businesses have found ethnographic research helpful in understanding how people live, use products and services, or need potential products or services. Ethnographic research methods provide a systematic and holistic approach so the information is valued by marketing researchers and product and service developers.

See *voice of the customer (VOC)*.

ETO – See *engineer to order*.

Euclidean distance – See *Minkowski distance*.

EurOMA – See *European Operations Management Association*.

European Operations Management Association (EurOMA) – Europe's leading professional society for operations management scholars and practitioners.

EurOMA was formed in the UK in 1984 and rapidly grew into Europe's leading professional association for those involved in operations management. The Europe-wide European Operations Management Association was founded in October 1993. EurOMA is an international network of academics and managers from around the world interested in developing operations management. It is a European-based network, with rapidly developing international links, where people can get together to communicate experience and ideas. It is also a network that bridges the gap between research and practice. EurOMA publishes the ***International Journal of Operations & Production Management*** (***IJOPM***). The website for EurOMA is www.euroma-online.org.

See *operations management (OM)*.

EVA – See *Economic Value Added (EVA)*.

Everyday Low Pricing (EDLP) – A pricing strategy and practice designed to create a more level (more stable) demand by keeping prices at a constant low price rather than using sporadic temporary pricing promotions; closely related to value pricing.

EDLP often promises customers the lowest available price without coupons, pricing promotions, or comparison shopping. This practice tends to reduce the seller's administrative cost to change prices and process coupons, reduce safety stock inventory (due to lower variability of demand), and increase customer loyalty.

See *bullwhip effect, forward buy, safety stock*.

executive sponsor – See *champion*.

expatriate – (1) Noun: A person who has taken residence in another country; often shortened to expat. (2) Verb: To force out or move out a country.

The word "expatriate" comes from the Latin expatriātus (from ex "out of") and patriā ("country, fatherland"). An expatriate is any person living in a country where he or she is not a citizen. The term is often used to describe professionals sent abroad by their companies. In contrast, a manual laborer who has moved to another country to earn money is called an "immigrant" or "migrant" worker.

See *offshoring, repatriate*.

expedite – See *expediting*.

expediting – The process of assigning a higher priority to a job (order or task) so it gets started and done sooner; de-expediting is the process of assigning a lower priority to a job.

When priorities for jobs change, some jobs should be given higher priority. However, when all jobs are given a higher priority, expediting has no value. Schedulers should realize that expediting one job will de-expedite all other jobs. For example, when an ambulance comes down a highway with its lights and sirens on, all other vehicles must move to the side. Expediting the ambulance, therefore, de-expedites all other vehicles on the road at that time.

See *buyer/planner, dispatching rules, job shop scheduling*.

experience curve – See *learning curve*.

experience economy – See *experience engineering*.

experience engineering – The process of understanding and improving customer sensory and emotional interaction and reaction to a service or a product.

Two quotes highlight the main point of experience engineering:
- "Consumer preference and motivation are far less influenced by the functional attributes of products and services than the subconscious sensory and emotional elements derived by the total experience." – Professor Gerald Zaltman, Harvard University, Procter & Gamble's Future Forces Conference, Cincinnati, Ohio 1997 (Berry, Carbone, & Haeckel 2002).
- "We need to look at our business as more than simply the building and selling of personal computers. Our business is the delivery of information and lifelike interactive experiences." – Andrew Grove, Chairman, Intel, 1996 COMDEX computer show (Pine & Gilmore 1998).

Joe Pine and James Gilmore, founders of the management consulting firm Strategic Horizons, wrote many of the early articles on this subject (Pine & Gilmore 1998). Pine and Gilmore used the term "**experience economy**" rather than the term "experience engineering." They argue that economies go through four phases:

Producers can use each phase to differentiate their products and services. As services become commoditized, organizations look to the next higher value (experiences) to differentiate their products and services. Although experiences have always been at the heart of the entertainment business, Pine and Gilmore (1998, 1999) argue that all organizations **stage an experience** when they engage customers in personal and memorable ways. Many of the best organizations have learned from the Walt Disney Company and have found that they can differentiate their services by staging experiences with services as the stage and goods as the props. The goal is to engage individuals to create memorable events.

Pine and Gilmore (1999) offer five design principles that drive the creation of memorable experiences:
1. Create a consistent theme that resonates throughout the entire experience.
2. Reinforce the theme with positive cues (e.g., easy-to-follow signs).
3. Eliminate negative cues, which are visual or aural messages that contradict the theme (e.g., dirty floors).
4. Offer memorabilia that commemorate the experience for the user (toys, dolls, etc.).
5. Engage all five senses (sight, sound, smell, taste, and touch) to heighten the experience and make it more memorable (e.g., the fragrant smell of a great restaurant).

The website for Pine and Gilmore's consulting firm, Strategic Horizons, is www.strategichorizons.com.

Carbone (2004), who coined the term "experience engineering," presents two types of **clues** customers pick up in their customer experience – **functional clues** and **emotional clues**. These are compared in the table below.

Functional clues	Emotional clues

• Actual functioning of the good or service.
 • Interpreted primarily by the logic part of the brain.
 • The minimum requirement to enter the game.
 • Example: Did the plumber fix the leak?
	• Smells, sounds, sights, tastes, and textures.
	 • The environment in which it is offered.
	 • Two types of emotional clues:
	   • *Mechanics* – Clues emitted by things (signs, facilities, etc.)
	   • *Humanics* – Clues emitted by people (gestures, comments, dress, voice tone)
	 • Examples: Feel of leather upholstery, sound and smell of a steak on a grill, tone of the service rep.

Carbone argues that emotional clues can work synergistically with functional clues to create customer value. He further proposes that customer value is equal to the functional benefits plus the emotional benefits less the financial and non-financial costs. He concludes that organizations should manage the emotional component of their products and services with the same rigor that they bring to managing product and service functionality. Carbone's firm, Experience Engineering, has a website at http://expeng.com.

See *facility layout*, *mass customization*, *service blueprinting*, *service management*, *service quality*.

expert system – A computer system that is designed to mimic the decision processes of human experts.

An expert system uses knowledge and reasoning techniques to solve problems that normally require the abilities of human experts. Expert systems normally have a domain-specific knowledge base combined with an inference engine that processes knowledge from the knowledge base to respond to a user's request for advice.

See *Artificial Intelligence (AI)*, *knowledge management*, *turing test*.

exponential distribution – A continuous probability distribution often used to model the time between arrivals for random events, such as a machine breakdown or customer arrival to a system; also known as the negative exponential distribution.

Parameter: The exponential distribution has only one parameter (β), which is the mean.

Density and distribution functions: The density and distribution functions for $x > 0$ are $f(x) = (1/\beta)e^{-x/\beta}$ and $F(x) = 1 - e^{-x/\beta}$.

Statistics: Range $[0, \infty)$, mean β, variance β^2, mode 0, and coefficient of variation $c = 1$. An indicator of an exponentially distributed random variable is a sample coefficient of variation (sample mean/sample standard deviation) close to one.

Graph: The graph below is the exponential density function with a mean of 1.

Estimating the parameter: The parameter (β) can be estimated as the sample mean.

Excel: In Excel, the exponential density and distribution functions are EXPONDIST(x, β, FALSE) and EXPONDIST(x, β, TRUE) and the equivalent Excel formulas are $(1/\beta)\text{EXP}(-x/\beta)$ and $1 - \text{EXP}(-x/\beta)$, respectively. Excel does not have an inverse for the exponential, but the Excel function GAMMAINV(p, β, 1) and the Excel formula $-\beta \ln(\text{RAND}())$ can be used for the inverse. In Excel 2010, EXPONDIST has been replaced by EXPON.DIST.

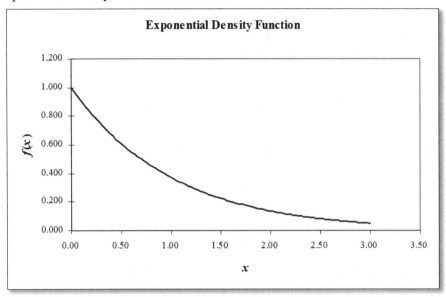

Excel simulation: In an Excel simulation, exponentially distributed random variates X can be generated with the inverse transform method using $X = -\beta \ln(1 - \text{RAND}())$. Note that the negative sign in this equation is correct because the natural log of a random number in the range $(0,1]$ is negative. Note that RAND() is in the range $[0,1)$, but $1 - \text{RAND}()$ is in the range $(0,1]$, which avoids the possibile error of taking the natural log of zero.

Relationships to other distributions: The exponential distribution is a special case of the gamma, Erlang, and Weibull. The exponential distribution is the only continuous distribution that has the memory-less property (i.e., $P(X > t + s \mid X > t) = P(X > s)$ for all $t, s > 0$).

See *coefficient of variation, Erlang distribution, gamma distribution, inverse transform method, Poisson distribution, probability density function, probability distribution, queuing theory, random number, Weibull distribution.*

exponential smoothing – A time series forecasting method based on a weighted moving average, where the weights decline geometrically with the age of the data; a graphical procedure that removes much of the random variation in a time series so that the underlying pattern is easier to see. ✪

Exponential smoothing is a popular time series extrapolation forecasting technique. It can also be used as a data smoothing technique. The focus here is the use of exponential smoothing for forecasting.

An exponentially smoothed average is a **weighted moving average** that puts more weight on recent demand data, where the weights decline **geometrically** back in time. (Note: Technically, exponential smoothing should have been called geometric smoothing[16].) With simple exponential smoothing, the smoothed average at the end of period t is the forecast for the next period and all other periods in the future. In other words, the one-period-ahead forecast is $F_{t+1} = A_t$ and the n-period-ahead forecast is $F_{t+n} = A_t$. Exponential smoothing can be extended to include both trend and seasonal patterns.

Simple exponential smoothing – The most basic exponential smoothing model uses a simple equation to update the exponentially smoothed average at the end of period t. The exponentially smoothed average at the end of period t is the exponentially smoothed average at the end of period $t - 1$ plus some fraction (α) of the

---

[16] *Exponential decay is defined for continuous time while geometric decay is only defined for discrete values. Exponential decay is defined as $y(t) = a \exp(-\beta t)$, where t is a real number, and geometric decay is defined as $y_n = an^{-b}$, where n is an integer.*

forecast error. The constant α (alpha) is called the smoothing constant and is in the range $0 < \alpha < 1$. The updating equation can be written as $A_t = A_{t-1} + \alpha E_t$, where the forecast error is $E_t = D_t - F_t$ and D_t is the actual demand (sales) in period t. The updating equation can be rewritten algebraically as $A_t = A_{t-1} + \alpha E_t = A_{t-1} + \alpha(D_t - A_{t-1}) = \alpha D_t + (1-\alpha)A_{t-1}$.

This suggests that the new exponentially smoothed average is a linear combination of the new demand and the old average. For example, when $\alpha = 0.1$, the new average is 10% of the new demand plus 90% of the old average. The A_{t-1} term in the above equation can be defined in terms of the average at the end of period $t-2$, i.e., $A_{t-1} = \alpha D_{t-1} + (1-\alpha)A_{t-2}$. The equation for A_{t-2} can be further expanded to show that $A_t = \alpha D_t + (1-\alpha)A_{t-1} = \alpha D_t + \alpha(1-\alpha)D_{t-1} + \alpha(1-\alpha)^2 D_{t-2} + \cdots + \alpha(1-\alpha)^k D_{t-k}$. This means that the exponentially smoothed average at the end of period t is a weighted average with the weight for demand at lag k of $\alpha(1-\alpha)^k$. For example, when $\alpha = 0.1$, the weight for the demand $k = 5$ periods ago is $0.1(1-0.1)^5 = 0.059$. These weights decline geometrically as the time lag k increases, which suggests that exponential smoothing should have been called geometric smoothing[17].

Exponential smoothing with trend – When a trend component is included, the one-period-ahead forecast is $F_{t+1} = A_t + T_t$, where T_t is the exponentially smoothed trend at the end of period t. The n-period-ahead forecast is then $F_{t+n} = A_t + nT_t$. The apparent trend in period t is the change in the exponentially smoothed average from period $t-1$ to period t (i.e., $A_t - A_{t-1}$). The trend, therefore, can be smoothed in the same way as the average demand was smoothed using the equation $T_t = \beta(A_t - A_{t-1}) + (1-\beta)T_{t-1}$, where β (beta) is the smoothing constant for the trend with $0 < \beta < 1$. When a trend component is included, the updating equation for the exponentially smoothed average should be $A_t = \alpha D_t + (1-\alpha)(A_{t-1} + T_{t-1})$. Exponential smoothing with trend is called **double exponential smoothing** because it is smoothing the difference between the smoothed averages.

Dampened trend – Gardner (2005) and others suggest that the trend be "dampened" (reduced) for multiple-period-ahead forecasts because almost no trends continue forever. The dampened one-period-ahead forecasting equation is then $F_{t+1} = A_t + \phi T_t$, where $0 \le \phi \le 1$ is the dampening factor. For n-period-head forecasts, the equation is $F_{t+n} = A_t + T_i \sum_{k=1}^{n} \phi^k$ where $\phi < 1$. The dampening parameter ϕ can be estimated from historical data.

Exponential smoothing with seasonality – Exponential smoothing can be extended to handle seasonality by using a multiplicative seasonal factor. The one-period-ahead forecast is the underlying average times the seasonal factor (i.e., $F_{t+1} = A_t \cdot R$, where R is the multiplicative seasonal factor). The seasonal factors are generally in the range (0.3, 3.0), indicating that the lowest demand period is about 30% of the average and the highest demand period is about 300% of the average.

The one-period-ahead forecast is defined as $F_{t+1} = A_t R_{t+1-m}$, where A_t is the underlying deseasonalized average and the multiplicative seasonal factor (R_{t+1-m}) inflates or deflates this average to adjust for seasonality. The seasonal factor for the forecast in period $t+1$ has the subscript $t+1-m$ to indicate that it was last updated m periods ago, where m is the number of periods in a season. For example, $m = 12$ for monthly forecasts. The seasonal factor for a forecast made in January 2012 for February 2012 uses the seasonal factor that was last updated in February 2011. The n-period-ahead forecast with seasonality is then $F_{t+n} = A_t R_{t+n-m}$, where F_{t+n} is the forecast n periods ahead and R_{t+n-m} is the exponentially smoothed multiplicative seasonal factor for period $t + n$.

---

[17] *The weights going back in time follow a geometric progression with initial value α and a common ratio of* $(1 - \alpha)$. *The sum of the weights from lag 1 to infinity is 1.*

The updating equation for the deseasonalized smoothed average is $A_t = \alpha D_t / R_{t-m} + (1-\alpha)A_{t-1}$. Multiplying by R_{t+n-m} inflates or deflates for seasonality, so dividing by R_{t+n-m} deseasonalizes the demand. Therefore, the term D_t / R_{t-m} is the deseasonalized demand in period t. Seasonal factors can be smoothed using the equation $R_t = \gamma D_t / A_t + (1-\gamma)R_{t-m}$, where D_t / A_t is the apparent deseasonalized demand in period t and γ (gamma) is the smoothing constant for seasonality with $0 < \gamma < 1$.

Exponential smoothing with trend and seasonality – Exponential smoothing with trend and seasonality is known as the Winters' Model (Winters 1960), the Holt-Winters' Model, and triple exponential smoothing. The forecast equation is $F_{t+n} = (A_t + nT_t)R_{t+n-m}$, where F_{t+n} is the forecast n periods ahead, T_t is the exponentially smoothed trend at the end of period t, and R_{t+n-m} is the exponentially smoothed multiplicative seasonal factor for period $t + n$. The equations for the Winters' Model must be implemented in this order:

Update smoothed deseasonalized average $\qquad A_t = \alpha D_t / R_{t-m} + (1-\alpha)(A_{t-1} + T_t)$

Update smoothed trend $\qquad T_t = \beta(A_t - A_{t-1}) + (1-\beta)T_{t-1}$

Update smoothed seasonal factor $\qquad R_t = \gamma D_t / A_t + (1-\gamma)R_{t-m}$

Make n-period-ahead forecast $\qquad F_{t+n} = (A_t + nT_t)R_{t-m+n}$

Forecasting lumpy demand – Exponential smoothing does a poor job of forecasting when the demand is "lumpy" (i.e., has many zeros between demands). A good rule of thumb is that an item with a coefficient of variation of demand greater than 1 has "lumpy" demand and therefore should not be forecasted with exponential smoothing methods. Croston (1972) suggests a method for forecasting the time between "lumps" and the size of the lumps, but few firms have used this approach. The best approach for lumpy demand is often to increase the size of the time buckets to avoid zero demand periods.

See *Box-Jenkins forecasting, centered moving average, coefficient of variation, Croston's Method, dampened trend, demand, demand filter, forecast error metrics, forecasting, geometric progression, lumpy demand, Mean Absolute Percent Error (MAPE), moving average, Relative Absolute Error (RAE), reorder point, seasonality, time bucket, time series forecasting, tracking signal, trend, weighted average.*

eXtensible Markup Language – See *XML*.

external failure cost – See *cost of quality*.

external setup – Activities done to prepare a machine to run a new job while the machine is still running the current job; also called an off-line or running setup.

Whereas external setups are done while a process is running, internal setups are done while a machine is idle. Therefore, moving the setup time from internal to external reduces downtime for the process and reduces cycle time for work in process.

See *internal setup, lean sigma, setup, setup time reduction methods*.

extranet – The use of Internet/Intranet technology to serve an extended enterprise, including defined sets of customers or suppliers or other partners.

An extranet is typically behind a firewall, just as an intranet usually is, and closed to the public (a "closed user group"), but is open to the selected partners, unlike a pure intranet. More loosely, the term may apply to mixtures of open and closed networks.

See *corporate portal, e-business, intranet*.

extrinsic forecasting model – See *forecasting*.

extrusion – (1) A manufacturing process that makes items by forcing materials through a die. (2) An item made by an extrusion process.

Materials that can be extruded include plastic, metal, ceramics, foods, and other materials. Many types of products are created through an extrusion process, including tubes, pipes, noodles, and baby food. Most materials that pass through extruders come out in a long uniform solid or hollow tubular shape. Extrusions often require additional machining processes, such as cutting. The three types of extrusion processes are hot (850-

4000F, 454-2204C), warm (800-1800F, 427-982C), and cold at room temperature (70-75F, 21-24C). Cracking is the most common problem with extrusion and can be caused by improper temperature, speed, or friction.
See *manufacturing processes*.

F

fabrication – A manufacturing process that transforms materials to make parts to go into an assembly.

Fabrication includes manufacturing processes (such as molding, machining, forming, or joining) and not assembly. Small businesses that specialize in metal fabrication are called **fab shops**. A semiconductor fabrication facility is called a **wafer fab** and makes integrated circuits (silicon chips).
See *assembly line, manufacturing processes, respond to order (RTO)*.

facility layout – The physical organization of processes in a facility. ✪

The layout of a factory should minimize the total cost of moving materials between workcenters. Some processes must be located next to each other, while others cannot be located next to each other due to heat, sound, or vibration. Other issues include cycle time, waste, space efficiency, communications, safety, security, quality, maintenance, flexibility, customer waiting time, aesthetics for workers, and aesthetics for customers.

The layout problem is not unique to manufacturing. Service businesses, such as hospitals and banks, have the same issues. Retailers use **planograms** to help layout retail stores. Similar layout problems are common in other design contexts, such as laying out an integrated circuit. **Experience engineering** issues are important when the customer contact is high.

The three basic types of facility layouts include the **process layout** (functional layout), the **product layout**, and the **fixed-position (project) layout**. Each of these is discussed briefly below.

Process layout (functional layout) – A layout that groups similar activities together in departments or workcenters according to the process or function that they perform. For example, all drills might be located together in the drill workcenter. The process layout is generally used in operations that are required to serve a wide variety of customer needs, so the equipment must serve many purposes and the workforce needs to be highly skilled. Although process layouts offer high flexibility, they are relatively inefficient because of long **queues**, long **cycle times**, and high materials handling costs. The best example of a process layout is a **job shop**. The major concerns in a process layout are cycle times, utilization, order promising, routing, and scheduling.

Traditional industrial engineering approaches to improving a process layout include process analysis, graphical methods, computer simulation, and computer optimization. CRAFT (Computerized Relative Allocation of Facilities Technique) is a heuristic approach developed by Buffa, Armour, and Vollmann (1964) that uses a **heuristic** (non-optimal) approach to solving a quadratic assignment formulation of the facility layout problem.

Product layout – A product layout arranges activities in the sequence of steps required to manufacture or assemble a product. Product layouts are suitable for mass production or repetitive operations in which demand is relatively steady and volume is relatively high. Product layouts tend to be relatively efficient, but not very flexible. The best example of a product layout is an **assembly line**. The major concern in a product layout is balancing the line. In designing an assembly line, many tasks (elements) need to be assigned to workers, but these assignments are constrained by the target cycle time for the product and precedence relationships between the tasks (i.e., some tasks need to be done before others). The **line balancing** problem is to assign tasks to workstations to minimize the number of workstations required while satisfying the cycle time and precedence constraints. Many operations researchers have developed sophisticated mathematical computer models to solve this problem[18]. The line balancing problem becomes less important when the organization can use cross-trained workers who can move between stations as needed to maximize flow. **Cellular manufacturing** is a powerful approach for converting some equipment in a process layout into a product layout for families of parts. **Mixed model assembly** allows some firms to justify having product layouts that are not dedicated to a single product. See the *cellular manufacturing* and *mixed model assembly* entries.

---

[18] *The webpage www.wiwi.uni-jena.de/Entscheidung/alb provides a video and an overview of the research on this problem.*

Fixed-position layout (project-layout) – A fixed-position layout is used in projects where the workers, equipment, and materials go to the production site because the product is too large, fragile, or heavy to move. This type of layout is also called a project layout because the work is usually organized around projects. The equipment is often left on-site because it is too expensive to move frequently. Due to the nature of the work, the workers in a fixed position layout are usually highly skilled. The most familiar examples of a fixed position layout are the construction of building or house. However, a fixed position layout is also used in shipbuilding and machine repair. The major concerns with a fixed-position layout are meeting the project requirements, within budget, and within schedule. See the *project management* entry.

The Theory of Constraints literature suggests that the focus for all layouts should be on the bottleneck process. See the *Theory of Constraints (TOC)* entry.

See *5S, assembly line, cellular manufacturing, continuous flow, CRAFT, cross-training, experience engineering, flowshop, focused factory, job order costing, job shop, lean thinking, line balancing, mixed model assembly, planogram, plant-within-a-plant, process design, process map, product-process matrix, project management, spaghetti chart, Theory of Constraints (TOC), workcenter.*

facility location – The physical site for a building. ✪

The facility location problem is to find the best locations for the organization's facilities (warehouses, stores, factories, offices). The facility location problem is often defined in terms of minimizing the sum of the incoming and outgoing transportation costs. In a retail context, the problem is often defined in terms of maximizing revenue. In the service context, the problem is defined in terms of meeting some service criterion, such as customer travel time or response time for customer needs.

Facility location theory suggests that the problem can be broken into finite and infinite set location models. The finite set location models evaluate a limited number of locations and determine which one is best. The infinite set location models find the best x-y coordinates (or latitudes and longitudes) for a site (or sites) that minimize some mathematical objective function. The center-of-gravity and numeric-analytic location models are infinite set location models. The gravity model for competitive retail store location and the Kepner-Tregoe Model are finite set location models.

Some location models assume that vehicles can travel directly across any geography, while others assume that vehicles are constrained to existing transportation networks. Some models assume that cost is proportional to the distance or time traveled, whereas others include all relevant costs, including tariffs, duties, and tolls.

See *center-of-gravity model for facility location, gravity model for competitive retail store location, great circle distance, greenfield, Kepner-Tregoe Model, numeric-analytic location model, process design, supply chain management, tariff, warehouse.*

factor analysis – A multivariate statistical method used to reduce the number of variables in a dataset without losing much information about the correlation structure between the variables.

Factor analysis originated in psychometrics and is used in behavioral sciences, social sciences, marketing, operations management, and other applied sciences that deal with large datasets. Factor analysis describes the variability of a number of observed variables in terms of a fewer number of unobserved variables called factors, where the observed variables are linear combinations of the factors plus error terms. To use an extreme example, a study measures people's height in both inches and centimeters. These two variables have a correlation of 100% and the analysis can be simplified by combining the variables into one "factor" without losing any information.

Factor analysis is related to **Principal Component Analysis (PCA)**. Because PCA performs a variance-maximizing rotation of the variable space, it takes into account all variability in the variables. In contrast, factor analysis estimates how much of the variability is due to common factors. The two methods become essentially equivalent if the error terms in the factor analysis model can be assumed to all have the same variance.

Cluster analysis and factor analysis are both data reduction methods. Given a dataset with rows that are cases (e.g., respondents to a survey) and columns that are variables (e.g., questions on a survey), cluster analysis groups cases into clusters and factor analysis groups variables into factors. Using the survey example, cluster analysis groups similar respondents and factor analysis groups similar variables.

See *cluster analysis, Principal Component Analysis (PCA).*

factorial – A mathematical function denoted as $n!$ and defined as the product of all positive integers less than or equal to n; in other words, $n! = n \cdot (n-1) \cdot (n-2) \cdots 2 \cdot 1$.

The factorial function is important in many fields of mathematics and statistics. For example, a sequence of items is called a **permutation** and a set of n items can be ordered in $n!$ different ways (permutations). The exclamation symbol (!) is called the "factorial" operator. Note that $0! = 1$ is a special case. For example, $5! = 5 \cdot 4 \cdot 3 \cdot 2 \cdot 1 = 120$. The factorial function is not defined for negative numbers. The definition of the factorial function can be extended to non-integer arguments using the **gamma function**, where $n! = \Gamma(n+1)$. The *gamma function* entry covers this subject in more detail.

Most computers cannot accurately compute values over $170!$ In Excel, $n! = \text{FACT}(n)$. Excel reports an integer overflow error for $\text{FACT}(n)$ when $n \geq 171$. For large n, $n!$ can be computed (approximately) in Excel with $\text{EXP}(\text{GAMMALN}(n+1))$ and the ratio of two large factorials can be computed approximately as $m!/n! = \text{EXP}(\text{GAMMALN}(m+1) - \text{GAMMALN}(n+1))$.

See *combinations, gamma function.*

Fagan Defect-Free Process – A formal process for reviewing products that encourages continuous improvement.

Fagan (2001) created a method of reviews and inspections for "early detection" of problems in software development while working at IBM. Fagan argues that the inspection process has two goals: (1) find and fix all defects and (2) find and fix all defects in the process that created the defects. The process specifies specific roles for a team of four people: Moderator, Reader, Author, and Tester.

See *agile software development, early detection, New Product Development (NPD), scrum.*

fail-safe – See *error proofing.*

Failure Mode and Effects Analysis (FMEA) – A process that identifies the possible causes of failures (failure modes), scores them to create a risk priority number, and then mitigates risk starting with the most important failure mode. ✪

Failure Mode and Effects Analysis (FMEA) was invented by NASA early in the U.S. Apollo space program. NASA created the tool to alleviate the stress between two conflicting mottos: "Failure is not an option" and "Perfect is the enemy of good." The first meant successfully completing the mission and returning the crew. The second meant that failure of at least some components was unavoidable.

FMEA is a simple process that identifies the possible causes of failures (failure modes), scores them on three dimensions (severity, occurrence, and detection) to create a risk priority number, and then mitigates risk starting with the most important failure mode. The first step in FMEA is to identify all potential failure modes where a failure might occur. Once these failure modes have been identified, FMEA then requires that each one be scored on three dimensions: severity, occurrence, and detection. All three dimensions are scored on a 1 to 10 scale, where 1 is low and 10 is high. These three scores are then multiplied to produce a Risk Priority Number (RPN). The failure models can then be prioritized based on the RPNs and risk mitigation efforts can then be designed for the more important failure modes.

Many organizations have found FMEA to be a powerful tool for helping them prioritize risk mitigation efforts. At 3M and other firms, FMEA is a required tool for all lean sigma projects.

Whereas Root Cause Analysis (RCA) identifies contributors to an adverse event after the fact, FMEA is intended to be a proactive (before the fact) tool. Ideally, FMEA anticipates all adverse events before they occur.

The scoring part of an FMEA requires the subjective evaluation of three dimensions for each failure mode, where each dimension is scored on a 1 to 10 scale:

Severity – Impact of the failure. If failure occurred, what is the significance of the harm of this failure in terms of cost, time, quality, customer satisfaction, etc.?

Occurrence – Frequency of occurrence. What is the probability that this failure will occur? (This is sometimes called the probability of occurrence.)

Detection – Ability to detect the problem and avoid the impact. Can the failure be detected early enough that it does not have a severe impact? (Important note: A 10 on detection means that it is hard to detect.)

Risk Priority Number (RPN) = (Severity) x (Occurrence) x (Detection)

It is easy to create an Excel workbook for FMEA. The following is a typical format. These actions usually target the likelihood of occurrence, but should also seek to make detection easier and reduce severity. After creating the workbook, the user can sort the rows by the RPN to prioritize the "actions to reduce risk."

Failure Model and Effects Analysis (FMEA) example

Process step	Failure mode	Failure causes	Failure effects	Severity (1-10)	Occurrence (1-10)	Detection (1-10)	Risk priority number (RPN)	Project/ actions to reduce risk
Surgery preparation	Wrong side surgery	Chart is incorrect	Patient agony. Law suits. Brand damage.	9	2	3	45	Have second MD check.
Surgery close up	Surgical tool left in patient	Lack of attention to tools remaining in patient	Patient agony. Law suits. Brand damage.	6	3	2	36	Have RN count tools before close up.

Source: Professor Arthur V. Hill

See the *Design Failure Mode and Effects Analysis (DFMEA)* entry for information about how FMEA can be applied to design.

See *Business Continuity Management (BCM), causal map, critical path, Design Failure Mode and Effects Analysis (DFMEA), error proofing, fault tree analysis, Hazard Analysis & Critical Point Control (HACCP), impact wheel,* lean *sigma, operations performance metrics, Pareto Chart, Pareto's Law, prevention, risk, risk assessment, risk mitigation, robust, Root Cause Analysis (RCA), work simplification.*

family – See *product family.*

FAS – See *Final Assembly Schedule (FAS).*

Fast Moving Consumer Goods (FMCG) – Any product sold in high volumes to end customers.

FMCG companies are firms that manufacture, distribute, or sell packaged consumer goods, food, hygiene products, grocery items, cleaning supplies, paper products, toiletries, soft drinks, diapers, toys, pharmaceuticals, and consumer electronics. These products are generally sold at low prices. FMCG seems to be synonymous with consumer packaged goods. The opposite of FMCG (and consumer packaged goods) is durable goods. Books and CDs are not FMCGs because consumers usually only buy them once.

See *category captain, category management, consumer packaged goods, durable goods, Efficient Consumer Response (ECR).*

fast tracking – See *critical path.*

fault tree analysis – A graphical management tool for describing the cause and effect relationships that result in major failures; a causal map usually used to identify and solve the causes for a specific actual historical problem.

Fault tree analysis is a causal map drawn from the top down. The actual historical fault or major failure being analyzed is identified as the "top event." All possible causes of the top event are identified in a tree. The main distinguishing feature of a fault tree compared to other types of causal maps is the use of "OR" nodes for independent causes and "AND" nodes for multiple causes that must exist concurrently for a failure to occur.

See *causal map, error proofing, Failure Mode and Effects Analysis (FMEA), risk assessment, risk mitigation, Root Cause Analysis (RCA), root cause tree.*

faxban – A pull signal for a kanban system that is sent via fax.

Faxban uses fax communication rather than physical kanban cards to send a pull signal. Faxban can reduce the delay between the time that pull is needed and the time that the pull signal is sent. An e-kanban is similar, except that the signal is sent via e-mail, EDI, or through the Web.

See *kanban.*

FED-up model – See *service quality.*

field service – Repair and preventive maintenance activities performed by service technicians at the customer site.

Field service technicians (techs) often travel from their homes to customer sites to perform repairs. Techs usually carry inventory in their vehicles and often replace this inventory from a central source of supply on a use-one-order-one basis. Tech performance is often measured by average response time and customer satisfaction. Service calls can be under a warranty agreement or can be for time and materials. Hill (1992) presented a number of models for planning field service territories and tech truck stock inventory.

See *response time, reverse logistics, Service Level Agreement (SLA), service parts.*

FIFO – See *First-In-First-Out (FIFO).*

fill rate – See *service level*.

Final Assembly Schedule (FAS) – A schedule for the respond to order (RTO) customer interface of a manufacturing process.

For assemble to order (ATO), make to order (MTO), and RTO products, the Master Production Schedule (MPS) is a materials plan for longer-leadtime materials, subassemblies, and components that are kept in inventory until customer orders arrive. The MPS, therefore, is a statement of a longer-term plan for longer-leadtime inventoried materials based on a demand forecast. MRP uses this MPS to create a detailed materials plan that schedules the manufacturing and purchasing activities needed to support the materials plan for these master-scheduled items.

In contrast, the Final Assembly Schedule (FAS) is a short-term (e.g., 1-2 week) materials plan based on actual customer orders. The final assembly process might include assembly or other finishing operations, such as adding accessories, labeling, and packing. The push-pull boundary separates items that are in the MPS and the FAS. The *Master Production Schedule (MPS)* entry provides more information on this topic.

See *assemble to order (ATO), bill of material (BOM), make to order (MTO), Master Production Schedule (MPS), push-pull boundary*.

financial performance metrics – Economic measures of success. ✪

All managers need to have a good understanding of financial performance metrics to make good decisions regarding capital investments, such as new plants and equipment, and also for process improvement projects. In virtually all public organizations and in most privately owned organizations, the financial performance metrics are the main goal. However, the operations performance metrics are often the "drivers" of the financial metrics. The cross-references below include most of the financial metrics that managers need to know.

See *asset turnover, balance sheet, Balanced Scorecard, break-even analysis, Compounded Annual Growth Rate (CAGR), cost of goods sold, DuPont Analysis, EBITDA, Economic Value Added (EVA), goodwill, income statement, Internal Rate of Return (IRR), Net Present Value (NPV), operations performance metrics, payback period, performance management system, Return on Assets (ROA), Return on Capital Employed (ROCE), Return on Investment (ROI), Return on Net Assets (RONA), sunk cost, total cost of ownership, Y-tree.*

finished goods inventory – The inventory units (or dollars) that are "finished" (completed) and ready for shipment or sale to a customer; sometimes abbreviated FG or FGI. ✪

Other types of inventory include raw materials, Work-in-Process (WIP), Maintenance-Repair-Operations (MRO), and pipeline (in-transit) inventory.

See *Maintenance-Repair-Operations (MRO), Work-in-Process (WIP) inventory*.

finite loading – See *finite scheduling*.

finite population queuing model – See *queuing theory*.

finite scheduling – Creating a sequence of activities with associated times so that no resource (person, machine, tool, etc.) is assigned more work time than the time available.

The opposite of finite scheduling is infinite loading, which ignores capacity constraints when creating a schedule. Hill and Sum (1993) developed the following terms for finite scheduling: A **due-date-feasible schedule** satisfies all due date requirements for all tasks (orders or operations). A **start-date-feasible schedule** does not have any tasks (orders or operations) scheduled before the current time. A **capacity-feasible schedule** does not require any resource to work more time than is available in any period.

Most finite scheduling systems begin with the current due date and therefore will always create start-date feasible schedules. However, if the capacity is insufficient, these systems will not be able to create due-date feasible schedules.

In contrast, MRP systems plan backward from the due date and therefore always create due-date feasible schedules. However, MRP systems are infinite loading systems and ignore capacity when creating a schedule, which means they create schedules that are often not capacity feasible. MRP systems will "schedule" some orders in the "past-due" time bucket, which means that the orders should have been started before the current time. When MRP systems create orders in the "past-due" bucket, the schedule is not start-date feasible, but is still "due-date" feasible.

Although many ERP systems and project management tools have finite scheduling capabilities, few firms use these tools. Most firms use infinite loading for both ERP and project management and then resolve resource contention issues after the plan (schedule) has been created. Finite scheduling was one of the main needs that motivated the development of Advanced Planning and Scheduling (APS) systems.

See *Advanced Planning and Scheduling (APS), backward loading, closed-loop MRP, forward scheduling, infinite loading, load, load leveling, Materials Requirements Planning (MRP), project management, time bucket.*

firm order – In the manufacturing context, a customer order that has no uncertainty with respect to product specifications, quantity, or due date; also called a customer order or firm customer order.

In contrast a "soft order" is a forecast or a planned order sometimes provided to suppliers via EDI.

See *Electronic Data Interchange (EDI), Master Production Schedule (MPS), Materials Requirements Planning (MRP).*

firm planned order – A manufacturing order that is frozen in quantity and time and is not affected by the MRP planning system.

Firm planned orders are created manually by planners and only planners can change the date or quantity for a firm planned order. When an MRP system regenerates materials plans for all items, firm planned orders are not changed. Firm planned orders give planners the ability to adjust schedules to handle material and capacity problems. The order quantities in a master production schedule are often called firm planned orders. A firm planned order is similar to, but not identical to, a firm customer order.

See *buyer/planner, manufacturing order, Master Production Schedule (MPS), time fence.*

first article inspection – The evaluation of the initial item in an order to confirm that it meets all specifications.

Approval to run additional parts is contingent on this first item meeting all specifications.

See *inspection.*

first mover advantage – The benefit sometimes gained by the first significant company to enter a new market.

Amazon is a good example of a firm that gained competitive advantage by being the first significant firm to enter the online book market. Although other firms sold books on the Internet before Amazon, it was the first firm to do so with appropriate systems and capitalization. Now that Amazon has established itself as the largest Internet book retailer, it has the economies of scale to offer low transaction costs (through good information systems and order fulfillment operations) and the economies of scope (and the network effect) to offer superior value to publishers and authors. The same arguments can be made for eBay in the on-line auction market.

Of course, the first firm in a market is not always able to establish a long-term competitive advantage. Dell Computer currently has the largest market share for personal computers, but many other firms, such as IBM, Apple, and Compaq, entered this market long before Dell.

See *market share, operations strategy.*

first pass yield – See *yield.*

first pick ratio – Percentage of items successfully retrieved from the initial warehouse storage location recommended on the pick list.

This is a performance measure for inventory accuracy and warehouse efficiency.

See *operations performance metrics, picking.*

First-In-First-Out (FIFO) – Using the arrival date as the priority for processing or as an accounting rule.

First-In-First-Out (FIFO) has several similar meanings:

Service priority – The customer who arrived first is serviced first. This is a common practice in walk-in clinics and restaurants.

Production scheduling – The customer order that was received first is processed first. Most lean systems use the FIFO rule. Although FIFO is the "fairest" rule, other dispatching rules often have better shop performance in terms of the average time in system.

Stock rotation – The method of picking goods from inventory that have been in inventory for the longest time.

Stock valuation – The method of valuing stocks that assumes that the oldest stock is consumed first and thus issues are valued at the oldest price.

See *dispatching rules, inventory valuation, Last-In-First-Out (LIFO), queuing theory, warehouse.*

fishbone diagram – See *causal map*.

five forces analysis – An industry analysis tool used to better understand a competitive environment.

Michael Porter's five forces analysis (Porter 1988) can be used by any strategic business unit to evaluate its competitive environment. This analysis looks at five key areas: threat of entrants to the market, the power of buyers, the power of suppliers, the threat of substitutes, and competitive rivalry. The model is shown below.

See *competitive analysis*, *industry analysis*, *operations strategy*, *SWOT analysis*.

Porter's Five Forces

Threat of new entrants

Bargaining power of suppliers → Competitive rivalry ← Bargaining power of buyers

Threat of substitute products

Porter, M.E. (1985). *Competitive Advantage*, Free Press, London.

five S – See *5S*.

fixed order quantity – The policy of using a constant (fixed) lotsize in a production or inventory planning system.

The Economic Order Quantity (EOQ) is a special case of a fixed order quantity. SAP and most other ERP/MRP systems will order in multiples of the fixed order quantity if the net requirements require more than the fixed order quantity.

See *Economic Order Quantity (EOQ)*, *lotsize*, *lotsizing methods*.

fixed price contract – A contract to complete a job at a predefined and set cost; also called a fixed-cost contract.

The contractor is obligated to finish the job, no matter how much time or cost is actually incurred. In other words, the contractor takes all the risk.

See *buy-back contract*, *purchasing*, *risk sharing contract*.

fixed storage location – The practice of storing items in a storage area that is labeled with the item ID.

With fixed storage locations, each item has a home location with the item's identification (part number, item number, SKU) on the shelf. Fixed storage locations are generally inefficient and hard to maintain because the space requirements for products in storage usually change over time as the demand patterns change. These changes require that the organization frequently reallocate the fixed location assignments or have excessive amounts of extra space allocated to each product.

On the positive side, fixed storage locations make it easy for people to find products. Most firms find that a mixture of fixed and random storage locations systems makes sense. The fixed storage locations are used for high-volume products where people are frequently picking items. These locations are replenished often from random storage locations that hold larger bulk quantities of items.

See *locator system*, *random storage location*, *supermarket*, *Warehouse Management System (WMS)*, *zone storage location*.

fixture – A device used to hold a work piece securely in the correct position relative to the tool while work is being done on the work piece.

Unlike a fixture, a jig can guide the tool.

See *jig*, *manufacturing processes*, *tooling*.

flexibility – The ability to change (adapt) quickly and efficiently in response to a change in the internal or external environment. ✪

Although the term "flexibility" is used very commonly in business, it is often used inconsistently and has several very different definitions. A major contributing factor to this ambiguity is that organizations face a wide variety of uncertainties and therefore need to have many types of flexibility. However, when managers and researchers discuss flexibility, they often fail to specify which type of flexibility they have in mind. Flexibility can be viewed both strategically and tactically. From a strategic point of view, flexibility can be defined as:

Volume flexibility – The ability to quickly and efficiently increase or decrease the production rate. This is sometimes called scalability and is about having economies of scale or at least avoiding diseconomies of scale.

Mix flexibility – The ability to efficiently handle a wide variety of products in one facility. Other authors define mix flexibility slightly differently. Schroeder, Meyer Goldstein, and Rungtusanatham (2011) defined it as the time to change the mix of products and services; Sethi and Sethi (1990) defined it as the ability of the manufacturing system to produce a set of part types without major setups; and Dixon (1992) defined it as the ability to manufacture a variety of products within a short period of time and without major modifications of existing facilities. Mix flexibility is closely related to product range.

Customization flexibility – The ability to quickly and efficiently provide a wide range of "respond to order" products. This is sometimes called mass customization and is fundamentally about having economies of scope or at least avoiding diseconomies of scope.

New product development flexibility – The ability to quickly and efficiently bring new products to market.

All four of the above flexibilities require the flexibility to be efficient. Unless the organization can "flex" efficiently, it is not truly flexible. For example, it might be possible for a firm to reduce its volume from 100 units per day to 50 units per day, but it is not considered to have volume flexibility if the cost per unit doubles.

Sethi and Sethi (1990) provide a research review article on this subject.

See *diseconomy of scale, mass customization, New Product Development (NPD), production planning, resilience, respond to order (RTO), scalability*.

Flexible Manufacturing System (FMS) – An integrated set of machines that have automated materials handling between them and are controlled by an integrated information system.

See *automation, cellular manufacturing, manufacturing processes, product-process matrix*.

float time – See *slack time*.

floater – A direct labor employee used to fill in on a production line when the regular worker is absent.

floor planning – An arrangement used by a retailer to finance inventory where a finance company buys the inventory, which is then held in trust for the user.

floor stock – Inventory stored close to a production process so workers can use it without an inventory transaction.

The labor cost of handling inventory transactions for lower cost items, such as fasteners, can sometimes be more than the cost of the items themselves. This is also true for bulk items, such as liquids in drums or wire on rolls. This is often solved by moving materials to floor stock as either **bulk issued** or **backflushed** items.

With **bulk issues**, the inventory balance in the warehouse inventory is reduced by the quantity issued and the floor stock account is increased by the same amount. The floor stock inventory is considered out of the system and the system may immediately call for a new reorder. In contrast, with **backflushing**, the MRP system considers the floor stock as available inventory and the floor stock inventory is reduced when the product is shipped. The backflush quantity is based on the "quantity per" in the bill of material (BOM).

See *backflushing*.

flow – The movement of products and customers through a process with minimum time wasted in waiting, processing, and non-value-adding activities, such as rework or scrap.

In the lean philosophy, one of the main goals is to improve flow by reducing lotsizes, queues, and rework. Improving flow reduces cycle time, which increases visibility and exposes waste.

See *lean, time-based competition*.

flow rack – Warehouse shelving that is tilted with rollers so cases roll forward for picking.

With a flow rack, only one case needs to be on the pick face, which means that many items can be available in a small area. Flow racks allow for high item density, which decreases travel time and increases picks per hour.

See *picking, warehouse*.

flow time – See *cycle time*.

flowchart – A diagram showing the movement of information and objects over time; also called a flow chart and a process flowchart.

The term "flowchart" has historically been used primarily for information flow. Most process improvement leaders now use the term "process map" when creating a diagram to show the steps in a process. See the *process map* entry for much more detail.

See *process map, seven tools of quality*.

flowshop – An academic research term used to describe a process that involves a sequence of machines where jobs move directly from one machine to the next.

Dudek, Panwalkar, and Smith (1992) recognized that "there is no precise definition of a flowshop," but they pointed out that "the following general assumptions are common in the literature. Jobs are to be processed in *m* stages sequentially. There is one machine at each stage. Machines are available continuously. A job is processed on one machine at a time without preemption and a machine processes no more than one job at a time."

See *facility layout, job shop, job shop scheduling.*

FMCG – See *Fast Moving Consumer Goods (FMCG).*

FMEA – See *Failure Mode and Effects Analysis (FMEA).*

FMS – See *Flexible Manufacturing System.*

FOB – A common freight/shipping acronym meaning "free on board."

When a buyer purchases something and pays for it with terms "FOB origin," the responsibility of the seller stops when the goods are delivered to the transporting company in suitable shipping condition. It is then the buyer's responsibility to pay for transportation. In addition, if something gets lost or is damaged during transport, it is settled between the buyer and the transportation company. FOB is an official Incoterm.

See *Cash on Delivery (COD), Incoterms, terms, waybill.*

focus group – A qualitative research technique that collects ideas from a small group of people.

Focus groups are often used as a marketing research tool to assess customer reactions to product ideas, but they can also be used for other purposes such as collecting employee opinions and gathering process improvement ideas. It is generally a good idea to have an experienced facilitator lead the focus group. Focus groups often use structured brainstorming methods such as the Nominal Group Technique (NGT).

See *brainstorming, Nominal Group Technique (NGT).*

focused factory – A process that is "aligned with its market" and therefore requires a limited range of operations objectives. ✪

The concept of a focused factory was originally developed by Harvard Business School Professor Wickham Skinner (1974) in his seminal article entitled "The Focused Factory." Skinner stated "The focused factory will out-produce, undersell, and quickly gain competitive edge over the complex factory." Skinner's article argues that a factory can excel at no more than one or two operations tasks, such as quality, delivery reliability, response time, low cost, customization, or short life cycle products.

"You can't be everything to everyone" is an old phrase that suggests that people (and firms) cannot do everything well, at least not in one process. A focused factory is a means of implementing a strategic direction for an operation. A firm can have several "focused factories" in any one factory building or location.

Schroeder and Pesch (1994) define a focused factory as one with "a limited and consistent set of demands that originate from its products, processes, and customers, enabling the factory to effectively support the business strategy." They state that "many manufacturing executives define focus simply as having a limited number of products ... but this definition is too narrow ... the key is to limit the demands placed on manufacturing by limiting the number of processes and customers as well as the number of products." Schroeder (2008) notes that the types of focus could be based on products, processes, technologies, sales volume, customer interface (make to stock versus make to order), or product maturity.

A focused factory, therefore, is not necessarily a factory that produces only one product, but a factory that reduces the variability or range of process requirements so the factory can excel at its key operations tasks. Focused factories align their processes to their markets and to the operations tasks required for those markets. This approach has implications for many process design issues, such as workforce (skill levels, salaried versus direct, customer-facing skills, etc.), performance metrics, customer interface, planning and control systems, cost accounting systems, facility layout, and supplier relationships. For example, the table below compares an operationally excellent make to stock "focused factory" making high volumes of standard products to an engineer to order "focused factory" developing innovative new products in response to customer orders.

Make to stock focused (MTS) factory versus engineer to order (ETO) focused factory

	Operationally excellent focused factory	Product leadership engineer to order focused factory
Workforce	Mostly direct labor, low wages	Many salaried workers, high wages
Performance metrics	Inventory, cost, cycle time	Time to market, on-time delivery
Customer interface	Make to stock/Assemble to order	Engineer to order/Make to order
Planning and control	Pull systems, MRP	Project management

Cost accounting	Throughput accounting, standard costs	Job-order costing, project costing
Facility layout	Product layout	Project layout, process layout
Supplier relationships	Many suppliers for commodities purchased at lowest cost	Few strategic "partners" who supply technologies as well as components
Main concern	Cost reduction, reliable delivery	Innovation, time to market
Main strategy	Lean manufacturing	Innovation, technology leadership

When a factory focuses on just a few key manufacturing tasks, it will be smaller, simpler, and more successful than a factory attempting to be all things to all customers. A focused factory can often deliver superior customer satisfaction to a vertical market, which allows it to dominate that market segment.

Some factories are unfocused originally because designers fail to recognize the limits and constraints of technologies and systems. Other factories start out highly focused, but lose focus over time due to product proliferation. In a sense, losing focus is "scope creep" for a factory.

See *cellular manufacturing, core competence, facility layout, functional silo, handoff, operations strategy, plant-within-a-plant, product proliferation, scope creep, standard products, throughput accounting.*

fool proofing – See *error proofing.*

force field analysis – A brainstorming and diagramming technique useful for gaining a shared understanding of the "tug of war" between the forces (factors) that drive (motivate) change toward a goal and the forces that restrain (block) change and support the status quo; force field analysis is supported by the force field diagram.

Force field analysis was developed by Kurt Lewin (1943), who saw organizations as systems where some forces were trying to change the status quo and some forces were trying to maintain it. A factor can be individual people, groups, attitudes, assumptions, traditions, culture, values, needs, desires, resources, regulations, etc. Force field analysis can be used by individuals, teams, and organizations to identify the relevant forces and focus attention on ways of reducing the hindering forces and encouraging the helping forces. The tool helps build a shared understanding of the relevant issues and then helps build an action plan to address the issues.

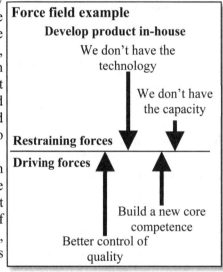

The figure on the right is an example of a force field "tug of war" on the issue of keeping new product development inside a firm. The equilibrium line separates the driving and restraining forces. (Note that the equilibrium line can be either vertical or horizontal.) The lengths of the arrows represent the strength of the forces. After the diagram is drawn, the team should focus on finding ways to strengthen or add driving forces and reduce or remove restraining forces.

See *Analytic Hierarchy Process (AHP), brainstorming, decision tree, Kepner-Tregoe Model, Lewin/Schein Theory of Change, Pugh Matrix, stakeholder analysis.*

force field diagram – See *force field analysis.*

force majeure – Events (or forces) beyond the control of the parties of a contract that prevent them from complying with the provisions of the contract; from French meaning superior force.

Typical forces that might be included in such a contract include governmental actions, restraints by court, wars or national emergencies, acts of sabotage, acts of terrorism, protests, riots, civil commotions, fire, arson, explosions, epidemics, lockouts, strikes or other labor stoppages, earthquakes, hurricanes, floods, lightning, embargos, blockades, archeological site discoveries, electrical outages, and interruptions of supply. The term "force majeure" is often used as the title of a standard clause in contracts exempting the parties for non-fulfillment of their obligations as a result of conditions beyond their control. In some cases, an industry shortage is considered a justifiable reason for a supplier to declare a force majeure and put customers on allocation.

Here is an example of a force majeure paragraph from naturalproductsinsider.com/ibg/terms.asp (November 27, 2005): "Neither party shall be deemed in default of this Agreement to the extent that performance of their obligations or attempts to cure any breach are delayed or prevented by reason of any act of God, fire, natural disaster, accident, act of government, shortages of materials or supplies, or any other causes beyond the control of such party, provided that such party gives the other written notice thereof properly and, in any event, within fifteen days of discovery thereof and uses its best efforts to cure the delay (force majeure). In the event of such force majeure, the time of performance or cure shall be extended for a period equal to the duration of the Force."

See *leadtime syndrome*.

forecast accuracy – See *forecast error metrics*.

forecast bias – The average forecast error over time, defined mathematically as $\frac{1}{T}\sum_{t=1}^{T} E_t$, where E_t is the forecast error in period t and T is the number of observations available.

The ideal forecasting system has a zero forecast bias, which means that it has an average forecast error of zero. When the forecast bias is zero, the positive and negative forecast errors "balance each other out." Bias is not the same as forecast accuracy. It is possible that a forecasting system with low accuracy (high mean absolute error) has zero forecast bias, and conversely, a forecasting system with a high accuracy (low mean absolute error) has high forecast bias. Forecast bias is a measure of the average performance of the forecasting system, whereas forecast accuracy is a measure of the reliability of the forecast.

Good forecasting systems have built-in exception reporting systems that trigger a "tracking signal" report when the forecast bias is large. See the *tracking signal* entry.

In practice, forecast bias can be tracked with three approaches: the moving average, the running sum of the errors, or the exponentially smoothed average error. The moving average approach defines the forecast bias as the average over the last T periods. The running sum of the errors approach uses the simple equation $R_t = R_{t-1} + E_t$, where R_t is the running sum of the forecast error at the end of period t. With this approach, a small consistent bias will become large over many periods. The exponentially smoothed average uses the equation $SE_t = SE_{t-1} + \alpha E_t$, where SE_t is the smoothed average error at the end of period t and α is the smoothing constant ($0 < \alpha < 1$). This is probably the best approach because it puts more weight on the most recent data.

See *alignment, bias, demand filter, forecast error metrics, Mean Absolute Deviation (MAD), Mean Absolute Percent Error (MAPE), mean squared error (MSE), tracking signal*.

forecast consumption – A method for reducing forecasted demand as the actual demand is realized.

See *forecasting, Materials Requirements Planning (MRP)*.

forecast error metrics – Mathematical measures used to evaluate forecast bias and accuracy. ✪

Forecast error is defined as the actual demand minus the forecast in a period. Using standard mathematical notation, $E_t = D_t - F_t$, where E_t is the forecast error in period t, D_t is the demand in period t, and F_t is the forecast made for period t. Given that the demand is rarely known, most organizations use actual sales as an estimate of demand. The following table is a summary of many forecast error metrics collected by this author. The symbol (◄) indicates metrics recommended by the author.

Forecast bias metrics for a single item
- Average error, $\overline{E}$ ◄
- Smoothed error, SE_t
- Mean Percent Error, MPE
- Mean Error Scaled by the Mean Demand,
- Running Sum of the Forecast Errors, RSE_t
- Tracking Signal, TS_{1t}, TS_{2t} ◄

Forecast accuracy metrics for a single item
- Mean Absolute Deviation (Mean Absolute Error), MAD
- Smoothed Mean Absolute Deviation, $SMAD_t$
- Mean Absolute Deviation as percent of average demand, $MADP$
- Mean Absolute Percent Error (Winsorized 1), $MAPE$
- Smoothed Mean Absolute Percent Error, $SMAPE_t$
- Relative Absolute Error – Random Walk, RAE_{rw}
- Relative Absolute Error – Exponential Smoothing, RAE_{es}
- Mean Absolute Scaled Error, $MASE$ ◄
- Thiel's U, U_1, U_2, U_3
- Mean Squared Error, MSE
- Smoothed Mean Squared Error, $SMSE_t$
- Root Mean Squared Error, $RMSE$
- Forecast Attainment, FA
- Demand Filter, DF_t ◄

Forecast bias metrics for a group of items

- Count or percentage of items with positive forecast error, *PPFE*

Forecast accuracy metrics for a group of items

- Weighted Mean Absolute Percent Error (Winsorized at 1), *WMAPE*
- Weighted Mean Absolute Scaled Error, *WMASE* ◄
- Median *MAPE*, *MdMAPE*
- Geometric Mean of the *MAPE*, *GMMAPE*

Other forecast error metrics

- Sample variance, standard deviation, $\hat{\sigma}^2$, $\hat{\sigma}$
- Sample correlation, coefficient of determination, r, r^2

- Weighted Average Forecast Error, *WAFE*
- Forecast Attainment, *FA* ◄

- Weighted Relative Absolute Error, *WRAE*
- Median *RAE*, *MdRAE*
- Geometric Mean *RAE*, *GMRAE*
- Forecast Attainment, *FA*
- Weighted Absolute Percent Error, *WAPE*
- Percent Better, *PB*

- Regression, a, b, r^2
- Sample autocorrelation at lag k, $\hat{\rho}_k$

See *bias*, *Box-Jenkins forecasting*, *correlation*, *demand filter*, *exponential smoothing*, *forecast bias*, *forecast horizon*, *forecast interval*, *forecasting*, *geometric mean*, *linear regression*, *Mean Absolute Deviation (MAD)*, *Mean Absolute Percent Error (MAPE)*, *Mean Absolute Scaled Error (MASE)*, *mean squared error (MSE)*, *Median*, *Median Absolute Percent Error (MdAPE)*, *operations performance metrics*, *Relative Absolute Error (RAE)*, *standard deviation*, *Thiel's U*, *tracking signal*, *weighted average*, *Winsorizing*.

forecast horizon – The number of time periods into the future that are forecasted.

For example, if a firm regularly makes forecasts that cover the next six months, it has a six-month forecast horizon. If a firm has a six-month manufacturing leadtime, it should clearly forecast at least six months into the future. Forecast error increases rapidly with the forecast horizon. It is often more practical and more economical to spend money to reduce the manufacturing leadtime (and the corresponding forecast horizon) than it is to find a better forecasting method to improve the forecast error for a given forecast horizon.

See *all-time demand*, *forecast error metrics*, *forecast interval*, *forecasting*, *forward visibility*.

forecast interval – The highest and lowest reasonable values for a forecast.

This is usually set as the forecast (which is usually an expected value) plus or minus z standard deviations of the forecast error. A reasonable value is $z = 3$. A forecast interval is very similar to a confidence interval, but it is not exactly the same. It is important to understand that the forecast interval is strongly influenced by the forecast horizon, where the forecast interval increases with the forecast horizon.

See *forecast error metrics*, *forecast horizon*, *forecasting*, *forward visibility*, *geometric mean*.

forecasting – Predicting the future values of a variable. ✪

Almost all organizations need to forecast sales or demand on a regular basis. Organizations also need to forecast the cost of materials, the availability of labor, the performance of a technology, etc. The two main types of forecasting methods are **quantitative** and **qualitative** methods. Quantitative methods can be further broken into time series methods and causal methods.

Time series methods (also called intrinsic forecasting methods) seek to find historical patterns in the data and then extrapolate those into the future. The simplest time series models are an average, moving average, and weighted moving average. Exponential smoothing forecasting models create forecasts with a weighted moving average, where the weights decline geometrically with the time lag. The Winters' and Holt-Winters' models for exponential smoothing (Winters 1960) add trend and seasonality. The Box-Jenkins method is a much more sophisticated model for time series forecasting (Box, Jenkins, & Reinsel 1994).

Causal methods (also called extrinsic or econometric forecasting methods) are nearly always multiple regression methods, where the model predicts one variable (the dependent variable) from one or more other independent lagged variables. See the *linear regression* and *econometric forecasting* entries.

Qualitative methods are subjective methods used to collect estimates from people. See the *Delphi* and *technological forecasting* entries for more information on qualitative models.

All time series can be **decomposed** into a **seasonal pattern** (tied to the calendar or a clock), a **trend**, **cyclical** (irregular patterns), and what is left over (random noise). See the *seasonality*, *trend*, and *time series* entries.

Forecast error is defined as the actual value minus the forecasted value. Most forecasting models assume that the random error is normally distributed. See the *forecast error metrics* entry for more detail.

Demand forecasts are better when:
- Expressed as a point estimate (a single number) and a forecast interval rather than just a point estimate.
- Aggregated across product families, regions, and periods.
- Made for a short horizon.
- Based on many periods of historical data.
- Supplemented by human intelligence.
- Clearly differentiated from a plan.
- Carefully aligned with reward systems.
- Created collaboratively by the supply chain.
- Used by everyone without modification.

Fundamental forecasting principles:
- Forecasting is difficult (especially if it is about the future).
- The only thing we know for sure about a forecast is that it is wrong.
- Separate forecasting and planning – forecast ≠ plan.
- It is easier to fit a model to historical data than it is to create accurate forecasts.
- Use lean to reduce cycle times and forecast horizons.
- Use information systems to replace inventory and improve service.
- Share demand information to reduce forecast error and coordinate the supply chain.
- Use leading indicators to reduce forecast error.
- Use demand management to balance supply and demand.
- Use yield management to maximize revenue.
- Use demand filters and tracking signals to control forecasts.
- Use the Bass Model for product life cycle forecasting, particularly at the beginning of the product life cycle.
- Use the geometric time series model for end-of-life forecasting.

Two misunderstandings of forecasting are common. Each of these is discussed below.

Confusing forecasting and planning – Many firms use the term "forecast" for their production plan. As a result, they lose important stockout (opportunity cost) information and create confusion and muddled thinking throughout their organizations. In a typical business context, the firm needs a forecast of the demand for its products without consideration of the firm's capacity or supply. In response to this "unfettered" (unconstrained) demand forecast, the firm should make its production and inventory plans. In some periods, the firm might plan to have inventory greater than demand; in other periods, the firm might plan to have inventory short of demand.

Confusing sales and demand history – Many people use the terms "sales" and "demand" interchangeably. However, they are not the same. Technically, demand is sales plus lost sales. Most firms keep a sales history, which they sometimes call the "demand history." (SAP uses the term "consumption" history.) This is a "censored" time series because sales will be less than demand when sales are lost due to lack of inventory. This distinction is important when using historical sales (not demand) to forecast future demand. Some retailers try to use information on the "in-stock position" to inflate the sales history to estimate the demand history.

The website www.forecastingprinciples.com provides a dictionary, bibliography, and other useful information on forecasting. *The Principles of Forecasting* is a free Web-based book by J. Scott Armstrong that can be found at www.forecastingprinciples.com/content/view/127/10 (April 18, 2011).

See *all-time demand, anchoring, Bass Model, Box-Jenkins forecasting, censored data, coefficient of variation, Collaborative Planning Forecasting and Replenishment (CPFR), Croston's Method, Delphi forecasting, demand, demand filter, demand management, econometric forecasting, elasticity, exponential smoothing, forecast consumption, forecast error metrics, forecast horizon, forecast interval, forward visibility, inventory management, leading indicator, linear regression, lumpy demand, Mean Absolute Deviation (MAD), Mean Absolute Percent Error (MAPE), moving average, Sales & Operations Planning (S&OP), seasonality, supply chain management, technological forecasting, Theta Model, time bucket, time series forecasting, tracking signal, trend.*

forecasting lifetime demand – See *all-time demand.*

forging – A manufacturing process that shapes metal by heating and hammering.

Forging usually involves heating metal (below the melting point) and then using hammering or pressure to shape the metal. Forged parts usually require additional machining. Forging can be cold, warm, or hot.

See *manufacturing processes.*

for-hire carrier – A common carrier or contract carrier trucking firm that transports goods for monetary compensation.

See *carrier, common carrier, logistics.*

forklift truck – A vehicle used in warehouses, factories, and distribution centers to lift, move, stack, and rack loads (usually on pallets); also called a lift truck, fork lift, and hi-low.

A forklift may have a special attachment on the front for handling certain specialized products.

See *cross-docking, logistics, materials handling, pallet, warehouse.*

forming-storming-norming-performing model – A model that explains the progression of team development.

This model of group development was first proposed by Tuckman (1965), who maintained that all four phases are necessary for a team to be successful. Tuckman and Jensen (1977) added "adjourning" in 1970, which some call "mourning."

- **Forming** – In this first stage, the team has high dependence on the leader for guidance. The team has little agreement on goals other than what the leader has defined. Individual roles and responsibilities are unclear. Processes are often ignored and team members often test the boundaries of the leader. The leader directs.
- **Storming** – Team members contend to establish their position relative to those of other team members and the leader and decision making is difficult. Informal alliances form and power struggles are common. The team needs to be focused on goals and compromises may be required to enable progress. The leader coaches.
- **Norming** – The team begins to develop consensus and clarify roles and responsibilities. Smaller decisions may be delegated to individuals or smaller teams. The team may engage in fun and social activities. The team begins to develop processes. The leader facilitates and enables.
- **Performing** – The team has a shared understanding of its vision and is less reliant on the leader. Disagreements are resolved positively and process changes are made easily. Team members might ask for assistance from the leader with personal and interpersonal development. The leader delegates and oversees.
- **Adjourning (Mourning)** – The team's work is complete when the task is successfully completed and the team members can feel good about their work. The leader should conduct a post-project review to ensure that individuals learn and that organizational learning is captured and shared.

Stage	Description	Leader's role
Forming	Team tests leader while team orients.	Directs
Storming	Team has conflict and contention for position in the team.	Coaches
Norming	Team spirit develops and processes and roles are clarified.	Facilitates and enables
Performing	Structural issues are resolved and roles become more flexible.	Delegates and oversees
Adjourning/ Mourning	Members are sad. This is a good opportunity for learning.	Conducts post-project review

See *brainstorming, mission statement, post-project review, project management.*

formulation – A list of the quantities of each ingredient needed to make a product, typically used for chemicals, liquids, and other products that require mixing; also called a recipe.

See *bill of material (BOM).*

forward buy – The practice of purchasing materials and components in excess of the short-term anticipated demand; the use of forward buys is called forward buying.

Forward buying is often motivated by trade promotions (temporary price reductions) or anticipation of a potential price increase. Although forward buying might reduce the acquisition cost for the customer, it can increase inventory carrying cost for the customer and increase the variability of the demand for the supplier. Everyday low pricing (EDLP) is a way to encourage customers to reduce forward buying and stabilize demand.

See *acquisition, bullwhip effect, Everyday Low Pricing (EDLP), futures contract, loss leader, promotion, purchasing.*

forward integration – See *vertical integration*.

forward loading – See *forward scheduling*.

forward pass – See *forward scheduling*.

forward pick area – A space within a warehouse used for storing and picking higher-demand items; this space is resupplied from a larger reserve storage area; sometimes called a golden zone.

This area usually has fixed storage locations so that pickers can remember where the items are located. Using a forward pick area can reduce unproductive travel time by order pickers but must be replenished from a bulk storage (reserve storage) area somewhere else in the warehouse. A forward pick area usually has small quantities of high-volume parts stored in carton flow racks positioned near a conveyor, shipping area, or the loading dock. Forward pick areas are common in distribution centers in North America, especially those supporting retail sales. Bartholdi (2011) provided more information in his free on-line book and Bartholdi and Hackman (2008) developed a mathematical model for optimizing the space allocated to a forward pick area.

See *picking, reserve storage area, slotting, warehouse, Warehouse Management System (WMS)*.

forward scheduling – A finite scheduling method that begins with the start date (which could be the current time) and plans forward in time, never violating the capacity constraints; also called forward loading or forward pass.

The start date and task times are the primary inputs to a forward scheduling algorithm. The planned completion date is an output of the process. Forward scheduling is quite different from **back scheduling**, which starts with the due date (planned completion date) and plan backward to determine the planned start date. The **critical path method** uses forward scheduling to determine the early start and early finish for each activity in the project network. See the *finite scheduling* entry for more detail.

See *back scheduling, Critical Path Method (CPM), finite scheduling*.

forward visibility – Giving information on future demand and production plans to internal and external suppliers.

Customers can give their suppliers forward visibility by sharing their **forecasts** and **production plans**. This allows suppliers to plan their production to better meet their customers' requirements.

See *Electronic Data Interchange (EDI), forecast horizon, forecast interval, forecasting, Materials Requirements Planning (MRP)*.

foundry – A facility that pours hot metal into molds to create metal castings.

A **casting** is any product formed by a **mold** (British, mould), which is a hollow cavity with the desired shape. The casting can be either ejected or broken out of the mold. Castings do not always require heat or a foundry. For example, plaster may be cast. Sand casting uses sand as the mold material.

A foundry creates castings by heating metal in a furnace until it is in liquid form, pouring the metal into a mold, allowing the metal to cool and solidify, and finally removing the casting from the mold. Castings often require additional operations before they become products sold to customers. Castings are commonly made from aluminum, iron, and brass. Castings are used in many products, such as engines, automobiles, and machine tools.

See *manufacturing processes, mold*.

Fourth Party Logistics (4PL) provider – See *Third Party Logistics (3PL) provider*.

fractile – A selection portion of a probability distribution.

For example, the lower quartile is the lower 25% of the cumulative probability distribution and the top decile is the top 10% of the cumulative probability distribution.

See *interquartile range, newsvendor problem*.

Free-on-Board (FOB) – See *FOB*.

freight bill – Invoice for the transportation charges of goods shipped or received. See *logistics*

freight forwarder – An independent business that handles export shipments for compensation.

See *logistics*.

front office – See *back office*.

frozen schedule – See *time fence*.

FTE – See *Full Time Equivalent*.

fuel surcharge – An extra charge added to the cost of a shipment to cover the variable cost of fuel.

fulfillment – The process of shipping products to customers in response to customer orders; also called fulfillment operations.

The fulfillment process almost always involves **order entry**, **picking** items from a warehouse or distribution center, **packaging**, and **shipping**. In addition, fulfillment may also involve:

- **Supplier-facing activities** – Placing replenishment orders, managing in-bound logistics, providing information on current inventory status to suppliers, and expediting.
- **Other customer-facing activities** – Tracking orders, sending automated e-mails to customers to let them know their packages are in transit, satisfying customer requests for information, handling returns, and providing help desk support for products.
- **Financial activities** – Processing credit card transactions, invoicing customers, and paying suppliers.

The term "fulfillment" is most often associated with e-commerce and other operations that ship many small orders to end customers rather than operations that process shipments to other manufacturers, wholesalers, or resellers. Examples of fulfillment operations include fulfillment operations for mail-order catalogs, Internet stores, and service parts. A **fulfillment house** is a third party that performs outsourced storage, order picking, packaging, shipment, and other similar services for others.

See *customer service, help desk, order entry, replenishment order, Third Party Logistics (3PL) provider, warehouse, Warehouse Management System (WMS)*.

Full Time Equivalent (FTE) – A labor staffing term used to equate the salary or work hours for a number of part-time people to the number of "equivalent" full-time people.

For example, three people working half-time is equal to 1.5 FTEs.

full truck load – See *less than truck load (LTL)*.

functional build – A design and manufacturing methodology that de-emphasizes individual part quality and focuses on system quality.

Conventional design and manufacturing processes sequentially check each part being produced against design specifications utilizing C_p and C_{pk} metrics. This requires that all critical dimensions of a part be within specification limits. An example is an auto manufacturer checking 1,400 points on a door die. If any of these are out of tolerance, they would be reworked to achieve proper specifications. With a functional build, if the part is close to passing, it is used in the assembly and the overall assembly is held to tighter tolerances. In contrast, the functional build process checks fewer points and fixes only the ones necessary to bring the door assembly (system) into tolerance. The result is a higher quality assembly, which is what the customer really cares about, at a substantially lower cost.

A study conducted by CAR found that Japanese automobile manufacturers had the lowest quality doors as measured by C_{pk} for individual parts, but had high customer scores for the door assembly, while American manufacturers had higher door component C_{pk} values, but lower customer scores (adapted from "The Quest for Imperfection," Charles Murray, **Design News**, October 10, 2005, www.designnews.com).

See *process capability and performance, Taguchi methods*.

functional silo – A functional group or department in an organization, such as marketing, operations, accounting, and finance, that is overly focused on its own organization and point of view, which results in inefficient and ineffective processes.

A silo is a tall cylindrical tower used for storing grain, animal feed, or other material. The photo on the right shows a series of six silos on an American farm. The metaphor here is that organizations often have "silos" where people in functional groups are overly focused on their own functions, do not coordinate with other functions, do not share information with other functions, and do not have constructive interactions with other functions. The functional departments are usually pictured as vertical lines, whereas processes serving each market segment are drawn as horizontal lines that cross multiple silos. The result of the functional silo problem is inefficient processes, poor customer service, and lack of innovation.

For example, a customer order begins with a salesperson who hands it off to order entry, but neglects to include some information. The order entry person enters the sales order data into the information system, but accidentally enters the promise date incorrectly. The manufacturing organization makes the product to the customer's requirements, but misses one important unusual customer need. The shipping people accidently ship the product to the billing address rather than to the point of need. It is easy for information to get lost in this process because each "silo" (department) has different goals and information systems. It is hard for any one process to "own" this customer order because the process is too far from the voice of the customer.

The **lean** answer to this issue is to create organizations around value streams that are aligned with market segments. A focus on value streams instead of silos reduces waste, cycle time, cost, and defects. In the operations strategy literature, this is called a **focused factory**.

See *Deming's 14 points*, *focused factory*, *lean thinking*, *mass customization*, *order entry*, *value stream*.

future reality tree – A theory of constraints term for a type of causal map used to show the relationships needed to create the future state desirable effects.

See *causal map*, *current reality tree*, *Theory of Constraints (TOC)*.

futures contract – An agreement to purchase or sell a commodity for delivery in the future with (1) a price determined at initiation of the contract, (2) terms that obligate each party to fulfill the contract at the specified price, (2) the purpose of assuming or shifting price risk, and may be satisfied by delivery or offset; also called futures.

A futures contract is a standardized, transferable, exchange-traded contract that requires delivery of a commodity, bond, currency, or stock index, at a specified price, on a specified future date. Unlike options, futures convey an obligation to buy. The risk to the holder is unlimited, and because the payoff pattern is symmetrical, the risk to the seller is unlimited. Money lost and gained by each party on a futures contract is equal and opposite. In other words, futures trading is a **zero sum game**. Futures contracts are forward contracts, meaning they represent pledges to make certain transactions at future dates. The exchange of assets occurs on the date specified in the contract. Futures are distinguished from generic forward contracts in that they contain standardized terms, trade on formal exchanges, are regulated by overseeing agencies, and are guaranteed by clearinghouses. To insure that payment will occur, futures also have a margin requirement that must be settled daily. Finally, by making an offsetting trade, taking delivery of goods, or arranging for an exchange of goods, futures contracts can be closed. Hedgers often trade futures for the purpose of keeping price risk in check.

See *commodity*, *forward buy*, *purchasing*, *zero sum game*.

fuzzy front end – The process for determining customer needs or market opportunities, generating ideas for new products, conducting necessary research on the needs, developing product concepts, and evaluating product concepts up to the point that a decision is made to proceed with development.

This process is called the fuzzy front end because it is the most unstructured part of product development. Preceding the more formal product development process, it generally consists of three tasks: strategic planning, concept generation, and pre-technical evaluation. These activities are often chaotic, unpredictable, and unstructured. In comparison, the subsequent new product development process is typically structured, predictable, and formal, with prescribed sets of activities, questions to be answered, and decisions.

Adapted from www.pdma.org (April 18, 2011).

See *New Product Development (NPD)*.

G

Gage R&R – See *Gauge R&R*.

gainsharing – An incentive program that provides financial benefits to employees based on improvements in quality or productivity; also called pay for performance.

See *Balanced Scorecard*, *human resources*, *job design*, *pay for skill*, *piece work*.

game theory – A branch of mathematics that models the strategic interactions among competitors to determine the optimal course of action.

Business can be viewed as a "game" between the competitors in a market. A decision (move) by one player motivates a move by another player. Historically, game theory can be traced back to the Talmud and Sun Tzu's writings. John von Neumann and Oskar Morgenstern are credited with the mathematical development of modern-day game theory in their book **Theory of Games and Economic Behavior** (Neumann & Morgenstern 1944). In the early 1950s, John Nash generalized these results and created the basis for the modern field of mathematical game theory[19]. The most widely known example of game theory is the prisoners' dilemma.

A major issue with game theory is the trade-off between realism and simplicity. The most common assumptions in game theory are (1) rationality (i.e., people take actions likely to make them happier, and they know what makes them happy) and (2) common knowledge (i.e., everyone else is trying to make themselves happy, potentially at our expense).

See *co-opetition (co-competition)*, *prisoners' dilemma*, *zero sum game*.

gamma distribution – A continuous probability distribution often used to model task times and other variables that have a left tail bounded by zero.

The gamma distribution has shape parameter α and scale parameter β. Important special cases of the gamma distribution include the exponential, k-Erlang, and chi-square distributions. The k-Erlang is a special case of the gamma with an integer shape parameter.

Gamma density and distribution functions: The gamma density function is $f(x) = \beta^{-\alpha} x^{\alpha-1} e^{-x/\beta} / \Gamma(\alpha)$ for $x > 0$; $f(x) = 0$ otherwise, where $\Gamma(\alpha) = \int_{t=0}^{\infty} t^{\alpha-1} e^{-t} dt$ is the gamma function. The gamma function does not have a closed form when α is not an integer, which means that the gamma density and distribution functions must be approximated numerically. The *gamma function* entry presents the VBA code for the gamma function.

Graph: The graph below shows a gamma density function with a range of α parameters and scale parameter $\beta = 1$. Note that if X is a gamma distributed random variable with shape α and scale 1, then βX is a gamma distributed random variable with shape α and scale β.

Statistics: Mean $\mu = \alpha\beta$, variance $\sigma^2 = \alpha\beta^2$, mode $\beta(\alpha-1)$ if $\alpha \geq 1$ and 0 otherwise, skewness $2/\sqrt{\beta}$, and coefficient of variation $c = \sqrt{\alpha}/\alpha$.

Parameter estimation: Many authors, such as Fisher and Raman (2010), use the method of moments to estimate $\alpha = \bar{x}^2 / s^2$ and $\beta = s^2 / \bar{x}$, where $\bar{x}$ and s are the sample mean and standard deviation. Law (2007) presented a maximum likelihood estimation procedure that requires numerical methods. Minka (2002, p. 2) claimed that the approach in Law "can be quite slow, requiring around 250 iterations if $\alpha = 10$" and presented an MLE approach that converges in about four iterations. All MLE approaches are based on the fact that the MLE estimate for beta is $\beta = \bar{x} / \alpha$.

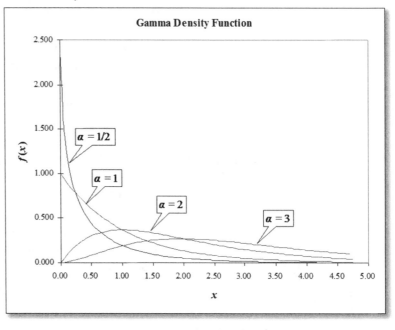

Gamma Density Function

Excel: In Excel, the natural log of the gamma function is GAMMALN(α), which means that the gamma function is EXP(GAMMALN(α)). The gamma density and distribution functions are GAMMADIST(x, α, β, FALSE) and GAMMADIST(x, α, β, TRUE). The inverse distribution function is GAMMAINV(p, α, β). In

---

[19] *John Nash was awarded the Nobel Prize in Economics in 1994 and was the subject of the film **A Beautiful Mind** in 2001.*

Excel 2010, the gamma distribution function is renamed GAMMA.DIST(x, α, β, TRUE), and the gamma inverse function is renamed GAMMA.INV(p, α, β).

Excel errors: The GAMMADIST and GAMMAINV functions in Excel 2003 and Excel 2007 will return #NUM for some combinations of input parameters. Knüsel (2005) stateed that the GAMMADIST function "can have numerical problems just in the most important central part of the distribution." Evidently, these problems have been fixed in Excel 2010.

Excel simulation: An Excel simulation can generate gamma distributed random variates with the inverse transform method using x = GAMMAINV(1-RAND(), α, β).

Partial expectation function: $H(x) = \mu F_{Gamma}(x \mid \alpha + 1, \beta)$.

Related distributions: If $X \sim$ Gamma$(1, \beta)$, then $X \sim$ Exponential(β), where β is the mean. If $X \sim$ Gamma(k, β), then $X \sim$ Erlang(k, β), where k is an integer. If $X \sim$ Gamma$(k/2, 2)$, then $X \sim$ Chi-square with k degrees of freedom. See Law (2007) for more details. The gamma, Weibull, and log-normal distributions are special cases of the generalized gamma distribution (Wikipedia 2010). The gamma converges to the normal distribution as the shape parameter (α) approaches infinity.

See *beta distribution, chi-square distribution, Erlang distribution, exponential distribution, gamma function, inverse transform method, negative binomial distribution, partial expectation, probability density function, probability distribution.*

gamma function – A mathematical extension of the factorial function to real and complex numbers.

The gamma function is $\Gamma(\alpha) = \int_{t=0}^{\infty} t^{\alpha-1} e^{-t} dt$ for $\alpha > 0$. When α is a non-negative integer, $\alpha! = \Gamma(\alpha + 1)$.

Note that $\Gamma(1/2) = \sqrt{\pi}$. In Excel, the gamma function can be computed as exp(GAMMALN(x)).

The gamma function is used in several probability distributions, including the beta, F, gamma, chi-square, and Weibull, and is also useful for evaluating ratios of factorials. The factorial of a positive integer n is defined as $n! = n \cdot (n-1) \cdot (n-2) \cdots 1$, where $0! \equiv 1$. The gamma function generalizes this to all non-negative real numbers where $\alpha! = \Gamma(\alpha + 1)$.

The gamma function provides a practical tool for evaluating ratios of factorials, such as $n!/m!$, that are common in probability, statistics, and queuing theory. When n or m is large, the factorial results in integer overflow problems. (The largest factorial that Excel can handle is 170!) Given that $n!/m! = \Gamma(n+1)/\Gamma(m+1)$, we know that $\ln(n!/m!) = \ln(\Gamma(n+1)/\Gamma(m+1)) = \ln(\Gamma(n+1)) - \ln(\Gamma(m+1))$. Defining $GLN(x) = \ln(\Gamma(x))$, then $\ln(n!/m!) = GLN(n+1) - GLN(m+1)$ and $n!/m! = \exp(GLN(n+1) - GLN(m+1))$. This procedure can be done in double precision and eliminates the risk of integer overflow problems. However, this procedure can have rounding problems. This method is comparable to cancelling out common terms in the ratio $n!/m!$ before doing the division. In Excel, the function for the natural log of the gamma function is GAMMALN(x).

The following table illustrates this point in Excel. From basic algebra, we know that $y = (n+1)!/n!$ is equal to $n+1$. The table shows that for n = 2, 4, and 169, the factorial and gamma function approaches both provide the correct values. However, for $n > 170$, the factorial method has integer overflow problems. In contrast, the gamma function provides the correct answer within the limits of computer precision.

Table comparing the factorial approach to the gamma approach

		n	2	3	169	170	3000
Input data		Exact answer ($n + 1$)	3	4	170	171	3001
Factorial approach		$n!$	2	6	4.2691E+304	7.2574E+306	Integer overflow
		$(n + 1)!$	6	24	7.2574E+306	Integer overflow	Integer overflow
		$y = (n + 1)!/n!$	3	4	170	Integer overflow	Integer overflow
		Overflow problems	No	No	No	Yes	Yes

Gamma function approach	g_1 = gammaln(n + 1)	0.6931472	1.7917595	701.4372638	706.5730622	21,024.0248530
	g_2 = gammaln(n + 2)	1.7917595	3.1780538	706.5730622	711.7147258	21,032.0315539
	$d = g_2 - g_1$	1.0986123	1.3862944	5.1357984	5.1416636	8.0067008
	$y = \exp(d)$	3	4	170	~171	~3001
	Overflow problems	No	No	No	No[20]	No

Source: Professor Arthur V. Hill

The gamma function has no closed form, but accurate and efficient approximate numerical methods are available. The following VBA code was written by this author based on the algorithm in Press et al. (2002). This was tested in Excel and found to be identical to the Excel function GAMMALN() in every case tested.

```
Function gamma_ln(xx As Double) as double
Dim x As Double, y As Double, tmp As Double, ser As Double, j As Integer
Static cof(0 To 5) As Double
    cof(0) = 76.1800917294715: cof(1) = -86.5053203294168
    cof(2) = 24.0140982408309: cof(3) = -1.23173957245015
    cof(4) = 1.20865097386618E-03: cof(5) = -5.395239384953E-06
    x = xx: y = x: tmp = x + 5.5: tmp = tmp - (x + 0.5) * Log(tmp): ser = 1.00000000019001
    For j = 0 To 5
        ser = ser + cof(j) / (y + j + 1)
    Next j
    gamma_ln = -tmp + Log(2.506628274631 * ser / x)
End Function
```

According to Wikipedia, Stirling's approximation is said to be good for large factorials. However, this author's implementation found that it had overflow problems for $n > 170$. The Wikipedia entry suggests Nemes approximation as an alternative, where $\ln \Gamma(z) \approx \frac{1}{2}\left(\ln(2\pi) - \ln z\right) + z\left(\ln\left(z + \frac{1}{12z - 0.1/z}\right) - 1\right)$. The author has tested this approximation and found it to be very precise for all values of z. Interestingly, the average of the gamma function approach and Nemes approach was consistently better than either approach in these tests.

See *algorithm*, *beta distribution*, *beta function*, *chi-square distribution*, *combinations*, *error function*, *factorial*, *gamma distribution*, *hypergeometric distribution*, *Student's t distribution*.

Gantt Chart – A graphical project planning tool that uses horizontal bars to show the start and end dates for each task. ✪

The simple Gantt Chart example on the right shows the start and end dates for five tasks. Although a Gantt Chart is a useful tool for communicating a project schedule (plan), it does not usually show precedence relationships between tasks and therefore is not a good project planning tool for large projects.

Microsoft Project, the most popular project planning software on the market today, uses Gantt Charts to communicate project schedules. Unlike most Gantt Charts, this software can use arrows to show precedence relationships between tasks.

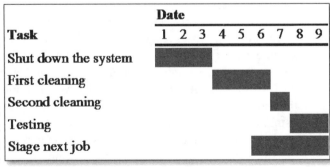

See *bar chart*, *Critical Path Method (CPM)*, *project management*, *waterfall scheduling*.

gap model – See *service quality*.

gate – See *project management*, *stage-gate process*.

---

[20] *For n = 170, the Excel value was y ≈ 171.000000000540; for n = 3000, y ≈ 3001.000000006510.*

gateway workcenter – The location in a facility where a manufacturing order has its first operation.

See *CONWIP, pacemaker*.

GATT – See *General Agreement on Tariffs and Trade (GATT)*.

gauge – An instrument used for measurement or testing; also spelled gage.

The word "gauge" is often spelled "gage," but according to the **New Merriam-Webster Pocket Dictionary** (G. & C. Merriam Co. 1971), "gauge" is the proper spelling.

An old management proverb says, "You cannot manage what you cannot measure." This is particularly true for managing process improvement. It is impossible to reduce variation in a process (and the products that are produced by that process) without a reliable measurement system.

Many people assume that the term "gauge" is confined to mean a micrometer, but in the context of Gauge R&R, the term "gauge" can mean any measurement device. In fact, "Gauge R&R" can be used for any measurement tool and can even be used for surveys and other non-factory measurement tools. The following list of common measurement and test equipment includes a broad range of measuring devices:

- Hand tools (calipers, micrometers, linear scales)
- Gauges (pins, thread, custom gauges)
- Optical tools (comparators, profiles, microscopes)
- Coordinate measuring machines
- Electronic measuring equipment (digital displays, output)
- Weights, balances and scales
- Hardness testing equipment
- Surface plate methods and equipment
- Surface analyzers (optical flats, roughness testers)
- Force measurement tools (torque wrenches, tensiometers)
- Angle measurement tools (protractors, sine bars, angle blocks)
- Color measurement tools (spectrophotometer, color guides, light boxes)
- Gauge maintenance, handling, and storage

See *Gauge R&R, manufacturing processes, Measurement System Analysis (MSA), metrology*.

Gauge R&R – A statistical tool that measures the variation in measurements that arises from (a) measurement device variability (repeatability) and (b) operator variability (reproducibility); also called Gage R&R.

The measurement system is a key part of understanding and improving process capability and Gauge R&R is a key part of the measurement system. In many lean sigma and lean manufacturing applications, Measurement System Analysis (MSA) is conducted in the Measure step of the DMAIC process. MSA is also a key part of the Control step (the "C") in DMAIC.

Gauge R&R measures two different types of variation in the measurement process:

- **Repeatability** – The ability of a device (gauge) to produce consistent results. It is a measure of the "within" variability between repeated measurements for one device, with one operator, on one part.
- **Reproducibility** – The ability of the appraiser (operator) to produce consistent results. It is the variation between different operators who measure the same part with the same device.

In addition, most Gauge R&R studies also measure the interaction between the gauge and the operator. For example, out of several inspectors, one might have a tendency to read one gauge differently than others.

The two most common methods used for Gauge R&R are the (1) **Average and Range** method and (2) **Analysis of Variance** (ANOVA). The Average and Range method, like many classical SPC methods, is based on ranges, which are easy to calculate manually. ANOVA is more accurate, but the Range and Average method is simpler and therefore has been more widely used. With the increased availability of statistical software tools for ANOVA, it is likely that ANOVA-based Gauge R&R will become the method of choice in the future.

Although the most obvious application of Gauge R&R is for tools, it can be applied to any type of measurements. For example, it can be applied to customer satisfaction and employee engagement surveys.

Some of the material above was adapted from e-mail correspondence with Gary Etheridge, Staff Engineer at Seagate, and from the website for the Automotive Industry Action Group (www.aiag.org). DeMast and Trip (2005) is a good reference on Gauge R&R.

See *Analysis of Variance (ANOVA), Design of Experiments (DOE), DMAIC, gauge, lean sigma, Measurement System Analysis (MSA), metrology, tooling*.

gemba – A Japanese term for the actual place where "real" work takes place; sometimes spelled genba.

The Japanese word "gemba" is frequently used for the shop floor or any place where value-adding work actually occurs. The main idea communicated by the term is that improvement really only takes place with (1) engagement of the people who work the process and (2) direct observation of the actual current conditions. For example, standardized work cannot be documented in the manager's office, but must be defined and revised in the "gemba." According to one source[21], the more literal translation is the "actual spot" and was originally adapted from law enforcement's "scene of the crime."

The Japanese characters are 現場 (from www.fredharriman.com/resources/documents/FHcom_Kaizen_ Terminology_03.pdf (January 27, 2009).

See *3Gs, checksheet, kaizen workshop, lean thinking, management by walking around, waste walk.*

gemba walk – See *waste walk.*

General Agreement on Tariffs and Trade (GATT) – A set of rules created by the United Nations to promote freer trade by limiting or eliminating tariffs and import quotas between signatory countries.

GATT is now supervised by the World Trade Organization (WTO), which expanded its scope from only traded goods to include services and intellectual property rights.

See *antitrust laws, purchasing, tariff.*

genetic algorithm – A heuristic search procedure that finds solutions to optimization problems by generating an initial solution and then permuting solutions until a stopping condition is found.

See *heuristic, operations research (OR), optimization.*

geometric decay – See *all-time demand, geometric progression.*

geometric mean – A measure of the central tendency appropriate for the product of two or more values.

The arithmetic mean (i.e., the average) is relevant for quantities that are added together and answers the question, "If all quantities had the same value, what value is needed to achieve the same total?" In contrast, the geometric mean is relevant for quantities that are multiplied together and answers the question, "If all quantities had the same value, what value is needed to achieve the same product?"

Example 1 – The area of a rectangle can be found by multiplying the length (L) and the width (W). In other words, $A = LW$. When $L = 10$ feet and $H = 6$ feet, the area is $A = 60$ square feet. What are the dimensions of a square with $L = W$ that has the same area? The answer is the geometric mean which is equal to $G = (LW)^{1/2} = (10 \cdot 6)^{1/2} = \sqrt{60} \approx 7.746$ feet. The arithmetic mean for this problem is $(10+6)/2 = 8$ feet and the geometric mean is less than the arithmetic mean (i.e., $7.746 < 8$ feet).

Example 2 – The volume of a room can be found by multiplying the length (L), depth (D), and height (H) together. In other words, $V = LDH$. When $L = 10$ feet, $D = 12$ feet, and $H = 8$ feet, then $V = 960$ cubic feet. What are the dimensions of a room that is a perfect cube with $L = D = H$ that has the same volume? The answer is the geometric mean, which is equal to $G = (LDH)^{1/3} = (10 \cdot 12 \cdot 8)^{1/3} = 960^{1/3} \approx 9.87$ feet. The arithmetic mean is $(10+12+8)/3 = 10$ feet and the geometric mean is less than the arithmetic mean (i.e., $9.87 < 10$ feet).

Example 3 – The geometric mean is an appropriate measure of the central tendency when an average growth rate is required. For example, suppose that in three successive years the return on an investment was 5%, 20%, and −4%. The "average" rate of return for these three years can be found as the geometric mean $G = (1.05 \cdot 1.20 \cdot 0.96)^{1/3} \approx 1.065$. Therefore, the average rate of return (Compound Annual Growth Rate or CAGR) is 6.5%. To prove this, we see that $1.065^3 \approx 1.05 \cdot 1.20 \cdot 0.96 = 1.2096$. The arithmetic means for these three values is $(1.05 + 1.2 + 0.96)/3 = 1.07$, which is more than the geometric mean.

The geometric mean is closely related to the CAGR. If sales grow from s_i to s_j over $n = j - i + 1$ years, the CAGR during this period is $(s_j / s_i)^{1/n} - 1$. For example, if sales grew from \$10 to \$16 million over a five-year period, the CAGR during this period is $(16/10)^{1/5} - 1 = 0.10$ or 10%.

The arithmetic mean is $A_n = \sum_{i=1}^{n} x_i$ and the geometric mean is $G_n = (x_1 \cdot x_2 \cdots x_n)^{1/n} = \left(\prod_{i=1}^{n} x_i \right)^{1/n}$, where x_i is the i-th value and n is the number of values. The geometric mean is always less than or equal to the arithmetic

---

[21] *http://elsmar.com/Forums/showthread.php?t=30789, June 14, 2010.*

mean (i.e., $G_n \leq A_n$). The arithmetic and geometric means are equal (i.e., $G_n = A_n$) only if $x_1 = x_2 = \ldots = x_n$. The logarithm of the geometric mean is the arithmetic mean of the log transformed data (i.e., $\log(G_n) = (1/n)\sum_{i=1}^{n} \log(x_i)$).

Excel – Excel uses the function GEOMEAN(*number1, number2,...*) for the geometric mean. The CAGR can be computed with the Excel function XIRR(*values, dates*).

See *Compounded Annual Growth Rate (CAGR), forecast error metrics, geometric progression, Internal Rate of Return (IRR), mean, skewness.*

geometric progression – A sequence of terms in which each term is a constant factor times the previous one.

The *n*-th term in a geometric progression is $d_n = \beta d_{n-1}$ (in recursive form) and $d_n = \beta^n d_0$ (in closed form). The β parameter is called the common ratio and is defined as $\beta = d_n / d_{n-1}$. The example below has $d_0 = 100$ and $\beta = 0.8$. In this example, $d_6 = \beta d_5 \approx 0.8 \cdot 32.77 \approx 26.21$ and $d_6 = d_0\beta^6 \approx 26.21$ (values are rounded).

Term index n	0	1	2	3	4	5	6
Value d_n	100.00	80.00	64.00	51.20	40.96	32.77	26.21
Finite sum, S_n		80.00	144.00	195.20	236.16	268.93	295.14

When $|\beta| < 1$, the sum of a geometric progression (a geometric series) has a closed-form expression. The sum of the first *n* terms (after term 0) is $S_n = d_1 + d_2 + \ldots + d_n = \beta d_0 + \beta^2 d_0 + \ldots + \beta^n d_0$. Multiplying both sides by β yields $\beta S_n = \beta^2 d_0 + \beta^3 d_0 + \ldots + \beta^{n+1} d_0$, and then subtracting this new equation from the first one yields $S_n - \beta S_n = \beta d_0 - \beta^{n+1} d_0$, which simplifies to $(1-\beta)S_n = d_0\beta(1-\beta^n)$. Given that $\beta < 1$, it is clear that $1 - \beta \neq 0$, which means it is possible to divide both sides by $1 - \beta$, which yields $S_n = d_0\beta(1-\beta^n)/(1-\beta)$. At the limit as $n \to \infty$, $\beta^n \to 0$ and the infinite sum (after term 0) is $S_\infty = d_0\beta/(1-\beta)$. In summary, the sum of an infinite geometric progression (starting at $n = 1$) is $S_\infty = d_0\beta/(1-\beta)$ and the finite sum of the first *n* terms is $S_n = d_0\beta(1-\beta^n)/(1-\beta)$. The finite sum from terms *m* to *n* is then $S_{m,n} = d_0(\beta^{n+1} - \beta^m)/(\beta-1)$.

For the above example, the infinite sum is $S_\infty = d_0\beta/(1-\beta) = 100 \cdot 0.8/(1-0.2) = 400$ and the sum of the first six terms (after term 0) is $S_6 = d_0\beta(1-\beta^6)/(1-\beta) = 100 \cdot 0.8 \cdot (1-0.8^6)/(1-0.8) \approx 295.14$.

The initial value (d_0) is called the scale factor and the constant factor (β) is called the common ratio. The sequence of values ($d_0, d_1, \ldots, d_n$) is called a geometric progression and the sum of a geometric progression ($d_0 + d_1 + \ldots + d_n$) is called a geometric series. The product of a geometric progression is $\prod_{i=0}^{n} d_0\beta^i = (d_1 d_n)^{(n+1)/2}$ if $\beta > 0$ and $d_0 > 0$.

See *all-time demand, exponential smoothing, geometric mean.*

geometric series – See *geometric progression.*

Getting Things Done (GTD) – A philosophy for managing a personal task list, filing system, and e-mails in a disciplined way; the name of a popular book on personal time management by David Allen (2001).

See the entry for the two-minute rule for what is probably Allen's most famous principle.

See *personal operations management, two-minute rule, two-second rule, tyranny of the urgent.*

Global Data Synchronization Network (GDSN) – An initiative designed to overcome product data inaccuracies and increase efficiencies among trading partners and their supply chains.

GDSN is a network of certified data pools that enable product information to be captured and exchanged in a secure environment conforming to global standards. Different versions of product information in the supply chain can cause serious business issues. Global Data Synchronization (GDS) ensures that trading partners always use the same version of the data. This empowers the supplier to manage the information flow in the supply chain and not rely on the trading partner or other third parties to manipulate their data. The foundational principles of GDS include:

- Product data is updated consistently between trading partners.
- Data is validated against standards and business rules.
- Trading partners classify their products in a common, standardized way.
- Trading partners have a single point of entry through their chosen data pool, reducing the cost of using multiple vendors.
- The uniqueness of items is guaranteed through the GS1 Global Registry.

The standards body that governs the GDSN is GS1, an organization dedicated to the design and implementation of global standards and solutions to improve the efficiency and visibility of supply and demand chains globally and across sectors. The GS1 system of standards is the most widely used supply chain standards system in the world and has been used for more than 30 years in multiple sectors and industries.

Global Positioning System (GPS) – A satellite-based technology that can be used to determine the current latitude and longitude for a device.

GPS technology can be a very helpful tool for collecting information in a transportation system.

See *logistics*, *telematics*.

global sourcing – See *sourcing*.

goal tree – See *Y-tree*.

gold parts – A phrase used in the Theory of Constraints for parts that have passed through the bottleneck.

These parts are much more valuable because the organization has invested time in them from its most valuable resource (the bottleneck).

See *inspection*, *Theory of Constraints (TOC)*.

golden zone – See *forward stocking area*.

Goldratt – See *Theory of Constraints (TOC)*.

Gompertz Curve – See *logistic curve*.

Good Manufacturing Practices (GMP) – Quality guidelines and general principles for producing and testing products developed by the U.S. Food and Drug Administration (the FDA) covering pharmaceuticals, diagnostics, foods, and medical devices; also called Current Good Manufacturing Practices (CGMP).

All guidelines follow the following basic principles:

- Manufacturing processes are clearly defined and controlled. All critical processes are validated to ensure consistency and compliance with specifications.
- Manufacturing processes are controlled and any changes to the process are evaluated. Changes that have an impact on the quality of the drug are validated as necessary.
- Instructions and procedures are written in clear and unambiguous language.
- Operators are trained to carry out and document procedures.
- Records are made manually or with instruments that demonstrate that all the steps required by the defined procedures and instructions were, in fact, taken and that the quantity and quality of the drug was as expected. Deviations are investigated and documented.
- Records of manufacture (including distribution) that enable the complete history of a batch to be traced are retained in a comprehensible and accessible form.
- The distribution of the drugs minimizes any risk to their quality.
- A system is available for recalling any batch of drug from sale or supply.
- Complaints about marketed drugs are examined, the causes of quality defects are investigated, and appropriate measures are taken with respect to the defective drugs and to prevent recurrence.

Adapted from http://en.wikipedia.org/wiki/Good_manufacturing_practice (March 19, 2011).

See *process validation*, *quality management*.

goodness-of-fit tests – See *chi-square goodness of fit test*, *Kolmogorov-Smirnov test (KS test)*.

goodwill – (1) In any business context: The value of a good relationship between a business and its customers. (2) In a business acquisitions context: An intangible asset equal to the cost to acquire a business over the fair market value of all other assets. (3) In an interpersonal context: A cheerful, friendly, kind attitude toward others.

In any business context, goodwill is the **reputational capital** of the firm. Goodwill is lost when the company cannot fulfill its service promises, runs out of inventory, or has poor product or service quality. Lost goodwill can lead to lost sales, lower margins, and loss of brand equity. Goodwill is very difficult to measure.

In a business acquisition context, goodwill is the difference between the fair market value of a company's assets (less its liabilities) and the market price or asking price for the overall company. In other words, goodwill is the amount in excess of the firm's book value that a purchaser would be willing to pay to acquire it. If a sale is realized, the new owner of the company lists the difference between book value and the price paid as goodwill in financial statements.

See *Economic Value Added (EVA)*, *financial performance metrics*, *quality management*, *safety stock*, *service level*, *stockout*.

GPS – See *Global Positioning System (GPS)*.

gravity flow rack – See *flow rack*.

gravity model for competitive retail store location – A mathematical model for locating one or more new retail stores relative to the competing stores in a region.

The basic concept of the gravity model is that the "gravitational pull" for a store on customers is directly proportional to the size of the store and inversely proportional to the travel time squared. In other words, customers will be attracted to larger close-by stores much more than they will be to smaller far-away stores. This model is an application of **Newton's Law**, which states that the gravitational pull between two planets is directly proportional to their mass and inversely proportional to the square of the distance between them.

The goal is to find the best location for one or more new stores from a set of potential locations, assuming that the new stores will have to compete for customers with the other stores in the region. The model allocates the revenue in the market to each of the stores based on the "pull," which is a function of store size (bigger is better) and travel time (closer is much better). The model can be used to evaluate all reasonable alternatives and select the store locations that maximize the total expected revenue.

The algorithm allocates all revenue in a region to the m stores. Store j is characterized by its size S_j and by a competitive index c_j, which is used to adjust for weak and strong competitors in the market. The region has n population areas (census blocks). The travel time from census block i to store j is t_{ij}. The "pull" for store j with competitive index c_j on census block i is directly proportional to the size of the store and inversely proportional to the travel time to the ρ power. Pull, therefore, is defined as $pull_{ij} = c_j S_j / t_{ij}^{\rho}$. The ρ parameter can be determined empirically, but is usually close to $\rho = 2$.

The probability that a resident of census block i will shop at store j is the normalized pull, which is given by $p_{ij} = \dfrac{pull_{ij}}{\sum_{k=1}^{m} pull_{ik}}$. Census block i has m_j customers with average revenue per customer of r_i. The expected revenue for store j, therefore, is $R_j = \sum_{i=1}^{n} p_{ij} r_i m_i$. The best location for a store (or set of stores) can be found by using the model to evaluate all reasonable alternative configurations and selecting the one that has the largest expected revenue.

See *center-of-gravity model for facility location*, *facility location*, *great circle distance*, *numeric-analytic location model*.

gray market – See *gray market reseller*.

gray market reseller – A broker that sells products through distribution channels other than those authorized or intended by the manufacturer; spelled "grey" outside the United States[22].

---

[22] *"Gray" with an "a" is used in America and "grey" with an "e" is used in England and everywhere else outside the U.S.*

Gray market resellers typically buy used equipment or clearance products on the open market and resell them to end-user customers at prices lower than those desired by the manufacturer. These resellers sell outside the normal distribution channels, typically have no relationship with the manufacturer, and typically provide no aftersales service. In some cases, the warranty is no longer valid.

Gray market products are usually (but not always) legal and are usually (but not always) bought and sold at prices lower than the prices set by the manufacturer or regulatory agency. These are often products that were sold in one national market and then exported and sold in another national market at a lower price. For example, a dealer might buy a car at a reduced price in one country and then sell it in another country at a lower price.

See the *diversion* entry for more information on the problems with this practice.

See *broker, diversion*.

great circle distance – The shortest distance between any two points on a sphere.

Given that the earth is approximately spherical, the great circle distance can be used to estimate the travel distance between any two points defined by their **latitude** and **longitude coordinates**. Now that Global Positioning Systems (GPS) and geographical databases are widely available, the great circle distance is a practical means to estimate distances for a wide variety of logistics and transportation planning problems.

The Spherical Law of Cosines computes the **great circle angle** (a_{ij}) between the points i and j on the earth using $a_{ij} = \text{acos}(\sin(x_i)\sin(x_j) + \cos(x_i)\cos(x_j)\cos(y_j - y_i))$, where (x_i, y_i) and (x_j, y_j) are the latitude and longitude coordinates for the two points expressed in radians. Convert the great circle angle into a great circle distance using $d_{ij} = r \cdot a_{ij}$, where r is the average radius of the earth, which is $r \approx 3958.76$ miles or $r \approx 6371.01$ km. If latitude and longitude are expressed in hours, minutes, and seconds ($h{:}m{:}s$), convert them to decimal degrees using *decimal_degrees = h + m*/60 + *s*/60/60, and then convert to radians using *radians = π · decimal_degrees*/180.

The Excel formula for the Spherical Law of Cosines is r*ACOS(SIN(x1)*SIN(x2)+ COS(x1)*COS(x2)*COS(y2-y1)) for earth radius *r* and coordinates (x1,y1) and (x2,y2) expressed in radians. When using the arc cosine function (ACOS), the absolute value of the argument must be less than one. It is useful, therefore, to implement this distance function in VBA to conduct this check. The following VBA code developed by this author implements the Law of Cosines great circle distance function in VBA using a derived arc cosine. It is important to use double precision for all variables in this code.

```
Global Const pi As Double = 3.14159265358979
Function distf(ByVal x1 As Double, ByVal y1 As Double,
    ByVal x2 As Double, ByVal y2 As Double) As Double     ' input lat/long data in decimal degrees
Const r_miles As Double = 3958.76  ' average radius of the earth in miles.
Dim a As Double
' convert decimal degrees to radians for lat/long coordinates (x1, y1) and (x2, y2).
    x1 = CDbl(x1 * pi / 180): y1 = CDbl(y1 * pi / 180): x2 = CDbl(x2 * pi / 180): y2 = CDbl(y2 * pi / 180)
    a = Sin(x1) * Sin(x2) + Cos(x1) * Cos(x2) * Cos(y2 - y1)   'apply law of cosines
    If a < -1 Then a = -1        ' the argument for the arc cosine cannot be less than -1.
    If a > 1 Then a = 1          ' the argument for the arc cosine cannot be greater than 1.
    distf = Atn(-a / Sqr(-a * a + 1)) + pi / 2      ' compute the arc cosine of a in radians.
    distf = r_miles * distf       ' convert radians to miles.
End Function
```

The above VBA code finds that the distance between Seattle (47:36:00,122:20:00) and Miami (25:45:00, 80:11:00) is 2732.473 miles and the distance between the Nashville International Airport (N 36°7.2', W 86°40.2') and the Los Angeles International Airport (N 33°56.4', W 118°24.0') is 1793.555 miles.

Love, Morris, and Wesolowsky (1988) suggest inflating intracity travel distances by a factor of roughly 1.18 to account for the fact that travel distances between intracity points is, on average, greater than the straight-line distance due to road structures.

See *facility location, gravity model for competitive retail store location, Manhattan square distance, numeric-analytic location model*.

green belt – See *lean sigma*.

green manufacturing – Manufacturing that is environmentally conscious and ideally more profitable; closely related to "sustainability."

The number of computers and other electronic devices on our planet appears to be increasing according to Moore's Law and are having a negative impact on our environment. According to Greenpeace, demand for new technology creates 4,000 tons of waste an hour, which often ends up in large piles in India, Africa, and China.

With take-back programs, customers return used technology to manufacturers that recycle the parts for new products. Many European nations have legal requirements for return logistics. The U.S. has few such laws, but many firms are voluntarily implementing such programs. For example, in 2004, Dell Computer recovered 40,000 tons of unwanted equipment for recycling, up 93% from 2005.

Ideally, organizations can improve the environment and improve their profits at the same time. Here are several good examples adapted from the article www.fastcompany.com/magazine/120/50-ways-to-green-your-business.html (October 25, 2007):

- **General Mills** – In the past two years, General Mills has turned its solid waste into profits. Take its oat hulls, a Cheerios by-product. The company used to pay to have them hauled off, but realized they could be burned as fuel. Now customers compete to buy the waste. In 2006, General Mills recycled 86% of its solid waste, earning more selling the waste than it spent on disposal. In 2006, General Mills redesigned packaging and shaved off 20% of the paperboard box without shrinking contents. The result was 500 fewer distribution trucks on the road each year.
- **General Electric** – Trains were already the cleanest way to move massive amounts of freight long distances, but General Electric raised the game with its Evolution locomotives, diesel engines launched in 2005 that cut fuel consumption by 5% and emissions by 40% compared to locomotives built just a year earlier. GE has plans for a GE hybrid diesel-electric locomotive that captures energy from braking (like the Toyota Prius) and improves mileage by another 10%. According to GE, the energy dissipated in braking a 207-ton locomotive during the course of a year is enough to power 160 homes for the same period.
- **Walmart** – Walmart is providing funding to the biggest truck manufacturers (ArvinMeritor, Eaton, International, and Peterbilt) to develop the first heavy-duty diesel-hybrid 18-wheeler. Walmart has pushed the liquid-laundry-detergent industry to cut bottle sizes by 50% or more by concentrating the liquid. Thus, Unilever's triple-concentrated All Small & Mighty detergent has saved 1.3 million gallons of diesel fuel, 10-million pounds of plastic resin, and 80 million square feet of cardboard since 2005. This fall, Procter & Gamble is converting its entire collection of liquids to double concentration.
- **C3 Presents** – Austin-based concert promoter C3 Presents made news when it banned Styrofoam cups from the sixth annual Austin City Limits Music Festival. Following the model the company created for Lollapalooza, C3 took a holistic approach to greening nearly every aspect of ACL, from bamboo-based concert T-shirts to gel sanitizer in the bathrooms to bio-diesel power generators.
- **Philadelphia Eagles** – Starting in 2006, the team's "Go Green" environmental campaign has its stadium cleaning crew making two full sweeps after each game, one to pick up recyclables and another for trash.
- **Tesco** – Some retailers have introduced product labels that encourage customers to weigh their carbon. The British grocery giant Tesco has a program to label all 70,000 of its products with carbon breakdowns.
- **Unilever** – Unilever has reconfigured the plastic bottles for its billion-dollar Suave shampoo brand, saving the plastic equivalent of about 15 million bottles a year.

The concept of the "green supply chain" extends green manufacturing concepts to the entire supply chain. Using green supply chain concepts, organizations find ways to reduce emissions, avoid toxic wastes, reduce total waste, improve energy efficiency, and otherwise improve their impact on the environment.

See *cap and trade, carbon footprint, energy audit, Moore's Law, remanufacturing, reverse logistics, sustainability, triple bottom line.*

green supply chain – See *green manufacturing.*

greenfield – The concept of building a new plant (or other facility) in a new location, which is often a field with no existing buildings on it.

This is often an opportunity for the firm to start with a fresh perspective on facility layout, process technology, and organization. In contrast, older facilities and land are sometimes called **brownfields**. These are often abandoned, idled, or under-used industrial or commercial facilities. Some brownfield locations also have problems with industrial contamination.

>See *facility location.*

gross profit margin – An ambiguous term that relates gross profit to sales, measured as (1) a dollar amount (i.e., revenue less cost of goods sold), or (2) a percentage (i.e., 100(gross profit margin in dollars)/revenue); also called gross margin.

>The first definition is the margin in dollars, while the second definition is the margin as a percentage. The second definition is sometimes called the gross margin percentage.

>See *cost of goods sold.*

gross requirement – The total demand for an item, including both independent and dependent demand.

>Unlike the gross requirement, the net requirements consider both on-hand inventory and open orders.

>See *Materials Requirements Planning (MRP).*

gross weight – (1) Packaging context: The total weight of a package (including packaging) and its contents. (2) Shipping/logistics context: The total weight of a vehicle and its contents.

>See *logistics, net weight, tare weight.*

group technology – (1) A methodology for classifying parts (items) based on similar production processes and required resources. (2) A manufacturing cell (cluster of machines, equipment, and workers) dedicated to making a set of parts that share similar routings.

>See *Computer Aided Design (CAD), cellular manufacturing.*

groupware – Software that helps groups of people work together on a common task; also called workgroup support systems, group support systems, and workflow software.

>Groupware supports communication, collaboration, and coordination and therefore can help improve productivity of people working in groups. Groupware functionality can include e-mail, group calendars, address books, video conferencing, audio conferencing, shared documents, shared databases, and task scheduling. Groupware is particularly helpful when the workers are not all in the same location. Friedman (2005) emphasized the importance of groupware (workflow software) in enabling firms to outsource.

>See *Decision Support System (DSS), outsourcing, project management.*

Growth-Share Matrix – See *cash cow.*

GTD – See *Getting Things Done (GTD).*

H

HACCP – See *Hazard Analysis & Critical Point Control (HACCP).*

half-life curve – A mathematical model that shows the relationship between a performance measure (such as defects) and the time required to reduce (cut) the performance measure in half. ✪

>The half-life curve was popularized by Ray Stata, founder of Analog Devices, Inc. (Stata 1989). Whereas the learning curve assumes that learning is driven by production volume, the half-life curve assumes that learning is driven by time. The half-life concept suggests that the performance measure will be cut in half every h periods, where h is a constant. For example, if the unit cost at time zero is $100 and the half-life is six months, the unit cost will be $50 at six months, $25 at 12 months, and so forth.

>Any performance variable with an ideal point of zero can be used in this model. For example, the performance variable could be cost/unit, time/unit, defects, cycle time, percent on-time delivery, etc.

>The basic equation for the half-life curve is $y(t) = ae^{bt}$, where $e \approx 2.718281$. The performance variable $y(t)$ is the performance at time t. The constants are $a = y(0)$ and $b = -\ln(2)/h$, where the half-life (in periods) is $h = -\ln(2)/b$. For example, if the half-life is 6 months, and the defect rate is 10% at time zero, at month 6 the defect rate should be 5%, and at month 12 the defect rate should be 2.5%.

>The graph below is an example of a half-life curve with parameters $h = 2$, $y(0) = 100$, and $b = -0.347$. Note that unlike the learning curve, the half-life curve is continuous and is defined for all values of t.

The easiest way to estimate b is to find the value that fits the first and last historical points $b = \ln(y(t)/y(0))/t$. A more accurate (but more complicated) approach for estimating b is to apply linear regression on transformed historical data. To apply linear regression, take the natural log transform of both sides of the half-life equation to find $\ln(y(t)) = \ln(a) + bt$, use linear regression to estimate the $\ln(a)$ and b parameters, and then use the model to estimate the performance variable at some time t in the future. Use the equation $h = -\ln(2)/b$ to estimate the half-life from the b parameter. This regression approach will not work if any $y(t)$ is zero and is also adversely affected by autocorrelation in the data.

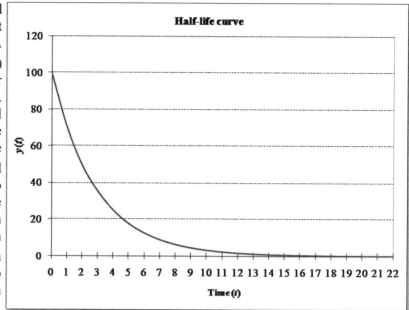

See *learning curve, learning organization, linear regression, Moore's Law, operations performance metrics.*

handoff – A point in a process where work or information is transferred from one individual or organization to another; also written hand-off.

From a lean manufacturing perspective, handoffs can lead to waste because each handoff has the potential to lose information and create a queue of materials waiting to be picked up. Reducing the number of handoffs will usually reduce the amount of information that is lost, reduce the number of queues, and reduce queue time, which results in better quality, service, and cycle time.

Handoffs can also present problems because the reward systems in different organizations and for different people might not be the same. For example, in a service organization, the customer-facing organization is usually rewarded based on customer satisfaction, but the back-office organization might be rewarded based on efficiency. Work enlargement seeks to combine these jobs into one job so that proper trade-offs can be made between customer service and efficiency.

See *addition principle, cellular manufacturing, focused factory, job enlargement, process map, service quality, single point of contact.*

hard currency – A freely convertible currency that is not expected to depreciate in value in the foreseeable future.

Hawthorne Effect – The concept that the act of showing attention to workers encourages better job performance.

The Hawthorne Studies (experiments) were conducted from 1927 to 1932 at the Western Electric Hawthorne Works in Chicago, where Harvard Business School professor Elton Mayo examined the relationships between work conditions and productivity. Mayo wanted to study the effects of fatigue and monotony on productivity and how rest breaks, work hours, temperature, and humidity affected productivity. In the process, Mayo stumbled upon the concept that the mere act of showing concern for people often spurs them on to better job performance. (Note: Several different interpretations of the Hawthorne Effect can be found in the literature.)

For example, if the leadership of an organization gives management training to a new employee, the employee will feel valued and will likely be motivated to work harder. The motivation is independent of the particular skills or knowledge gained from the training. This is the Hawthorne Effect at work.

The Hawthorne Effect has been called the "Somebody Upstairs Cares Syndrome." To generalize the concept, when people have a sense of belonging and being part of a team, they are more productive.

See *human resources, job design.*

Hazard Analysis & Critical Point Control (HACCP) – Regulations issued by the U.S. Food and Drug Administration (FDA) to drive standardization in food safety.

Concepts center on building quality into food manufacturing processes rather than relying only on inspections and sampling. HACCP involves seven principles:

1. **Analyze hazards** – Identify potential hazards associated with a food and establish measures to control those hazards. The hazard could be biological (e.g., microbes), chemical (e.g., toxin), or physical (e.g., ground glass or metal fragments).

2. **Identify critical control points** – These are points in food production from the raw state through processing and shipping to consumption by the consumer at which the potential hazard can be controlled or eliminated. Examples are cooking, cooling, packaging, and metal detection.

3. **Establish preventive measures with critical limits for each control point** – For a cooked food, for example, this might include setting the minimum cooking temperature and time required to ensure the elimination of any harmful microbes.

4. **Establish procedures to monitor the critical control points** – Such procedures might include determining how and by whom cooking time and temperature should be monitored.

5. **Establish corrective actions to be taken when monitoring shows that a critical limit has not been met** – For example, food should be reprocessed or disposed if the minimum cooking temperature is not met.

6. **Establish procedures to verify that the system is working properly** – For example, testing time and temperature recording devices should be used to verify that a cooking unit is working properly.

7. **Establish effective recordkeeping to document the HACCP system** – This includes records of hazards and their control methods, the monitoring of safety requirements, and actions taken to correct potential problems.

See *error proofing, Failure Mode and Effects Analysis (FMEA), hazmat, sustainability*.

hazmat – A hazardous material; also called HAZMAT and dangerous goods.

Hazmat or HAZMAT is any solid, liquid, or gas that can harm people, other living organisms, property, or the environment. The term "hazardous material" is used in this context almost exclusively in the U.S. The equivalent term in the rest of the English-speaking world is dangerous goods. A hazardous material may be radioactive, flammable, explosive, toxic, corrosive, biohazardous, oxidizing, asphyxiating, or allergenic, or it may have other characteristics that make it hazardous in specific circumstances (source: http://en.wikipedia.org/wiki/HAZMAT, October 1, 2006).

See *Hazard Analysis & Critical Point Control (HACCP), sustainability*.

headhaul – A carrier's primary trip, bringing a shipment to its destination.

See *logistics*.

hedging – Any transaction designed to reduce financial risk.

Hedging usually deals with reducing the risk of loss from price fluctuations. Hedging is usually done for defensive purposes. It is often a combination of "bets" (transactions) such that if one bet loses, another wins (i.e., taking two positions that will offset each other if prices change). In operations, hedging is commonly used to reduce the risk of a price increase for raw materials. For example, Southwest Airlines, the only major airline to remain consistently profitable shortly after the 9/11 tragedy in 2001, used a hedging strategy that allowed it to buy jet fuel for 38% less than the market price (Schlangenstein 2005). Unlike arbitrage, a hedge does not carry the implication of having an edge. Note that the word "hedge" can be used as a noun or a verb.

See *arbitrage*.

heijunka – A Japanese technique used to smooth production over time; also called load leveling, linearity, and stabilizing the schedule.

平準化

HEI JUN KA
Production Smoothing

Dennis (2002) defined heijunka as "distribution of volume and mix evenly over time." The Japanese word heijunka (pronounced "hey-june-kah") literally means to "make flat and level." Taiichi Ohno (1978) at Toyota defined heijunka as **production leveling**. Heijunka is considered one of the main pillars of the Toyota Production System (TPS) and is closely related to lean production. It is very similar to the concepts of production smoothing and load leveling. The following is a simple example of production smoothing.

Week	Demand		Weekly production
1	900		500
2	200	Average = 500 units/week →	500
3	700		500
4	200		500
5	500		550
6	500	Average = 550 units/week →	550
7	400		550
8	800		550

One of the main concepts for smoothing production is frequent changes of the model mix to be run on a given line. Instead of running large batches of one model after another, TPS advocates small batches of many models over short periods of time. This is called **mixed model assembly**. This requires quick changeovers, but results in smaller lots of finished goods that are shipped frequently.

The main tool for heijunka is a visual scheduling board known as a heijunka box, which is generally a wall schedule with rows dedicated to each product (or product family) and columns for each time period (e.g., 20-minute periods). Colored production control kanban cards representing individual jobs are placed in the slots in proportion to the number of items to be built of a given product type during a time interval. The heijunka box makes it easy to see what types of jobs are queued for production. Workers remove the kanban cards from the front of the schedule as they process the jobs.

The **heijunka box** consistently levels demand by short time increments (20 minutes in this example). This is in contrast to the mass-production practice of releasing work for one shift, one day, or even a week to the production floor. Similarly, the heijunka box consistently levels demand by mix. For example, it ensures that Product C and Product D are produced in a steady ratio in small batch sizes.

Production process stability introduced by leveling makes it considerably easier to introduce lean techniques ranging from standard work to continuous flow cells. Muda (waste) declines as mura (unevenness in productivity and quality) and muri (overburden of machines, managers, and production associates) decline. When processes are leveled in volume and mix, employees are no longer overburdened, customers get better on-time delivery, and manufacturers reduce cost when muda, mura, and muri are reduced.

Although production leveling tools can be used to level the load (hours of work for the factory), demand management tools can be used to level the demand, which makes it easier to level the load.

See *chase strategy, demand management, dispatching rules, job shop scheduling, kanban, lean thinking, level strategy, load, load leveling, mixed model assembly, takt time*.

heijunka box – See *heijunka*.

help desk – A resource that provides problem-solving advice for internal or external customers.

Corporations often provide help desk support to their customers via toll-free phone numbers, faxes, websites, and e-mail. The help desk is often the part of a call center that handles support for technical products. Help desk workers sometimes use decision support software and knowledge bases to answer questions.

See *call center, fulfillment, knowledge management, service management*.

Herbie – The bottleneck in a process.

The question, "Where's your Herbie?" is asking, "Where is your bottleneck?" This is based on the popular Goldratt Institute film and book entitled *The Goal* (Goldratt 1992), where one boy (Herbie) in the Boy Scout troop slowed down the entire troop on a long march through the woods. The teaching point here was that organizations need to "go find their Herbie and help him with his load."

See *bottleneck, Theory of Constraints (TOC)*.

heuristic – A simple rule of thumb (procedure) used to solve a problem.

For example, when a vehicle schedule is created, the next location selected for the vehicle might be the one closest to the last one selected. This is called the "closest customer" heuristic. Heuristics often produce very good and sometimes even the mathematically best (optimal) solutions. However, the problem with heuristics is that users seldom know how far the heuristic solution is from the optimal solution. In other words, a heuristic procedure might produce a good solution, but the solution is not guaranteed to be the optimal (best) solution. All heuristic procedures are said to be algorithms; however, not all algorithms are heuristics, because some algorithms always guarantee an optimal (mathematically best) solution. For some heuristics, it is possible to mathematically derive the "worst case" performance, the average case performance, or both.

See *algorithm, genetic algorithm, operations research (OR), optimization, simulated annealing, Traveling Salesperson Problem (TSP).*

hidden factory – A term for either rework or non-value-adding transactions in a system.

Rework – Armand Feigenbaum, a well-known quality expert, coined the term "hidden factory" to describe the vast amount of work needed to correct the mistakes made by others. He estimated that the hidden factory might be as much as 40% of the total cost (Feigenbaum 2004).

Non-value-added transactions – Miller and Vollmann (1985) identified a different type of "hidden factory" that processed vast numbers of internal transactions that added little or no value to customers. This is often true when a firm reduces lotsizes to move toward lean production without using visual control systems.

Eliminating both types of hidden factories (waste) is a key part of lean thinking.

See *Activity Based Costing (ABC), lean thinking, rework, yield.*

High Performance Work Systems (HPWS) – A form of workgroup that typically emphasizes high employee involvement, empowerment, and self-management.

HPWS generally incorporate the following features:

- More job complexity, multi-tasking, and multi-skilling.
- Increased employee qualifications.
- Ongoing skill formation through enterprise training.
- A minimum of hierarchy.

- Greater horizontal communication and distribution of responsibility (often through teams).
- Compensation incentives for performance and skill acquisition.
- Increased focus on "core activities."

Firms that use HPWS often seek to improve organization performance through six synergistic strategies:

- Leadership that empowers others.
- Relentless focus on strategy and results.
- Open sharing of relevant information.

- Borderless sharing of power.
- Team-based design.
- Teamwork reinforced through rewards.

Unfortunately, the definition of HPWS is ambiguous, and practices vary widely between firms. HPWS is closely related to employee involvement, employee empowerment, high involvement, people involvement, high commitment systems, mutual gains enterprises, socio-technical systems, participative management, self-management, boss-less systems, self-directed work teams, and empowered work teams.

Adapted from a contribution by Aleksandar Kolekeski, ISPPI Institute, Skopje, Macedonia, kolekeski@msn.com, September 19, 2005.

See *empowerment, human resources, job design, New Product Development (NPD), organizational design, productivity, self-directed work team.*

histogram – A graphical approach for displaying frequency data as a bar chart.

Histograms can be shown vertically or horizontally. The histogram is one of the seven tools of quality. See the *Pareto Chart* entry to see an example of a vertical histogram.

See *bar chart, Pareto Chart, seven tools of quality.*

hockey stick effect – A pattern of sales or shipments that increase dramatically at the end of the week, month, or quarter.

This pattern looks like a hockey stick because it is low at the beginning of the period and high at the end. The hockey stick effect is nearly always a logical result of reward systems based on sales or shipments. The large changes cause variance in the system, which often results in increased inventories, stockouts, overtime, idle capacity, frustrated workers, and other significant problems. Clearly, the best solution is to change the reward system to motivate workers to produce and sell at the market demand rate.

One creative potential solution is to have different sales regions with offset quarters so one region has a quarter ending in January, another ending in February, etc. Another creative solution is to shorten the reporting reward period from quarters to months or even weeks. This gives the organization less time to change between the extreme priorities, and therefore provides motivation to avoid the hockey stick.

See *carrying charge, carrying cost, production planning, seasonality.*

holding cost – See *carrying charge, carrying cost*.

hoshin planning – A systematic planning methodology developed in Japan for setting goals and aligning the organization to meet those goals; also called hoshin kanri and policy deployment. 方針 管理

Hoshin is short for "hoshin kanri." The word "hoshin" is from "ho," which means direction, and "shin," which means needle. Therefore, the word "hoshin" could translate into direction needle or compass. The word "kanri" is from "kan," which means control, and "ri," which means reason or logic. Taken altogether, hoshin kanri means management and control of the organization's direction needle or focus. Hoshin planning is like a management compass that points everyone in the organization toward a common goal.

Hoshin kanri planning passes (deploys) policies and targets down the management hierarchy. At each level, the policy is translated into policies, targets, and actions for the next level down. "Catchball" is played between each level to ensure that the plans are well-understood and can be executed (see the entry *catchball*).

Hoshin operates at two levels: (1) the strategic planning level to define long-range objectives and (2) the daily management level to address routine aspects of business operations.

Hoshin plans should be regularly reviewed against actual performance. This review can be organized in a "hoshin review table," which should show the owner, time frame, performance metrics, target, and results. Any difference between the target and actual results should be explained. The review tables should cascade upward.

The **X-Matrix**, the main tool of hoshin planning, works backward from desired **results**, to **strategies**, to **tactics**, to **processes**. See the simple example below. The planning process begins with the results, which are driven by strategies, which are driven by tactics, which are achieved by process improvements. The "correlation" cells identify causal relationships using the symbols: ◉ = strong relationship, O = important relationship, and △ = weak relationship. The accountability columns indicate roles and responsibilities for individuals, teams, departments, and suppliers. See Jackson (2006) for more details.

Simple X-Matrix example

The X-Matrix is similar to Management by Objectives (MBO), developed by Drucker (1954), except that it focuses more on organizational rather than individual goals. The X-Matrix is also similar to the **strategy**

mapping concepts developed by Kaplan and Norton (1990), the Y-tree concept used at 3M, and the causal mapping tools as presented by Hill (2011c). A strategy map requires the causal linkages: learning & growth → internal → customer → financial. In contrast, the X-Matrix requires the causal linkages: process → tactics → strategies → results. In this author's view, an X-Matrix is more general than a strategy map, a Y-tree is more general than an X-Matrix, and a causal map is more general than a Y-tree. However, some industry experts argue that hoshin planning is unlike other strategic planning methods because it has more accountability and more "catchball" interaction between levels in the organization.

See *alignment, balanced scorecard, catchball, causal map, lean thinking, Management by Objectives (MBO), mission statement, PDCA (Plan-Do-Check-Act), strategy map, Y-tree.*

house of quality – See *Quality Function Deployment (QFD).*

hub-and-spoke system – A distribution system used by railroads, motor carriers, and airlines to consolidate passengers or shipments to maximize equipment efficiency.

Many passenger airlines in North America, such as Delta and United, have hub-and-spoke networks, where the hub is a central airport and the spokes are the routes that bring passengers to and from the hub. In contrast, the direct route (or point-to-point) system does not use a central hub airport. In North America, Southwest Airlines is an example of a direct route system. The hub-and-spoke system is an important distribution strategy. For example, FedEx, a delivery service, has a hub in Memphis, with all FedEx shipments going through this hub.

See *consolidation, logistics.*

human resources – (1) The employees in an organization. (2) The organizational unit (department) charged with the responsibility of managing employee-related processes such as hiring, orientation, training, payroll, benefits, compliance with government regulations, performance management (performance management, performance reviews), employee relations, employee communications, and resource planning; sometimes called the personnel organization; often abbreviated HR.

See *absorptive capacity, addition principle, back office, business process outsourcing, cost center, cross-training, delegation, division of labor, empowerment, Enterprise Resources Planning (ERP), ergonomics, gainsharing, Hawthorne Effect, High Performance Work Systems (HPWS), job design, job enlargement, job rotation, labor grade, lean sigma, learning curve, learning organization, multiplication principle, on-the-job training (OJT), operations management (OM), organizational design, outsourcing, pay for skill, productivity, RACI Matrix, Results-Only Work Environment (ROWE), scientific management, self-directed work team, Service Profit Chain, service quality, standardized work, subtraction principle, unfair labor practice, value chain, work measurement, work simplification, workforce agility.*

hypergeometric distribution – A discrete probability distribution widely used in quality control and auditing.

The hypergeometric distribution is useful for determining the probability of exactly x defective units found in a random sample of n units drawn from a population of size N that actually contains m defective units. It is a particularly useful distribution for acceptance sampling and auditing. The normal, Poisson, and binomial distributions are often used as approximations for the hypergeometric distribution.

The hypergeometric distribution can be used to create confidence limits on the number of errors in a population based on a sample. For example, an auditor can take a sample and then conclude with a 95% confidence level that the true percentage of errors in the population is no more than p percent. The auditor can also use this distribution to estimate the sample size required to achieve a desired confidence limit. Most statistics textbooks recommend using the normal distribution for the proportion defective; however, this is an approximation for the hypergeometric distribution and will be inaccurate when the error rate is small.

Parameters: Population size N and sample size n.

Probability mass function: $P(X = x) = p(x, N, n, m) = \binom{m}{x}\binom{N-m}{n-x} \bigg/ \binom{N}{n}$, where x is the number of successes in the sample, n is the sample size, m is the number of successes in the population, and N is the size of the population. The distribution function is simply the summation of the mass function.

Statistics: Range $[a,b]$ where $a = \max(0, n-(N-m))$ and $b = \min(m,n)$, mean πn, variance $\pi(1-\pi)n(N-n)/(N-1)$, where $\pi = m/N$. The mode has no closed form.

Graph: A jar has a population of $N = 100$ balls, with $m = 20$ red balls and $(N - m) = 80$ white balls. Samples of $n = 5$ balls are drawn randomly from the jar. The graph below is the hypergeometric probability mass function for x, which is the number of red balls found in a sample.

Excel: In Excel, the probability mass function is HYPGEOMDIST(x, n, m, N), where x is the number of successes in the sample, n is the size of the sample, m is the number of successes in the population, and N is the size of the population. Excel does not have distribution or inverse functions for the hypergeometric distribution. The natural log of the gamma function (GAMMALN(x)) is useful for software implementation of this distribution. In Excel 2010, HYPGEOMDIST has been replaced by HYPGEOM.DIST, but still uses the same arguments.

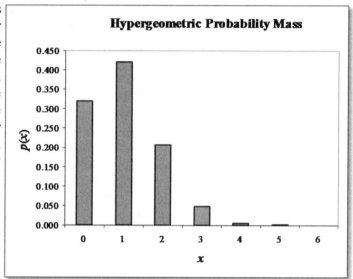

Relationships with other distributions: The standard deviation for the hypergeometric distribution is equal to that of the binomial distribution times the finite population correction factor (i.e., $\sigma_h = \sigma_b \sqrt{(N - n)/(N - 1)}$). Therefore, when the population size N is large compared to the sample size (i.e., $N \gg n$), the correction factor is close to 1 (i.e., $\sqrt{(N - n)/(N - 1)} \approx 1$) and the hypergeometric distribution can be approximated reasonably well with a binomial distribution with parameters n (number of trials) and $p = m/N$. A reasonable rule of thumb is that the hypergeometric distribution may be approximated by the binomial when $N/n \geq 20$. (The binomial differs from the hypergeometric distribution in that sampling is done with replacement.) The Poisson distribution is often used as an approximation for the hypergeometric in the auditing profession. The normal distribution can be used as an approximation for the hypergeometric when $N/n \geq 50$ and $np(1-p) \geq 10$.

See *binomial distribution, gamma function, Poisson distribution, probability distribution, probability mass function, sampling, Statistical Quality Control (SQC)*.

hypothesis – In the operations management context, a suggested explanation for a problem; a statement of what could be true; a proposition for how a problem might be solved.

A hypothesis consists of a statement of what could be true, often with some accompanied explanation and justification. A hypothesis requires more work by the investigator to attempt to disprove it. When attempting to address an operations problem, the best consultants work with their clients to quickly generate a large number of hypotheses about how the problem might be solved. Much of the remainder of the consulting engagement is then dedicated to testing if the hypotheses are true.

Most scientists require that a hypothesis be falsifiable, which means that it is possible to test if the statement is false. Failing to falsify a hypothesis does not prove that the hypothesis is true. A hypothesis cannot ever be accepted or confirmed because no human will ever have infinite knowledge. However, after a hypothesis has been rigorously tested and not falsified, it may form the basis for theory and for reasonable action.

See *issue tree, Minto Pyramid Principle, strategy map*.

I

I2 – A software vendor of Advanced Planning and Scheduling (APS) systems.
See *Advanced Planning and Scheduling (APS)*.

ideation – A group brainstorming process that seeks to generate innovative thinking for new product development from of a group of people.

According to Graham and Bachmann (2004), ideation is done in the conceptual phase (the fuzzy front end) of the design process. Ideation has strict disciplines but allows for free-wheeling imagination. The process identifies the specific issue in need of rethinking, rethinks it in a fresh way, and evaluates the practical advisability of the resulting ideas.

See *brainstorming, causal map, Kano Analysis, New Product Development (NPD), Nominal Group Technique (NGT), TRIZ.*

IDOV – See *Design for Six Sigma (DFSS), lean sigma.*

IIE – See *Institute of Industrial Engineers.*

impact wheel – A graphical brainstorming tool that can be used to help a group identify and address the effects of a decision, action, or potential event.

An impact wheel exercise is a causal mapping exercise that seeks to identify the impact of an event. In some sense, the impact wheel is the opposite of a Root Cause Analysis (RCA) because a RCA seeks to identify factors that caused an event, whereas the impact wheel seeks to identify the effects that will be caused by an event.

The impact wheel is a simple structured brainstorming approach designed to help managers fully explore the potential consequences of specific events and decisions. The impact wheel can help managers uncover and manage unexpected and unintended consequences of a decision. It is a powerful tool for exploring the future that will be created by decisions made today.

The impact wheel process begins with the facilitator writing down the name for a change (event or decision) on a Post-it Note and placing it on the wall. The facilitator then engages the participants in a discussion of (1) the "impacts" extending out from the change (drawn like the spokes of a wheel), (2) the likelihood for each impact, and (3) implications of each impact (costs, benefits). The group then focuses on each of the critical impacts and repeats the process around each one. This approach can be supported by environmental scanning (to consider external issues), scenario development (to consider best-case, worst-case, status-quo, and wild-card scenarios), and expert interviews (to gain insights from subject matter experts). More detailed risk analysis might follow with a formal Failure Mode and Effects Analysis (FMEA) for each impact.

The figure on the right is a simple example of an impact wheel in a bank that is considering adding more workers. The first round identified "more difficult scheduling" as one impact of hiring more workers. The second round further identified the need to buy new software and hire a new scheduler.

See *5 Whys, brainstorming, causal map, Failure Mode and Effects Analysis (FMEA), issue tree, lean sigma, Nominal Group Technique (NGT), Root Cause Analysis (RCA).*

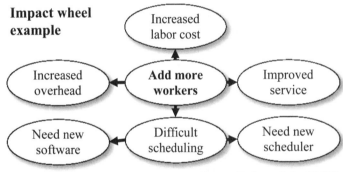

Impact wheel example

Source: Professor Arthur V. Hill

implementation – The process of turning a plan into reality.

The term "implementation" is often used in the context of setting up a new computer-based information system (e.g., an ERP system), implementation of a new program or policy in an organization (e.g., a process improvement program), or converting the conceptual design for a computer code into the actual computer code. Implementations that require major changes often require strong leadership and cross-disciplinary project teams. In the systems context, a number of implementation approaches are discussed in practice:

- **Full cutover** – The old system is turned off and the new system is turned on at the same time. As a joke, this is sometimes called "cold turkey."
- **Phased cutover** – Functions are tested and turned on sequentially.
- **Parallel** – The organization runs both the old and new systems at the same time to compare performance. This approach is not practical when the systems require decisions to be made or when a significant amount of manual data entry is required.
- **Conference room pilot** – The organization creates a realistic test database and then uses it to test the system and train users before the system is implemented. A pilot can be used with any of the above approaches.

The best approach (or combination of approaches) depends on the specific situation.

See *Enterprise Resources Planning (ERP), lean sigma, pilot test, post-project review, project charter, RACI Matrix, Software as a Service (SaaS), stakeholder analysis, turnkey.*

implied shortage cost – See *shortage cost.*

inbound logistics – See *logistics.*

See *logistics, Over/Short/Damaged Report, Third Party Logistics (3PL) provider, Transportation Management System (TMS), value chain.*

income statement – A standard financial statement during a certain accounting period (usually quarterly or annually) that summarizes how much money came in to a firm (income or revenue), how much money was paid out (expenses), and the difference (net income or profit) after taxes.

See *balance sheet, EBITDA, financial performance metrics.*

incoming inspection – The process of checking the quality and quantity of an order received from a supplier.

Incoming inspection can be done for both internal and external sources of supply. Incoming inspection samples items based on inspection policies and determines if the incoming order (batch) is acceptable or not. If it is not acceptable, the materials are reworked, returned to the vendor, or scrapped. Well-managed firms charge their suppliers for the time and materials cost of handling defective materials and use supplier scorecards to communicate assessments of their supplier's performance.

A **chargeback** is a customer-assessed penalty on the supplier when the shipment is late, has poor quality, or has improper packaging. One company visited by this author received a batch of cartons that were defective. They did not know that they were defective until they started to fill the cartons with ice cream. They stopped production immediately when the problem was found, but still had significant product loss. As a result, they did not pay for the defective cartons and charged the supplier a fee for the ice cream lost due to the defective cartons.

See *Acceptable Quality Level (AQL), acceptance sampling, Advanced Shipping Notification (ASN), dock-to-stock, inspection, Lot Tolerance Percent Defective (LTPD), quality management, receiving, Statistical Process Control (SPC), Statistical Quality Control (SQC), supplier scorecard.*

Incoterms – Rules for trade contracts published by the International Chamber of Commerce (ICC) and widely used in international and domestic commercial transactions; also known as International Commercial terms.

Incoterms are accepted by governments and firms around the world for use in international trade, transportation, and distribution. These terms support trade by reducing ambiguity in trading relationships. Free on Board (FOB) is an example. The Incoterms in effect on January 1, 2011 can be found at www.iccwbo.org/incoterms.

See *FOB, terms.*

incremental cost – See *marginal cost.*

indented bill of material – See *bill of material (BOM).*

independent demand – (1) The demand from external customers rather than a higher-level assembly or company-run stocking location. (2) Demand that must be forecasted rather than planned because it cannot be planned based on the plans for other items under the organization's control.

Examples of independent demand include consumer demand for a retailer, customer orders arriving at a distributor warehouse, and demand for an end item for a manufacturing firm. Internal demand for a component that goes into an end item is considered dependent demand because this demand is planned based on the production plan for the end item.

In the 1980s, this term clearly meant demand from external customers and therefore had to be forecasted. Today, however, the term is less clear because many firms now receive detailed demand information from their customers via electronic communications, such as EDI.

See *demand, dependent demand, inventory management.*

indirect cost – See *overhead.*

indirect labor – See *overhead.*

indirect materials – See *overhead.*

inductive reasoning – Inductive reasoning is making inferences about a larger subject based on specific examples.

In contrast, deductive reasoning begins with a general "theory" or concept that makes inferences about specific applications or situations. Arguments based on experience or observation are best expressed inductively, while arguments based on laws, rules, or other widely accepted principles are best expressed deductively.

Consider the following pair of examples. John: "I've seen that when I throw a ball up in the air, it comes back down. So I guess that the next time I throw the ball up, it will come back down." Mary: "I know from Newton's Law that everything that goes up must come down. And so, if you throw the ball up, it must come down." John is using inductive reasoning, arguing from observation, while Mary is using deductive reasoning, arguing from the Law of Gravity. John's argument is from the specific (he observed balls being thrown up and coming back down) to the general (the prediction that similar events will result in similar outcomes in the future). Mary's argument is from the general (the Law of Gravity) to the specific (this throw).

The difference between inductive and deductive reasoning is mostly in the way the arguments are expressed. Any inductive argument can also be expressed deductively, and any deductive argument can also be expressed inductively. John's inductive argument was supported by his previous observations, while Mary's deductive argument was supported by her reference to the Law of Gravity. John could provide additional support by detailing his observations, without any recourse to books or theories of physics, while Mary could provide additional support by discussing Newton's law.

Both inductive and deductive reasoning are used in business. However, lean sigma programs often emphasize **data-based decision making**, which is inductive (based on hard data) rather than deductive.

See *lean sigma*, *Minto Pyramid Principle*, *paradigm*.

industrial engineering – The branch of engineering that deals with the design, implementation, and evaluation of integrated systems of people, knowledge, equipment, energy, and material to produce products and services in the most efficient way. ✪

Industrial engineers draw upon the principles and methods of engineering analysis and synthesis, operations research, and the physical and social sciences to design efficient methods and systems. Industrial engineers work to eliminate wastes of time, money, materials, energy, and other resources. Typical industrial engineering issues include plant layout, analysis and planning of workers' jobs, economical handling of raw materials, flow of materials through the production process, and efficient control of the inventory. Industrial engineers work not only in manufacturing, but also in service organizations, such as hospitals and banks. The field of industrial engineering has expanded in recent years to consider many issues across the supply chain.

See *Institute of Industrial Engineers (IIE)*, *standard time*, *systems engineering*.

industry analysis – A methodology used to study and evaluate economic trends in an industry.

Industry analysis involves a study of the economic, socio-political, and market factors that determine the future of a sector of an economy. Major factors include relative buyer and supplier power and the likelihood of new entrants to the market. Whereas industry analysis focuses on the underlying economic factors of an entire industry, competitive analysis focuses on specific competitors and their competitive positions in the market. Porter's Five Forces are often used as the basis for an industry analysis.

See *competitive analysis*, *five forces analysis*, *operations strategy*, *SWOT analysis*.

infinite capacity planning – See *infinite loading*.

infinite loading – Creating a production plan based on planned manufacturing leadtimes without regard to available production capacity; also called infinite capacity planning and infinite scheduling.

Most Materials Requirement Planning (MRP) systems use fixed planned leadtimes that are independent of the amount of work-in-process (WIP) inventory in the system. This approach implicitly assumes that all resources have "infinite" capacity and that capacity constraints will not affect the schedule. However, most MRP systems provide load reports that managers can use to see when load exceeds the capacity.

See *Advanced Planning and Scheduling (APS)*, *finite scheduling*, *load*, *Materials Requirements Planning (MRP)*, *project management*.

INFORMS – See *Institute for Operations Research and the Management Sciences (INFORMS)*.

infrastructure – See *operations strategy*.

input/output control – A production planning and control method that monitors planned and actual inputs and planned and actual outputs for a resource, such as a workcenter.

If the planned input is greater than the planned output, the planned queue of work-in-process (WIP) inventory will increase. The same is true for actual input, output, and WIP. If actual WIP grows, actual throughput time will increase. Therefore, it is important to keep the planned input and output at about the same level so that WIP and throughput time do not change.

Input/output control example

	Period			
	1	2	3	4
Planned input	10	10	11	11
Actual input	10	10	11	13
Planned output	11	10	12	12
Actual output	11	9	12	12
Queue = 3	2	3	2	3

The example input/output report on the right shows the queue (backlog) starting at 3 units, shrinking when the actual input is less than the actual output, and growing when the actual output is greater than the actual input. When the planned and actual values are not the same, management should identify the cause of the differences and take action when needed.

See *capacity, Capacity Requirements Planning (CRP), load.*

in-sourcing – See *outsourcing.*

inspection – The process of checking units to ensure that they are free from defects. ✪

Inspection can be done for **batch control** (i.e., accept or reject a batch of parts (batch control) or **process control** (i.e., check if a process is in control). Inspection can use **source inspection** (i.e., the operator checks his or her own work), **successive check** (the next person in the process, or **final inspection** (the final produce is inspected), or some combination of the above.

Ideally, inspection is done at the source so the process has immediate feedback and has a sense of ownership of quality. Common slogans for this concept include **quality at the source** and **early detection of defects**. Most firms also conduct final inspection before products are put into finished goods inventory or delivered to customers. Inspection should also be done just before a **bottleneck** so valuable bottleneck time is not wasted on defective parts. More attention should be given to the **gold parts** that have gone through the bottleneck because valuable bottleneck capacity has been invested in these parts.

Successive check is a quality inspection system where each person checks the work done by the previous process (Shingo 1986). Theoretically, successive checks can accomplish 100% inspection by a "disinterested" person and provide almost immediate feedback and action. If successive checks are done throughout a process, the probability of a failure getting through is low, but the opportunity for repeated low-value work is high. Successive inspection requires time, which usually means that these inspections can only be done on a few potential defects. Also, successive checks may not be able to provide immediate feedback to those who made the error. The management of Andersen Corporation's Menomonie, Wisconsin, plant measured **escapes** as well as defects, where an escape is defined as passing a bad part to the next workcenter and is measured by successive step inspections. Management measured escapes to identify opportunities to reduce defects.

Self check is a quality inspection system where each person checks his or her own work (Shingo 1986). In some sense, this is the ideal inspection because it means that no waste is generated for the next step in the process, and errors are found and fixed immediately. Self check can be 100%, especially when it is assisted by a poke-yoke (error-proof) device. Self check is a good example of quality at the source.

Many firms are able to eliminate incoming inspection by having suppliers certify that materials meet certain quality standards. This saves money and time for both parties. An ideal process has no inspection because products and processes are so carefully designed that inspection, a non-value-adding activity, is not needed.

See *acceptance sampling, attribute, Computer Aided Inspection (CAI), cost of quality, Deming's 14 points, error proofing, first article inspection, gold parts, incoming inspection, quality at the source, quality management, Statistical Process Control (SPC), Statistical Quality Control (SQC), supplier qualification and certification, Total Quality Management (TQM).*

Installation Qualification (IQ) – See *process validation.*

instantaneous replenishment – Instantaneous replenishment is a materials management term that describes situations in which the entire lotsize is received all at one time.

Instantaneous replenishment is common when ordering from an outside supplier that ships the entire order quantity at one time. This is also the situation when a distribution center places an order to an internal plant because the entire order is shipped to the distribution center at one time.

In contrast, with **non-instantaneous replenishment**, the production batch (lot) does not arrive all at the same time. This is a common situation when ordering from an internal plant. As shown in the graph on the right, inventory grows when the product is being produced and declines when not being produced. When being produced, inventory grows at rate $p - d$, where p is the production rate and d is the demand rate. When not being produced, the inventory declines at the demand rate d. The average lotsize inventory

Graph for non-instantous replenishment

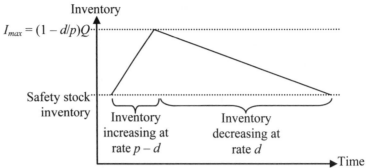

for non-instantaneous replenishment is the $(1 - d/p)Q/2$ and the optimal lotsize is $\sqrt{\dfrac{2DS}{ic(1-d/p)}}$. As expected,

as production rate p approaches infinity, d/p approaches zero, the average lotsize inventory approaches $Q/2$, and the optimal lotsize approaches the instantaneous *EOQ*.

See *cycle stock, Economic Order Quantity (EOQ), lotsizing methods.*

Institute for Operations Research and the Management Sciences (INFORMS) – The largest professional society in the world for professionals in the field of operations research (O.R.).

INFORMS was established in 1995 with the merger of the Operations Research Society of America (ORSA) and The Institute for Management Sciences (TIMS). The society serves the scientific and professional needs of educators, investigators, scientists, students, managers, and consultants, as well as the organizations they serve, by such services as publishing 12 scholarly journals that describe the latest O.R. methods and applications and a membership magazine with news from across the profession. The society organizes national and international conferences for academics and professionals as well as members of the society's special interest groups.

INFORMS publishes many scholarly journals, including ***Management Science***, ***Operations Research***, ***Manufacturing & Service Operations Management*** (***MSOM***), ***Decision Analysis***, ***Information Systems Research***, ***INFORMS Journal of Computing***, ***Interfaces***, ***Marketing Science***, ***Mathematics of OR***, ***Organizational Science***, and ***Transportation Science***. The INFORMS website is www.informs.org.

See *Manufacturing and Service Operations Management Society (MSOM), operations management (OM), operations research (OR).*

Institute for Supply Management (ISM) – A professional society for supply management professionals.

Founded in 1915, the Institute for Supply Management (ISM) claims to be the largest supply management association in the world. ISM's mission is to lead the supply management profession through its standards of excellence, research, promotional activities, and education. ISM's membership base includes more than 40,000 supply management professionals with a network of domestic and international affiliated associations.

Formerly known as the National Association of Purchasing Management, the organization changed its name to Institute for Supply Management in May 2001 to reflect the increasing strategic and global significance of supply management. ISM has a certification process for the Certified Purchasing Manager (C.P.M.) designation. The process requires a passing grade on the CPM exam. ISM provides many publications to its members, including the ***Journal of Supply Chain Management***, a publication for purchasing professionals and educators.

The ISM website is www.ism.ws.

See *operations management (OM), purchasing, supply chain management.*

Institute of Industrial Engineers (IIE) – The world's largest professional society dedicated solely to the support of the industrial engineering profession and individuals involved with improving quality and productivity.

Founded in 1948, IIE is an international, non-profit association that provides leadership for the application, education, training, research, and development of industrial engineering.

IIE publishes two academic journals (***IIE Transactions*** and ***The Engineering Economist***), a monthly news magazine (***IE Magazine***), and a practitioner management journal (***Industrial Management***).

The IIE website is www.iienet2.org.

See *industrial engineering, operations management (OM)*.

in-stock – See *service level*.

integer programming (IP) – A type of linear programming where the decision variables are restricted to integer values.

The term "integer programming" is short for integer linear programming. Mixed integer programming (MIP) has some decision variables that are continuous and some that are integer.

See *assignment problem, knapsack problem, linear programming (LP), mixed integer programming (MIP)*.

Integrated Product Development (IPD) – The practice of systematically forming teams of functional disciplines to integrate and concurrently apply all necessary processes to produce an effective and efficient product that satisfies the customer's needs.

IPD is nearly synonymous with simultaneous engineering and concurrent engineering. Benefits claimed for IPD include less development time, fewer engineering changes, less time to market, higher quality, and higher white collar productivity.

See *concurrent engineering, Engineering Change Order (ECO), New Product Development (NPD), simultaneous engineering*.

intellectual capital – The sum of an organization's collective knowledge, experience, skills, competences, and ability to acquire more; also called knowledge capital.

At least one source defined intellectual capital as the difference between book value and market value. Although this might be too strong, most management experts agree that the balance sheet and other financial statements do not reflect intellectual capital and that intellectual capital is the most valuable asset for many firms.

See *intellectual property (IP), knowledge management, learning organization*.

intellectual property (IP) – An intangible asset based on knowledge work.

Commercial forms of IP include software, product designs, databases, chemical compounds, drugs, and inventions. Artistic forms of IP include books, music, plays, photography, images, and movies. Organizations and individuals often use patents, trademarks, and copyrights to try to protect IP, but often the best protection for IP is avoiding unauthorized access.

See *contract manufacturer, intellectual capital, knowledge management, learning organization, offshoring, outsourcing, sourcing, technology transfer*.

interchangeability – See interchangeable parts.

interchangeable parts – Identical components that can be selected at random for an assembly; interchangeability is a closely related term.

Before the 18th century, highly skilled workers made parts for products, such as guns, using imprecise equipment and methods, which resulted in each product being different. The principle of interchangeable parts was developed throughout the 18th and 19th centuries. Interchangeable parts were used as early as 1814 for clocks in Switzerland.

Firms with interchangeable parts can make high volumes of identical parts and easily assemble them into products. Interchangeable parts are made to conform to standard specifications, which were made possible by the development of machine tools, templates, jigs, fixtures, gauges, measuring tools (e.g., calipers and micrometers), and industry standards (e.g., screw threads). Interchangeable parts enabled the assembly line and mass production, which were developed in the early 20th century.

Interchangeability has many benefits compared to the old craft approach to manufacturing, including (1) reduced assembly labor time and cost by allowing easy assembly and repair without custom fitting, (2) reduced repair time and cost, (3) reduced labor rates and training costs because the assembly process requires less skill, (4) easier field repair due to interchangeable parts, and (5) reduced materials cost because parts are more likely to work in the assembly.

See *commonality, standard parts, standard products*.

intermittent demand – See *lumpy demand*.

intermodal shipments – A transportation term used to describe the movement of goods by more than one mode of transportation (e.g., rail, truck, air, and ocean).

Intermodal shipments usually involve movement of goods by railroad (in a trailer or container) that originate and terminate with either a motor carrier or ocean shipping line. For example, an ocean container might be picked up by a truck, delivered to a port, transported by a ship, and then picked up by another truck in another country. In the trucking industry, intermodal often refers to the combination of trucking and rail transportation.

See *logistics, mode, multi-modal shipments, trailer, Transportation Management System (TMS)*.

Internal Rate of Return (IRR) – The discount rate at which the net present value of the future cash flows of an investment equals the cost of the investment.

The *IRR* has to be found by trial and error (numerical) methods. It is the discount rate at which the net present value is zero. Given cash flows $(C_1, C_2, …, C_N)$ in periods $1, 2, …, N$, the *IRR* is the rate of return r such that $NPV = \sum_{n=0}^{N} \frac{C_n}{(1+r)^n} = 0$. The *Compounded Annual Growth Rate (CAGR)* entry provides much more detail.

See *Compounded Annual Growth Rate (CAGR), financial performance metrics, geometric mean, investment center*.

internal setup – Work done to prepare a machine for production while the machine is down.

One of the first and most important setup reduction activities is to reduce or eliminate internal setup tasks. This is done by performing external setups, which is doing the setup work while the machine is still working.

See *external setup, setup, setup time reduction methods*.

interoperability – The ability of two or more diverse systems to work together.

Interoperability is the ability of two or more systems to communicate, exchange information, and use the information that has been exchanged without modification or development of custom interfaces and tools. Interoperability is often a challenge when systems are made by different manufacturers. One key to interoperability is compliance with technical specifications and standards.

See *commonality, modular design (modularity), network effect*.

interplant orders – Transfer of materials from one manufacturing or distribution location to another inside the same organization.

See *manufacturing order, purchase order (PO)*.

interpolated median – A measure of the central tendency used for low resolution data (such as surveys, student grades, and frequency data) where several values fall at the median; the interpolated median is equal to the median plus or minus a correction factor that adjusts for a non-symmetrical (skewed) distribution when many observations are equal to the median.

Many experts consider the median to be a better measure of central tendency than the mean because the median, unlike the mean, is not influenced by extremely low or high values. Some people consider the interpolated median to be a better measure of central tendency than the median when many values are equal to the median (computed in the standard way) and the distribution is non-symmetrical (skewed). However, some statistical experts assert that the interpolated median does not have a good theoretical basis and was just "made up by someone who could not decide between the mean and the median."[23]

When the distribution is skewed, the interpolated median adjusts the median upward or downward according to the number of responses above or below the median. A right-skewed distribution will have a positive correction factor and a left-skewed distribution will have a negative correction factor.

Define the following parameters for a data set: N is the number of observed values, *im* is the interpolated median, m is the median computed in the standard way, n_b is the number of values below (less than) m, n_e is the number of values equal to m, and n_a is the number of values above (greater than) m. The equation for the interpolated median is then $im = m$ for $n_e = 0$; otherwise $im = m + (n_a - n_b)/(2n_e)$. If $n_b = n_a$, the distribution is not skewed, the correction factor is zero, and the interpolated median will be equal to the median (i.e., $im = m$). (Note: $n_b = n_a$ will always be true when $n_e \leq 1$.) If $n_b < n_a$, the distribution is right-skewed, the correction factor is positive, and the interpolated median is greater than the median; conversely, if $n_b > n_a$, the distribution is left-skewed, the correction factor is negative, and the interpolated median is less than the median. If the number of

---

[23] *Private conversation with Professor Chris Nachtscheim, Carlson School of Management, University of Minnesota.*

values equal to the median (n_e) is equal to zero or one, the number of values above and below the median will always be equal and the correction factor will be zero.

For example, a sample of $N = 7$ responses for a five-point Likert survey was $x_i = \{1,3,3,3,5,5,5\}$ with a median of $m = 3$. (See the histogram below.) The number of observations below the median is $n_b = 1$, the number above the median is $n_a = 3$, and the number equal to the median is $n_e = 3$. The interpolated median is then $i_m = 3.33$, which is higher than the median of 3 because $n_a > n_b$. The right-skewed distribution "pulls" the interpolated median above the median, but only slightly.

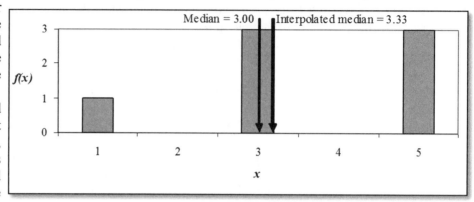

Gretchen Donahue and Corrie Fiedler, instructors at the University of Minnesota, noted that the above equation is for a five-point Likert scale and recommend using the following equations for student grades on a four-point scale: $im = m$, for $n_e = 0$; $im = m - 1/6 + (N/6 - n_b/3)/n_e$, for $n_e > 0$. With this equation the interpolated median for the above example is 3.11, which is less than the 3.33 found above, but still greater than the median.

See *mean, median, skewness, trimmed mean.*

interquartile range – A statistics term for the 50% of the observations included from the top of the lowest quartile to the bottom of the highest quartile of a distribution.

The interquartile range (*IQR*) is defined by the points at the 75th and 25th percentile of the data, and therefore, is the range that includes the middle 50% of the observations. Because the *IQR* uses the middle 50%, it is not affected by outliers or extreme values in the top or bottom quartiles.

See *box plot, fractile, outlier, range.*

interval notation – A mathematical convention for writing the range for a variable.

The interval notation uses brackets [or] when endpoints are included and parentheses (or) when end points are not included. The symbols ∞ and $-\infty$ are used for positive and negative infinity and the union sign $\cup$ is used to combine sets. For example, the range $[5, \infty)$ includes the number 5 and all values greater than 5. The range $(5,7)$ includes all values between 5 and 7, but not the endpoints (i.e., $5 < x < 7$). The range $(-\infty, -2] \cup (1,\infty)$ includes all negative values less than or equal to -2 and all positive values strictly greater than 1 with 1 not included in the range. Infinity never has an endpoint, which means that the infinity symbol is always accompanied by a parenthesis and never by a bracket. Random number generators, such as the Excel function RAND(), create a stream of values in the range $[0,1)$, which means that it is possible (though unlikely) to get a value of 0, but never a value of one. In Excel, the random number $1 - \text{RAND}()$ will be in the range $(0,1]$.

See *random number, range.*

interval scale – See *scales of measurement.*

intranet – An application of Internet technology, software, and applications within for use within an enterprise.

An intranet is a private network as opposed to the Internet, which is the public network. An intranet may be entirely disconnected from the public Internet, but is usually linked to it and protected from unauthorized access by security firewall systems. More loosely, the term may also include extranets. An intranet involves Web-based technologies and is typically used within an organization's internal network to centralize applications or data. It is usually segmented into data or applications that all employees have access to and data or applications that are restricted to only authorized users.

See *corporate portal, e-business, extranet.*

in-transit inventory – The quantity of goods shipped but not yet received.

In-transit inventory may belong to either the shipper or the customer, depending on the terms of the contract. See *inventory management, logistics*.

intrinsic forecasting model – See *forecasting*.

Inventory Dollar Days (IDD) – A Theory of Constraints (TOC) measure of investment in inventory.

The **Theory of Constraints (TOC)** promotes Inventory Dollar Days (IDD) as a measure of things done ahead of schedule and **Throughput Dollar Days (TDD)** as a measure of things done behind schedule. A dollar day is one dollar held in inventory for one day. When an individual borrows money from a bank, the interest payment is based on how many dollars are borrowed and for how long, which means that interest is based on dollar days. When a firm is holds inventory, the cost to the firm is based on the dollar days of inventory. The IDD can be calculated as IDD = (unit cost) x (quantity on hand) x (days in the system). For example, if a manufacturing order for 100 units has been waiting at a workcenter for five days and the unit cost is $2, the workcenter has 100 x 5 x 2 = $1000 dollar days for that order.

Similarly, when a firm is late, the time value of money is lost during the delay. The cost to the firm, therefore, is based on the dollar days late. TDD measures the value of each late shipment multiplied by the number of days it was late (i.e., a $1-million order five days late becomes five-million TDD).

Phillip Brooks, president and owner of H. Brooks and Company, a St. Paul, Minnesota distributor of fresh fruits and vegetables, shared the following quote with the author: "We began measuring dollar days of inventory last winter, with an item ranking and overall totals by buyer and vendor. You will find that this number will be surprisingly large and will create an insight followed by instant action – and focus on inventory items that are unneeded. In the last eight months, we have cut this measure by about 50%."

The IDD for a set of items during a planning period is the sum of the unit cost for each item times the number of days in inventory for each item. Therefore, IDD is a time-integrated sum. Any time-integrated sum can be turned into a time-integrated average by dividing by the number of periods. Therefore, IDD divided by the number of days in the planning period is the average inventory investment. For example, if a set of items has an IDD of 30,000 dollar days during a 30-day month, the average inventory investment for the month is $1000. With a monthly carrying charge of 1%, the carrying cost for these items is $10.

See *carrying cost, inventory turnover, operations performance metrics, periods supply, Theory of Constraints (TOC), throughput accounting, Throughput Dollar Days (TDD)*.

inventory management – Inventory management involves planning and control of all types of inventories. ✪

Inventory management involves forecasting demand, placing purchase and manufacturing orders, and filling sales orders. Inventory management requires two decisions that must be made frequently: when to order, and how much to order. A less frequent inventory management decision is deciding if an item should be stocked. If an item is not stocked, the firm must make, assemble, or buy the item in response to customer demand.

Inventory managers may be responsible for all types of inventory:

- **Raw materials/purchased components inventory** – Purchased materials from outside suppliers.
- **In-transit inventory** – Inventory shipped, but not yet received.
- **Work-in-process inventory (WIP)** – Products started in manufacturing, but not yet complete.
- **Manufactured components/subassemblies** – Parts and subassemblies built and then stored in inventory until needed for higher-level products or assemblies.
- **Finished goods inventory** – Products that are complete, but not yet shipped to a customer.
- **Supplies/consumables inventory** – Supplies needed for the manufacturing process, but do not become a part of any product (e.g., cleaning supplies for a machine). These are often called Maintenance, Repair, & Operating Supplies (MRO) items. (Note: MRO has many similar names, including "Maintenance, Repair, and Operations" and "Maintenance, Repair, and Overhaul.")
- **Scrap inventory** – Defective products that will be reworked, recycled, or scrapped.
- **Consignment inventory** – Products owned by one party, but held by another party until sale.

Inventory control systems must determine when to order (order timing) and how much to order (order quantity). Order timing can be based on a reorder point (R) or a fixed schedule (every P time periods). Order quantity can be a fixed quantity Q (possibly the EOQ) or a variable quantity based on an order-up-to level (T). With an order-up-to (base stock) policy, the order quantity is set to $T - I$, where I is the inventory position.

The table below summarizes the main inventory management approaches with respect to order timing and order quantity policies. The variable names include: P the periodic review period, Q the order quantity, T the order-up-to level, R the reorder point, S the order cost, i carrying charge, c unit cost, A annual demand in units, I current inventory position, s safety stock in units, μ_X mean demand during leadtime, μ_D mean demand per period, and μ_L mean leadtime.

Summary of the inventory control models

		Order quantity		Equations
		Fixed order quantity (Q)	Order-up-to level (T)	
Order timing	Continuous review $P = 0$	Order point system (R, Q)	Min/Max system (R, T)	$R = \mu_X + s$
	Periodic review[24] $P > 0$	Milk delivery system (P, Q)	Periodic review system (P, T)	$P = \sqrt{\dfrac{2S}{icA}}$
Equations		$Q^* = \sqrt{\dfrac{2AS}{ic}}$	$T = (P + \mu_L)\mu_D + s$ $Q = T - I$	

See *ABC classification, active item, aggregate inventory management, carrying cost, consignment inventory, continuous replenishment planning, continuous review system, dependent demand, distribution, distributor, Economic Order Quantity (EOQ), forecasting, independent demand, in-transit inventory, inventory position, inventory turnover, joint replenishment, logistics, lotsizing methods, materials handling, materials management, Materials Requirements Planning (MRP), min-max inventory system, on-hand inventory, on-order inventory, order cost, order-up-to level, periodic review system, periods supply, pull system, purchasing, random storage location, raw materials, reorder point, safety stock, service level, square root law for safety stock, square root law for warehouses, supply chain management, vendor managed inventory (VMI), Warehouse Management System (WMS), zero inventory.*

inventory position – The amount of inventory available to fill future orders; defined as on-hand plus on-order minus allocated and minus backordered inventory quantities; also called stock position. ✪

On-hand inventory is the material that is physically located in the plant or warehouse. On-order inventory includes the materials that have been ordered but not yet received. Allocated inventory and backorders have been promised to customers or other orders and therefore are not available for use. Many textbooks and training programs simplify the definition to just on-hand plus on-order.

See *allocated inventory, backorder, continuous review system, inventory management, on-hand inventory, on-order inventory, open order, order-up-to level, reorder point, supply chain management.*

inventory shrink – See *shrinkage.*

inventory turnover – The number of times that the inventory is replaced during a time period (usually a year). ✪

The standard accounting measure for inventory turnover is the cost of goods sold divided by the average inventory investment. For example, if a firm has an annual cost of goods sold of $10 million and an average inventory investment of $5 million, the firm has two turns per year. Inventory turnover (T) can also be defined as $52d/I$, where d is the average demand in units per week and I is the average inventory in units.

If the current inventory investment is close to the average and the historical rate of consumption is close to the current rate of consumption, the inverse of the inventory turnover ratio for any inventory is approximately the periods supply. The inverse of the inventory turnover ratio for work-in-process inventory (WIP) is an estimate of the dollar-weighted cycle time for a product.

Some students confuse inventory turnover with other turnover measures. Employee turnover is the number of times that employees are replaced during a period (usually a year). Outside of the U.S., turnover usually means sales or revenue.

Hill and Zhang (2010) identified six "fallacies" regarding inventory turnover: the ratio fallacy, the end-of-period inventory fallacy, the different numerator/denominator units fallacy, the different demand fallacy, the industry average fallacy, and the common turnover (days supply) fallacy.

---

[24] *The names for periodic review systems are not standard in the literature.*

It is good management to have a target turnover or periods supply for a group of items. However, this well-intended policy can easily cascade down the organization and become the target for each plant, product, and raw material. Good managers should not allow this to happen.

See *aggregate inventory management, asset turnover, balanced scorecard, carrying charge, carrying cost, cost of goods sold, cycle time, DuPont Analysis, employee turnover, Inventory Dollar Days (IDD), inventory management, inventory valuation, operations performance metrics, periods supply, turnover.*

inventory turns – See *inventory turnover.*

inventory valuation – The process of assigning a financial value to on-hand inventory.

Inventory valuation is based on the standard cost and the selected accounting convention, which may be First-In-First-Out (FIFO), Last-In-First-Out (LIFO), average list price, or some other method.

See *First-In-First-Out (FIFO), inventory turnover, Last-In-First-Out (LIFO).*

inventory/order interface – See *push-pull boundary.*

inverse transform method – A simulation procedure for generating random variates from a particular theoretical or empirical cumulative probability distribution.

The distribution function $F(x)$ for a random variable x is defined such that $F(x_0) = P(x < x_0)$. The inverse distribution function is defined such that $x = F^{-1}(p)$ is the x value associated with the probability p for this distribution function. In other words, if $p = F(x)$, then $x = F^{-1}(p)$. The inverse transform method generates random variates using $x = F^{-1}(r)$, where r is a uniformly distributed random variable in the interval $(0, 1]$.

In Excel, the inverse transform method should use r = 1-RAND(), where r is uniformly distributed in the interval $(0,1]$. This is because RAND() is in the interval $[0,1)$, which means it can generate a value of zero, which causes problems with most cumulative distribution functions.

See *Erlang distribution, exponential distribution, gamma distribution, interval notation, lognormal distribution, normal distribution, random number, simulation, uniform distribution, Weibull distribution.*

investment center – An accounting term for an area of responsibility that is held accountable for revenues, expenses, and invested capital.

See *cost center, Internal Rate of Return (IRR), profit center, revenue center.*

invoice – (Noun) An itemized statement issued by the seller to the buyer that indicates the products, quantities, prices, taxes, and payment terms for products or services the seller has provided to the buyer; also called a bill or statement. (Verb) To prepare and send such an invoice; also called billing.

Invoices are often delivered to the buyer at the time of delivery of the goods or services.

See *Accounts Receivable (A/R), Electronic Data Interchange (EDI), purchase order (PO), purchasing, supplier, terms.*

IPD – See *Integrated Product Development.*

Ishikawa Diagram – See *causal map.* ✪

islands of automation – Robotic or other automated systems that function independently of other systems.

This phrase is often used in arguments to justify more integrated systems.

See *automation.*

ISO – International Organization for Standardization.

ISO 14001 – Certification standards created by the International Organization for Standardization related to environmental impact.

The ISO 14001 standards specify the requirements for an environmental management system to enable an organization to formulate a policy and objectives, taking into account legislative requirements and information about significant environmental impacts. It applies to those environmental aspects that the organization can control and over which it can be expected to have influence.

See *quality management.*

ISO 16949 quality standard – See *TS 16949 quality standard.*

ISO 9000 – See *ISO 9001:2008.*

ISO 26000 – A systematic approach developed by the International Organization for Standardization (ISO) that organizations can use to address social responsibility issues; also known as the SR standard.

Unlike ISO 9001 and ISO 14000, ISO 26000 is a guidance standard rather than a certifiable management system. It covers seven SR subjects: governance, human rights, labor practices, environment, operating practices, consumer rights, and community rights (Bowers and West 2011).

See *ISO 9001:2008*.

ISO 9001:2008 – A family of standards for quality management systems published by the International Organization for Standardization (ISO) that is designed to help organizations better meet the needs of their customers and other stakeholders; also called ISO 9001:2008.

According to the ISO website[25], "The ISO 9000 family of standards represents an international consensus on good quality management practices. It consists of standards and guidelines relating to quality management systems and related supporting standards. ISO 9001:2008 is the standard that provides a set of standardized requirements for a quality management system, regardless of what the user organization does, its size, or whether it is in the private or public sector. It is the only standard in the family against which organizations can be certified – although certification is not a compulsory requirement of the standard. The other standards in the family cover specific aspects, such as fundamentals and vocabulary, performance improvements, documentation, training, and financial and economic aspects."

The ISO standards can be used in three ways: (1) The standard requires the organization to audit its own quality system to verify that it is managing its processes effectively, (2) the organization may invite its clients to audit its quality system, and (3) the organization may engage the services of an independent quality system certification body to obtain an ISO 9001:2008 certificate of conformity. Note that certification is done by certification bodies and not ISO itself. An ISO certificate must be renewed at regular intervals, usually around three years. More than one-million organizations worldwide are certified.

ISO standards are based on eight principles:

1. **Customer focus** – Organizations should understand current and future customer needs, should meet customer requirements, and should strive to exceed customer expectations.
2. **Leadership** – Leaders establish unity of purpose and direction of the organization. They should create and maintain an internal environment in which people can become fully involved in achieving the organization's objectives.
3. **Involvement of people** – People at all levels are the essence of the organization and their full involvement enables their abilities to be used for the organization's benefit.
4. **Process approach** – A desired result is achieved more efficiently when activities and related resources are managed as a process.
5. **System approach to management** – Identifying, understanding, and managing interrelated processes as a system contributes to the organization's effectiveness and efficiency in achieving its objectives.
6. **Continual improvement** – Continual improvement of the organization's overall performance should be a permanent objective of the organization.
7. **Factual approach to decision making** – Effective decisions are based on the analysis of data and information.
8. **Mutually beneficial supplier relationships** – An organization and its suppliers are interdependent and a mutually beneficial relationship enhances the ability of both to create value.

Many firms using ISO can claim significant financial benefits (Naveh and Marcus 2005) and significant operational benefits (Hendricks and Singhal 2001). Some of the benefits claimed for ISO include efficiency, increased productivity, improved employee motivation, improved customer satisfaction, and increased profit.

Some critics suggest that ISO can be summarized as "document what you do and do what you document." If that is true, a firm could be carefully following a well-documented process that is consistently producing poor quality products. Other criticisms focus on the bureaucratic overhead and the fact that many firms pursue certification purely for marketing and sales reasons without regard to actual quality.

See *ISO 26000, lean sigma, lean thinking, Malcolm Baldrige National Quality Award (MBNQA), quality management, standardized work, TS 16949 quality standard.*

---

[25] *www.iso.org/iso/iso_catalogue/management_and_leadership_standards/quality_management/iso_9000_essentials.htm,* *February 24, 2011.*

issue – (1) In an inventory context: To physically move material from a stocking location and make the transaction for this move. (2) In a problem-solving context: A topic that deserves further attention.

See *allocated inventory, backflushing*.

issue log – A project management tool that records problems identified during a project and then monitors them to make sure that they are resolved.

Issue logs are usually created and maintained in an Excel file, using the following columns:
- Issue ID (optional number or code)
- Issue name (very short description)
- Description (longer description)
- Priority (A = top priority, D = low priority)
- Author (optional)
- Date created
- Due date
- Date resolved (blank until the issue is closed)
- Owner (once it has been assigned)
- Notes/actions (optional)

The issue log should be "owned" by one person, often the project manager (or admin), and should be brought to each meeting. Project team meetings should prioritize outstanding issues and make sure someone owns each of the high-priority issues. Project team meetings should also hold people accountable to complete the issues they own. Resolved issues are usually also kept in the issue log, but sorted at the bottom of the list or moved to another worksheet in the Excel workbook.

See *Nominal Group Technique (NGT), project management*.

issue tree – A mapping tool used to break a problem into its component issues.

In their book ***The McKinsey Mind***, Rasiel and Friga (2001) defined an issue tree as "the series of questions or issues that must be addressed to prove or disprove a hypothesis." Issue trees are used by many consulting firms to structure their approach to a client's problem. Like detective work, the process starts with a set of potential solutions (hypotheses) expressed as questions. For each of the main questions (hypotheses), the issue tree starts with the question on the far left and moves to the right to identify additional questions that need to be answered to address that question. The process continues with more detailed questions on the right. Each question should guide the project team's data collection, inquiry, and research. Ideally, the issues at any one level in the tree are "mutually exclusive and collectively exhaustive" (MECE) so that all possibilities are explored. (See the *MECE* entry.) If the answer is "no" to any question, further inquiry along that branch is usually not needed.

The figure below is an example of a simple issue tree that "explodes" the problem into a set of sub-issues (questions) that the consulting project needs to answer. A much larger example can be found at http://interactive.cabinetoffice.gov.uk/strategy/survivalguide/skills/s_issue.htm (March 25, 2011).

Issue trees are closely related to the Minto Pyramid Principle (Minto 1996) used by many consulting firms to structure arguments in a consulting presentation. Issue trees are similar to mindmaps and are a special case of a logic tree.

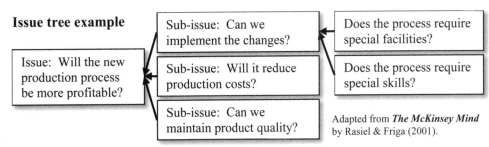

Issue tree example

Adapted from ***The McKinsey Mind*** by Rasiel & Friga (2001).

It is more important that issues be independent than MECE. For example, an outgoing shipment could be late because of mechanical problems with a truck or because the products were not ready to ship. These two events are not mutually exclusive (because they both could be true), but they can be studied independently.

Issue trees are usually drawn from left to right and are often created in Microsoft Excel or Visio. Phil Miller, Professional Director of the Carlson Consulting Enterprise at the University of Minnesota, uses an Excel workbook with these column headings from left to right: Governing question, sub-questions, sub-questions (for the sub-questions), and analysis.

See *causal map, decision tree, hypothesis, impact wheel, MECE, mindmap, Minto Pyramid Principle, Root Cause Analysis (RCA), Y-tree*.

item master – See *bill of material (BOM)*.

item number – See *Stock Keeping Unit (SKU)*.

J

JCAHO – See *Joint Commission*.

jidoka – The Toyota Production System practice of designing processes and empowering workers to shut down a process when an abnormal condition occurs; sometimes called autonomation. ✪

The Japanese word "jidoka" is often translated as "autonomation," which is a contraction of the words "autonomous" and "automation." Jidoka is sometimes translated as "automation with a human touch (or human mind)." According to Ohno (1978), the original jidoka device was a loom developed by Sakichi Toyoda (1867-1930), the founder of the Toyota Motor Company. This loom stopped instantly if any one of the threads broke so defective products were not built and so problems could be seen immediately. According to Ohno (1979), Toyota sold the patent for his loom in 1930 to the Platt Brothers in England for $500,000, and then invested this money in automobile research, which later led to the creation of the Toyota Motor Company.

Originally, jidoka focused on automatic methods for stopping a process when an error condition occurred; however, it is now used to describe both automated and human means for stopping a process when a problem occurs. For example, a process can use limit switches or devices that will automatically shut down the process when the required number of pieces has been made, a part is defective, or the mechanism jams. This same process can be operated with policies that allow the operators to shut down the machine when a warning light goes on.

Quality benefits of jidoka – Jidoka causes work to stop immediately when a problem occurs so defective parts are never created. In other words, Jidoka conducts 100 percent inspection, highlights the causes of problems, forces constant process improvement, and results in improved quality. Whereas automation focuses on labor reduction, jidoka (autonomation) focuses on quality improvement. Note that jidoka is closely related to Shigeo Shingo's concept of poka yoke.

Cost benefits of jidoka – Jidoka frees equipment from the necessity of constant human attention, makes it possible to separate people from machines, allows workers to handle multiple operations, and prevents equipment breakdowns. Ideally, jidoka stops the line or machine automatically, which reduces the burden of workers to monitor the process. In fact, many sources define jidoka as stopping production automatically when a problem occurs.

Jidoka is often implemented with a signal to communicate the status of a machine. For example, a production process might use **andon lights** with a green light if everything is okay, a yellow light to signal an abnormal condition, and a red light if the process is stopped.

See *andon light, automation, autonomation, empowerment, error proofing, lean thinking, multiple-machine handling, Toyota Production System (TPS)*.

jig – A mechanical device that holds a work piece securely in the correct position or has the capability of guiding the tool during a manufacturing operation.

See *fixture, manufacturing processes, tooling*.

JIT – See *Just-in-Time (JIT)*.

JIT II – A practice of having supplier representatives work at a customer location to better facilitate product design or production coordination activities.

The JIT II concept was developed by Lance Dixon at Bose Corporation (Porter & Dixon 1994). JIT II is essentially vendor managed inventory (VMI), early supplier involvement, and co-location of personnel. The term does not appear to be widely used.

See *co-location, Early Supplier Involvement (ESI), lean thinking, vendor managed inventory (VMI)*.

job – (1) In a general context: Any work that needs to be done by an individual or a machine. (2) In a manufacturing context: Work that is done to create a batch of an item in response to a customer request; also known as an order, manufacturing order, or production order.

See *job order costing, job shop, lotsize*.

job design – The process of defining and combining tasks to create work for an individual or a group of individuals; also called work design and socio-technical design. ✪

Job design usually results in a job description, which defines the set of tasks and responsibilities for an individual worker. Job design should consider organizational requirements, individual worker attributes, health, safety, and ergonomics. Taylor's **scientific method** tended to view job design as a pure engineering problem; however, the human relations movement broadened the scope to consider job satisfaction, motivation, and interpersonal issues.

Organizations can better achieve their objectives by designing work that motivates workers to achieve their full potential. A deep understanding of job design requires an understanding of behavioral science, organizational behavior, organizational design, psychology, human resources management, economics, operations, and engineering.

Socio-technical design considers the interaction between people and the technological processes in which they work. Socio-technical design is important in almost every operations management topic. For example, visual control, a key lean manufacturing concept, is a good socio-technical design because when processes are made more visual, workers can understand them better and be more productive.

See *addition principle, cellular manufacturing, cross-training, division of labor, empowerment, ergonomics, gainsharing, Hawthorne Effect, High Performance Work Systems (HPWS), human resources, job enlargement, job rotation, labor grade, lean thinking, multiplication principle, New Product Development (NPD), on-the-job training (OJT), organizational design, pay for skill, productivity, RACI Matrix, Results-Only Work Environment (ROWE), scientific management, self-directed work team, Service Profit Chain, single point of contact, standardized work, subtraction principle, work measurement, work simplification, workforce agility*.

job enlargement – Adding more tasks to a job; increasing the range of the job duties and responsibilities. ✪

The management literature does not have consistent definitions of the terms "job enlargement" and "job enrichment." However, most experts define the terms as follows:

Job enlargement – This is also called horizontal job enlargement and adds similar tasks to the job description. In other words, the worker is assigned more of a co-worker's job. For example, the worker who cleans sinks also is assigned to clean the toilets.

Job enrichment – This is sometimes called vertical job enlargement and adds more decision rights and authority to the job. In other words, the worker is assigned some of the boss' job. For example, the worker might be given the added responsibilities of scheduling and inspecting the bathroom cleaning process for other workers.

Job enlargement can have many benefits for an organization. Some of these include:

Reduced cycle time – When workers have broader skills, they can be moved to where they are needed. This reduces queue time and cycle time.

Fewer queues – When a worker is assigned to do two steps instead of one, the queue between the steps is eliminated, and much of the associated wait time is eliminated.

Improved process improvement capability –Workers with broader experience are better able to help the organization improve processes, which means that the organization can accelerate "learning."

Improved worker morale and retention – Enlarged jobs are often more interesting, which improves worker morale and retention.

See *addition principle, Business Process Re-engineering (BPR), cross-training, division of labor, empowerment, handoff, human resources, job design, job rotation, learning organization, organizational design, pay for skill, standardized work, work simplification*.

job enrichment – See *job enlargement*.

job order costing – A cost accounting approach that accumulates costs for a job as it passes through the system; also known as job costing.

A job order costing system will accumulate the standard (or actual) direct labor, direct materials, and overhead costs as a job passes through each step in a process. This type of system makes the most sense for a process layout, such as a job shop.

See *backflushing, facility layout, job, job shop, overhead, target cost.*

job rotation – The movement of workers between different jobs in an organization.

This policy can be an effective method for cross-training and can improve communications, increase process understanding, and reduce stress and boredom. Job rotation can also prevent muscle fatigue and reduce workplace injuries.

Job rotation also makes sense for managers. The vice president of Emerson/Rosemount in Eden Prairie, Minnesota, had been the vice president of Engineering, vice president of Manufacturing, and vice president of Marketing before being named the president of the division. This executive was well prepared for a general management role because of his job rotation experiences.

See *cross-training, human resources, job design, job enlargement, learning organization, pay for skill, workforce agility.*

job shop – A manufacturing facility (or department in a facility) that groups similar machines in an area and makes customized products for customers. ✪

A **job shop** makes customized products with a make to order (MTO) customer interface in a **process layout**. This customization is accomplished by moving customer orders through one or more departments (workcenters) to complete all of the steps (operations) on the routing. Job shops typically have long customer leadtimes, long queues, highly skilled workers, and general purpose machines. One of the main challenges for a job shop is promising completion dates to customers and then scheduling orders to reliably deliver the jobs on or before the promised date.

For example, a machining job shop might have drills, lathes, and grinding machines in separate workcenters. Almost every order going through the job shop is unique in terms of the engineering specifications, routings, and order sizes. The job shop has a long queue of orders waiting at each machine in order to maintain reasonably high utilization of the equipment and skilled machine operators.

In contrast, a **product layout** organizes people and equipment in the sequence required to make the product. For example, an **assembly process** is often organized in a straight line in the sequence required to build the product. Assemblies are moved one at a time from one assembly step to the next. Some workers may require tools and machines for their step in the process. All products go through exactly the same sequence, very little product variety is allowed, no queues are allowed between steps, and parts are moved very short distances by hand in lotsizes of one unit.

See *batch process, discrete manufacturing, dispatching rules, facility layout, flowshop, job, job order costing, job shop scheduling, makespan.*

job shop scheduling – The process of creating a schedule (or sequence) for jobs (orders) that will be processed in a job shop.

Job shops must make order date promises to customers when the jobs arrive. However, the uncertainty in queue times, setup times, and run times makes it difficult to predict when an order will be completed. One of the main performance metrics used in most job shops is the percentage of orders that are on time with respect to the original promise date. Although many managers agree that it would be better to measure against the original customer request date, few firms use this policy. Some firms follow the poor management practice of allowing the promise date to be changed after the promise was made to the customer, and then measure their performance against the revised promised date.

Academic research in job shop scheduling divides problems into two classes: static and dynamic. In the static problem, the set of jobs is given and does not change. The static problem is usually defined as minimizing the average flow time or the makespan (the ending time for the last job). Historically, the academic research in job shop scheduling has focused on simulation experiments that compare dispatching rules and developing both exact and heuristic finite scheduling algorithms that create schedules that do not violate the capacity constraints. Exact methods often require inordinate amounts of computing time, but guarantee the optimal (mathematically best) solution; heuristic methods are computationally fast, but do not guarantee the optimal solution. See the *dispatching rules* entry for more detail.

Most **Advanced Planning and Scheduling (APS)** systems, such as I2, Manugistics, and SAP APO, have scheduling capabilities for job shop scheduling. However, in this author's experience, these systems are often difficult to understand, implement, and maintain because of the data requirements, complexity of the problems, and complexity of the systems.

See *Advanced Planning and Scheduling (APS), algorithm, dispatching rules, expediting, flowshop, heijunka, job shop, makespan, service level, shop floor control, slack time.*

jobber – See *wholesaler.*

Joint Commission – An independent, not-for-profit organization that sets healthcare quality standards and accredits healthcare organizations in the United States; formerly called the Joint Commission on Accreditation of Healthcare Organizations (JCAHO), but now officially called The Joint Commission" and abbreviated TJC.

The Joint Commission is an independent, not-for-profit organization in the U.S. that is governed by a board of physicians, nurses, and consumers. It evaluates and accredits more than 15,000 healthcare organizations and programs in the U.S. Its mission is "To continuously improve the safety and quality of care provided to the public through the provision of healthcare accreditation and related services that support performance improvement in health care organizations." Its "positioning statement" is "Helping Health Care Organizations Help Patients." The Joint Commission's standards address an organization's performance in key functional areas. Each standard is presented as a series of "Elements of Performance," which are expectations that establish the broad framework that its surveyors use to evaluate a facility's performance.

The Joint Commission's homepage is www.jointcommission.org.

See *adverse event, sentinel event.*

joint replenishment – The practice of ordering a number of different products on a purchase or manufacturing order to reduce the ordering (setup) cost.

In the purchasing context, inventory management cost can often be reduced by ordering many items from a supplier on the same purchase order so the transaction and shipping costs are shared by many items. One simple joint replenishment policy is to trigger a purchase order for all items purchased from a supplier when one item reaches a reorder point. Order quantities can be determined using an order-up-to level policy subject to minimum order quantities and package size multiples. **In a manufacturing context**, joint replenishment is important when a process has **major setups** between families of products and **minor setups** between products within a family. When one product needs to be made, the firm makes many (or all) products in the family.

See *inventory management, lotsizing methods, major setup cost, order-up-to level, purchasing, setup cost.*

joint venture – A legal entity formed between two or more parties to undertake an activity together; commonly abbreviated as JV.

JVs normally share profits, risk, information, and expertise. JVs are common in oil exploration and international market entry. Many JVs are disbanded once the activity is complete.

See *Third Party Logistics (3PL) provider, vertical integration.*

just do it – A very small process improvement task or project; also called quick hits.

Most process improvement projects are able to identify a number of small "just do it" improvement tasks. These just do it tasks can be done by one person, require less than a day, do not normally require sign-offs by quality control or higher-level managers, and do not require significant coordination with other people. The "just do it" slogan is a trademark of Nike, Inc., and was popularized by Nike shoe commercials in the late 1980s.

Examples of just do it tasks include calling a supplier to request that they avoid deliveries over the noon hour, improving safety by attaching a power wire to a wall, or adding a sign to a storage area.

Process improvement teams should quickly implement these small improvements and not waste time prioritizing or discussing them. However, it is important that project teams document the benefits of these tasks so leaders can learn about the improvement opportunities and implement similar ideas in other areas, and include the benefits of the just do it tasks when evaluating the contributions of the project team.

See *lean sigma, project management, quick hit.*

Just-in-Time (JIT) – A philosophy developed by Toyota in Japan that emphasizes manufacturing and delivery of small lotsizes only when needed by the customer. ✪

JIT primarily emphasizes the production control aspects of lean manufacturing and the Toyota Production System (TPS). For all practical purposes, the term "JIT manufacturing" has disappeared from common usage in North America. The concept of "lean manufacturing" is now considered more current and larger in scope.

See *kanban, lean thinking, Toyota Production System (TPS)*.

K

kaikaku – A Japanese word meaning radical change, breakthrough improvement, transformation, or revolution.

Kaikaku is a major, significant improvement that occurs after many small, incremental improvements (kaizen events). Kaikaku should come naturally after completing many kaizens. The kaizens make kaikaku possible because they simplify the process and make it more visible. Kaizen is essential for a long-term lean transformation, but kaikaku is sometimes necessary to achieve breakthrough performance.

See *Business Process Re-engineering (BPR), kaizen, kaizen workshop*.

kaizen – A Japanese word meaning gradual and orderly continuous improvement or "change for the better." ✪

The English translation is usually continuous (or continual) improvement. According to the kaizen philosophy, everyone in an organization should work together to make improvements. It is a culture of sustained continuous improvement focusing on eliminating waste in all systems and processes of an organization. Kaizen is often implemented through **kaizen events** (also called **kaizen workshops**), which are small process improvement projects usually done in less than a week. The Lean Enterprise Institute dictionary (Marchwinski & Shook 2006) teaches that kaizen has two levels:

1. System or flow kaizen focusing on the overall value stream. This is kaizen for management.
2. Process kaizen focusing on individual processes. This is kaizen for work teams and team leaders.

The Japanese characters for kaizen (改善) mean change for the good (source: http://en.wikipedia.org/wiki/Kaizen, May 10, 2011).

See *kaikaku, kaizen workshop, lean thinking*.

kaizen event – See *kaizen workshop*.

kaizen workshop – The lean practice of using short (one to five day) projects to improve a process; also known as a kaizen event, kaizen blitz, and rapid process improvement workshop (RPIW). ✪

A kaizen workshop uses various lean tools and methods to make the problem visible, and then uses formal root cause analysis and other means to identify and correct the problem at the source. The result is rapid process improvement that can result in lower costs, higher quality, lower cycle time, and better products and services. Although kaizen has historically been applied in manufacturing, many service businesses are also now applying kaizen. One notable example is the Park Nicollet Health Systems, headquartered in St. Louis Park, Minnesota.

A kaizen workshop is not a business meeting or a typical process improvement project. It is a hands-on, on-the-job, action learning, and improvement activity led by a skilled facilitator. The process involves identifying, measuring, and improving a process. Unlike many approaches to process improvement, kaizen achieves rapid process improvement in many small steps.

Kaizen teams include people who work the process and also heavily involve other people who work the process. Therefore, workers usually feel consulted and involved, which goes a long way in overcoming resistance to change. On this same theme, kaizen workshops often try many small "experiments," again with the workers involved, which drives rapid learning and system improvement while maintaining strong "buy-in" from the people who work the process everyday.

Compared to DMAIC, a kaizen workshop has a number of disadvantages and advantages as listed in the table on the right. One challenge of kaizen workshops is managing the activities before and after

Kaizen workshop

Disadvantages	Advantages
• Disruption of business • Sometimes not enough time for data-based decision making • Items on the "30-day list" for more than 30 days • Sometimes hasty decisions are bad ones	• Quick business results • Disruption limited to the event • Rapid experiments in the gemba • Involvement of the gemba • Workers own the process and the results

Source: Professor Arthur V. Hill

the event. Some organizations prepare for a month before a workshop and then have a month of work after the workshop. However, it is fairly common for items on the "30-day list" to be on the list for more than 30 days.

See *5 Whys, 5S, A3 Report, DMAIC, gemba, kaikaku, kaizen, lean thinking*.

kanban – A lean signaling tool developed by Toyota that indicates the need for materials or production. ✪

Kanban is the Japanese word for sign, signboard, card, instruction card, visible record, doorplate, or poster. In manufacturing, a kanban is usually a card, cart, or container. A **kanban square** is a rectangle marked with tape on a table or on the floor. A **kanban card** is often attached to a storage and transport container. Ideally, kanban signals are physical in nature (containers, cards, etc.), but they can also take the form of a fax (a faxban), an e-mail, or even a computer report.

A kanban signal comes from the customer (downstream) workcenter and gives a workcenter authority to start work. If a workcenter does not have a kanban signal such as a card, container, or fax, it is **blocked** from doing any more work. For example, when a kanban square is full, the workcenter is not allowed to produce any more.

A kanban system was formerly called a "**just-in-time**" system because production is done just before the need of a downstream workcenter. However, the term "just-in-time" and the related JIT acronym have fallen out of favor in North America.

A kanban system is a "pull system" because the kanban signal is used to "pull" materials from upstream (supplier) workcenters. In contrast, an MRP system (or any schedule-based system) is a push system. Push systems use a detailed production schedule for each part. Parts are "pushed" to the next production stage as required by the schedule.

Push systems, such as MRP, require demand forecasts and estimated production leadtimes. To be "safe," most firms use planned leadtimes that are much longer than the average actual time. Unfortunately, long planned leadtimes invariably result in poor forecasts, which result in excess inventory and long actual leadtimes. Long actual leadtimes drive management to further increase leadtimes and compound the problem. **Pull systems** tend to work better than push systems for repetitive manufacturing as long as the demand is relatively level and cycle times are small.

Toyota uses a **dual-card kanban system** with two main types of kanban cards – the production kanban and the withdrawal kanban. The production kanban signals (indicates) the need to produce more parts. No parts may be produced without a production kanban. If no production kanban cards are at the workcenter, the workcenter must remain idle and workers perform other duties. Containers for each specific part are standardized, and they are always filled with the same (ideally, small) quantity. The withdrawal kanban signals (indicates) the need to withdraw parts from one workcenter and deliver them to the next workcenter.

The number of kanban cards between two workcenters determines the maximum amount of work-in-process inventory between them. Production must stop if all kanban cards are attached to full containers. When a kanban card is removed, the maximum level of work-in-process inventory is reduced. Removing kanban cards can continue until a shortage of materials occurs. A shortage indicates a problem that was previously hidden by excessive inventory. Once the problem is found, corrective action is taken so the system can function at a lower level of work-in-process inventory.

According to http://en.wikipedia.org/wiki/Kanban, the kanji characters for kanban are 看板.

See *blocking, CONWIP, faxban, heijunka, Just-in-Time (JIT), lean thinking, POLCA (Paired-cell Overlapping Loops of Cards with Authorization), pull system, standard products, starving, upstream*.

Kano Analysis – A quality measurement tool used to categorize and prioritize customer requirements based on their impact on customer satisfaction; also called the Kano Model, Kano Diagram, and Kano Questionnaire.

Kano Analysis was developed by the Japanese quality expert Dr. Noriaki Kano of Tokyo Rika University to classify customer perceptions of product characteristics. Kano defines five categories of product attributes:

- **Must-have attributes (also called must-be or basic/threshold attributes)** – The basic functions and features that customers expect of a product or service. For example, an airline that cannot meet airport noise regulations will not succeed in the marketplace.
- **Performance attributes (one-dimensional quality attributes)** – These attributes result in satisfaction when fulfilled and dissatisfaction when not filled. The better the performance, the greater the customer satisfaction. For example, an airline that provides more entertainment options will be perceived as having better service.

- **Delighter attributes (also called attractive quality attributes)** – These are the unexpected "extras" that can make a product stand out from the others. For example, an airline that offers free snacks in the waiting area would be a welcome surprise. Delighters vary widely between customers and tend to change over time. This point is consistent with the popular service quality expression, "Today's delight is tomorrow's expectation."
- **Indifferent attributes (reverse quality attributes)** – These attributes do not affect customer satisfaction.

For example, when customers pick up rental cars at an airport, they will likely have different attitudes about seats, checkout speed, and global positioning systems. Customers will always expect seats in the car and will be completely dissatisfied with a car without seats. Seats, therefore, are a must-have feature. Customers expect the check-in process to take about 15 minutes, but are happier if it takes only 10 minutes. Satisfaction, therefore, increases with check-in speed. Lastly, many customers are delighted if their rental cars have a Global Positioning System (GPS). A GPS, therefore, is a "delighter" feature.

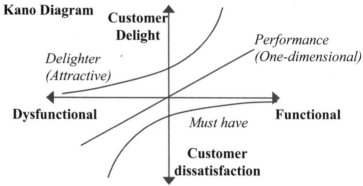

Kano Analysis uses a graphical approach as shown in the Kano Diagram on the right. The x-axis ("dysfunctional/functional") of the diagram measures the level of a particular product attribute (i.e., checkout speed) and the y-axis ("delight/dissatisfaction") measures customer satisfaction. For example, checkout speed is a performance attribute and is drawn as a 45-degree straight line. Must-have features (e.g., seats) are drawn so that high functionality brings satisfaction up to zero. When a "delighter" feature (e.g., a GPS) is not present, satisfaction is still at or above zero, but increasing a "delighter" can increase satisfaction significantly.

Kano Analysis begins by identifying all possible customer requirements and uses a survey to measure customer perceptions about each requirement. The following is a simple example of a Kano Questionnaire:

Kano questionnaire example

If the radio antenna automatically retracts when the radio is turned off, how do you feel? (Note: This is the functional form of the question.)	1. I like it that way. 2. It must be that way. 3. I am neutral. 4. I can live with it that way. 5. I dislike it that way.
If the radio antenna automatically does not retract when the radio is turned off, how do you feel? (Note: This is the dysfunctional form of the question.)	1. I like it that way. 2. It must be that way. 3. I am neutral. 4. I can live with it that way. 5. I dislike it that way.

Each question has two parts (1) "How do you feel if that feature is present in the product?" and (2) "How do you feel if that feature is not present in the product?" The responses for the two questions are then translated into curves on the graph.

A Kano Analysis can be used to classify and prioritize customer needs. This is useful because customer needs are not all the same, do not all have the same importance, and are different for different subpopulations. The results of a Kano Analysis can be used to identify customer segments, prioritize customer segments, design products for each segment, and guide process improvement efforts.

Walden et al. (1993) have written a good review article on Kano Analysis.

See *Analytic Hierarchy Process (AHP), ideation, New Product Development (NPD), Pugh Matrix, service quality, voice of the customer (VOC)*.

keiretsu – A Japanese term for a set of companies with interlocking business relationships and shareholdings.

The big six keiretsu are Mitsui, Mitsubishi, Sumitomo, Fuyo (formed primarily from the old Yasuda zaibatsu), Sanwa, and Dai-Ichi Kangyo. The keiretsu were established after World War II, following the dissolution of the family-owned conglomerates known as zaibatsu by the American Occupation authorities. It was the belief of many Americans that they could hasten the spread of democracy in Japan by reducing the concentration of wealth and hence economic power. Shares of companies owned by the zaibatsu were distributed to employees and local residents. As a result that when the stock market reopened in 1949, 70 percent of all listed shares were held by individuals.

Unfortunately, the zaibatsu dissolution was done in a haphazard manner. Often a single factory that merely assembled products for its group became an independent company, lacking a finance department, marketing department, or even a procurement department. To deal with this precarious situation, companies within the former zaibatsu banded together through a system of cross-shareholding, whereby each company owned shares in all other group members' companies. Within this structure, the major shareholders tended to be banks, a general trading company, and a life insurance company. Today, the "Big Six" keiretsu are all led by their respective banks, which are the largest in Japan.

Because listed companies bought and held onto shares in other listed companies, the ratio of shares owned by individuals in Japan steadily declined to around 20 percent by 2003. There has also never been a hostile takeover of a listed Japanese company, simply because its shareholders have refused to sell at any price. This has made management rather complacent and has greatly reduced shareholders' rights. Annual shareholders' meetings in Japan tend to be held on the exact same day, and usually end quickly without any questions.

In the 1990s, when the Japanese stock market was in decline, stable shareholding began to decline. Banks needed to sell their shareholdings to realize gains to cover their credit costs. Life insurers had to sell to realize higher returns to pay their policyholders.

The keiretsu concept is rarely used by Western companies. One exception is the venture capital firm of Kleiner, Perkins, Caufield & Byers, which encourages transactions among companies in which it holds a stake.

See *Just-in-Time, lean thinking, Toyota Production System (TPS)*.

Kepner-Tregoe Model – A systematic scoring approach used to evaluate alternatives in a decision-making process and win organizational approval for the decisions that come out of the process.

The Kepner-Tregoe (KT) Model was developed by Charles H. Kepner and Benjamin B. Tregoe in the 1960s. KT is particularly effective when the organization has to evaluate a number of qualitative issues that have significant trade-offs between them. The KT Model has been "discovered" by many people and is very similar to Criteria Based Matrix, Pugh Matrix, Multi-Attribute Utility Theory (MAUT), and other methodologies.

The steps in the Kepner-Tregoe methodology are:
1. Clearly define the problem at a high level.
2. Establish strategic requirements (musts), operational objectives (wants), and constraints (limits).
3. Rank objectives and assign relative weights.
4. Generate alternatives.
5. Assign a relative score for each alternative on an objective-by-objective basis.
6. Calculate the weighted score for each alternative and identify the top two or three alternatives.
7. List adverse consequences for each top alternative and evaluate the probability (high, medium, low) and severity (high, medium, low).
8. Make a final, single choice between the top alternatives.

The Kepner-Tregoe entry in Wikipedia provides a paired-comparison approach for developing the weights for the KT Model. Each of the criteria is listed on both the columns and the rows. Experts are then asked to independently compare all pairs of criteria in the matrix and to put a "1" when the row criterion is more important than the column criterion. Ties are not allowed. The main diagonal of the matrix is filled with all "1"s. The rows are then summed and divided by the sum of the values in the matrix, which will always be $s = n + n(n-1)/2$, where n is the number of criteria that are evaluated.

For example, a location decision has three criteria: cost, distance to markets, and availability of suppliers. The matrix is fort his example is shown below.

Kepner-Tregoe paired-comparison example

	Cost	Markets	Suppliers	Sum	Sum/s	Rank
Cost	1	1	1	3	50%	1
Distance to markets	0	1	1	2	40%	2
Availability of suppliers	0	0	1	1	10%	3
			Sum (s)	6	100%	

For the above analysis, $n = 3$, which means that $s = n + n(n-1)/2 = 6$. This is a good check to help avoid data entry errors. It can be seen in this analysis that the cost dimension clearly dominates the other two criteria. This matrix is only used to compute the weights for the criteria that are used for inputs to the KT Model.

The following is a simple example of the KT Model used for a new plant location decision where management has collected both quantitative and qualitative data, and needs to make difficult decisions regarding trade-offs between costs, risks, quality, etc. All dimensions are scored on a 10-point scale, where 10 is very desirable and 1 is very undesirable. (The values in this table are completely hypothetical.) Of course, many other criteria could also be used in this analysis and a much more detailed cost model should be used to support this type of decision. Many factors such as risk are hard to quantify in the cost model. In this example, China has better cost, but Mexico has better (shorter) distance to makets and greater availability of suppliers. The Mexico site, therefore, appears to be slightly more desirable.

Kepner-Tregoe example	Weight	China	Mexico
Cost	50%	7	6
Distance to markets(days)	40%	6	7
Availability of suppliers[a]	10%	4	6
	100%	6.3	6.4

[a] Reverse scaled so that 1 is good and 10 is bad.

Source: Professor Arthur V. Hill

The final weighted score seldom "makes" the final decision. The scoring process informs the process and helps stimulate a useful debate that supports the final decision, which must be made (and owned) by the management team. It is wise to ask the people who make the decision to create the weights and score the alternatives so they "own" the inputs as well as the results.

Some have criticized the KT Model because it does not explicitly consider risk and uncertainty issues. It is a good practice to include a risk dimension as one of the qualitative factors. In addition, KT tends to focus on consensus, which can lead to group-think and limit creative and contradictory points of view.

The Kepner-Tregoe consulting firm's website is www.kepner-tregoe.com.

See *affinity diagram, Analytic Hierarchy Process (AHP), C&E Matrix, decision tree, facility location, force field analysis, Nominal Group Technique (NGT), Pugh Matrix, TRIZ.*

Key Performance Indicator (KPI) – A metric of strategic importance.

See *balanced scorecard, dashboard, Key Process Output Variable (KPOV), operations performance metrics.*

Key Process Input Variable (KPIV) – See *Key Process Output Variable (KPOV).*

Key Process Output Variable (KPOV) – A term commonly used in lean sigma programs to describe an important output variable controlled by one or more Key Process Input Variables (KPIVs); also called Critical to Quality (CTQ).

All processes have both inputs and outputs. KPIVs include both controlled and uncontrolled variables. Organizations can change controlled input variables, but cannot change the uncontrolled variables. An example of a controlled input variable is the temperature of an oven; an example of an uncontrolled input variable may be the humidity of the room. Many uncontrolled KPIVs can become controlled if the organization decides to make the investment. For example, room humidity can be controlled with an investment in humidity control equipment.

Key Process Output Variables (KPOVs) are variables that are affected by the KPIVs. KPOVs are usually variables that either internal or external customers care about, such as units produced per hour, defects per million opportunities, and customer satisfaction.

See *C&E Matrix, Critical to Quality (CTQ), Key Performance Indicator (KPI), lean sigma.*

kickback – See *bribe.*

kiosk – A small store located in the common area of an enclosed mall or in a larger store.

KISS principle – The acronym "Keep It Simple Stupid," used to admonish people to eliminate unnecessary complexity.

> Wikipedia suggests the more polite version "Keep It Short and Simple."
>
> See *lean thinking, Occam's razor.*

kitting – The manufacturing practice of gathering items for assembly or distribution, typically in boxes or bags.

> Kitting is often a good way to ensure that all parts are available and easy to reach. In a manufacturing context, **kits** of parts are often put together in boxes and given to workers to assemble. In a distribution context, kits are prepared to be packed and shipped. If inventoried, kits should have their own part numbers.
>
> Some consultants argue that kitting is a bad idea because it tends to increase inventory, increase cycle times, and is often a non-value-added step in a process. They advocate that firms should have **logical kitting**, where they use their MRP systems to ensure that all parts are available. **Staging** is a similar idea.
>
> See *knock-down kit, Materials Requirements Planning (MRP), staging.*

KJ Method – A technique for building affinity diagrams named after Kawakita Jiro; also known as KJ Analysis.

> The key principle of the KJ Method is that everyone works together in silence to allow for individual creativity and to keep focused on the problem rather than getting sidetracked in discussion. The *Nominal Group Technique (NGT)* entry includes most of the main ideas for both affinity diagrams and the KJ Method.
>
> See *affinity diagram, Nominal Group Technique (NGT).*

knapsack problem – An important operations research problem that derives its name from the problem of finding the best set of items that can fit into a knapsack (backpack).

> The knapsack problem is to select the items to put into a knapsack (known as a backpack to most students today) that will maximize the total value subject to the constraint that the items must fit into the knapsack with respect to the knapsack's maximum weight or volume. The knapsack problem is a one of the best-known combinatorial optimization problem in operations research.
>
> Given a set of n items that each have value v_i and weight (or volume) w_i, the knapsack problem is to find the combination of items that will fit into the knapsack to maximize the total value. Stated mathematically, the knapsack problem is to maximize the total value, $\sum_{i=1}^{n} v_i x_i$, subject to the constraint that the items fit into the knapsack, i.e., $\sum_{i=1}^{n} w_i x_i < W$, where W is the maximum weight (or volume) for the knapsack, and the decision variables x_i are restricted to either zero or one (i.e., $x_i \in \{0,1\}$ for all i). The "bounded knapsack problem" allows for up to c_i copies of each item. The mathematical statement of the problem is the same except that the domain for the decision variables changes to $x_i \in \{0,1,...,c_i\}$. The "unbounded knapsack problem" places no upper bound on the number of copies for each kind of item.
>
> The knapsack problem can be solved to optimality with dynamic programming. Although no polynomial-time algorithm is known, fairly large knapsack problems can be solved to optimality quickly on a computer.
>
> See *algorithm, integer programming (IP), operations research (OR).*

knock-down kit – A kit or box of parts that can be used to assemble a product; also known as Complete Knocked Down (CKD) or Semi-Knocked Down (SKD).

> Knock-down kits are commonly used in the automotive industry. The manufacturer sells knock-down kits to a foreign affiliate to avoid paying import taxes or to receive tax preferences for having higher local content. For example, the General Motors factory in northern Hungary received knock-down kits in large wooden boxes from Opal in Germany and assembled them into cars using Hungarian workers. The automobiles assembled in this plant had sufficient local labor content to qualify for tax advantages from the Hungarian government[26].
>
> See *kitting.*

knowledge capital – See *knowledge management.*

---

[26] *This observation was made by the author from a plant tour in the early 1990s.*

knowledge management – Practices and systems used by organizations to identify, create, represent, and distribute knowledge for reuse, awareness, and learning across the organization.

Hansen, Nohria, and Tierney (1999) defined two knowledge management strategies:

Codification strategy – In some organizations, knowledge management centers on the computer. Knowledge is carefully codified and stored in databases where it can be accessed and used easily by anyone in the company. This is called a codification strategy.

Personalization strategy – In other organizations, knowledge is closely tied to the person who developed it and is shared mainly through direct person-to-person contact. The purpose of the computer for these companies is to help people communicate knowledge, not just store it. This is called the personalization strategy.

A good information systems infrastructure is an important success factor for a good knowledge management system. However, the biggest problem in knowledge management is usually not the information system, but rather the lack of proper incentives for people to add knowledge to the knowledge database. People are busy and often do not have time to add new information that might be valuable to others. Some people are also concerned that if they put their private information into the knowledge management system, their jobs could be at risk and they might, in fact, diminish their value to the firm.

See *business intelligence, call center, expert system, help desk, intellectual capital, intellectual property (IP), knowledge capital, knowledge worker, learning organization, Product Data Management (PDM), technology transfer, tribal knowledge.*

knowledge work – Jobs that deal primarily with transforming information.

See *knowledge worker.*

knowledge worker – A person whose primary job is to use his or her intellectual capability with supporting information systems to acquire, accumulate, process, analyze, synthesize, create, develop, use, manage, distribute, and communicate information.

The term "knowledge worker" was first used by Peter Drucker in his book ***Landmarks of Tomorrow*** (1959) to describe workers who use their intellectual capacities rather than their manual or physical skills. Knowledge workers are typically involved in tasks such as planning, acquiring, searching, analyzing, organizing, storing, programming, distributing, marketing, or otherwise adding value by transforming information into more valuable information. Knowledge workers include those with information intensive jobs, such as lawyers, scientists, academics, teachers, engineers, medical professionals, programmers, systems analysts, writers, and reporters.

See *knowledge management, knowledge work, personal operations management.*

Kolmogorov-Smirnov test (KS test) – A non-parametric statistical test that is usually used to determine if a set of observations differs from a hypothesized continuous probability distribution.

The KS test can be used to determine if a particular continuous theoretical distribution (such as the uniform, normal, lognormal, exponential, Erlang, gamma, beta, or Weibull) is a good fit with the data. The KS test compares the empirical cumulative distribution with the hypothesized cumulative distribution function. More generally, the KS test can be used to determine if any two datasets differ significantly without any assumptions about the distribution of data.

The KS test is based on the largest "error" between the actual and theoretical cumulative distribution functions. Given n independent samples arranged in numerical order $x_1 \leq x_2 \leq \dots \leq x_n$, define $F_s(x)$ as the cumulative distribution for the sample. $F_s(x_j) = (j+1)/n$, therefore, is the fraction of the n observations that are less than or equal to x. Define $F(x)$ as the hypothesized theoretical cumulative distribution. The "one-sided" KS statistics are then $D_n^+ = \max(F_s(x_j) - F(x_j))$ and $D_n^- = \max(F(x_j) - F_s(x_j))$.

Critical values for the D_n statistic are tabulated in many statistics textbooks and are available in many statistical software packages. Unfortunately, Excel does not support the KS test without add-in software, such as Crystal Ball. For large sample sizes, $P(D_n > x/\sqrt{n}) \approx 1 - 2\sum_{i=1}^{\infty}(-1)^{i-1}e^{-2i^2x^2}$.

Technically, the KS test is only appropriate when all parameters of the distribution are known with certainty. However, in nearly all cases, it is necessary to estimate the parameters from the data. The chi-square test is more appropriate than the KS test for discrete distributions.

Failure to reject the null hypothesis of no difference should not be interpreted as "accepting the null hypothesis." For smaller sample sizes, goodness-of-fit tests are not very powerful and will only detect major differences. On the other hand, for a larger sample size, these tests will almost always reject the null hypothesis because it is almost never exactly true. As Law and Kelton (2002) stated, "This is an unfortunate property of these tests, since it is usually sufficient to have a distribution that is nearly correct."

The KS test was developed by Russian mathematicians Andrey Nikolaevich Kolmogorov (Андре́й Никола́евич Колмого́ров, 1903-1987) and Vladimir Ivanovich Smirnov (Владимир Иванович Смирнов, 1887-1974).

See *chi-square goodness of fit* test.

KPI – See *Key Performance Indicator (KPI)*.

KPOV – See *Key Process Output Variable (KPOV)*.

kurtosis – A statistical measure of the "peakedness" of a probability distribution.

Higher kurtosis means more of the variance is the result of infrequent extreme deviations, as opposed to frequent modestly sized deviations. The sample kurtosis is $g = \dfrac{m_4}{m_2^2} - 3 = \dfrac{S_4/n}{S_2^2/n^2} - 3$, where $S_4 = \sum_{i=1}^{n}(x_i - \overline{x})^4$

and $S_2 = \sum_{i=1}^{n}(x_i - \overline{x})^2$ and where x_i is the i-th value, $\overline{x}$ is the sample mean, m_2 is the second sample moment about the mean (the sample variance), and m_4 is the fourth sample moment about the mean. The Excel KURT function uses the equation $g = \dfrac{(n+1)n(n-1)S_4}{(n-2)(n-3)S_2^2} - \dfrac{3(n-1)^2}{(n-2)(n-3)}$, which is an unbiased estimator.

See *mean, skewness, variance*.

L

labor grade – A classification system that groups jobs together that have approximately the same market value; also called pay grade or job class.

Labor grades are usually based on skills, experience, education, duties, budget responsibilities, level of independence, or leadership responsibilities and indicate pay ranges.

See *human resources, job design, pay for skill*.

labor intensive – An adjective used to describe products or services that require significant labor time and cost but relatively little capital.

Examples of labor intensive businesses include consulting, accounting, barber shops, teaching, and call centers. Labor intensive products and services are sometimes good candidates for outsourcing to lower labor cost economies. In some situations, labor intensive processes can be automated to reduce unit cost and improve quality, but often at the expense of more capital, higher fixed costs, and less flexibility.

See *automation, capital intensive, outsourcing, service management, value added ratio*.

labor management systems – See *work measurement*.

labor standards – See *work measurement*.

lagging indicator – See *leading indicator*.

LAI – See *Lean Advancement Initiative (LAI)*.

landed cost – An inventory costing term for the actual or standard procurement, transportation, duties, taxes, broker fees, and other costs required to "land" a product at a location.

The term "landed cost" is usually used in the context of an imported purchased item.

See *logistics, offshoring, outsourcing*.

Last-In-First-Out (LIFO) – (1) In an inventory management or queue management context: A priority rule based on the last arriving item, unit, or customer. (2) In an accounting context: A method for assigning costs based on the cost for the most recently manufactured or purchased items.

In inventory management with LIFO, the last unit put into inventory (or queue) will be the first to go out. This practice can result in some inventory being in inventory for a long time. In contrast, with First-In-First-Out (FIFO), the first unit put into the inventory will be the first to go out. The same statements are true in the context of a queue discipline. With the LIFO queue discipline, the last arriving customer is serviced first.

In accounting, LIFO is used to determine the cost of goods sold where the most recent units purchased from suppliers are assumed to be sold first. Most U.S.-based companies use LIFO to reduce income tax in times of inflation.

Note that inventory management and accounting policies can be different. It is quite common for the warehouse to use FIFO to manage inventory, where the accounting system uses LIFO to assign costs.

See *cost of goods sold, dispatching rules, First-in-First-Out (FIFO), inventory valuation, queuing theory.*

late configuration – See *postponement*.

late customization – See *postponement*.

lateness – See *service level*.

Law of Large Numbers – A fundamental concept in probability and statistics that describes how the average of a randomly selected sample from a large population is likely to grow closer to the true average of the whole population as the number of observations increases.

For example, the average weight of 10 apples randomly selected from a barrel of 100 apples is probably closer to the true average weight of all 100 apples than the average weight of 3 apples taken from that same barrel.

The weak Law of Large Numbers states that as the sample size grows larger, the difference between the sample mean and the population mean will approach zero. The strong Law of Large Numbers states that as the sample size grows larger, the probability that the sample and population means will be equal approaches one.

One of the most important conclusions of the Law of Large Numbers is the Central Limit Theorem, which describes how sample means tend to occur in a normal distribution around the mean of the population regardless of the shape of the population distribution, especially as sample sizes get larger.

See *Central Limit Theorem*

layout – See *facility layout*.

LCL (less than container load) – See *less than container load (LCL)*.

leading indicator – A variable that changes in advance of a new trend or condition and therefore can be used to predict another variable one or more periods ahead.

Examples of leading indicators include economic variables, such as the number of building permits, non-residential housing, mobile phones shipped, unemployment insurance claims, money supply, and inventory changes. Policy makers often watch many of these leading indicators to decide what to do about interest rates.

In contrast, coincident indicators change at the same time as the variable of interest and lagging indicators change after the variable of interest. These variables, therefore, are of no use for predictive purposes, but can sometimes confirm the existence of a condition or trend.

See *balanced scorecard, econometric forecasting, forecasting.*

leadtime – The planned replenishment time for an order; often written as two words (lead time); also called production leadtime, manufacturing leadtime, and planned leadtime. ✪

The planned leadtime is a planning factor used in both MRP and reorder point systems for the planned time required to replenish inventory from a supplier (a purchase order) or from a plant (a manufacturing order). This planning factor is called the "replenishment leadtime" in SAP.

Ideally, the planned leadtime is a reliable forecast of the expected (average) actual replenishment time in the future. In other words, the planned leadtime should not include any cushion or buffer to handle situations where the actual leadtime is longer than average. The buffer should be handled by the safety stock and should not be imbedded in the planned leadtime.

The planned leadtime for a manufacturing order is the sum of the planned leadtimes for all steps in the routing for the order. For each operation, this typically includes (a) the queue time before the operation begins, (b) the setup time to get the machine ready for production, (c) the run time to process the order, and finally (d) the post-operation time to wait for the order to be picked up and moved to the next workcenter.

The term "leadtime" is often used as a synonym for throughput time, cycle time, flow time, and customer leadtime. However, the prefix "lead" suggests that the term "leadtime" should be used primarily as a planning factor for the time to "lead" the event rather than as the actual throughput time. It is better, therefore, to use the terms "throughput time," "cycle time," or "flow time" rather than "leadtime" when describing actual throughput times. (See the *cycle time* entry to better understand the two conflicting definitions of cycle time.)

The planned leadtime is a constant, but the actual throughput time (sometimes called cycle time) is a random variable and has a minimum, maximum, mean, standard deviation, median, etc. Note that the safety stock calculation should use either an estimate of the longest leadtime or the more complicated safety stock equation that includes both the mean and standard deviation of the leadtime. (See the *safety stock* entry for more detail.)

The promised customer leadtime is the promised customer wait time for an order. The actual customer leadtime is the actual wait time (a random variable) experienced by the customer.

It is important to understand that the planned leadtime, actual leadtime (throughput time, flow time), promised customer leadtime, and actual customer leadtime might all be different. Therefore, it is important for managers, engineers, and students of operations management to be very clear when they use these terms. When a manager reports that the factory has a leadtime of two weeks, this could mean a two-week planned leadtime, two-week average leadtime, two-week minimum leadtime, two-week modal leadtime, two-week promised customer leadtime, etc.

The *cycle time* entry provides more insights into these and other closely related issues.

See *cumulative leadtime, customer leadtime, cycle time, demand during leadtime, leadtime syndrome, manufacturing order, purchase order (PO), purchasing, purchasing leadtime, push-pull boundary, reorder point, routing, run time, takt time, time in system, turnaround time.*

leadtime syndrome – A vicious cycle where a supplier's quoted leadtime gets longer, which results in customers ordering more to cover their planned leadtime, which results in the supplier quoting an even longer leadtime.

The cycle can be described as follows:
1. A manufacturer increases the quoted leadtime. This could be for any reason, such as a vacation, a machine problem, a slight increase in demand, etc.
2. The customer learns about the increased leadtime and releases orders earlier to cover the demand during the planned leadtime. Note that the customer's true average demand did not change in this scenario.
3. The manufacturer receives the larger order, adds it to the order backlog, and further increases the quoted leadtime. The leadtime syndrome continues back to step 1.

The solution to the leadtime syndrome is for customers to communicate their true demand to their suppliers to give their suppliers forward visibility of their true demand and for suppliers to avoid increasing quoted leadtimes, even when the demand increases. The leadtime syndrome is closely related to the bullwhip effect. George Plossl (1985) discussed the leadtime syndrome in his books and seminars in the 1980s.

See *bullwhip effect, force majeure, leadtime, Parkinson's Laws.*

Lean Advancement Initiative (LAI) – A learning and research community that brings together key aerospace stakeholders from industry, government, and academia; formerly called the Lean Aerospace Initiative.

LAI is a consortium-guided research program headquartered at the Massachusetts Institute of Technology (MIT) Department of Aeronautics and Astronautics, in close collaboration with the Sloan School of Management. LAI is managed under the auspices of the Center for Technology, Policy and Industrial Development, an interdisciplinary research center within the Engineering Systems Division. LAI was born out of practicality and necessity. Declining procurement budgets, rising costs, and overcapacity prompted the defense acquisition strategy to stress affordability rather than just performance at any cost. LAI was formally launched in 1993, when leaders from the U.S. Air Force, MIT, labor unions, and defense aerospace businesses forged a trail-blazing partnership to transform the industry, reinvigorate the workplace, and reinvest in America by applying lean manufacturing principles. Most of the above comes from LAI's website (http://lean.mit.edu).

See *lean thinking.*

Lean Aerospace Initiative – See *Lean Advancement Initiative (LAI).*

lean design – Lean design is a set of tools for reducing the new product development cost and time with a focus on reducing variation, addressing bottlenecks, eliminating rework, and managing capacity.

See *lean thinking, New Product Development (NPD).*

Lean Enterprise Institute (LEI) – A nonprofit education and research organization founded by Jim Womack in 1997 to promote and advance the principles of lean thinking in every aspect of business and across a wide range of industries.

LEI develops and teaches lean principles, tools, and techniques designed to enable positive change. A major LEI objective is to create a complete toolkit for lean thinkers to use in transforming businesses. The lean toolkit is intended to be a dynamic and continually evolving means of sharing knowledge among lean thinkers. One of the more important publications of the LEI is the **Lean Lexicon**, edited by Chet Marchwinski and John Shook (2009). The LEI website is www.lean.org.

See *8 wastes*, *lean thinking*.

lean manufacturing – See *lean thinking*.

lean production office – See *lean promotion office*.

lean promotion office – The program "office" (team) that manages the lean implementation.

This team provides leadership, training, and support for implementing a lean manufacturing program.

See *lean thinking*, *program management office*.

lean sigma – A formal process improvement program that combines six sigma and lean thinking principles; also called lean six sigma. ✪

Six sigma versus lean – Lean sigma process improvement programs are widely used in larger firms throughout North America and Europe. These programs grew out of the six sigma program, which was developed by Motorola and expanded and popularized by GE. In recent years, nearly all six sigma programs have changed their names to lean sigma to reflect the fact that they now embrace many lean principles and tools. The George Group, a North American consultancy that owns the trademark to the name "lean sigma," argues that six sigma programs historically focused on reducing variation, whereas lean programs focused on reducing the average cycle time (George, Rowlands, & Kastle 2003; George 2003). However, this dichotomy is too simplistic given that many organizations use six sigma tools, such as process mapping, to reduce the average cycle time and waste and many organizations use lean principles, such as error proofing and small lotsizes, to reduce variation and defects. Clearly, both lean and six sigma seek to reduce variation, defects, waste, and cycle time.

How to combine six sigma and lean – Paul Husby, retired senior vice president at 3M, and other thought leaders have argued that six sigma tends to rely on statistical methods, whereas lean is more of a philosophy of how a firm should be managed, with emphasis on simplicity, visibility, standardized work, and accountability. He suggests the following simple rule: If the cause is unknown or difficult to determine, use the six sigma DMAIC approach, but otherwise use lean.

According to Scot Webster, former vice president of Quality and Supply Chain at Medtronic[27], "Six sigma makes a science of process capability and lean makes a science of process flow and both are implemented with the DMAIC approach." Webster argued that the standard six sigma equation $Y = f(x_1, x_2, \ldots, x_N)$ works for both six sigma and for lean. The only difference is that for six sigma, the challenge is to find the vital few x_i variables among a large number of possible variables; for lean, the challenge is to find the vital few from only 18 potential tools. He listed 11 of the 18 tools in his publicly available talk: transfer lot size, process lot size, options, rework, downtime, external set up, internal set up, attended machine, unattended machine, move, and labor. He summarized his talk on lean sigma by arguing that both six sigma and lean are about leadership development and asserted that lean sigma was 70 percent leadership development and 30 percent process improvement.

One of the best ways to combine lean and six sigma principles in a lean sigma program is to use the six sigma program framework to provide an organizational structure for process improvement projects. This structure helps the firm align projects with the organization's strategies and goals, staff appropriately, and have proper accountability. Many six sigma projects use lean manufacturing principles and tools (cycle time reduction, lotsize reduction, etc.). The six sigma DMAIC approach can be used for all projects, but experts such as Husby argue that DMAIC is not needed for most lean projects because the problem and the solution are already well understood.

---

[27] *These quotes are from a talk given by Scot Webster in the Carlson School of Management on October 27, 2004.*

Five views of lean sigma – Zhang, Hill, and Gilbreath (2010) identify five different views of lean sigma programs as shown in the figure on the right. From the **metric point of view**, lean sigma is about maximizing the "sigma level" (minimizing the defect rate or some other process capabilities metrics), often with the target of six sigma (or 3.4 defects per million opportunities). From the **tool point of view**, lean sigma is about applying managerial tools (e.g., brainstorming) and statistical tools (e.g., design of experiments) to problem solving. From the **project point of view**, lean sigma is about defining and executing lean sigma projects with black belt or green belt project leaders using the DMAIC five-step problem solving methodology. From the **program point of view**, lean sigma is about a program management office that finds and prioritizes problems that need to be addressed and then charters and resources projects to address those problems. From the **philosophy point of view**, lean sigma is about building a sustainable culture of leaders who are relentless about continuously improving processes to eliminate waste and defect.

Source: Professor Arthur V. Hill

Metric View

Tool View

Project View

Program View

Philosophy View

DMAIC – Lean sigma projects often use the six sigma five-step process called DMAIC – Define, Measure, Analyze, Improve, and Control. These five steps are described in more detail in the *DMAIC* entry. Lean sigma projects are often driven by an understanding of the "entitlement" (i.e., the best possible performance) for a process. However, the target may be different from the entitlement.

Key roles in a lean sigma program – Lean sigma identifies five key roles for its successful implementation (Harry & Schroeder 2000). Certification programs for most of these roles are available from many sources. Some of the content below is adapted from the ASQ.org site. The executive leadership and champion work at the program level, whereas master black belts, black belts, green belts, and yellow belts work at the project level.

- **Executive Leadership:** Provide overall leadership for the program office by aligning lean sigma projects with corporate and business unit strategies. They also ensure that proper resources are allocated to the program. The leadership should include the CEO and other key top executives. They are responsible for setting the vision for the lean sigma program. They also empower the other role holders with the freedom and resources to explore new ideas for breakthrough improvements.
- **Champion:** Lead the lean sigma program. The champion is selected by the Executive Leadership and is usually a member of the executive team. The champion must translate the company's strategies and goals into projects. He or she also identifies resources and removes barriers to program and project success. The champions also acts as a mentor to the master black belts and black belts. At GE, this level of certification is now called Quality Leader. The champion usually manages the project selection process and the project hopper (the set of potential projects) and also selects people to become black belts.
- **Master black belts:** Assist champions in program management and train and coach black belts and green belts in project management. They are usually full-time resources for the lean sigma program. Master black belts should be experienced black belts.
- **Black belts:** Lead problem-solving projects and train and coach team members with help from master black belts. Black belts usually have between four and eight weeks of training and are normally assigned to manage projects full-time for a limited period (normally 2-3 years). They focus primarily on lean sigma project execution, whereas champions and master black belts focus on identifying projects.
- **Green belts:** Assist black belts on black belt projects and lead green belt projects while maintaining full-time job responsibilities. Green belts usually have between two and four weeks of training.
- **Yellow belts:** Participate as project team members and review process improvements that support the project. Many lean sigma programs do not use this designation.
- **White belts:** Understand basic lean sigma concepts and work on local problem-solving teams that support overall projects but may not be part of a lean sigma project team. Few programs use this designation.

Lean sigma training programs – The following is a list of topics that are often included in lean sigma training programs. Almost all of these topics can be found in this encyclopedia.

Program management skills

• Roles and responsibilities for executive leadership • Roles and responsibilities for the program champion • Roles and responsibilities for master black belts, black belts, green belts, project sponsors, and process owners • Project generation (finding potential projects for the project hopper)	• Project hopper (portfolio) management (project prioritization and selection) • Human resource development (selecting and training resources with the leadership development view) • Project staffing (assigning people to projects) • Program communication plan • Program performance measurement

Project management tools

• Brainstorming methods (affinity diagrams, nominal group technique) • Project charters • Project team selection (engagement plan) • Leading effective meetings (agenda, schedules, frequency, notes, task assignments) • Managing for change (conflict management, stakeholder analysis, RACI Matrix) • Project communication plan • Issue trees	• Work breakdown structure (WBS) • Project scheduling and reporting • Project reviews • DMAIC • Kaizen workshops • Project closing (project completion notice, post-project review, project closing report) • Microsoft Project or Excel (for project management) • Microsoft PowerPoint (for project presentations)

Use of process metrics

• Balanced scorecard concepts (Better, Faster, Cheaper) • Cost of quality (prevention cost, detection cost, internal failure, external failure) • Process capability and performance metrics (DPMO, sigma level, yield, first-pass yield, C_p, C_{pk}, P_p, P_{pk}) • Cycle time measurement (cost of long cycle times, quality, time elasticity of demand) • Inventory turnover measurement • Marginal versus full cost • Cost of carrying inventory • Waiting time measurement (mean time in system and in queue, utilization, Little's Law)	• Customer satisfaction measurement • Forecast error measurement tools • Measurement System Analysis (MSA) • Gauge R&R • Overall Equipment Effectiveness (OEE) • Labor efficiency and productivity (includes methods time measurement studies) • Learning measurement (trend line, learning curve, half-life curve, Moore's Law) • Supplier scorecards • Standard red/yellow/green scorecard dashboards • See the *operations performance metrics* entry for more details on this subject.

Process diagnostic tools

• The 8 wastes • Process mapping • Value stream mapping • SIPOC analysis • Causal mapping	• Knowledge mapping (also called mindmapping) • Root cause analysis • Theory of Constraints (identifying and protecting the bottleneck, the bottleneck as the pacemaker) • Microsoft Visio and Excel (for process mapping)

Lean sigma and lean process improvement tools

• FMEA (Failure Mode and Effects Analysis) • Error proofing (mistake proofing, poke yoke) • 5S • Standardized work and writing standard operating instructions • Setup and lotsize reduction tools (SMED)	• Pull versus push • Lean scheduling tools focusing on the pacemaker workcenter • Queue management concepts • Cellular manufacturing (benefits of cells, Chaku Chaku, justification of cells, etc.)

Statistical tools

• Descriptive statistics (mean, median, mode, range, standard deviation, etc.) • Exploratory data analysis • Pareto analysis	• Confidence intervals • Sampling plans (sample size calculations, stop and go rules, dollar unit sampling) • Hypothesis testing

• Graphical analysis (histograms, scatter plots, box plots, etc.) • Statistical process control (x-bar charts, r-charts, c-charts, p-charts, run charts) • Regression analysis	• Design of experiments (Taguchi methods, full factorial, factional factorial, ANOVA) • Non-parametric statistics • Microsoft Excel (for simple statistical analysis) • Minitab, SAS, or SPSS (for statistical analysis)
Voice of the customer tools	
• Customer satisfaction surveys • Marketing research surveys • Quality Function Deployment/House of Quality	• Kano analysis • Conjoint analysis • Pugh matrix
New product development tools	
• Design for Six Sigma (DFSS) • Design for manufacturing (plus other DFx concepts, such as Design for Assembly, Design for Disassembly, Design for Environment, Design for Reliability, etc.) • IDOV and DMADV • TRIZ	• Taguchi methods • New product development organization (e.g., heavyweight NPD teams) • Service blueprinting • Service guarantees • Experience engineering • Designing and managing a NPD stage-gate process

Source: Professor Arthur V. Hill

See *benchmarking, brainstorming, C&E Diagram, C&E Matrix, Capability Maturity Model (CMM), causal map, champion, control chart, control plan, Critical to Quality (CTQ), cross-functional team, defect, Defects per Million Opportunities (DPMO), Deming's 14 points, deployment leader, Design for Six Sigma (DFSS), Design of Experiments (DOE), DMAIC, entitlement, external setup, Failure Mode and Effects Analysis (FMEA), Gauge R&R, human resources, impact wheel, implementation, inductive reasoning, ISO 9001:2008, just do it, Key Process Output Variable (KPOV), lean thinking, linear regression, Metrology, PDCA (Plan-Do-Check-Act), post-project review, process, process capability and performance, process improvement program, process map, program management office, project charter, project hopper, Pugh Matrix, quality management, quality trilogy, quick hit, RACI Matrix, sigma level, stage-gate process, stakeholder analysis, Statistical Process Control (SPC), statistical quality control (SQC), strategy map, Taguchi methods, Total Quality Management (TQM), transactional process improvement, value chain, value stream map, voice of the customer (VOC), zero defects.*

lean six sigma – See *lean sigma.*

lean thinking – A philosophy and set of practices originally developed at Toyota that seeks to eliminate waste; also known as lean manufacturing or just lean. ✪

A brief history of lean – Lean concepts were first introduced at Toyota by Taiichi Ohno in Japan (Ohno 1978). Richard Schonberger played an important role in popularizing "just-in-time" (JIT) concepts in the U.S. in the 1980s, which emphasized the material flow aspects of lean (Schonberger 1982, 1986). The term "lean" was coined by John Krafcik[28] in the MIT International Motor Vehicles Program, but popularized in the book *The Machine That Changed the World* (Womack, Jones, & Roos 1991). More recently, Jim Womack at LEI has led a resurgence of interest in lean thinking with a view of lean that goes well beyond materials flow and manufacturing (Womack & Jones 2003). Today, the term "lean thinking" is used to emphasize that lean is more of a philosophy than a set of tools and that lean principles can be applied in services, government, and other non-manufacturing contexts.

Benefits of lean – Lean thinking focuses on reducing waste though a high level of engagement of the people in the "gemba" (the place that real work is done). Many firms that embraced lean thinking have been able to achieve significant benefits, such as reduced cycle time, inventory, defects, waste, and cost while improving quality and customer service and developing workers.

The basic concepts of lean – Many lean experts argue that promoters of lean sigma programs "just don't get it." They argue lean sigma programs use some lean tools but miss the lean philosophy, which means they do not truly understand lean. Clearly, lean is much more than a set of tools.

---

[28] *Interestingly, John Krafcik was named President and CEO of Hyundai North America in 2008. Under his leadership, Hyundai increased its marketshare by 50% (source: http://www.hyundainews.com/Executive_Bios.asp, April 23, 2011).*

Many lean consultants teach that lean is about simplifying processes, but then over-complicate lean by using too many Japanese words and focusing more on lean tools than on lean philosophy. After 25 years of study, this author believes that lean thinking can be summarized in just five words as shown in the simple diagram below.

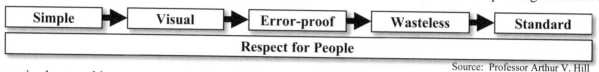

| Simple | → | Visual | → | Error-proof | → | Wasteless | → | Standard |

Respect for People

Source: Professor Arthur V. Hill

Lean is about making processes simple and visual. Once processes are simple and visual, it becomes easier for people in the "gemba" to make them error-proof and to eliminate waste. Once processes are simple, visual, error-proof, and wasteless, it is important to make them standard so that the benefits are sustainable. Lastly, respect for people before, during, and after the process improvement activity is critical to success.

The house of lean – The popular **house of lean** figure shown below is often used to teach the fundamentals of lean thinking. A similar figure appears in the Ohno (1978) book. This figure is adapted from Pascal (2002). The left side focuses on managing materials, the right side focuses on managing the manufacturing process, and the bottom focus on the fundamentals. Definitions for the terms in this figure can be found in this encyclopedia.

The house of lean

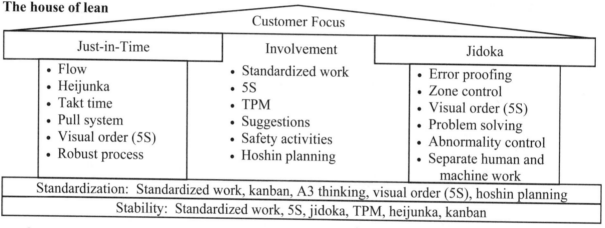

Customer Focus

Just-in-Time	Involvement	Jidoka
• Flow • Heijunka • Takt time • Pull system • Visual order (5S) • Robust process	• Standardized work • 5S • TPM • Suggestions • Safety activities • Hoshin planning	• Error proofing • Zone control • Visual order (5S) • Problem solving • Abnormality control • Separate human and machine work

Standardization: Standardized work, kanban, A3 thinking, visual order (5S), hoshin planning

Stability: Standardized work, 5S, jidoka, TPM, heijunka, kanban

Lean for process improvement – The "virtuous cycle of lean" is shown in the figure below.

The virtuous cycle of lean

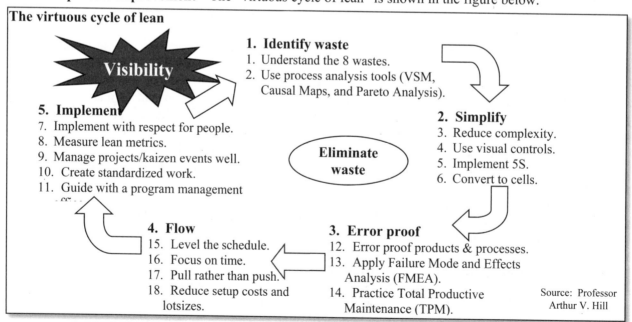

Visibility

1. Identify waste
1. Understand the 8 wastes.
2. Use process analysis tools (VSM, Causal Maps, and Pareto Analysis).

2. Simplify
3. Reduce complexity.
4. Use visual controls.
5. Implement 5S.
6. Convert to cells.

5. Implement
7. Implement with respect for people.
8. Measure lean metrics.
9. Manage projects/kaizen events well.
10. Create standardized work.
11. Guide with a program management

Eliminate waste

3. Error proof
12. Error proof products & processes.
13. Apply Failure Mode and Effects Analysis (FMEA).
14. Practice Total Productive Maintenance (TPM).

4. Flow
15. Level the schedule.
16. Focus on time.
17. Pull rather than push.
18. Reduce setup costs and lotsizes.

Source: Professor Arthur V. Hill

The cycle begins by identifying waste using the 8 wastes framework, value stream mapping, causal maps (or Ishikawa Diagrams), and Pareto Analysis. Once waste has been identified, it is eliminated (or at least reduced)

by making the process simpler, more visible, and more error-proof. Flow is then achieved by leveling the schedule, reducing cycle time, using a pull system, and reducing setup costs, setup times, and lotsizes (one-piece flow is the ideal). Finally, implement changes with respect for people (the gemba), focusing on lean metrics, such as the value added ratio, using well-executed kaizen events, and creating standardized work, all guided by a strong program management office. The virtuous cycle is self-reinforcing because the new improvement process will be even more visible, which makes it easier to see and eliminate waste. This figure was developed by this author and has been validated from first-hand experience with many factory and hospital lean implementations.

Spear and Bowen's five rules – Spear and Bowen (1999) defined five rules that capture much of the lean philosophy at Toyota. They emphasized that lean is more of a philosophy than a set of tools. These four rules are briefly described as follows:

- **Rule 1. Specifications document all work processes and include content, sequence, timing, and outcome** – Each process should be clearly specified with detailed work instructions. For example, when workers install seats with four bolts, the bolts are inserted and tightened in a set sequence. Every worker installs them the same way every time. While lean thinking shows respect for people and values experimentation (using PDCA), individual workers do not change processes. Teams work together to experiment, analyze, and change processes. Workers need problem-solving skills to their support teams in improving standard processes over time.
- **Rule 2. Connections with clear yes/no signals directly link every customer and supplier** – Lean uses kanban containers (or squares) that customers use to signal the need for materials movements or production.
- **Rule 3. Every product and service travels through a single, simple, and direct flow path** – Toyota's U-shaped workcells are the ultimate manifestation of this rule. This improves consistency, makes trouble shooting easier, and simplifies material handling and scheduling.
- **Rule 4. Workers at the lowest feasible level, guided by a teacher (Sensei), improve their own work processes using scientific methods** – Rule 4 is closely tied with Rule 1 and engages the entire workforce in the improvement efforts.
- **Rule 5. Integrated failure tests automatically signal deviations for every activity, connection, and flow path** – This is the concept of jidoka or autonomation. It prevents products with unacceptable quality from continuing in the process. Examples include detectors for missing components, automatic gauges that check each part, and visual alarms for low inventory. The andon light is a good example of this rule.

See *3Gs, 5S, 8 wastes, A3 Report, absorption costing, agile manufacturing, agile software development, andon light, batch-and-queue, blocking, Capability Maturity Model (CMM), catchball, cellular manufacturing, champion, continuous flow, cross-training, defect, demand flow, Drum-Buffer-Rope (DBR), facility layout, flow, functional silo, gemba, heijunka, hidden factory, hoshin planning, ISO 9001:2008, jidoka, JIT II, job design, Just-in-Time (JIT), kaizen, kaizen workshop, kanban, Keiretsu, KISS Principle, Lean Advancement Initiative (LAI), lean design, Lean Enterprise Institute (LEI), lean promotion office, lean sigma, milk run, muda, multiplication principle, one-piece flow, Overall Equipment Effectiveness (OEE), overhead, pacemaker, pitch, process, process improvement program, program management office, project charter, pull system, Quick Response Manufacturing, red tag, rework, scrum, sensei, Shingo Prize, Single Minute Exchange of Dies (SMED), stakeholder analysis, standardized work, subtraction principle, supermarket, takt time, Theory of Constraints (TOC), Toyota Production System (TPS), transactional process improvement, true north, two-bin system, value added ratio, value stream, value stream manager, value stream map, visual control, waste walk, water spider, zero inventory.*

learning curve – A mathematical model that relates a performance variable (such as cost per unit) to the number of units produced, where the performance variable decreases as the cumulative production increases, but decreases at a slower rate; also called experience curve. ✪

All systems can improve over time, and the rate of improvement can and should be measured. This learning can take place at any level: the machine, individual, department, plant, business unit, and firm. Some authors use the term "experience curve" for more complex systems, such as factories or firms; however, there is no practical difference between the learning curve and experience curve concepts.

The performance variable is usually the cost per unit or time per unit, but could be any variable that has an ideal point of zero. For example, other possible variables could be the defect rate (defects per million opportunities, DPMO), customer leadtime, etc. Variables, such as yield and productivity, are not appropriate performance variables for the learning curve because they do not have an ideal point of zero.

The graph below is an example of a learning curve with $k = 80\%$, $y_1 = 100$, and a learning parameter of $b = 0.322$. Learning curve graphs are only defined for integer values of n.

"Satisficing" is the practice of meeting the minimum requirements rather than seeking to improve over time. People tend to "satisfice" if not given an appropriate goal. The learning curve, therefore, can be used to set appropriate goals for improvement. The learning rate can also be used to benchmark organizational learning across organizational boundaries. Every measure in a balanced scorecard could have a complementary measure for its rate of learning.

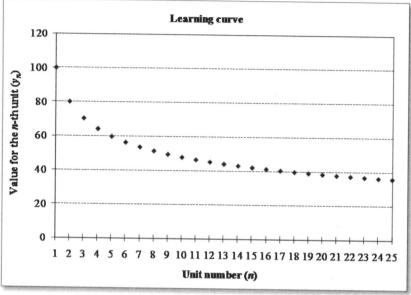

With the learning curve, every time the cumulative production volume doubles, the cost goes down by a fixed percentage. (The remainder of this discussion will assume that the performance variable is cost.) For example, with an 80% learning curve, the cost goes down by 20% every time the cumulative production doubles. If the unit cost for unit 1 is $100, the unit cost for unit 2 is $80, the unit cost for unit 4 is $64, etc.

The equation for the learning curve model is $y_n = y_1 n^{-b}$, where n is the unit number, y_n is the cost for the n-th unit, y_1 is the value for the first unit, and b is the learning parameter. The model requires that $b \geq 0$ and uses a negative sign in the model. Many textbooks present the model without a negative sign and have $b \leq 0$.

For a k-percent learning curve, the cost goes down by $(1-k)\%$ every time the cumulative production doubles. If the learning rate parameter k is known, the learning curve is given by $b = -\ln(k)/\ln(2)$. Conversely, if the learning parameter b is known, the learning rate parameter is $k = 2^{-b}$.

For example, for an 80% learning curve, $k = 0.8$ and $b = 0.322$. With $y_1 = 100$, the unit cost for the first 8 units is 100, 80, 70, 64, 60, 56, 53, and 51. (Note that these values are rounded to the nearest integer.)

The cumulative cost through the n-th unit is given by the following approximation (Camm, Evans, & Womer 1987; Badiru 1992): $Y_n = \sum_{i=1}^{n} y_i \cong \frac{y_1}{1-b}\left((n+\tfrac{1}{2})^{(1-b)} - (\tfrac{1}{2})^{(1-b)}\right)$. This approximation was tested for $k = 0.8$ and was found to have an absolute percentage error of less than 2% when $n = 1$. The error approaches zero as n increases, with an error of less than 0.03% for $n > 100$. This equation can be used to estimate the average cost through the n-th unit as $A_n = Y_n/n$.

The easiest approach for estimating the learning parameter from historical data is to find the value that fits the curve to the first and last observed historical values $b = -\ln(y_n/y_1)/\ln(n)$. The parameter y_1 for this model is set to the first observed historical value. However, this approach places too much weight on the first and last values and ignores the historical data in between.

Another approach recommended by some is to estimate the model parameters b and y_1 with linear regression on log transformed historical data. We first apply the natural log transform to both sides of the basic learning curve equation to find $\ln(y_n) = a - b\ln(n)$, where $a = \ln(y_1)$. We then apply linear regression to the transformed data to estimate the intercept ($a = \ln(y_1)$) and slope (b) for the line. We then estimate the intercept $y_1 = \exp(a)$ and learning rate $k = 2^{-b}$. However, linear regression poses some serious technical problems due to autocorrelation in the data. Several methods, such as first differences, can be used to try to compensate for the autocorrelation problem, but that is beyond the scope of this document. Note that the required transformation is not possible if the performance variable is zero for any historical observation.

See *autocorrelation, balanced scorecard, half-life curve, human resources, learning organization, linear regression, Moore's Law, operations performance metrics, satisficing, workforce agility.*

learning organization – An organization that has the ability to learn from its environment and improve its ability to compete over time. ✪

Most organizations today find that their current products and processes will become obsolete in a fairly short period of time. Jack Welch, former chairman of the board and CEO of General Electric, emphasized this point in his famous quote, "When the rate of change outside the company is greater than the rate of change inside the company, then we are looking at the beginning of the end" (Caroselli 2003, page 137).

It is necessary, therefore, for managers to lead their organizations in such a way that their organizations have built-in systems for improving (learning) over time. Learning organizations have the ability to transform their organizational experiences into improved products, processes, and knowledge.

Organizations can learn from many sources, including:

- **Customers** – To learn about customer's needs and desires as they change over time.
- **Suppliers** – To learn about new materials, technologies, and processes.
- **Research labs and technology suppliers** – To learn about new product and process technologies being developed by research labs, universities, and suppliers.
- **Workers** – To document new processes and make tacit knowledge explicit.

Senge (1990) argues that learning organizations exhibit five main characteristics: systems thinking, personal mastery, mental models, a shared vision, and team learning. This author has created the following list of strategies that organizations can deploy to nurture and accelerate learning. Most of these described are described in other entries in this encyclopedia.

- **Create knowledge management systems** – To leverage information systems to codify and share knowledge.
- **Measure learning** – To assess and reward learning based on measurable performance improvement. The learning curve and the half-life curve can be used for this.
- **Offer service guarantees** – To reward customers for sharing their complaint information.
- **Pursue early supplier involvement** – To get suppliers more involved in product design.
- **Benchmark best-in-class processes and products** – To capture standards and processes to use as a basis of comparison. See *benchmarking*.
- **Use cross-training, job rotation, job enlargement, and job enrichment to develop workers** – To disseminate learning within the firm.
- **Use co-location** – To improve learning across different functions and firms. See *co-location*.
- **Implement cycle counting** – To find the source of data integrity problems. See *cycle counting*.
- **Use post-project reviews** – To evaluate what went well (reinforce behavior) and what could have been done better (to identify new behaviors) when a project is completed. See *post-project review*.
- **Conduct root cause analysis after every adverse event** – To learn what could have been done to prevent a specific situation with an undesired (or desired) effect. See *Root Cause Analysis (RCA)*.

See *balanced scorecard, business intelligence, co-location, cross-training, cycle counting, half-life curve, human resources, intellectual capital, intellectual property (IP), job enlargement, job rotation, knowledge management, learning curve, Moore's Law, operations performance metrics, post-project review, Root Cause Analysis (RCA), satisficing, workforce agility.*

legacy system – An existing computer-based information system that is only being used until a newer system is fully operational.

The term "legacy" often implies that the old system has been in use for a long time and is becoming obsolete. Legacy systems are often expensive to maintain because they are difficult to interface with new systems.

See *Enterprise Resources Planning (ERP)*.

less than container load (LCL) – A shipment of a container that is not full; LCL can also refer to a customer's freight that is combined with others to produce a full container load.

See *less than truck load (LTL), logistics, shipping container, truck load.*

less than truck load (LTL) – A shipment that does not fill the truck or a shipment with less than the weight needed to qualify for a truck load quantity discount.

LTL shipments do not qualify for full truck load (FTL) rates based on weight or volume and normally have a longer delivery time due to consolidation with other LTL shipments. LTL is usually used to designate shipments weighing between 100 and 10,000 pounds. These shipments are usually not economical to ship via parcel shippers or FTL carriers and fall somewhere in between. This quantity of freight also involves more intermediate handling than does truck load freight.

A typical LTL carrier collects freight from various shippers, consolidates that freight onto trailers, and sends the shipment for line-haul. For delivery, a similar process is followed, where the freight from the line-haul trailer is unloaded, re-sorted, and sent for delivery. In most cases, drivers make deliveries first and then pick up from shippers once the trailer is empty. Therefore, most pickups are made in the afternoon and most deliveries are performed in the morning.

The main advantage of using an LTL carrier is that a shipment may be transported for a fraction of the cost of hiring an entire truck and trailer for an exclusive shipment. A number of additional services are also available from LTL carriers that are not typically offered by FTL or parcel carriers. These services include liftgate service at pickup or delivery, residential (also known as "non-commercial") service at pickup or delivery, inside delivery, notification prior to delivery, freeze protection, and others. These services are usually billed at a predetermined flat fee or for a weight-based surcharge calculated as a rate per pound or per hundred-weight.

See *carrier, consolidation, cross-docking, less than container load (LCL), logistics, quantity discount, shipping container, trailer, truck load.*

level – See *bill of material (BOM).*

level loading – See *load leveling.*

level of service – See *service level.*

level production – See *chase strategy, Heijunka, level strategy.*

level strategy – A production planning approach that keeps the workforce level constant and satisfies seasonal demand with inventories built during the off season, overtime, or subcontracting.

The level strategy maintains a constant workforce level and meets demand with inventory (built in the off season), overtime production, subcontracting, or some combination thereof. In contrast with a chase strategy, the workforce level is changed to meet (chase) demand.

Many firms are able to economically implement a chase strategy for each product and a level employment overall strategy by offering counter-seasonal products. For example, a company that makes snow skis might also make water skis to maintain a constant workforce without building large inventories in the off season. Other examples of counter-seasonal products include snow blowers and lawn mowers (e.g., Toro) and snowmobiles and all terrain vehicles (e.g., Polaris Industries).

See *chase strategy, heijunka, load, load leveling, Master Production Schedule (MPS), production planning, Sales & Operations Planning (S&OP), seasonality, subcontracting.*

leverage the spend – Combine purchasing from multiple units in an organization to justify negotiation for lower prices from a supplier.

An organization can "leverage the spend" with a supplier by combining all purchases across multiple departments, plants, and divisions into one negotiated contract. This allows the organization to buy in larger quantities, which gives it the power to bargain for a lower price. One common example is for Maintenance, Repair and Operations (MRO) items (such as office supplies) purchased by a large multi-divisional organization. Many organizations used to allow each department, location, plant, and division to buy its own MRO supplies. The firm can often get a much better price from suppliers by combining "the spend" (all purchases) across all divisions and all departments. The same concept can be used for many direct materials (non-MRO items). Many consulting firms have made this concept a major part of their consulting services.

See *consolidation, Maintenance-Repair-Operations (MRO), purchasing, spend analysis, Supply Chain Management.*

Lewin/Schein Theory of Change – A three-stage model developed by Kurt Lewin and Edgar Schein that describes how individuals change; the three stages are unfreeze, change, and refreeze.

Kurt Lewin developed a three-stage model of change that has come to be known as the unfreeze-change-refreeze model. Edgar Schein provided further detail for a more comprehensive model of change that he called "cognitive redefinition." The combined model is often called the Lewin/Schein Theory of Change or the Lewin/Schein Change Model (Schein 1992). The three stages are described briefly below.

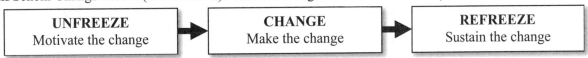

Unfreeze (motivate the change) – Change requires adding new forces for change or removing some of the existing factors that are at play in perpetuating the current behavior. This unfreezing process has three sub-processes that relate to a readiness and motivation to change:

- **Disconfirmation** – Learning and change begins with dissatisfaction or frustration, such as not meeting personal goals.
- **Survival anxiety** – When people accept the disconfirming information as valid, they feel "survival anxiety" or guilt. However, this may not be sufficient to prompt change if "learning anxiety" is present.
- **Psychological safety** – Learning anxiety triggers defensiveness and resistance due to the pain of having to unlearn what had been previously accepted. Three stages occur in response to learning anxiety: (1) denial, (2) scapegoating and passing the buck, and (3) maneuvering and bargaining. It is necessary to move past the possible anxieties for change to progress. This can be accomplished by either having the survival anxiety be greater than the learning anxiety or, preferably, by reducing learning anxiety. Change agents can create psychological safety by having people work in groups, providing positive visions for the learner, breaking the learning process into small steps, providing coaching, etc.

Move (change what needs to be changed) – Once sufficient dissatisfaction with the current conditions and a sincere desire to change exists, it is necessary to identify exactly what needs to be changed. Three possible impacts from processing new information are: words take on new or expanded meaning, concepts are interpreted within a broader context, and the scale used to evaluate new input is adjusted. A concise view of the new state is required to clearly identify the gap between the present and proposed state. Activities that aid in making the change include imitation of role models and looking for personalized solutions through trial-and-error learning.

Refreeze (making the change permanent) – Refreezing is the final stage where new behavior becomes habitual, which includes developing a new self-concept and identity and also establishing new interpersonal relationships. In the process improvement program literature, this is called the "control plan."

The ADKAR model is very similar, but somewhat easier to understand and apply.

See *ADKAR Model for Change, change management, control plan, force field analysis.*

life cycle cost – See *total cost of ownership.*

life cycle planning – See *product life cycle management.*

lifetime demand – See *all-time demand.*

LIFO – See *Last-In-First-Out (LIFO).*

Likert scale – A psychometric scale commonly used in survey instruments.

When responding to a Likert-scaled item on a survey, respondents typically specify their level of agreement to a statement. The following is an example of a five-point Likert scale often used by this author and his research colleagues: 1 = Disagree strongly, 2 = Disagree, 3 = Neutral, 4 = Agree, 5 = Agree strongly. Note that each phrase in this scale starts with either Disagree or Agree.

The Likert scale is named after Rensis Likert, who published a report describing its use (Likert 1932). The proper pronunciation is "lick-urt" rather than "lie-kurt."

line balancing – The problem of assigning tasks to workstations to minimize the number of workstations required while still satisfying the cycle time and precedence constraints.

A perfectly balanced process will have all steps in the process working at exactly the same rate. This will result in no idle time for any step and no inventory between steps. When designing an assembly line, many tasks (elements) need to be assigned to workstations. These assignments are constrained by the cycle time for the line (i.e., one completion every five minutes) and the precedence relationships between the tasks (i.e., some tasks need to be done before others). Many operations researchers have developed sophisticated mathematical computer models to solve this problem. The line balancing problem is less important when the organization can use cross-trained workers who can move between workstations as needed to maximize flow.

See *assembly line, cross-training, facility layout.*

line extension – A new product that is a variation of an existing product.

Line extensions are not significantly different from the original product and almost always share the same brand. Examples include a new package size, a new flavor, or a new ingredient. For example, Cheerios cereal now comes in many variants, with different flavors and package sizes.

See *New Product Development (NPD).*

line fill rate – See *service level.*

line of visibility – The line that separates a service operation into back office operations (that take place without the customer) and front office operations (that are in direct contact with the customer).

See *back office, service blueprinting, service management, service quality.*

linear programming (LP) – A mathematical approach for finding the optimal value of a linear function of many variables constrained by a set of linear equations of the same set of variables.

LP is one of many optimization techniques used in mathematical programming, which is one of the main tools used in operations research. A linear program must have a single **objective function**, which is the linear equation for the variable to be optimized. The LP must also have a set of linear constraints that must be satisfied.

LP has been applied to many operations problems. The most important problems are as follows:

The assignment problem – Match the items needing assignment with the possible assignments (locations) to minimize the total cost subject to the constraint that each item must have exactly one location and each location must have exactly one item. See the *assignment problem* entry for more detail.

The transportation problem – Find the amount of a product to send from plant i to market j to minimize total cost. Constraints include (a) the need to exactly satisfy the market demand and (b) the requirement that all available product be shipped somewhere. This problem can easily be extended to handle multiple periods (where the product is "shipped" from one period to the next) and multiple products (commodities). Special-purpose algorithms called network algorithms can solve the multiple-period, single-commodity problem very efficiently. See the *transportation problem* entry for more detail.

The blending problem – Find the optimal blend of ingredients to minimize the total cost while still meeting nutritional constraints.

The product mix problem – Find the optimal product mix to maximize the contribution to profit while still meeting capacity and other constraints.

Mathematically, a linear program is expressed as: Minimize $\sum_{j=1}^{n} c_j x_j$ subject to the constraints $\sum_{j=1}^{N} a_{ij} x_j \le b_i$

for constraints $i = 1, 2, \ldots, M$. The x_j are the decision variables, the c_j are the coefficients of the objective function, and the b_i are the "right hand side" constraint coefficients.

The solution to a linear program provides the optimal values for each of the decision variables (the x_i variables). In addition, the solution also provides "shadow prices" for each constraint. The shadow price is the value added by relaxing a constraint by one unit. Shadow prices allow users to conduct "sensitivity analysis" to experiment with a variety of what-if scenarios, such as increasing or decreasing resources.

Efficient computer code is available to solve linear programs with tens of thousands of variables. The Excel Solver can solve smaller linear programs. Closely related mathematical programming tools include integer programming (IP), mixed-integer programming (MIP), zero-one programming, network optimization, stochastic programming, chance constrained programming, and goal programming.

See *algorithm, assignment problem, integer programming (IP), mixed integer programming (MIP), network optimization, Newton's method, operations research (OR), optimization, product mix, production planning, sensitivity analysis, transportation problem, Traveling Salesperson Problem (TSP), what-if analysis.*

linear regression – A standard statistical technique that is used to find an approximate linear relationship between one or more independent (predictor) variables and a single dependent variable; also called regression and regression analysis. ✪

Linear regression is a powerful tool for both forecasting and understanding the relationships between two or more variables. Linear regression fits a linear equation to a set of historical data points to minimize the sum of the squared errors between the fitted linear equation and the historical data points.

The simplest type of regression is a **trend line** that relates the time period t to the dependent variable y_t. The parameters for the linear model $y_t = a + bt + \varepsilon_t$ can be estimated to minimize the sum of the squared errors $\sum_{t=1}^{n} \varepsilon_t^2$ with the equations $\hat{b} = \dfrac{6}{n(n-1)}\left(\dfrac{2}{n+1}\sum_{t=1}^{n} t y_t - \sum_{t=1}^{n} y_t\right)$ and $\hat{a} = \dfrac{1}{n}\sum_{t=1}^{n} y_t - \hat{b}(n+1)/2$. The equation for the $\hat{b}$ parameter must be solved before the equation for the $\hat{a}$ parameter. In Excel, the formula INDEX(LINEST(y_range),1,1) returns the slope and INDEX(LINEST(y_range),1,2) returns the intercept for a trend line and TREND(y_range,,n+k) returns the k-th value ahead in the y_range time series with n values. (Note that the two commas indicate that the x_range is not used.)

For **simple linear regression with two variables**, the input data consists of n observations on a single independent variable $(x_1, x_2, \ldots, x_n)$ and a single dependent variable $(y_1, y_2, \ldots, y_n)$. The parameters for the linear model $y_i = a + bx_i + \varepsilon_i$ can be estimated to minimize the sum of the squared errors $\sum_{i=1}^{n} \varepsilon_i^2$ using

$$\hat{b} = \frac{n\sum_{i=1}^{n}(x_i y_i) - \sum_{i=1}^{n} x_i \sum_{i=1}^{n} y_i}{n\sum_{i=1}^{n} x_i^2 - \left(\sum_{i=1}^{n} x_i\right)^2} \quad \text{and} \quad \hat{a} = \frac{1}{n}\sum_{i=1}^{n} y_i - \frac{\hat{b}}{n}\sum_{i=1}^{n} x_i.$$

The $\hat{b}$ parameter must be solved before the $\hat{a}$ parameter.

The Excel function TREND(y_range, x_range, new_x_range) is useful for projecting trends into the future. Excel charts can also show a trend line. The Excel formula INDEX(LINEST(y_range, x_range),1,1) calculates the slope and INDEX(LINEST(y_range, x_range),1,2) calculates the intercept for a trend line.

For **multiple regression**, the input data consists of M observations on a single dependent variable (y_i, $i = 1$, 2, ..., M) and the N independent variables $(x_{i1}, x_{i2}, \ldots, x_{iN})$. The goal is to estimate the β_j parameters for the linear model $y_i = \beta_0 + \beta_1 x_{1i} + \beta_2 x_{2i} + \ldots + \beta_N x_{Ni} + \varepsilon_i$ that minimize the sum of the squared errors, where ε_i is the error for the i-th observation. In other words, the least squares fit minimizes the sum $\sum_{i=1}^{M} \varepsilon_i^2$. Multiple regression uses matrix algebra to estimate the β_j parameters and evaluate the fit of the model.

Simple and multiple linear regression can also be done in Excel with Tools/Data Analysis/Regression. (If Data Analysis is not listed under Tools, then go to Add-ins and check the Analysis ToolPak to load this feature into your version of Excel.) A more direct approach for simple linear regression is to use INDEX(LINEST(y_range, x_range),1,1) to return the slope and INDEX(LINEST(y_range, x_range),1,2) to return the intercept. It is easy to extend this approach to access all the parameters and statistics for both simple and multiple regression. See Excel's Help menu for more details.

Although Excel can be used for most simple statistical analyses, its multiple regression capability is limited because the input range must consist of contiguous (adjacent) columns of x variables. Most people involved in serious statistical analysis use dedicated statistical software packages, such as Minitab, SPSS, SAS, or Jump.

See any standard statistics textbook for more information on this subject.

See *Analysis of Variance (ANOVA)*, *Bass model*, *Box-Jenkins forecasting*, *correlation*, *dampened trend*, *discriminant analysis*, *Durbin-Watson Statistic*, *econometric forecasting*, *forecast error metrics*, *forecasting*, *half-life curve*, *lean sigma*, *learning curve*, *logistic regression*, *outlier*, *scatter diagram*, *Theta Model*, *time series forecasting*, *trend*.

linearity – See *heijunka*.

line-haul – The longest leg of a shipment; also, the movement of freight between terminals. See *logistics*.

Little's Law – A fundamental queuing theory principle developed by MIT Professor John D. C. Little (Little 1961) that shows that the relationship between the average time in system (W_s), the average arrival rate (λ), and the average number in system (L_s) is given by $L_s = \lambda W_s$ for a system in steady state. ✪

In other words, the average number of customers (units, calls, etc.) in the system in steady state is equal to the product of the average arrival rate and the average time in system. For example, if a bank has an average arrival rate of $\lambda = 10$ customer/hour and the average time in system is $W_s = 1$ hour, the average number in system is $L_s = 10$ customers. Similarly, the relationship between the average time in queue, average arrival rate, and average number in queue is $L_q = \lambda W_q$, which means that the number of customers waiting in queue is the average arrival rate times the average time in queue. Both forms of the equation are considered Little's Law.

Little's Law can also be written as $W_s = L_s / \lambda$ to find the average time in system. For example, if a factory has an average demand rate (λ) of 10 orders per day and the current work-in-process inventory (L_s) is 100 orders, the average time in system (W_s) for an order will be $W_s = L_s / \lambda = 100/10 = 10$ days.

The average time in system is the sum of the average time in queue plus the average service time. This is written mathematically as $W_s = W_q + 1/\mu$, where μ is the mean service rate and $1/\mu$ is the mean service time.

See *capacity, cycle time, periods supply, queuing theory, time in system, wait time, Work-in-Process (WIP) inventory*.

load – (1) In a production planning context: The amount of work (demand) planned for a resource in a given time period; the requirements (in hours of work) for a resource in a time period. (2) In a logistics/transportation context: Anything that is to be moved from one location to another.

In the production planning context, load is usually expressed in terms of standard hours of work. Load is a measure of the actual (or forecasted) requirements for a resource. Therefore, load is used to determine if a resource is in an under- or over-capacity situation.

A load report shows the number of planned hours of work in each time period (e.g., day) and compares it to the capacity for that same time period. A load report is a simplified version of an input/output control report.

See *Advanced Planning and Scheduling (APS), backward loading, capacity, finite scheduling, heijunka, infinite loading, input/output control, level strategy, load leveling, project management, standard time*.

load leveling – The practice of attempting to even out the requirements for machines, people, and other key resources over time; also called level loading.

In both the project planning and manufacturing contexts, the goal is often to have a level (even) workload for key resources (machines, people, etc.) over time. **Production smoothing** (also called production linearity) is a key concept in lean manufacturing. (See the *heijunka* entry for more on production smoothing.) Some **finite planning manufacturing systems** and some project management systems attempt to create schedules that require about the same amount of a resource in every period. With **finite loading**, available capacity is an input, whereas with load leveling, the average capacity requirement is an output.

See *Advanced Planning and Scheduling (APS), Critical Path Method (CPM), finite scheduling, heijunka, level strategy, load, project management*.

load report – See *load*.

location analysis – See *facility location*.

locator system – An information system that (1) identifies storage locations where items are currently stored and (2) finds appropriate storage locations for items that are going into storage.

A locator system is a fundamental tool in all modern Warehouse Management Systems (WMS). Locator systems have several potential benefits, including:

- **Maximize space utilization** by assigning items to storage bins that are neither too small nor too large and by allowing for random storage of items (instead of fixed storage locations) where any one SKU can be stored in more than one location. (See the *random storage location* entry for more information.)
- **Improve productivity** by locating fast-moving products closer to more accessible locations and locating items so they can be picked efficiently.
- **Increase record accuracy** by separating similar items.

Location systems require a logical location naming convention for warehouses, zones within warehouses, aisles (or racks) within zones, bays or sections in an aisle, shelves (or levels) in a bay, and bins (for a specific SKU). Real-time locator systems use RFID technology to help find items.

See *fixed storage location, part number, random storage location, real-time, slotting, warehouse, Warehouse Management System (WMS), zone storage location.*

lockbox – A secure location used to receive checks in the mail, process them, and then transfer funds.

Lockboxes are more secure than typical business offices and can focus on receiving, capturing, and truncating[29] checks and then transferring payments to the appropriate bank accounts. For example, Allianz, a global insurance firm, uses a number of lockbox operations to process premium payments for insurance polices. Lockbox services are often offered by larger banks. A well-run lockbox operation will be efficient and secure and have minimal float (uncollected balances).

See *Optical Character Recognition (OCR).*

logistic curve – A growth curve that has an "S" shape as the market demand reaches a saturation point.

The logistic curve is $y(t) = a / (1 + c \exp(-bt))$, where t is the time since introduction, $y(t)$ is the cumulative sales to time t, a is the saturation point (the maximum total market demand), and b is the coefficient of imitation. The **Richards Curve**, a generalization of the logistic curve, is $y(t) = d + a / (1 + c \exp(-b(t - m)))^{1/c}$. The additional parameters include d as the lower asymptote, b as the average growth rate, and m as time of maximum growth. The **Gompertz Curve** has a similar shape and is given by $y(t) = a \exp(-ce^{-bt})$, where t is the time since introduction and a is the upper asymptote. Many researchers consider the **Bass Model** to be better than the above models. Note that the logistic curve has nothing to do with logistics management.

See *Bass Model.*

logistic regression – Logistic regression is a statistical modeling approach used to predict a binary dependent variable (the y response variable) based on a set of independent variables (the x variables); also called Binary Logistic Regression.

The y variable is binary, which means that it can be either a zero or a one. The model can also be used to estimate the probability that $y = 1$ for a given set of x values. Logistic regression can be a useful tool in the area of quality for understanding the impact of variables on defects. Other applications include credit scoring (determining which customers are worthy of credit), donor screening (determining which potential donors might be more likely to donate), and niche marketing (determining which customers should receive a mailing).

For a single x variable, the logistic regression model has the form $\hat{p}(x) = \dfrac{e^{\beta_0 + \beta_1 x}}{1 + e^{\beta_0 + \beta_1 x}}$, where $\hat{p}(x)$ is the estimated probability that $y = 1$ for the given x value. The parameters β_0 and β_1 are usually estimated using a Maximum Likelihood Estimation approach to provide the best fit with historical data. The model can be extended to handle multiple x variables.

Logistic regression is closely related to Probit Analysis. Many statistical packages, such as SPSS, SAS, and MINITAB, have logistic regression capabilities.

Note that logistic regression has nothing to do with logistics.

See *cluster analysis, data mining, data warehouse, discriminant analysis, linear regression.*

logistics – The organizational function responsible for managing a company's total distribution, transportation, and warehousing needs. ✪

---

[29] *Check truncation is the process of taking an image of the check, using Optical Character Recognition (OCR) to convert the information into digital form, and storing the checks until no longer needed.*

A **logistics network** is a system of suppliers, plants, warehouses, distribution centers, and transportation providers used to produce, store, and move products from suppliers of suppliers to customers of customers. Logistics management is responsible for the flow of materials and the associated flows of information and cash through this network. Logistics is closely associated with transportation, warehousing, inventory management, and customer services activities. The logistics function is often responsible for negotiating contracts with suppliers of transportation, warehousing, and other services.

For any one facility, **inbound logistics** involves the systems, policies, and procedures used to track and manage materials coming in from suppliers or returned goods from customers. In contrast, **outbound logistics** includes systems, policies, and procedures used to track and manage products moving from suppliers and manufacturing plants to distribution centers, distributors, and customers. In the military, logistics also involves the movement of personnel. Logistics plays a major role in delivering the "nine rights" to customers:

- The right product
- The right quantity
- The right time
- The right quality
- The right place
- The right form
- The right price
- The right packaging
- The right information

See *backhaul, Boxcar, cargo, carrier, common carrier, cross-docking, deadhead, dimensional weight, distribution, distribution center (DC), distribution channel, distribution network, Distribution Requirements Planning (DRP), distributor, dock, dock-to-stock, drop ship, dunnage, for-hire carrier, forklift truck, freight bill, freight forwarder, Global Positioning System (GPS), gross weight, headhaul, hub-and-spoke system, intermodal shipments, in-transit inventory, inventory management, landed cost, less than container load (LCL), less than truck load (LTL), line-haul, materials handling, materials management, milk run, mode, multi-modal shipments, net weight, numeric-analytic location model, Over/Short/Damaged Report, pallet, premium freight, private carrier, purchasing, repositioning, reverse logistics, supply chain management, tare weight, telematics, Third Party Logistics (3PL) provider, ton-mile, trailer, Transportation Management System (TMS), transportation problem, Traveling Salesperson Problem (TSP), truck load, value chain, warehouse, Warehouse Management System (WMS)*.

logistics network – See *logistics*.

lognormal distribution – A continuous probability distribution used to model random variables that are always non-zero and have a long right tail, such as the time to perform a task or the demand for a product.

The lognormal is appropriate for random variables that are the product of other variables. The shape of the distribution is similar to the gamma and Weibull distributions, but tends to have a larger spike for low values.

Parameters: The parameters (μ, σ) are the mean and standard deviation of the underlying normal distribution and not of the lognormal distribution itself. See the parameter estimation section below.

Density and distribution functions: The lognormal density function for $x > 0$ is $f(x) = \dfrac{1}{x\sigma\sqrt{2\pi}}\exp\left(\dfrac{-(\ln x - \mu)^2}{2\sigma^2}\right)$. Like the normal distribution, the lognormal distribution function has no closed form. $F_{LN}(x) = F_u((\ln(x)-\mu)/\sigma)$, where F_{LN} is the lognormal CDF and F_u is the standard normal CDF.

Statistics: Range $[0,\infty)$, mean $\exp(\mu+\sigma^2/2)$, median $\exp(\mu)$, mode $\exp(\mu-\sigma^2)$, variance $\exp(2\mu+\sigma^2)(\exp(\sigma^2)-1)$, and coefficient of variation $c = \sqrt{\exp(\sigma^2)-1}$.

Graph: The graph below is the lognormal density function with (μ,σ) = (0,1), which means $\mu_{LN} \approx 1.6487$ and $\sigma_{LN} \approx 2.1612$. The median for this distribution is 1. At the tails, $F^{-1}(0.05) = 0.193$ and $F^{-1}(0.95) = 5.180$.

Parameter estimation: According to Law and Kelton (2000), with n observations of a lognormally distributed random variable x_i, the maximum likelihood estimators for the parameters of the underlying normal distribution are $\hat{\mu} = \frac{1}{n}\sum_{i=1}^{n}\ln(x_i)$ and

$\hat{\sigma} = \sqrt{\frac{1}{n}\sum_{i=1}^{n}\ln(x_i - \hat{\mu})^2}$. Blumenfeld (2010) presented the method of moments estimators $\hat{\mu} = \ln(\overline{x}) - \frac{1}{2}\ln(1 + s_x^2/\overline{x}^2)$ and $\hat{\sigma} = \sqrt{\ln(1 + s_x^2/\overline{x}^2)}$, where $\overline{x}$ and s_x^2 are the sample mean and variance of the lognormally distributed random variable. However, in this

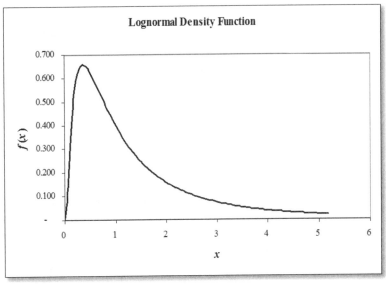

Lognormal Density Function

author's experience, these are not as precise as the equations from Law and Kelton. When given the mean and variance of the lognormal distribution (μ_{LN}, σ_{LN}), the parameters for the underlying normal distribution are

$\sigma = \sqrt{\ln(1 + \sigma_{LN}^2/\mu_{LN}^2)}$ and $\mu = \ln(\mu_{LN}) - \sigma^2/2$. The lognormal is degenerate when $\sigma_{LN} \leq \mu_{LN}/\sqrt{e}$.

Excel: In Excel, the function LOGNORMDIST(x, μ, σ) can be used for the cumulative lognormal. Excel 2003 and 2007 do not have a function for the lognormal density function, but it can be calculated with 1/($x*\sigma*$SQRT(2*PI()))*EXP(-((LN(x)-μ)^2/(2*σ^2))). Note that all parentheses in this formula are required. The cumulative inverse function in Excel is LOGINV(p, μ, σ). The Excel functions LOGNORMDIST(x, μ, σ) and LOGINV(p, μ, σ) use the mean and standard deviation of the underlying normal distribution rather than the mean (μ_{LN}) and standard deviation (σ_{LN}) of the lognormal distribution itself. Excel 2010 renamed LOGNORMDIST as LOGNORM.DIST(x, μ, σ, *cumulative*) and LOGINV as LOGNORM.INV(p, μ, σ).

Excel simulation: In an Excel simulation, lognormally distributed random variates can be generated with the inverse transform method with x = LOGINV(1-RAND(), μ, σ). Alternatively, pairs of normally distributed random variates X_{N1} and X_{N2} can be generated with the Box-Muller method and then transformed into lognormally distributed random variates with $X_{LN} = \exp(\mu + \sigma X_N)$. See the *normal distribution* entry for more information on the Box-Muller method.

Relationships to other distributions: If a random variable x_i is lognormally distributed, the random variable $\ln(x_i)$ is normally distributed.

See *error function, inverse transform method, normal distribution, probability density function, probability distribution*.

Lorenz Curve – A graphical representation used in economics and business to show the proportion of a distribution accounted for by the top x percent of the units; often used to show the cumulative distribution of income accounted for by the top x% of households.

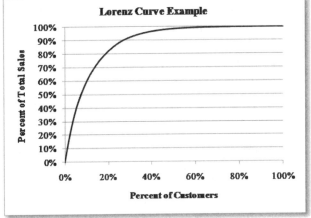

Lorenz Curve Example

An equal distribution is represented by a line at a 45-degree angle. In inventory management, the ABC analysis is an example of a Lorenz Curve.

For example, a firm has n customers with annual sales s_i, i = 1, 2, ..., n sorted from highest to lowest (i.e., $s_1 \geq s_2 \geq ... \geq s_n$). Define $x_i = i/n$, $S_i = \sum_{j=1}^{i} s_j$, $y_i = S_i/S_n$, and $(x_0, y_0) = (0, 0)$. The Lorenz Curve is the piecewise linear curve that connects the points (x_i, y_i), for $i = 0, 1, ..., n$. The graph above shows that the top 20% of the customers generate about 80% of total sales.

See *ABC classification*, *Pareto's Law*.

loss leader – A product offered at a low price to attract customers; known as a "key value item" in the United Kingdom.

A loss leader is a product sold at a low price (even at a loss) to stimulate profitable sales of other products. A loss leader is a kind of sales promotion. In the U.S., loss leaders are sometimes constrained by state minimum-price laws.

Some automobile dealerships use the loss leader as a **bait and switch** strategy. They offer an automobile for a very low price (the loss leader) but might have only one vehicle available for sale at that price. Some dealers follow the unscrupulous practice of having no vehicles available at the low price. When customers arrive, they lie to customers by telling them that the low price vehicle was already sold.

The following statements are generally true about loss leaders:

- In a retail store context, loss leaders, such as milk, are often placed at the back of a store to force shoppers to walk past other more profitable products on the way.
- Loss leaders are often products that customers purchase frequently, so they are aware that the loss leader prices are a good value. This leads customers to believe the entire store has good prices.
- Items offered as loss leaders are often limited or have a short product life, which discourages stockpiling (forward buying) by customers.

A closely related strategy involves using a loss leader to make it hard for customers to switch to other systems or standards. In other words, the loss leader reduces the initial cost for customers, but increases their switching cost, which "locks" them into a particular technology or service provider. Examples of this practice include:

- Razors sold at a low margin (or even a negative marging) to sell highly profitable disposable razor blades.
- Game consoles sold below cost to sell games.
- Inkjet printers sold below cost to sell consumables.
- Cell phones sold below cost to sell cell phone contracts.

In summary, a loss leader is a common marketing strategy to increase customer traffic and revenue at the cost of lost gross margin on just a few products. Some of the above concepts were adapted from the Wikipedia entry for loss leader.

See *forward buy*, *switching cost*.

lot – See *lotsize*.

Lot Tolerance Percent Defective (LTPD) – The maximum level of percent defective that is acceptable in a production batch.

The LTPD of a sampling plan is the level of quality routinely rejected by the sampling plan. It is generally defined as the percent defective that the sampling plan will reject 90% of the time. In other words, this is also the percent defective that will be accepted by the sampling plan at most 10% of the time. This means that lots at or worse than the LTPD are rejected at least 90% of the time and accepted at most 10% of the time.

See *Acceptable Quality Level (AQL)*, *acceptance sampling*, *consumer's risk*, *incoming inspection*, *quality management*, *sampling*, *tolerance*.

lot traceability – See *traceability*.

lot tracking – See *traceability*.

lot-for-lot – A simple lotsizing rule that sets the lotsize quantity equal to the net requirement in a period (usually a day); also known as a "discrete lotsize."

When planning using lot-for-lot order quantity, the system uses the exact net requirement quantity (i.e., requirements minus available stock) as the order quantity for the period. The system will group requirement quantities from the same period (usually one day) together in one lotsize. This lotsizing rule is available in nearly all MRP systems.

Contrary to some sources, lot-for-lot does not necessarily match the production lotsize with an individual customer order. Lot-for-lot is equivalent to a one period supply.

See *lotsize*, *lotsizing methods*, *Materials Requirements Planning (MRP)*, *periods supply*.

lotsize – The quantity that is ordered; also called batch size, order size, and run length.

The lotsize is called the order size for purchase orders and the lotsize, batchsize, or run length for manufacturing orders. The optimal lotsize for stationary demand is the Economic Order Quantity (EOQ).

See *cycle stock, Economic Order Quantity (EOQ), fixed order quantity, job, lot-for-lot, lotsizing methods, periods supply.*

lotsize inventory – See *cycle stock.*

lotsizing methods – Techniques for determining the quantity to order on a purchase or manufacturing order. ✪

The basic lotsizing methods (algorithms) include the following:

- **Fixed lotsize** – A constant quantity is ordered every time. Note that multiples of the fixed lotsize may be required if the net requirements exceed the fixed lotsize.
- **Economic Order Quantity (EOQ)** – The EOQ is a special case of a fixed lotsize. Again, multiples of the fixed lotsize may be required if the net requirements exceed the EOQ.
- **Period order quantity** – The lotsize is set equal to a fixed number of periods of net requirements (e.g., a 4 week supply).
- **Lot-for-lot** (discrete lotsize) – The lotsize is set to what is needed for the next period. Lot-for-lot is a special case of the period order quantity, where the number of periods is one.
- **Dynamic lotsizing procedures** – These procedures are similar to the period order quantity in that they define the lotsize in terms of the number of periods of net requirements that will be added to define the lotsize. However, the number of periods used in the lotsize can change for each order. The procedures attempt to find the optimal (minimum cost) lotsizes for the net requirements over the planning horizon. Examples of dynamic lotsizing procedures include Least Unit Cost, Least Period Cost, Least Total Cost (also called Part Period Balancing), and Wagner-Whitin.

Most **ERP systems**, such as SAP or Oracle, also allow for **order size modifiers** that are used to adjust order sizes. Modifiers are of three types: the minimum order size (either quantity or days supply), the maximum order size (either quantity or days supply), and multiples of a user-defined quantity. The multiples approach is appropriate when the lotsizes are constrained by delivery, packaging, or shipping units. For example, if the package size is 100 units per carton and the unit of measure is "each" (one unit), the order size has to be a multiple of 100 units.

Many firms, such as retailers and distributors, often buy many products from a single supplier. Many items can be ordered on one order and therefore can share the ordering cost. This is called **joint replenishment**. See the *joint replenishment* entry for discussion on this issue.

Many firms have found that the analysis of a single item in an inventory has little value, but an **aggregate analysis** of a large set of items can have a significant impact. See the *aggregate inventory analysis* entry.

See *aggregate inventory management, algorithm, Economic Lot Scheduling Problem (ELSP), Economic Order Quantity (EOQ), fixed order quantity, instantaneous replenishment, inventory management, joint replenishment, lot-for-lot, lotsize, manufacturing order, Period Order Quantity (POQ), purchase order (PO), safety stock, Time Phased Order Point (TPOP), time-varying demand lotsizing problem, transfer batch, Wagner-Whitin lotsizing algorithm.*

low level code – See *bill of material (BOM), Materials Requirements Planning (MRP).*

LP – See *linear programming (LP).*

LTL – See *less than truck load (LTL).*

LTPD – See *Lot Tolerance Percent Defective (LTPD).*

lumpy demand – An intermittent sales pattern that has sales separated by many periods with no sales; also known as intermittent demand and sporadic demand; used to describe the demand pattern for slow moving inventory.

For example, the following demand stream is said to be lumpy: 2000, 0, 0, 0, 0, 0, 0, 0, 1000, 0, 0, 0, 5000. Lumpy demand is often caused by having a small set of customers who often have large lotsizes. For example, one of 3M's international operations in Europe would only order from a plant in North America once every six months. The demand stream for this was (0, 0, 0, 0, 0, B), where "B" was a big number.

Lumpy demand often creates significant problems for forecasting, inventory management, and scheduling. Lumpy demand is common for spare parts, MRO items, make to order items, and low-demand items. Many retailers and wholesalers find that more than half their SKUs are slow moving items.

The coefficient of variation is a practical way to measure lumpiness. A good rule of thumb is that demand with a coefficient of variation greater than one is considered to be lumpy demand.

Exponential smoothing forecasting methods are not good at forecasting lumpy demand. Croston's Method for forecasting was designed for lumpy demand. Often the best way to handle lumpy demand is to increase the size of the time "buckets" (e.g., increase the time period from weeks to months or from months to quarters) so that a period with zero demand is rare.

See *coefficient of variation, Croston's Method, exponential smoothing, forecasting, Maintenance-Repair-Operations (MRO)*.

M

MAD – See *Mean Absolute Deviation (MAD)*.

maintenance – The work of keeping something in proper condition, upkeep, or repair.

Maintenance activities can be divided into three types: emergency maintenance, preventive maintenance, and predictive maintenance. **Emergency maintenance** is an unplanned maintenance problem that often results in lost productivity and schedule disruption.

Preventive maintenance is the practice of checking and repairing a machine on a scheduled basis before it fails; also called preventative maintenance. The maintenance schedule is usually based on historical information on the time between failures for the population of machines. In contrast, emergency maintenance is where maintenance is done after the machine fails. In the practice of dentistry, preventive maintenance is the annual checkup and cleaning; emergency maintenance is the urgent trip to the dentist when the patient has a toothache. The old English saying, "a stitch in time saves nine" suggests that timely preventive maintenance will save time later. In other words, sewing up a small hole in a piece of clothing will save more stitching later.

Predictive maintenance is the practice of monitoring a machine with a measuring device that can anticipate and predict when it is likely to fail. Whereas preventive maintenance is based on a schedule or a counting mechanism, predictive maintenance is based on the information from a measurement device that reports the status of the machine. Predictive maintenance is often based on vibration analysis. Predictive maintenance should be targeted at equipment with high failure costs and should only be used when the predictive tools are reliable (McKone & Weiss 2002).

See the *Total Productive Maintenance (TPM)* entry for more information on this topic.

See *autonomous maintenance, availability, bathtub curve, Maintenance-Repair-Operations (MRO), Mean Time Between Failure (MTBF), Mean Time to Repair (MTTR), reliability, reliability engineering, Reliability-Centered Maintenance (RCM), robust, Total Productive Maintenance (TPM), work order*.

Maintenance-Repair-Operations (MRO) – Purchased "non-production" items not used directly in the product; also called Maintenance, Repair, and Operating supplies, Maintenance, Repair, and Operations, and Maintenance, Repair, and Overhaul.

MRO is typically divided between manufacturing MRO (cutting oil, sandpaper, etc.) and non-manufacturing MRO (travel, office supplies, etc.). Manufacturing MRO includes electrical and mechanical, electronic, lab equipment and supplies, and industrial supplies. These items are generally not handled by the firm's ERP system, but are often a significant expense for many firms. General and Administrative (G&A) expenses include computer-related capital equipment, travel and entertainment, and MRO. MRO is usually the most significant and most critical of these expenses.

Many consulting firms have had success helping large multi-division firms "leverage their MRO spend" across many divisions. They save money by getting all divisions to buy from the same MRO suppliers, which gives the buying firm more leverage and volume discounts. For example, they get all divisions to use the same airline and negotiate significantly lower prices. This may also reduce transaction costs.

See *business process outsourcing, consolidation, consumable goods, finished goods inventory, leverage the spend, lumpy demand, maintenance, overhead, purchasing, service parts, spend analysis, supplier, Total Productive Maintenance (TPM).*

major setup cost – The changeover cost from one family of products to another family of products; the "between-family" changeover cost.

A **minor setup** involves changing over a process from one product to another in the same product family. In contrast, a major setup is involves changing over a process from a product in one product family to a product in another product family. In other words, a minor setup is **within family** and a major setup is **between families**, and therefore requires more time and cost. Both major and minor setup costs can be either sequence-dependent or sequence-independent.

See *joint replenishment, sequence-dependent setup time, setup cost.*

make to order (MTO) – A process that produces products in response to a customer order. ✪

MTO processes typically produce products that (1) are built in response to a customer order, (2) are unique to a specific customer's requirements, and (3) are not held in finished goods inventory. However, statements (2) and (3) are not always true:

MTO products are not always unique to a customer – It is possible (but not common) to use an MTO process for standard products. For example, the publisher for this book could have used an MTO process called Print on Demand that prints a copy of the book after the customer order is received. This is an example of a "standard product" produced in response to a customer order.

MTO products are sometimes held in finished goods inventory – Many descriptions of MTO state that MTO never has any finished goods inventory. However, an MTO process may have a small amount of temporary finished goods inventory waiting to be shipped. An MTO process may also have some finished goods inventory when the customer order size is smaller than the minimum order size. In this case, the firm might hold residual finished goods inventory, speculating that the customer will order more at a later date.

The *respond to order (RTO)* entry discusses these issues in much greater depth.

See *build to order (BTO), engineer to order (ETO), Final Assembly Schedule (FAS), mass customization, pack to order, push-pull boundary, respond to order (RTO), standard products.*

make to stock (MTS) – A process that produces standard products to be stored in inventory. ✪

The main advantage of the make to stock (MTS) customer interface strategy over other customer interface strategies, such as assemble to order (ATO), is that products are usually available with nearly zero customer leadtime. The main challenge of an MTS strategy is to find the balance between inventory carrying cost and service, where the service level is measured with a fill rate metric, such as the unit fill rate or order cycle fill rate.

See *assemble to order (ATO), push-pull boundary, respond to order (RTO), service level, standard products.*

make versus buy decision – The decision to either manufacture an item internally or purchase it from an outside supplier. ✪

Managers in manufacturing firms often have to decide between making a part (or product) internally or buying (outsourcing) it from a supplier. These decisions require careful use of accounting data and often have strategic implications. The guiding slogan is that "**a firm should never outsource its core competence.**"

One of the most difficult aspects of this decision is how to handle overhead. If overhead is completely ignored and the focus is on only direct labor and materials, the decisions will generally opt for "insourcing." If overhead is fully allocated (including overhead that will remain even after outsourcing is complete), decisions will generally opt for outsourcing and can lead the firm into the **death spiral** where everything is outsourced. (See the figure above.) In the death spiral, the firm outsources and then finds itself with the same overhead but fewer units, which means that overhead per unit goes up, which leads the firm to pursue more outsourcing.

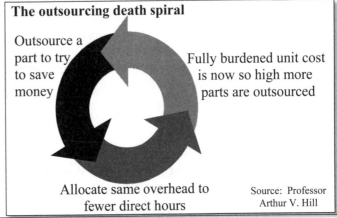

The outsourcing death spiral

Outsource a part to try to save money

Fully burdened unit cost is now so high more parts are outsourced

Allocate same overhead to fewer direct hours

Source: Professor Arthur V. Hill

See *burden rate, business process outsourcing, outsourcing, overhead, standard cost, supply chain management, vertical integration.*

makespan – The time that the last job finishes for a given set of jobs.

The static job shop scheduling problem involves scheduling a set of jobs on one or more machines. One of the common objectives in the static job shop scheduling problem is to minimize makespan, which means to minimize the maximum completion time of jobs. In other words, the goal is to assign jobs to machines and sequence (or schedule) to minimize the completion time for the last job completed.

See *job shop, job shop scheduling.*

Malcolm Baldrige National Quality Award (MBNQA) – An annual award established in 1987 to recognize Total Quality Management in American industry. ✪

The MBNQA was named after Malcolm Baldrige, the U.S. Secretary of Commerce from 1981 to 1987. It represents the U.S. government's endorsement of quality as an essential part of a successful business strategy. The MBNQA is based on the premise that competitiveness in the U.S. economy is improved by (1) helping stimulate American companies to improve quality and productivity, (2) establishing guidelines and criteria in evaluating quality improvement efforts, (3) recognizing quality improvement achievements of companies, and (4) making information available on how winning companies improved quality. The MBNQA scoring system is based on seven categories illustrated below.

Organizations can score themselves or be scored by external examiners using the following weights for each area: leadership (120), strategic planning (85), customer focus (85), measurement, analysis, and knowledge management (90), workforce focus (85), operations focus (85), and results (450). The total adds to 1000 points.

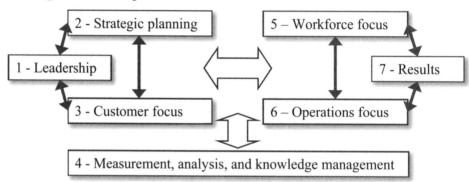

Baldrige criteria for performance excellence framework

See http://www.nist.gov/baldrige for more information.

See *American Society for Quality (ASQ), benchmarking, ISO 9001:2008, quality management, Shingo Prize, Total Quality Management (TQM).*

Management by Objectives (MBO) – A systematic method for aligning organizational and individual goals and improving performance.

Management by Objectives (MBO), developed by Drucker (1954), is a goal setting and performance management system. With MBO, senior executives set goals that **cascade** down the organization so every individual has clearly defined objectives, with individuals having significant input in setting their own goals. Performance evaluation and feedback is then based on these objectives. Drucker warned of the **activity trap**, where people were so involved in their day-to-day activities that they forgot their primary objectives.

In the 1990s, Drucker put MBO into perspective by stating, "It's just another tool. It is not the great cure for management inefficiency … MBO works if you know the objectives [but] 90% of the time you don't" (Mackay 2007, p. 53). Deming (2000) teaches that the likely result of MBO is suboptimization because of the tendency of reward systems to focus on numbers rather than on the systems and processes that produce the numbers. He argues that employees will find ways to give management the numbers, often by taking actions that are not in the best interests of the organization.

See *balanced scorecard, Deming's 14 points, hoshin planning, performance management system, suboptimization, Y-tree.*

management by walking around – A management concept that encourages management to walk, observe, and communicate with workers; sometimes abbreviated MBWA.

David Packard and William Hewlett, founders of Hewlett-Packard (HP), coined the term "management by walking around" to describe an active management style used at HP. MBWA was popularized by Peters and Austin (1985). The bigger idea is that management needs to be engaged with the workers and know and understand the "real" work that is being done. Japanese managers employ a similar concept called the **3Gs** (Gemba, Genbutsu, and Genjitsu), which mean the "actual place," "actual thing," and "actual situation."

See *3Gs, gemba, one-minute manager, waste walk.*

Manhattan square distance – A distance metric on an *x-y* plane that limits travel to the *x* and *y* axes.

The Manhattan square distance is a good estimate for many intracity travel distances where vehicles can only travel in certain directions (e.g., north/south or east/west) due to the layout of the roads. The equation for the Manhattan square distance is $d_{ij} = |x_i - x_j| + |y_i - y_j|$. This metric is named after the densely populated borough of Manhattan in New York City that is known for its rectangular street layout. The **Minkowski distance** metric is a general form of the Manhattan square distance.

See *cluster analysis, great circle distance, Minkowski distance metric.*

manifest – A customs document listing the contents loaded on a means of transport, such as a boat or aircraft.

See *Advanced Shipping Notification (ASN), bill of lading, packing slip.*

MANOVA (Multivariate Analysis of Variance) – See *Analysis of Variance (ANOVA).*

Manufacturing and Service Operations Management Society (MSOM) – A professional society that is a division of the Institute for Operations Research and the Management Sciences (INFORMS), which promotes the enhancement and dissemination of knowledge, and the efficiency of industrial practice, related to the operations function in manufacturing and service enterprises.

According to the MSOM website, "The methods which MSOM members apply in order to help the operations function add value to products and services are derived from a wide range of scientific fields, including operations research and management science, mathematics, economics, statistics, information systems and artificial intelligence. The members of *MSOM* include researchers, educators, consultants, practitioners and students, with backgrounds in these and other applied sciences."

MSOM publishes the ***M&SOM Journal*** as an INFORMS publication. The website for MSOM is http://msom.society.informs.org.

See *Institute for Operations Research and the Management Sciences (INFORMS), operations management (OM), operations research (OR).*

manufacturing cell – See *cellular manufacturing.*

Manufacturing Cycle Effectiveness (MCE) – See *value added ratio.*

Manufacturing Execution System (MES) – An information system that collects and presents real-time information on manufacturing operations and prioritizes manufacturing operations from the time a manufacturing order is started until it is completed; often called a shop floor control system.

Shop floor control has been an important topic in the production planning and control literature for decades, but the term "MES" has only been used since 1990. Whereas MRP systems plan and control orders for an item with order sizes, launch dates, and due dates, MESs plan and control the operations in the routing for an item. Most MESs are designed to integrate with an ERP system to provide **shop floor control** level details.

MES provides for production and labor reporting, shop floor scheduling, and integration with computerized manufacturing systems, such as **Automated Data Collection (ADC)** and computerized machinery. Specifically, MES functions include resource allocation and status, dispatching production orders, data collection/acquisition, quality management, maintenance management, performance analysis, operations/detail scheduling, labor management, process management, and product tracking and genealogy. Some MESs will also include document control systems that provide work instructions, videos, and drawings to operators on the shop floor.

The benefits claimed for an MES include (1) reduced manufacturing cycle time, (2) reduced data entry time, (3) reduced Work-in-Process (and increase inventory turns), (4) reduced paper between shifts, (5) reduced leadtimes, (6) improved product quality (reduced defects), (7) reduced lost paperwork and blueprints, (8) improved on-time delivery and customer service, (9) reduced training and changeover time, and, as a result, (10) improved gross margin and cash flow. See MESA International website at www.mesa.org for more information.

See *Automated Data Collection (ADC)*, *Materials Requirements Planning (MRP)*, *real-time*, *routing*, *shop floor control*, *shop packet*, *Total Productive Maintenance (TPM)*.

manufacturing leadtime – See *leadtime*.

manufacturing order – A request for a manufacturing organization to produce a specified number of units of an item on or before a specified date; also called shop order, production order, and production release. ✪

All orders should include the order number, item (material) number, quantity, start date, due date, materials required, and resources used. The order number is used in reporting material and labor transactions.

See *firm planned order*, *interplant order*, *leadtime*, *lotsizing methods*, *Materials Requirements Planning (MRP)*, *planned order*, *purchase order (PO)*, *work order*.

manufacturing processes – Technologies used in manufacturing to transform inputs into products. ✪

The following list presents a taxonomy of manufacturing processes developed by the author. This taxonomy omits many types of processes, particularly chemical processes.

- **Processes that remove materials and/or prepare surfaces** – Cutting (laser, plasma, water jet), drilling, grinding, filing, machining (milling, planning, threading, rabbeting, routing), punching, sawing, shearing, stamping, and turning (lathe, drilling, boring, reaming, threading, spinning).
- **Forming processes** – Bending (hammering, press brakes), casting (metal, plaster, etc.), extrusion, forging, hydroforming (hydramolding), molding, and stamping.
- **Temperature related processes** – Cooling (cryogenics) and heating (ovens).
- **Separating processes** – Comminution & froth flotation, distillation, and filtration.
- **Joining processes** – Adhesives, brazing, fasteners, riveting, soldering, taping, and welding.
- **Coating processes** – Painting, plating, powder coating, printing, thermal spraying, and many others.
- **Assembly processes** – Assembly line, mixed model assembly, and manufacturing cells.

Computer Numerically Controlled (CNC) machines and Flexible Manufacturing Systems (FMS) can do a variety of these activities. Manufacturing cells can be used for many activities other than just assembly. Machines used in manufacturing are often supported by tooling (e.g., fixtures, jigs, molds) and gauges.

See *assembly*, *assembly line*, *Computer Numerical Control (CNC)*, *die cutting*, *extrusion*, *fabrication*, *fixture*, *Flexible Manufacturing System (FMS)*, *forging*, *foundry*, *gauge*, *jig*, *mixed model assembly*, *mold*, *production line*, *stamping*, *tooling*.

Manufacturing Resources Planning (MRP) – See *Materials Requirements Planning (MRP)*.

manufacturing strategy – See *operations strategy*.

Manugistics – A software vendor of Advanced Planning and Scheduling (APS) systems.

See *Advanced Planning and Scheduling (APS)*.

MAPD (Mean Absolute Percent Deviation) – See *Mean Absolute Percent Error (MAPE)*.

MAPE (Mean Absolute Percent Error) – See *Mean Absolute Percent Error (MAPE)*.

maquiladora – A Mexican corporation that operates under a maquila program approved by the Mexican Secretariat of Commerce and Industrial Development (SECOFI).

A maquila program entitles the maquiladora company to foreign investment and management without needing additional authorization. It also gives the company special customs treatment, allowing duty-free temporary import of machinery, equipment, parts, materials, and administrative equipment, such as computers and communications devices, subject only to posting a bond guaranteeing that such goods will not remain in Mexico permanently.

Ordinarily, a maquiladora's products are exported, either directly or indirectly, through sale to another maquiladora or exporter. The type of production may be the simple assembly of temporarily imported parts, the manufacture from start to finish of a product using materials from various countries, or any combination of manufacturing and non-manufacturing operations, such as data-processing, packaging, and sorting coupons.

The legislation now governing the industry's operation is the "Decree for Development and Operation of the Maquiladora Industry," published by the Mexican federal Diario Oficial on December 22, 1989. This decree described application procedures and requirements for obtaining a maquila program and the special provisions that apply only to maquiladoras (source: www.udel.edu/leipzig/texts2/vox128.htm, March 28, 2011).

See *outsourcing*, *supply chain management*.

marginal cost – An economics term for the increase (or decrease) in cost resulting from an increase (or decrease) of one unit of output or activity; also called incremental cost.

Operations managers can make sound economic decisions based on the marginal cost or marginal profit by ignoring **overhead** costs that are fixed and irrelevant to a decision. This is true for many production and inventory models.

For example, the marginal cost of placing one more purchase order (along with the associated receiving cost) may be very close to zero. At the same time the firm might have large buying and receiving departments that have significant overhead (e.g., building space, receiving space), which means that the average cost per order is high. When making decisions about the optimal number of purchase orders per year, the firm should ignore the average costs and make decisions based on the marginal (incremental) cost. All short-term decisions should be based on the marginal cost, and long-term decisions should be based on the average (or full) cost. As many accountants like to say, "All costs are variable in the long run."

Marginal revenue is the additional revenue from selling one more unit. Economic theory says that the maximum total profit will be at the point where the marginal revenue equals marginal cost.

See *carrying charge, carrying cost, Economic Order Quantity (EOQ), economy of scale, numeric-analytic location model, order cost, safety stock, sunk cost.*

market pull – See *technology push.*

market share – The percent of the overall sales (dollars or units) of a market (local, regional, national, or global) that is controlled by one company.

One insightful question to ask a senior executive is, "What is your market share?" When he or she answers, then ask, "Of what?" Many managers are caught by this trick question and report their market share for their regional or national market instead of the global market. This question exposes a lack of global thinking.

See *cannibalization, core competence, disruptive technology, first mover advantage, product proliferation, target market, time to market.*

mass customization – A business model that uses a routine approach to efficiently create a high variety of products or services in response to customer-defined requirements. ✪

Some people mistakenly assume that mass customization is only about increasing variety at the same cost. However, some of the best examples of mass customization focus on reducing cost while maintaining or even reducing variety. For example, AbleNet manufactures a wide variety of products for disabled people, such as the electrical switch shown on the right. The product comes in a number of different colors and with a wide variety of features (e.g., push once, push twice, etc.). When AbleNet created a **modular design**, it was able to provide customers with the same variety as before, but dramatically reduced the number of products it produced and stored. It was able to mass customize by postponing the customization by using decals and cover plates that could be attached to the top of the button. It also moved much of the feature customization to the software, allowing the hardware to become more standard. As a result, AbleNet significantly improved service, inventory, and cost while keeping the same variety for its customers.

Pine (1993) argues that mass customization strategies should be considered in markets that already have many competitors and significant variety (i.e., markets that clearly value variety). According to Kotha (1995), the competitive challenge in this type of market is to provide the needed variety at a relatively low cost.

Products and services can be mass customized for a channel partner (e.g., a distributor), a customer segment (e.g., high-end customers), or an individual customer. Customization for an individual is called **personalization**.

One of the primary approaches for mass customization is **postponement**, where customization is delayed until after the customer order is received. For example, IBM in Rochester, Minnesota, builds the AS400 using "vanilla boxes," which are not differentiated until after the customer order has been received. IBM customizes the vanilla boxes by inserting hard drives, modems, and other modular devices into slots on the front of the box.

Eight strategies can be used for mass customization:[30]

1. Design products for mass customization – Make the products customizable.
2. Use robust components – Commonality is a great way to improve customization.
3. Develop workers for mass customization – Mass customization and flexibility are fundamentally a function of the flexibility and creativity of the workers.
4. Apply lean/quality concepts – Lean thinking (and short cycle times) and high quality are essential prerequisites for mass customization.
5. Reduce setup times – Long setup times (and large lotsizes) are the enemy of mass customization.
6. Use appropriate automation – Many people equate mass customization with automation; however, many of the best mass customization concepts have little to do with automation.
7. Break down functional silos – Functional silos contribute to long cycle times, poor coordination, and high costs, all of which present obstacles to mass customization.
8. Manage the value chain for mass customization – Some of the best examples of mass customization use virtual organizations and supply chain management tools to increase variety and reduce cost.

Pine and Gilmore (1999) have extended mass customization concepts to "experiences," where the goal is to create tailored memorable experiences for customers.

See *agile manufacturing, assemble to order (ATO), commonality, configurator, economy of scope, engineer to order (ETO), experience engineering, flexibility, functional silo, make to order (MTO), modular design (modularity), operations strategy, pack to order, postponement, print on demand, product mix, product proliferation, product-process matrix, push-pull boundary, respond to order (RTO), robust, sand cone model, virtual organization.*

Master Production Schedule (MPS) – A high-level plan for a few key items used to determine the materials plans for all end items; also known as the master schedule. ✪

As shown in the figure on the right, the manufacturing planning process begins with the **strategic plan**, which informs the **business plan** (finance) and the **demand plan** (marketing and sales), which in turn, inform the **production plan** (manufacturing). The **Sales & Operations Planning Process (S&OP)** then seeks to reconcile these three plans. **Resource Requirements Planning (RRP)** supports this reconciliation process by evaluating the production plan to make sure that sufficient resources (labor and machines) are available. RRP is a high-level evaluation process that only considers aggregate volume by product families (often in sales dollars or an aggregate measure of capacity, such as shop hours) and does not consider specific products, items, or resources.

Once the production plan is complete, the **master scheduling process** combines the production plan, **firm customer orders**, and managerial insight to create the MPS, which is a schedule for end items. **Rough Cut Capacity Planning (RCCP)** then evaluates the master schedule to make sure that sufficient capacity is available. RCCP is more detailed than RRP, but only considers the small set of end items in the master production schedule. Many firms consider major assemblies to be make to stock end items. The Final Assembly Schedule (FAS) is then used to schedule specific customer orders that pull from this inventory. Although the MPS is based on forecast (demand plan) information, it is a plan rather than a forecast, because it considers capacity limitations. Even though the MPS has the word "schedule" in it, it should not be confused with a detailed schedule.

Once the MPS is complete, the **Materials Requirements Planning (MRP)** process converts the MPS into a **materials plan**, which defines quantities and dates for every production and purchase order for every item. MRP

---

[30] Source: *Professor Arthur V. Hill's PowerPoint talk on Mass Customization.*

uses a **gross-to-net** process to subtract on-hand and on-order quantities and a **back scheduling** process to account for **planned leadtimes**. **Capacity Requirements Planning (CRP)** then evaluates the materials plan to make sure that sufficient capacity is available. CRP is more detailed than RCCP and considers the capacity requirements for every operation in the routing for every production order in the materials plan. Although this capacity check is more detailed than the others, it is still fairly rough, because it uses daily time buckets and uses planned leadtimes based on average queue times. **Advanced Planning and Scheduling (APS)** systems can be used to conduct even more detailed scheduling.

Once the materials plan is complete, **planners** and **buyers** (or **buyer/planners**) review the materials plan and determine which manufacturing orders to release (send) to the factory and which purchase orders to release to suppliers. The planners and buyers may also reschedule open orders (orders already in the factory or already with suppliers) to change the due dates (pull in or push out) or the quantities (increase or decrease).

The planning above the MPS determines the overall **volume** and is often done in dollars or aggregate units for product families. In contrast, the planning at the MPS level and below is done in date-quantity detail for specific items and therefore determines the **mix** (Wallace & Stahl 2003).

Many firms do not have the information systems resources to conduct RRP, RCCP, and CRP.

All of the above plans (the production plan, master production schedule, and materials plan) have a companion **inventory plan**. If the planned production exceeds the planned demand, planned inventory will increase. Conversely, if planned production is less than the planned demand, planned inventory will decrease.

For example, the high-level production plan (aggregate plan, sales and operations plan) for a furniture company specifies the total number of chairs it expects to need for each month over the next year. The MPS then identifies the number of chairs of each type (by SKU) that are needed each week. MRP then builds a detailed materials plan by day for all components and determines the raw materials needed to make the chairs specified by the MPS.

The figure below shows three types of **bill of materials**. The **assembly BOM** starts with many components (at the bottom of the BOM) and converts them into a few end products (at the top). The final product is a standard product and typically has a make to stock customer interface. The **modular BOM** starts with many components assembled into a few **modules** (subassemblies) that are mixed and matched to create many end items. This is typically an **assemble to order** customer interface. The disassembly[31] BOM starts with a raw material, such as oil, and converts it into many end items, such as motor oil,

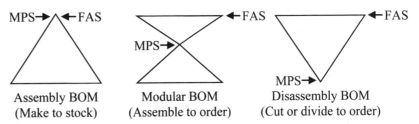

| Assembly BOM (Make to stock) | Modular BOM (Assemble to order) | Disassembly BOM (Cut or divide to order) |

gasoline, and plastic. This is typically a make to order customer interface, but could also be make to stock.

The **Theory of Constraints (TOC)** literature labels the processes for making these three BOMs as the A-plant, T-plant, and V-plant. See the *VAT analysis* entry for more detail.

The MPS is said to be "top management's handle on the business," because the MPS includes a very limited number of items. Therefore, the MPS process should focus on the narrow part of the BOM, which suggests that master scheduling should be done for end items for an assembly BOM, for major components for the modular BOM, and for raw materials for a disassembly BOM. **Safety stock** should be positioned at the same level as the MPS so that it is balanced between materials. In other words, a safety stock of zero units of item A and ten units of item B is of little value to protect against demand uncertainty if the end item BOM requires one unit of each. The **Final Assembly Schedule (FAS)** is a short-term schedule created in response to customer orders for the modular BOM. The **push-pull boundary** is between the items in the master schedule and in the FAS.

See *assemble to order (ATO)*, *Available-to-Promise (ATP)*, *back scheduling*, *bill of material (BOM)*, *Bill of Resources*, *Business Requirements Planning (BRP)*, *Capacity Requirements Planning (CRP)*, *chase strategy*, *Final Assembly Schedule (FAS)*, *firm order*, *firm planned order*, *level strategy*, *Materials Requirements Planning (MRP)*, *on-hand inventory*, *on-order inventory*, *production planning*, *push-pull boundary*, *Resource*

---

[31] *The term "disassembly" was selected by this author. This term is not widely used in the literature.*

Requirements Planning (RRP), Rough Cut Capacity Planning (RCCP), safety leadtime, Sales & Operations Planning (S&OP), time fence, VAT analysis.

master schedule – The result of the master production scheduling process.

See *Master Production Schedule (MPS)*.

master scheduler – The person responsible for creating the master production schedule.

See *Master Production Schedule (MPS)*.

material delivery routes – See *water spider*.

Material Review Board (MRB) – A standing committee that determines the disposition of items of questionable quality.

materials handling – The receiving, unloading, moving, storing, and loading of goods, typically in a factory, warehouse, distribution center, or outside work or storage area.

Materials handling systems use four main categories of mechanical equipment: storage and handling equipment, engineered systems (e.g., conveyors, handling robots, AS/RS, AGV), industrial trucks (e.g., forklifts, stock chasers), and bulk material handling (e.g., conveyor belts, stackers, elevators, hoppers, diverters).

See *forklift truck, inventory management, logistics, materials management, receiving, supply chain management.*

materials management – The organizational unit and set of business practices that plans and controls the acquisition, creation, positioning, and movement of inventory through a system; sometimes called materials planning; nearly synonymous with logistics.

Materials management must balance the conflicting objectives of marketing and sales (e.g., have lots of inventory, never lose a sale, maintain a high service level) and finance (e.g., keep inventories low, minimize working capital, minimize carrying cost). Materials management often includes purchasing/procurement, manufacturing planning and control, distribution, transportation, inventory management, and quality.

If a firm has both logistics and materials management functions, the logistics function will focus primarily on transportation issues and the materials in warehouses and distribution centers and the materials management function will focus on procurement and the materials inside plants.

See *carrying cost, inventory management, logistics, materials handling, purchasing, service level, supply chain management, Transportation Management System (TMS), warehouse, Warehouse Management System (WMS).*

materials plan – See *Materials Requirements Planning (MRP)*.

Materials Requirements Planning (MRP) – A comprehensive computer-based planning system for both factory and purchase orders; a major module within Enterprise Resources Planning Systems; also called Manufacturing Resources Planning. ✪

MRP is an important module within **Enterprise Requirements Planning (ERP)** systems for most manufacturers. MRP was originally called **Materials Requirements Planning** and focused primarily on planning purchase orders for outside suppliers. MRP was then expanded to handle **manufacturing orders** sent to the shop floor, and some software vendors changed the name to Manufacturing Resources Planning.

MRP plans level by level down the **bill of material (BOM)**. MRP begins by **netting** (subtracting) any on-hand and on-order inventory from the **gross requirements**. It then schedules backward from the **due date** using fixed **planned leadtimes** to determine **order start dates**. **Lotsizing methods** are then applied to determine order quantities. Lotsizes are often defined in terms of the number of days of **net requirements**. With **MRP regeneration**, a batch computer job updates all records in the database. With **MRP net change generation**, the system updates only the incremental changes.

MRP creates **planned orders** for both manufactured and purchased materials. The set of planned orders (that can be changed by MRP) and **firm orders** (that cannot be changed by MRP) is called the **materials plan**. Each order is defined by an order number, a part number, an order quantity, a start date, and a due date. MRP systems use the planned order start date to determine priorities for both shop orders and purchase orders. MRP is called a **priority planning system** rather than a scheduling system, because it backschedules from due dates using planned leadtimes that are calculated from the average queue times.

Nearly all MRP systems create detailed materials plans for an item using a **Time Phased Order Point (TPOP)** and fixed planned leadtimes. Contrary to what some textbooks claim, MRP systems rarely consider available capacity when creating a materials plan. Therefore, MRP systems are called **infinite loading systems** rather than **finite loading systems**. However, MRP systems can use **Rough Cut Capacity Planning (RCCP)** to check the **Master Production Schedule (MPS)** and **Capacity Requirements Planning (CRP)** to create load reports to check materials plans. These capacity checks can help managers identify situations when the plant load (planned hours) exceeds the capacity available. **Advanced Planning and Scheduling (APS)** systems are capable of creating detailed materials plans that take into account available capacity; unfortunately, these systems are hard to implement because of the need for accurate capacity, setup, and run time data.

See *Advanced Planning and Scheduling (APS), allocated inventory, Available-to-Promise (ATP), bill of material (BOM), Business Requirements Planning (BRP), Capacity Requirements Planning (CRP), closed-loop MRP, dependent demand, Distribution Requirements Planning (DRP), effectivity date, Engineering Change Order (ECO), Enterprise Resources Planning (ERP), finite scheduling, firm order, forecast consumption, forward visibility, gross requirements, infinite loading, inventory management, kitting, low level code, Manufacturing Execution System (MES), manufacturing order, Master Production Schedule (MPS), net requirements, on-hand inventory, on-order inventory, pegging, phantom bill of material, planned order, production planning, purchase order (PO), purchasing, routing, time bucket, time fence, Time Phased Order Point (TPOP), where-used report.*

matrix organization – An organizational structure where people from different units of an organization are assigned to work together under someone who is not their boss.

In a matrix organization, people work for one or more leaders who are not their bosses and who do not have primary input to their performance reviews. These people are "on loan" from their home departments. A matrix organization is usually (but not always) a temporary structure that exists for a short period of time. An example of a matrix organization is an architectural firm where people from each discipline (e.g., landscape architecture, heating, and cooling) temporarily report to a project manager for a design project.

See *performance management system, project management.*

maximum inventory – See *periodic review system.*

maximum stocking level – An SAP term for the target inventory.

See *periodic review system.*

MBNQA – See *Malcolm Baldrige National Quality Award.*

MCE (Manufacturing Cycle Effectiveness) – See *value added ratio.*

mean – The average value; also known as the arithmetic average. ✪

The mean is the arithmetic average of a set of values and is a measure of the central tendency. For a sample of n values $\{x_1, x_2, \ldots x_n\}$, the **sample mean** is defined as $\bar{x} = \dfrac{1}{n}\sum_{i=1}^{i=n} x_i$. For the entire population of N values, the **population mean** is the expected value and is defined as $\mu_x = \dfrac{1}{N}\sum_{i=1}^{i=N} x_i$. Greek letter μ is pronounced "mu."

For a continuous distribution with density function $f(x)$, the mean is the expected value $\mu_x = E(X) = \displaystyle\int_{x=-\infty}^{\infty} x\,f(x)dx$, which is also known as the **complete expectation** and the **first moment**. The **partial expectation**, an important inventory theory concept, is defined as $H(z) = \displaystyle\int_{x=-\infty}^{z} x\,f(x)dx$.

The **median** is considered to be a better measure of central tendency than the mean when the data is likely to have outliners. The median is said to be an "error resistant" statistic.

See *box plot, geometric mean, interpolated median, kurtosis, median, mode, partial expectation, skewness, trim, trimmed mean.*

Mean Absolute Deviation (MAD) – A measure of the dispersion (variability) of a random variable; defined as the average absolute deviation from the mean. ✪

The mathematical definition of the *MAD* for a random variable x_i with mean μ is $\frac{1}{n}\sum_{i=1}^{n}|x_i - \mu|$. The standard deviation for a normally distributed random variable is theoretically exactly equal to $\sqrt{\pi/2}\,MAD$ (approximately $1.25MAD$). This is true asymptotically[32], but will rarely be true for any sample.

Brown (1967) implemented this approach widely at IBM, because early computers could not take square roots. However, by 1970, Brown argued that "*MAD* is no longer appropriate to the real world of computers. It never was the correct measure of dispersion" (Brown 1970, p. 148).

Other experts, such as Jacobs and Wagner (1989), argue that *MAD* is a still good approach, because absolute errors are less sensitive to outliers than the squared errors used in the variance and standard deviation. The *MAD* approach continues to be used in many major inventory management systems, including SAP.

In a forecasting context, the average error is often assumed to be zero (i.e., unbiased forecasts). In this context, $MAD = (1/T)\sum_{t=1}^{T}|E_t|$. The *MAD* can be smoothed at the end of each period with the updating equation $SMAD_t = \alpha|E_t| + (1-\alpha)SMAD_{t-1}$. The smoothed *MAD* is sometimes called the smoothed absolute error or *SAE*.

See *forecast bias, forecast error metrics, forecasting, Mean Absolute Percent Error (MAPE), mean squared error (MSE), Median Absolute Percent Error (MdAPE), outlier, Relative Absolute Error (RAE), robust, standard deviation, tracking signal, variance.*

Mean Absolute Percent Deviation (MAPD) – See *Mean Absolute Percent Error (MAPE).*

Mean Absolute Percent Error (MAPE) – A commonly used (but flawed) measure of forecast accuracy that is the average of the absolute percent errors for each period; also called the Mean Absolute Percent Deviation (MAPD). ✪

MAPE is defined mathematically as $MAPE = \frac{1}{T}\sum_{t=1}^{T}\frac{|E_t|}{D_t}$, where E_t is the forecast error in period t, D_t is the actual demand (or sales) in period t, and T is the number of observed values. Many firms multiply by 100 to rescale the *MAPE* as a percentage. Note that the *MAPE* is not the *MAD* divided by the average demand.

The *MAPE* has three significant problems. First, when the demand is small, the absolute percent error in a period ($APE_t = |E_t|/D_t$) can be quite large. For example, when the demand is 10 and the forecast is 100, the APE_t for that period is $90/10 = 9$ (or 900%). These very large values can have an undue influence on the *MAPE*. Second, when the demand is zero in any period, the *MAPE* is undefined. Third, it is conceptually flawed. The *MAPE* is the average ratio, when it should be the ratio of the averages. In the opinion of many experts, the **Mean Absolute Scaled Error (*MASE*)** is a better metric than the *MAPE* because it avoids the above problems.

One way to try to fix the *MAPE* is to **Winsorize** (bound) the ratio in each period at 100%, which means that the *MAPE* is defined in the range [0%, 100%]. See the *Winsorizing* entry for details. However, in this author's view, this "fix" only treats the symptoms of the problem.

The average *MAPE* can be misleading as an aggregate measure for a group of items with both low and high demand. For example, imagine a firm with two items. One item is very important with high demand, high unit cost, and low *MAPE* (e.g., 10%), and the other is a very unimportant item with low demand, low unit cost, and high *MAPE* (e.g., 90%). When these two *MAPE* values are averaged, the overall *MAPE* is 50%. However, this gives too much weight to the low-demand item and not enough to the important item. The weighted *MAPE* avoids this problem. The **weighted average *MAPE*** is defined as $\sum_{i=1}^{N} w_i MAPE_i / \sum_{i=1}^{N} w_i$, where w_i is the importance weight for item i of N items. The annual cost of goods sold is the best weight to use in this equation.

---

[32] *The difference between the sample standard deviation and $\sqrt{\pi/2} \approx 1.25$ times the sample MAD will approach zero as the sample size goes to infinity.*

Like many time series forecasting statistics, the *MAPE* can be smoothed with the updating equation $SMAPE_t = \alpha |E_t| / D_t + (1-\alpha)SMAPE_{t-1}$. Be sure to Winsorize the APE_t when implementing this equation.

See *demand filter, exponential smoothing, forecast bias, forecast error metrics, forecasting, Mean Absolute Deviation (MAD), Mean Absolute Scaled Error (MASE), mean squared error (MSE), Median Absolute Percent Error (MdAPE), Relative Absolute Error (RAE), Thiel's U, tracking signal, Winsorizing.*

Mean Absolute Scaled Error (MASE) – A forecast performance metric that is the ratio of the mean absolute deviation for a forecast scaled by (divided by) the mean absolute deviation for a random walk forecast.

Hyndman and Koehler (2006) proposed the *MASE* as a way to avoid many of the problems with the **Mean Absolute Percent Error (*MAPE*)** forecast performance metric. The *MASE* is the ratio of the **mean absolute error** for the forecast and the mean absolute error for the random walk forecast. Whereas the *MAPE* is the average of many ratios, the *MASE* is the ratio of two averages.

In the forecasting literature, the mean absolute error for the forecast error is called the **Mean Absolute Deviation (MAD)** and is defined as $MAD = \frac{1}{T}\sum_{t=1}^{T}|D_t - F_t|$, where D_t is the actual demand and F_t is the forecast for period t. The **random walk forecast** for period t is the actual demand in the previous period (i.e., $F_t = D_{t-1}$); therefore, the Mean Absolute Deviation for the random walk is $MAD_{RW} = \frac{1}{T}\sum_{t=1}^{T}|D_t - D_{t-1}|$. This assumes a one-period-ahead forecast, but it can easily be modified for a k-period-ahead forecast. The *MASE*, therefore, is defined as $MASE = MAD / MAD_{RW}$.

The *MASE* will only have a divide-by-zero problem when the demand does not change over the entire horizon, but that is an unlikely situation. When *MASE* < 1, the forecasts are better than the random walk forecast; when *MASE* > 1, the forecasts are worse than the random walk forecast. A forecasting model with a *MASE* of 20% has a forecast error of 20% of the forecast error of the simplistic random walk forecast. A *MASE* of 95% is only slightly better than a simplistic random walk forecast.

The **Mean Absolute Scaled Accuracy (MASA)** is the companion accuracy measure for the *MASE* and is defined as $1 - MASE$. *MASA* can be interpreted as the percent accuracy of the forecast relative to the accuracy of the random walk forecast. When *MASA* = 0, the forecasts are no better than the random walk forecast; when *MASA* < 0, the forecasts are worse than the random walk forecast; and when *MASA* = 60%, the average absolute forecast error is 40% of the average absolute forecast error for the random walk forecast. *MASE* and *MASA* are better measures of forecast accuracy than *MAPE* because they measure accuracy against an objective standard, which is the random walk forecast.

Hyndman and Koehler (2006, p. 13) assert that measures based on scaled measures (such as the *MASE*) "should become the standard approach in comparing forecast accuracy across series on different scales." However, the *MASE* has two organizational challenges. First, it is not always easy to explain to managers. Second, when changing from *MAPE* to *MASE*, those responsible for forecasting will have to explain why the reported forecast accuracy decreases dramatically.

Dan Strike at 3M has suggests a very similar metric that uses a **12-month moving average** as the scaling factor. This metric is even simpler than *MASE* to explain, but may be slightly harder to implement.

Thiel's U_3 metric is the mean squared error scaled by the mean squared error for the random walk forecast. Therefore, it can be argued that the "new" *MASE* scaling concept is just an adaption of Thiel's metric that uses the *MAD* rather than the mean squared error (*MSE*).

MASE can be implemented with simple moving averages or with **exponential smoothing** for both the numerator (the smoothed *MAD*) and the denominator (the smoothed *MAD* for a random walk forecast).

See *forecast error metrics, Mean Absolute Percent Error (MAPE), Relative Absolute Error (RAE).*

mean squared error (MSE) – The expected value of the square of the difference between an estimator and the parameter.

The *MSE* measures how far off an estimator is from what it is trying to estimate. In forecasting, the *MSE* is a measure of the forecast error that is the average of the squared forecast errors and is defined mathematically as

$MSE = \dfrac{1}{T}\sum_{t=1}^{T} E_t^2$, where E_t is the forecast error in period t and T is the number of observed values. The *MSE* is an estimate of the variance of the forecast error and is approximately equal to the variance when the forecast bias is close to zero. Like most time series statistics, the *MSE* can be smoothed with the updating equation $SMSE_t = (1-\alpha)SMSE_{t-1} + \alpha E_t^2$. The **root mean squared error (*RMSE*)** is the square root of the *MSE* and is an estimate of the standard deviation of the forecast error. In fact, the *RMSE* will be equal to the standard deviation of the forecast error if the forecast is unbiased. Variances are additive, but standard deviations are not; therefore, *RMSE* is not normally smoothed.

See *forecast bias, forecast error metrics, Mean Absolute Deviation (MAD), Mean Absolute Percent Error (MAPE), standard deviation, tracking signal, variance.*

Mean Time Between Failure (MTBF) – A maintenance and reliability term for the average time that a component is expected to work without failing.

The *MTBF* is a good measure of **product reliability**. The *MTBF* is often modeled with the **bathtub curve** that has higher failure rates at the beginning and end of the product life cycle. The **Mean Time For Failure (MTFF)** is the average time to the first failure and is sometimes used for non-repairable products.

See *availability, bathtub curve, maintenance, Mean Time to Repair (MTTR), New Product Development (NPD), reliability, Total Productive Maintenance (TPM).*

Mean Time to Repair (MTTR) – A maintenance and reliability term for the average time required to fix something, such as a machine.

The *MTTR* is a measure of the complexity and cost of a repair job and a measure of the **maintainability** of a product (Schroeder 2007). The *MTTR* should not be used as the only performance measure for service techs because the best service techs are often assigned the most difficult repair jobs, which means they will have the highest *MTTR*. The same is true for doctors and other skilled professionals.

See *availability, maintenance, Mean Time Between Failure (MTBF), New Product Development (NPD), serviceability, Total Productive Maintenance (TPM).*

Measurement System Analysis (MSA) – An approach for verifying the accuracy and precision of a data measurement system using statistical analysis tools, such as Gauge R&R, attribute Gauge R&R, and the P/T ratio.

See *Gauge, Gauge R&R, metrology.*

MECE – The concept that an analysis should define issues and alternatives that are mutually exclusive and collectively exhaustive; pronounced "me-see."

MECE thinking is widely used by strategy consulting firms, such as McKinsey, Bain, and BCG, to create both issue trees and decision trees (Rasiel 1998). In fact, the case interview method these firms use to screen applicants is designed to test MECE thinking.

Mutually exclusive means that the ideas or alternatives are distinct and separate and do not overlap. **Collectively exhaustive** means that the ideas or alternatives cover all possibilities. The Venn diagram below shows two sets (A and B) that overlap and therefore are not mutually exclusive. The union of sets A, B, and C is collectively exhaustive because it covers all possibilities.

In most anlysies, it is far more important that issues be separable than MECE. For example, an outgoing shipment could be late because of mechanical problems with a truck or because the products were not ready to ship. These two events are not mutually exclusive, because they both could be true, but they can and should be studied separately.

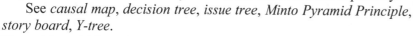

See *causal map, decision tree, issue tree, Minto Pyramid Principle, story board, Y-tree.*

median – The middle value of a set of sorted values. ✪

The median, like the mean, is a measure of the **central tendency**. The calculation of the median begins by sorting the values in a list. If the number of values is odd, the median is the middle value in the sorted list. If the number of values is even, the median is the average of the two middle values in the sorted list. For example, the median of {1, 2, 3, 9, 100} is 3, and the median of {1, 2, 3, 9, 100, 200} is (3 + 9)/2 = 6.

The median is often a better measure of central tendency than the mean when the data is highly skewed. For example, consider the following selling prices for houses (in thousands): $175, $180, $200, $240, $241, $260, $800, and $2400. The mean is $562, but the median is only $240.5. In this case, the mean is "pulled up" by the two high prices.

Excel provides the function MEDIAN(*range*) for computing the median of a range of values.

Some people consider the **interpolated median** to be better than the median when many values are at the median and the data has a very limited number of possible values. For example, the interpolated median is often used for Likert survey questions on the 1-5 or 1-7 scale and also for grades in the U.S. that are translated from A, A-, B+, etc. to a 4.0 scale.

See *box plot, forecast error metrics, interpolated median, mean, Median Absolute Percent Error (MdAPE), mode, skewness, trimmed mean.*

Median Absolute Percent Error (MdAPE) – The middle value of all the percentage errors for a data set when the absolute values of the errors (negative signs are ignored) are ordered by size.

See *forecast error metrics, Mean Absolute Deviation (MAD), Mean Absolute Percent Error (MAPE), median.*

mergers and acquisitions (M&A) – The activity of one firm evaluating, buying, selling, or combining with another firm.

Whereas an **acquisition** is the purchase of one company by another, a **merger** is the combination of two companies to form a new company. In an acquisition, one firm will buy another to gain market share, create greater efficiency through economies of scale, or acquire new technologies or resources.

The goal for both mergers and acquisitions is to **create shareholder value**. The success of a merger or acquisition depends on whether this synergy is achieved from (1) growing revenues through synergies between products, markets, or product technologies or (2) economies of scale through headcount reduction, purchasing leverage, IT systems, HR, and other functional synergies. Unfortunately, planned synergies are not always realized, and in some cases revenues decline, morale sags, costs increase, and share prices drop.

See *acquisition, antitrust laws, economy of scale.*

Metcalfe's Law – See *network effect.*

Methods Time Measurement (MTM) – See *work measurement.*

metrology – The science of measurement; closely related to Measurement System Analysis (MSA).

Metrology attempts to validate data obtained from test equipment and considers precision, accuracy, traceability, and reliability. Metrology, therefore, requires an analysis of the uncertainty of individual measurements to validate instrument accuracy. The dissemination of traceability to consumers (both internal and external) is often performed by a dedicated calibration laboratory with a recognized quality system.

Metrology has been an important topic in commerce since people started measuring length, time, and weight. For example, according to *New Unger's Bible Dictionary*, the cubit was an important measure of length among the Hebrews (Exodus 25:10) and other ancient peoples. It was commonly measured as the length of the arm from the point of the elbow to the end of the middle finger, which is roughly 18 inches (45.72 cm).

The scientific revolution required a rational system of units and made it possible to apply science to measurement. Thus, metrology became a driver of the Industrial Revolution and was a critical precursor to systems of mass production. Modern metrology has roots in the French Revolution and is based on the concept of establishing units of measurement based on constants of nature, thus making measurement units widely available. For example, the meter is based on the dimensions of the Earth, and the kilogram is based on the mass of a cubic meter of water. The Système International d'Unités (International System of Units or SI) has gained worldwide acceptance as the standard for modern measurement. SI is maintained under the auspices of the Metre Convention and its institutions, the General Conference on Weights and Measures (CGPM), its executive branch, the International Committee for Weights and Measures (CIPM), and its technical institution, the International Bureau of Weights and Measures (BIPM). The U.S. agencies with this responsibility are the National Institute of Standards and Technology (NIST) and the American National Standards Institute (ANSI).

See *gauge, Gauge R&R, lean sigma, Measurement System Analysis (MSA), reliability.*

milestone – An important event in the timeline for a project, person, or organization.

A milestone event marks the completion of a major deliverable or the start of a new phase for a project. Therefore, milestones are good times to monitor progress with meetings or more formal "stage-gate" reviews that require key stakeholders to decide if the project should be allowed to continue to the next stage. In project scheduling, milestones are activities with zero duration.

See *deliverables, project management, stage-gate process, stakeholder.*

milk run – A vehicle route to pick up materials from multiple suppliers or to deliver supplies to multiple customers.

The traditional purchasing approach is for customers to send large orders to suppliers on an infrequent basis and for suppliers to ship orders to the customer via a common carrier. With a milk run, the customer sends its own truck to pick up small quantities from many local suppliers on a regular and frequent basis (e.g., once per week). Milk runs speed delivery and reduce inventory for the customer and level the load for the supplier, but at the expense of additional transactions for both parties. Milk runs are common in the automotive industry and are a commonly used lean practice. Hill and Vollmann (1986) developed an optimization model for milk runs.

See *lean thinking, logistics, Vehicle Scheduling Problem (VSP).*

min/max inventory system – See *min-max inventory system.*

mindmap – A diagram used to show the relationships between concepts, ideas, and words that are connected to a central concept or idea at one or more levels.

A mindmap is a graphical tool that can be used by an individual or a group to capture, refine, and share information about the relationships between concepts, ideas, words, tasks, or objects that are connected to a central concept or idea at one or more levels in a hierarchy. Mindmaps can be used to:

- Generate ideas
- Capture ideas
- Take course notes
- Provide structure to ideas
- Review and study ideas
- Visualize and clarify relationships
- Help plan meetings and projects
- Organize ideas for papers
- Create the storyboard for a presentation
- Stimulate creativity
- Create a shared understanding
- Create the agenda for a meeting
- Communicate ideas with others
- Teach concepts to others
- Document ideas
- Help make decisions
- Create a work breakdown structure
- Create a task list
- Prioritize activities
- Solve problems

A mindmap represents how one or more people think about a subject. The spatial organization on the paper (or screen) communicates the relationship between the nodes (ideas, concepts, objects, etc.) in the creator's mind. Creating a mindmap helps the creators translate their thinking about a subject into more concrete ideas, which helps them clarify their own thinking and develop a **shared understanding** of the concepts. Once created, a mindmap is an excellent way to communicate concepts and relationships to others.

Methods – The concepts on a mindmap are drawn around the central idea. Subordinate concepts are then drawn as branches from those concepts. Buzan and Buzan (1996) recommend that the mindmaps should be drawn by hand using multiple colors, drawings, and photos. This makes the mindmap easier to remember, more personal, and more fun. They argue further that the mindmap should fit on one piece of paper, but allowed it to be a large piece of paper. Many powerful software packages are now available to create mindmaps, including Mind Manager (www.mindjet.com), Inspiration (www.inspiration.com), and many others.

Relationship to other mapping tools – A mindmap is similar to a causal map, except the links in a mindmap usually imply similarity rather than causality. A strategy map is a special type of causal map. A project network shows the time relationships between the nodes and therefore is not a mindmap. A bill of material (BOM) drawing and a work breakdown structure are similar to mindmaps in that they show relatedness and subordinated concepts.

Mindmap example – The example below was created by the author with Mindjet Mind Manager software to brainstorm both the work breakdown structure and the issue tree for a productivity improvement project. The symbol (+) indicates that additional nodes are currently hidden from view.

In conclusion, mindmaps are a powerful tool for visualizing, structuring, and communicating concepts related to a central idea. This author predicts that mindmapping software will become as popular as Microsoft's process mapping tool (Microsoft Visio) and project management tool (Microsoft Project Manager).

See *causal map, issue tree, process map, project network, strategy map, Work Breakdown Structure (WBS)*.

Minkowski distance metric – A generalized distance metric that can be used in logistics/transportation analysis, cluster analysis, and other graphical analysis tools.

If location i has coordinates (x_i, y_i), the Euclidean (straight-line) distance between points i and j is

$$d_{ij} = \sqrt{(x_i - x_j)^2 + (y_i - y_j)^2},$$

which is based on the **Pythagorean Theorem**. The **Manhattan square distance** only considers travel along the x-axis and y-axis and is given by $d_{ij} = |x_i - x_j| + |y_i - y_j|$. The Minkowski distance generalizes these metrics and defines the

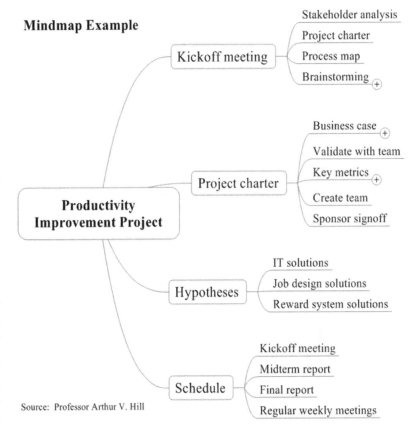

Mindmap Example

Source: Professor Arthur V. Hill

distance as $d_{ij} = (|x_i - x_j|^r + |y_i - y_j|^r)^{1/r}$. The Minkowski distance metric is equal to the Euclidean distance when $r = 2$ and the Manhattan square distance when $r = 1$. Minkowski distance can be defined in multi-dimensional space. Consider item i with K attributes (dimensions) (i.e., $x_{i1}, x_{i2}, \ldots, x_{iK}$). The Minkowski distance between items i and j is then defined as $d_{ij} = \left(\sum_{k=1}^{K} |x_{ik} - x_{jk}|^r \right)^{1/r}$.

The **Chebyshev distance** (also called the maximum metric and the L_∞ metric) sets the distance to the longest dimension (i.e., $d_{ij} = \max(|x_i - x_j|, |y_i - y_j|)$) and is equivalent to the Minkowski distance when $r = \infty$.

See *cluster analysis, Manhattan square distance, Pythagorean Theorem*.

min-max inventory system – An inventory control system that signals the need for a replenishment order to bring the inventory position up to the maximum inventory level (target inventory level) when the inventory position falls below the reorder point (the "min" or minimum level); known as the (*s,S*) system in the academic literature, labeled (*R,T*) in this book. ✪

As with all **reorder point systems**, the reorder point can be determined using statistical analysis of the **demand during leadtime distribution** or with less mathematical methods. As with all **order-up-to systems**, the order quantity is the order-up-to level minus the current **inventory position**, which is defined as (on-hand + on-order – allocated – backorders).

A special case of a min-max system is the (*S* − 1, *S*) system, where orders are placed on a "one-for-one" basis. Every time one unit is consumed, another unit is ordered. This policy is most practical for low-demand items (e.g., service parts), high-value items (e.g., medical devices), or long leadtime items (e.g., aircraft engines).

See *inventory management, order-up-to level, periodic review system, reorder point*.

minor setup cost – See *major setup cost, setup cost*.

Minto Pyramid Principle – A structured approach to building a persuasive argument and presentation developed by Barbara Minto (1996), a former McKinsey consultant.

The Minto Pyramid Principle developed by Barbara Minto (1996) can improve almost any presentation or persuasive speech. Minto's main idea is that arguments should be presented in a pyramid structure, starting with the fundamental question (or hypothesis) at the top and cascading down the pyramid, with arguments at one level supported by arguments at the next level down. At each level, the author asks, "How can I support this argument?" and "How do I know that this is true?" The presentation covers all the arguments at one level, and then moves down to the next level to further develop the argument.

For example, a firm is considering moving manufacturing operations to China. (See the figure below.) At the top of the pyramid is the hypothesis, "We should move part of our manufacturing to China."

Example of the Minto Pyramid Principle

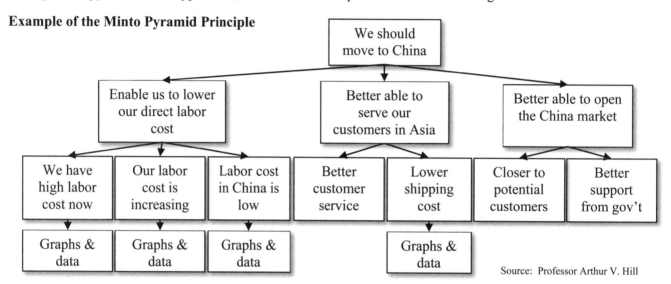

Source: Professor Arthur V. Hill

From this, the team doing the analysis and making the presentation asks, "Why is it a good idea to move to China?" The answer comes at the next level with three answers: (1) We will have lower labor cost in China, (2) we can better serve our customers in Asia, and (3) locating in China will eventually open new markets for the company's products in China. The team then asks "Why?" for each of these three items and breaks these out in more detail at the next level. The "enable us to lower our direct labor cost" argument is fully developed before the "better able to serve our customers in Asia" is started.

Minto recommends that the presentation start with an opening statement of the thesis, which consists of a factual summary of the current situation, a complicating factor or uncertainty that the audience cares about, and the explicit or implied question that this factor or uncertainty raises in the audience's mind and that the presenter's thesis answers. The closing consists of a restatement of the main thesis, the key supporting arguments (usually the second row of the pyramid), and finally an action plan.

See *hypothesis*, *inductive reasoning*, *issue tree*, *MECE*, *story board*.

mission statement – A short statement of an organization's purpose and aspirations, intended to provide direction and motivation.

Most organizations have a **vision statement** or **mission statement** that is intended to define their purpose and *raison d'être*[33]. However, for many organizations, creating a vision or mission statement is a waste of time. Vision and mission statements are published in the annual report and displayed prominently on the walls, but they are understood by few, remembered by none, and have almost no impact on anyone's thinking or behavior. Yet this does not have to be the case. Vision and mission statements can be powerful tools for aligning and energizing an entire organization.

---

[33] *Raison d'être is a French phrase that means reason to be or justification for existence. This phase is often written in English as "raison d'etre" without the ê.*

Although scholars do not universally agree on the difference between vision and mission statements, most view the vision statement as the more strategic longer-term view and argue that the mission should be derived from the vision. A vision statement should be a short, succinct, and inspiring statement of what the organization intends to become at some point in the future. It is the mental image that describes the organization's aspirations for the future without specifying the means to achieve those aspirations. The table below presents examples of vision statements that have worked and others that probably would not have worked.

Worked	Would not work
Put a man on the moon by the end of the decade − President John F. Kennedy	To be an aeronautical leader and apply ingenuity and innovation in our work as we value our taxpayers and government employees.
Put a computer on every desk in America − Bill Gates	Be a leader in the field of software development in the American market by making software that is easy to use. We also will provide a good return on investment for our shareholders.
Be number one or number two in every market we compete in. − Jack Welch, CEO, GE	Be an industry leader by providing quality products to our customers, using the talents of our employees, and providing above average returns to our shareholders.
Revolutionize the way people do financial work. – Intuit (Quicken)	Be a preferred seller of financial software for our customers and provide superior returns to our investors.

Of course, having a vision, mission, goals, and objectives is not enough. Organizations need to further define competitive strategies and projects to achieve them. A competitive strategy is a plan of action to achieve a competitive advantage. Projects are a means of implementing strategies. Projects require goals and objectives, but also require a project charter, a team, and a schedule. Strategies and projects should be driven by the organization's vision and mission. The *hoshin planning*, *Y-tree*, and *strategy mapping* entries present important concepts on how to translate a strategy into projects and accountability.

The mission statement translates the vision into more concrete and detailed terms. Many organizations also have values statementS dealing with integrity, concern for people, concern for the environment, etc., where the values statement defines constraints and guides all other activities. Of course, the leadership must model the values. Enron's motto was "Respect, Integrity, Communication and Excellence" and its vision and value statement declared "We treat others as we would like to be treated ourselves … We do not tolerate abusive or disrespectful treatment. Ruthlessness, callousness and arrogance don't belong here" (source: http://wiki.answers.com, May 8, 2011). However, Enron's leadership obviously did not live up to it.

Goals and **objectives** are a means of implementing a vision and mission. Although used interchangeably by many, most people define goals as longer term and less tangible than objectives. The table below on the left shows the Kaplan and Norton model (2004), which starts with the mission and then follows with values and vision. This hierarchy puts mission ahead of values and vision. The table below on the right is a comprehensive hierarchy developed by this author that synthesizes many models.

Kaplan and Norton hierarchy	
Mission	Why we exist.
Core values	What is important to us.
Vision	What we want to be.
Strategy	Our game plan.
Strategy map	Translate the strategy.
Balanced scorecard	Measure and focus.
Target and initiatives	What we need to do.
Personal objectives	What I need to do.

Source: Kaplan & Norton (2004), p. 33.

Comprehensive hierarchy	
Values	Our core beliefs that guide all that we do.
Vision	What we want to become in the future.
Mission	What we want to achieve with our vision.
Strategies	How we will achieve our mission with clearly defined goals.
Projects & priorities	How we implement strategies with clearly defined objectives.
Alignment	How individuals and departments will contribute to our mission.

Source: Professor Arthur V. Hill

In conclusion, vision and mission statements can be powerful tools to define the organization's desired end state and to energize the organization to make the vision and mission a reality. To be successful, these statements need to be clear, succinct, passionate, shared, and lived out by the organization's leaders. They should be supported by a strong set of values that are also lived out by the leadership. Lastly, the vision and mission need to be supported by focused strategies, which are implemented through people and projects aligned with the strategies and mission.

See *Balanced Scorecard, forming-storming-norming-performing model, hoshin planning, SMART goals, strategy map, true north, Y-tree.*

mistake proofing – See *error proofing.*

mix flexibility – See *flexibility.*

mixed integer programming (MIP) – A type of linear programming where some decision variables are restricted to integer values and some are continuous; also called mixed integer linear programming.

See *integer programming (IP), linear programming (LP), operations research (OR).*

mixed model assembly – The practice of assembling multiple products in small batches in a single process.

For example, a firm assembled two products (A and B) on one assembly line and used large batches to reduce changeover time with sequence AAAAAAAAAAAAAAABBBBBBBBBBBBBBB. However, the firm was able to reduce changeover time and cost, which enabled it to economically implement mixed model assembly with sequence ABABABABABABABABABABABABABABAB.

The advantages of mixed model assembly over the large batch assembly are that it (1) reduces inventory, (2) improves service levels, (3) smoothes the production rate, and (4) enables early detection of defects. Its primary disadvantage is that it requires frequent changeovers, which can add complexity and cost.

See *assembly line, early detection, facility layout, heijunka, manufacturing processes, service level, setup time reduction methods.*

mizusumashi – See *water spider.*

mode – (1) In a statistics context: The most common value in a set of values. (2) In a transportation context: The method of transportation for cargo or people (e.g., rail, road, water, or air).

In the statistics context, the mode is a measure of central tendency. For a discrete distribution, the mode is the value where the probability mass function is at its maximum value. In other words, the mode is the value that has the highest probability. For a continuous probability distribution, the mode is the value where the density function is at its maximum value. However, the modal value may not be unique. For symmetrical distributions, such as the normal distribution, the mean, median, and mode are identical.

In the transportation context, the mode is a type of carrier (e.g., rail, road, water, air). Water transport can be further broken into barge, boat, ship, ferry, or sailboat and can be on a sea, ocean, lake, canal, or river. Intermodal shipments use two or more modes to move from origin to destination.

See *intermodal shipments, logistics, mean, median, multi-modal shipments, skewness.*

modular design (modularity) – Organizing a complex system as a set of distinct components that can be developed independently and then "plugged" together. ✪

The effectiveness of the modular design depends on the manner in which systems are divided into components and the mechanisms used to plug components together. Modularity is a general systems concept and is a continuum describing the degree to which a system's components can be separated and recombined. It refers to the tightness of coupling between components and the degree to which the "rules" of the system architecture enable (or prohibit) the mixing and matching of components. Because all systems are characterized by some degree of coupling between components and very few systems have components that are completely inseparable and cannot be recombined, almost all systems are modular to some degree (Schilling 2000).

See *agile manufacturing, commonality, interoperability, mass customization.*

modularity – See *modular design.*

mold – A hollow cavity used to make products in a desired shape.

See *foundry, manufacturing processes, tooling.*

moment of truth – A critical or decisive time on which much depends; in the service quality context, an event that exposes a firm's authenticity to its customers or employees. ✪

A moment of truth is an opportunity for the firm's customers (or employees) to find out the truth about the firm's character. In other words, it is a time for customers or employees to find out "who we really are." This is a chance for employees (or bosses) to show the customers (or employees) that they really do care about them and to ask customers (or employees) for feedback on how products and services might be improved. These are special moments and should be managed carefully.

When creating a **process map**, it is important to highlight the process steps that "touch" the customer. A careful analysis of a typical service process often uncovers many more moments of truth than management truly appreciates. Such moments might include a customer phone call regarding a billing problem, a billing statement, and an impression from an advertisement.

People tend to remember their first experience (primacy) and last experience (recency) with a service provider. It is important, therefore, to manage these important moments of truth with great care.

The book *Authenticity* (Pine & Gillmore 2007) argues that in a world increasingly filled with deliberately staged experiences and manipulative business practices (e.g., frequent flyer programs), consumers often make buying decisions based on their perception of the honesty, integrity, and transparency of a service provider. This definition of authenticity is closely related to the concept of a moment of truth.

See *primacy effect, service blueprinting, service management, service quality.*

Monte Carlo simulation – See *simulation.*

Moore's Law – A prediction made by Intel cofounder Dr. Gordon E. Moore in 1965 stating that the number of components on an integrated circuit will double every 12 months (or 18 months or 24 months).

In 1975, Moore revised his 12 months to 24 months. Other people have revised the law to the widely quoted number of 18 months, which is an average of the 12 and 24 months. Moore's Law is really not a "law." It is simply an empirical observation that the number of components on a circuit was growing at an exponential rate.

Moore was not the first person to make this kind of observation. In 1751, Benjamin Franklin noted in his essay "Observations Concerning the Increase of Mankind, Peopling of Countries, etc.," that "This million doubling, suppose but once in 25 years, will, in another century, be more than the people of England, and the greatest number of Englishmen will be on this side of the water."

Moore's Law is an **exponential growth model** of a continuous variable that can be applied to many fast-growth contexts, such as millions of instructions per second (MIPS) for the fastest computer, the number of Internet users, and the mosquito population in Minnesota.

The mathematical model for exponential growth is identical to the exponential decay half-life "time-based learning" model, and both use the form $y(t) = ae^{bt}$. Unlike the learning curve model that has discrete time periods, the exponential growth (or decay) model is expressed in continuous time. Whereas the performance variable for exponential growth doubles every h time periods, the performance variable for the half-life curve "halves" every h time periods. The constants for both models are $a = y(0)$, $b = \ln(2)/h$, and $h = \ln(2)/b$, but the signs for b and h are opposite those of the half-life model.

See *green manufacturing, half-life curve, learning curve, learning organization.*

moving average – An average over the last n periods often used as a short-term forecast; also called a rolling average, rolling mean, or running average. ✪

The moving average can be used to make forecasts based on the most recent data. It can also be used to smooth data for graphing purposes.

An n-period moving average is the arithmetic average of the last n periods of a time series. For a time series $(d_1, d_2, ..., d_T)$, the moving average is $\sum_{t=T-n+1}^{T} d_t / n$. In other words, a moving average is a weighted average with equal weights that sum to one for the last n periods and zero weights for all values more than n periods old.

An **exponentially smoothed average** (sometimes called an exponential moving average) is like a moving average in that it is also a weighted average and an average of the recent data for a time series. Whereas a moving average uses equal weights for the last n periods and zero weights for all values more than n periods old, an exponentially smoothed average uses weights that decline geometrically with the age of the data. When the demand is stationary, an n-period moving average can be proven to have the same expected value as a simple exponential smoothed average with smoothing constant $\alpha = 2/(n+1)$.

See *Box-Jenkins forecasting, centered moving average, exponential smoothing, forecasting, time series forecasting, weighted average.*

MPS – See *Master Production Schedule.*

MRB – See *Material Review Board.*

MRO – See *Maintenance-Repair-Operations (MRO).*

MRP – See *Materials Requirements Planning (MRP).*

MTBF – See *Mean Time Between Failure (MTBF).*

MTM (Methods Time Measurement) – See *work measurement.*

MTO – See *make to order (MTO).*

MTS – See *make to stock (MTS).*

MTTR – See *Mean Time to Repair (MTTR).*

ムダ

MU DA

muda – A Japanese word for waste used to describe any activity that does not add value. ✪

In conversational Japanese, "muda" means useless, futile, or waste. In popular lean manufacturing terminology, muda is any type of waste. All eight of the "8 wastes" are examples of muda: over-production, waiting, conveyance, processing, inventory, motion, correction, and wasted human potential.

According to the Lean Enterprise Institute, "muda," "mura," and "muri" are three Japanese terms often used together in the Toyota Production System to describe wasteful practices that should be eliminated.

- **Muda** (Non-value-added) – Any activity that consumes resources without creating value for the customer.
- **Mura** (Imbalance) – Unevenness in an operation; for example, an uneven work pace in an operation causing operators to hurry and then wait.
- **Muri** (Overload) – Overburdening or causing strain on equipment or operators.

See *8 wastes, error proofing, lean thinking, Toyota Production System (TPS).*

multi-modal shipments – Moving goods using two or more modes of transportation; also called multi-modal transport.

An example is a container picked up from the shipper by truck, loaded onto the rail, shipped by rail to a port, and then loaded onto a vessel. Multi-modal shipments help optimize supply chain efficiency, but can make tracking difficult because of the need for coordination between the modes.

See *intermodal shipments, logistics, mode, shipping container.*

multiple source – See *single source.*

multiple-machine handling – The practice of assigning workers to operate more than one machine at a time.

This is a common Japanese manufacturing practice that is made possible by the application of jidoka and error proofing principles. **Chaku-Chaku** is an application of this principle.

See *Chaku-Chaku, error proofing, jidoka.*

multiplication principle – Investing strategically in process improvements that can be "multiplied" (i.e., used) over many transactions.

Love (1979) challenged people to invest time and money to improve processes, particularly when a one-time investment can be multiplied over many transactions. Good examples include creating checklists, writing standard operating procedures, reducing setup time, automating a process, creating a standard legal paragraph, and applying 5S. The multiplication principle suggests that organizations should focus their process improvement efforts on those repetitive activities that cost the most.

See *5S, addition principle, automation, checklist, human resources, job design, lean thinking, setup time reduction methods, subtraction principle.*

mura – See *muda.*

muri – See *muda.*

Murphy's Law – A humorous and pessimistic popular adage often stated as, "If anything can go wrong, it will" or "Anything that can go wrong will go wrong." ✪

Murphy's Law is similar to the **Second Law of Thermodynamics** (sometimes called the law of entropy), which asserts that all systems move to the highest state of disorder (the lowest possible state of energy) and tend to stay there unless energy is supplied to restore them. O'Toole's commentary on Murphy's Law is "Murphy was an optimist." The website http://userpage.chemie.fu-berlin.de/diverse/murphy/murphy2.html (April 1, 2011) offers many similar types of "laws."

See *error proofing, Parkinson's Laws, project management.*

N

NAFTA – See *North American Free Trade Agreement (NAFTA)*.

nanotechnology – The study of the control of materials on an atomic or molecular scale; also called nanotech.

"Nano" means a billionth. A nanometer is one-billionth of a meter. Nanotechnology generally deals with structures of the size of 100 nanometers or smaller.

See *disruptive technology*.

NAPM (National Association of Purchasing Management) – See *Institute for Supply Management (ISM)*.

National Association of Purchasing Management (NAPM) – See *Institute for Supply Management (ISM)*.

NC machine –See *Numerically Controlled (NC) machine*.

near miss – See *adverse event*.

nearshoring – The practice of moving work to a neighboring country; also called near shore outsourcing.

U.S. firms nearshore to Canada and Mexico as well to Central and South America and the Caribbean. Firms in Western Europe nearshore to central and Eastern Europe. Whereas **offshoring** means to move work to any other country (possibly across an ocean), nearshoring means to move work to another country in the same region. The term "nearshoring" often implies **outsourcing** to another firm, but technically, it is possible for a firm to nearshore to a plant owned by the firm in another nearby country. The advantages of keeping the work in a nearby region can include better communication (particularly if the countries share the same language), better cultural understanding (leading to trust), less travel distance (leading to reduced cost and more frequent visits and tighter controls), and fewer time zones (leading to easier and more frequent communication).

See *offshoring, outsourcing, sourcing*.

necessary waste – See *8 wastes*.

negative binomial distribution – A discrete probability distribution that counts the number of successes (or failures) in a sequence of independent Bernoulli trials (each with probability of success p) before the r-th failure (or success); also known as the Pascal distribution, Pólya distribution, and gamma-Poisson distribution.

The negative binomial is the discrete analog to the gamma distribution and therefore can take on many shapes. Like the gamma and Poisson, the negative binomial is only defined for non-negative values (i.e., $x \geq 0$).

The Poisson distribution is the most commonly used discrete probability distribution in inventory theory, but has only one parameter and is only appropriate when the mean and variance are approximately equal. The negative binomial distribution is a good alternative to the Poisson when the data is "dispersed" (i.e., $\sigma^2 > \mu$).

Parameters: $r > 0$ is the number of failures and p is the probability of success on each experiment.

Probability mass and cumulative distribution functions: $p(x) = \binom{x+r-1}{r-1} p^r (1-p)^x$, where x is a non-negative integer, p is a probability, and r is an integer for the Pascal version but can be any real positive number for the Pólya version. For the Pólya version with non-integer r, $p(x) = \dfrac{\Gamma(r+x)}{x!\,\Gamma(r)} p^r (1-p)^x$, where $\Gamma(.)$ is the gamma function. Note that this distribution can be parameterized in many ways, so care must be taken to not confuse them. The CDF has no closed form, but can be written as $F(x) = I(p; r, x+1)$, where $I(p; r, x+1)$ is the regularized beta function. (See the *beta function* entry for more information.)

Statistics: Range $x \in \{0, 1, 2, \dots \}$, mean $\mu = r(1-p)/p$, variance $\sigma^2 = rp/(1-p)^2 = \mu/(1-p)$, and mode $\lfloor (r-1)p/(1-p) \rfloor$ if $r > 1$; 0 otherwise.

Graph: The graph below is the negative binomial probability mass function with $r = 5$ trials of a fair coin ($p = 0.5$).

Parameter estimation: The method of moments parameters are $p = 1 - \mu/\sigma^2$ and $r = \mu(1-p)/p$. Many authors recommend a Maximum Likelihood Estimator (MLE) approach over the method of moments estimators.

Excel: In Excel, the probability mass function is NEGBINOMDIST(x, r, p) and is interpreted as the probability of x failures before the r-th success when the probability of a success on any one trial is p.

Excel simulation: An Excel simulation can use the inverse transform method to generate negative binomial random variates using a direct search for the inverse cumulative CDF function.

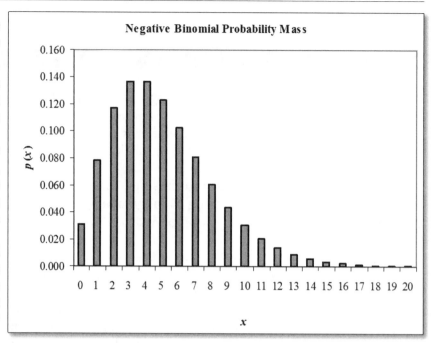

Negative Binomial Probability Mass

Relationships to other distributions: The geometric distribution is a special case of the negative binomial distribution for $r = 1$. The sum of r independent geometric(p) random variables is a negative binomial (r, p) random variable. The sum of n negative binomial random variables with parameters (r_i, p) is a negative binomial with parameters (Σr_i, p). The negative binomial converges to the Poisson as r approaches infinity, p approaches 1, and μ is held constant. The Pascal distribution (after Blaise Pascal) and Pólya distribution (after George Pólya) are special cases of the negative binomial. The convention among statisticians and engineers is to use the negative binomial (or Pascal) with an integer-valued r and use Pólya with a real-valued r. The Pólya distribution more accurately models occurrences of "contagious" discrete events, such as tornado outbreaks, than does the Poisson distribution.

See *Bernoulli distribution, beta function, gamma distribution, Poisson distribution, probability distribution, probability mass function.*

negative exponential distribution – See *exponential distribution.*

net change MRP – See *Materials Requirements Planning (MRP).*

Net Present Value (NPV) – The future stream of benefits and costs converted into equivalent values today. ✪

The NPV is calculated by assigning monetary values to benefits and costs, discounting future benefits and costs using an appropriate discount rate, and subtracting the sum total of discounted costs from the sum total of discounted benefits. Mathematically, NPV is defined as $NPV = \sum_{t=1}^{n} \dfrac{C_t}{(1+r)^t} - C_0$, where t is the time period, n is the number of periods, r is the discount rate, C_t is the net cash flow in period t, and C_0 is the initial cash outlay.

See *financial performance metrics.*

Net Promoter Score (NPS) – A simple but useful loyalty metric based on customers' willingness to recommend.

The Net Promoter Score (NPS) is a relatively new **loyalty** metric developed by Frederick Reichheld (2003). It is derived from the "willingness to recommend metric," which is a survey instrument with the single item (question), "How likely is it that you would recommend us to a friend or colleague?"

Customers are asked to respond using a 0-10 **Likert rating scale** with 0 anchored on the extreme negative end and 10 on the extreme positive end. Customers are then divided into three categories: (1) promoters (9 or 10) are loyal enthusiasts who keep buying from a company and urge their friends to do the same; (2) passives (7 or 8) are satisfied but unenthusiastic customers who can be easily wooed by the competition; and (3) detractors (0 to 6) are unhappy customers. The NPS is the percentage of promoters minus the percentage of detractors. Reichheld (2003) compared the NPS to a financial net worth that takes the assets minus the liabilities, where the assets are the promoters and the liabilities are the detractors.

Reichheld (2003) claims that the NPS is the single best predictor of customer loyalty. He argues that the NPS is highly correlated with growth rates and that it is the single most reliable indicator of a company's ability to grow. The consulting firm Satmetrix offered a short white paper on this subject found at www.satmetrix.com/pdfs/NetPromoterWPfinal.pdf, May 16, 2011.

Dixon, Freeman, and Toman (2010) claim that the **Customer Effort Score (CES)** is more predictive of customer loyalty in a call center context than either the NPS or customer satisfaction.

Hill, Hays, and Naveh (2000) develop a concept similar to the NPS based on an economic model showing that loyalty is related to the ratio (not the difference) of satisfied and dissatisfied customers; i.e., $\Pi_s / (1 - \Pi_s)$, where Π_s is the percent satisfied. This suggests that loyalty might be a function of the ratio Π_p / Π_d, where Π_p is the percent promoters and Π_d the percent detractors, rather than the difference $\Pi_p - \Pi_d$. This concept has not yet been tested empirically.

See *Customer Effort Score (CES)*, *operations performance metrics*, *service management*, *service quality*.

net requirements – The number of units still needed to satisfy the materials plan in a Materials Requirements Planning (MRP) system.

In the MRP planning process, the net requirement is calculated as the gross requirements (units needed by higher-level items) plus allocations (units already promised to an order), less on-hand inventory (units that are available now), less open orders (scheduled receipts that will soon be available), less safety stock (desired number of units on-hand at all times).

See *Materials Requirements Planning (MRP)*, *open order*.

net weight – (1) In a packaging context: The weight of a product without packaging. (2) In a shipping/logistics context: The weight of a vehicle without its fuel, cargo, personnel, pallets, containers, or straps.

See *gross weight*, *logistics*, *tare weight*.

network effect – An economics term that describes a situation where the value of a product or service increases with the number of adopters, thereby encouraging an increasing number of adopters; also called a network externality.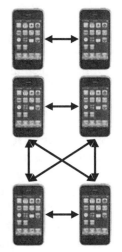

The network effect can be illustrated with cell phones. If the world had only one cell phone that used a particular communication technology, it would be of no value. However, this cell phone would become much more valuable if two of them existed, even more valuable if four of them existed, and far more valuable if nearly everyone had one.

Economists call this a **network externality** because when new consumers join the network, they have a beneficial external impact on consumers already in the network. The network effect produces a self-reinforcing cycle, with more buyers attracting more buyers.

Metcalfe's Law states, "The value of a telecommunications network is proportional to the square of the number of users of the system (n^2)" (Shapiro & Varian 1999). Metcalfe's Law explains many of the network effects of communication technologies and networks, such as the Internet, social networking, and Wikipedia. It is related to the fact that the number of unique connections in a network with n nodes is $n(n-1)/2$. Briscoe, Odlyzko, and Tilly (2006) argues that Metcalfe's Law is wrong and proposes $n \log(n)$ as an alternative growth model. With both models, the value of the network grows faster than a linear growth rate. If cost grows linearly with n and value grows faster than linear, the value will eventually exceed the cost.

The network effect is enabled by the **interoperability** of the network. The network effect is often the result of **word-of-mouth testimonials**. In other words, people may adopt a service because "everyone" uses it. Over time, positive network effects can create a "bandwagon effect" as the network becomes more valuable. This is related to the **Bass Model**.

The expression network effect nearly always refers to **positive network externalities**, as in the case of the telephone. **Negative network externalities** can also occur where more adopters make a product less valuable. This is sometimes referred to as "congestion," as in automobile congestion on the road.

With **economy of scale**, the supply side of a business becomes more efficient as it grows. With the network effect, the demand side of a business becomes more valuable as it grows. The network effect, therefore, is essentially a demand side economy of scale.

See *Bass Model, economy of scale, interoperability.*

network optimization – An operations research term for an efficient approach for modeling and solving a class of linear programming problems.

Many problems can be modeled as a network optimization problem, including the assignment problem, the transportation problem, and the transshipment problem. Most network optimization problems can be represented by a set of notes with arrows connecting them (a directed graph). The user must define the minimum flow, maximum flow, and cost per unit flow that can pass along each arc in the network. The fundamental rule is conservation of flow, which states simply that the flow coming into a node must equal the flow going out of a node. Only one type of commodity (product) can be modeled. More general methods, such as linear and integer programming, can handle multiple commodity flows.

The Ford and Fulkerson "out-of-kilter" algorithm is the most famous approach for solving this problem, but primal network algorithms are much more efficient. Several variants of the Ford and Fulkerson algorithm are available in the public domain and are efficient enough to handle many practical problems.

See *algorithm, assignment problem, linear programming (LP), operations research (OR), optimization, transportation problem, transshipment problem.*

neural network – A computer program that can "learn" over time; often called an "artificial neural network."

A neural network is a program that creates a computer network designed to function in a similar way to natural neural structures, such as a human brain. They can be used to model complex relationships between inputs and outputs or to find patterns in data. Neural networks are sometimes used in data mining applications to try to find relationships between inputs and outputs.

For example, neural networks might be helpful in identifying which customers have high credit risk based on history with other customers. In another example, a neural network approach was used at the University of Minnesota to try to identify how much of a particular polymer was found in a microscopic digitized photo. The program was "trained" by hundreds of photos that had many variables describing each pixel in the photo. Over time, the neural net program was able to develop a simple set of decision rules that could be used to correctly classify future pixels most of the time.

See *Artificial Intelligence (AI), data mining.*

never event – See *sentinel event.*

New Product Development (NPD) – The process of generating new product and service concepts, creating designs, and bringing new products and services to market; also called product development. ✪

The NPD process is often divided into three steps:

The fuzzy front end – The activities that generate and select concepts to be started into product development. Organizations should only start concepts that have a high probability of financial success.

New product development – The process of translating product concepts into specific designs that can be manufactured and brought to market.

Commercialization – The process of managing a new product through pilot production, production ramp-up, and product launch into the channels of distribution.

One of the key issues for NPD is forming the NPD project team. The following four tables compare the NPD team structure for four types of organizations: functional, lightweight, heavyweight, and autonomous. A good reference on this subject is Clark and Wheelwright (1992).

Functional

Description	• Members are grouped by discipline. • Entire project is divided into independent functional responsibilities.
Advantages	• Good means of evaluating functional performance. • Functional managers bring experience and knowledge.
Disadvantages	• Project tends to move sequentially through functional areas • No one directly involved in the project is responsible for results.
Best when	• Deep expertise is available.

Lightweight

Description	• Members still reside in their functional areas and are not dedicated to the team. • The team depends on the technical functions to get the work accomplished. • Liaison (middle or junior level manager) coordinates the project committee.
Advantages	• Greater coordination and better scheduling
Disadvantages	• Speed and coordination advantages are seldom realized.
Best when	• The focus is on derivative products.

Heavyweight

Description	• Dedicated team leader with large responsibility. • Team members report to the team leader. • The core group is co-located with its heavyweight project leader but still has a reporting relationship with functional bosses. • Core team "contract."
Advantages	• Focused task objectives. • Handle cross-functional integration very well. • Rapid and efficient development of new products and processes.
Disadvantages	• May raise conflicts with the functional management. • Teams want control over secondary activities. • May inhibit development of deep functional excellence. • Possibly requires more testing and quality assurance.
Best when	• A system solution is required.

Autonomous (sometimes called tiger teams)

Description	• Similar to heavyweight team. • No functional reporting relationships.
Advantages	• Few conflicts with functional management.
Disadvantages	• Teams want control over secondary activities. • May inhibit development of deep functional excellence. • Possibly requires more testing and quality assurance.
Best when	• A radical new concept is required.

Product Development and Management Association (PDMA) and the Product Development Institute (PDI) are two of the leading professional societies for NPD professionals in North America.

The Toyota approach to NPD appears to be quite different from that used in Western Europe and North America. Morgan and Liker (2006) provided a good overview of the Toyota NPD process.

See *absorptive capacity, adoption curve, Analytic Hierarchy Process (AHP), autonomous workgroup, breadboard, clockspeed, commercialization, Computer Aided Design (CAD), concurrent engineering, configuration management, Design for Six Sigma (DFSS), disruptive technology, Early Supplier Involvement (ESI), Fagan Defect-Free Process, flexibility, fuzzy front end, High Performance Work Systems (HPWS), ideation, Integrated Product Development (IPD), job design, Kano Analysis, lean design, line extension, Mean Time Between Failure (MTBF), Mean Time to Repair (MTTR), phase review, planned obsolescence, platform strategy, postponement, process design, Product Data Management (PDM), project charter, project management, prototype, Pugh Matrix, Quality Function Deployment (QFD), reliability, reverse engineering, scrum, serviceability, simultaneous engineering, stage-gate process, technology road map, time to market, time to volume, TRIZ, voice of the customer (VOC), waterfall scheduling.*

new product flexibility – See *flexibility.*

newsvendor model – A mathematical model that solves the newsvendor problem, which is an important problem where the decision maker must decide how much to purchase given the probability distribution of demand, the cost of under-buying one unit, and the cost of over-buying one unit; formerly called the newsboy model or the newsboy problem. ✪

The newsvendor problem appears in many business contexts, such as buying for a one-time selling season, making a final production run, setting safety stocks, setting target inventory levels, and making capacity decisions. These contexts all have the same problem structure: a single policy parameter, such as the order quantity, the presence of random demand, and known unit overage and unit underage costs.

The newsvendor model is fundamental to solving many important operations problems. The intuition obtained from the model can also be helpful. Explicitly defining the over-buying and under-buying cost and calculating the critical ratio can lead managers and analysts to better decisions.

The optimal order quantity is the demand associated with the critical ratio (also called the critical fractile), which is $R = c_u/(c_u + c_o)$, where c_u is the cost of having one unit less than the realized demand, and c_o is the unit cost of having one unit more than the realized demand. In the simplest retail environment, c_u is price minus unit cost (the gross margin), and c_o is unit cost minus salvage value. The optimal order quantity is $Q^* = F^{-1}(R)$, where $F^{-1}(R)$ is the inverse of the cumulative distribution function evaluated at the critical ratio.

For example, a grocery store owner needs to buy newspapers every Monday. If the owner buys one newspaper more than the demand, the store loses the cost of the newspaper (c_o = unit cost = $0.10). If the owner buys one newspaper less than the demand, the store loses the margin on the newspaper (c_u = unit price – unit cost = $0.50 – $0.10 = $0.40). The critical ratio, therefore, is $R = c_u/(c_u + c_o) = 0.4/(0.4 + 0.1) = 90\%$, and the optimal order quantity is at the 90th percentile of the cumulative demand distribution (CDF).

For the normal distribution, the Excel function for the optimal order quantity is NORMINV(critical ratio, mean, standard deviation). For example, if we have a newsvendor problem with normally distributed demand with a mean of 4 units, a standard deviation of 1 unit, and costs c_o = $100 and c_u = $1000, the critical ratio is $R = 0.91$, and the optimal order quantity is $Q^* = $ NORMINV(0.91, 4, 1) = 5.34 units.

See *anchoring, bathtub curve, capacity, fractile, Poisson distribution, purchasing, safety stock, seasonality, slow moving inventory, stockout, triangular distribution.*

newsvendor problem – See *newsvendor model.*

Newton's method – An important numerical method for "finding the roots" of the function; also known as the Newton-Raphson iteration.

The roots of a function $f(x)$ are the x values where $f(x) = 0$. Newton's method uses the Newton step $x_{k+1} = x_k - f(x_k)/f'(x_k)$ to find a better x value with each iteration. For "well-behaved" functions, Newton's method usually converges very quickly, usually within five to ten steps. However, the choice of the starting point x_0 is important to the speed of convergence. The method will converge when df/dx and d^2f/dx^2 do not change signs between x_0 and the root of $f(x) = 0$. Cheney and Kincaid (1994) identified three possible situations where Newton's procedure will not converge. These are the runaway problem, the flat spot problem, and the cycle problem.

See *linear programming (LP), operations research (OR).*

NGT – See *Nominal Group Technique (NGT).*

no fault receiving – A way of inventory accounting used in retailing where store employees are only required to "count boxes" and put the items away; employees are not required to account for the item count in each box.

See *receiving.*

nominal capacity – See *capacity.*

Nominal Group Technique (NGT) – A planning tool that helps a group organize and prioritize issues and gain buy-in through the process. ✪

Originally developed as an organizational planning technique by Delbecq, Van de Ven, and Gustafson in 1971, the nominal group technique can be used as an alternative to both the focus group and the Delphi techniques. It presents more structure than the focus group, but still takes advantage of the synergy created by group participants. The NGT helps build agreement on the issues in the process. This author uses the following approach for facilitating NGT brainstorming sessions:

1. **Prepare** – The leader in the organization should define **the main question**, find a skilled facilitator, select a group of participants, instruct the participants to come prepared to address the main question, arrange for a room with some empty walls, get marking pens (to make it hard for people to write too small) and Post-it Notes (at least 20 per participant). The 3M lined 4x6 Super-Sticky Post-it Notes work well.

2. **Kickoff** – The facilitator should open the meeting by clearly defining the main question (e.g., "How can we reduce waiting times for our customers?") and the scope of the discussion (e.g., "Our scope will not include information system issues."). The facilitator should this question on the whiteboard or easel and then ask the participants if they have any questions about the main question or scope before beginning.

3. **Generate** – Participants should then spend about five to ten minutes thinking quietly and creatively about the main question and generating a number of ideas to address the question. (In this author's experience, very few workgroups are disciplined enough to prepare their notes before the meeting.) Each participant should write each idea on a separate Post-it Note, with a one-to five word title in very large (one-inch high) letters on the top half of the note. Notes must be readable from the other side of the room. The facilitator should instruct participants to put their markers down when done. The facilitator should move on to the next step when about three quarters of the participants have their markers down.

MONDAY STAFFING

4. **Share** – Each participant is asked to share just one note for each round. The facilitator should add each note to the wall, trying to group them logically. For smaller groups, it works well to have everyone stand at the wall during this process. Discussion is not allowed during this time, except to ask short clarification questions. Participants should share their duplicate notes first and then add one new idea (note) to the wall. Participants should feel free to pass and then jump back in if they think of other contributions. The process should continue around the room until all notes are on the wall.

5. **Group** – The facilitator should ask for two or three volunteers to come to the wall and organize the notes into groups while other participants take a short break.

6. **Regroup** – When people return from break, they should come to the wall and study the groups. They can move a note from one group to another, combine two or more groups, add a new group, add new notes, and make copies of notes that belong to more than one group.

7. **Arrange** – With help from the participants, the facilitator should arrange groups in logical order on the wall (e.g., time order or in some sort of hierarchy). Some groups might become subgroups of larger groups. This process may require additional title notes.

8. **Vote** – Each participant should vote on the top three groups he or she believes is worthy of further discussion and action. (The facilitator should only allow two votes per person if the number of groups is less than four.)

9. **Assign** – Organizing the ideas into groups and prioritizing them is usually just the starting point. It is now necessary to determine the next steps. It is important to decide who has ownership for a particular issue or solution and to clearly define the next steps for that person. In some cases, it is also a good idea to begin to create a formal project to address the top issues.

   Advantages of the NGT process over typical brainstorming include:

- Shows respect for all participants and their ideas.
- Does not allow "high-verbal" or "high-control" participants to dominate the discussion.
- Collects many ideas from the participants along with detailed documentation of these ideas.
- Efficiently creates a set of notes to document the ideas using the participants' own words.
- Very quickly and efficiently groups and prioritizes ideas.
- Results in good solutions.
- Creates a shared understanding of the problems and the solutions.
- Builds a strong sense of ownership of the results.

   See *affinity diagram, brainstorming, causal map, focus group, ideation, impact wheel, issue log, Kepner-Tregoe Model, KJ Method, parking lot, Root Cause Analysis (RCA), seven tools of quality.*

nominal scale – See *scales of measurement.*

non-instantaneous replenishment – See *instantaneous replenishment.*

normal distribution – A continuous probability distribution commonly used to model errors (for both forecasting and regression models) and also for the sum of many independent random variables. ✪

   Parameters: Mean μ and standard deviation σ.

Density and distribution functions: The density function for the normal distribution has a bell shape and is written mathematically as $f(x) = \dfrac{1}{\sqrt{2\pi}\sigma} e^{-(x-\mu)^2/(2\sigma^2)}$. The distribution function is the integral of the density function and has no closed form, but is tabulated in many books.

Statistics: Range $(-\infty, \infty)$, mean (μ) = mode = median, variance (σ^2). The inflection points for the density function are at $\mu \pm \sigma$. The standard normal distribution has mean $\mu = 0$ and standard deviation $\sigma = 1$.

Graph: The graph on the right is the normal probability density function (PDF) with $\mu = 10$ and $\sigma = 2$.

Parameter estimation: The sample mean and standard deviation are unbiased estimators of μ and σ.

Excel: In Excel, the standard normal distribution function evaluated at z is NORMSDIST(z). This is the probability that a standard normal random variable will be less than or equal to z. Excel normal density and distribution functions are NORMDIST(x, μ, σ, FALSE) and NORMDIST(x, μ, σ, TRUE). NORMINV(p, μ, σ) is the inverse distribution function, which returns the value of x that has cumulative probability p. Excel 2010 renames the functions as NORM.DIST, NORM.S.DIST, NORM.INV, and NORM.S.INV, but continue to use the same parameters.

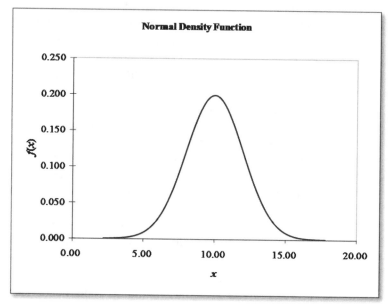

Excel simulation: In an Excel simulation, normally distributed random variates can be generated by the inverse transform method with x = NORMINV(1-RAND(), μ, σ). Another approach, based on the central limit theorem, is to sum 12 random numbers. The sum minus 12 is approximately standard normal. The Box-Muller method is a special-purpose approach for generating independent normal random deviates from a stream of random numbers and is more efficient and precise than other methods. The Box-Muller VBA code follows:

```
Function normal_rv_bm(mu, sigma) as double
Const twopi As Double = 6.28318530717959
Dim ncall As Long, u1 As Double, u2 As Double, z As Double, z2 As Double
    ncall = ncall + 1
    If ncall Mod 2 <> 0 Then
        u1 = Rnd(): u2 = Rnd()
        z = Sqr(-2 * Log(u1)) * Cos(twopi * u2): z2 = Sqr(-2 * Log(u1)) * Sin(twopi * u2)
    Else
        z = z2
    End If
    normal_rv_bm = z * sigma + mu
End Function
```

Approximation for $F(z)$: The following VBA code is an accurate approximation for the standard normal distribution function based on the algorithm in Press et al. (2002)[34]. The author compared this approximation to NORMSDIST(z) for z in the range $[-6, 6]$ and found a maximum absolute deviation of 7.45061×10^{-8} at $z = 0.72$.

---

[34] *This is algorithm 26.2.17 from Abramowitz and Stegun (1964), which claims a maximum absolute error $< 7.5 \cdot 10^{-8}$. The VBA implementation above increases the number of significant digits for the $c2 = 1/\sqrt{2\pi}$ parameter and uses the "if-then" condition provided in Press but not in Abramowitz and Stegun.*

```
Function normsdistF(z As Double) As Double
Const c2 = 0.398942280401433, p = 0.2316419, b1 = 0.31938153, b2 = -0.356563782
Const b3 = 1.781477937, b4 = -1.821255978, b5 = 1.330274429: Dim t As Double, b0 As Double
   t = 1 / (1 + p * Abs(z)): b0 = c2 * Exp((-z) * (z / 2))
   normsdistF = 1 - b0 * ((((b5 * t + b4) * t + b3) * t + b2) * t + b1) * t
   If z < 0 Then normsdistF = 1 - normsdistF
End Function
```

Approximation for the inverse distribution function $F^{-1}(p)$: The following is an approximation for the inverse of the standard normal distribution function: $x = F^{-1}(p) \approx 5.06329114(p^{0.135} - (1-p)^{0.135})$ or in Excel =5.06329114*(p ^0.135-(1-p)^0.135). This approximation was tested in Excel in the range $p = (0.50400, 0.99997)$ and was found to have a maximum absolute percent error of 4.68% at $p = 0.99997$. For p in the range (0.504, 0.9987), the maximum absolute percent error was 0.67% at $p = 0.10$. Computer code for the inverse normal with a relative absolute error less than 1.15×10^{-9} for $x = F^{-1}(p) \geq -38$ can be found at http://home.online.no/~pjacklam/notes/invnorm (April 7, 2011).

See *binomial distribution, central limit theorem, confidence interval, error function, inverse transform method, lognormal distribution, probability density function, probability distribution, random number, sampling, Student's t distribution.*

normal time – A work measurement term from the field of industrial engineering used for the time to complete a task as observed from a time study, adjusted for the performance rating. ✪

The steps in estimating a normal time are as follows:

1. **Compute the average task time for each operator** – Collect several random observations on task times, and compute the average observed task time $\overline{t_i}$ for each operator i.

2. **Estimate the performance rating for each operator** – Make subjective estimates of the performance rating (r_i) for each operator i, where $r_i = 1.10$ for someone working 10% faster than normal.

3. **Calculate the standard time** – Calculate the standard time as the product of the allowance (A) and the average observed times adjusted by the performance ratings (r_i), i.e., $T_{std} = (1+A)\frac{1}{N}\sum_{i=1}^{N} r_i \overline{t_i}$. The allowance ($A$) is for personal needs, fatigue, and unavoidable delays. The allowance should depend on work environment issues, such as temperature, dust, dirt, fumes, noise, and vibration and is usually about 15%.

See *performance rating, standard time, time study, work measurement, work sampling.*

normalization – An information systems term for the process of reducing redundancies and anomalies in a database; once normalization is done, the database is said to be normalized.

See *data warehouse.*

North American Free Trade Agreement (NAFTA) – An agreement that formed a free trade area between the U.S., Canada, and Mexico. It went into effect on January 1, 1994.

np-chart – A statistical process control chart used to monitor the number of non-conforming units in a sample.

The np-chart is similar to a p-chart. The only major difference is that the np-chart uses count data rather than proportions. The control limits are typically set at $np \pm 3\sqrt{np(1-p)}$, where p is the estimate of the long-term process mean. The np-chart plots the number of non-conforming units.

See *control chart, p-chart, Poisson distribution, Statistical Process Control (SPC).*

NPD – See *New Product Development (NPD).*

numerically controlled (NC) machine – See *Computer Numerically Controlled (CNC) machine.*

numeric-analytic location model – An iterative method that guarantees the optimal solution to the single facility infinite set location problem.

A firm needs to locate a single warehouse to serve n customers. Each customer (j) has coordinates (x_j, y_j), demand or weight (w_j), and a transportation cost of c_j per unit per mile. The single warehouse facility is to be located at the coordinates (x_0, y_0). The travel distance from the warehouse to customer j is assumed to be

Pythagorean (straight-line) distance defined by $d_j = \sqrt{(x_0 - x_j)^2 + (y_0 - y_j)^2}$. The goal is to find the (x_0, y_0) coordinates for the warehouse that minimize the total incremental cost (*TIC*) defined as $TIC = \sum_{j}^{n} c_j w_j d_j$. The center-of-gravity solution for this problem is $x_0 = \sum_{j=1}^{n} c_j w_j x_j$ and $y_0 = \sum_{j=1}^{n} c_j w_j y_j$. This solution is sometimes called the "center of mass" or "centroid." Although the center-of-gravity method is quite simple, it is not necessarily optimal and can be far from optimal.

See *center-of-gravity model for facility location, facility location, gravity model for competitive retail store location, great circle distance, logistics, marginal cost, Pythagorean Theorem, warehouse.*

O

objective function – See *linear programming.*

obsolescence – See *obsolete inventory.*

obsolete inventory – Inventory that can no longer be sold because of lack of market demand, outdated technology, degradation of quality, or spoilage; also called "dead and excess" inventory and "dead stock."

Most firms try to remove obsolete inventory to free up space and take a tax **write-off** earlier rather than later. Firms often use simple rules to determine if inventory is **dead**. These rules are usually based on how much time has passed with no sales. Some firms, particularly retailers, can "clear" nearly obsolete inventory by selling it at a discounted price. Gupta, Hill, and Bouzdine-Chameeva (2006) presented a pricing model for clearing **end-of-season** retail inventory. Most firms have a **financial reserve** for obsolete inventory based on sales, current inventory investment, age, historical trends, and anticipated events.

See *ABC classification, all-time demand, carrying charge, red tag, shrinkage, slow moving inventory, termination date.*

OC curve – See *operating characteristic curve.*

Occam's Razor – A principle in science and philosophy that recommends selecting the competing hypothesis that makes the fewest assumptions; also called the law of parsimony; also spelled Ockham's Razor.

This principle is interpreted to mean that the simplest of two or more competing theories is preferable and that an explanation for unknown phenomena should first be attempted in terms of what is already known.

See *KISS principle, parsimony.*

Occupational Safety and Health Administration (OSHA) – A U.S. government agency created by the Occupational Safety and Health Act of 1970 to ensure safe and healthful working conditions for working men and women by setting and enforcing standards and by providing training, outreach, education and assistance.

OSHA is part of the U.S.Department of Labor. The administrator for OSHA is the assistant secretary of labor for occupational safety and health. OSHA's administrator answers to the secretary of labor, who is a member of the cabinet of the president of the United States.

See *DuPont STOP, error proofing, risk management, safety.*

Ockham's Razor – See *Occam's Razor.*

OCR – See *Optical Character Recognition (OCR).*

ODM (Original Design Manufacturer) – See *contract manufacturer.*

OEE – See *Overall Equipment Effectiveness.*

OEM (Original Equipment Manufacturer) – See *original equipment manufacturer.*

off-line setup – See *setup reduction.*

offshoring – Developing a supplier in another country with either vertically integrated or external suppliers.

Whereas **outsourcing** refers to the use of another party regardless of that party's location, offshoring refers to the location of the source of supply. A firm could offshore and own the offshore vertically integrated supplier.

The primary issues that should be considered in an offshore decision include (1) expertise in managing remote locations, (2) quality of the workforce, (3) cost of labor, (4) language skills, (5) telecom bandwidth, (6) cost and reliability, (7) infrastructure, (8) political stability, (9) enforceability of intellectual property rights and business contracts, (10) general maturity of the business environment, and (11) risk related to weather (earthquakes, hurricanes, tornadoes, typhoons, and volcanoes).

See *expatriate, intellectual property (IP), landed cost, nearshoring, operations strategy, outsourcing, supply chain management.*

one-minute manager – A simple managerial coaching concept that involves three one-minute interactions between a manager and an employee.

The One Minute Manager (Blanchard & Johnson 1982) presented three simple ways for managers to interact with their subordinates – goal setting, praise, and reprimand. All three of these interactions require about one minute, though the time may vary based on the situation. The main point is that these three interactions can and should be short, simple, and regular. These three interactions are briefly described below:

One-minute goal setting – One-minute managers regularly ask employees to review their goals with a script such as, "What are your goals for this month?" This process helps the manager and employees confirm that they are in complete agreement on goals and priorities.

One-minute praise – When one-minute managers catch their employees doing something right, they give their employees immediate praise and tell them specifically what they did right. Just saying "good job" is not specific. After giving a praise, the manager should pause for a moment to allow the employee to feel good and then remind the employee how his or her actions help the organization. The managers should finish by shaking hands and encouraging the employee to keep up the good work.

One-minute reprimand – One-minute managers provide immediate, specific, and clear feedback to employees. The goal of the reprimand is not to punish, but rather to help employees better achieve their goals. Following a reprimand, the manager should shake hands and remind the employee that he or she is important and that it was the employee's behavior that did not meet the standard.

The three one-minute interactions are closely interrelated. One-minute goal setting clarifies goals, one-minute praise reinforces behavior consistent with the goals, and one-minute reprimand gives negative feedback for behavior inconsistent with the goals.

See *management by walking around, SMART goals.*

one-piece flow – A lean manufacturing practice of making only one part at a time (a batch size of one) before moving the part to the next step in the process; also called single-piece flow, make-one-move-one, and one-for-one replenishment.

This lean ideal is not always achievable. Single Minute Exchange of Dies and other setup time reduction methods are critical for helping organizations reduce setup cost (and ordering cost) and move toward this ideal.

See *batch-and-queue, continuous flow, lean thinking, setup time reduction methods, Single Minute Exchange of Dies (SMED), zero inventory.*

on-hand inventory – The quantity shown in the inventory records as being physically in the inventory. ✪

Whereas on-hand inventory is the current physical quantity in stock, the inventory position is the quantity on-hand plus on-order, less allocated, less backordered.

See *allocated inventory, backorder, cycle counting, inventory management, inventory position, Master Production Schedule (MPS), Materials Requirements Planning (MRP), on-order inventory, open order, perpetual inventory system.*

on-order inventory – The amount of inventory that has been ordered from a supplier (internal or external) but not yet received. ✪

The inventory position is the quantity on-hand, plus on-order, less allocated, less backordered.

See *inventory management, inventory position, Master Production Schedule (MPS), Materials Requirements Planning (MRP), on-hand inventory, open order, perpetual inventory system.*

on-the-job training (OJT) – A method for training employees by involving them in the work.

Workers develop skills simply by working, ideally under the watchful eye of a supervisor or mentor, and usually during the normal workday.

See *cross-training, human resources, job design.*

on-time and complete – See *on-time delivery*.

on-time delivery (OTD) – A customer delivery/service metric that is measured as the percentage of orders received by the promised date (within an allowable time window); also known as on-time and complete.

See *blanket purchase order (PO), dispatching rules, operations performance metrics, service level, supplier scorecard, Transportation Management System (TMS)*.

open-book management – Sharing key financial information openly with employees and other stakeholders.

The phrase "open-book management" was coined by John Case of *Inc. Magazine* in 1993 (Aggarwal & Simkins 2001) to describe the practice of providing employees with all relevant information about their company's financial performance. Some firms take it a step further and share financial information with customers and suppliers. In this author's experience, this concept is rarely used in North America.

See *stakeholder*.

open order – An order sent to a supplier (either internal or external) but not yet received by the customer; also called a scheduled receipt. ❂

When an order is sent to a supplier, it is said to be released. Open orders are included in the inventory position (but not the on-hand balance) and used with both internal and external suppliers. The on-order balance for an item is the sum of the order quantities for all open orders for that item.

See *bullwhip effect, Business Requirements Planning (BRP), inventory position, net requirements, on-hand inventory, on-order inventory*.

operating characteristic curve – A graphical approach for understanding the parameters of a lot acceptance sampling plan.

The operating characteristic curve (OC) plots the probability of accepting a lot on the *y*-axis and the lot fraction or percent defectives on the *x*-axis.

See *acceptance sampling, consumer's risk, producer's risk, quality management, sampling, Statistical Process Control (SPC), Statistical Quality Control (SQC)*.

operation – (1) In a general context: Any manufacturing or service process, no matter how large or small. (2) In a Materials Requirements Planning (MRP) or shop floor control context: A specific step in the routing required to make an item.

In the MRP context, the routing specifies the sequence of operations required to make an item. Each operation is defined by the operation sequence number, the workcenter, required materials, standard setup time, and standard run time per part.

See *dispatching rules, operations management (OM), routing, shop floor control*.

operation overlapping – See *transfer batch*.

operations management (OM) – Management of the transformation process that converts labor, capital, materials, information, and other inputs into products and services for customers. ❂

Operations management is a core subject taught in all business schools, along with accounting, finance, marketing, human resources, management information systems, and general management/strategy. The preface of this encyclopedia presents a framework for operations management. Many colleges and universities are now using the broader term "**supply chain and operations management**."

The **operations management framework** below was developed through an extensive survey of operations management professors and practitioners (Hays, Bouzdine-Chameeva, Meyer Goldstein, Hill, & Scavarda 2007). (The figure below is an adaption of that framework.) An organization's operations strategy is derived from its business strategy and should guide and inform decisions in the four "pillars" of operations management: product & process design, capacity & demand management, supply chain management, and process improvement. These four pillars are supported by quality and people management, systems management, analytical tools, and performance metrics. All terms in this framework are presented in detail elsewhere in this encyclopedia.

Operations management framework

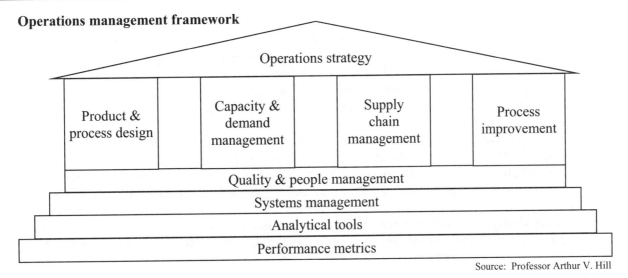

Source: Professor Arthur V. Hill

The operations management profession is supported by many academic and professional societies, including:

- American Society for Quality (ASQ), www.asq.org
- APICS - The Association for Operations Management, www.apics.org
- Association for Manufacturing Excellence (AME), www.ame.org
- Council of Supply Chain Management Professionals (CSCMP), www.cscmp.org
- Decision Sciences Institute (DSI), www.decisionsciences.org
- European Operations Management Association (EurOMA), www.euroma-online.org
- Institute for Operations Research and the Management Sciences (INFORMS), www.informs.org
- Institute for Supply Management (ISM), www.ism.ws
- Institute of Industrial Engineers (IIE), www.iienet2.org
- International Federation of Operational Research Societies (IFORS), www.ifors.org
- Lean Enterprise Institute (LEI)[35], www.lean.org
- Manufacturing and Service Operations Management Society (MSOM), http://msom.society.informs.org
- Operational Research Society, www.orsoc.org.uk
- Production and Operations Management Society (POMS), www.poms.org
- Project Management Institute (PMI), www.pmi.org
- Society of Manufacturing Engineers (SME), www.sme.org
- Supply Chain Council (SCC)[36], www.supply-chain.org

A short description for each of these societies is presented in this encyclopedia. This list omits many other important professional societies in related disciplines inside and outside North America.

See *American Society for Quality (ASQ), APICS (The Association for Operations Management), Association for Manufacturing Excellence (AME), Council of Supply Chain Management Professionals (CSCMP), Decision Sciences Institute (DSI), European Operations Management Association (EurOMA), human resources, Institute for Operations Research and the Management Sciences (INFORMS), Institute for Supply Management (ISM), Institute of Industrial Engineers (IIE), Manufacturing and Service Operations Management Society (MSOM), operation, operations research (OR), operations strategy, Production Operations Management Society (POMS), Project Management Institute (PMI), Society of Manufacturing Engineers (SME), Supply Chain Council.*

operations performance metrics – Variables used to evaluate any process. ✪

As noted in the *balanced scorecard* entry, it is important that the performance metrics be balanced. One way to balance metrics is to use both financial and operations performance metrics. Operations performance metrics are often the key means for achieving the financial performance metrics, because the operations performance metrics usually "drive" the financial metrics.

---

[35] *Like the other organizations in this list, LEI is a non-profit; however, it is not a professional society like the others.*
[36] *The Supply Chain Council is closely identified with the SCOR model.*

With respect to operations performance metrics, many firms have at least one metric in each of these three categories: **better** (quality related metrics), **faster** (time and flexibility related metrics), and **cheaper** (cost related metrics). Many operations experts argue that the cheaper metrics are improved by improving the better and faster metrics. This author has added **stronger** as a fourth category of metrics to include risk management and strategic alignment. Many operations performance metrics are used in practice. This encyclopedia provides clear definitions for nearly all of the following operations performance metrics:

Better metrics:

- **Product performance metrics** – These depend on the specific product (e.g., the specifications for an automobile will define how long it takes to accelerate from 0 to 60 miles per hour).
- **Customer satisfaction and loyalty metrics** – Customer satisfaction, intention to repurchase (willingness to return), willingness to recommend, Net Promoter Score (NPS), Customer Effort Score (CES), and actual customer loyalty.
- **Process capability and performance metrics and quality metrics** – Yield, defects, defects per million units, defects per million opportunities, parts per million, rolled throughput yield, sigma level metric, process capability (C_p), process capability index (C_{pk}), process performance (P_p), and the process performance index (P_{pk}).
- **Service related metrics** – Service level, cycle service level, unit fill rate, order fill rate, line fill rate, perfect order fill rate, on-time delivery (OTD), percent on-time and complete, average response time, premium freight, stockout cost, and shortage cost.

Faster metrics:

- **Time metrics** – Cycle time[37], order to cash cycle time, throughput time, customer leadtime, time to market, average wait time, average time in system, Mean Time to Repair (MTTR), Mean Time Between Failure (MTBF).
- **Learning rate metrics** – Learning rate (learning curve), half-life, and percent improvement.
- **Theory of Constraints metrics** – Inventory Dollar Days (IDD), Throughput Dollar Days (TDD), and Throughput dollars.
- **Lean metrics** – Value added ratio (also called manufacturing cycle effectiveness)[38].

Cheaper metrics:

- **Inventory metrics** – Inventory turnover, periods supply (days on-hand), inventory investment, and inventory carrying cost.
- **Forecast error metrics** – Mean Absolute Percent Error (MAPE), Mean Absolute Scaled Error (MASE), bias, and forecast attainment.
- **Equipment metrics** – Utilization, availability, downtime, first-pass yield, Mean Time Between Failure (MTBF), Mean Time to Repair (MTTR), and Overall Equipment Effectiveness (OEE).
- **Traditional cost accounting metrics** – Productivity (output/input), efficiency (standard time)/(actual time), utilization, sales, gross margin, overhead variance (fixed and variable), labor variance, labor efficiency variance, direct material variance, direct material price variance, and cost per part.
- **Warehouse metrics** – First pick ratio, inventory accuracy, capacity utilization, cube utilization, mispicks.
- **Transportation metrics** – Freight cost per unit shipped, outbound freight costs as percentage of net sales, inbound freight costs as percentage of purchases, average transit time, claims as percentage of freight costs, freight bill accuracy, percent of truckload capacity utilized, average truck turnaround time, on-time pickups.

Stronger metrics:

- **Strategic alignment** – Gap between goals and performance on highest level strategic performance metrics.
- **Risk assessment metrics** – Risk priority number (in the context of an FMEA), expected loss, probability of failure.
- **Safety metrics** – Number of days since last injury, number of serious accidents per time period, number of near misses, time to fix safety issues.

---

[37] *This term has multiple meanings. See the cycle time entry for more details.*

[38] *Lean could be classified as "better" (because it reduces defects), "faster" (because it reduces cycle time), and "cheaper" (because it reduces waste and cost). The same is true for several other types of metrics.*

- **Triple bottom line metrics** – People (human capital) metrics, planet (natural capital) metrics, and profit (economic benefit for all stakeholders) metrics.

See *balanced scorecard, benchmarking, Capability Maturity Model (CMM), cube utilization, Customer Effort Score (CES), cycle time, dashboard, Data Envelopment Analysis (DEA), downtime, efficiency, Failure Mode and Effects Analysis (FMEA), financial performance metrics, first pick ratio, forecast error metrics, half-life curve, Inventory Dollar Days (IDD), inventory turnover, Key Performance Indicator (KPI), learning curve, learning organization, Net Promoter Score (NPS), on-time delivery (OTD), Overall Equipment Effectiveness (OEE), performance management system, process capability and performance, productivity, queuing theory, robust, sand cone model, scales of measurement, service level, service management, sigma level, standard time, strategy map, supplier scorecard, Throughput Dollar Days (TDD), utilization, wait time, work measurement, yield, Y-tree.*

operations research (OR) – The science that applies mathematical and computer science tools to support decision making. ✪

Operations research (OR) draws on many mathematical disciplines, such as optimization, statistics, stochastic processes (queuing theory), decision theory, simulation, graph theory (network optimization), and game theory. Optimization can be further broken down into constrained and unconstrained optimization, each of which can be broken down further into linear, non-linear, and discrete optimization. Simulation appears to be a field of growing importance with a number of powerful software tools, such as Arena, that are available for creating complex stochastic models of real-world systems.

During its formative years shortly after World War II, OR professionals argued that OR projects should be multi-disciplinary. However, most OR people today are trained as mathematicians, computer scientists, or industrial engineers. OR is considered by most experts to be synonymous with management science. The largest professional organization for operations research is INFORMS (www.informs.org).

See *algorithm, assignment problem, decision tree, genetic algorithm, heuristic, Institute for Operations Research and the Management Sciences (INFORMS), knapsack problem, linear programming (LP), Manufacturing and Service Operations Management Society (MSOM), mixed integer programming (MIP), network optimization, Newton's method, operations management (OM), optimization, sensitivity analysis, simulated annealing, simulation, transportation problem, transshipment problem, Traveling Salesperson Problem (TSP).*

operations strategy – A set of policies for using the firm's resources to support the business unit's strategy to gain competitive advantage; also called manufacturing strategy. ✪

Operations objectives – Operations strategy is usually defined in terms of the operations objectives of cost, quality, flexibility, and service. Other variants of this list also include delivery (instead of service), time or speed (as a part of service or flexibility), and customization (as a type of flexibility). Some lists also include safety, sustainability, environmental issues, and development of human capital. The Andersen Corporation Menomonie plant uses safety, quality, delivery, cost, and morale. This encyclopedia uses better, faster, cheaper, and stronger, where stronger means more robust and better aligned with strategy.

Trade-offs – Firms can often gain competitive advantage by making the best tradeoffs and by avoiding trade-offs between operations objectives. For example, Dell Computer was able to "change the rules of the game" and gain competitive advantage by being the first to successfully offer low cost assemble-to-order customized computers through direct mail (providing customization and quality without cost). Similarly, FedEx was one of the first to offer reliable overnight package delivery at a reasonable price (providing reliable fast delivery at a reasonable price).

Explicit versus implicit – The operations strategy may be explicit or implicit. An implicit strategy is not written down, and senior executives may not be able to articulate it, but it becomes apparent with an objective evaluation of the management's consistent approach to decision making and the firm's position in the market.

Operations strategy process versus content – Researchers in the operations management field often make a distinction between the operations strategy process and content. The process is the methodology that the organization uses to create its operations strategy, whereas the content is the substance of the strategy.

Structure versus infrastructure decisions – The most effective operations organization is not necessarily the one that has the maximum efficiency, responsiveness, or flexibility, but rather the one that best fits the strategic requirements of the business. In other words, the operations organization should always strive to make decisions that are consistent with the competitive strategy being pursued by the strategic business unit. Hayes and Wheelwright (1984, p. 31) developed the following list of "manufacturing strategy decision categories" and divided the list into two sets – structure and infrastructure:

Structure
- Capacity – Amount, timing, type
- Facilities – Size, location, specialization
- Technology – Equipment, automation, linkages
- Vertical integration – Direction, extent, balance

Infrastructure
- Workforce – Skill level, wage policies, employment security
- Quality – Defect prevention, monitoring, intervention
- Production planning/materials control – Sourcing policies, centralization, decision rules
- Organization – Structure, control/reward systems, role of staff groups

Whereas structural decisions are physical, longer term, and more difficult to change, infrastructural decisions are more tactical and require less visible capital investments (but can still be difficult to change). Hayes and Wheelwright argue that these eight decision areas are closely interrelated and that "it is this pattern of structural and infrastructural decisions that constitutes the manufacturing strategy of a business unit" (Hayes & Wheelwright 1984, p. 32). This framework is closely related to the McKinsey *7S Model*.

Other entries in the *EOM* – The *balanced scorecard*, *strategy map*, and *causal map* entries discuss strategy process issues in more detail. The *strategy map* entry presents the time-based competition strategy. The *mass customization* entry presents customization as a potential component of an operations strategy. *Outsourcing* to achieve lower cost is also a component of an operations strategy. A *focused factory* is an important manufacturing strategy, and the *Service Profit Chain* is an important service operations strategy. The *push-pull boundary* and *postponement* entries deal with the customer interface, leadtime, and customization issues.

See *7S Model, agile manufacturing, balanced scorecard, blue ocean strategy, cash cow, catchball, competitive analysis, core competence, first mover advantage, five forces analysis, focused factory, industry analysis, mass customization, offshoring, operations management (OM), order qualifier, outsourcing, plant-within-a-plant, postponement, push-pull boundary, resource based view, respond to order (RTO), robust, sand cone model, Service Profit Chain, strategy map, supply chain management, sustainability, SWOT analysis, technology push, time-based competition, vertical integration, virtual organization.*

opportunity cost – The value of an alternative (opportunity) that was not taken. ✪

When people have a choice between two or more alternatives, they will generally choose the best one. However, choosing the best alternative means that they cannot choose the next best alternative. The opportunity cost is the value of the next best alternative that must be sacrificed, i.e., "the value of the road not taken."

For example, a firm can only make one product in a factory and decides to build product A instead of B. Although it makes a profit on product A, it gave up the profit on product B. The forgone profit on product B is called the opportunity cost.

For a more specific example, consider a factory that has one large machine (the bottleneck) that constrains the plant's production rate. The firm makes $1,000 per hour in gross revenue every hour the machine is running. The firm currently has a setup time on this machine of one hour per day, which means that the firm could make $1,000 more per day if the setup could be eliminated. The standard costing system assigns direct labor and overhead to this machine at a rate of $200 per machine hour. However, the true cost of the setup is much more than $200 per hour because of the opportunity cost (i.e., the lost gross margin).

See *carrying cost, economics, overhead, setup cost, stockout, Theory of Constraints (TOC).*

Optical Character Recognition (OCR) – A technology that enables a machine to translate images into text.

See *Automated Data Collection (ADC), Electronic Product Code (EPC), lockbox.*

optimization – An operations research term for mathematical techniques that find the best solution to a problem.

Optimization techniques can be classified as either **unconstrained** or **constrained** optimization. Unconstrained optimization methods include **calculus** and **numerical methods** (search methods). Constrained optimization methods include **linear programming**, **integer programming**, and many other mathematical programming methods. Optimization techniques can also be classified as **deterministic** (has no uncertainty) or **stochastic** (allows for uncertainty). For example, finding the optimal safety stock is usually modeled as an unconstrained stochastic optimization problem, and finding the minimum cost allocation of products to warehouses in a distribution network is usually modeled as a constrained deterministic optimization problem.

Although many students use the term "optimize" to describe any situation where they are attempting to find the best solution, most professors prefer to reserve the word to only describe situations where the mathematically best solution is guaranteed to be found by a mathematical optimization procedure.

Excel provides useful optimization tools with (1) **Goal Seek** (for unconstrained optimization) and (2) the **Solver** (for both unconstrained and constrained optimization). Excel can be used with the Solver (and VBA as needed) to develop practical decision support systems for many important supply chain and operations management optimization problems (Winston & Albright 2011).

See *Advanced Planning and Scheduling (APS)*, *algorithm*, *Decision Support System (DSS)*, *genetic algorithm*, *heuristic*, *linear programming (LP)*, *network optimization*, *operations research (OR)*, *simulated annealing*.

order backlog – See *backlog*.

order cost – The marginal cost of placing one more purchase or manufacturing order; synonymous with setup cost.

Order cost increases with the number of orders. It includes costs related to the work of preparing, shipping, releasing, monitoring, receiving inspection, and put away. The *setup cost* entry provides more details.

See *inventory management*, *marginal cost*, *setup cost*.

order cycle – The time between receipts for the orders of an item; also called the replenishment cycle.

The number of order cycles per year can be estimated as D/Q, where D is the forecasted annual demand and Q is the average order quantity. The *reorder point* entry presents a graph that shows several order cycles.

See *reorder point*, *safety stock*, *service level*, *stockout*.

order cycle service level – See *safety stock*.

order entry – The process (and the related organizational unit) of receiving customer sales order information and entering it into a fulfillment system.

Order entry systems communicate important information to customers, such as prices, terms, availability, promise dates, technical product information, and payment options (cash, credit, credit card, etc.). People taking orders (customer service representatives) may act as salespersons and pursue opportunities to **cross-sell** complimentary products and **up-sell** more expensive products. After the order has been entered into the system, the system will create information for picking, shipping, and invoicing.

See *call center*, *configurator*, *cross-selling*, *customer service*, *fulfillment*, *functional silo*.

order fill rate – See *fill rate*.

order fulfillment – See *fulfillment*.

order penetration point – See *push-pull boundary*.

order picking – See *picking*.

order point system – See *reorder point*.

order qualifier – An attribute of a product or service that is necessary for customers to consider buying; also called an order loser.

An **order qualifier** is a characteristic that customers use to screen products for further evaluation. In contrast, an **order winner** makes a critical difference in the buyer's decision process. In other words, the order qualifier "gets the salesperson in the door" to be considered by the potential buyer and the order winner "gets the salesperson out the door with the order in hand" (i.e., seals the deal and beats out the competition).

For example, the order qualifier for some buyers looking for a watch might be a price under $100. However, the order winner might be other product characteristics, such as the warranty or the wristband.

See *operations strategy*.

order quantity modifier – See *lotsizing methods*.

order size – See *lotsize*.

order winner – See *order qualifier*.

order-to-cash – The time between the receipt of the order from the customer and the receipt of the payment from the customer.

See *cycle time*, *respond to order (RTO)*.

order-up-to level – An inventory control term for a maximum inventory level; also called base stock, target inventory, max, maximum, model stock, and par level; in academic literature, often called an S system.

An inventory system using an order-up-to level policy calculates the order quantity as the order-up-to level minus the current inventory position. The optimal order-up-to level is the optimal safety stock plus the average demand per period times leadtime plus review period (i.e., $T = SS + \mu_d(L+P)$). With a continuous review system, the review period is zero.

See *inventory management, inventory position, joint replenishment, min-max inventory system, periodic review system, reorder point.*

ordinal scale – See *scales of measurement.*

organizational design – (1) The structure that defines the duties, goals, decision rights, policies, and reporting relationships for individuals or groups of people in an organization. (2) The process of creating such a structure.

Organizational design structure – Although an organizational design is reflected in an organizational chart, it is much more than a chart. Some examples of organizational design structures include:

- Centralized structure – Decision rights are concentrated in the top management, and tight control is exercised over departments and divisions.
- Decentralized structure – Decision rights are distributed, and the departments and divisions have more autonomy.
- Hierarchical structure – A common centralized structure where clear reporting lines are drawn, with each manager typically having several direct reports.
- Functional structure – Organizations are divided along areas of expertise, such as engineering and marketing. This structure is usually efficient within functional areas.
- Divisional (product) structure – An example of a decentralized structure, where the organization is divided into geographical or product-based divisions.
- Matrix structure – A structure that uses cross-functional and cross-divisional teams to deliver products, where team members often report to both a functional boss and a project leader outside their function.

Organizational design process – Organizational design is the process of aligning the people in an organization to meet its strategic objectives. Organizational design activities start with the organization's goals and take into account the current organizational structure, skills and abilities of its people, job functions, and uncertainty in the external environment. The process seeks to form the organization into a structure that best suits its value proposition.

See *absorptive capacity, cross-functional team, High Performance Work Systems (HPWS), human resources, job design, job enlargement, RACI Matrix, self-directed work team, virtual organization, workforce agility.*

organizational structure – See *organizational design.*

Original Design Manufacturer (ODM) – See *contract manufacturer.*

Original Equipment Manufacturer (OEM) – An organization that sells products made by other organizations under its own name and brand.

Contrary to what the name "original equipment manufacturer" suggests, the OEM is not the manufacturer, but rather the re-seller of the equipment to the end user. More fitting terms include "original equipment customizer," "original equipment designer," or "original equipment concept designer." The OEM is usually the customizer or designer of the product and usually handles marketing, sales, and distribution. The OEM usually offers its own warranty, support, and licensing of the product.

In many cases, the OEM merely brands the equipment with its own logo. The OEM's name is either placed on the devices by the manufacturer that makes the equipment or by the OEM itself. In some cases, the OEM does add value. For example, an OEM might purchase a computer from a company, combine it with its own hardware or software, and then sell it as a turnkey system (see *Value Added Reseller*).

Some firms specialize in OEM manufacturing but never sell anything under their own brands (see *contract manufacturer*). Many manufacturing companies have separate OEM divisions for goods that are private labeled.

The entry *contract manufacturer* discusses Electronics Manufacturing Services (EMS) and Contract Electronics Manufacturing Services (CEMS), which are special types of OEMs.

See *contract manufacturer, private label, turnkey, Value Added Reseller (VAR).*

OSHA – See *Occupational Safety and Health Administration (OSHA)*.

outbound logistics – See *logistics*.

outlier – A statistical term used to describe an observed value that is out of the ordinary and therefore should not be included in the sample statistics.

Outliers can have a significant impact on the sample mean and variance. They can be attributed to either special causes (such as measurement error) or a heavy-tailed distribution. When outliers can be attributed to special causes, they should be removed from the sample. For example, this author set up a forecasting system for a firm that had a once-per-year shipment to Belgium. Removing this large planned shipment from the data made it easier to forecast the demand. A reasonable rule of thumb is to exclude observations that are above (below) the mean plus (minus) three standard deviations. However, it is foolish to exclude outliers from a sample unless the analyst has good theory behind doing so. In many cases, outliers provide important information about the distribution and the variable in question.

One approach for dealing with outliers is to use robust (error-resistant) statistics, such as the median. Unlike the mean, the median is not affected by a few outliers in the data. Other robust statistics include trimmed and Winsorized estimators and the interquartile range.

See *control chart, interquartile range, linear regression, Mean Absolute Deviation (MAD), run chart, special cause variation, trim, trimmed mean, Winsorizing*.

outsourcing – Buying products and services from an independent supplier. ✪

Many popular articles imply that "outsourcing" is buying products or services from Asia or from some other part of the world. However, the correct definition of outsourcing is buying product or services from any outside firm. Sourcing products and services from a wholly owned subsidiary on another continent should be called "**offshoring**" rather than outsourcing; buying products or services from another firm on another continent should be called "**offshore outsourcing**."

A good example of outsourcing is Boston Scientific's clean room gowns. Boston Scientific's core competence is designing, manufacturing, marketing, and selling implantable medical devices – not managing gowns. However, its gown supplier has a clear focus on clean room gowns and is "world class" at that business. Therefore, Boston Scientific outsources its gown management. An example of outsourcing services is Best Buy, which outsourced many of its IT and human resources functions to other firms.

Nearly all consultants and management professors argue that firms should not outsource their **core competence**. However, this statement is not always helpful, because many managers have trouble identifying their organization's core competence and find that their core competence changes over time.

Some penetrating questions that managers should ask with respect to outsourcing include:

- **If this process is a core competency, why are we making it only for ourselves?** If a firm has a truly world-class process, then why not leverage that expertise (and overhead)? The answer to this question is often, "Well, the process is really not that good," which suggests that the process is not a true core competence after all.
- **If the process is not a core competency, why not buy it from someone who has this core competency?** If a process is clearly not a core competence and never will be, then management should ask why not outsource it from another organization that has a core competency in this area?
- **Are we ready to become dependent on others for this process?** When outsourcing manufacturing, management is, in effect, deciding that the process is not a core competency and is creating dependency on other firms. When a firm outsources, it will no longer have those 20-year veterans who know everything there is to know about esoteric materials, equipment, and testing. The firm gives up the equipment, tools, and expertise. Over time, the firm may even erode its ability to talk intelligently to its suppliers and customers. This is not a significant problem as long as the process is clearly not a core competency and the firm has good suppliers who have this core competency.
- **Do we understand the switching costs?** Switching is often difficult and costly and involves many systems, such as machines, tooling, people, expertise, information systems, coordination, transportation, production planning, and costing. Moreover, switching back may be just as costly if management changes its mind.

Many firms find that they can improve both cost and quality if they can find an outside supplier that has a core competence in a particular area. For example, historically many firms have outsourced the manufacturing of components. More recently, we have seen firms outsourcing final assembly, new product development, and many services, such as IT and human resources.

Given that outsourcing often increases inventories, outsourcing can go against lean principles. For example, if a firm outsources a component to China and dramatically increases leadtimes, inventory and the associated carrying cost will also increase dramatically. Some experts consider Dell to be an example of successful lean outsourcing, because it outsources nearly all its component manufacturing and yet carries nearly zero component inventory[39]. If managed properly, outsourcing, in combination with smart supplier agreements and Vendor Managed Inventories, can sometimes result in a significant decrease in inventories and provide excellent synergies with lean manufacturing.

Many firms fail to understand that many overhead costs do not go away (at least, not in the short term) with an outsourcing decision. Some of the "surprise" overhead costs that come with an outsourcing decision include:

- Overhead costs allocated to production in the high-wage location, which must be re-allocated to remaining products. In other words, some of the fixed costs do not go away in outsourcing, and the internal burden rates go up and the volume goes down. (See the *make versus buy decision* entry.)
- Carrying cost of the additional inventory of goods in transit (the square root law).
- Cost of additional safety stocks to ensure uninterrupted supply.
- Cost of expedited shipments.
- Cost of scrap-related quality issues.
- Cost of warranty claims if the new facility or supplier has a long learning curve.
- Cost of engineer visits to set up the operation or straighten out problems.
- Cost of stockouts and lost sales caused by long leadtimes.
- Cost of obsolete parts.

Outsourcing decisions sometimes also fail to properly account for currency risks, country risks, connectivity risks, and competitive risks when a supplier becomes a competitor.

Contracts are not always enforceable across international borders, particularly in countries that do not have well-developed legal systems. Therefore, the manufacturer will assume some risk with both the intellectual property (product designs and process designs) and during the order-to-cash cycle for any order. However, all business relationships involve risk, so it comes down to developing trust between the business partners. If the supplier wants to keep the manufacturer as a customer, it needs to prove itself trustworthy. Firms, on the other hand, need to weigh this risk against the risk of global competitors coming to the market with a significantly cheaper and better product.

The World Is Flat (Friedman 2005) identified ten forces that flattened the world and made offshore outsourcing much easier: (1) the fall of the Berlin Wall (11/9/89), (2) Netscape (8/9/95), (3) workflow software, (4) open-sourcing (blogs, wikis) allowing people to upload and collaborate, (5) outsourcing, (6) offshoring, (7) supply-chaining, (8) insourcing (B2B services)[40], (9) in-forming, and (10) wirelessness.

See *absorptive capacity, Activity Based Costing (ABC), burden rate, business process outsourcing, carrying cost, contract manufacturer, co-packer, core competence, delegation, groupware, human resources, intellectual property (IP), labor intensive, landed cost, make versus buy decision, maquiladora, nearshoring, offshoring, operations strategy, overhead, purchasing, Service Level Agreement (SLA), sourcing, subcontracting, supply chain management, switching cost, vendor managed inventory (VMI), vertical integration.*

Over/Short/Damaged Report – A transportation management report that highlights any items that were received but unexpected (i.e., more than what was ordered), expected but not received (i.e., short of what was ordered), or received in damaged condition; also called the OS&D report.

An Over/Short/Damaged report is commonly run for a single inbound trailer or for a day's worth of inbound trailers to gauge the quality of the shipments. Ideally, an OS&D report should be completely empty with no unexpected, missing, or damaged items.

The OS&D report is typically created by the Transportation Management System or Warehouse Management System. The OS&D report is created by comparing the list of items the firm expected to receive (typically from

---

[39] *Some experts argue that Dell is not lean because their suppliers carry much of their inventory.*

[40] *Friedman uses the term "insourcing" here very differently than the way most supply chain managers use the term.*

the Advanced Shipping Notification) with the actual receipts as recorded by the warehouse personnel who handled the receiving. Often this OS&D report is created by comparing the barcode scans of the wireless devices used during receiving with the ASN file that defines what should have been in the trailer.

The OS&D report is important to managers for several reasons:

- **Overage items will probably need manual intervention** – Normally, in a cross-dock or warehousing scenario, each incoming item has an ultimate destination (typically another warehouse or some end shipping point). This destination is indicated in the ASN file. If an unexpected item is received in a high-volume cross-dock or warehousing environment, manual intervention will be required to determine the appropriate ultimate destination of the item.
- **Missing items will need manual intervention** – In normal circumstances, each item has an ultimate destination. If items are missing, warehouse managers may need to alert downstream warehouses or customers of missing goods.
- **Proper recording of damages limits liability** – In many logistics scenarios, the company takes ownership of the items only after they have been received in good condition. Any damage to items after receipt will be the responsibility of the recipient. Therefore, if damaged items are received, it is important that the damage be noted immediately. Good wireless Transportation Management Systems (TMS) and Warehouse Management Systems (WMS) make it easy for warehouse personnel to record damaged goods upon receipt.

From a high-level management perspective, the OS&D report can be used to evaluate the overall effectiveness of the relationship between the originator of the shipment and the recipient of the shipment.

See *Advanced Shipping Notification (ASN), cross-docking, Electronic Data Interchange (EDI), logistics, receiving, shortage report, Transportation Management System (TMS), Warehouse Management System (WMS).*

Overall Equipment Effectiveness (OEE) – A lean operations/TPM metric defined as the product of three variables – the availability rate, performance rate, and yield (or quality) rate.

Overall Equipment Effectiveness (OEE) is considered by many to be a key metric for lean operations management. OEE is used extensively in Total Productivity Management (TPM) applications, particularly in large firms, such as 3M, that have large capital intensive operations. OEE is the product of three variables: (Availability Rate) x (Performance Rate) x (Yield Rate). Each of these three variables is defined as follows:

- **Availability rate** = (Operating time less downtime)/(Total operating time). This measures downtime losses due to changeovers, equipment failures, and startup losses. Availability is not the same as utilization. Availability captures downtime losses from emergency maintenance, setups, and adjustments.
- **Performance rate** = (Total output)/(Potential output at rated speed). This measures speed losses due to idling and minor stoppages or reduced speed operation.
- **Yield (or quality) rate** = (Good output)/(Total output). This measures defects and rework. The yield rate for OEE is sometimes called the quality rate or first-pass yield rate.

If OEE is applied to a non-bottleneck machine, care must be taken to avoid maximizing utilization and building inventory long before it is needed. It does not make sense to maximize one asset (a machine) to create another asset (inventory) that sits idle for a long time. When properly implemented, OEE will maximize availability (which is not the same as utilization).

See *capacity, downtime, effectiveness, efficiency, lean thinking, operations performance metrics, process capability and performance, productivity, rework, Total Productive Maintenance (TPM), utilization, value added ratio, yield.*

overhead – Business costs that cannot be meaningfully and easily assigned to individual products or services; sometimes called indirect cost or burden. ✪

Overhead costs include all costs to conduct business except for direct labor and direct materials. These costs include indirect labor, indirect materials, selling expenses, general and administrative expenses, depreciation, setup costs, quality costs, cleanup costs, fringe benefits, payrolls taxes, and insurance. Examples of overhead costs include the building and machine depreciation, building utilities (power, water, sewer), MRO supplies (e.g., sandpaper), office supplies (pens and paper), and supervisory labor. Manufacturing overhead is often allocated to products based on direct labor hours.

See *absorption costing, Activity Based Costing (ABC), burden rate, carrying cost, commonality, cost of goods sold, direct cost, direct labor cost, job order costing, lean thinking, Maintenance-Repair-Operations*

(MRO), make versus buy decision, opportunity cost, outsourcing, period cost, setup cost, standard cost, Theory of Constraints (TOC), throughput accounting, variable costing, work measurement, Work-in-Process (WIP) inventory.

overhead rate – See *burden rate.*

overlapping – See *transfer batch.*

overproduction – Producing more than what is needed at the time.

   See *8 wastes, batch-and-queue.*

P

pacemaker – (1) In a manufacturing context: The lean manufacturing concept of using a single workcenter to set the pace (speed) for the entire process; also called a pacing process. (2) In a medical context: A medical device used to set the pace of a patient's heart.

   In the lean manufacturing context, the pacemaker should be used to level-load the system over time and to set the pace for the other processes in the system. Ideally, the pace for the pacing process should be determined by the takt time, which is the cycle time determined by the market demand rate. Processes before the pacemaker (upstream) should produce only when they receive a pull signal from the next downstream process or directly from the pacemaker. This helps prevent overproduction and keeps the pacemaker from being starved. Processes after the pacemaker (downstream) should not block the pacemaker, should push materials in small order quantities (possibly using transfer batches), and should not be allowed to have inventories except in supermarkets or finished goods inventory. The pacemaker is normally the assembly process in a make to stock system. In make to order systems, the pacemaker is typically the process step where the product becomes unique.

   Using a pacemaker simplifies scheduling, maintains a level output, focuses on the bottleneck, and prevents overproduction. The pacemaker concept is similar to the Drum-Buffer-Rope concept (Theory of Constraints) and to the CONWIP concept.

   See *CONWIP, Drum-Buffer-Rope (DBR), gateway workcenter, lean thinking, supermarket, takt time, Theory of Constraints (TOC), transfer batch, upstream.*

pacing process – See *pacemaker.*

Pack to order – A customer interface strategy that collects components and packs them into a box or some other shipping container in response to a customer order.

   Pack to order is similar to assemble to order, because it is "assembling" the shipment, which includes one or more products, packaging, and shipping information, in response to a customer order. Boston Scientific's "pack to demand" process fills orders from inventory by attaching a country- and language-specific label to the box before shipping.

   See *make to order (MTO), mass customization, respond to order (RTO).*

packing slip – The paperwork that accompanies a shipment and describes its contents, including information such as order numbers, item numbers, and quantities.

   See *Advanced Shipping Notification (ASN), bill of lading, manifest.*

Paired-cell Overlapping Loops of Cards with Authorization – See *POLCA.*

pallet – A portable horizontal, rigid platform used as a base for storing, stacking, and transporting a load of goods.

   Pallets are designed to be picked up and moved by a forklift truck. Pallets vary with respect to size, design, strength, and materials. Most pallets are made from wood, but they can also be made from plastic or steel. A two-way pallet allows a forklift truck to enter from the front or the back, whereas a four-way pallet is designed so a forklift can enter the pallet from any side. The most common pallet in the U.S. is the Grocery Manufacturer's Association (GMA) grocery pallet, which is a 4-way pallet that is 40 inches (101.6 cm) wide, 48 inches (121.92) deep, and 5 inches (12.7 cm) high. A skid is a pallet that does not have bottom deck boards.

   See *forklift truck, logistics, warehouse.*

paradigm – A way of thinking; a frame of thought.

An old paradigm can inhibit creative thinking about a new problem. A new paradigm (also called a "paradigm shift") can be a powerful new way of thinking about an old problem. For example, in the Soviet factory management paradigm, bigger and heavier machines were usually better. This influenced reward systems and machine design in many negative ways. The quality management field has seen a paradigm shift from thinking that quality and cost are always trade-offs to understanding that improved conformance quality usually leads to lower cost.

See *bounded rationality, inductive reasoning.*

parent item – See *bill of material (BOM).*

Pareto analysis – See *Pareto Chart.*

Pareto Chart – A histogram (bar chart) that helps identify and prioritize the most common sources of errors or defects. ✪

The Pareto Chart, named for Vilfredo Pareto, was popularized as a quality management tool by Joseph M. Juran and Kaoru Ishikawa. The basic concept is based on Pareto's Law, which teaches that each system has an "important few and a trivial many" (often called the 80-20 principle). A Pareto Chart highlights the important few by displaying the frequencies for the causes of a problem, sorted from highest to lowest.

For example, an analysis of work stoppages on a production line is shown in the table on the right, presented here from highest to lowest frequency. These data were graphed to create the Pareto Chart below, which highlights the need to focus on the causes of human errors.

Cause of stoppage	Frequency	Relative frequency	Cumulative
Human error	12	41%	41%
Defective materials	8	28%	69%
Machine breakdown	4	14%	83%
Misplaced tooling	3	10%	93%
Other problems	2	7%	100%
Total	29	100%	

The line shows the cumulative frequency and shows the total percent of the causes up to and including that cause. Fixing the first two causes (human error and defective materials) will remove 69% of the stoppage problems, whereas fixing the last two will remove only 17%.

Pareto Charts can easily be generated in Microsoft Excel. When selecting the chart type, go to "custom types" and select "Line – Column on 2 Axes."

See *ABC classification, bar chart, causal map, checksheet, Failure Mode and Effects Analysis (FMEA), histogram, Pareto's Law, Root Cause Analysis (RCA), seven tools of quality.*

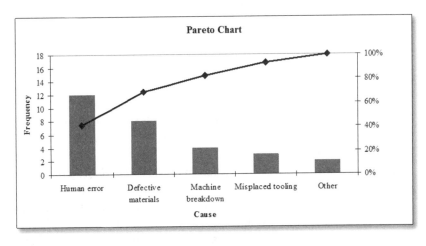

Pareto efficiency – See *Pareto optimality.*

Pareto optimality – An economics concept developed by the Italian economist Vilfredo Pareto that describes a situation where no one individual can be made better off without making other individuals worse off; also called Pareto efficiency.

Given an initial allocation of goods among a set of individuals, a **Pareto improvement** is a reallocation that makes at least one individual better off without making any others worse off. An allocation is **Pareto optimal (Pareto efficient)** when no other Pareto improvements can be made. Pareto efficiency does not necessarily result in a socially desirable distribution of resources and makes no statement about equality or the overall well-being of a society.

See *economics, Pareto's Law.*

Pareto's Law – The principle that most systems have a vital few and a trivial many; also called the 80-20 rule or principle. ✪

Pareto's Law teaches that most of the consequences in a system come from just a few of the causes. Some popular expressions of Pareto's Law include, "Don't sweat the small stuff," "Major on the majors," and "the vital few and the trivial many." Juran preferred to say "the vital few and the *useful* many" to emphasize that the less important causes should not be ignored. The implication of Pareto's Law is that people need to find and focus on the important few causes (issues, items, people, customers, problems) and not spend too much time on the many causes that do not matter as much. Pareto's Law is written as two numbers, where the first number represents the percentage of the consequences (e.g., cost, errors) and the second number is the percentage of objects (e.g., causes). Note that the two numbers do not need to add up to 100.

Examples of Pareto's Law include the ABC classification (manage the high dollar volume items), FMEA (manage the high risk failure modes), Theory of Constraints (manage the bottleneck), dispatching rules (start high-priority jobs first), critical path and critical chain analysis (manage the most important path and tasks in a project), supplier management (just a few suppliers account for most of the spend), customer sales distribution (few customers account for most of the sales), quality control (most of the defects can be attributed to just a few causes), human relations (most of the problems are caused by just a few people), sports (just a few players make most of the points), medicine (most people die from one of a few causes), and international relations (most of the problems in the world are caused by just a few rogue nations).

Alfredo Pareto was an Italian economist who lived in France in the early 1900s. In studying the distribution of wealth in Milan (Milano), he found that 20% of the people earned about 80% of the wealth. Although developed by the same man, Pareto's Law is unrelated to the economics concept of Pareto efficiency. A **Pareto Chart** is a useful way to show a frequency count and highlight the higher priority issues.

See *ABC classification, causal map, cycle counting, error proofing, Failure Mode and Effects Analysis (FMEA), Lorenz Curve, Pareto Chart, Pareto Optimality, Root Cause Analysis (RCA), Theory of Constraints (TOC).*

parking lot – A meeting facilitation tool used to store discussion items not immediately relevant to the agenda.

Meeting participants often raise issues that are not immediately relevant to the current topic. When this happens, the meeting leader and other participants should keep the focus on the current agenda by (1) suggesting adding the item to the parking lot, (2) quickly adding the idea to the parking lot list if others agree, and (3) immediately returning to the current agenda item. The parking lot list is often written on a whiteboard or flip chart. If Post-it Notes are being used to brainstorm ideas, the parking lot can be a set of Post-its on a side wall. Ideally, the facilitator and participants will show respect for the person, show respect for the idea, and capture potentially important ideas for future discussions. Just before the meeting adjourns, the facilitator should ensure that someone records the parking lot issues and that the items will be addressed appropriately. In many cases, parking lot items should be added to the agenda for the next meeting.

See *affinity diagram, brainstorming, causal map, Nominal Group Technique (NGT), personal operations management, two-second rule.*

Parkinson's Laws – Laws written by Professor C. Northcote Parkinson in the book *Parkinson's Law* (1958). ✪

A 20th century British author and professor of history, Cyril Northcote Parkinson (1909-1993) wrote some sixty books, including his famous satire of bureaucratic institutions. Parkinson's most famous law is often quoted as "Work expands to fill the time allotted to it"; however, Parkinson's actual wording was, "Work expands so as to fill the time available for its completion." Here are some other examples of Parkinson's laws:

- Expenditure rises to meet income.
- Expansion means complexity, and complexity decay.
- Policies designed to increase production increase employment; policies designed to increase employment do everything but.
- When something goes wrong, do not "try, try again." Instead, pull back, pause, and carefully work out what organizational shortcomings produced the failure. Then, correct those deficiencies. Only after that, return to the assault.
- Delay is the deadliest form of denial.
- The matters most debated in a deliberative body tend to be the minor ones where everybody understands the issues.
- Deliberative bodies become decreasingly effective after they pass five to eight members.

This author has written a few 21st century operations management corollaries to Parkinson's Laws:

- Inventory expands to fill the space allotted to it.
- The best way to improve on-time delivery is to reduce cycle time so that customers have taken delivery before they have time to change their minds.
- Lying begets[41] lying. If a firm lies to its customers about expected delivery dates, customers will lie to the firm about the actual need date.
- The later a project becomes, the more unlikely it is that the project manager will inform the customer of the project's lateness.
- The pi rule for project management: Poorly managed projects require approximately pi (3.1416) times more time than originally planned.

See *bullwhip effect, leadtime syndrome, Murphy's Law, project management*.

PARM (Perishable Asset Resource Management) – See *yield management*.

parsimony – Adoption of the simplest assumption in the formulation of a theory or in the interpretation of data, especially in accordance with the rule of Occam's Razor.

See *Occam's Razor*.

part number – A unique identification number (or alphanumeric string) that defines an item for inventory management purposes; also called Stock Keeping Unit (SKU), item number, material, product code, or material. ✪

Historically, APICS and other professional societies in North America have used the terms "item number" or "part number." However, SAP, the most widely used **Enterprise Resources Planning (ERP)** system, uses the term "material." Retailers often use the term "**Stock Keeping Unit (SKU).**" In some cases, a part number is used to identify the "generic" item, and the SKU is used for the inventory count for that part number at a specific location. A **serial number** is an identifier for a specific unit.

It is better to use **all numeric** part numbers (0-9) and not mix alpha (A-Z) and numeric characters. This is because many numbers and letters are easily confused in both reading and writing. For example, the number 1 and the letter l, the number 5 and the letter S, and the number 0 and the letter O are easy to confuse on a computer screen and in handwriting. In addition, many letters sound the same. For example, K and A, M and N, and Y and I sound alike. If letters are used, they should not be case-sensitive.

A **significant (meaningful) part number** uses characters, or groups of characters, coded to describe item attributes, such as the product family, commodity, location, or supplier. A **semi-significant part number** is an identifier that uses a portion of the number that is meaningful. Significant part numbers rarely work very well because product attributes change over time and part numbers require too many characters to be truly meaningful. It is good practice, therefore, to use short (seven digits or less) non-meaningful part numbers to reduce data entry time and errors and then use additional codes for item attributes. The use of **Automated Data Collection (ADC)** systems, such as barcoding and RFID, has made these issues less important.

Check digits are often added to the base part number to make it possible to conduct a quick validity check. See the *check digit* entry for more information.

In manufacturing, some items might exist for a short period of time in the assembly process. These items are sometimes called **phantom items**. However, if these items are not inventoried, they should usually not be given part number identifiers.

See *active item, Automated Data Collection (ADC), barcode, bill of material (BOM), check digit, Electronic Product Code (EPC), locator system, phantom bill of material, product family, Radio Frequency Identification (RFID), raw materials, traceability, unit of measure, Universal Product Code (UPC), warehouse*.

part period balancing – See lotsizing.

partial expectation – The partial first moment of a random variable; also called partial moment.

The partial expectation for a probability distribution is an important property used in inventory theory and risk management. The complete expectation (first moment) for continuous random variable X is the expected

---

[41] *The word "begets" is an old English word that means to bring about, create, or father.*

value $\mu_X = \int\limits_{x=-\infty}^{\infty} xf(x)dx$. The partial expectation evaluated at x_0 is $H(x_0) = \int\limits_{x=-\infty}^{x_0} xf(x)dx = \mu_X - \int\limits_{x=x_0}^{\infty} xf(x)dx$.

Blumenfeld (2010) and others defined the partial expectation as the weighted tail of the distribution $H'(x_0) = \int\limits_{x=x_0}^{\infty} xf(x)dx = \mu_X - H(x_0)$. The partial expectation is related to the conditional expectation with

$$H(x_0) = E(X \mid X < x_0)P(X < x_0) \text{ or } H(x_0) = \mu - E(X \mid X > x_0)(1 - F(x_0)).$$

The partial expectation functions for several distributions are presented in the table on the right. These equations were derived by the author from the tail conditional expectation functions in Landsman and Valdez (2005). Winkler, Roodman, and Britney (1972) presented closed-form expressions for the partial expectations for several distributions.

See *gamma distribution, mean, probability density function, safety stock.*

partial moment – See *partial expectation.*

Partial expectations for continuous distributions:

Normal	$H(x) = \mu F_u(z) - \sigma f_u(z)$, where $z = (x-\mu)/\sigma$
Lognormal	$H(x) = e^{\mu+\sigma^2/2}(1 - F_u((\mu+\sigma^2 - \ln(x))/\sigma))$
Exponential	$H(x) = \mu - (x+\mu)e^{-x/\mu}$
Gamma	$H(x) = \mu F_{Gamma}(x \mid \alpha+1, \beta)$

Partial expectations for discrete distributions:

Poisson	$H(x) = \mu F_{Poisson}(x-1)$
Binomial	$H(x) = \mu F_{Binomial}(x-1 \mid p, n-1)$
Negative binomial	$H(x) = \mu F_{NB}(x-1 \mid p, \alpha+1)$

Note: f_u and F_u are the pdf and CDF for the standard normal distribution.

Parts per Million (PPM) – See *Defective Parts per Million (DPPM).*

pay for performance – See *gainsharing.*

pay for skill – A compensation policy that rewards employees for developing new capabilities; also called skill-based pay, pay for knowledge, and pay for learning.

The organization provides training on a set of skills and increases the hourly pay rate for workers who can demonstrate that they have acquired new skills. For example, an employee who learns to use a laser welder might be paid an extra $0.25 per hour.

Some of the benefits of a pay for skill program include (1) allowing employers to cover for an absent worker, (2) reducing inventory and cycle time when workers can move to where the work is, (3) reducing boredom and increasing employee engagement, and (4) giving workers a broader perspective of the process, which gives them insights that can be used to improve the process.

On the negative side, pay for skill will not achieve greater performance for the employee if the skill is not needed or not used. **Job rotation** can also achieve many of the same benefits. A one-time bonus might make more sense in some cases. A similar approach is to create a labor grade (pay grade) system in which employees get promoted to new pay grades after mastering new skills.

See *gainsharing, human resources, job design, job enlargement, job rotation, labor grade, piece work.*

payback period – The time required to break even on an investment.

Payback ignores the time value of money and is regarded to be a crude and imprecise analysis. Much better methods include Net Present Value (NPV) and Economic Value Added (EVA). However, payback is still a commonly used approach for "quick and dirty" investment analysis.

See *break-even analysis, financial performance metrics.*

p-chart – A quality control chart used to monitor the proportion of units produced in a process that are defective; a unit is considered defective if any attribute of the unit does not conform to the standard.

To set up a p-chart, estimate $\overline{p}$, the long-term percent defective, from a large sample while the process is under control. Then set the **upper and lower control limits** at $UCL = \overline{p} + 3\sqrt{\overline{p}(1-\overline{p})/n}$ and $LCL = \max(\overline{p} - 3\sqrt{\overline{p}(1-\overline{p})/n}, 0)$.

To use a p-chart, sample *n* units from the process every so many lots, units, or time periods. The sample proportion is $p = x/n$, where *x* is the number of defective units found in the sample. Plot the sample proportion on the p-chart and determine if the process is "**under control**."

The p-chart is based on the **binomial distribution**, which is the sum of *n* independent **Bernoulli** distributed binary (0-1) random variables with mean $\overline{p}$ and standard deviation of the estimate $\sqrt{\overline{p}(1-\overline{p})/n}$. The normal distribution is a reasonable estimate of the binomial when $n\overline{p} \geq 10$ and $n\overline{p}(1-\overline{p}) \geq 10$.

Whereas the p-chart plots the proportion defective for any sample size, the np-chart plots the number of defective units for a fixed sample size.

See *attribute, Bernoulli distribution, binomial distribution, control chart, np-chart, Statistical Process Control (SPC), Statistical Quality Control (SQC)*.

PDCA (Plan-Do-Check-Act) – A well-known four-step approach for process improvement; also called PDSA (Plan-Do-Study-Act), the Deming Cycle, and the Shewhart Cycle. ✪

The PDCA cycle is made up of four steps:

- **PLAN** – Recognize an opportunity and plan the change. Plan to improve operations first by finding out what things are going wrong and then generate ideas for solving these problems. Decide what actions might reduce process variation.
- **DO** – Test the change. Make changes designed to solve the problems on a small or experimental scale first. This minimizes disruptions while testing whether the changes will work.
- **CHECK** – Review the test, analyze the results, and identify learning. Use data to determine if the change was effective in reducing variation. Check whether the small-scale or experimental changes are achieving the desired result or not. Also, continuously check nominated key activities (regardless of any experimentation going on) to provide information on the quality of the output at all times and to identify new problems that might appear.

- **ACT** – Take action based on what you learned in the check step. If the change was successful, implement the change and identify opportunities to transfer the learning to other opportunities for improvement. Implementation will likely require involvement of other persons and organizations (departments, suppliers, or customers) affected by the change. If the change was not successful, document that plan and go through the cycle again with a different plan.

Upon completion of a PDCA cycle, the cycle is repeated to test another idea. The repeated application of the PDCA cycle to a process is known as continuous quality improvement.

The PDCA cycle was developed by Shewhart (1939). Shewhart said the cycle draws its structure from the notion that constant evaluation of management practices, as well as the willingness of management to adopt and disregard unsupported ideas, is the key to the evolution of a successful enterprise. W. Edwards Deming first coined the term "Shewhart cycle" for PDCA, naming it after his mentor and teacher at Bell Laboratories in New York. Deming promoted PDCA as a primary means of achieving continued process improvement. He also referred to the PDCA cycle as the PDSA cycle ("S" for study) to emphasize the importance of learning in improvement. Deming is credited with encouraging the Japanese to adopt PDCA in the 1950s.

The Japanese eagerly embraced PDCA and other quality concepts, and to honor Deming for his instruction, they refer to the PDCA cycle as the Deming cycle. Many lean thinking programs use PDCA concepts.

Most quality improvement projects today use a similar five-step approach called DMAIC, which comes from the lean sigma movement. Most people (including this author) find DMAIC more intuitive and easier to follow than the PDCA or PDSA approaches.

See *DMAIC, hoshin planning, lean sigma, quality management, Total Quality Management (TQM)*.

PDF – See *probability density function*.

PDM – See *product data management*.

PDSA (Plan-Do-Study-Act) – See *PDCA*.

pegging – The process of identifying the sources of the gross requirements for an item in the MRP materials plan.

Single-level pegging for a gross requirement goes up one level in the bill of material (BOM). Full-level pegging goes all the way up to the top level. Pegging is an important tool for helping production planners identify the impact that a late order might have on higher-level orders and customers. Pegging is like a where-used report, but is only used for those parent items that determine the gross requirements for the item.

See *bill of material (BOM)*, *bill of material implosion*, *Materials Requirements Planning (MRP)*, *where-used report*.

percentage bill of material – See *bill of material (BOM)*.

perfect order fill rate – See *fill rate*.

performance management system – A set of policies and procedures with a supporting information system used to help create and maintain alignment between the organizational and employee goals.

A good performance management system is built on four main activities:
- **Planning** – The manager and direct reports collaboratively establish goals, objectives, outcomes, and training requirements for the direct report.
- **Coaching** – The manager trains, observes, and provides feedback to direct reports to improve performance.
- **Appraisal** – The manager provides performance feedback to direct reports and documents performance for both the pay and promotion decision processes.
- **Rewards** – The organization provides rewards in the form of recognition, pay raises, bonuses, and promotions.

Although performance measurement focuses only on evaluating performance, performance management takes a broader view, with more emphasis on intentional performance development. A good performance management system will align and coordinate individual behavior with the organization's strategic objectives.

Culbert (2010) made 12 arguments against performance reviews:[42]
- Focus on finding faults and placing blame.
- Focus on deviations from some ideal as weaknesses.
- Focus on comparing employees.
- Create competition between boss and subordinate.
- Create one-sided-accountability and too many boss-dominated monologues.
- Create "thunderbolts from on high," with the boss speaking for the company.
- Cause the subordinate to suffer if they make a mistake.
- Create an environment that allow the big boss to go on autopilot.
- Focuse on scheduled events.
- Give human resource people too much power.
- Do not lead to anything of substance.
- Are hated, and managers and subordinates avoid doing them until they have to.

Culbert (2010) went on to propose a collaborative constant dialog between the manager and employee built on trust and respect and where they are both responsible for success. Part of this dialog includes a "Performance Preview" that Culbert claimed holds people accountable, gives both managers and employees helpful feedback, and gives the company more of what it needs. He proposed three questions: (1) What are you getting from me that you like and find helpful? (2) What are you getting from me/the company that gets in your way and that you would like to have stopped? (3) What are you not getting from me/the company that you think would make you more effective? Tell me how that would help you specifically to do your job better?

Coens and Jenkins (2002) make similar arguments against performance reviews and suggest that managers should (1) provide honest feedback to employees by maintaining daily, two-way communication; (2) empower employees to be responsible for their careers, for receiving feedback, and for holding themselves accountable for the work to be done; (3) have the freedom to choose for themselves the most effective ways of working with people; (4) move away from an individual performance company to an organizational improvement company; and (5) create a culture to support the above.

See *financial performance metrics*, *Management by Objectives (MBO)*, *operations performance metrics*, *work measurement*.

---

[42] *These are reworded slightly here.*

performance quality – See *product design quality*.

performance rating – A subjective estimate of a worker's pace of work.

A 120% performance rating means that the observer estimated that the worker was working 20% faster than a normal worker. The performance rating is used to adjust the observed time to compute the normal time.

See *normal time, standard time, time study, work measurement*.

performance-based contracting – A legal relationship that allows organizations (usually governmental organizations) to acquire services via contracts that define what is to be achieved rather than how it is to be done.

In many situations, performance-based contracting provides good value products and services. In addition, performance-based contracting gives firms the freedom to bring new approaches to their customers.

See *service guarantee, Service Level Agreement (SLA)*.

period cost – Expenses based on the calendar rather than the number of units produced; also called period expense.

Period costs include selling and administrative costs, depreciation, interest, rent, property taxes, insurance, and other fixed expenses based on time. Period costs are expensed on the income statement in the period in which they are incurred and not included in the cost of goods sold.

See *overhead*.

Period Order Quantity (POQ) – A simple lotsizing rule that defines the order quantity in terms of periods supply[43]; also known as the Periodic Order Quantity, days supply, weeks supply, and months supply.

The POQ is implemented in MRP systems by setting the lotsize to the sum of the next POQ periods of net requirements after the first positive net requirement. The optimal POQ is the Economic Order Quantity (EOQ) divided by the average demand per period. The POQ is $\sqrt{2S/(icD/365)}$ days, where D is the expected annual demand, S is the ordering (or setup) cost, i is the carrying charge, and c is the unit cost.

See *Economic Order Quantity (EOQ), lotsizing methods, periods supply, time-varying demand lotsizing problem*.

periodic review system – An order-timing rule used for planning inventories; also known as a fixed-time period model, periodic system, fixed-order interval system, and *P*-model. ✪

A periodic review system evaluates the **inventory position** every P time periods and considers placing an order. Unlike a **reorder point system** that triggers an order when the inventory position falls below the reorder point, a periodic review system only considers placing orders at the end of a predetermined time period, the review period (P). The graph below shows the periodic review system through two review periods.

The periodic review system makes good economic sense when the firm has economies of scale in transportation cost. In other words, the periodic review system should be used when the firm can save money by shipping or receiving many different items at the same time. The optimal review period is the perod order quantity (POQ), which is EOQ/μ_D, where EOQ is the economic order quantity and μ_D is the average demand per period. However, in most situations, the review period is determined by other factors, such as the transportation schedule.

The periodic review system can be implemented with either a fixed order quantity, such as the EOQ, or with an order-up-to lotsizing rule. The order-up-to rule is also known as a **base stock system**. This rule orders a quantity that brings the inventory position up to a **target** inventory at the end of each review period. The target inventory level is also called the base stock level. The optimal target inventory is $T = SS + \mu_D(L+P)$, where μ_D is the average demand per period, L is the replenishment leadtime, and P is the review period. The **safety stock** is $SS = z\sigma_D\sqrt{L+P}$ units, where σ_D is the standard deviation of demand per period and z is the **safety factor**. The average lotsize is $\overline{Q} = \mu_D P$, and the average inventory is $SS + \overline{Q}/2$. Compared to the reorder point system, the periodic system requires more safety stock inventory, because it must protect against stockouts during the review period plus the replenishment leadtime ($L + P$) rather than just during the replenishment leadtime (L).

---

[43] *It is not clear if this term should be plural (periods), plural possessive (periods' supply), or singular possessive (period's supply). The plural is used here based on the assumption that this expression is short for periods of supply.*

Periodic review system graph

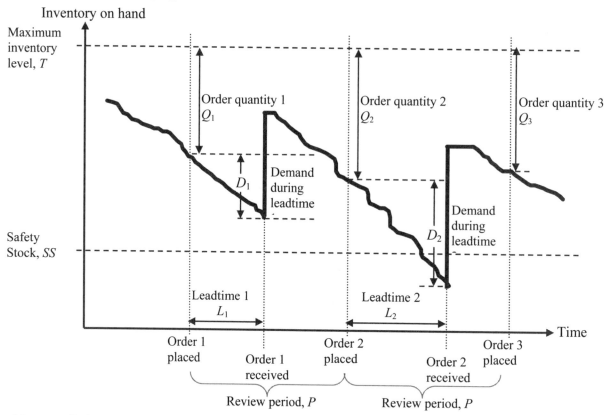

Most retail chains use a periodic review system to replenish their stores. Each store has a target inventory level (base stock level) for each stock keeping unit (SKU). Every week the stores order enough to bring their inventory positions up to the base stock level, and trucks move the orders from regional warehouses to the stores.

See *continuous review system, inventory management, min-max inventory system, order-up-to level, perpetual inventory system, reorder point, safety stock, slow moving inventory, supermarket, warehouse.*

periods supply – The "time quantity" for an inventory; also known as days on hand (DOH), days supply, days of inventory, days in inventory (DII), inventory days, inventory period, coverage period, weeks supply, and months supply. ✪

The periods supply[44] is the expected time remaining before the current inventory goes to zero, assuming that the current average demand rate does not change. The periods supply metric is often preferable to the **inventory turnover metric**, because it is easier to understand and can easily be related to procurement and manufacturing leadtimes.

Periods supply is estimated by taking the current inventory and dividing by some estimate of the current (or future) average demand. The current average demand might be a simple moving average, an exponentially smoothed average, or an exponentially smoothed average with trend. For example, a professor has 100 pounds of candy in his office and is consuming 20 pounds per day. Therefore, the professor has five-days supply.

The periods supply metric and the inventory turnover metric measure essentially the same inventory performance. However, periods supply is based on the current average or forecasted demand, and inventory turnover is based on historical actual demand or cost of goods sold over a specified time period. If demand is relatively stable, one can easily be estimated from the other. The relationships between inventory turnover (T) and days on hand are $T = 365/DOH$ and $DOH = 365/T$. Inventory Dollar Days (IDD) is the unit cost times DOH.

---

[44] *It is not clear if this term should be plural (periods), plural possessive (periods' supply), or singular possessive (period's supply). The plural is used here based on the assumption that this expression is short for periods of supply.*

The days supply for work-in-process (WIP) inventory can also be used as an estimate of the cycle time. For example, a firm with 10-days supply of WIP inventory has a cycle time of about 10 days. This concept is based on Little's Law (Little 1961), which states that the average inventory is the demand rate times the cycle time. Written in queuing theory terms, this is $L = \lambda W$, where L is the number in system (the work-in-process), λ is the mean arrival rate (the demand rate), and W is the time in system (the cycle time). Note that when days supply is calculated from financial measures, this estimate of the average cycle time is a dollar-weighted average.

See *cycle time, Inventory Dollar Days (IDD), inventory management, inventory turnover, Little's Law, lot-for-lot, lotsize, Period Order Quantity (POQ), weighted average.*

Perishable Asset Resource Management (PARM) – See *yield management.*

permutations – See *combinations.*

perpetual inventory system – An inventory control system that keeps accurate inventory records at all times.

In a perpetual inventory system, records and balances are updated with every receipt, withdrawal, and inventory balance correction. These systems often provide real-time visibility of inventory position (inventory on-hand and inventory on-order). In contrast, an inventory system could update inventory records periodically. However, with modern computers it makes little sense to use a periodic updating system.

See *on-hand inventory, on-order inventory, periodic review system, real-time.*

personal operations management – A philosophy and set of practices for applying operations management principles to help individuals (particularly knowledge workers) become more productive.

The term "personal operations management" was coined in by the author (Hill, 2011a). The book adapts and applies lean principles to personal time and life management.

See *6Ps, delegation, Getting Things Done (GTD), knowledge worker, parking lot, SMART goals, time burglar, two-minute rule, two-second rule, tyranny of the urgent.*

PERT – See *Project Evaluation and Review Technique.*

phantom – See *phantom bill of material.*

phantom bill of material – A bill of material coding and structuring technique used primarily for transient (non-stocked) subassemblies; phantom items are called blow-through (or blowthrough) or transient items.

A phantom bill of material represents an item that is physically built but rarely stocked before being used in the next level in the bill of material. **Materials Requirements Planning (MRP)** systems do not create planned orders for phantom items and are said to "blow through" phantom items.

See *bill of material (BOM), Materials Requirements Planning (MRP), part number.*

phase review – A step in the new product development process where approval is required to proceed to the next step; also called stage-gate review and tollgate review.

See the *stage-gate process* entry for more detail.

See *DMAIC, New Product Development (NPD), stage-gate process.*

phase-in/phase-out planning – A planning process that seeks to coordinate the introduction of a new product with the discontinuation of an existing product.

New products typically offer updated features and benefits that make the current product obsolete. The phase-in of the new product and the phase-out of the current product is complicated by many factors, such as forecasting the demand for both products, planning the consumption and disposal of the inventory of the current product, filling the distribution channel with the new product, giving proper incentives to the sales force for both the current and new products, coordinating end-of-life policies for all related products and consumables, carefully designing a pricing strategy that maximizes contribution to profit, and last, but not least, creating an effective market communication program. With respect to market communications, some firms have found themselves in trouble when information about a new product becomes public and the market demand for the current product to decline rapidly.

For example, the demand for the Apple iPad 2 will decline rapidly once the Apple iPad 3 is announced. Hill and Sawaya (2004) discuss phase-in/phase-out planning in the context of the medical device industry.

See *product life cycle management.*

physical inventory – The process of auditing inventory balances by counting all physical inventory on-hand.

A physical inventory is usually done annually or quarterly and usually requires that all manufacturing operations be stopped. **Cycle counting** is better than the physical inventory count, because it (1) counts important items more often, (2) fixes the record-keeping process rather than just fixing the counts, and (3) maintains record accuracy during the year.

See *cycle counting*.

pick face – The storage area immediately accessible to the order picker.

See *picking, warehouse*.

pick list – A warehouse term for an instruction to retrieve items from storage; also called a picking list.

A pick list gives stock pickers the information they need to pick the right items, in the right quantities, from the right locations, in the right sequence (route). These items may be for a specific production order, sales order, or interplant order, or, alternatively, they may be for a group of orders. If the pick list is for a group of orders, the orders need to be consolidated (assembled) from the items that are picked.

See *backflushing, picking, warehouse*.

picking – The process of collecting items from storage locations to meet the requirements of an order. ✪

Warehouses usually have more outgoing shipments (customer orders) than incoming shipments (purchase orders). This is particularly true for warehouses that serve retailers, because these warehouses are often used to break out large orders from a few manufacturers into small orders sent to many retailers. The picking process, therefore, has a significant impact on overall supply chain efficiency. **Mispicks** (errors in picking) directly impact customers and customer satisfaction.

The ideal picking system will have low purchase and implementation cost, low operating cost, low cycle time per pick, and high accuracy. The efficiency of the picking system is highly dependent upon the warehouse system and policies for locating SKUs in the warehouse.

The type of picking process depends on many factors, such as product characteristics (weight, volume, dimensions, fragility, perishability), number of transactions, number of orders, picks per order, quantity per pick, picks per SKU, total number of SKUs, shipping requirements (piece pick, case pick, or full-pallet loads), and value-added services, such as private labeling, cutting, or packaging. A **pick to clear** rule selects item locations with the smallest quantities first to empty the bins more quickly. A **pick to light** system uses LED lights for each bin and uses these lights to guide the picker to the next bin to be picked.

Picking is closely connected to the **slotting policies**, which are the rules used to guide employees to a bin (or bins) when putting materials away. All **Warehouse Management Systems (WMS)** provide functionality for both slotting and picking rules.

Voice picking (voice recognition) uses speech recognition and speech synthesis technologies to allow workers to communicate with the WMS. Warehouse workers use wireless, wearable computers with headsets and microphones to receive instructions by voice and verbally confirm their actions back to the system. The wearable computer, or voice terminal, communicates with the WMS via a radio frequency local area network (LAN). **Directed RF picking** uses radio frequency technologies to transmit picking, put away, replenishment, and cycle count instructions to warehouse personnel using either handheld or truck-mounted devices.

See *batch picking, carousel, discrete order picking, first pick ratio, flow rack, forward pick area, pick face, pick list, private label, random storage location, reserve storage area, slotting, task interleaving, voice picking, warehouse, Warehouse Management System (WMS), wave picking, zone picking*.

picking list – See *pick list*.

piece work – Pay for performance based on the number of units produced rather than on the number of hours worked or a salary; also called piece rate.

See *gainsharing, pay for skill*.

pilot test – A method used to test new software or a production process before it is fully implemented; for information systems, a pilot test is also called a conference room pilot.

In the software context, the purpose of the pilot test may be to (1) evaluate for purchase, (2) evaluate for implementation, (3) evaluate if the database and settings in the software are ready for implementation, and (4) train users how to use the software. Ideally, the pilot test is conducted with actual data by actual decision makers in conditions as close as possible to actual operating conditions. The pilot uses realistic test data, but the system is not "live," which means that no data are changed and no decisions are made that affect actual operations. In a manufacturing context, a pilot run is done to test the capabilities of the system before ramping up production.

See *beta test, implementation, prototype*.

pipeline inventory – The number of units (or dollars) of inventory currently being moved from one location to another.

See *supply chain management, Work-in-Process (WIP) inventory*.

pitch – The time allowed to make one container of a product.

Pitch is used to check if actual production is keeping up with takt time requirements. Pitch is a multiple of takt time based on the container size. For example, if the container size is 60 units and the takt time is 10 seconds, pitch is 60 x 10 = 600 seconds (or 10 minutes) for each container. Pitch can also be expressed as a rate. For example, if pitch (as a time) is 10 minutes per container, pitch (as a rate) is 6 containers per hour.

See *cycle time, lean thinking, takt time*.

Plan-Do-Check-Act – See *PDCA*.

Plan-Do-Study-Act – See *PDCA*.

planned leadtime – See *cycle time, leadtime*.

planned obsolescence – A strategy of designing products to become obsolete or non-functional after a period of time; also known as built-in obsolescence.

Firms sometimes use planned obsolescence to motivate customers to buy replacement products. **Obsolescence of desirability** refers to a marketing strategy of trying to make the previous model appear to be obsolete from a psychological standpoint (e.g., automobile style and other fashion goods). **Obsolescence of function** refers to a strategy of making the product cease to be functional after some period of time or number of uses (e.g., products with built-in, non-replaceable batteries).

See *New Product Development (NPD), product life cycle management*.

planned order – An MRP term for a recommended purchase order or manufacturing order generated by the planning system.

MRP systems create planned orders to meet the net requirements for higher-level products, assemblies, and subassemblies. Planned orders are deleted and replaced by new planned orders every time MRP recalculates the materials plan. When planners convert a planned order to a firm planned order, it can no longer be changed by the MRP system. Capacity Requirements Planning (CRP) uses planned orders, firm planned orders, and open (released) orders to determine the requirements (load) on each workcenter for each day.

See *Capacity Requirements Planning (CRP), manufacturing order, Materials Requirements Planning (MRP), purchase order (PO), time fence*.

planning bill of material – See *bill of material (BOM)*.

planning horizon – The span of time that the master schedule extends into the future.

In a manufacturing context, the planning horizon for the master production schedule should extend beyond the cumulative (stacked) leadtime for all components.

See *cumulative leadtime, time fence*.

planning versus forecasting – See *forecasting demand*.

planogram – A diagram used to specify how products are to be displayed in a retail space; also called plano-gram, plan-o-gram, and POG.

A good planogram allows inexperienced employees to properly maintain the retail shelf stock and appearance. A good planogram system will help the retailer (1) control inventory investment, (2) maximize inventory turnover, (3) minimize labor cost, (4) satisfy customers, (5) maximize sales, (6) maximize profit, and (7) maximize return on investment for the space.

See *assortment, category captain, facility layout*.

plant stock – An SAP term for on-hand inventory in a particular plant location.

plant-within-a-plant – A relatively autonomous process ("a plant") located within a facility that allows for more focus and accountability; sometimes called a focused factory.

Each plant-within-a-plant (or focused factory) will likely have unique operations objectives (cost, quality, delivery, etc.) and unique workforce policies, production control methods, accounting systems, etc. This concept was promoted by Professor Wickham Skinner at Harvard Business School in a famous article on the focused factory (Skinner 1974). See the *focused factory* entry for more details.

See *facility layout, focused factory, operations strategy*.

platform strategy – A new product development strategy that plans new products around a small number of basic product designs (platforms) and allows for many final products with differing features, functions, and prices.

A platform strategy is commonly used in the automotive industry, where the platform is a chassis/drive-train combination upon which different models are built (e.g., Chevrolet, Buick, Cadillac). This concept is used in many other industries, such as personal computers (e.g., Dell), white goods (e.g., Whirlpool), and medical devices (e.g., Medtronic).

See *New Product Development (NPD), white goods*.

point of use – The lean manufacturing practice of storing materials, tools, and supplies in a manufacturing facility close to where they are needed in the manufacturing process.

Point of use reduces non-value-added walking and searching time.

See *5S, dock-to-stock, receiving, water spider*.

PMI – See *Project Management Institute (PMI)*.

PO – See *purchase order*.

Point-of-Sale (POS) – A data collection device located where products are sold; usually a scanning and cash register device in a retail store.

POS data collection provides a rich source of data that can be used to (1) provide real-time sales information for the entire supply chain, (2) help maintain accurate inventory records, (3) automatically trigger replenishment orders as required, (4) provide data for detailed sales analysis, and (5) provide in-store information to shoppers.

See *category captain, real-time, Universal Product Code (UPC)*.

Poisson distribution – A discrete probability distribution useful for modeling demand when the average demand is low; also used for modeling the number of arrivals to a system in a fixed time period.

Like the exponential distribution, the Poisson distribution only has one parameter. Unlike the exponential, the Poisson is a discrete distribution, which means that it is only defined for integer values. The mean of the Poisson distribution is λ (lambda), and the variance is equal to the mean. The probability mass function $p(x)$ is the probability of x and is only defined for integer values of x.

Parameter: The Poisson has only one parameter (λ), which is the mean.

Probability mass and distribution functions:

$$p(x,\lambda) = \begin{cases} \dfrac{e^{-\lambda}\lambda^x}{x!} & \text{if } x \in \{0,1,\ldots\} \\ 0 & \text{otherwise} \end{cases} \quad \text{and} \quad P(x,\lambda) = \sum_{i=0}^{\lfloor x \rfloor} p(x,\lambda) = \begin{cases} e^{-\lambda}\sum_{i=0}^{\lfloor x \rfloor}\dfrac{\lambda^i}{i!} & \text{if } x \geq 0 \\ 0 & \text{otherwise} \end{cases}$$

Partial expectation function: The partial expectation for the Poisson distribution is

$$H(x) = \sum_{j=0}^{x} jp(x,\lambda) = \lambda P(x-1,\lambda) \text{ for } x \geq 1 \text{ (Hadley \& Whitin 1963)}. \text{ This is a useful tool for inventory models.}$$

Statistics: Range non-negative integers {0, 1, … }, mean λ (note that λ need not be an integer), variance λ, mode $\lambda - 1$ and λ if λ is an integer and $\lfloor \lambda \rfloor$ otherwise, where the $\lfloor x \rfloor$ rounds down to the nearest integer. Median $\approx \lfloor \lambda + 1/3 - 0.02/\lambda \rfloor$. Coefficient of variation $c = 1/\sqrt{\lambda}$. Skewness $1/\sqrt{\lambda}$. Kurtosis $3 + 1/\sqrt{\lambda}$.

Graph: The graph below shows the Poisson probability mass function with mean $\lambda = 3$.

Excel: The Excel function for the Poisson probability mass function is POISSON(x, λ, FALSE). The Microsoft Excel function for the cumulative Poisson distribution is POISSON(x, λ, TRUE), which returns the probability that the random variable will be less than or equal to x given that the mean of the Poisson distribution is λ. Excel does not provide an inverse Poisson distribution function.

Excel simulation: In an Excel simulation, it is necessary to use Excel formulas or a VBA function to generate Poisson distributed random variates, because Excel does not have an inverse function for the Poisson distribution. Law and Kelton (2000) presented a simple and fast algorithm, which is implemented in the VBA code below. Law and Kelton (2000) also noted that the inverse transform method with a simple search procedure can also perform well. Given that the Poisson distribution is typically used only for distributions with a low mean (e.g., $\lambda < 9$), a simple search procedure is reasonably fast.

Poisson Probability Mass

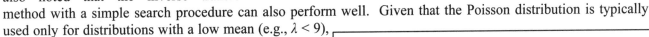

Relationships to other distributions: The Poisson and exponential distributions are unique in that they have only one parameter. If the number of arrivals in a given time interval [0,t] follows the Poisson distribution, with mean λt, the interarrival times follow the exponential distribution with mean $1/\lambda$. (See the *queuing theory* entry.) If $X_1, X_2, ..., X_m$ are independent Poisson distributed random variables with mean λ_i, then

```
Function poisson_random_number(lambda)
Dim L As Double, p As Double, k As Integer
    L = Exp(-lambda): k = 0: p = 1
    Do: k = k + 1: p = p * Rnd()
    Loop While (p > L)
    poisson_random_number = k - 1
End Function
```

$X_1 + X_2 + ... + X_m$ is Poisson distributed with mean $\lambda_1 + \lambda_2 + ... + \lambda_m$. The Poisson distribution is a good approximation of the binomial distribution when $n \geq 20$ and $p \leq 0.05$ and an excellent approximation when $n \geq 100$ and $np \leq 10$. For large values of λ (e.g., $\lambda > 1000$), the normal distribution with mean λ and variance λ is an excellent approximation to the Poisson. The normal distribution is a good approximation for the Poisson when $\lambda \geq 10$ if the continuity correction is used (i.e., replace $P(x)$ with $P(x + 0.5)$). Haley and Whitin (1963) presented several pages of equations related to the Poisson distribution that are useful for inventory models.

History: The French mathematician Siméon Denis Poisson (1781-1840) introduced this distribution.

See *bathtub curve, binomial distribution, c-chart, dollar unit sampling, exponential distribution, hypergeometric distribution, negative binomial distribution, newsvendor model, np-chart, probability distribution, probability mass function, queuing theory, slow moving inventory, u-chart.*

poka-yoke – See *error proofing.*

POLCA (Paired-cell Overlapping Loops of Cards with Authorization) – A hybrid push/pull production control system for low-volume manufacturing developed by Professor Rajan Suri at the University of Wisconsin.

Suri and Krishnamurthy (2003, p. 1) describe POLCA as follows: "It is a hybrid push-pull system that combines the best features of card-based pull (Kanban) systems and push (MRP) systems. At the same time, POLCA gets around the limitations of pull systems in high-variety or custom product environments, as well as the drawbacks of standard MRP, which often results in long lead times and high WIP."

See *CONWIP, Drum-Buffer-Rope (DBR), kanban.*

Pollaczek-Khintchine formula – A relatively simple queuing formula that relates the standard deviation of the service time to the mean number of customers in queue for a single server queuing system.

The formula itself can be found in the *queuing theory* entry.

See *queuing theory*.

POMS – See *Production Operations Management Society*.

pooling – A practice of combining servers to reduce customer waiting time or combining inventory stocking locations to reduce inventory.

Operations managers often have to decide if it is better to have separate channels (each with its own queue) or to combine them into one queue (waiting line). Similarly, operations managers often have to decide if it is better to hold inventory in separate stocking locations or to combine them into a single stocking location. This is called the pooling problem. An queuing example is used here to explore the benefits of pooling.

A firm has two technical experts, with one on the East Coast and one on the West Coast. Customers on the West Coast are only allowed to call the West Coast expert; and the same is true for the East Coast. The average interarrival time[45] for customers calling the technical experts is $a = 0.4$ hours on both coasts. The average service time for the two identical experts is $p = 0.3$ hours. The utilization for each expert is $\rho = p / a = 0.3/0.4 = 75\%$. (Be careful to not confuse ρ and p.) The coefficient of variation for the interarrival time is 1, and the coefficient of variation for the service time is also 1 (e.g., $c_a = 1$ and $c_s = 1$). Each expert is analyzed separately, which means that the number of servers is $s = 1$. Using the approximate G/G/s model (see the *queuing theory* entry), the average queue time is:

$$W_q = \left(\frac{p}{s}\right)\left(\frac{\rho^{\sqrt{2(s+1)}-1}}{1-\rho}\right)\left(\frac{c_a^2 + c_p^2}{2}\right) = \left(\frac{0.3}{1}\right)\left(\frac{0.75^{\sqrt{2(1+1)}-1}}{(1-0.75)}\right)\left(\frac{1^2+1^2}{2}\right) = 0.9 \text{ hours}$$

Therefore, customers will have to wait about 0.9 hours on average for each expert.

If the organization were to combine the two lines to form just one line for the experts, it would "pool" the systems and have only one line. In this case, the interarrival time for the combined system is half that of the separate systems (i.e., $a = 0.2$ hours), but the average service time remains the same ($p = 0.3$ hours). Again, using the approximate G/G/s model but with $s = 2$ servers, the average queue time for this system is:

$$W_q = \left(\frac{p}{s}\right)\left(\frac{\rho^{\sqrt{2(s+1)}-1}}{1-\rho}\right)\left(\frac{c_a^2 + c_p^2}{2}\right) = \left(\frac{0.3}{2}\right)\left(\frac{0.75^{\sqrt{2(2+1)}-1}}{(1-0.75)}\right)\left(\frac{1^2+1^2}{2}\right) = 0.395 \text{ hours}$$

Therefore, customers in the "pooled" system have to wait about 0.4 hours on average. In this case, pooling reduced the average waiting time by about one-half (from 0.9 hours to 0.4 hours), a very significant difference.

Why is the pooled system so much better? The answer is that in the old system, one expert could be idle while the other had customers waiting in line. In other words, the pooled system makes better use of the experts.

The benefits of pooling are often significant. The main point here is not the queuing model, but rather the fact that many systems can often be improved by pooling resources. Pooled systems can often make better use of resources, reduce the waiting time for customers, and reduce the risk of long waiting times.

Examples of this pooling concept can be found in many contexts:

- The dean of a business school centralized all tech support people for the school into one office instead of having one assigned to each department. The pooled resource provided faster and better support.
- Delta Airlines shares parts with other airlines in Singapore. This reduces the risk of any airline not having a needed part and reduces the required investment.
- Xcel Energy shares expensive power generator parts with many other firms in the Midwestern U.S.
- A large service firm reduced average waiting time by consolidating its call centers in one location.

Pooling also has disadvantages. When a service firm consolidates its call centers, some local customers might not experience service that is culturally sensitive, particularly if the call center is moved to another country. Also, large call centers can experience diseconomies of scale. Putting all operations in one location can be risky from a business continuity standpoint, because a disaster might put the entire business at risk. Finally, in

---

[45] *This is the average time between arrivals for customers.*

a queuing context, if the mean service times for the customer populations are very different from one another, the pooled coefficient of variation of the pooled service time will increase and the average time in queue will also increase (Van Dijk & Van Der Sluis 2007).

See *addition principle, call center, consolidation, diseconomy of scale, postponement, queuing theory, slow moving inventory.*

POQ – See *Period Order Quantity.*

portal – See *corporate portal.*

Porter's Five Forces – See *five forces analysis.*

POS – See *Point-of-Sale.*

post-mortem review – See *post-project review.*

post-project review – The practice of appraising a project after it has been completed to promote learning for (1) the members of the project team, (2) the sponsoring organization, and (3) the wider organization; also called post-mortem review, project retrospective, and post-implementation audit.

Organizations should seek to learn from their successes and failures. Organizations that do not do this are doomed to repeat their mistakes over and over again. This is a critical activity for successful project management. Gene Heupel of GMHeupel Associates recommends that process improvement project teams conduct three activities at the end of a project: (1) create a project completion notice, (2) conduct a post-project review, and (3) create a project closing report. Each of these is discussed briefly below.

The **project completion notice** is serves several purposes, including (1) verifying that the deliverables in the project charter have been completed, (2) defining the plan to sustain the implementation, and (3) releasing the team and establishing the end-of-project activities. Heupel recommends that the project team have the project sponsor sign this document.

The **post-project review** is a comprehensive review conducted by the project team to ensure that the team and the organization have learned as much as they can from the project. Lessons learned from this review are documented in the project closing report. It is important to remember that the purpose of this review is not to blame people, but rather to help the organization learn from the project experience so that going forward it will retain the good practices and improve the poor ones.

The **project closing report** contains all of the significant documents related to the project as well as lessons learned from the post-project review. This report becomes an important part of the organization's knowledge base going forward. The project is not complete until the sponsor has signed off on the project closing report.

In many contexts, the post-project review might also (1) assess the level of user satisfaction, (2) evaluate the degree to which the stated goals were accomplished, and (3) list further actions required.

See *deliverables, forming-storming-norming-performing model, implementation, lean sigma, learning organization, project charter, project management, sponsor.*

postponement – The principle of delaying differentiation (customization) for a product as long as possible to minimize complexity and inventory; also called delayed differentiation, late customization, and late configuration. ✪

Forecasting the demand for standard products is relatively easy, and the **inventory carrying cost** for these products is relatively low. However, forecasting demand for products differentiated for a particular channel or customer is much harder, and the carrying cost is often high due to obsolescence. Firms will likely have too much inventory for some differentiated products and too little for others. If a firm can delay the differentiation of the products until after the customer order has been received, the finished goods inventory is eliminated. Postponement is a form of **pooling**, where the organization pools the inventory as long as possible before the customer order requires differentiation.

Postponement is a foundational principle for **mass customization**. Postponement principles often allow an organization to change from make to order to assemble to order or configure to order, which allows the firm to reduce customer leadtime or increase customization. The point at which products are customized for customers is called the **push-pull boundary**.

For example, HP was able to standardize its printers and put all country-specific power management technology in the cord. This allowed for lower inventory and better customer service.

See *agile manufacturing, customer leadtime, mass customization, New Product Development (NPD), operations strategy, pooling, push-pull boundary, respond to order (RTO), standard products.*

predatory pricing – The practice of selling a product or service at a very low price (even below cost) to drive competitors out of the market and create barriers to entry for potential new competitors.

After a company has driven its competitors out of the market, it can recoup its losses by charging higher prices in a monopoly relationship with its customers. Predatory pricing is against the law in many countries.

See *antitrust laws, bid rigging, bribery, price fixing.*

predictive maintenance – See *maintenance.*

premium freight – Additional charges paid to a transportation provider to expedite shipments.

Premium freight can be used for bringing purchased materials into a facility and delivering products to customers. Premium freight is used when the normal freight method cannot provide needed materials in time for a production schedule. An increase in premium freight for purchased materials suggests that the firm should consider freezing more of the master production schedule (i.e., move out the time fence).

Similarly, premium freight is used when the normal freight method cannot deliver finished goods to customers by the promised delivery dates. An increase in premium freight for delivering products to customers suggests that the firm may be over-promising on its delivery dates to its customers.

See *logistics, time fence.*

prevention – Work to design and improve products and processes so defects are avoided.

Prevention cost is the cost associated with this work and includes product design, process design, work selection, worker training, and many other costs. The **cost of quality** suggests that investing in prevention will generally reduce appraisal (inspection) cost, internal failure cost, and external failure cost. However, many firms find that prevention cost is the hardest component of the cost of quality to measure.

See *cost of quality, error proofing, Failure Mode and Effects Analysis (FMEA), rework, sentinel event.*

preventive maintenance – See *maintenance.*

price elasticity of demand – See *elasticity.*

price fixing – Agreement between competitors to set an agreed-upon minimum price.

Price fixing inhibits competition and therefore forces customers to pay more than they would in a competitive environment. Price fixing is an illegal practice in many countries.

See *antitrust laws, bid rigging, bribery, predatory pricing, purchasing.*

price of non-conformance – See *cost of quality.*

primacy effect – A concept from psychology and sociology that suggests that people assign disproportionate importance to initial stimuli or observations.

For example, if a subject reads a long list of words, he or she is more likely to remember words read toward the beginning of the list than words read in the middle. The phenomenon is due to the fact that short-term memory at the beginning of a sequence of events is far less "crowded," because fewer items are being processed in the brain.

The **recency effect** is a similar concept from psychology and sociology that suggests that people assign disproportionate importance to final stimuli or observations.

In summary, the primacy and recency effects predict that people will remember the items near the beginning and the end of the list. Lawyers scheduling the appearance of witnesses for court testimony and managers scheduling a list of speakers at a conference take advantage of these effects when they put speakers they wish to emphasize at the beginning or end. In measuring customer satisfaction, it is well-known that customers place undo emphasis on their first and most recent customer experiences ("moments of truth").

See *moments of truth, service quality.*

primary location – See *random storage location.*

Principal Component Analysis (PCA) – A statistical tool that transforms a number of possibly correlated variables into a smaller number of uncorrelated variables called principal components.

The first principal component accounts for as much of the variability in the data as possible, and each subsequent component accounts for as much of the remaining variability as possible.

See *cluster analysis, factor analysis.*

print on demand – A customer interface strategy of printing books, manuals, and other materials in response to a customer order rather than creating an inventory; also called POD, publish on demand, and print to order.

Print on demand requires a printing process that can efficiently handle small printing batch sizes. Print on demand is a mass customization strategy made possible by computer-based printing technologies. Ideally, print on demand has nearly zero setup time, setup cost, finished goods inventory, and obsolete inventory.

See *mass customization, respond to order (RTO)*.

print to order – See *print on demand*.

prisoners' dilemma – A conflict situation ("game") in which two players can decide to either cooperate or cheat.

The prisoner's dilemma is a classic scenario in the game theory literature that received its name from the following hypothetical situation (Axelrod 1984). Imagine two criminals, A and B, arrested under suspicion of having committed a crime together. However, the police do not have sufficient proof to convict them. The police separate the prisoners and offer each of them the same deal. If one testifies for the prosecution against the other and the other remains silent, the betrayer goes free, and the silent accomplice receives the full 10-year sentence. If both stay silent, both prisoners are sentenced to only six months in jail for a minor charge due to lack of evidence. If each betrays the other, each receives a two-year sentence. Each prisoner must make the choice of whether to betray the other or remain silent. However, neither prisoner knows what choice the other prisoner will make. The game is summarized in the following table.

The gain for mutual cooperation in the prisoners' dilemma is kept smaller than the gain for one-sided betrayal so that players are always tempted to betray. This economic relationship does not always hold. For example, two wolves working together can kill an animal that is more than twice as large as what either of them could kill alone.

Prisoner's dilemma

		Prisoner B	
		B stays silent	B betrays
Prisoner A	A stays silent	Both serve 6 months	A serves 10 years B goes free
	A betrays	A goes free B serves 10 years	Both serve 2 years

The prisoners' dilemma is meant to study short-term decision making where the actors do not have any specific expectations about future interactions or collaborations (e.g., in the original situation of the jailed criminals). Synergy usually only gets its full power after a long-term process of mutual cooperation, such as wolves hunting deer. If two entities repeatedly face a prisoners' dilemma with each other, a fairly good strategy for each one is sometimes called tit for tat, which means that if you cheated on the previous move, I'll cheat on this move; if you cooperated on the previous move, I'll cooperate on this move.

See *game theory, zero sum game*.

private carrier – A shipper that transports its goods in truck fleets that it owns or leases.

See *common carrier, logistics*.

private label – A product or service created by one organization but sold by another organization under the seller's brand name.

The most common example is when a large retailer (e.g., Target) contracts with a manufacturer to make a generic version of its product sold under the Target brand. Private label is a common practice in consumer packed goods and white goods.

See *category captain, category management, consumer packaged goods, Original Equipment Manufacturer (OEM), picking, white goods*.

privatization – The process of moving from a government owned and controlled organization to a privately owned and controlled for-profit organization; spelled privatisation in most of the world outside of the U.S.

pro bono – To work for the public good without charging a fee; short for the Latin *pro bono publico*, which means "for the public good."

When lawyers, consultants, and other professionals work "*pro bono*," they work without charging a fee. Some organizations provide *pro bono* services, but then prominently mention the gift in their marketing communications. Technically, this is *gratis* (free of charge) rather than *pro bono*, because it is part of the organization's advertising, promotion, and branding strategy and not truly intended only for the public good.

probability density function – A statistics term for a function that represents the probability for a continuous random variable as the area under the curve; usually written as $f(x)$; also called the density function and PDF. ✪

Only **continuous random variables** have probability density functions. **Discrete random variables** have a **probability mass function**, which defines the probability for each discrete (integer) value (e.g., $p(x) = P(X = x)$).

The integral of the PDF for the entire range of a continuous random variable is one (i.e., $\int_{t=-\infty}^{t=\infty} f(t)dt = 1$).

The **Cumulative Distribution Function** (also called the CDF or simply the distribution function) is the lower tail (left tail) cumulative probability (i.e., the integral of the PDF) and is the probability that a random variable is less than the specified value. This can be expressed mathematically as $P(X \le x) = F(x) = \int_{t=-\infty}^{t=x} f(t)dt$, where X is a continuous random variable, x is a specific value, and $f(x)$ is the density function evaluated at x.

The probability that a random variable is in the range $[a, b]$ is $P(a \le X \le b) = \int_{t=a}^{t=b} f(t)dt$. The **reliability function** is simply one minus the CDF. The PDF is the derivative of the cumulative distribution function (i.e., $dF(x)/dx = f(x)$).

See *beta distribution, chi-square distribution, Erlang distribution, exponential distribution, gamma distribution, lognormal distribution, normal distribution, partial expectation, probability distribution, probability mass function, random variable, reliability, sampling distribution, Student's t distribution, triangular distribution, uniform distribution, Weibull distribution*.

probability distribution – A mathematical or graphical description of how likely a random variable will be less than or equal to a particular value. ✪

Random variables are said to be either discrete (i.e., only integer values) or continuous (i.e., any real values). Discrete random variables have a **probability mass function** that defines the probability for each discrete (integer) value. Continuous random variables have a **Probability Density Function (PDF)**, where the probability is represented by the area under the curve. The **Cumulative Distribution Function (CDF)** evaluated at x is the probability that the random variable will attain a value less than or equal to x.

See *Bernoulli distribution, beta distribution, bimodal distribution, binomial distribution, chi-square distribution, Erlang distribution, exponential distribution, gamma distribution, hypergeometric distribution, lognormal distribution, negative binomial distribution, normal distribution, Poisson distribution, probability density function, probability mass function, random variable, sampling distribution, Student's t distribution, triangular distribution, uniform distribution, Weibull distribution*.

probability mass function – A probability theory term for an equation that can be used to express the probability that a discrete random variable will be exactly equal to a given value; usually denoted as $p(x)$.

A discrete random variable can only take on integer values. In contrast, a **probability density function** is used for continuous variables.

The probability mass is $p(x) = P(X = x)$. A probability mass function must sum to one (i.e., $\sum_{x=-\infty}^{\infty} p(x) = 1$).

See *Bernoulli distribution, bimodal distribution, binomial distribution, hypergeometric distribution, negative binomial distribution, Poisson distribution, probability density function, probability distribution, sampling distribution*.

Probit Analysis – See *logistic regression*.

process – A set of steps designed to achieve a particular goal. ✪

All processes have inputs and outputs. Ideally, processes will also have a feedback mechanism that evaluates the outputs and adjusts the inputs and the processes to better achieve the desired goal.

As mentioned in the preface to this book, this author uses the following framework to discuss process improvement:

- **Better** – How can we provide customers improved product quality, service quality, and value?
- **Faster** – How can we reduce cycle times to make our products and services more flexible and customizable?
- **Cheaper** – How can we reduce waste, lower cost, and better balance demand and capacity in a global supply chain?
- **Stronger** – How can we leverage our competitive strengths (core competences), mitigate risks by making processes more robust, and consider the triple bottom line (people, planet, and profits)?

Process improvement programs, such as lean sigma and lean, typically use tools, such as process mapping, error proofing, and setup time reduction methods, to reduce waste and add more value.

See *error proofing, lean sigma, lean thinking, process map, robust, setup time reduction methods, systems thinking.*

process capability and performance – A lean sigma methodology that measures the ability of a process to consistently meet quality specifications. ✪

Process capability and performance can be measured in many ways. The simplest approach is to measure the Defects per Million Opportunities (DPMO), where a defect is anything that does not meet the customer (or specification) requirements. A DPMO value can be translated into a sigma level, where the lower the DPMO, the higher the sigma level. (See the *sigma level* entry.)

Another approach is to use the statistical measures C_p and C_{pk} for measuring process capability and P_p and P_{pk} for measuring process performance. Process capability compares the process output for an "in-control" process with the customer's specification (tolerance limits) to determine if the common-cause variation is small enough to satisfy customer requirements.

The figure on the right shows a process with a process mean that is not centered between the lower tolerance limit (LTL) and the upper tolerance limit (UTL). Note that the mean μ is right of the center of the tolerance limits. Therefore, this process is not centered. This figure also shows that the process limits for common-cause variation ($\pm 3\sigma$) are well within the specification (tolerance) limits. Therefore, this process is said to be capable.

One humorous way to communicate this concept is to compare the specification limits to the width of a garage. The common-cause variation (the process width) is the size of a car that must fit into the garage. The specification width is the size

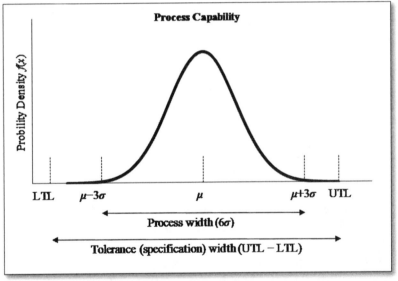

of the garage. If the garage is large (wide specification limits) and the car is small (tight process limits), the car will fit into the garage with no problem. However, if the garage is narrow and the car is large, the car will hit the sides of the garage (defects will be produced).

Several of the main process capability concepts are defined in more detail below.

Process Capability (C_p) – Process capability is the difference between the tolerance (specification) limits divided by the process width. In mathematical terms, this is $C_p = (UTL - LTL)/(6\sigma)$, where *UTL* is the Upper Tolerance Limit and *LTL* is the Lower Tolerance Limit. C_p should be at least 1.33 for the process to be considered capable. (This is a defect rate of 0.0063%.) The standard deviation for C_p can be estimated with moving range, range, or sigma control charts. The inverse of process capability is called the process capability ratio (C_r) and should be no greater than 75% for the process to be considered capable.

Process Capability Index (C_{pk}) – The process capability index (C_{pk}) measures the ability of a process to create units within specification limits. C_{pk} is the difference between the process mean and the closest specification limit over the standard deviation times three. The C_{pk} adjusts C_p for a non-centered distribution and therefore is preferred over C_p. For example, in target shooting, if shots hit the bottom right corner of the target and form a tight group, the process has a high C_p but a low C_{pk}. When the sight is adjusted so this tight group is centered on the bull's eye, the process also has a high C_{pk}. C_{pk} is the smaller of the capability of the upper half and the lower half of the process. In mathematical terms, $C_{pu} = (UTL - \mu)/(3\sigma)$, $C_{pl} = (\mu - LTL)/(3\sigma)$, and $C_{pk} = \min(C_{pl}, C_{pu})$. When the C_{pk} is less than one, the process is said to be incapable. When the C_{pk} is greater than or equal to one, the process is considered capable of producing a product within specification limits. The C_{pk} for a six sigma process is 2. The process capability index (C_{pk}) can never be greater than the process capability (C_p). They will be equal when the process average is exactly in the middle of the specification limits.

Process Performance (P_p) – Process performance is similar to C_p, except it is based on the sample standard deviation. The inverse of process performance is called the process performance ratio (P_r).

Process Performance Index (P_{pk}) – The process performance index is similar to C_{pk} except it is based on the sample standard deviation. Process performance is based on the sample standard deviation, whereas process capability is based on the long-term "common-cause" standard deviation determined from the moving range, range, or sigma control charts. Process performance, therefore, is the actual short-term performance of a system, whereas process capability is the system's long-term potential to perform when under control. The difference between the two is the potential for improvement. The table below compares these two metrics.

	Process Capability	Process Performance
Interpretation	A measure of the long-term potential or aptitude of the process.	A measure of recent short-term actual performance for a sample.
Measures	C_p, C_{pk}, C_r	P_p, P_{pk}, P_r
Time horizon	Long-term	Short-term
How to estimate the standard deviation	Estimated over a longer period of time using moving range, range, or sigma control charts.	Estimated from a sample standard deviation.

Source: Professor Arthur V. Hill

See *business capability, common cause variation, control chart, cost of quality, Defects per Million Opportunities (DPMO), Design for Six Sigma (DFSS), functional build, lean sigma, operations performance metrics, Overall Equipment Effectiveness (OEE), process validation, sigma level, specification limits, Statistical Process Control (SPC), Statistical Quality Control (SQC), tolerance, yield.*

process control – See *Statistical Process Control (SPC)*.

process design – The activities required to create a new manufacturing or service process. ✪

Process design includes facility location, facility layout, process planning, capacity planning, ergonomics, and work design. Process design should be simultaneous with product design and guided by the organization's strategy. One key component of process design is to error-proof the process.

See *capacity, ergonomics, error proofing, facility layout, facility location, New Product Development (NPD), service blueprinting.*

process flowchart – See *process map*.

process improvement program – A systematic approach for improving organizational performance that consists of practices, tools, techniques, and terminology and implemented as a set of process improvement projects. ✪

Many process improvement program concepts are presented in this book. The best-known programs are lean sigma and lean. In recent years, nearly all six sigma programs have been renamed "lean sigma."

See *benchmarking, Business Process Management (BPM), Business Process Re-engineering (BPR), error proofing, lean sigma, lean thinking, program management office, project hopper, project management, standardized work, Theory of Constraints (TOC), voice of the customer (VOC).*

process layout – See *facility layout*.

process map – A diagram showing the logical flow of steps required for a task; also called a flowchart, process flowchart, and business process map. ✪

The "as-is" process map shows how the process currently operates. The "should-be" process map shows the team's recommendations for how the process should operate in the future.

Guidelines for creating process maps – The following is a list of best practices for process mapping developed by this author.

- Engage the gemba to create the process map.
- Use Post-it Notes to brainstorm the steps.
- Use rectangles for process steps.
- Use diamonds for decision steps.
- Use ovals or rounded rectangles to start and end processes.
- Do not bother with more sophisticated shapes.
- Draw the map from left to right.
- Do not bother with complicated standards for how the arrows connect to the boxes.
- Be careful to have the right scope.
- Show all the flows.
- Start with the "as-is" before creating the "should-be" process map.
- Listen to the voice of the customer.
- Identify the pain points.
- Identify the handoffs.
- Identify the waits.
- Identify the setup (changeover) steps.
- Identify the "as-is" and "should-be" control points for monitoring the process.
- Identify the bottleneck.
- Identify the risk points (fail points).
- Identify the non-value-added steps.
- Identify the rework loops.
- Identify the moments of truth.
- Identify roles and responsibilities for the major steps in the process.
- Identify the line of visibility.
- Show the numbers.
- Use a hierarchical approach.
- Use normal-sized paper.
- Identify and prioritize opportunities for improvement.

Software tools for process mapping – Many software tools are available for process mapping. Although the most popular tool appears to be Microsoft Visio, Microsoft Excel can create process maps that are just as good. Simple process maps can also be created in Microsoft Word and Microsoft PowerPoint.

Getting the benefits of a value stream map with a process map – Although a value stream map is more visual than a process map, a process map is better than a value stream map from the standpoint of information value. A process map allows for decision points, but a value stream map does not. A value stream map requires a diagram of the physical system, which works well in a factory, but is difficult in a knowledge work process. This is particularly important for transactional processes in banks and other information-intensive organizations with many decision points. Therefore, nearly all the information in a value stream map can be included in a process map. To make the process map more visual, it is possible to add photos, drawings, and icons.

See *benchmarking, brainstorming, Business Process Management (BPM), causal map, facility layout, flowchart, handoff, lean sigma, mindmap, process, rework, service blueprinting, seven tools of quality, SIPOC Diagram, standardized work, upstream, value stream map.*

process performance qualification – See *process validation.*

process validation – A term used by the Food and Drug Administration (FDA) in the U.S. for establishing documented evidence that a process will consistently produce a product meeting specifications.

Process validation is a requirement of the Current Good Manufacturing Practices Regulations for Finished Pharmaceuticals and the Good Manufacturing Practice Regulations for Medical Devices. The following terms are important elements of process validation (source: www.fda.gov, April 19, 2011):

Installation Qualification (IQ) – Establishing confidence that process equipment and ancillary systems are capable of consistently operating within established limits and tolerances.

Process performance qualification – Establishing confidence that the process is effective and reproducible.

Product performance qualification – Establishing confidence through appropriate testing that the finished product has been produced according to the specified process and meets all requirements.

Prospective validation – Validation conducted prior to the distribution of a new product or a product made under a revised manufacturing process, where the revisions may affect the product's characteristics.

Retrospective validation – Validation of a process for a product already in distribution based upon accumulated production, testing, and control data.

Validation – Establishing documented evidence that provides a high degree of assurance that a specific process will consistently produce a product that meets pre-determined specifications and quality attributes.

Validation protocol – A written plan stating how validation will be conducted, including test parameters, product characteristics, production equipment, and decision points on what constitutes acceptable test results.

Worst case – A set of conditions encompassing upper and lower processing limits and circumstances, including those within standard operating procedures, which pose the greatest chance of process or product failure when compared to ideal conditions. Such conditions do not necessarily induce product or process failure.

See *Good Manufacturing Practices (GMP)*, *process capability and performance*, *quality assurance*, *Statistical Process Control (SPC)*, *Statistical Quality Control (SQC)*.

procurement – See *purchasing*.

producer's risk – The probability of rejecting a lot that should have been accepted.

The producer suffers when a lot with an acceptable quality level (AQL) is rejected. This is called a Type I error. The Greek letter α (alpha) is used for Type I risk with typical α values in range (0.2, 0.01).

See *Acceptable Quality Level (AQL)*, *acceptance sampling*, *consumer's risk*, *operating characteristic curve*, *quality management*, *sampling*, *Type I and II errors*.

Product Data Management (PDM) – The business function and associated software that creates, publishes, and manages detailed product information.

PDM manages all information related to a product and the components that go into a product. The data include current and historical specifications, the engineering change history (version control), the item master, bill of material (BOM), and routing databases.

The best PDM systems are Web-based collaborative applications for product development that allow enterprises to share business processes and product data with dispersed divisions, partners, and customers. PDM systems hold master data in a single secure vault where data integrity can be assured and all changes are monitored, controlled, and recorded (i.e., version control). Duplicate reference copies of the master data, on the other hand, can be distributed freely to users in various departments for design, analysis, and approval. The new data are then released back into the vault. When the database is changed, a modified copy of the data, signed and dated, is stored in the vault alongside the old data.

See *knowledge management*, *New Product Development (NPD)*, *product life cycle management*, *version control*.

product design quality – The degree to which the product design meets customer requirements; also called design quality and performance quality. ✪

Product design quality is the output of a team of knowledge workers in marketing, product design, quality assurance, operations, and sourcing, possibly with the help of suppliers. This design is stored and communicated in drawings (CAD files) and specifications.

For example, the marketing and R&D people in a firm decide that a watch should be designed to survive 100 meters under water based on focus groups with customers and salesforce feedback. This design is better than a watch designed to only survive 10 meters under water.

Although the product design standards might be high (e.g., survive 100m under water), it is possible that the manufacturing process is flawed and that products regularly fail to meet the standard (e.g., only survive 10m under water). In summary, product design (performance) quality is how well the design specifications meet customer requirements, and **conformance quality** is how well the actual product meets the design specifications.

See *conformance quality*, *quality management*, *warranty*.

product family – A group of items with similar characteristics; also called family or part family.

Product families can be created from many different points of view, including selling, sales planning, production planning, engineering, forecasting, capacity planning, financial planning, and factory layout. Product families may meet a common set of customer requirements (e.g., a product family sold to one market segment), may have similar manufacturing requirements (e.g., all items within a family require the same sequence of manufacturing steps), or may have similar product technologies or components (e.g., all use digital electronics).

See *bill of material (BOM)*, *cellular manufacturing*, *part number*, *Resource Requirements Planning (RRP)*, *Sales & Operations Planning (S&OP)*, *sequence-dependent setup time*, *setup cost*, *value stream*.

product layout – See *facility layout*.

product life cycle management – Managing a product through its entire life, from concept to design, development, commercialization, manufacturing, and finally, phase out.

Many firms struggle with the early and late phases of the product life cycle. During the start-up phase, the difficulties include forecasting (see the *Bass Model* entry) and commercialization. In the later phases, many firms fail to clearly state their end-of-life policies regarding when they will stop selling or supporting products.

As products mature and reach technical obsolescence, an end-of-life policy can help both the manufacturer and its customers. The manufacturer cannot afford to support products and technologies indefinitely. The end-of-life policy sets boundaries and manages expectations about the supply and support guidelines for a product. Many manufacturers provide support and replacement parts for up to five years after the date of sale, even for products that are removed from the market. For some critical products, the manufacturer takes the initiative to notify customers months in advance of the products' scheduled end-of-life.

Good product life cycle management is supported by a good product profitability analysis, which is based on **Activity Based Costing (ABC)**. This analysis can help balance the conflicting interests of manufacturing (that wants to eliminate obsolete products early) and sales (that wants to keep a full catalog of products).

Some of the key product life cycle events that need to be managed include:

- **End of Production** – The date that a product is no longer produced or shipped by a manufacturer.
- **End of Life** – The date that a product is no longer marketed or sold.
- **End of Support** – The last date that a product will be supported. Some customers might negotiate an extension for this date.

Some firms use a **termination date** policy for products and components. A product and its unique components[46] are no longer sold or supported after the termination date. The advantages of having a termination date policy include:

- Provides a clear plan for every functional area that deals with products (manufacturing, purchasing, inventory, service, engineering, and marketing) and supports an orderly, coordinated phase-out.
- Communicates to the salesforce and market that the product will no longer be supported (or at least no longer sold) after the termination date. This can provide incentive for customers to upgrade to a newer product.
- Allows manufacturing and inventory planners to bring down the inventories for all unique components needed for the product in a coordinated way.

Good implementation practices of a termination date policy include the following policies:

- Helps the organization plan many years ahead to warn all stakeholders, including marketing, sales, product management, purchasing, and manufacturing.
- Makes sure that all functions (and divisions) have "buy-in" to the termination date.

See *adoption curve, all-time demand, all-time order, Bass Model, bathtub curve, phase-in/phase-out planning, planned obsolescence, Product Data Management (PDM), stakeholder, technology road map, termination date, time to market, value engineering, version control*.

product mix – The variety of products that a firm offers to the market; also called product assortment.

Product mix usually refers to the length (the number of products in the product line), breadth (the number of product lines that a company offers), depth (the different varieties of products in the product line), and consistency (the relationship between products in their final destination) of product lines. Product mix is a strategic decision based on the industry, the firm's desired position in the market, and the firm's ability to offer more variety without adding cost (mass customization). By definition, specialty or niche firms have a limited product mix.

See *linear programming (LP), mass customization, product proliferation*.

product mix problem – See *linear programming (LP)*.

product performance qualification – See *process validation*.

product proliferation – The marketing practice of adding new products, product variants, and product extensions to the market; also called stock keeping unit (SKU) proliferation.

Product proliferation occurs when marketing and sales organizations offer new product variations through different color combinations, sizes, features, packaging, languages, regions, etc. Product line extensions can bring both benefits and problems.

---

[46] *The "unique" components are those that are needed only for the product being terminated. If a component is also needed in a product that is not being terminated, the component cannot be terminated.*

Benefits of product line extensions include:

- Meet the ever-changing customer needs.
- Increase sales and capture larger market share.
- Help firms explore new products and markets. Hamel and Prahalad (1991) argue for the use of "expeditionary marketing" to test new markets because of the difficulties of conducting marketing research.
- Create a barrier to entry for competitors.

Problems of product line extensions (and product proliferation) include:

- Products competing with one another in the same market.
- Consumer confusion about the products.
- Cannibalization of the existing product line of the company.
- Higher complexity, which increases costs and makes service more difficult throughout the product life cycle.

The marketing, sales, and R&D organizations are responsible for identifying new products and are held accountable for growing sales each year. However, as Mariotti (2008) points out, no organization within a firm is responsible for balancing the drive to increase (proliferate) the number of SKUs. His book argues persuasively that product proliferation leads to complexity that has significant hidden costs.

Product rationalization is the process of evaluating which products should be kept in a product portfolio. Product rationalization is based on several factors, such as sales, margin, product life cycle, support for complementary products, and similarity of product attributes. As mentioned above, it tends to be a difficult process in many firms because of goal misalignment between the sales and marketing organizations, which want a broad product line to satisfy a wide variety of customers and win new ones, and the manufacturing and supply chain organizations, which want to reduce cost, complexity, and inventory.

See *Activity Based Costing (ABC)*, *assortment*, *focused factory*, *market share*, *mass customization*, *product mix*, *standard products*.

product rationalization – See *product proliferation*.

product simplification – See *value engineering*.

product structure – See *bill of material (BOM)*.

production activity control – See *shop floor control*.

production function – A microeconomics concept that defines the relationship between an organization's inputs and outputs.

The production function is a mathematical model that indicates what outputs can be obtained from various amounts and combinations of factor inputs. In its most general mathematical form, a production function is expressed as $Q = f(x_1, x_2, ..., x_n)$, where Q is the quantity of output and $(x_1, x_2, ..., x_n)$ are the factor inputs, such as capital, labor, raw materials, land, technology, and management.

The production function can be specified in a number of ways, including an additive (linear) function $Q = a + b_1 x_1 + b_2 x_2 + ... + b_n x_n$ or a multiplicative (Cobb-Douglas) production function $Q = a x_1^{b_1} x_2^{b_2} ... x_n^{b_n}$. Other forms include the "constant elasticity of substitution" production function (CES), which is a generalized form of the Cobb-Douglas function, and the quadratic production function, which is a specific type of additive function. The best form of the equation and the best values of the parameters depend on the firm and industry.

See *Data Envelopment Analysis (DEA)*, *economics*.

production line – A manufacturing term for a sequence of workstations or machines that make a product (or family of products); most often used in a high-volume, repetitive manufacturing environment where the machines (workcenters) are connected by conveyers.

Levitt (1972) wrote an **HBR** article entitled the "Production-line approach to service" that used McDonald's as an example to support his argument that services should be managed more like factories with respect to standardization, technology, systems, and metrics.

See *assembly line*, *manufacturing processes*, *service management*.

production linearity – See *heijunka*.

Production Operations Management Society (POMS) – An international professional society representing the interests of production and operations management professionals from around the world.

The purposes of the society are to (1) extend and integrate knowledge that contributes to the improved understanding and practice of production and operations management (POM), (2) disseminate information on POM to managers, scientists, educators, students, public and private organizations, national and local governments, and the general public, and (3) promote the improvement of POM and its teaching in public and private manufacturing and service organizations throughout the world.

Professor Kalyan Singhal founded POMS on June 30, 1989, in collaboration with about three hundred professors and executives. The society held its first international meeting in Washington, D.C. in October 1990. The first issue of the POMS journal ***Production and Operations Management*** was published in March 1992.

The POMS website is www.poms.org.

See *operations management (OM)*.

production order – See *manufacturing order*.

production plan – See *production planning*.

production planning – The process of creating a high-level production plan, usually in monthly time buckets for families of items, and often measured in a high-level common unit of measure, such as units, gallons, pounds, or shop hours; called aggregate planning or aggregate production planning in the academic literature. ✪

In academic circles, the result of the aggregate production planning process is called the **aggregate plan**, whereas in many practitioner circles (including APICS) it is known simply as the **production plan**. Aggregate planning is particularly difficult for firms with seasonal demand for their products. Firms such as Polaris (a manufacturer of snowmobiles and ATVs) and Toro (a manufacturer of snow blowers and lawnmowers) have to build inventory in the off season in anticipation of seasonal demand.

Production planning is just one step in the Sales & Operations Planning (S&OP) process. S&OP is a broader and higher-level business process that includes sales, marketing, finance, and operations and that oversees the creation of the business plan, the sales plan, and the production plan. (See the *Sales & Operations Planning (S&OP)* entry for more information on this topic.)

Whereas the business plan is usually defined in dollars (profit, revenue, and cost), the production plan is usually defined by units or some other aggregate output (or input) measure, such as shop hours worked, gallons produced, crude oil started, etc. An aggregate measure is particularly useful when the production plan includes many dissimilar products.

The goal is to meet customer demand at the lowest cost. Relevant costs for production planning decisions include inventory carrying costs, capacity change costs (hiring, training, firing, facility expansion or contraction, equipment expansion or reduction), and possibly the opportunity costs of lost sales.

The linear programming formulation for the aggregate production planning problem has been in the operations management and operations research literature since the 1960s. It assumes that the demand is known with certainty over the T-period planning horizon. The problem is to find the optimal production plan, workforce plan, and inventory plan to meet the demand at the lowest cost. Mathematical statement of the problem is below.

The aggregate production planning problem

$$\text{Minimize } z = \sum_{t=1}^{T} (c_H H_t + c_F F_t + c_{OT} OT_t + c_W W_t + c_C I_t)$$

Subject to $I_t = I_{t-1} + P_t - D_t$, for $t = 1, 2, \dots, T$ $\qquad P_t = r(W_t + OT_t)$, for $t = 1, 2, \dots, T$

$OT_t \leq 1.5 W_t$, for $t = 1, 2, \dots, T$ $\qquad\qquad W_t = W_{t-1} + H_t - F_t$, for $t = 1, 2, \dots, T$

where,

T	Number of periods in the planning horizon.
t	Period index, $t = 1, 2, \dots, T$.
c_H	Cost of hiring one worker.
H_t	Number of workers hired in period t.
c_F	Cost of firing one worker.
F_t	Number of workers fired in period t.
c_{OT}	Cost of using one full-time equivalent worker to work overtime for one period.

OT_t Number of workers working over time in period t, expressed in full-time equivalents. (The constraint above assumes that overtime is limited to 1.5 times regular time.)

c_W Cost of employing one worker for one period.

W_t Number of workers employed in period t.

c_C Cost of carrying one unit for one period.

I_t Inventory (in units) at the end of period t.

P_t The production rate in period t. This is the number of units produced in period t.

D_t Number of units demanded in period t.

R Number of units produced by one worker per period.

The objective function is to minimize the sum of the hiring, firing, overtime, regular time, and carrying costs. The first constraint is the inventory balancing equation, which requires the new inventory at the end of period t to be equal to the old inventory plus what is produced minus what is sold. The second constraint defines the number of units produced in period t as a function of the number of workers working in that period. The third constraint limits overtime labor hours to 1.5 times the regular time labor hours. Finally, the fourth constraint defines the number of regular time workers as the old number plus the number hired less the number fired.

Although the model has been around for a long time, very few firms have found it useful. The basic model requires the assumption that demand is known with certainty, which is usually far from reality. The model also requires the estimation of a number of cost parameters, such as the firing cost, hiring cost, and carrying cost, which are often hard to estimate. Finally, the linear programming modeling approach does not seem to fit well with the organizational dynamics that surround such difficult decisions as firing employees or building inventory.

See *aggregate inventory management, anticipation inventory, Business Requirements Planning (BRP), carrying charge, carrying cost, chase strategy, flexibility, hockey stick effect, level strategy, linear programming (LP), Master Production Schedule (MPS), Materials Requirements Planning (MRP), Resource Requirements Planning (RRP), Rough Cut Capacity Planning (RCCP), Sales & Operations Planning (S&OP), seasonality, time bucket, unit of measure.*

production smoothing – See *heijunka.*

productivity – A measure of the value produced by a system for a given level of inputs. ✪

Productivity is normally defined and measured as the ratio of an output measure divided by an input measure (e.g., hamburgers created per hour). It is a measure of how well a country, industry, business unit, person, or machine is using its resources. Productivity for a firm can be compared to another firm or to itself over time.

Total factor productivity is measured in monetary units. Partial factor productivity is measured in individual inputs or monetary units. For example, **labor productivity** could be measured as units per labor hour. **Partial factor productivity** can be misleading because a decline in the productivity of one input may be due to an increase in the productivity of another input. For example, a firm might improve labor productivity by outsourcing production, but find that the overall cost per unit is up due to the high cost of managing the outsourcing partner.

Whereas total factor productivity is total output divided by total input, partial factor productivity can be defined as output/labor hour, output/capital, output/materials, output/energy, etc. Multi-factor productivity is defined as output/(labor + capital + energy), output/(labor + materials), etc.

Many firms define and report productivity in terms of cost/unit, which is really the inverse of productivity. This is not output divided by input, but rather input (cost) divided by output (units). For example, a firm consumed 2400 hours of labor to process 560 insurance forms. What is the labor productivity? Answer: 2400/560 = 4.29 forms/hour. However, the firm prefers to express this in terms of hours per form (e.g., 0.23 hours/form) and dollars/form (e.g., $4.67/form).

The above definition of productivity is indistinquishable from the economics definition of **efficiency**. However, the industrial definition of efficiency is quite different from the above definition of productivity.

See *Data Envelopment Analysis (DEA), earned hours, efficiency, High Performance Work Systems (HPWS), human resources, job design, operations performance metrics, Overall Equipment Effectiveness (OEE), Results-Only Work Environment (ROWE), utilization.*

product-process matrix – A descriptive model that relates the production volume requirements to the type of production process. ✪

The product-process matrix

		Product structure/product life cycle					Flexibility & unit cost
Production volume		Very low	Low	Medium	High	Very high	
Standardization		None	Very low	Low	High	Very high	
Number of products		Very high	Many	Many	Few	Very few	
Process structure/process life cycle	No flow (project layout)	Project (e.g., building, ship building)			NOT FEASIBLE	NOT FEASIBLE	High
	Jumbled flow (job shop)		Job shop (e.g., printer, restaurant)			NOT FEASIBLE	
	Disconnected line flow (batch)			Batch (e.g., heavy equipment)			
	Connected line flow (assembly line)	NOT FEASIBLE[47]			Assembly line (e.g., autos, Burger King)		
	Continuous flow (continuous)	NOT FEASIBLE[48]	NOT FEASIBLE			Continuous (e.g., refinery, consumer products)	Low

Adapted from Hayes & Wheelwright 1979a, 1979b

The product-process matrix was first introduced by Robert H. Hayes and Steven C. Wheelwright in two *Harvard Business Review* articles published in 1979 entitled "Link Manufacturing Process and Product Life Cycles" and "The Dynamics of Process-Product Life Cycles" (Hayes & Wheelwright 1979a, 1979b). The matrix consists of two dimensions, product structure/product life cycle and process structure/process life cycle. The process structure/process life cycle dimension describes the process choice (job shop, batch, assembly line, and continuous flow) and process structure (jumbled flow, disconnected line flow, connected line flow and continuous flow), while the product structure/product life cycle describes the four stages of the product life cycle (low to high volume) and product structure (low to high standardization).

Later writers have added an additional stage in the upper-left for the project layout. The product-process matrix is shown below with some examples along the main diagonal. Many authors argue that the ideal configuration is the main diagonal (the shaded boxes in the matrix) so that the product and process match. Others point out that mass customization and flexible manufacturing systems are strategies to move down the matrix while still offering product variety.

See *facility layout, Flexible Manufacturing System (FMS), mass customization*.

profit center – An accounting term for an area of responsibility held accountable for its contribution to profit.

Multi-divisional firms often hold each division responsible for its own profit. However, most public firms do not report profits for each profit center to external audiences.

See *cost center, investment center, revenue center*.

program – A set of projects that are coordinated to achieve certain organizational objectives.

A program is an on going activity with no set end date with a long-term goal, usually implemented with a series of many interrelated projects. Programs are often managed by a **program management office** (PMO)

---

[47] *In some cases, it is possible to still have an assembly line for low-volume products by using mixed model assembly.*

[48] *It is possible to have continuous flow for low-volume products by using automation and mass customization strategies.*

The Encyclopedia of Operations Management

with a dedicated leadership team. An example of a program might be a process improvement program, such as lean sigma, or a large-scale construction project, such as a nuclear reactor that requires years to complete.

See *program management office*, *project charter*, *project management*.

program management office – An individual or group of people who are charged with overseeing a set of projects intended to achieve some overarching objective; often called a PMO. ✪

One of the keys to success of process improvement programs, such as lean sigma, is managing the **hopper** of potential projects so the firm is carefully selecting the projects from a strategic point of view and matching them to resources (black belts and green belts) to develop the leadership capability in the firm. According to Englund, Graham, and Dinsmore (2003, p. xii), "The project office adds value to the organization by ensuring that projects are performed within procedures, are in line with organizational strategies, and are completed in a way that adds economic value to the organization."

A research project by Zhang, Hill, Schroeder, and Linderman (2008) found two keys to success for any process improvement program: **Strategic Project Selection (SPS)** and **Discipline Project Management (DPM)**. The research found a causal linkage from DPM to SPS to operating performance. SPS and DPM are both outcomes of a well-managed program management office.

Other related terms include project management office and project control (Englund, Graham, & Dinsmore 2003). Still other firms use the name of the program to name the office (e.g., lean sigma champion, lean promotion office, director of management information systems, etc.). These programs could be related to new product development projects, building projects, process improvement projects, or marketing research projects.

See *champion*, *lean promotion office*, *lean sigma*, *lean thinking*, *process improvement program*, *program*, *project charter*, *project hopper*, *project management*.

project – See *project management*.

project charter – A document that clearly defines the key attributes of a project, such as the purpose, scope, deliverables, and timeline; closely related to a statement of work (SoW). ✪

The charter is essentially an informal contract between the project sponsor and the project leader and team. Like a good product design or building blueprint, a well-designed project charter provides a strong foundation for a successful project.

The following project charter format has been developed over the course of several years by Gene Heupel and Professor Arthur Hill. Mr. Heupel was the Director of Project Control at Xcel Energy for many years and is now the president of GMHeupel Associates, a consultancy that provides process improvement and project management services. This framework draws from his experience, a large number of company examples, and the Project Management Institute's recommended format.

- **Project name:** Usually a short descriptive name.
- **Project number:** Often a budget number or project designator in the "portfolio" of projects.
- **Problem:** A clear and concise business case for the project. This statement should include enough background to motivate the project. (See the *business case* entry for detailed suggestions on how to write a business case.)
- **Objectives:** The targeted benefits (improvement) in cost, sales, errors, etc. This requires selection of the metrics to be used and the target values for these metrics. In some cases, the benefits may be hard to quantify (e.g., customer satisfaction); however, in general, it is best to define quantifiable objectives. Some firms require separate sections for "financial impact" and "customer impact."
- **Deliverables:** A list of products to be delivered (e.g., improved procedures, NPV analysis, training, implementation plan) and how these will be delivered to the project sponsor (e.g., workshop, PowerPoint presentation, Excel workbook, or training).
- **Scope:** A clear statement of the project boundaries, including clear and deliberate identification of what is out of scope. Many experts break this section into "inclusions" and "exclusions."
- **Assumptions:** Key beliefs about the problem (e.g., an assumption that the process improvement efforts will not require changes to the information systems).
- **Schedule:** A short list of the most important planned completion dates (milestones) for each of the main activities and deliverables in the project.
- **Budget:** The estimated labor hours and cost for key resources plus any other expenses.

- **Risk mitigation:** The barriers that might keep the project from being completely successful, including a statement about how these should be addressed. For example, a project might be at risk if one user group fails to embrace a new process. The mitigation for this might be to assign a key representative of this user group to the process design team and to provide training for all the users before the new process is implemented.
- **Team:** A list of the team members' names and titles along with their roles (e.g., team leader, team member, team support person). Some organizations add planned utilization, start dates, and end dates. Subject matter experts (SMEs) should also be listed with an explanation of their roles (e.g., advising, reviewing, etc.). SMEs are not formal team members and therefore can be included without increasing the size of the team.
- **Sponsor:** The name of the project sponsor or sponsors. Sponsors should be included from every organization that is significantly impacted by the project.
- **Approvals:** Signatures from all project sponsors before the project is started. It is important to revise the charter and get new approvals whenever the scope is changed. In some situations, such as new product development, signoffs are required at the end of each phase of the project.

A **statement of work (SoW)** is a description of the business need, scope, and deliverables for a project. The SoW usually follows the **project charter** and provides more detail. However, some organizations use a SoW in place of a project charter. At a minimum, the SoW should include the business need, scope, and deliverables. However, some experts insist that the SoW also include acceptance criteria and schedule. Still others include all the details of the project charter, including executive summary, background, objectives, staffing, assumptions, risks, scope, deliverables, milestones, and signatures.

See *A3 Report, business case, champion, change management, deliverables, implementation, lean sigma, lean thinking, New Product Development (NPD), post-project review, program, program management office, project management, RACI Matrix, scope creep, scoping, sponsor, stage-gate process, stakeholder, stakeholder analysis, Subject Matter Expert (SME).*

Project Evaluation and Review Technique (PERT) – A project planning and scheduling method developed by the U.S. Navy for the Polaris submarine project.

In its original form, PERT required each task to have three task time estimates: the optimistic task time (a), the most likely task time (m), and the pessimistic task time (b) (Malcolm, Roseboom, Clark, & Fazar, 1959). The **expected task time** is then estimated as $E(T) = (a + 4m + b)/6$ and the **task time variance** as $V(T) = (b - a)^2/36$. These equations were supposedly based on the beta distribution. Sasieni (1986) asserts that these equations have little scientific basis, but Littlefield and Randolph (1987) attempt to refute Sasieni's assertions. In this author's view, Sasieni was probably closer to the truth on this issue.

The expected critical path time is estimated by adding the expected times for the tasks along the critical path; similarly, the variance of the critical path time is estimated by adding the variances along the critical path. The earliest and latest project completion time are then estimated as the expected critical path time plus or minus z standard deviations of the critical path time.

This approach assumes that (1) the distribution of the project completion time is determined only by the critical path time (i.e., that no other path could become critical), (2) the project completion time is normally distributed, and (3) the equations for the mean and variance are correct. In reality, these assumptions are almost always incorrect. Few organizations find that the three-task time approach is worth the time, confusion, or cost.

See *beta distribution, critical chain, Critical Path Method (CPM), project management, slack time, work breakdown structure (WBS).*

project hopper – A simple tool that helps a process improvement program leader (champion) manage the set of current and potential projects.

The project hopper is a tool used to help store and prioritize potential process improvement projects. This is usually done with an Excel workbook. Ecolab and other firms prioritize potential projects based on two dimensions: (1) benefits (sales growth, cost reduction, improved service) and (2) effort (cost, resources, time to achieve benefits). Ecolab graphs each project on these two dimensions and uses that information as a visual tool to help managers prioritize potential projects[49]. Preliminary project charters are then written for the most

---

[49] *The is from a private conversation with Cathy Clements, former Vice President, Fueling the Future, Ecolab, in 2007.*

promising projects, and then the benefit and cost assessment is performed one more time to select which projects to charter, resource, and initiate.

See *lean sigma, process improvement program, program management office.*

project management – The planning, organizing, scheduling, directing, and controlling of a one-time activity to meet stakeholder-defined goals and constraints on scope, schedule, and cost. ✪

According to the Project Management Institute's ***Project Management Body of Knowledge*** (PMBOK 1996, p. 167), "A project is a temporary endeavor undertaken to create a unique product or service."

Key success factors for project management include conducting a careful **stakeholder analysis**, creating a clear **project charter** with well-defined roles and responsibilities (using the **RACI Matrix**), assigning a strong project leader, avoiding **scope creep**, and finally conducting a careful **post-project review** (also called a post-mortem review) so the organization learns from its project management mistakes and successes.

Well-managed projects also make proper trade-offs between the goals of time, cost, and scope (as illustrated by the **project management triangle**). The project management triangle emphasizes the point that all projects require trade-offs between scope (quality), cost, and time. See the *project management triangle* entry.

In most cases, the ideal project team will not have more than five or six members. If additional expertise is needed, Subject Matter Experts (SMEs) can assist the team, but need not be on the team. SMEs should be listed in the project charter. The project should have one or more clearly defined sponsors who have signed the charter.

This author has collected and adapted the following list of pessimistic project management "laws" (with a little humor) over many years. Of course, well-managed organizations do not have to be victims of these laws.

- **Murphy's Law:** If it can go wrong, it will.
- **Second Law of Thermodynamics (Law of Entropy):** All systems tend toward their highest state of disorder. (Murphy's Law is an application of this law.)
- **Parkinson's Law:** Work expands to fill the time allotted to it. (Parkinson's exact wording was "Work expands so as to fill the time available for its completion.") This is only one of many laws found in his book (Parkinson 1958).
- **The Pi Rule:** Poorly managed projects take pi ($\pi \approx 3.1416$.) times longer than originally planned. People tend to think that the path is across the diameter of the circle, when it is in fact the entire circumference.
- **The optimistic time estimate law:** Projects rarely do what was promised and are rarely completed on time, within budget, or with the same staff that started them. **Corollary a:** It is highly unlikely that your project will be the first exception. **Corollary b:** A carelessly planned project will take $\pi \approx 3.1416$ times longer to complete than expected, and a carefully planned project will take only $e \approx 2.7183$ times as long. **Corollary c:** When the project is going well, something will go wrong. **Corollary d:** When things cannot get any worse, they will. **Corollary e:** When things appear to be going better, you have overlooked something.
- **The last 10 percent law:** Projects progress rapidly until they are 90 percent complete. The last 10 percent takes about 50 percent of the time.
- **Brooke's Law:** Adding people to a late project generally makes it later.
- **The project employment law:** A project requiring more than 18 months tends to lose its identity as a project and becomes a permanent part of the organization. **Corollary:** If the project objectives are allowed to change freely, the team might unintentionally turn the project into guaranteed long-term employment.
- **The project charter law:** A project without a clearly written charter will experience scope creep and will help stakeholders discover their organization's worst political problems.
- **The project correction law:** The effort required to correct a project that is off course increases every day it is allowed to continue off course.
- **The matrix organization law:** Matrix organizations tend to be dysfunctional. All employees really have only one boss and that is the person who makes their next salary decision. (However, matrix organizations are essential in the modern firm, particularly for project management.)
- **The project leader law:** A great way to sabotage an important project is to assign whoever is completely available as the project leader.
- **The technical leadership law:** The greater the project's scope and organizational complexity, the less likely a technician is needed to manage it. **Corollary:** Get the best project manager who can be found. A good project manager will find the right technical people for the project.

- **The belief in the system law:** If the user does not believe in the system, a parallel informal system will be developed, and neither will work very well.
- **The post-project review law:** Organizations that do not have a disciplined post-project review process are doomed to repeat their mistakes over and over again.

Project Management Institute's ***Project Management Body of Knowledge*** (PMBOK) is the accepted standard for project management practices. Another source of project management knowledge is the ***Automotive Project Management Guide*** published by AIAG (Automotive Industry Action Group, www.aiag.org). AIAG publishes a set of books used by Ford, GM, and others for managing automotive projects and suppliers. Brown and Hyer (2009) wrote a good project management book entitled ***Managing Projects: A Team-Based Approach***.

See *6Ps, change management, co-location, committee, co-opt, critical chain, critical path, Critical Path Method (CPM), cross-functional team, Design Structure Matrix (DSM), Earned Value Management (EVM), facility layout, finite scheduling, forming-storming-norming-performing model, Gantt Chart, groupware, infinite loading, issue log, just do it, load, load leveling, matrix organization, milestone, Murphy's Law, New Product Development (NPD), Parkinson's Laws, post-project review, process improvement program, program, program management office, project charter, Project Evaluation and Review Technique (PERT), Project Management Institute (PMI), project management triangle, project network, scope creep, scoping, slack time, sponsor, stage-gate process, stakeholder, stakeholder analysis, steering committee, Subject Matter Expert (SME), waterfall scheduling, work breakdown structure (WBS).*

Project Management Institute (PMI) – The leading association for the project management profession.

Founded in 1969, PMI is one of the world's largest professional membership associations, with a half million members and credential holders in more than 180 countries. It is a not-for-profit organization that advances the project management profession through globally recognized standards and certifications, collaborative communities, an extensive research program, and professional development opportunities. PMI's Project Management Professional certification is the most widely recognized in the profession.

The latest version of PMI's ***A Guide to the Project Management Body of Knowledge*** can be purchased from the PMI website (www.pmi.org).

See *operations management (OM), project management.*

project management office – See *program management office.*

project management triangle – A graphic used to emphasize that projects require trade-offs between time, cost, and scope and that the project sponsor can usually only control two of these; also called the project triangle and the triple constraint.

The graphic on the right shows the three goals of most projects – time, cost, and scope. Scope is sometimes replaced by quality or features.

One humorous way to use this tool is to fold a piece of paper into a triangle and hand it to the project sponsor or user. The sponsor will invariably take it with two hands and grasp two sides. The point is then made that the sponsor can control two sides, but the third side must be under control of the project team.

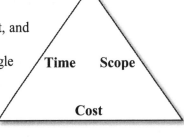

See *project management, scope creep, sponsor.*

project network – A database that shows the predecessor/successor relationships between the pairs of activities required to complete a project.

For the pair A → B, activity A is called the predecessor and B the successor. A predecessor activity usually needs to be completed before the successor can be started. However, four possible types of logical relationships are possible in most modern project management software packages:
- Finish-to-start – The "from" activity must finish before the "to" activity may start.
- Finish-to-finish – The "from" activity must finish before the "to" activity may finish.
- Start-to-start – The "from" activity must start before the "to" activity may start.
- Start-to-finish – The "from" activity must start before the "to" activity may finish.

See *Critical Path Method (CPM), mindmap, project management, slack time.*

project team – See *project management.*

promotion – (1) Marketing communications used in the marketplace (e.g., advertisements). (2) A temporary price reduction often accompanied by advertising.

Promotion is one of the four "P's" of the marketing mix (product, price, place, and promotion). Everyday low pricing (EDLP) avoids price reductions and encourages customers to reduce forward buying and stabilize demand.

See *forward buy*.

prospective validation – See *process validation*.

prototype – In the product development context, an example built for evaluation purposes.

A prototype is a trial model used for evaluation purposes or a standard for subsequent units produced. Prototypes are often built quickly to help users evaluate features and capabilities. In the software development context, prototyping is particularly important for getting user input before the final design is implemented. Prototyping is closely related to the software development concept of agile design.

A **beta test** is the test of new software by a user under actual work conditions and is the final test before the software is released. In contrast, an **alpha test** is the first test conducted by the developer in test conditions.

See *agile software development, beta test, breadboard, catchball, New Product Development (NPD), pilot test, scrum, sprint burndown chart*.

pseudo bill of material – See *bill of material (BOM)*.

public warehouse – See *warehouse*.

public-private partnership – A form of cooperation between government and private enterprise with the goal of providing a service to society through both private for-profit and not-for-profit organizations.

For example, PPL (http://www.pplindustries.org) is a public-private partnership in the city of Minneapolis, Minnesota, that has served Hennepin County for more than thirty years. The mission of PPL is to "work with lower-income individuals and families to achieve greater self-sufficiency through housing, employment training, support services, and education." One of PPL's main divisions is called "PPL Industries Disassembly and Reclamation," which employs hundreds of ex-convicts to disassemble tens of thousands of electronic products, such as televisions, stereos, telephones, VCRs, and computers collected by Hennepin County each year. This service provides value to society by giving jobs and job training to just-released convicts, and it also helps protect the environment.

See *triple bottom line*.

Pugh Matrix – A decision tool that facilitates a disciplined, team-based process for concept generation, evaluation, and selection.

The Pugh Matrix is a scoring matrix that defines the important criteria for a decision, defines the weights for each criterion, defines the alternatives, and then scores each alternative. The selection is made based on the consolidated scores. The Pugh Matrix allows an organization to compare different concepts, create strong alternative concepts from weaker concepts, and arrive at the best concept, which may be a variant of other concepts. This tool is very similar to the Kepner-Tregoe Model.

Several concepts are evaluated according to their strengths and weaknesses against a reference concept called the datum (base concept), which is the best current concept at each iteration of the methodology. The Pugh Matrix encourages comparison of several different concepts against a base concept, creating stronger concepts and eliminating weaker ones until an optimal concept is finally reached.

See *Analytic Hierarchy Process (AHP), decision tree, Design for Six Sigma (DFSS), force field analysis, Kano Analysis, Kepner-Tregoe Model, lean sigma, New Product Development (NPD), Quality Function Deployment (QFD), TRIZ, voice of the customer (VOC)*.

pull system – A system that determines how much to order and when to order in response to customer demand, where the customer may be either an internal or external customer. ✪

All production and inventory control systems deal with two fundamental decision variables: (1) when to order, and (2) how much to order. It is easiest to understand "push" and "pull" systems for managing these two variables in a logistics context. Suppose, for example, a factory supplies two warehouses. With a push system, the people at the factory decide when and how much to ship to each of the two warehouses based on forecasted demand and inventory position information. With a pull system, the problem is disaggregated so the people at each warehouse decide when and how much to order from the factory based on their needs. Of course, the factory might not have the inventory, so some of these orders might not be filled.

The following table compares push and pull systems.

A comparison of push and pull systems

Dimension	Push	Pull
Signal to produce more	Schedule or plan	Customer signal
Timing of signal	Advance of the need	At the time of the need
Typical signal	Paper or computer	Container, square, cart, or paper
Information scope	Global	Local only
Planning horizon	Fairly long	Very short
Level demand needed	No	Generally yes
Standard parts/products	Not necessary	Generally necessary
Large queues possible	Yes	No
Negatives	Too much inventory Not visual Requires more information Long planned leadtimes	No planning Misses customer demand at the beginning of the product life cycle and too much inventory at the end
Best for	Non-repetitive, batch, seasonal demand, short product life cycles Long leadtime purchasing	Repetitive, high-volume manufacturing, with stable demand
Visibility	Not visible	Visible
Stress to improve	Little	Much
Problems found from	Computer reports	Shop floor/visible signals

Source: Professor Arthur V. Hill

Hopp and Spearman (2004) provide a different perspective in their comparison of push and pull systems. They define a pull system as one that limits the amount of work in process that can be in the system and a push system as one that has no limit on the amount of work in process that can be in the system. They argue further that the definition of push and pull is largely independent of the make to order/make to stock decision.

See *CONWIP, inventory management, kanban, lean thinking, push-pull boundary, repetitive manufacturing, standard parts, two-bin system, warehouse.*

purchase order (PO) – A commercial document (or electronic communication) that requests materials or services; often abbreviated PO or P.O. ✪

Purchase orders usually specify the quantity, price, and terms for the purchase. A purchase order may request many different items, with each item having a separate "line."

See *Accounts Receivable (A/R), blanket purchase order, buyer/planner, Electronic Data Interchange (EDI), interplant order, invoice, leadtime, lotsizing methods, manufacturing order, Materials Requirements Planning (MRP), planned order, purchasing, requisition, service level, supplier.*

purchasing – The business function (department) responsible for selecting suppliers, negotiating contracts, and ensuring the reliable supply of materials; also known as procurement, supply management, supplier management, supplier development, strategic sourcing, and buying. ✪

The goals of a purchasing organization are usually defined in terms of on-time delivery, quality, and cost. Some purchasing organizations, particularly in the larger firms, also get involved helping their suppliers improve their performance. The *sourcing, supplier scorecard,* and *spend analysis* entries have much more information on this topic.

Purchasing practices in the U.S. are constrained by a number of important laws. Bribery, kickbacks, price fixing, and GATT rules are important issues for purchasing managers. See the *antitrust law* and *GATT* entries for more details.

See *Accounts Receivable (A/R), acquisition, antitrust laws, bill of lading, blanket purchase order, bribery, business process outsourcing, buy-back contract, buyer/planner, commodity, due diligence, Electronic Data Interchange (EDI), e-procurement, fixed price contract, forward buy, futures contract, General Agreement on Tariffs and Trade (GATT), Institute for Supply Management (ISM), inventory management, invoice, joint replenishment, leadtime, leverage the spend, logistics, Maintenance-Repair-Operations (MRO), materials management, Materials Requirements Planning (MRP), newsvendor model, outsourcing, price fixing, purchase order (PO), purchasing leadtime, reconciliation, Request for Proposal (RFP), requisition, reverse auction, right of first refusal, risk sharing contract, service level, single source, sourcing, spend analysis, supplier, supplier qualification and certification, supplier scorecard, supply chain management, tier 1 supplier, total cost of ownership, transfer price, vendor managed inventory (VMI).*

purchasing leadtime – The time between the release and receipt of a purchase order from a supplier; also known as purchase leadtime and replenishment leadtime.

The purchasing leadtime parameter in a Materials Requirements Planning (MRP) system should be the **planned purchasing leadtime**, which should be set to the average actual value. Safety stock and safety leadtime is then used to handle variability in the demand during the replenishment leadtime.

See *cycle time, leadtime, purchasing, safety leadtime, safety stock.*

push system – See *pull system.*

pushback – Active or passive resistance to an idea or new way of doing things.

This term is often used in the context of organization change. For example, when consultants states that they are getting "pushback on a proposal," it means the organization is resisting proposed changes.

See *stakeholder analysis.*

push-pull boundary – The point at which a supply chain (or firm) switches from building to forecast (push) to building to an actual customer order (pull); Hopp (2007) calls this the inventory/order (I/O) interface; Schroeder (2008) calls this the customization point; others call it the order penetration point, decoupling point, or customization process decoupling point.

The push-pull boundary is the point at which the customer order enters the system. For example, with an **assemble to order (ATO)** system, the point of entry is just before the final assembly. ATO systems, therefore, generally use a longer-term **Master Production Schedule (MPS)** to plan inventory for all major components, fasteners, etc., and a **Final Assembly Schedule (FAS)** to schedule the production of specific orders.

Moving the push-pull boundary to a point earlier in the process allows firms to be more responsive to customer demand and avoid mismatches in supply and demand. However, the customer leadtime will usually get longer. The push-pull boundary is closely related to **postponement** (postponed differentiation) and has strategic implications. See the *postponement* and *Respond-to-Order* entries for more detailed information.

One of the most successful examples of a firm moving the push-pull boundary for competitive advantage is Dell Computer, which assembles computers in response to customer orders. In contrast, many of Dell's competitors (e.g., Compaq Computer) built to finished inventory, sometimes with disastrous business results. By moving from MTS to ATO, Dell was able to reduce finished goods inventory and provide a more customized product. However, more recently, computers have become more of a commodity, which means that customization is less important. In response, Dell is now building standard computer to stock (MTS) and selling them through Best Buy.

See *cumulative leadtime, customer leadtime, Final Assembly Schedule (FAS), leadtime, make to order (MTO), make to stock (MTS), mass customization, Master Production Schedule (MPS), operations strategy, postponement, pull system, respond to order (RTO).*

put away – See *slotting.*

Pythagorean Theorem – In any right triangle, the area of the square with side c (the hypotenuse) is equal to the sum of the areas of squares with sides a and b; the Pythagorean equation is $c^2 = a^2 + b^2$.

See *cluster analysis, Minkowski distance metric, numeric-analytic location model.*

Q

QFD – See *Quality Function Deployment.*

QR – See *Quick Response.*

QRM – See *Quick Response Manufacturing.*

QS 9000 – A supplier development program developed by a Chrysler/Ford/General Motors supplier requirement task force.

The purpose of QS 9000 is to provide a common standard and a set of procedures for the suppliers of the three companies.

See *quality management*.

quadratic formula – A basic algebra approach for finding the roots of a second order polynomial of the form $y = ax^2 + bx + c = 0$.

The quadratic formula is $x = (-b \pm \sqrt{b^2 - 4ac})/(2a)$. For example, the roots (solution) of the equation $y = x^2 + 3x - 4 = 0$ are $x = -4$ and 1, which means that the graph of the equation crosses the x-axis (i.e., when $y = 0$) at both $x = -4$ and $x = 1$.

qualification – See *supplier qualification and certification*.

qualitative forecasting – See *forecasting*.

quality – See *quality management*.

quality assurance – The process of ensuring that products and services meet required standards.

Quality assurance is built on the following basic principles: (1) quality, safety, and effectiveness must be designed into the product, (2) quality cannot be inspected or tested into the product, (3) each step of the manufacturing process should be controlled to maximize the probability that the finished product meets all specifications, (4) humans tend to be unreliable at the inspection process, and (5) it is important to find the critical few points for inspection. Process validation is a key element in assuring that quality assurance goals are met.

See *process validation, quality management, Statistical Process Control (SPC), Statistical Quality Control (SQC)*.

quality at the source – The quality management philosophy that workers should be responsible for their own work and should perform needed inspections before passing their work on to others.

Quality at the source is an application of the **early detection of defects** philosophy to ensure that every step of a process only passes along perfect conformance quality to the next step. The opposite of this philosophy is to try to "inspect quality in" at the end of the process.

People who do the work should be responsible for ensuring their own conformance quality. This concept is often called **self check**. Checking quality in a later step tends to encourage workers to be lazy and careless, because they know that someone else will be checking their work.

Similarly, suppliers should check their own work. A good **supplier qualification and certification** program can eliminate incoming inspection and reduce cost for both the supplier and the customer.

Similarly, data entry personnel should ensure that every number is entered properly. Data entry should not have to be inspected by someone else. One good way to achieve this goal is to have the computer system validate every data item to ensure that it has a reasonable range of values. **Automated Data Collection (ADC)** is very useful because machines are much more reliable than people for routine tasks.

See *Automated Data Collection (ADC), conformance quality, early detection, inspection, quality management, supplier qualification and certification*.

quality circles – A small group of volunteers who meet to identify, analyze, and improve their processes and workplace environment.

Typical discussion topics include safety, product design, and process improvement. Unlike many process improvement teams, quality circles remain intact over time. Quality circles were popular in the 1980s and early 1990s in North America, but then fell out of favor.

See *brainstorming, quality management*.

Quality Function Deployment (QFD) – A structured method for translating customer desires into the design specifications of a product; also known as "house of quality," because the drawing often looks like a house. ✪

QFD uses cross-functional teams from manufacturing, engineering, marketing, and sourcing. The process begins with market research and other voice of the customer (VOC) tools to define current and future customer needs and then categorize them into customer requirements. Requirements are then prioritized based on their importance to the customer. Conjoint analysis can help with this process. QFD then compares product and product attributes in the competitive marketplace with respect to competitor market positions and demographics.

The four phases of QFD are:

Phase 1. Product planning using QFD – (1) Define and prioritize customer needs, (2) analyze competitive opportunities, (3) plan a product to respond to needs and opportunities, and (4) establish critical characteristic target values.

Phase 2. Assembly/part deployment – (1) Identify critical parts and assemblies, (2) identify critical product characteristics, and (3) translate into critical part/assembly characteristics and target values.

Phase 3. Process planning – (1) Determine critical processes and process flow, (2) develop production equipment requirements, and (3) establish critical process parameters.

Phase 4. Process/quality control – (1) Determine part and processes characteristics, (2) establish process control methods and parameters, and (3) establish inspection and test methods and parameters.

See *affinity diagram, concurrent engineering, conjoint analysis, cross-functional team, New Product Development (NPD), Pugh Matrix, quality management, voice of the customer (VOC)*.

quality management – The discipline that focuses on measuring and improving product and service performance and conformance to specifications. ✪

Quality is somewhat difficult to define. The standard textbook definitions include fitness for use, conformance to customer requirements, and conformance to specifications. Many sources begin with Garvin's eight dimensions of product quality (Garvin 1987):

- **Performance** – Measurable primary operating characteristics. Examples: Auto acceleration, TV reception.
- **Features** – Attributes available. Examples: Free drinks on airplanes, automatic tuners on a TV.
- **Reliability** – Probability that a product will malfunction within a given time period. Often measured by the Mean Time Between Failure (MTBF).
- **Conformance** – Degree to which a product meets established standards. Example: Many of the Japanese cars imported to the U.S. in the 1970s were good in conformance but not in durability.
- **Durability** – Measure of product life (until replacement)[50].
- **Serviceability** – Speed, courtesy, competence, and ease of repair. Measured by mean response time and Mean Time to Repair (MTTR).
- **Aesthetics** – Appeal of the product's look, feel, sound, taste, or smell based on personal judgment.
- **Perceived quality** – Reputation, indirect method of comparing products. Example: Sony (San Diego, California) and Honda (Marysville, Ohio) are reluctant to tell customers their products are made in the U.S.

The **cost of quality** is an important framework for understanding quality (Feigenbaum 1983). This concept is summarized briefly below. (See the *cost of quality* entry for more detail.)

- **Prevention costs** – Costs associated with designing products to be more robust (using design for manufacturing tools) and with preventing process problems from occurring (through error proofing).
- **Appraisal costs** – Costs related to inspection and testing.
- **Internal failure costs** – Costs associated with scrap (wasted materials), rework, repair, wasted capacity, and the opportunity cost of lost sales.
- **External failure costs** – Costs associated with lawsuits, returns, lost customer goodwill, complaint handling, and customer recovery, including the net present value of all future lost profit due to quality problems.

Another major concept in quality is the difference between **conformance quality** and **design quality** (also called performance quality). Conformance quality is simply the percentage of products that meet the product specifications and can be measured as a yield rate, first-pass yield, etc. In contrast, product design quality has to do with the design specifications. It is possible for a simple cheap product to have perfect conformance quality, but low design quality. Conversely, it is possible for a product to have a superior design (in terms of features and intended performance), but have poor conformance quality.

Quality control can be broken into two types: **Process control**, which asks "Is this process performing normally?" and **lot control** (acceptance sampling), which asks "Is this lot (batch) acceptable?"

---

[50] *In Garvin's framework, reliability and durability are practically synonymous.*

Inspection can be done by **variables** (using tools, such as the x-bar or r-chart) or by **attributes** (using tools, such as the p-chart or the c-chart). Inspection by variables is usually for process control; inspection by attributes is usually for lot control.

Basic quality principles include:

- Do not try to inspect quality into a product.
- Strive for quality at the source.
- Inspect before the bottleneck. (Take care of "golden parts" that have gone through the bottleneck.)
- Most defects are the result of management error.
- Human inspectors rarely detect more than 50-60% of defects.
- Processes have many sources of uncontrollable variation (common causes), but special (assignable) causes of variation can be recognized and controlled.

Quality management and service quality management are major themes in this encyclopedia.

See *Acceptable Quality Level (AQL), acceptance sampling, American Society for Quality (ASQ), attribute, causal map, common cause variation, conformance quality, consumer's risk, control chart, cost of quality, Critical to Quality (CTQ), defect, Defects per Million Opportunities (DPMO), Deming's 14 points, Design for Reliability (DFR), Design for Six Sigma (DFSS), durability, error proofing, Good Manufacturing Practices (GMP), goodwill, incoming inspection, inspection, ISO 14001, ISO 9001:2008, lean sigma, Lot Tolerance Percent Defective (LTPD), Malcolm Baldrige National Quality Award (MBNQA), operating characteristic curve, PDCA (Plan-Do-Check-Act), producer's risk, product design quality, QS 9000, quality assurance, quality at the source, quality circles, Quality Function Deployment (QFD), quality trilogy, reliability, service quality, seven tools of quality, special cause variation, stakeholder analysis, Statistical Process Control (SPC), Statistical Quality Control (SQC), supplier qualification and certification, tampering, Total Quality Management (TQM), TS 16949 quality standard, voice of the customer (VOC), yield, zero defects.*

quality trilogy – A concept promoted by Joseph Juran and the Juran Institute stating that quality consists of three basic quality-oriented processes: quality planning, quality control, and quality improvement.

Juran (1986) expanded on these three processes using the following guidelines:

Quality planning

• Identify both internal and external customers.	• Develop a process that can produce the needed product features.
• Determine customer needs.	
• Develop product features that correspond to customer needs. (Products include both goods and services.)	• Prove process capability (prove that the process can meet the quality goals under operating conditions).
• Establish quality goals that meet the needs of customers and suppliers alike, and do so at a minimum combined cost.	

Quality control

• Choose control subjects and what to control.	• Measure actual performance.
• Choose units of measurement.	• Interpret the difference (actual versus standard).
• Establish measurement.	
• Establish standards of performance.	• Take action on the difference.

Quality improvement

• Prove the need for improvement.	• Provide remedies.
• Identify specific projects for improvement.	• Prove that the remedies are effective under operating conditions.
• Organize to guide the projects.	
• Organize for diagnosis for discovery of causes.	• Provide for control to hold the gains.
• Diagnose to find the causes.	

See *lean sigma, quality management, Total Quality Management (TQM).*

quantitative forecasting methods – See *forecasting.*

quantity discount – A pricing mechanism that offers customers a lower price per unit when they buy more units.

Sellers often offer a lower price to customers when customers order in larger quantities. The difference between the normal price and the reduced price is called a price discount. Two policies are common in practice: the incremental units discount and the all-units discount.

The **incremental units discount policy** gives the customer a lower price only on units ordered above a breakpoint. For example, if a seller has a price breakpoint at 100 units and a customer orders 120 units, the price for the first 100 units is $10 and the price for the last 20 units is $9, for a total price of $1180.

In contrast, the **all-units discount policy** offers a lower price on *all* units ordered. For example, if a seller has a price breakpoint at 100 units and a customer orders 120 units, the price for all 120 units is lowered from $10 to $9, for a total price of $1080. With both policies, the optimal (minimum total cost) order quantity will always be at one of the price breakpoints (where the price changes) or at a feasible EOQ.

See *blanket purchase order, bullwhip effect, carrying cost, commonality, Economic Order Quantity (EOQ), less than truck load (LTL), risk sharing contract.*

quantity flexible contracts – See *risk sharing contracts.*

queue – See *waiting line.*

queue time – See *wait time.*

queuing theory – A branch of mathematics that deals with understanding systems with customers (orders, calls, etc.) arriving and being served by one or more servers; also known as queueing theory[51], waiting line theory, and stochastic processes. ✪

Managers and engineers often need to make important decisions about how much capacity to have, how many lines to have, and where to invest in process improvement. Intuition around these decisions is often wrong, and computer simulation is often too expensive to be of practical value. Queuing theory can give managers:

- A **powerful language** for describing systems with waiting lines (queues).
- Practical **managerial insights** that are critical to understanding many types of operations.
- Computationally fast **analytical tools** that can be implemented in Excel and used to help managers

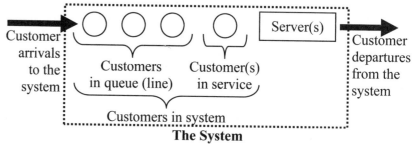

and engineers answer a wide variety of important "what-if" questions. For example, queuing models can help answer questions such as, "What would happen to our average waiting time if we added a server?"

Nearly all queuing theory models assume that the mean service rate and the mean arrival rate do not change over time. These models then evaluate the steady state (long-term) system performance with statistics, such as utilization, mean time in queue, mean time in system, mean number in queue, and mean number in system. Unfortunately, queuing models are often limited by the required assumptions that the mean arrival rate and mean service rate do not change over time; therefore, most queuing models are only approximations of the real world.

Customers arriving to the system can be people, orders, phone calls, ambulances, etc. The server (or servers) in the system can be machines, people, buildings, etc. Customers often spend time waiting in queue before they begin service. The customer's time in system is the sum of their waiting time in queue and their service time. The mean service (processing) time is the inverse of the mean service rate (i.e., $p = 1/\mu$ and $\mu = 1/p$) and the mean time between arrivals is the inverse of the mean arrival rate (i.e., $a = 1/\lambda$). Utilization is the percentage of the time that the servers are busy (i.e., $\rho = \lambda/\mu = p/a$).

One of the fundamental managerial insights from queuing theory is that the relationship between utilization and the mean time in system is highly non-linear. The graph below shows this relationship with commonly used assumptions. This particular graph has a mean arrival rate of $\lambda = 100$ customers per hour and one server with a mean service rate of $\mu = \lambda/\rho$ customers per hour, where ρ is the utilization. However, the shape of the graph is similar no matter which parameters are used. The practical implication of this insight is that managers who seek to maximize utilization might find themselves dramatically increasing the mean time in system, which might mean very long customer waiting times, poor service, and high inventory.

---

[51] *Both spellings "queuing" and "queueing" are found in the literature. It is not clear which one is preferred.*

The most basic queuing model has a single server ($s = 1$) and requires three assumptions: (1) the time between arrivals follows the negative exponential distribution, (2) service times also follow the negative exponential distribution, and (3) the service discipline is first-come-first-served. (Note: The negative exponential distribution is often called the exponential distribution.) The model also assumes that all parameters are stationary, which means that the mean arrival rate and mean service rate do not change over time and are not affected by the state of the system (i.e., a long waiting line will not affect the arrival rate). This model is known as the M/M/1 queue. The first "M" notation indicates that the arrival process is Markovian. The second "M" indicates that the service process is also **Markovian**. The "1" indicates that the system has one server. A Markovian arrival process has interarrival times that follow the exponential distribution. A Markovian service process has service times that also follow the exponential distribution. A Markovian process is also called a **Poisson process**.

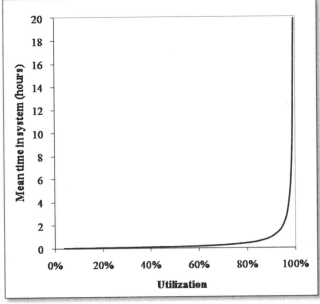

Define μ (mu) as the mean service rate (customers/period) and λ (lambda) as the mean arrival rate (customers/period). The steady state results for the M/M/1 queue are then:

Average utilization:	$\rho = \lambda / \mu$ (Note: ρ is the Greek letter "rho.")
Average time in system:	$W_s = 1 / (\mu - \lambda)$
Average time in queue:	$W_q = \rho W_s = \rho / (\mu - \lambda)$
Average number in system:	$L_s = \lambda / (\mu - \lambda)$
Average number in queue:	$L_q = \lambda^2 / (\mu(\mu - \lambda))$
Probability of n customers in system:	$P(n) = (1 - \rho)\rho^n$
Probability that $TIS > t$:	$P(TIS > t) = e^{-\mu(1-\rho)t}$ (TIS is the time in system.)
Probability that $TIQ > t$:	$P(TIQ > t) = \rho\, e^{-\mu(1-\rho)t}$ (TIQ is the time in queue.)
Little's Law:	$L_s = \lambda W_s$ and $L_q = \lambda W_q$

More detail and examples of Little's Law (Little 1961) can be found in the *Little's Law* entry. The *Pollaczek-Khintchine formula* entry presents the model for the M/G/1 queue, which is a Markovian (Poisson) arrival process for a single server with a general (G) service time distribution. When the number of servers is greater than one, the arrival process is not Markovian, or the service process is not Markovian, the "heavy-traffic" approximation can be used. See the *pooling* entry for an example of this model.

Erlang C formula can be used to estimate the required number of servers for a call center or any other system with random arrivals. The only two inputs to the model are the average (or forecasted) arrival rate and the average service time. The **service policy** is stated in terms of the probability $p*$ that an arriving customer will have to wait more than $t*$ time units (e.g., seconds). For example, the service policy might be that at least $p* = 90\%$ of customers will have to wait no more than $t* = 60$ seconds for a customer service representative to answer a call. This is written mathematically as $P(T \le t*) \ge p*$, where T is the waiting time for a customer, which is a random variable. Although this model has Erlang in its name, it does not use the Erlang distribution. This model is essentially the M/M/s queuing model with an exponentially distributed time between arrivals and exponentially distributed service times.

Finite population queuing models are used when the size of the calling population is small. For example, a finite queuing model should be used when the "customers" in the system are a limited number of machines in a factory. **State-dependent** queuing models are applied when the mean arrival rate or the mean service rate are dependent upon the state of the system. For example, when customers arrive to the system and see a long waiting line, they may become discouraged and exit the system.

See *balking, call center, capacity, exponential distribution, First-In-First-Out (FIFO), Last-In-First-Out (LIFO), Little's Law, operations performance metrics, Poisson distribution, Pollaczek-Khintchine formula, pooling, run time, time in system, utilization, value added ratio, wait time, what-if analysis.*

quick hit – A process improvement opportunity that can be realized without much time or effort; also called a "just do it" task and a "sure hit."

Lean sigma project teams are often able to identify and implement a number of process improvements very quickly. These improvements are often not the main focus of the project, but are additional benefits that come from the project and therefore should be included in the project report and credited to the process improvement project. These improvements often justify the entire project. Quick hits usually do not require a formal project plan or project team and can normally be done by one person in less than a day.

See *DMAIC, just do it, lean sigma.*

Quick Response (QR) – See *Quick Response Manufacturing.*

Quick Response Manufacturing – An approach for reducing leadtimes developed by Professor Rajan Suri, director of the Center of Quick Response Manufacturing, University of Wisconsin-Madison.

See *agile manufacturing, Efficient Consumer Response (ECR), lean thinking, time-based competition.*

R

RACI Chart – See *RACI Matrix.*

RACI Matrix – A matrix that identifies the roles and responsibilities for all stakeholders involved in any process; the activity of creating a before and after RACI Matrix is called responsibility charting or RACI Analysis; also called a RACI Chart, Responsibility Assignment Matrix, and Linear Responsibility Chart; RACI is pronounced *ray-see.*

When an organization is going through any type of change, it is important to identify the people involved in the process (the stakeholders) and understand how their roles and responsibilities change from the current process to the new process. The RACI Matrix can be used to ensure that all team members, managers, sponsors, and others know their roles for each step in the new process. The benefits of using the RACI Matrix include fewer misunderstandings, less time wasted in meetings, increased productivity and capacity, fewer disputes about responsibilities and authorities, and better ownership of roles and responsibilities. The RACI Matrix can also be used as the basis of a communication plan before the project and the control plan at the end of the project.

The matrix identifies the process steps down the left side and the individuals or functional roles on the columns across the top. For each step in the process, the matrix indicates the following roles ("decision rights") for each individual or function:

- **R = Responsible** – The person responsible for the actions and implementation of the change. Ideally, only one person is assigned to each task, and each row will have only one R cell.
- **A = Authority** – The person ultimately responsible and accountable for making sure that the task is completed. This person is ultimately answerable for the decision or activity and is usually the supervisor of the person responsible to do the task. This person has decision rights ("yes/no" authority) with respect to the important decisions. Only one person should be accountable for each task, which means that each row should have one and only one A cell. (Note: Most sources call this "Accountable." However, the terms "responsible" and "accountable" are easy to confuse. Therefore, many sources are now using the less ambiguous term "authority.")
- **C = Consulted** – This person should be consulted before, during, and after the task. This person should be "kept in the loop" with two-way communication. The rule here is "no surprises" for this critical person.
- **I = Informed** – This person should be informed when the task is completed. This person should be "kept in the picture" with one-way communication.

Many organizations add the letter "S" for the people who provide support for the responsible (R) role. The acronym for this form is RASCI and is pronounced *ras-see*. Some organizations assign colors based on the letter in the cell.

The project team has its own project RACI Matrix, and the process has both a before ("as is") and after ("should-be") RACI Matrix. Begin with the A for each task. Each row should have exactly one A, very few Rs, and only a few Cs and Is. Be careful that each column does not have too much work for any one individual. The *stakeholder analysis* entry discusses these issues further.

RACI Matrix wedding example

		Stakeholders			
		Bride	Groom	Mother of bride	Mother of groom
Tasks	Get wedding dress	AR		C	
	Get tuxedos	C	AR		I
	Arrange for groom's dinner	I	C	I	AR
	Arrange for church	AR	AR	I	I
	Get food for the reception dinner	A	C	R	I
	Gifts for the groomsmen	I	AR		

Source: Professor Arthur V. Hill

A simple hypothetical example of a RACI Matrix for a wedding is shown above. In this example, the bride is both responsible (R) and accountable (A) for the "get wedding dress" task. The mother is to be consulted (C) on this task, and the groom is not involved at all. The groom is both responsible and accountable for the "get tuxedos" task, and the bride is to be consulted. The "groom's dinner" task has both A and R for the mother of the groom, with others being informed or consulted.

Vertical analysis reveals that the bride has many responsibilities and raises concerns that she will be overwhelmed. This analysis suggests that she delegate some "R" tasks to others.

Horizontal analysis starts by ensuring that only one person is the authority (A) and only one person is responsible (R) for each task. This analysis finds no problems with this particular RACI Matrix.

See *change management, control plan, human resources, implementation, job design, lean sigma, organizational design, project charter, stakeholder, stakeholder analysis, workforce agility*.

rack jobber – See *wholesaler*.

Radio Frequency Identification (RFID) – The attachment of transponders to products, as an alternative to barcodes, to enable product identification using a scanner from some distance away. ✪

Transponders may be either read only or read/write. Although these technologies are generally used inside a plant, some interesting new options are now available through the Internet and even satellite technologies.

See *Automated Data Collection (ADC), barcode, Electronic Product Code (EPC), part number, Universal Product Code (UPC), warehouse, Warehouse Management System (WMS)*.

random number – A uniformly distributed value in the range (0, 1); often used in a computer simulation.

Random numbers can be generated on a computer using a **pseudo-random number generator**. These generators typically generate a recursive sequence of long integer values, where the next value in the sequence is computed from the previous value. These integers are then translated into the range (0, 1) by dividing by the largest possible integer. This is called a "pseudo" random number generator, because the values appear to be random from a statistical point of view but are not truly random.

For example, Von Neumann developed the simple, **mid-square** pseudo-random number generator in 1946. With a given seed integer, the next random integer is found by squaring the previous value and finding the middle integer value. The table below shows the sequence for the mid-square random number generator with a seed integer of 1111. The random number is the random integer divided by 10,000. The last column shows the random integer squared and uses square brackets [ ] and bold font to show the middle integer. The random integer 1111 squared is 1234321, which has a middle integer 2343, which becomes the second random integer. The third random integer is the middle integer of $(2343)^2$, which is 4896.

The initial value (the **random number seed**) uniquely identifies the entire sequence (stream) of random integers and random numbers. In other words, the entire sequence can be repeated exactly for multiple simulation experiments by using the same random number seed each time.

Although the mid-square random number generator is a good way to teach the concept of a random number generator, it has very poor cycle length (i.e., it repeats itself fairly quickly) and has poor statistical properties. In fact, the mid-square method in the example above begins to repeat every fifth value, starting with the 54th random number. As a result, the mid-square random number generator should never be used for any serious simulation analysis.

The **linear congruential random number generator** (LCG) can generate streams of millions of random numbers without repeating and also has good statistical properties vis-à-vis the runs test, serial correlation, and other tests. Law (2007) presents more details on LCGs.

Mid-square pseudo-random number generator

	Random Integer I	Random Number $r = I/10000$	I^2	Eight character text for I^2
Seed	1111	0.1111	1234321	01[2343]21
1	2343	0.2343	5489649	05[4896]49
2	4896	0.4896	23970816	23[9708]16
3	9708	0.9709	94245264	94[2452]64
4	2452	0.2452	6012304	06[0123]04
5	0123	0.0123	15129	00[0151]29

Source: Professor Arthur V. Hill

In Excel, random numbers can be generated with the formula RAND(). However, the RAND() function can return a value of zero, which causes serious problems with many cumulative distribution functions. Using interval notation, the range for RAND() is [0,1). A simple way around this problem is to use 1-RAND(), which is also a uniformly distributed random variable with range (0,1], and therefore will never return a value of zero[52].

The Excel function RANDBETWEEN(A,B) can be used to generate equally probable (uniformly distributed) random integers between A and B, including the endpoints (i.e., range [A, B]). The Excel formula A+RAND()*(B-A) can be used to generate continuous uniform values between A and B. In VBA, random numbers are generated with the Rnd() function. To generate a stream of random numbers in VBA with a user-defined random number seed, use Rnd(-1) immediately before using the Randomize[stream_number] statement.

Knüsel (2005) found that the random number generator in both Excel 2003 and Excel 2007 has a short cycle length and therefore should not be used in simulations or statistical analyses where accuracy is important. Microsoft has apparently fixed this problem in Excel 2010.

See *Erlang distribution, exponential distribution, interval notation, inverse transform method, normal distribution, random variable, runs test, simulation.*

random number generator – See *random number.*

random storage location – A warehouse policy that stores an item in one or more locations labeled with bin IDs rather than a single fixed storage location labeled with the item ID.

Storage locations in a **warehouse** can be either **fixed** or **random**. Fixed storage locations often do not work well over time, because the mix changes (items are added or removed) and the demand rates change (increase or decrease). These issues force the organization to reallocate space to the "fixed" storage locations.

A random storage location often allocates inventories to the first available location that has enough (but not too much) space. This approach will end up with most items stored in more than one location. Random storage makes better use of space and does not require that the fixed storage locations be changed; however, random storage systems require an information system to keep track of where items are stored. With random storage, it is almost impossible for people to remember where an item is stored.

Many warehouses use a combination of fixed and random storage systems. The fixed storage area is the **primary location (reserved location)** for the item, and the shelf is labeled with item ID. The primary location is the default stocking location and pick face and is used for receipts and picks for a given item. Items can be moved from random bulk storage to the fixed locations as needed.

See *fixed storage location, inventory management, locator system, picking, warehouse, Warehouse Management System (WMS), zone storage location.*

random variable – A quantity that can take on multiple values (or a continuum of values) with a probability specified by a probability distribution; also called a random variate; sometimes abbreviated RV.

Random variables can be either **discrete** (integer) or **continuous** (any real value). Discrete random variables have a **probability mass function** $p(x)$, which is the probability that random variable X equals the value x (i.e.,

---

[52] *The entry on interval notation explains the precise meaning of the brackets (, [,), and].*

$\text{Prob}(X = x) = p(x))$ and a **cumulative distribution function (CDF)**, which defines the probability that random variable X is less than or equal to the value x (i.e., $\text{Prob}(X \leq x) = F(x) = \sum_{i=-\infty}^{x} p(i)$). Continuous random variables have a **probability density function** $f(x)$ such that the cumulative distribution function (CDF) is

$$F(x) = \int_{t=-\infty}^{x} f(t)dt.$$

See *probability density function, probability distribution, random number.*

range – (1) In a statistics context: The difference between the maximum and the minimum of a set of observed values. (2) In a marketing context: The variety of products offered to a market.

In statistics, the range is a measure of the dispersion (or variability) of a random variable. The range for a sample is the difference between the highest and lowest value observations in the sample. For a normally distributed random variable, the range will be about 6σ. See the entry *interval notation* for an explanation of the mathematical notation for a range (or domain) for a variable or parameter.

In marketing, the **product range** is the variety of products offered to the market. See the *flexibility* entry.

See *box plot, interquartile range, interval notation, r-chart, standard deviation.*

Rapid Process Improvement Workshop (RPIW) – See *kaizen workshop.*

RASCI – See *RACI Matrix.*

rated capacity – See *capacity.*

ratio scale – See *scales of measurement.*

raw materials – Purchased items that are the basic inputs to a manufacturing process.

Raw materials are usually bulk or basic commodities, such as chemicals and metals, but may include commonly used parts, such as nuts, bolts, and screws. Some firms make a distinction between raw materials and purchased components, where purchased components are typically purchased assemblies or manufactured parts.

See *inventory management, part number.*

r-chart – A quality control chart that monitors the range (variability) of a process.

A sample of n parts is collected from the process every so many parts or time periods. The range (maximum minus minimum) of the sample is plotted on the control chart. If the sample range is smaller than the specification limits, the process is said to be "under control."

See *control chart, range, Statistical Process Control (SPC), Statistical Quality Control (SQC).*

reality tree – See *current reality tree.*

real-time – A adjective that describes any process that handles data immediately received rather than periodically in batches or with a delay.

See *Business Process Management (BPM), locator system, Manufacturing Execution System (MES), perpetual inventory system, Point-of-Sale (POS), Warehouse Management System (WMS).*

receiving – The organization and its supporting building space and equipment that process materials coming into a facility, such as a plant, warehouse, distribution center, or hospital.

When a shipment is received, the receiving organization verifies the contents, quality, and condition of the shipment against a purchase order, interplant order, or customer return (RMA). In some cases, extensive quality testing is done while the shipment is kept on hold. Once verified, the items are then moved either to inventory or directly to the point of use in the facility.

See *Advanced Shipping Notification (ASN), bill of lading, cross-docking, dock-to-stock, incoming inspection, materials handling, no fault receiving, Over/Short/Damaged Report, point of use, reconciliation, Return Material Authorization (RMA), supplier qualification and certification, Third Party Logistics (3PL) provider, warehouse, Warehouse Management System (WMS).*

recency effect – See *primacy effect.*

reconciliation – In the accounting/information systems context, the process of comparing two sets of records and resolving differences so the two sets are in agreement.

See *purchasing, receiving.*

red tag – A lean manufacturing practice used in the 5S "sort" step.

The term "red tag" is used as a verb to describe the process of labeling parts, tools, furniture, measurement instruments, office materials, books, magazines, scrap, etc., that are no longer needed. The term is also used as a noun for the tag placed on an item to signal that the item should be disposed and how it should be disposed (e.g., used in another location, stored, recycled, sold, or discarded).

The **sort step** in the **5S** process often finds many items in a work area that are not necessary for the job. These items might have some value, but make the work area less visible. If an item might have some value, it is **red tagged** to signal that it should be moved to the red tag area. If an item obviously has no value, it should be discarded, with special care for hazardous materials. The items in the red tag area should be reviewed regularly (e.g., every two weeks) by a cross-functional team of supervisors and engineers. Organizations often invite employees to peruse the red tag area for items they could use in their own areas or buy for their personal use. The result of a good red tag process is a more visible workplace, which is a main objective of lean thinking.

See *5S, cross-functional team, lean thinking, obsolete inventory, scrap.*

re-engineering – See *Business Process Re-engineering (BPR).*

refurb – See *refurbished.*

refurbished – Products that have been returned by the customer, disassembled, repaired, tested, and repackaged for sale; sometimes called refurb or refurbed products.

The refurbishing (**remanufacturing**) process often involves disassembly, replacement of some parts, and reassembly. In some cases, these products are marked as "refurb" products and sold at a discount with a shorter warranty. However, in some industries, refurb products are used interchangeably with new ones. Although this might seem unethical, these firms are typically using components that have a very long MTBF (Mean Time Between Failure), which means that this practice rarely affects product performance.

See *remanufacturing.*

regeneration – See *Materials Requirements Planning (MRP).*

regional sourcing – See *sourcing.*

regression – See *linear regression.*

reintermediation – See *disintermediation.*

Relative Absolute Error (RAE) – A forecasting performance metric that compares the actual forecast error to the forecast error of a very simple forecasting model; defined mathematically as the mean of the absolute values of the actual forecast errors divided by mean of the absolute values of the forecast errors from a naïve (simplistic) forecasting model.

The *RAE* is the forecast error expressed as a percent of the error from a very simple forecasting model. When this ratio is close to zero, the forecasting model is good; when this ratio is greater than one, the forecasting model is worse than the naïve forecasting model.

Armstrong and Collopy (1992) proposed a simple *RAE* metric that compares the forecast errors against the absolute error of a **random walk forecast**. A random walk uses the actual demand from the previous period as the forecast for this period. The equation for the *RAE* using the random walk forecast as the basis of comparison is $RAE_{rw} = \dfrac{1}{T}\sum_{t=1}^{T}\dfrac{|E_t|}{|D_t - D_{t-1}|}$, where E_t is the forecast error in period t, D_t is the actual demand (sales) in period t,

and T is the number of values collected so far. The difference $D_t - D_{t-1}$ is the change in the demand from the last period to this period.

One problem with this approach is that when the demand is constant for two successive periods (i.e., $|D_t - D_{t-1}| = 0$), the RAE_{rw} will have a divide-by-zero problem. Also, when this difference is small, the *RAE* ratio can be very large. Collopy and Armstrong (2006) suggest "Winsorizing" (bounding) the *RAE* in each period so the ratio does not exceed some maximum value. Many authors suggest a bound of 1. For example, if the demand is 0 and the forecast error is 20 units, $|E_t| / D_t$ should be set to 1. This means that *MAPE* is defined in the range (0, 100%).

A slightly more sophisticated approach is to generate the naïve forecast with a simple exponential smoothing model where $\alpha = 0.1$. Mathematically, this is expressed as $SA_{t-1} = 0.1D_{t-1} + 0.9SA_{t-2}$, where SA_{t-1} is the smoothed average demand at the end of period $t-1$ and is used as the naïve forecast for period t. One advantage of this method is that the smoothed average will almost never be zero.

Collopy and Armstrong (2006) argue persuasively that the Mean Absolute Scaled Error (MASE) metric is better than any *RAE* metric.

See *exponential smoothing, forecast error metrics, Mean Absolute Deviation (MAD), Mean Absolute Percent Error (MAPE), Mean Absolute Scaled Error (MASE), Thiel's U, Winsorizing.*

reliability – The probability that an item will continue to function at customer expectation levels during a specified period of time under stated conditions.

Mathematically, reliability is expressed as one minus the cumulative distribution function (CDF). In other words, $R(t) = P(T > t) = \int_{s=t}^{\infty} f(s)ds$, where T is a random variable that represents the life of the product (starting at time zero) and $f(t)$ is the density function for the time to failure.

See *availability, bathtub curve, commonality, Design for Reliability (DFR), downtime, maintenance, Mean Time Between Failure (MTBF), metrology, New Product Development (NPD), probability density function, quality management, reliability engineering, Total Productive Maintenance (TPM).*

reliability engineering – An engineering field and function that deals with the ability of a system, machine, product, or component to perform required tasks under stated conditions for a specified period of time.

Reliability engineering practices include the design, specification, assessment, and achievement of product or system reliability requirements. This involves aspects of prediction, evaluation, production, and demonstration.

See *maintenance, reliability, Total Productive Maintenance (TPM).*

Reliability-Centered Maintenance (RCM) – A maintenance approach that prioritizes machines and maintenance activities to increase system reliability.

The seven basic questions for RCM are:
1. What are the functions and associated performance standards of the asset in its present operating context?
2. In what ways does it fail to fulfill its functions?
3. What causes each functional failure?
4. What happens when each failure occurs?
5. In what way does each failure matter?
6. What can be done to predict or prevent each failure?
7. What should be done if a suitable proactive task cannot be found?

RCM emphasizes the use of predictive maintenance techniques in addition to traditional preventive measures. A well-run RCM program focuses scarce economic resources on the assets that would cause the most disruption if they were to fail.

See *maintenance, Total Productive Maintenance (TPM).*

remanufacturing – The process of repairing, refurbishing, or disassembling products into reusable components.

Remanufacturing often involves breaking a product down into modules, disposing of modules, replacing those that cannot be refurbished, repairing those that can, and then reassembling and testing the product. Remanufacturing is being driven by both economic and environmental interests. In some countries, remanufacturing is required by law. Examples of products that are often remanufactured include aircraft engines (Chua, Scudder, & Hill 1993), diesel engines, and other expensive equipment.

See *Design for Disassembly, green manufacturing, refurbished (refurb), reverse logistics.*

reorder point – An inventory management policy that orders more inventory when the inventory position hits a critical level called the reorder point; also called an order point system. ✪

The graph below shows the reorder point system through two order cycles. Whenever the inventory position (on-hand plus on-order minus allocated) goes below the reorder point, a new order is placed.

Reorder point system

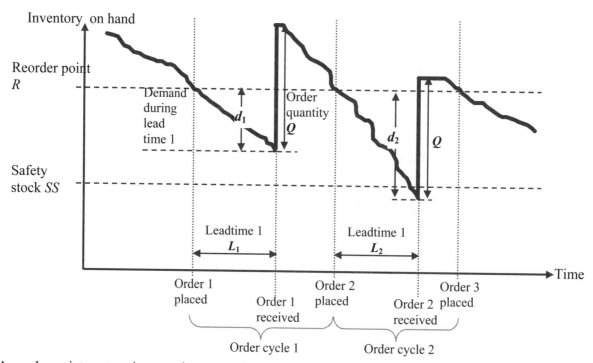

An order point system is a continuous review system, which means that it compares the inventory position with the reorder point after every transaction. The standard equation for the reorder point is $R = L\mu_D + SS$, where L is the constant planned leadtime, μ_D is the average demand per period, and SS is the safety stock in units. The safety stock is normally set to $SS = z\sqrt{L}\,\sigma_D$, where z is the safety factor, and σ_D is the standard deviation of demand per period. The *safety stock* entry explains how to select the safety factor z and the planned leadtime L to achieve a user-specified service level.

The first term of the reorder point ($L\mu_D$) is the expected (or forecasted) demand during leadtime, which could be a moving average, a simple exponentially smoothed average, or a more sophisticated forecast that also includes trend and seasonal factors. In contrast, the Time Phased Order Point (TPOP) system used in all MRP systems uses the planned requirements (consumption) from higher-level assemblies to forecast (or plan) the demand during leadtime. The second term of the reorder point is the safety stock.

See *continuous review system, demand during leadtime, exponential smoothing, inventory management, inventory position, leadtime, min-max inventory system, order cycle, order-up-to level, periodic review system, safety stock, service level, Time Phased Order Point (TPOP), two-bin system.*

repatriate – (1) To return to the country of birth, citizenship, or origin. (2) One who has been repatriated.

For example, a division of a multinational firm might need to repatriate funds to the firm's headquarters.

See *expatriate.*

repetitive manufacturing – A production process with large lotsizes (long runs) of standard products.

The term "repetitive manufacturing" is often used in the context of a pull system.

See *continuous flow, pull system.*

replenishment leadtime – See *purchasing leadtime, leadtime.*

replenishment order – A purchase or manufacturing order used to resupply an item.

See *continuous review system, demand during leadtime, fulfillment, safety stock, two-bin system, vendor managed inventory (VMI).*

repositioning – (a) Inventory context: Moving inventory to where it can better serve customers. (b) Transportation context: Moving empty ocean containers to where they will more likely be needed. (c) Marketing context: Changing the identity of a product relative to competing products.

See *backhaul, deadhead, logistics.*

request date – See *job shop scheduling, respond to order (RTO), service level.*

Request for Information (RFI) – See *Request for Proposal (RFP).*

Request for Proposal (RFP) – An invitation to prospective suppliers to submit a document that includes the price, schedule, technical specifications, and additional supporting information.

The RFP specifies the required product or service and the due date and time. RFPs request information, such as the technical specifications of the products and services, quantities, price, schedule, place of delivery, method of shipment, packaging, instruction manual requirements, data requirements, training, support, technical capabilities of the supplier, references (other customers), and financial information (so that financial stability of the supplier can be evaluated).

A well-run RFP process informs prospective suppliers about the customer's requirements, encourages them to make their best offers, collects factual proposals from a number of suppliers, and uses an objective and structured evaluation process to select the best supplier.

Similarly, many buyers submit a Request for Information (RFI) or a Request for Quotation (RFQ). An RFI is used to find suppliers that can meet the specifications. A buyer uses an RFI to discover supplier capabilities without having to reveal volume or service requirements. An RFP takes an RFI one step further by requesting that the supplier bid on specific items defined by specification, quantities, delivery locations, packaging, method of shipment, etc. An RFQ is used when a supplier is already familiar with the buyer's requirements and the focus is on price.

See *purchasing.*

Request for Quotation (RFQ) – See *Request for Proposal (RFP).*

requisition – A purchasing term for a formal request for materials or services sent from an organizational unit to the buying organization.

Requisitions are often used to replenish inventory, meet a particular customer need, conduct maintenance, acquire consulting services, or meet some other need. They usually take the form of a document or electronic record. Like purchase orders, requisitions specify a creation date, request date, requested items, and quantities; but unlike purchase orders, requisitions usually leave pricing and vendor selection to the buying organization.

See *purchase order (PO), purchasing.*

reserve storage area – A warehousing term for an area used to store inventory that is used to replenish forward pick areas; also called bulk storage, overflow storage, reserve locations, and backup storage.

See *forward pick area, picking, slotting, warehouse.*

resilience – The ability of an organization to reinvent business models and strategies as circumstances require.

A resilient organization has the power to prosper in almost any economic climate. To be resilient, organizations need management systems that facilitate innovation and experimentation. According to Hamel and Välikangas (2003, p. 62), "Battlefield commanders talk about getting inside the enemy's decision cycle. If you can retrieve, interpret, and act upon battlefield intelligence faster than your adversary you will be perpetually on the offensive, acting rather than reacting. In an analogous way, one can think about getting inside a competitor's renewal cycle. Any company that can make sense of its environment, generate strategic options, and realign its resources faster than its rivals will enjoy a decisive advantage. This is the essence of resilience. And it will prove to be the ultimate competitive advantage in the age of turbulence when companies are being challenged to change more profoundly, and more rapidly, than ever before."

They argue that managers can reduce the time to recognize the need to change a business model in three ways: (1) get first-hand evidence by visiting places where change happens first (e.g., talking to people under 18, visiting a research lab), (2) filter out the "filterers" who have a vested interest in continued ignorance, and (3) face up to the inevitability that your current strategy will decay.

See *agile manufacturing, Business Continuity Management (BCM), flexibility, robust, scalability, time-based competition.*

resource based view – A strategic point of view that firms can gain competitive advantage if and only if they have superior resources and those resources are protected by barriers to entry; sometimes called RBV.

A firm's unique combination of resources and organizational capabilities create the potential for competitive advantage to the extent to which they are valuable, rare, inimitable (hard to imitate), and non-substitutable. The resource based view holds that these resources and capabilities are the foundation of a firm's strategy, the primary source of the firm's profit, and the only stable basis of the firm's identity (Wu, Melnyk, & Flynn 2010).

See *core competence, operations strategy.*

Resource Requirements Planning (RRP) – A process used to check higher-level plans to ensure that sufficient resources are available; also called resource planning.

RRP is done at the product family/aggregate unit level before the master schedule is updated to ensure that the production plan does not exceed the available capacity.

See *Business Requirements Planning (BRP), capacity, Capacity Requirements Planning (CRP), Master Production Schedule (MPS), product family, production planning, Rough Cut Capacity Planning (RCCP), Sales & Operations Planning (S&OP).*

respond to order (RTO) – A customer interface strategy that postpones one or more value-adding activities in the supply chain until after the customer order has been received. ✪

The term "respond to order" was coined by this author to describe assemble to order (ATO), make to order (MTO), engineer to order (ETO), and other customer interface systems that support customization. The following table contrasts the make to stock (MTS) strategy with the three main RTO strategies.

RTO strategy	Concept	Inventory	Customer leadtime	Examples
Make to stock (MTS)	Standard products built to forecast and inventoried well before demand.	Large finished goods inventory. Usually also has WIP and raw materials.	Only the delivery time to get finished goods to the customer.	Medical devices, many consumer products.
Assemble to order (ATO)	Standard modules assembled in response to a customer order.	Inventory of modules. Usually also has WIP and raw materials.	Only the assembly and delivery time.	Dell computer ATO computers. Pack to order is a special case.
Make to order (MTO)	Raw materials are transformed into a final product in response to a customer order.	Usually inventories of raw materials. It is possible to implement with almost no inventory.	Fabrication, assembly, delivery, and possibly purchased raw material leadtime.	Customized clothing, injection-molded parts. Print on demand is a special case.
Engineer to order (ETO)	A design is developed and produced in response to a customer order.	Potentially no inventory. Might inventory standard components and raw materials.	Design, fabrication, assembly, and delivery time.	Custom home construction, customer circuit boards.

Source: Professor Arthur V. Hill

Similar RTO customer interface strategies include:

- Build to order (BTO) – Another name for make to order (MTO) or assemble to order (ATO). See Gunasekaran and Ngai (2005) for an article on BTO.
- Configure to order (CTO) – A customer interface strategy that adjusts parameters or adds modules to a product in response to a customer order.
- Pack to order – A customer interface strategy that collects components and packs them in a box or some other shipping container in response to a customer order.
- Print on demand – A customer interface strategy that prints books, manuals, and other materials in response to a customer order rather than creating an inventory of printed materials. This is commonly called "Print-on-Demand" in the publishing industry.

The *service level* entry presents metrics for all types of RTO strategies.

See *assemble to order (ATO), build to order (BTO), configure to order (CTO), customer leadtime, engineer to order (ETO), fabrication, flexibility, make to order (MTO), make to stock (MTS), mass customization, operations strategy, order-to-cash, pack to order, postponement, print on demand, push-pull boundary, service level, standard products.*

response time – The time between a request and the satisfaction of that request.

In the field service context, response time is usually defined as the time from the initial customer request for service until the technician appears at the customer site. In some cases, the technician might be delayed in getting to a machine after arriving at the site due to building security and walking time. Some field service organizations offer response time guarantees.

See *field service, service guarantee.*

responsibility charting – See *RACI Matrix.*

restocking charge – See *buy-back contract.*

Results-Only Work Environment (ROWE) – An employment policy co-created at Best Buy by Cali Ressler and Jodi Thompson that allows workers to choose when and where they work provided they achieve their required goals.

ROWE is a radical experiment designed to provide unparalleled freedom for employees to decide when, where, and how much they work (Ressler & Thompson, 2010). With ROWE, jobs are not defined in terms of showing up for work but rather in terms of the required outcomes. ROWE empowers individual workers to decide how they will achieve results. Workers are often not even required to attend meetings in person.

Although this program began only for salaried employees, it has been extended to hourly workers. Salaried employees are only required to work as much time as it takes to complete their goals. Hourly employees, however, have to work a set number of hours to comply with U.S. labor regulations, but they can still choose when they work.

Potential benefits of ROWE	Potential problems of ROWE
• Happier employees and greater productivity. • Greater loyalty to the company. • Lower employee turnover and less hiring expense. • Potential better work/life balance. • Better relationships with family and friends. • More focused and energized work. • More focus on results.	• Sometimes difficult to measure work outcomes. • Blurred distinction between work and personal time. • Concern that some people might be lazy. • Some people might work too much. • Potential for stress and conflict. • May be harder to manage. • Potentially less collaborative culture.

Source: Professor Arthur V. Hill

The developers' website is http://gorowe.com.

See *human resources, job design, productivity.*

retrospective validation – See *process validation.*

Return Goods Authorization (RGA) – See *Return Material Authorization (RMA).*

return logistics – See *reverse logistics.*

Return Material Authorization (RMA) – A document or electronic record provided by a supplier that gives a customer authority to return a product; also called Return Goods Authorization (RGA).

An RMA gives a customer permission to return a product for credit, repair, or disposal. The RMA gives the receiving location information about the product and instructions on how to process the return.

See *buy-back contract, receiving, return to vendor, reverse logistics.*

Return on Assets (ROA) – A financial measure of a company's after-tax profitability relative to its total assets.

ROA is calculated as (net income)/(total assets).

See *financial performance metrics.*

Return on Capital Employed (ROCE) – A measure of how effectively a firm is using its capital.

ROCE is calculated as EBIT divided by capital employed, where EBIT is earnings before interest and taxes and capital employed is total assets less current liabilities.

See *financial performance metrics.*

Return on Investment (ROI) – The rate of return of an investment over some time period.

ROI is calculated as net income divided by total assets.

See *financial performance metrics.*

Return on Net Assets (RONA) – A measure of the productivity of a company's invested capital regardless of the amount of financial leverage employed.

RONA is calculated as profit after tax divided by fixed assets plus working capital, where working capital is defined as current assets minus current liabilities.

See *DuPont Analysis, financial performance metrics*.

return to vendor – Purchased material found to be defective during receiving inspection or the production process and then designated to be returned to the supplier for credit or replacement.

For example, a regional dairy company found that some of its ice cream cartons were defective after it started the manufacturing process. The company immediately informed the carton supplier of the problem and then later charged the relevant costs to the supplier, including the cost of the cartons, the cost of the ice cream lost in the process, and the lost labor and machine capacity.

See *buy-back contract, Return Material Authorization (RMA), reverse logistics*.

revenue center – An accounting term for an area of responsibility that is only held accountable for its sales.

Revenue centers are almost always customer-facing organizations, such as the sales organization.

See *cost center, investment center, profit center*.

revenue management – See *yield management*.

revenue sharing contract – See *buy-back contract*.

reverse auction – An auction in which a buyer submits requests for quotations from suppliers for goods or services.

The buyer calls for bids for something that it needs to buy, and the suppliers quote the price and volume at which they are willing to supply the good or service.

For example, General Electric invites a group of qualified suppliers to participate in an electronic auction with a clearly defined date and product specification. At the time of the auction, participating bidders assemble at a common Internet site and bid for the General Electric contract.

See *Dutch auction, e-auction, e-business, e-procurement, purchasing, sniping*.

reverse engineering – The process of dismantling and studying a competitor's product to understand the strengths and weaknesses of the design to support the design effort for a similar product.

Reverse engineering can be used to better understand product technologies, materials, process technologies, assembly methods, and suppliers. Reverse engineering is a legal competitive strategy if the product is obtained legally and so long as no patents, trademarks, or copyrights are violated.

See *New Product Development (NPD), technology transfer*.

reverse logistics – The management of the flow of warranty returns, products, salvage, and waste from the customer back to the supplier; also called return logistics.

Reverse logistics returns materials to a manufacturer, distribution center, repair center, or disposal site to be reused, serviced, repaired, recycled, re-manufactured, or disposed. The materials can be either hazardous or non-hazardous. In some cases, firms integrate their forward and reverse logistics activities.

For example, 3M has its field service technicians manage the return of hazardous circuit boards for refurbishing or proper disposal. Likewise, Volkswagen takes back old cars to recycle and reuse some seat materials. Interest in reverse logistics is driven by both environmental concerns and cost-saving opportunities.

Many order management systems have reverse logistic modules that allow service reps to create **Return Merchandise Authorizations (RMAs)** to send to customers so items can be brought back into the retailer's supply chain and tracked appropriately.

See *distribution, field service, green manufacturing, logistics, remanufacturing, Return Material Authorization (RMA), return to vendor, upstream*.

revision control – See *version control*.

revision level – See *version control*.

rework – Any activity that attempts to fix, correct, or repair an unacceptable product or service.

In manufacturing, rework is often required to fix units that had defects in the manufacturing process. If rework cannot be done or is unsuccessful, the defective units are usually scrapped.

In the lean philosophy, rework is waste, because it adds cost, reduces capacity, takes up space, etc. Lean consultants are fond of saying that any word that starts with the letters "re" is evil. For example, readjust, reassemble, rebuild, recalibrate, recertify, recheck, recount, recreate, redo, reenter, reinstall, reopen, repack, repair, repeat, replan, reprint, resend, reset, reship, resort, restart, restate, retell, retest, retrace, return, retype, revisit, and rework are almost always wasteful. However, many "re" words are also good in operations. For example, record, recycle, redeem, reduce, refill, refine, relax, relate, remember, remove, repair, repent, replace, replenish, respect, and reuse.

See *8 wastes*, *hidden factory*, *lean thinking*, *Overall Equipment Effectiveness (OEE)*, *prevention*, *process map*, *scrap*.

RFID – See *Radio Frequency Identification (RFID)*.

RFP – See *Request for Proposal*.

Richards Curve – See *logistic curve*.

right of first refusal – A purchasing practice where a buyer's favored supplier sees bids of all other participating suppliers before announcing its own.

Elmaghraby, Goyal, and Pilehvar (2010) found that this practice has both qualitative and quantitative benefits for the buyer when the buyer has a second auction in the near future with the same participating suppliers. This outcome depends on the suppliers managing the information generated in the first auction to optimize the joint outcome of both auctions.

See *purchasing*.

risk – A source of danger.

The term "risk" is often used synonymously with "probability," but in professional risk assessments, risk takes into account both the probability of a negative event with how harmful that event might be. An event is said to be of high risk only if the probability and the impact are both high.

See http://en.wikipedia.org/wiki/Risk for a good summary on this topic.

See *Failure Mode and Effects Analysis (FMEA)*, *risk assessment*, *risk mitigation*.

risk assessment – The identification and evaluation of nearly all possible causes (modes) of failure.

For each possible failure mode, a thorough risk assessment considers (1) what can fail, (2) how likely is it to fail, and (3) the economic and social consequences of a failure. The *Failure Model and Effects Analysis (FMEA)* entry describes this process in more detail.

See *decision tree*, *Failure Mode and Effects Analysis (FMEA)*, *fault tree analysis*, *risk*, *risk management*, *risk mitigation*.

risk management – The assessment and mitigation of risk.

See *Occupational Safety and Health Administration (OSHA)*, *risk assessment*, *risk mitigation*, *safety*.

risk mitigation – Actions taken to reduce the probability or lessen the impact of an adverse event.

Ideally, risk mitigation completely prevents an adverse event. However, when total prevention is not possible, it is important to (a) reduce the probability of the event and (b) reduce the impact of the event if it does occur. Risk mitigation also planning how the recovery should be implemented.

See *error proofing*, *Failure Mode and Effects Analysis (FMEA)*, *fault tree analysis*, *risk*, *risk assessment*, *risk management*, *safety*.

risk sharing contract – An agreement between two parties to engage in a transaction where the payment is based on uncertain results.

The table on the right presents an interesting example of a risk sharing agreement (a revenue sharing agreement) between Blockbuster (a north American video rental chain) and the video manufacturers. In this example, Blockbuster pays a lower up-front charge, but gets more DVDs to rent. In exchange, the manufacturer gets a share of Blockbuster's rental revenue.

Cachon and Lariviere (2005) compared revenue sharing to a number of other supply

Video store revenue sharing (risk sharing) contract example

	Traditional	Cooperative
Number of DVDs purchased	10	30
Price per DVD	$60	$9
Purchase cost	$600	$270
Number of rentals	300	500
Total rental revenue	$900	$1500
Retailer's share of rental revenue	$900 (100%)	$750 (50%)
Retailer's profit	$300	$480
Supplier's share of rental revenue	$0 (0%)	$750 (50%)
Supplier's total revenues	$600	$1,020
Supplier's cost @$10/DVD	$100	$300
Supplier's profit	$500	$720
Total supply chain profit	$800	$1200

Adapted from Cachon and Lariviere (2001)

chain contracts, such as buy-back contracts, price-discount contracts, quantity-flexibility contracts, sales-rebate contracts, franchise contracts, and quantity discounts and found that revenue sharing is equivalent to buy-backs in the newsvendor case and equivalent to price discounts in the price-setting newsvendor case. They also identified several limitations of revenue sharing, which explain why it is not prevalent in all industries.

See *buy-back contract*, *fixed price contract*, *purchasing*, *quantity discount*, *service guarantee*, *supply chain management*.

Robinson-Patman Act – See *antitrust laws*.

robotics – The science, development, and application of self-contained, programmable, multifunctional electronic, electric, or mechanical devices called robots that can function without human intervention and can augment humans in their work.

Robots combine artificial intelligence software, mechanical manipulators, sensors, controllers, and computers to provide programmable automation. Czech writer Karel Čapek introduced the word "robot" in his play *R.U.R.* (*Rossuum's Universal Robots*) in 1921. The word "robot" comes from the Czech word "robota," which means "compulsory labor." The word was popularized by science fiction writer Isaac Asimov.

See *Artificial Intelligence (AI)*, *Automated Guided Vehicle (AGV)*, *automation*.

robust – (a) Hard to break; (b) Useful in a wide variety of situations; (c) Useful in the presence of high variation; sometimes called fault tolerant or error-proof; antonym: error-prone.

Robust design: A component or product design is said to be "robust" if it (1) can be used in a wide variety of products, (2) can be adapted to new requirements, (3) is reliable, sturdy, and almost never breaks (i.e., resilient and error resistant) in the presence of environmental variation, or (4) can be produced in the presence of variation without defects. Points (1) and (2) support **part commonality**.

Robust process: A process is said to be "robust" if it (1) can be used for a wide variety of products, (2) can adapt to new requirements, and (3) can withstand a wide variety of stresses and almost never fails (i.e., is error resistant).

See *Business Process Management (BPM)*, *commonality*, *Design of Experiments (DOE)*, *durability*, *error proofing*, *Failure Mode and Effects Analysis (FMEA)*, *maintenance*, *mass customization*, *Mean Absolute Deviation (MAD)*, *operations performance metrics*, *operations strategy*, *process*, *resilience*, *Taguchi methods*.

rolled throughput yield – See *yield*.

Root Cause Analysis (RCA) – A tool used to identify the contributors to an adverse event (or events) after the fact. ✪

Unlike **Failure Mode and Effects Analysis (FMEA)**, RCA is usually conducted after an adverse event rather than before. The purpose of RCA is to identify what caused the event and then improve the system so the problem does not reoccur. As the name implies, the goal is to track down and fix the root cause (or the system of causes) of the problem, not simply deal with the symptoms of the problem.

RCA is fundamental to all **process improvement programs**. Many tools are useful in RCA. The **5 Whys** and **Pareto analysis** are particularly useful starting points. **Causal maps**, **C&E Diagrams**, and **fishbone diagrams** go beyond the 5 Whys approach. These tools can be facilitated with a Nominal Group Technique (NGT) and affinity diagrams. If enough data is available, linear regression analysis and graphical tools, such as scatter diagrams, can often help identify the potential "problem drivers." The end result of RCA should be an action plan for fixing the system of causes of the problem.

The *causal map* entry argues that the term "root cause" can be misleading, because most problems have more than one cause. In fact, most problems have a system of causes that need to be understood, prioritized, and managed.

See *5 Whys*, *affinity diagram*, *C&E Diagram*, *causal map*, *error proofing*, *Failure Mode and Effects Analysis (FMEA)*, *fault tree analysis*, *impact wheel*, *issue tree*, *learning organization*, *Nominal Group Technique (NGT)*, *Pareto Chart*, *Pareto's Law*, *scatter diagram*, *sentinel event*, *service recovery*.

root cause tree – A causal map that begins with the undesired effect and tracks back to root causes.

A root cause tree is very closely related to causal maps, C&E Diagrams, and fault trees. Root cause trees usually put the undesired effect (the problem) at the top of the page, identify the main causes of the problem below it, and then identify the causes for each cause below that.

See *C&E Diagram*, *causal map*, *fault tree analysis*.

root mean squared error (RMSE) – See *mean squared error (MSE)*.

Rough Cut Capacity Planning (RCCP) – A process that checks if enough capacity is available to achieve a given Master Production Schedule (MPS).

The Rough Cut Capacity Planning (RCCP) process converts the **Master Production Schedule (MPS)** into a requirements plan for a few key resources using a **bill of resources**. If the required resources (the load) exceed the available resources (the capacity), production planners must find additional capacity or lower the load.

Some consultants use the term "rough cut capacity planning" to describe the process of checking the capacity for the highest-level **production plan**. However, according to the *APICS Dictionary* and other sources, **Resource Requirements Planning (RRP)** is used to compare load and capacity for the production plan (also known as the aggregate production plan), and RCCP is used to compare load and capacity for the MPS.

See *bill of resources, Business Requirements Planning (BRP), capacity, Capacity Requirements Planning (CRP), Master Production Schedule (MPS), production planning, Resource Requirements Planning (RRP), Sales & Operations Planning (S&OP)*.

routing – The sequence of manufacturing steps (operations) required to make an item.

Whereas the **bill of material (BOM)** defines which items are required to make a product, the **routing** defines the sequence of operations required to make each item (material, part number, item number, or SKU). Each operation is usually identified by a sequence number, workcenter, operation effectivity date, standard setup time, and standard run time per part. The routing information may also include tooling, special labor and machine resources, alternate routings or operations, and other specifications. Materials Requirements Planning (MRP), Capacity Resources Planning (CRP), and Manufacturing Execution Systems (MES) use routing information for planning purposes.

The **primary routing** defines the normal sequence of operations used to assemble or manufacture an item and therefore is normally used for capacity planning and standard cost estimation. The **alternate routing** is a sequence of steps used when the primary routing is not viable due to machine downtime or congestion.

See *bill of material (BOM), Capacity Requirements Planning (CRP), leadtime, Manufacturing Execution System (MES), Materials Requirements Planning (MRP), operation, run time, shop floor control, shop packet, Theory of Constraints (TOC), workcenter*.

R-squared – See *correlation, linear regression*.

RTO – See *respond to order (RTO)*.

run chart – A simple graph that displays data in time sequence; also known as a runs chart, time series graph, time series plot, trend chart, run-sequence plot, line graph, and run diagram.

The x-axis for a run chart is either time or the observation number. The y-axis is an output (performance) metric for a process. The mean or median of the performance variable is often included in the graph to show a horizontal reference line.

A run chart can be used to monitor a process to check for changes in the mean or trend and also to check for outliers. Unlike a control chart, the y variable for a run chart usually represents a single observation rather than a sample statistic (such as the mean or range of a sample) and does not show control limits.

See *control chart, outlier, scatter diagram, seven tools of quality*.

run time – The time required to produce a single part or product.

The total time for an operation is the setup time plus the batch size (lotsize) times the run time. The total time for an order is the sum of the operation times for all operations in the routing. The planned leadtime for an order should include queue time. In the queuing theory context, the average run time is called the average service time.

See *Economic Lot Scheduling Problem (ELSP), leadtime, queuing theory, routing, setup time, touch time*.

running setup – See *external setup*.

runs test – A statistical test that checks if a sequence of values is sequentially (serially) independent.

The runs test is a non-parametric statistics test used to answer questions about a time series such as:

- **Is this sequence data generated from a random process?** If the sequence is truly random, it should change directions fairly often, but not too often.

- **Is this process in control?** If a process is in control, the performance variable will have a constant mean and can be modeled as $y_t = \mu + e_t$, where y_t is the t-th observation, μ is the mean, and e_t is the error term in period t. If the sequence of errors is random, the errors should change signs fairly often, but not too often.
- **Is this model a good fit for the time series data?** If the model is a good fit for the data, the errors should be random and should change signs fairly often, but not too often.
- **Does this time series have serial correlation?** If successive values are correlated (e.g., $COR(x_t, x_{t-1}) > 0$), the time series has serial correlation and is not serially (sequentially) independent.
- **Can we assume that values from two different sources come from the same underlying population?** If we have values from two different sources (locations, firms, subpopulations), are they from the same distribution or are they different?

The above questions involve a sequence that can be coded (represented) as a sequence of 0 and 1 values. All sequences can be coded as a binary variable using methods such as:

- Code an increase from period to period as a 1 and a decrease as a 0.
- Code a value greater than the mean (or median or mode) as a 1 and below as a 0.
- Code a value greater than zero (or some other cut point value) as a 1 and below as a 0.
- Combine the sequences from the two sources, rank them from lowest to highest values, and label the data from the first source with a 0 and the second source with a 1.

A run is defined as a sequence of one or more binary variables (0 or 1) that have the same value. For example, the sequence {0, 0, 1, 1, 1, 0, 0, 0, 1, 0, 0, 1, 1, 1, 0, 0} has seven runs. We can use probability theory to calculate the probability that a sequence has exactly r runs given the number of 1's and 0's in the sequence. If the number of runs in the sequence is far less or far more than expected, the sequence is judged to be not sequentially independent. For example, when flipping a coin, the sequence HHHHHTTTTT would be considered just as unexpected as HTHTHTHTHT. The runs test is called a "non-parametric" test, because it can make inferences from the data without making any statements about the parameter values and requires no assumptions about the distribution of the data.

See *autocorrelation, Durbin-Watson Statistic, random number.*

S

S&OP – See *Sales & Operations Planning (S&OP).*

SaaS – See *Software as a Service (SaaS).*

safety – Freedom from the occurrence or risk of injury, danger, or loss.

See *DuPont STOP, error proofing, Occupational Safety and Health Administration (OSHA), risk management, risk mitigation.*

safety capacity – Capacity that is available in case of an emergency; sometimes called a capacity cushion.

Safety capacity is planned "extra" capacity and can be measured as the difference between the **planned capacity** and **planned demand**. Examples include a medical doctor "on call," a supervisor who can help in time of need, or capacity for overtime. Safety capacity is not just having too much capacity; it is capacity that is not actually working but can be called to work in case of emergency. Although safety capacity, **safety stock**, and **safety leadtime** can both be used to protect a firm from uncertain demand and supply, they are not identical concepts.

See *capacity, safety leadtime, safety stock.*

safety factor – See *safety stock.*

safety leadtime – The difference between the planned and average time required for a task or manufacturing order; called safety time by Wallace and Stahl (2003).

Safety leadtime is the "extra" planned leadtime used in production planning and purchasing to protect against fluctuations in leadtime. The same concept can be used in project scheduling. Safety leadtime should absorb the variability in the leadtimes. Whereas safety stock should be used to absorb variability in the demand and yield, safety leadtime should be used to protect against uncertainty in leadtimes or task times. Critical chain scheduling uses a buffer time to protect tasks assigned to constrained resources so they are almost never starved for work.

For example, if it takes a student an average of 30 minutes to get to school, and the student plans to leave 35 minutes before a class begins, the student will arrive 5 minutes early on average. This means that the student will have a safety leadtime of 5 minutes.

See *critical chain, Master Production Schedule (MPS), purchasing leadtime, safety capacity, safety stock, sequence-dependent setup time, slack time.*

safety stock – The planned or actual amount of "extra" inventory used to protect against fluctuations in demand or supply; the planned or actual inventory position just before a replenishment order is received in inventory; sometimes called buffer stock, reserve stock, or inventory buffer. ✪

The business case for safety stock: Safety stock is management's primary control variable for balancing carrying cost and service levels. If the safety stock is set too high, the inventory carrying cost will be too high. If safety stock is set too low, the shortage cost will be too high. Safety stock is needed in nearly all systems to protect against uncertain demand, leadtime, and yield that affect demand, supply, or both demand and supply.

Definition of safety stock: Managers often confuse safety stock with related concepts, such as an order-up-to level (for determining the lotsize), a reorder point (a "minimum" inventory for triggering a new order), or the average inventory. Safety stock is the average inventory when a new order is received. It is not the minimum, maximum, or average inventory. The figure below shows the safety stock as the lowest point on each of the three order cycles. The actual safety stock over this time period is the average of these three values.

Cycle inventory and safety stock inventory

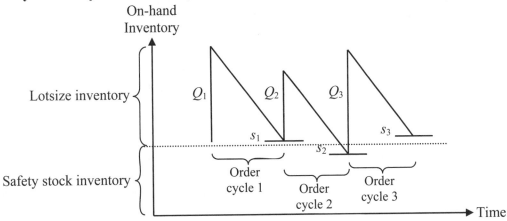

For stationary demand, the average inventory is the safety stock plus the average lotsize inventory. Given that the average lotsize inventory is half the average lotsize, the average inventory is $\overline{I} = SS + \overline{Q}/2$ units, where SS is the safety stock and $\overline{Q}$ is the average lotsize. Therefore, safety stock can be estimated as $SS = \overline{I} - \overline{Q}/2$.

Safety stock in different types of systems: The reorder point system, the order-up-to (target) inventory system, the Time Phased Order Point (TPOP) system, and MRP systems manage inventory with a planned (or forecasted) demand during the replenishment leadtime. Safety stock protects the organization from demand during the leadtime that is greater than planned. Therefore, safety stock should be based on the standard deviation of demand during leadtime and not just the average demand during leadtime.

Safety stock and days supply: It is a common practice to define safety stock in terms of a constant days supply. Although it is fine to communicate safety stocks in terms of days supply, it is a bad idea to use a constant days supply to set safety stock, unless all items have the same leadtime, average demand, standard deviation of demand, yield, and stockout cost.

The equation for safety stock: Define X as the demand during the replenishment leadtime. Safety stock is then $SS = z\sigma_X$, where z is the safety factor, which is usually between 1 and 4, and σ_X is the estimated standard deviation of demand during replenishment leadtime. Assuming that demand is serially independent, the standard deviation of demand during the leadtime is $\sigma_X = \sqrt{L}\sigma_D$, where L is the fixed planned replenishment leadtime and σ_D is the standard deviation of demand per period. Safety stock is then $SS = z\sqrt{L}\sigma_D$.

Safety stock and the leadtime parameter L: The basic safety stock model assumes that leadtime (L) is constant. More complicated models treat leadtime as a random variable and use the average leadtime and the standard deviation of the leadtime. Therefore, leadtime can be handled in the safety stock model in three ways: (1) use a constant leadtime at the average, (2) use a constant leadtime at a value well above the average, or (3) use the safety stock based on the standard deviation of the leadtime, e.g., $\sigma_X = \sqrt{\mu_L \sigma_D^2 + \mu_D^2 \sigma_L^2}$. When the review period P is greater than zero, the equation is $\sigma_X = \sqrt{(\mu_L + P)\sigma_D^2 + \mu_D^2 \sigma_L^2}$ (Silver, Pyke, and Peterson 1998).

Safety stock versus safety leadtime: As a general rule, safety stock should be used to absorb the variability in the demand (or yield), and safety leadtime should be used to protect against uncertainty in leadtimes. Whereas safety stock requires more inventory, safety leadtime requires that inventory arrive earlier.

The safety factor parameter z: The safety factor (z) determines the service level, where the service level increases as z increases. Many academic textbooks are imprecise on this subject. At least three approaches can be used to calculate the safety factor: (1) the order cycle service level approach, (2) the unit fill rate approach, and (3) the economic approach. Each of these approaches is described briefly below.

The *order cycle service level approach* is commonly taught in texts and implemented in major software systems (including SAP). This approach defines the service level as the probability of a shortage event on one order cycle. An order cycle is defined as the time between placing orders, and the average number of order cycles per year is A/Q, where A is the annual demand in units, and Q is the average order quantity. The safety factor for this approach is based on the standard normal distribution (i.e., $z = F^{-1}(SL)$). This z value can be easily calculated in Excel using NORMSINV(SL). The order cycle service level approach does not consider how many order cycles are expected per year or how many units might be short in a stockout event and is therefore not recommended.

The *unit fill rate service level approach* for setting the safety factor defines the service level as the expected percentage of units demanded that are immediately available from stock. This approach defines safety stock closer to the actual economics; however, this approach is much more complicated than the order cycle service level approach. No matter which service level approach is used, it is not clear how to set the best service level.

The *economic approach* for setting the safety factor z requires an estimate of the shortage or stockout cost per unit short (stocked out). If management is able to estimate this cost, the newsvendor model can be used to determine the safety factor that will minimize the expected total incremental cost (carrying cost plus shortage cost). This model balances the cost of having to carry a unit in safety stock inventory and the cost of having a unit shortage. Unfortunately, it is difficult to estimate the cost of a shortage (or a stockout) for one unit at the retail level. It is even more difficult to translate a shortage (or a stockout) into a cost at a distribution center, factory warehouse, or finished goods inventory.

The periodic review system: For a periodic review system with a time between reviews of P time periods, L should be replaced with $L + P$ in all equations. In other words, when ordering only every P time periods, the safety stock is $SS = z\sqrt{L + P}\,\sigma_D$. Note that $P = 0$ for a continuous review system.

The Time Phased Order Point (TPOP) system: If a firm places replenishment orders based on a TPOP system (based on forecasts), the safety stock should be defined in terms of the standard deviation of the forecast error rather than the standard deviation of demand. Unfortunately, many managers, systems designers, professors, students, and textbooks do not understand this important concept.

See *aggregate inventory management, autocorrelation, cycle stock, demand during leadtime, Economic Order Quantity (EOQ), Everyday Low Pricing (EDLP), goodwill, inventory management, lotsizing methods, marginal cost, newsvendor model, order cycle, partial expectation, periodic review system, purchasing leadtime, reorder point, replenishment order, safety capacity, safety leadtime, service level, square root law for safety stock, stockout, Time Phased Order Point (TPOP), warehouse.*

Sales & Operations Planning (S&OP) – A business process used to create the Sales & Operations Plan, which is a consensus plan involving Marketing/Sales, Operations/Logistics, and Finance that balances market demand and resource capability; also called Sales, Inventory & Operations Planning (SI&OP). ✪

S&OP is an important process in virtually all firms, but it is particularly critical in manufacturing firms. Fundamentally, S&OP is about finding the right balance between demand and supply. If demand is greater than supply, customers will be disappointed, customer satisfaction will decline, and sales will be lost. If supply is greater than demand, cost will be high.

The diagram below presents an example of an S&OP process. This diagram is based on concepts found in Wallace (2004) and Ling and Goddard (1995). However, it should be noted that each firm will implement S&OP in a different way. Most experts recommend that the S&OP process be repeated each month. Step 1 usually begins with statistical forecasts at either a product or product family level. These forecasts are then modified with market intelligence from sales management, usually for each region. However, some experts argue that providing statistical forecasts to sales management gives them an easy way out of doing the hard work of creating the forecasts. Statistical forecasts are useful for the majority of products, and most experts consider it a waste of time to not use the statistical forecasts as a starting point.

In step 2, the product management and the management of the Strategic Business Unit (SBU) work with the demand management organization to convert the sales forecasts into an unconstrained demand plan, which factors in higher-level issues, such as industry trends, pricing, and promotion strategy. The demand plan is expressed in both units and dollars. In step 3, operations and logistics have the opportunity to check that the supply (either new production or inventory) is sufficient to meet the proposed demand plan. If major changes need to be made, they can be made in steps 4 or 5. In step 4 (parallel to step 3), finance reviews the demand plan to ensure that it meets the firm's financial objectives (revenues, margins, profits) and creates a financial plan in dollars. In step 5, the demand management organization coordinates with the other organizations to put together a proposed Sales & Operations Plan that is a consensus plan from the demand plan, supply plan, and financial plan. Finally, in step 6, the executive team meets to finalize the S&OP plan. At every step in the process, assumptions and issues are identified, prioritized, and passed along to the next step. These assumptions and issues play important roles in steps 5 and 6.

An example S&OP process

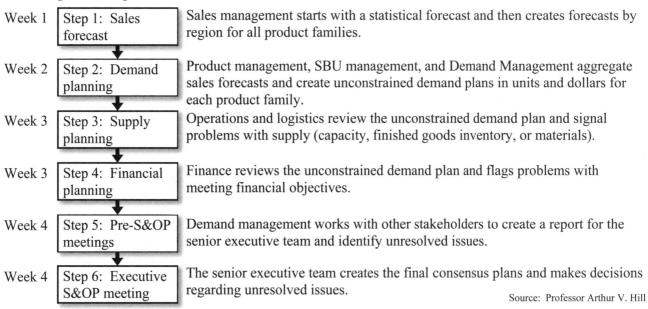

Week 1	Step 1: Sales forecast	Sales management starts with a statistical forecast and then creates forecasts by region for all product families.
Week 2	Step 2: Demand planning	Product management, SBU management, and Demand Management aggregate sales forecasts and create unconstrained demand plans in units and dollars for each product family.
Week 3	Step 3: Supply planning	Operations and logistics review the unconstrained demand plan and signal problems with supply (capacity, finished goods inventory, or materials).
Week 3	Step 4: Financial planning	Finance reviews the unconstrained demand plan and flags problems with meeting financial objectives.
Week 4	Step 5: Pre-S&OP meetings	Demand management works with other stakeholders to create a report for the senior executive team and identify unresolved issues.
Week 4	Step 6: Executive S&OP meeting	The senior executive team creates the final consensus plans and makes decisions regarding unresolved issues.

Source: Professor Arthur V. Hill

See *aggregate inventory management, Business Requirements Planning (BRP), Capacity Requirements Planning (CRP), chase strategy, closed-loop MRP, demand management, forecasting, level strategy, Master*

Production Schedule (MPS), product family, production planning, Resource Requirements Planning (RRP), Rough Cut Capacity Planning (RCCP), time fence.

Sales Inventory & Operations Planning (SI&OP) – See *Sales & Operations Planning (S&OP)*.

salvage value – The value of an item when it is scrapped instead of sold; also known as scrap value.

Retailers and manufacturers can usually find salvage firms or discounters to buy obsolete inventory. Some companies use salvage firms to buy unsold electronic parts. The salvage firm pays a low price (e.g., $0.01 per pound) and keeps the parts in inventory for years. In the rare case of a demand, the salvage firm sells the parts back at the original book value. Large retailers often discount older products in their stores, but if that strategy does not work, they often turn to branded and unbranded Internet sales channels.

See *scrap*.

sample size calculation – A statistical method for estimating the number of observations that need to be collected to create a confidence interval that meets the user's requirements.

Managers and analysts often need to estimate the value of a parameter, such as an average time or cost. However, with only a few observations, the estimates might not be very accurate. Therefore, it is necessary to know both the estimated mean and a measure of the accuracy of that estimate.

Confidence intervals can help with this problem. A confidence interval is a statement about the reliability of an estimate. For example, a confidence interval on the time required for a task might be expressed as "25 hours plus or minus 2 hours with a 95% confidence level," or more concisely "25 ± 2 hours." The first number (25) is called the "sample mean." The second number (2) is called the "half-width" of the confidence interval. The "95% confidence" suggests that if we were to make this estimate many times, the true mean would be included ("covered") in the confidence interval about 95% of the time. It is sometimes stated as, "We are 95% sure that the confidence interval contains the mean."

Sometimes some observations have already been collected, and the goal is to develop a confidence interval from these observations. At other times, the required half-width is known, and it is necessary to find the number of observations needed to compute this half-width with a certain degree of confidence. It is also possible to express the half-width as a percentage. The five most common problems related to confidence intervals are:

- Problem 1: Create a confidence interval given that n observations are available.
- Problem 2: Find the sample size needed to create the desired confidence interval with a prespecified half-width.
- Problem 3: Find the sample size needed to create the desired confidence interval with a prespecified half-width expressed as a decimal percentage.
- Problem 4: Find the sample size needed to create the desired confidence interval on a proportion with a prespecified half-width percentage.
- Problem 5: Develop a confidence interval for a stratified random sample.

The entry in this encyclopedia on confidence intervals addresses Problem 1. For Problem 2, the goal is to find the smallest sample size n that is necessary to achieve a two-tailed $100(1 - \alpha)\%$ confidence interval with a prespecified half-width of h units.

Step 0. **Define parameters** – Specify the desired half-width h (in units), the estimated size of the population N, and the confidence level parameter α. If the size of N is large but unknown, use an extremely large number (e.g., $N = 10^{10}$). Compute $z_{\alpha/2} = \text{NORMSINV}(1 - \alpha / 2)$.

Step 1. **Take a preliminary sample to estimate the sample mean and standard deviation** – Take a preliminary sample of n_0 observations, where $n_0 \geq 9$ observations, and estimate the sample mean and standard deviation ($\overline{x}$ and s) from this sample.

Step 2. **Estimate the required sample size** – Compute $n^* = (z_{\alpha/2} s / h)^2$. Round up to be conservative. If the sample size n is large relative to the total population N (i.e., $n^*/N > 0.05$), use $n^* = (z_{\alpha/2} s)^2 / (h^2 + (z_{\alpha/2} s)^2 / N)$ instead. (This assumes that $n^* \geq 30$, so it is appropriate to use a z value; otherwise use the t value.)

Step 3. **Take additional observations** – If $n^* > n_0$, take $n^* - n_0$ additional observations.

Step 4. **Recompute the sample mean and sample standard deviation** – Recompute $\overline{x}$ and s from the entire n observations.

Step 5. **Compute the half-width and create the confidence interval** – Compute the half-width $h' = z_{\alpha/2}\, s / \sqrt{n}$. If the sample size n is large relative to the total population N (i.e., $n/N > 0.05$), use $h' = \left(z_{\alpha/2}\, s / \sqrt{n} \right) \sqrt{1 - n/N}$ instead. The confidence interval is then $\overline{x} \pm h'$.

Step 6. **Check results** – Make sure that $h \ge h'$; if not, repeat steps 2 to 6.

The larger the number of observations (n), the smaller the confidence interval. The goal is to find the lowest value of n that will create the desired confidence interval. If n observations are selected randomly many times from the population, the confidence interval ($\overline{x} \pm h'$) will contain the true mean about $100(1-\alpha)\%$ of the time.

See *central limit theorem, confidence interval, dollar unit sampling, sampling, standard deviation.*

sampling – The selection of items from a population to help a decision maker make inferences about the population.

Sampling is frequently used when it is impossible, impractical, or too costly to evaluate every unit in the **population**. Sampling allows decision makers to make **inferences** (statements) about the population from which the sample is drawn. A random sample provides characteristics nearly identical to those of the population.

One major issue in developing a sampling plan is the determination of the number of observations in the sample (**the sample size**) needed to achieve a desired **confidence level** and maximum allowable error. See the *sample size calculation* entry for more details.

Probability sampling includes simple random sampling, systematic sampling, stratified sampling, probability proportional to size sampling, and cluster or multistage sampling. **Stratified sampling** (also known as stratification) defines groups or strata as independent subpopulations, conducts random samples in each of these strata, and then uses information about the population to make statistical inferences about the overall population. Stratified sampling has several advantages over simple random sampling. First, stratified sampling makes it possible for researchers to draw inferences about groups that are particularly important. Second, stratified sampling can significantly tighten the confidence interval on the mean and reduce the sample size to achieve a predefined confidence interval. Finally, different sampling approaches can be applied to each stratum.

See *acceptance sampling, Analysis of Variance (ANOVA), central limit theorem, confidence interval, consumer's risk, dollar unit sampling, hypergeometric distribution, Lot Tolerance Percent Defective (LTPD), normal distribution, operating characteristic curve, producer's risk, sample size calculation, sampling distribution, standard deviation, t-test, work sampling.*

sampling distribution – The probability distribution for a statistic, such as the sample mean, based on a set of randomly selected units from a larger population; also called the finite-sample distribution.

A sampling distribution can be thought of as a relative frequency distribution from a number of samples taken from a larger population. This relative frequency distribution approaches the sampling distribution as the number of samples approaches infinity. For discrete (integer) variables, the heights of the distribution are probabilities (also called the probability mass). For continuous variables, the intervals have a zero width, and the height of the distribution at any point is called the probability density.

The standard deviation of the sampling distribution of the statistic is called the **standard error**. According to the **central limit theorem**, the standard error for the sample mean is always $s / \sqrt{n-1}$, where s is the standard deviation for the sample. Other statistics, such as the sample median, sample maximum, sample minimum, and the sample standard deviation, have different sampling distributions.

For example, an analyst is trying to develop a confidence internal on the average waiting time for a call center where the waiting time follows an exponential distribution. The analyst collects $n = 101$ sample waiting times and finds the sample mean and standard deviation are $(\overline{x}, s) = (5.5, 1.2)$ minutes. According to the central limit theorem, the sampling distribution for the sample mean is the normal distribution regardless of the underlying distribution. The sampling distribution for the sample mean, therefore, is normal with mean and standard deviation $(\overline{x}, s/\sqrt{n-1}) = (5.5, 0.12)$ minutes with a 95% confidence interval of $(5.26, 5.74)$ minutes.

See *central limit theorem, confidence interval, probability density function, probability distribution, probability mass function, sampling.*

sand cone model – An operations strategy model that suggests a hierarchy for the operations capabilities of quality, reliability, speed, and cost, where the quality is the base of the sand cone, followed by reliability, speed, and cost.

In the short-term, organizations often have to make trade-offs between **cost**, **speed**, **reliability**, and **quality**. For example, speed can sometimes be increased by using premium freight, which adds cost. However, Ferdows and De Meyer (1990) argue that in the longer run, firms can avoid trade-offs and build cumulative capabilities in all four areas. They argue that management attention and resources should first go toward enhancing quality, then dependability (reliability), then speed (flexibility), and finally cost (efficiency). They argue further that capabilities are built one on top of the other like a sand cone, where each lower layer of sand must be extended to support any increase for a higher layer. The drawing above depicts this relationship.

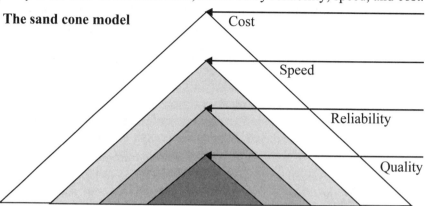

The sand cone model

Adapted from Ferdows, K. & A. De Meyer (1990).

Pine (1993) makes a similar argument in his book on mass customization but changes the order to cost → quality → flexibility. He argues that in the life cycle of a product, such as 3M's Post-it Notes, the first priority was to figure out a way to make it profitable. The first small batch of Post-it Notes probably cost 3M about $50,000; but during the first year, 3M was able to find ways to automate production and bring the cost down substantially. The second priority was then to increase conformance quality to ensure the process was reliable. Some could argue that this was essentially a continuation of the effort to reduce cost. The third and last priority was to increase variety from canary yellow[53] in three sizes to many colors and sizes.

See *mass customization, operations strategy, premium freight.*

SAP – A leading Enterprise Resources Planning (ERP) software vendor; the full name is SAP AG; SAP is the German acronym for Systeme, Andwendungen, Produkte in der Datenverarbeitung, which translated to English means Systems, Applications, Products in Data Processing.

SAP was founded in Germany in 1972 by five ex-IBM engineers. SAP is headquartered in Walldorf, Germany, and has subsidiaries in more than 50 countries. SAP America, which has responsibility for North America, South America, and Australia, is headquartered just outside Philadelphia.

See *ABAP (Advanced Business Application Programming), Advanced Planning and Scheduling (APS), Enterprise Resources Planning (ERP).*

satisfaction – See *service quality.*

satisficing – The effort needed to obtain an outcome that is good enough but is not exceptional.

In contrast to satisficing action, **maximizing action** seeks the biggest and **optimizing action** seeks the best. In recent decades, doubts have been expressed about the view that in all rational decision making the agent seeks the best result. Instead, some argue it is often rational to seek to satisfice (i.e., to get a good result that is good enough although not necessarily the best). The term was introduced by Simon (1957). (Adapted from *The Penguin Dictionary of Philosophy*, ed. Thomas Mautner, found at www.utilitarianism.com/satisfice.htm, April 1, 2011.)

See *bounded rationality, learning curve, learning organization.*

SBU – See *Strategic Business Unit (SBU).*

scalability – The ability to increase capacity without adding significant cost, or the ability to grow with the organization.

For example, software is said to be "scalable" if it can handle a significant increase in transaction volume.

See *agile manufacturing, flexibility, resilience.*

---

[53] *Humorous aside: 3M has a copyright on the color canary yellow.*

scale count – An item count based on the weight determined by a scale.

A scale count is often more economical than performing an actual physical count. This is particularly true for small inexpensive parts where slight inaccuracy is not important. Counting accuracy depends on the scale accuracy, the variance of the unit weight, and the variance of the container tare weight. Of course, the container tare weight should be subtracted from the total weight.

See *cycle counting, tare weight*.

scales of measurement – The theory of scale types.

According to Wikipedia, psychologist Stanley Smith Stevens developed what he called levels of measurement that include:

- **Nominal scale** – Categorical, labels (however, some critics claim that this is not a scale).
- **Ordinal scale** – Rank order.
- **Interval scale** – Any quantitative scale, such as temperature, that has an arbitrary zero point; although differences between values are meaningful, ratios are not.
- **Ratio scale** – Any quantitative scale, such as a weight, that does not have an arbitrary zero point; ratios are meaningful.

See *operations performance metrics*.

scatter diagram – A graphical display of data showing the relationship between two variables; also called scatterdiagram and scatterplot.

The scatter diagram is usually drawn as a set of points on a graph. When the points appear to fall along a line (e.g., from bottom left to top right), the user might hypothesize a linear relationship.

See *linear regression, Root Cause Analysis (RCA), run chart, seven tools of quality*.

scheduled receipt – See *open order*.

scientific management – An approach to management and industrial organization developed by Frederick Winslow Taylor (1856-1915) in his monograph ***The Principles of Scientific Management*** (Taylor 1911).

Taylor believed that every process had "one best way" and developed important industrial engineering and operations management approaches, such as the time and motion studies, to find that best way. For example, in one of Taylor's most famous studies, he noticed that workers used the same shovel for all materials. His research found that the most effective load was 21.5 pounds, which led him to design different shovels for each material for that weight.

Taylor made many important contributions to the field of operations management, emphasizing time and motion studies, division of labor, standardized work, planning, incentives, management of knowledge work, and selection and training. Taylor also influenced many important thought leaders, including Carl Barth, H. L. Gantt, Harrington Emerson, Morris Cooke, Hugo Münsterberg (who created industrial psychology), Frank and Lillian Gilbreth, Harlow S. Person, and James O. McKinsey and many important organizations, such as Harvard University's Business School, Dartmouth's Amos Tuck School, University of Chicago, Purdue University, McKinsey (an international consulting firm), and the American Society of Mechanical Engineers. His work also influenced industrial development in many other nations, including France, Switzerland, and the Soviet Union.

One criticism of scientific management is that it separated managerial work (e.g., planning) and direct labor. This led to jobs where workers were not expected to think. In contrast, many successful Japanese firms stress the need to gather suggestions from workers and require managers begin their careers on the shop floor.

See *best practices, division of labor, human resources, job design, standardized work, time study, work measurement*.

scope – See *project management, scope creep*.

scope creep – The tendency for project boundaries and requirements to expand over time, often resulting in large, unmanageable, and never-finished projects.

Scope creep is reflected in subtle changes in project requirements over time. For example, a software project might start out as a simple table that needs to be accessed by just a single type of user. However, as the user group becomes engaged in the project, the "scope" increases to include a larger and more complicated database with multiple tables and multiple types of users.

One of the main keys to successful project management is avoiding scope creep. If the users want to increase the scope of a project, they should be required to either go back and change the charter (and get the appropriate signed approvals) or defer the changes to a new project. If management does not manage scope creep, the project will likely not be completed on time or within budget.

In a consulting context, scope creep is additional work outside the project charter that the client wants for no additional charge. If the client is willing to change the charter and pay for the work, it is an "add-on sale" and is not considered scope creep.

See *focused factory*, *project charter*, *project management*, *project management triangle*, *scoping*.

scoping – The process of defining the limits (boundaries) for a project.

Defining the project scope is a critical determinant of the success of a project. When scoping a project, it is just as important to define what is not in scope as it is to define what is in scope.

See *project charter*, *project management*, *scope creep*.

SCOR Model – A process reference model that has been developed and endorsed by the Supply-Chain Council as the cross-industry, standard, diagnostic tool for supply-chain management, spanning from the supplier's supplier to the customer's customer; acronym for Supply-Chain Operations Reference. ✪

The SCOR Model

The SCOR Model allows users to address, improve, and communicate supply chain management practices within and between all interested parties. The SCOR framework attempts to combine elements of business process design, best practices, and benchmarking. The basic SCOR model is shown above.

The SCOR Model was developed to describe the business activities associated with all phases of satisfying a customer's demand. It can be used to describe and improve both simple and complex supply chains using a common set of definitions. An overview of the SCOR Model can be found on the Supply Chain Council webpage http://supply-chain.org. Some of the benefits claimed for the SCOR Model include (1) standardized terminology and process descriptions, (2) predefined performance measures, (3) best practices, and (4) basis for benchmarking a wide variety of supply chain practices.

See *benchmarking*, *bullwhip effect*, *Supply Chain Council*, *supply chain management*, *value chain*.

scrap – Material judged to be defective and of little economic value.

Scrap is any material that is obsolete or outside specifications and cannot be reworked into a sellable product. Scrap should be recycled or disposed of properly according to environmental laws. A **scrap factor** (or yield rate) can be used to inflate the "quantity per" to allow for yield loss during a manufacturing process. The **scrap value** (or **salvage value**) is credited to factory overhead or the job that produced the scrap.

See *conformance quality*, *cost of quality*, *red tag*, *rework*, *salvage value*, *yield*.

scree plot – See *cluster analysis*.

scrum – A method of implementing agile software development, where teams meet on a daily basis, and computer code is delivered in two to four week "sprints."

Scrum is similar to **lean thinking** in many ways. The fundamental concept of scrum is that the organization produces computer code in small "chunks" (like small lotsizes) that can be quickly evaluated and used by others. This allows for early detection of defects, a key operations management concept. This is consistent with the lean concept of reducing lotsizes and "one-piece flow." Scrum is also similar to lean in that it requires short stand-up meetings and clear accountabilities for work. Scum defines three roles and three meetings:

The three roles:
1. **Product owner** – This person manages the product's requirements and divides the work among team members and among sprints.
2. **Scrum master** – This person runs the daily scrum meeting.
3. **Team members** – These are the software developers responsible for delivering code that meets the requirements.

The three meetings:
1. **Sprint Planning Meeting** – The product owner and team members meet at the start of a sprint to plan this period's work and identify any issues that may impact the program.
2. **Daily Scrum Meeting** – This 15-minute meeting is led by the scrum master, and each team member is expected to answer three questions: "What did you accomplish since yesterday's scrum meeting?", "What will you accomplish before tomorrow's scrum meeting?", and "What roadblocks may impede your progress?" The sprint burndown chart, a measure of the team's progress, is updated during this meeting. Attendees at scrum meetings are expected to stand, rather than sit, during the 15 minutes. This is to keep the meeting concise and on time.
3. **Sprint Review Meeting** – The product owner holds this meeting at the conclusion of a sprint, to review the state of the deliverables, and cross-check them against the stated requirements for that sprint.

   See *agile software development, deliverables, early detection, Fagan Defect-Free Process, lean thinking, New Product Development (NPD), prototype, sprint burndown chart, waterfall scheduling.*

search cost – The cost of finding a supplier that can provide a satisfactory product at an acceptable price.

   See *switching cost, total cost of ownership, transaction cost.*

seasonal factor – See *seasonality.*

seasonality – A recurring pattern in a time series that is based on the calendar or a clock.

   The demand for a product is said to have seasonality if it has a recurring pattern on an annual, monthly, weekly, daily, or hourly cycle. For example, retail demand for toys in North America is significantly higher during the Christmas season. The demand for access to major highways is much higher during the "rush hours" at the beginning and end of a workday. For some firms, sales tend to increase at the end of the quarter due to sales incentives. This is known as the "hockey stick effect."

   Most forecasting models apply a multiplicative seasonal factor to adjust the forecast for the seasonal pattern. The forecast, therefore, is equal to the underlying average times the seasonal factor. For example, a toy retailer might have a seasonal factor for the month of December (i.e., the Christmas season) of 4, whereas a low demand month such as January, might have a seasonal factor of 0.6. Demand data can be "deseasonalized" by dividing by the seasonal factor. Although it is not recommended, it is also possible to use an additive seasonal factor.

   See *anticipation inventory, Box-Jenkins forecasting, chase strategy, exponential smoothing, forecasting, hockey stick effect, level strategy, newsvendor model, production planning, time series forecasting, trend.*

self check – See *inspection.*

self-directed work team – Work groups that have significant decision rights and autonomy.

   See *High Performance Work Systems (HPWS), human resources, job design, organizational design.*

sensei – A reverent Japanese term for a teacher or master.

   In the **lean manufacturing** context, a sensei is a master of lean knowledge with many years of experience. In traditional lean environments, it is important for the sensei to be a respected and inspirational figure. Toyota uses a Japanese-trained sensei to provide technical assistance and management advice when it is trying something for the first time or to help facilitate transformational activities.

   See *lean thinking.*

sensitivity analysis – The process of estimating how much the results of a model will change if one or more of the inputs to the model are changed slightly.

   Although the concept of sensitivity analysis can be used with any model, it is a particularly powerful part of **linear programming** analysis. For example, in linear programming, the analyst can determine the additional profit for each unit of change in a constraint. The economic benefit of changing the constraint by one unit is called the "shadow price" of the constraint.

   See *linear programming (LP), operations research (OR).*

sentinel event – A healthcare term used to describe any unintended and undesirable occurrence that results in death or serious injury not related to the natural course of a patient's illness; sometimes called a "never event."

   A sentinel is a guard or a lookout. Serious **adverse healthcare events** are called sentinel events because they signal the need for a "sentinel" or "guard" to avoid them in the future. Examples of sentinel healthcare events include death resulting from a medication error, suicide of a patient in a setting with around-the-clock care, surgery on the wrong patient or body part, infection-related death or permanent disability, assault or rape, transfusion death, and infant abduction.

Following a sentinel event (or potential sentinel event), nearly all healthcare organizations conduct a **root cause analysis** to identify the causes of the event and then develop an action plan to mitigate the risk of the event reoccurring. The Joint Commission (formerly called JCAHO) tracks statistics on sentinel events.

See *adverse event, causal map, error proofing, Joint Commission, prevention, Root Cause Analysis (RCA).*

sequence-dependent setup cost – See *sequence-dependent setup time.*

sequence-dependent setup time – A changeover time that changes with the order in which jobs are started.

A sequence-dependent setup time (or cost) is a **changeover time** (or cost) that is dependent on the order in which jobs are run. For example, it might be easy to change a paint-making process from white to gray, but difficult to change it from black to white. Sometimes, setups are not sequence-dependent between items within a **product family**, but are sequence-dependent between families of products. In this case, setups between families are sometimes called **major setups**, and setups within a family are called **minor setups**.

When setup times (or costs) are sequence-dependent, it is necessary to have a "from-to" table of times (or costs), much like a "from-to" travel time table on the back of a map. Creating a schedule for sequence-dependent setup times is a particular type of combinatorial optimization problem that is nearly identical to the **traveling salesperson problem**.

See *batch process, major setup cost, product family, safety leadtime, setup, setup cost, setup time, Traveling Salesperson Problem (TSP).*

serial correlation – See *autocorrelation.*

serial number traceability – See *traceability.*

service blueprinting – A process map for a service that includes moments of truth, line of visibility, fail points, and additional information needed to create the right customer experience.

The main idea of service blueprinting is to get customers' perspectives into the service design and improvement process. During the process design stage, business process managers, architects, interior designers, marketing managers, operations managers, and IT professionals use the service blueprint to guide the design process. After the design is completed and implemented, the blueprint defines the required features and quality of the service for the service managers. Some recommended steps for service blueprinting include:

1. **Clearly identify the target customer segment.**
2. **Develop a process map from the customer's point of view** – This should include the choices the customers need to make when they buy and use the service. It should also include all activities, flows, materials, information, failure points, customer waiting points (queues), risk points, pain points, and handoffs.
3. **Map employee actions both onstage and backstage** – This involves drawing the lines of interaction and visibility and then identifying the interactions between the customer and employee and all visible and invisible employee actions.
4. **Link customer and contact person activities to needed support functions** – This involves drawing the line of internal interaction and linking the employee actions to the support processes.
5. **Add evidence of service at each customer action step** – This involves showing evidence of the service that the customer sees and receives at each point of the service experience.

The service blueprint should show all points of interaction between the customer and service providers (known as "moments of truth"), identify "fail points" and the "line of visibility," and include fairly precise estimates of the times required for each step, including the queue times. The line of visibility separates a service operation into back office operations that take place without the customer's presence and front office operations in direct contact with the customer. Some people argue that the only difference between a process map and a service blueprint is the identification of the fail points and the demarcation of the line of visibility.

A service blueprint is better than a verbal description because it is more formal, structured, and detailed and shows the interactions between processes. The blueprint provides a conceptual model that facilitates studying the service experience prior to implementing it and also makes the implementation easier.

See *experience engineering, line of visibility, moment of truth, process design, process map, service failure, service guarantee, service management.*

service failure – A situation when a service provider does not provide satisfactory service. ✪

The best service organizations pay a great deal of attention to these situations and try to recover dissatisfied customers before they become "terrorists" and give a bad report to a large number of potential customers. (Note: The word "terrorists" has been used in this context by service quality experts for decades; however, in light of recent events, many experts are now shying away from using such a strong and emotionally charged word.)

For example, when this author was traveling through Logan Airport in Boston on the way to Europe, an airport restaurant served some bad clam chowder that caused him to get very sick (along with at least one other traveler on the same flight). As a form of **service recovery**, the restaurant offered a free coupon for more food. This form of service recovery was not adequate and he became a "terrorist" who reported this service failure to thousands of people. (Note: This restaurant is no longer in business in the Logan Airport.)

See *service blueprinting*, *service guarantee*, *service management*, *service quality*, *service recovery*.

service guarantee – A set of two promises offered to customers before they buy a service. The first promise is the level of service provided and the second promise is what the provider will do if the first promise is not kept. ✪

Hays and Hill (2001) found empirically that a service guarantee often has more value for operations improvement than it does for advertising. A carefully defined service guarantee can have the following benefits:

- Defines the value proposition for both customers and employees.
- Supports marketing communications in attracting new customers, particularly those who are risk-adverse.
- Helps the service firm retain "at-risk" customers.
- Lowers the probability that dissatisfied customers will share negative word-of-mouth reports with others.
- Motivates customers to provide useful process improvement ideas.
- Motivates service firm employees to learn from mistakes and improve the service process over time.
- Clearly predefines the service recovery process for both customers and employees.
- Ensures that the service recovery process does not surprise customers.

A service guarantee is usually applied to organizations serving external customers, but it can also be applied to internal customers. Service guarantees are not without risk (Hill 1995). Offering a service guarantee before the organization is ready can lead to serious problems. Announcing the withdrawal of a service guarantee is tantamount to announcing that the organization is no longer committed to quality.

A service guarantee is a promise related to the intangible attributes of the service (e.g., timeliness, results, satisfaction, etc.), whereas a **product warranty** is a promise related to the physical attributes of the product (durability, physical performance, etc.). Product warranties are similar to service guarantees from a legal perspective and have many of the same benefits and risks.

Hill (1995) developed the figure below to show the relationship between a service guarantee and **customer satisfaction**. The numbers in the figure are for illustrative purposes only. The three arrows show that a service guarantee can increase **Service guarantees, service failures, and customer satisfaction**

the percent of customers who complain (by rewarding them to complain), the percent recovered (by having a predefined service recovery process and payout), and the percent satisfied (by motivating learning from service

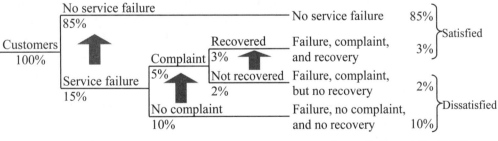

Source: Professor Arthur V. Hill (1995)

failures). Organizations never want to increase the percent of dissatisfied customers, but they should want to increase the percent of dissatisfied customers who complain so they hear all customer complaints. Service guarantees inflict "pain" on the organization, which motivates the organization to learn faster.

From 1973-1980, Domino's Pizza offered a "30-minutes or it's free" guarantee. Unfortunately, Domino's settled major lawsuits for dangerous driving in 1992 and 1993, which led the firm to abandon its on-time delivery guarantee and replace it with an unconditional satisfaction guarantee (source: Wikipedia, March 28, 2011).

A **Service Level Agreement (SLA)** is essentially a service guarantee for commercial customers. See the *Service Level Agreement (SLA)* entry for a comparison of service guarantees, SLAs, and product warranties.

See *brand, caveat emptor, durability, performance-based contracting, response time, risk sharing contract, service blueprinting, service failure, Service Level Agreement (SLA), service management, service quality, service recovery, SERVQUAL, value proposition, warranty*.

service level – A measure of the degree to which a firm meets customer requirements. ✪

Service level is often measured differently for **make to stock (MTS)** and **respond to order (RTO)** products. It is possible, however, to define a general service level metric for both MTS and RTO. The following three sections describe these three types of service level metrics.

Service level metrics for make to stock (MTS) products – Retailers, distributors, and manufacturers that make and or sell products from inventory (from stock) need a service level measure that reflects the availability of inventory for customers. For make to stock (MTS) products, the service level is usually measured as a **fill rate metric**. The **unit fill rate** is the percentage of units filled immediately from stock; the **line fill rate** is the percentage of lines filled immediately from stock; and the **order fill rate** is the percentage of orders filled immediately from stock. The terms "fill rate" and "service level" are often used synonymously in many make to stock firms.

Many textbooks, such as Schroeder et al. (2011) and most major ERP systems (e.g., SAP) define the service level for MTS products as the **order cycle service level**, which is the probability of not having a stockout event during an **order cycle**. However, this is a poor service metric because it does not take into account the number of order cycles per year or the severity of a stockout event. See the *safety stock* entry for more detail.

Best Buy and other retail chains measure service level with the **in-stock position**, which is the percentage of stores in the chain (or the percentage of items in a store) that have the **presentation quantity**[54]. The presentation quantity is the minimum number of units needed to create an attractive offering for customers. The calculation of in-stock for an item is (Number of stores that have the presentation minimum on-hand)/(Total number of stores stocking that item).

Service level metrics for respond to order (RTO) products – Respond to order products are assembled, built, fabricated, cut, mixed, configured, packaged, picked, customized, printed, or engineered in response to a customer's request (order). The service level for these products is usually measured as the percent of orders that are filled on time, otherwise known as **on-time delivery (OTD)**, which is the percent of orders shipped (or received) complete within the promise date (or request date).

Ideally, firms should compute OTD based on the customer **request date**, because the **promise date** may or may not satisfy the customer's requirements. However, most firms find it difficult to use the request date because customers can "game" the request date to get a higher priority. Measuring OTD is further complicated by the fact that the supplier can update the promise date as the situation changes so orders are rarely late. Firms should compute OTD from the customer's perspective. Therefore, firms should measure OTD based on the customer receipt date rather than the manufacturer's ship date. However, most firms do not have access to the customer receipt date, and therefore measure OTD against their shipping dates, and then hold their distribution/transportation partners responsible for their portion of the customer leadtime.

OTD can be improved by either (1) making safer promises (e.g., promise three weeks instead of two weeks) or (2) reducing the mean or variance of the manufacturing leadtime. The first alternative can have a negative impact on demand. The second alternative requires lean sigma thinking to reduce the mean and variability of the customer leadtime. Hill and Khosla (1992) and Hill, Hays, and Naveh (2000) develop models for the leadtime elasticity of demand and for finding the "optimal" customer leadtime to offer to the market.

The **customer leadtime** for an RTO product is the actual time between the order receipt and the delivery to the customer. Customer leadtime, therefore, is a random variable that has a mean, mode, standard deviation, etc. The planned leadtime (or planned customer leadtime) is usually a fixed quantity, which may be conditioned on some attribute of the order (quantity, complexity, routing, materials, size, etc.). For example, a firm might offer a two-week leadtime for standard products and a three-week leadtime for non-standard products.

---

[54] *Source: Personal conversations with Best Buy management in 2009.*

Some academics define additional performance metrics for RTO products, such as the mean and standard deviation of lateness, earliness, and tardiness. Define A as the actual delivery date (or time) and D as the due date (or time) for a customer order. **Lateness** is then defined as $D - A$, **earliness** is defined as $\max(D-A, 0)$, and **tardiness** is defined as $\max(A-D, 0)$. Lateness can be either positive or negative. Negative lateness means that the delivery was early. Neither earliness nor tardiness can be negative. Earliness is zero when an order is on time or late and tardiness is zero when an order is on time or early. **Average earliness** is commonly calculated only for early orders and **average tardiness** is commonly calculated only for tardy orders. Using more sophisticated mathematical notation, earliness is $(D - A)^+$ and tardiness is $(A - D)^+$, where $(x)^+ = \max(x, 0)$. Some systems prioritize orders based on lateness.

General service level metrics for both MTS and RTO products − It is possible to use a service level metric for both MTS and RTO products by defining the fill rate as the percent of units, lines, or orders shipped by the due date. Some firms call this **on-time and complete**. Some members of the Grocery Manufacturing Association in North America use a fill rate metric called the **perfect order fill rate**, which is the percent of orders shipped on time, to the correct customer, to the correct place, complete (right quantity), free of damage, in the right packaging, with the correct documentation, and with an accurate invoice. However, some firms have backed away from the perfect order fill rate because it may be more demanding than customers expect, which means that it is more expensive than customers need. This suggests that firms should customize their perfect order metric to the needs of their market.

See *aggregate inventory management, carrying cost, commonality, customer service, delivery time, dispatching rules, goodwill, inventory management, job shop scheduling, make to stock (MTS), materials management, mixed model assembly, on-time delivery (OTD), operations performance metrics, order cycle, purchase order (PO), purchasing, reorder point, respond to order (RTO), safety stock, Service Level Agreement (SLA), service management, slow moving inventory, stockout.*

Service Level Agreement (SLA) − An arrangement between a service provider and a customer that specifies the type and quality of services that will be provided.

A Service Level Agreement (SLA) is usually a legally binding contract, but it can also be an informal agreement between two parties. The SLA is an effective means for the customer and supplier to engage in a serious discussion at the beginning of a relationship to determine what is important to the customer and clearly specify expectations. The service provider is usually obliged to pay the customer a penalty if any condition in the SLA is not satisfied. SLA conditions often include a definition of services, performance measurement, problem management, customer duties, warranties, disaster recovery, and termination of agreement. SLAs are also used to monitor a supplier's performance and force the supplier to take corrective action when the conditions of the agreement are not met.

An SLA is essentially a **service guarantee** for a commercial (B2B) market. Service guarantees are usually designed for consumers (B2C) and are very short (e.g., as short as one sentence). In contrast, SLAs are usually designed for commercial customers (B2B) and usually require several pages of legal terminology. An Operating Level Agreement (OLA) is essentially an SLA within a firm. OLAs are often the key tool for achieving SLAs. A **warranty** is essentially a legally binding SLA for product performance rather than service performance.

Examples of an SLA: (1) A number of capital equipment firms offer a range of options (a menu) of field service SLAs to their customers that allow customers to make trade-offs between the price and service quality as measured by equipment downtime, technician response time, etc. (2) The best-known SLAs are in the telecommunications markets where the service provider might provide SLAs that specify uptime requirements. (3) Many firms use SLAs in an outsourcing relationship to clarify the business requirements for both parties.

See *business process outsourcing, downtime, field service, outsourcing, performance-based contracting, service guarantee, service level, service management, service quality, warranty.*

service management − A product that is simultaneously produced and consumed. ✪

Services are said to be **intangible**, which means that the service is not a physical "thing." However, many (if not most) services have **facilitating goods**. For example, a dinner at a nice restaurant will have comfortable chairs, nice plates, and good food. However, the chairs, plates, and food are not the service; they are only the facilitating goods for the service. Services **cannot be inventoried**, which means that they cannot be stored. For example, a flight from London to Paris at noon on July 4, cannot be "stored" in inventory until July 5. Once the aircraft has taken off, that capacity is gone forever.

Although most services are **labor intensive** (e.g., haircuts, surgery, and classroom instruction), some are **capital intensive** (e.g., power generation). Many services require that the customer have intensive **customer contact** in the process throughout the production of the service (e.g., surgery), others require limited contact with the customer at the beginning and end of the process (e.g., car repair), and some require no customer involvement at all (e.g., police protection). Using McDonald's as an example, Levitt (1972) argue that both labor intensive and capital intensive services should be managed more like factories with respect to standardization, technology, systems, and metrics.

See *Application Service Provider (ASP), back office, business process outsourcing, call center, Customer Effort Score (CES), experience engineering, help desk, labor intensive, line of visibility, Net Promoter Score (NPS), operations performance metrics, production line, service blueprinting, service failure, service guarantee, service level, Service Level Agreement (SLA), Service Profit Chain, service quality, service recovery, SERVQUAL, Software as a Service (SaaS), transactional process improvement.*

service marketing – See *service management.*

service operations – See *service management.*

service parts – Components, parts, or supplies used to maintain or repair machinery or equipment; spare parts.

Service parts are sometimes called **spare parts**, but the term "spare" implies that they are not needed, which is often not the case (Hill 1992). Service parts are usually considered to be Maintenance-Repair-Operations (MRO) items. The *slow moving inventory* entry presents an inventory model based on the Poisson distribution for managing service parts.

See *aftermarket, bathtub curve, field service, Maintenance-Repair-Operations (MRO), slow moving inventory.*

Service Profit Chain – A conceptual model for service management that relates employee satisfaction to customer satisfaction, revenue and profit.

The Service Profit Chain, developed by Heskett, Jones, Loveman, Sasser, and Schlesinger (1994) and Heskett, Sasser, and Schlesinger (1997), begins with "internal service quality," which involves workplace design and job design for employees. The central concept is that if employees are satisfied, they will have lower labor turnover (higher employee retention) and better productivity. Higher employee satisfaction, retention, and productivity then translate into better "external service value" and satisfaction for the customer. This higher customer satisfaction then translates into higher customer loyalty, revenue, and ultimately into sales growth and profitability for the firm. This model is promoted by several consulting firms, including Heskett's firm, the Service Profit Chain Institute (www.serviceprofitchain.com). The figure below shows the Service Profit Chain.

The Service Profit Chain

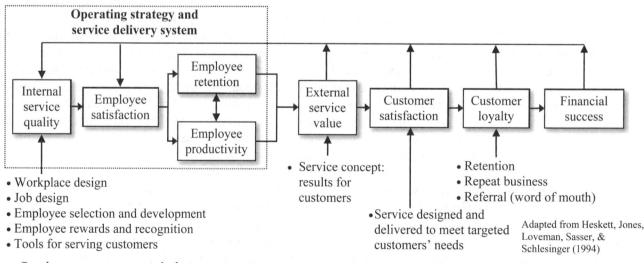

See *human resources, job design, operations strategy, service management, service quality.*

service quality – A customer's long-term overall evaluation of a service provider. ✪

Hays and Hill (2001) defined service quality as a customer's long-term overall evaluation of a service provider and **customer satisfaction** as the customer's evaluation of a specific service episode (a service event). However, some authors reverse these definitions. Service quality is perceived differently based on three types of product attributes: search qualities, experience qualities, and credence qualities.

Search qualities – Product attributes that can be fully evaluated prior to purchase. For example, the color of a dress purchased in a store can easily be evaluated before purchase. Color, style, price, fit, and smell are generally considered to be search qualities.

Experience qualities – Product attributes that cannot be evaluated without the product being purchased and consumed (experienced) by the customer. For example, the flavor of a food product cannot be evaluated until it is consumed. Given that the customer cannot fully evaluate the quality of the product until it is purchased, customers often have to rely more on personal recommendations for products that have experience qualities.

Credence qualities – Product attributes that cannot easily be evaluated even after purchase and consumption. For example, the quality of the advice from lawyers, doctors, and consultants is often hard to evaluate even after the advice has been given, because it is often quite subjective.

Zeithaml, Parasuraman, and Berry (1988) and many others define the service quality "gap" as the difference between the expectations and the delivery for a particular service episode. However, this model suggests that service quality (or customer satisfaction) is high when customers expect and receive mediocre service. In response to this problem, this author created the simple **FED-up model**, which states that F equals E minus D, where F = Frustration, E = Expectation, and D = Delivery. When $F = 0$, the customer is not necessarily satisfied; the customer is just not frustrated. In other words, no gap between expectation and delivery is not satisfaction, but rather the absence of dissatisfaction.

The **critical incidents method** is a good approach for identifying potential service quality dimensions. (See the *critical incidents method* entry.) The gap model is a good structure for measuring these dimensions on a survey, because it measures both importance and performance for each dimension of service quality. The gap model defines the gap as importance minus performance. Thus, if a service quality dimension has high importance but has low performance, it has a large gap and should be given high-priority.

Many hotels use three questions to measure customer satisfaction and service quality:

- Willingness to return – Do you intend to return to our hotel in the next year?
- Willingness to recommend – Would you recommend our hotel to your friends and family?
- Overall satisfaction – Overall, were you satisfied with your experience at our hotel?

More recently, many hotels have simplified the measurement process and now use the **Net Promoter Scale** developed by Reichheld (2003), which is a modification of the "willingness to recommend" question above. Dixon, Freeman, and Toman (2010) claim that the **Customer Effort Score (CES)** is a better predictor of customer loyalty in call centers than either the NPS or direct measures of customer satisfaction.

A common consultant's exhortation to service leaders is to "delight our customers!" However, great care should be taken in applying this slogan. For example, when this author traveled to Europe several years ago, an airline agent allowed him the option of using a domestic upgrade coupon to upgrade from coach to business class. He was delighted to be able to sit in business class for the eight-hour flight. However, a couple of weeks later, he flew the same route and was denied the same upgrade and therefoe was quite disappointed. The principle here is that **today's delight is tomorrow's expectation**. Service providers should not delight customers unless they can do so consistently, and when they do perform a "one-off" special service, they should manage the customer's expectations for the future.

Pine and Gillmore's (2007) book on "Authenticity" argues that in a world increasingly filled with deliberately staged experiences and manipulative business practices (e.g., frequent flyer miles), consumers choose to buy based on how real and how honest they perceive a service provider to be. This is related to the **moment of truth** concept.

It is sometimes possible to improve service quality by changing customer perception of waiting time using one of Maister's (1985) eight factors that affect customer perceptions of wait time:

- **Unoccupied waits seem longer than occupied waits** – An unoccupied wait is one where the customer has nothing to do or to entertain them; in other words, the customer is bored.

- **Pre-process waits seem longer than in-process waits** – For example, a patient might feel better waiting in the exam room (in-process wait) than in the waiting room (pre-process wait).
- **Anxiety makes waits seem longer.**
- **Uncertain waits seem longer than waits of a known duration** – Therefore, manage customer expectations.
- **Unexplained waits seem longer than explained waits.**
- **Unfair waits seem longer than equitable waits.**
- **The more valuable the service, the longer people will be willing to wait.**
- **Waiting alone seems longer than waiting with a group** – This is an application of the first factor.

ASQ has a Service Quality Division that has developed *The Service Quality Book of Knowledge*. More information on this book can be found on ASQ's website http://asq.org.

See *critical incidents method, Customer Effort Score (CES), customer service, empathy, empowerment, experience engineering, human resources, Kano Analysis, line of visibility, moment of truth, Net Promoter Score (NPS), primacy effect, quality management, service failure, service guarantee, Service Level Agreement (SLA), service management, Service Profit Chain, SERVQUAL, single point of contact, triage.*

service recovery – Restoring customers to a strong positive relationship with the firm after they have experienced a service failure. ✪

The service recovery principle (slogan) is, "It is much easier to keep an existing customer than it is to find a new one." Many consultants make unsubstantiated claims about this by stating that "It costs about ten times more to win a new customer than it does to keep an existing customer." The **customer acquisition cost** is the cost of finding a new customer and the **service recovery cost** is the cost of keeping a customer. Customer acquisition cost includes costs related to sales calls, advertising, direct mail, and other marketing communications, all of which can be quite expensive. Some firms measure the annual customer acquisition cost as the advertising budget divided by the number of new customers during a year. This analysis regularly finds good support for the claim that customer acquisition cost is high. Service recovery cost is the cost of compensating customers for a service failure plus some administrative cost, both of which are usually modest compared to the life-time value of the customer.

The **six steps to service recovery** are (1) listen, (2) apologize and show empathy, (3) ask the service recovery question "What can we do to completely satisfy you?" (4) fix the problem quickly (prioritize customers and escalate if needed), (5) offer symbolic atonement (something tangible the customer will appreciate), and (6) follow up to ensure that the relationship is fixed. Steps 3 and 5 of this process are particularly important, because they ensure the customer has been completely restored to a healthy relationship with the service provider.

This author developed the **three fixes of service quality**, which are (1) ensure the customer's specific problem is fixed, (2) ensure the customer relationship is fixed so he or she will return, and (3) ensure the system is fixed so this problem never recurs. Step (3) here requires root cause analysis and error proofing.

See *acquisition, error proofing, Root Cause Analysis (RCA), service failure, service guarantee, service management.*

serviceability – The speed, courtesy, competence, and ease of repair.

Serviceability is often measured by mean response time and Mean Time to Repair (MTTR).

See *Mean Time to Repair (MTTR), New Product Development (NPD).*

SERVQUAL – A service quality instrument (survey) that measures the gap between customer expectations and perceptions after a service encounter.

The SERVQUAL instrument developed by Parasuraman, Zeithaml, and Berry (1988) has been used in numerous service industries. The instrument is organized around five dimensions of customer service:

Tangibles – Physical facilities, equipment, and appearance of personnel

Reliability – Ability to perform the promised service dependably and accurately

Responsiveness – Willingness to help customers and provide prompt service

Assurance – Competence, courtesy, credibility, and security

Empathy – Access, communication, and understanding

The diagram below is the SERVQUAL model (Zeithaml, Parasuraman, and Berry 1988) with several adaptations made by this author. Customers get their expectations from their own past experiences with the service provider, experiences with other service providers, their own intrinsic needs, and from communications from the service provider. The basic concept of the model is that Gap 5 (the service quality gap) exists when the perceived service does not meet the expected service. This gap is the result of one or more other gaps. Gap 1 (the product design gap) is a failure to understand the customer's needs and expectations. Gap 2 (the process design gap) is a failure to design a process consistent with the product design. Gap 3 (the production gap) is a failure to actually deliver (produce) a service that meets the needs of a specific customer. Gap 4 (the perjury gap) is a failure to communicate to set and manage customer expectations. In summary, service providers should avoid the product design, process design, production, and perjury gaps in order to avoid the service quality gap and consistently deliver satisfying customer experience.

Teas (1994) and others challenge SERVQUAL in a number of ways. One of the main criticisms is that it defines quality as having no gap between expectation and delivery. However, some argue that service quality is not a function of the gap, but rather a function of the delivered value, which has no connection with the gap. For example, if someone hates McDonald's hamburgers and goes to a McDonald's restaurant and buys a hamburger, the customer gets what he or she expects. However, the customer will not perceive this as good quality. See the discussion of the FED-up model in the *service quality* entry for a simple model that addresses this issue.

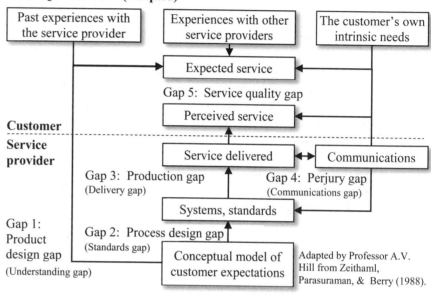

SERVQUAL Model (Adapted)

Adapted by Professor A.V. Hill from Zeithaml, Parasuraman, & Berry (1988).

See *customer service, empathy, service guarantee, service management, service quality*.

setup – The activity required to prepare a process (machine) to produce a product; also called a changeover.

A setup is a common term in a factory where the tooling on a machine has to be changed to start a new order. However, setups are an important part of all human activity. For example, a surgical operation has a setup time and setup cost to prepare the operating room for a surgery. A racecar has a changeover when it goes in for a pit stop on a racetrack. Adding a new customer to a database is also a setup process.

See *batch process, external setup, internal setup, sequence-dependent setup time, setup cost, setup time, setup time reduction methods*.

setup cost – In a manufacturing context, the cost to prepare a process (e.g., a machine) to start a new product; in a purchasing context, the cost to place a purchase order; also known as the changeover cost or order cost. ✪

The setup cost (or **ordering cost**) is an important parameter for managerial decision making for manufacturers, distributors, and retailers. This cost is particularly important when making **order sizing** (lotsizing, batchsize) decisions. If the ordering cost is close to zero, the firm can justify small lotsizes (order sizes) and approach the ideal of **just-in-time (one-piece flow)**. In a purchasing context, the ordering cost is the cost of placing and receiving an order. In a manufacturing context, the setup cost is the cost of setting up (changing over) the process to begin a new batch. This cost is usually called the "setup" or "changeover" cost.

In both the purchasing and manufacturing contexts, the ordering cost should reflect only those costs that vary with the number of orders. For example, most overhead costs (such as the electricity for the building) are not relevant to lotsizing decisions and therefore should be ignored. The total annual ordering cost is dependent only on the number of orders placed during the year.

The typical **standard costing** approach used in many firms includes allocated overhead in the order cost. In a manufacturing context, the number of standard labor hours for the machine setup is multiplied by the "burden" (overhead) rate. For many firms, the burden rate is more than $200 per shop hour. Many accountants make the argument that "all costs are variable in the long run," and therefore the overhead should be included in the ordering cost. Although this argument is probably true for product costing, it is not true for estimating the ordering cost for determining lotsizes. Inventory theorists argue that the ordering cost (setup cost) should be treated as a marginal cost, which means overhead costs should be ignored.

In the **purchasing context**, the cost components include the following:

- Order preparation component – Computer processing, clerical processing.
- Order communication component – The marginal cost of mailing, faxing, or electronic communication of the order to the supplier.
- Supply order charge – Any order processing charge from the supplier.
- Shipping cost component – The fixed portion of the shipping cost (note that the per unit shipping cost should be considered part of the unit cost and not part of the ordering cost).
- Receiving cost – Cost of handling the receipt of an order. This cost includes the accounting costs, the per order (not per unit) inspection costs, and the cost of moving the order to storage. Again, costs that vary with the number of units should not be included here.

In the **manufacturing context**, the cost components included in the setup cost include the following:

- Order preparation component – Computer processing and clerical processing.
- Order communication component – Sending the order paperwork or electronic information to the shop floor.
- Setup labor cost component – The incremental labor cost of setting up the machine. This cost should include the workers' hourly wage and fringe, but should not be assigned any other factory overhead (burden).
- Opportunity cost of the machine time lost to setup – At a bottleneck machine, time lost to a setup has tremendous value. In fact, for every hour that the bottleneck is sitting idle, the entire plant is also idle. Therefore, the opportunity cost of the capacity at the bottleneck is the opportunity cost of lost capacity for the entire plant. For example, if a plant is generating $10,000 in gross margin per hour, one hour lost to a setup at the bottleneck has an opportunity cost of $10,000. The opportunity cost for time lost to a setup at a non-bottleneck machine is zero. Goldratt and Cox (1992) and Raturi and Hill (1988) expand on these ideas.
- Shop floor control cost component – The cost of handling data entry activities associated with the order. Again, this is the cost per order that is handled.

Many plants have large setups between families of parts and small setups between parts within a family. The setups between families are sometimes called **major setups** and the setups between parts within a family are called **minor setups**.

A **sequence-dependent** setup time (or cost) is a changeover time (or cost) that is dependent on the order in which jobs are run. For example, it might be easy to change a paint-making process from white to gray, but difficult to change from black to white. Sometimes, setups are not sequence-dependent between items within a product family, but are sequence-dependent between families of products. When setup times (or costs) are sequence-dependent, it is necessary to have a "from-to" table of times (or costs), much like a "from-to" travel time table on the back of a map. Creating a schedule for sequence-dependent setup times is a particular type of combinatorial optimization problem that is nearly identical to the traveling salesperson problem.

See *batch process, burden rate, carrying charge, carrying cost, continuous process, joint replenishment, major setup cost, opportunity cost, order cost, overhead, product family, sequence-dependent setup time, setup, setup time, Single Minute Exchange of Dies (SMED), standard cost, Theory of Constraints (TOC), Traveling Salesperson Problem (TSP).*

setup time – The time required to prepare a machine for the next order; also called changeover time. ✪

See *batch process, continuous process, downtime, Economic Lot Scheduling Problem (ELSP), run time, sequence-dependent setup time, setup, setup cost, setup time reduction methods, Single Minute Exchange of Dies (SMED).*

setup time reduction methods – Procedures used to reduce the time and cost to change a machine from making one type of part or product to another; also called Single Minute Exchange of Die and rapid changeovers. ✪

For many processes, the key to process improvement is to reduce the setup time and cost. Setup time does not add value to the customer and is considered "waste" from the lean manufacturing point of view. Reducing setup times often provides significant benefits, such as less direct labor time, less direct labor cost, more available capacity, better customer service, better visibility, less complexity, and easier scheduling. Setup reduction also enables **small lotsizes**, which in turn reduces the variability of the processing time, reduces queue time, reduces cycle time, and ultimately improves quality through early detection of defects. In addition, setup reduction helps an organization strategically, because fast setups allow for quick response to customer demands.

Many firms have setups simply because they do not have enough volume to justify dedicating a machine to a particular part or product. In some cases, if a firm can reduce setup costs, it can function as though it has the same economies of scale as a much larger firm.

One of the best methods for reducing setup time is to move setup activities **off-line**, which is setup time done while the machine is still running. Another name for this is an **external setup**. This author uses the more descriptive term **running setup**, because the next job is being set up while the machine is still running. The figure below is a timeline that shows that external (off-line) setup is done while the machine is working, both before and after the internal (on-line) setup time.

Timeline showing external and internal setup time

Machine is running (cycle time)	Machine is idle (setup time)	Machine is running (cycle time)
External setup time (off-line setup time)	Internal setup time (on-line setup time)	External setup time (clean up, put away)
	Setup time for machine scheduling	
Total setup time for setup team labor and tool scheduling		

Time →

Source: Professors Arthur V. Hill and John P. Leschke

For example, at the Indianapolis 500 race, the crew will prepare the tires, fuel, and water for the race car while the car is still going around the track. When the racecar arrives in the pit area, the crew changes all four tires, adds fuel, and gives the driver water. All of this is done in about 18 seconds. Another example is a surgical procedure in a hospital where the nurses prepare a patient while another patient is still in surgery.

Setup teams can also reduce setup times. When a setup is needed, a signal (e.g., a light) indicates that all members of the setup team should converge on the machine. The setup team then quickly does its job. Some people who do not understand managerial accounting might challenge the economics of using a team. However, for a bottleneck process, the labor cost for the setup team is often far less than the cost of the capacity lost to a long setup. In other words, the increased capacity for the **bottleneck** and the plant is often worth more than the cost of the setup team.

Tooling, fixtures, and jigs also need to be managed well to reduce setup time. Buying **dedicated tools** can often be justified with an analysis of the

Source: Bert van Dijk /Wikimedia Commons

economic benefits of setup reduction. Using a setup cart that is carefully managed with 5S principles can also help reduce setup time.

Managers and engineers have only a limited time available for setup reduction. Therefore, it is important that setup reduction efforts be prioritized. Goldratt (1992) emphasizes that the priority should be on the bottleneck capacity. Leschke (1997a, 1997b) and Leschke and Weiss (1997) emphasize that some setups are shared by many items and therefore deserve higher priority in a setup reduction program.

See *agile manufacturing, cycle stock, early detection, external setup, internal setup, mixed model assembly, multiplication principle, one-piece flow, process, running setup, setup, setup time, Single Minute Exchange of Dies (SMED), staging, Theory of Constraints (TOC).*

seven tools of quality – A set of seven fundamental tools used to gather and analyze data for process improvement: histogram, Pareto Chart, checksheet, control chart, fishbone (Ishikawa) diagram, process map (flowchart), and scatter diagram (scatterplot). ✪

Many sources use the above seven tools, but some sources, such as the ASQ and Wikipedia websites replace process map with **stratification**, while others, such as Schroeder (2007), replace the checksheet with the **run chart**. This author argues that a process map is far more important than stratification, and a checksheet is more practical than a run chart. This author argues further that a **causal map** is better than a fishbone diagram and that other tools, such as **FMEA**, **error proofing**, and the **Nominal Group Technique**, should be added to the list.

Other technical quality tools include design of experiments (DOE), multiple regression (and other multivariate statistical techniques), statistical hypothesis testing, sampling, and survey data collection. Non-technical quality tools include project management, stakeholder analysis, brainstorming, and mindmapping. All of the above tools are described in this book.

See *C&E diagram, causal map, checksheet, control chart, flowchart, histogram, Nominal Group Technique (NGT), Pareto Chart, process map, quality management, run chart, scatter diagram, Statistical Process Control (SPC), Statistical Quality Control (SQC)*.

seven wastes – See *8 wastes*.

shadow board – A visual indicator of where tools should be stored on a wall or in a drawer; usually in the form of an outline similar to a shadow.

Shadow boards are a standard practice in the set-in-order step of 5S to organize tools and materials. Shadow boards call immediate attention to a failure to follow the discipline of "a place for everything and everything in its place," which is fundamental to 5S and lean thinking.

In work areas where several people share a set of tools, it is a good idea to require workers to "sign out" tools by putting cards with their names on the board where the tools are normally stored. In this way, everyone knows who has the tool. This simple visual approach is a good example of the application of lean thinking.

See *5S, error proofing, lean thinking, visual control*.

shadow price – See *sensitivity analysis*.

Shingo Prize – An annual award given to a number of organizations by the Shingo Prize Board of Governors based on how well they have implemented lean thinking; an organization headquartered at and sponsored by Utah State University that manages the Shingo Prize evaluation process, conferences, and training events.

According to the Shingo Prize website, "The Shingo Prize is regarded as the premier manufacturing award recognition program for North America. As part of the Shingo Prize mission and model, the Prize highlights the value of using lean/world-class manufacturing practices to attain world-class status." Similar to the Malcolm Baldrige Award, the Shingo Prize has developed a model (framework) that can be used prescriptively to evaluate the performance of an organization.

The prize is named after the Japanese industrial engineer **Shigeo Shingo**, who distinguished himself as one of the world's leading experts in improving manufacturing processes. According to the Shingo Prize website, Dr. Shingo "has been described as an engineering genius who helped create and write about many aspects of the revolutionary manufacturing practices which comprise the renowned Toyota Production System."

The Shingo Prize website homepage is http://bigblue.usu.edu/shingoprize.

See *lean thinking, Malcolm Baldrige National Quality Award (MBNQA)*.

shipping container – (1) Anything designed to carry or hold materials in transit. (2) A large metal shipping box of a standard size that is used to securely and efficiently transport goods by road, ship, or rail, without having to be repacked; also called ocean container.

In 2006, 20 million shipping containers were in use. Although containers are essential for international trade and commerce, no single system governs the international movement of containers, which makes it difficult to effectively track a container through the supply chain.

The International Organization for Standardization (ISO) regulates container sizes to ensure some consistency throughout the world. The standard external dimensions for containers are a width of 8 feet (2.44 m), height of 8.5 feet (2.59 m) or 9.5 feet (2.9 m), and length of 20, 40, or 45 feet (6.1 m, 12.2 m, or 13.7 m). For inside dimensions, deduct 4 inches (10.16 cm) from the width, 9 inches (22.9 cm) from the height, and 7 to 9 inches (17.8 cm to 22.9 cm) from the length. Common types of containers include:

General purpose (dry cargo) container – This is the most commonly used shipping container and can carry the widest variety of cargo. It is fully enclosed, weatherproof, and equipped with doors either on the end wall (for end loading) or the side wall (for side loading.) The most common lengths of general purpose containers are 20 feet and 40 feet. Containers are measured in 20-foot equivalent units (TEU), meaning that a 20-foot container is 1 TEU and a 40-foot container is 2 TEU. Other general purpose container sizes include a 10-foot length (mostly used in Europe and by the military) and the high-cube container, which is for oversized freight.

Thermal container (reefer) – This is a container with insulated walls, doors, roof, and floor, which helps limit temperature variation. The thermal container is used for perishable goods, such as meat, fruits, and vegetables. This type of container often has a heating or cooling device.

Flat rack (platform) – This is not an actual container, but rather a means for securing oversize cargo that will not fit into a regular container. The flat rack is equipped with top and bottom corner fittings that hold the cargo in place on the top deck of the vessel and is generally used for machinery, lumber, and other large objects.

Tank container – This type of container is used for bulk gases and liquids.

Dry bulk container – This is a container used to ship dry solids, such as bulk grains and dry chemicals. It is similar to the general purpose container, except that it is usually loaded from the top instead of from the side or the end. Each container has its own identification code with four letters that identify which ocean carrier owns the container (such as CSCL for China Shipping Container Lines) plus several numbers. After a container is loaded and sealed, the seal is assigned a number that is valid only for that shipment.

Container vessels vary greatly in size and capacity. A small container vessel might carry as few as 20 TEU, but most modern vessels carry 1,000 TEU or more. At the time of this writing, the largest container vessel in the world has a capacity of 8,063 TEU. Typical vessels load containers in tall slots that extend from three to six containers below deck to three to six containers above deck. The containers are locked at the corners.

See *cargo, cube utilization, less than container load (LCL), less than truck load (LTL), multi-modal shipments, trailer.*

shipping terms – See *terms.*

shop calendar – A listing of the dates available for material and capacity planning.

Materials Requirements Planning (MRP) systems need the shop calendar to backschedule from the order due date to create the order start date (Hamilton 2003). MRP systems also require the shop calendar to create capacity requirements planning reports.

See *Capacity Requirements Planning (CRP), job shop scheduling, Manufacturing Execution System (MES), Manufacturing Requirements Planning (MRP).*

shop floor control – The system used to schedule, release, prioritize, track, and report on operations done (or to be done) on orders moving through a factory, from order release to order completion; also known as production activity control. ✪

Major functions of a shop floor control system include:
- Assigning priorities for each shop order at each workcenter.
- Maintaining work-in-process inventory information.
- Communicating shop-order status information.
- Providing data for capacity planning and control purposes.
- Providing shop order status data for both WIP inventory and accounting purposes.
- Measuring efficiency, utilization, and productivity of labor and machines.
- Supporting scheduling and costing systems.

See *backflushing, dispatching rules, job shop scheduling, Manufacturing Execution System (MES), operation, routing.*

shop packet – A set of documents that move with an order through a manufacturing process; also called a traveler.

The shop packet might include bill of material, routing, pick slip, work instructions, production and labor reporting tickets, move tickets, and other support forms.

See *bill of material (BOM), Manufacturing Execution System (MES), routing.*

shortage – See *stockout.*

shortage cost – See *stockout.*

shortage report – A list of items not available to meet requirements for customer orders or production orders; also called a shortage list.

See *Over/Short/Damaged Report*.

shrinkage – (1) In an inventory context: Inventory lost due to deterioration or shoplifting (theft from "customers"), breakage, employee theft, and counting discrepancies. (2) In a call center context: The non-revenue generating time as a percentage of the total paid time; also called staff shrinkage.

In the inventory context, shrinkage is usually discovered during a cycle count. In the call center context, shrinkage is the percentage of paid working time that is unproductive. Unproductive time includes breaks, meetings, training, benefit time (sick, vacation, etc.), and other off-phone member service activities.

See *call center, carrying charge, carrying cost, cycle counting, obsolete inventory*.

SIOP – See *Sales & Operations Planning (S&OP)*.

sigma level – A metric that measures the defect rate for a process in terms of the standard normal distribution with an assumed shift in the mean of 1.5 standard deviations.

The sigma level metric is often taught in lean sigma programs as a measure of effectiveness for a process. The estimation process usually assumes that the control limit is set based on a standard normal random variable with mean 0 and standard deviation 1, but that the true process has a standard deviation of 1 and mean of 1.5 (instead of 0). The sigma level metric uses this model to estimate the number of defects per million opportunities (DPMO). The table below shows the DPMO for a range of sigma level and assumed mean shift values.

The well-known "3.4 defects per million opportunities" can be found in the top right cell of the table. For a sigma level of $SL = 6$ and mean shift $MS = 1.5$, the probability of a defect in the right tail is 0.000003398, the probability of a defect in the left tail is practically 0, and the overall probability of a defect is 0.000003398. Therefore, the total expected DPMO is $3.3977 \approx 3.4$.

Four-sigma represents an average performance level across many industry sectors. If the entire world operated on a four-sigma standard, the world would have some serious problems:

- 20,000 lost articles of mail per hour
- Unsafe drinking water 15 minutes per day
- 5,000 surgical errors per week   Two bad aircraft landings per day
- 200,000 wrong prescriptions each year
- No electricity 7 hours each month

The Excel formula for converting a "sigma level" (SL) with a mean shift (MS)

DPMO by sigma level and assumed mean shift

Sigma level (SL)	Assumed shift in the mean (MS)			
	$MS = 0.0$	$MS = 0.5$	$MS = 1.0$	$MS = 1.5$
6.0	0.0	0.0	0.3	3.4
5.6	0.0	0.2	2.1	20.7
5.2	0.2	1.3	13.3	108
4.8	1.6	8.6	72.4	483
4.4	10.8	48.6	337	1,866
4.0	63.3	236	1,350	6,210
3.6	318	988	4,663	17,865
3.2	1,374	3,575	13,917	44,567
2.8	5,110	11,208	36,003	96,809
2.4	16,395	30,582	81,094	184,108
2.0	45,500	73,017	160,005	308,770
1.6	109,599	153,530	278,914	461,140
1.2	230,139	286,529	434,644	621,378
0.8	423,711	478,889	615,190	768,760
0.4	689,157	723,888	806,504	893,050

Source: Professor Arthur V. Hill

into a defect rate (per million opportunities) is = (NORMDIST(-SL, MS, 1, TRUE) + 1 - NORMDIST(SL, MS, 1, TRUE))*1000000. As noted above, it is commonly assumed that the mean is shifted by $MS = 1.5$ sigma.

Contrary to the hyperbole found in many popular practitioner publications, six sigma may not be the optimal sigma level. The optimal sigma level may be lower or higher than six sigma and should be based on the cost of a defect relative to the cost of preventing a defect.

See *defect, Defective Parts per Million (DPPM), Defects per Million Opportunities (DPMO), DMAIC, lean sigma, operations performance metrics, process capability and performance, specification limits*.

simple exponential smoothing – See *exponential smoothing*.

simulated annealing – A heuristic search method used for combinatorial (discrete) optimization problems.

Simulated annealing is analogous to how the molecular structure of metals is disordered at high temperatures but ordered (crystalline) at low temperatures. In simulated annealing, the "temperature" starts out high, and the search for a better solution has a high probability of accepting an inferior solution. This allows the procedure to jump out of locally optimal solutions and potentially find a better solution. As the temperature is lowered, this probability decreases, and the best solution found so far becomes "frozen."

See *heuristic*, *operations research (OR)*, *optimization*.

simulation – A representation of reality used for experimentation purposes; some types of simulations are called Monte Carlo simulations. ✪

In operations management, a computer simulation is often used to study systems, such as factories or service processes. The computer simulation model allows the analyst to experiment with the model to find problems and opportunities without having to actually build or change the real system.

Simulation models can be categorized as either **deterministic** or **stochastic**. Deterministic simulations have no random components and therefore will always produce exactly the same results. Deterministic simulations, therefore, only need to be "run" once. On the other hand, stochastic simulations generate random variables and allow the user to explore the variability of the system. For example, a financial planning model might specify the mean and standard deviation of demand and the mean and standard deviation of the unit cost. The simulation model might be run for many replications to compute the net present value of a number of different strategies.

Stochastic simulations are also known as **Monte Carlo simulations**. Although Monte Carlo simulations can have a time dimension, most do not. For example, a Monte Carlo simulation could be used to cast two die (random integers in the range [1, 6]) several million times to get a distribution of the product of the two values.

Computer simulations can be further classified as either being **discrete**, **continuous**, or **combined discrete and continuous**. A discrete simulation processes distinct **events**, which means that the computer logic moves to a point in time (i.e., an event time), changes one or more of the system state variables, and then schedules the next event. In other words, the simulation model skips from one time point (event) to the next, and the system status changes only at these points in time. In contrast, a continuous simulation model represents the movement of continuous variables changing over time (e.g., the course of a rocket in flight).

The inverse transform method can be used to generate a random variable from any distribution with a known distribution function. More computationally efficient special-purpose generators are available for several probability distributions, such as the normal distribution. See the *random number* entry for more detail.

Many analysts new to simulation make several common errors in their simulation modeling efforts. Some of these errors include:

Not conducting a proper statistical analysis – Many new simulation users are tempted to let the simulation run for a few thousand observations and then compare the mean performance for the different alternatives considered in the experiment. The problem with this approach is that the means might not be statistically different due to the variability of the system.

Improper start-up conditions – Simulation models often need user-defined start-up conditions, particularly for queuing systems. Starting a system "empty and idle" will often cause serious bias in the average results.

Creating improper confidence intervals – Simulation statistics, such as the average number of customers (or units) in the system, are highly correlated over time. This is called autocorrelation or serial correlation. In other words, the number in system at time t is highly correlated with the number in system at time $t + 1$. As a result, many simulation analyses underestimate the variability and create confidence intervals on the mean that are far too small (narrow). The proper approach is to use batch means (the means over long time intervals) and then treat each batch mean as a single observation for computing a confidence interval. This often has significant implications for the number of observations that are needed.

Not considering all sources of variability – A research study done at the University of Michigan many years ago found that the biggest shortfall of most simulation models was the missing variables. For example, an inventory simulation might do a good job of handling the normal variability of the demand during the leadtime. However, this same simulation might ignore catastrophic events, such as fire in a supplier's plant, which might shut down the entire firm for a month.

Not taking advantage of common random number streams – Most simulation languages, such as Arena, allow the user to run multiple simulations on the "same track" with respect to the sequence of random values. This is done by dedicating a random number seed to each random process (e.g., the demand quantity, time between arrivals, etc.). This approach allows the analyst to have far more comparable results.

Simulation modeling has come a long way in the last 20 years. Commercial simulation software, such as Arena, makes simulation modeling easy. Unfortunately, it is just as easy today as it was 20 years ago to make serious errors in modeling and analysis. As an old saying goes, "Simulation should be the method of last resort." In other words, common sense and simple queuing models should be used before a simulation is attempted.

See *confidence interval, Decision Support System (DSS), inverse transform method, operations research (OR), random number, systems thinking, Turing test, what-if analysis.*

simultaneous engineering – A systematic approach to the integrated concurrent design of products and their related processes, including manufacturing and support.

Benefits of simultaneous engineering include reduced time to market, increased product quality, and lower product cost. Simultaneous engineering is closely related to **Design for Manufacturing (DFM)**. Simultaneous engineering appears to be synonymous with concurrent engineering and Integrated Product Development (IPD).

See *concurrent engineering, Integrated Product Development (IPD), New Product Development (NPD).*

single exponential smoothing – See *exponential smoothing.*

Single Minute Exchange of Dies (SMED) – A lean manufacturing methodology for reducing setup time to less than a single digit (e.g., less than 10 minutes); also called Single Minute Exchange of Die and rapid changeover.

This term was coined by Shigeo Shingo in the 1950s and 1960s. The term is used almost synonymously with **quick changeovers and setups**. The changeover time is the time from the last good part for one order to the first good part of the next order. A single-digit time is not required, but is often used as a target value. The *setup time reduction methods* entry has more information on this subject.

See *lean thinking, one-piece flow, setup cost, setup time, setup time reduction methods.*

single point of contact – A service quality principle suggesting that a customer should have to talk to only one person for the delivery of a service.

The single point of contact is summarized nicely with the slogan "one customer, one call, one relationship." This slogan emphasizes that each customer should only have to make one phone call and should only have to establish a relationship with one service provider. Unfortunately, the opposite of this occurs in many service organizations when a customer waits a long time in queue only to be told by the unfriendly service workers (or the phone system) that they will have to talk to someone else. The customer never builds a relationship with any service worker, and no service worker ever takes any "ownership" of the customer's needs.

Advantages of the single point of contact principle include (1) the firm builds a closer relationship with the customer, (2) the customer does not have to wait in multiple queues, (3) the customer's expectations are better managed, (4) much less information is lost in the "handoffs" between multiple service workers, (5) the job design is more satisfying for the service worker because they get to "own" the entire set of the customer's needs, and (6) the company may benefit from a reduced cost of service delivery in a "once and done" environment.

However, the single point of contact model is not without cost. In many cases, the single point of contact increases the cost of service, because workers require more training and one worker might have a long queue while another is idle. In other words, from a queuing theory standpoint, the single point of contact dedicates each server to a particular set of customers. If not managed carefully, this can increase average waiting time and decrease overall system performance.

See *handoff, job design, service quality.*

single sampling plan – See *acceptance sampling.*

single source – The practice of using only one supplier for an item or service even though one or more other suppliers are qualified to be suppliers.

With a single source supplier, a firm still has other qualified sources of supply that it could use in case of emergency. In contrast, with a sole source supplier, the firm has one and only one source of supply that is capable of supplying the item or service. A sole source supply is in essence a monopoly situation and can be risky for the customer. However, in some situations, a sole source relationship is unavoidable. For example, a music CD is usually sold by only one "label" (the artist's one and only distribution company). Music retailers, such as Best Buy have no choice but to have a sole source of supply if it wants to carry that artist's music.

With a dual source (or multiple source) relationship, the buying organization has two or more suppliers qualified to supply a material or component and actually uses two or more of these suppliers. A dual source relationship is a multiple source relationship with exactly two suppliers. Dual (or multiple) sourcing makes the most sense for commodity items, such as grain, salt, metals, or chemicals. Many firms have multiple sources of supply for a group of items (a commodity group) but still use a single source for each item in that group.

See *commodity, dual source, purchasing, sourcing.*

single-piece flow – See *one-piece flow.*

SIOP – See *Sales & Operations Planning (S&OP).*

SIPOC Diagram – An acronym for Suppliers, Inputs, Process, Outputs, and Customers, which is a tool used to identify all relevant elements of a process for the purposes of process improvement.

Suppliers ▶ Inputs ▶ Process ▶ Outputs ▶ Customers

All process improvement projects should consider all five of these elements. Note that this is a useful tool for all process improvement projects, not just supply chain projects.

See *process map, supply chain management, systems thinking, value chain.*

six sigma – See *lean sigma.*

skewness – A statistical measure of the asymmetry of the probability distribution of a random variable.

If a probability distribution has no skewness, it is symmetric on both sides of the mean, and the mean = median = mode. Mathematically, skewness is defined as the third standardized moment. For a sample of n observations, Wikipedia defines sample skewness as $g = \frac{1}{n}\sum_{i=1}^{n}(x_i - \overline{x})^3 \Big/ \left(\frac{1}{n}\sum_{i=1}^{n}(x_i - \overline{x})^2\right)^{3/2}$ where, $\overline{x}$ is the sample mean. The Excel formula SKEW(*range*) uses $g = \frac{n}{(n-1)(n-2)}\sum_{t=1}^{n}\left(\frac{x_t - \overline{x}}{s_x}\right)^3$, the ***Engineering Statistics Handbook*** (NIST 2010) uses $g = \frac{1}{n-1}\sum_{t=1}^{n}\left(\frac{x_t - \overline{x}}{s_x}\right)^3$, and von Hippel (2005) uses $g = \frac{1}{n}\sum_{t=1}^{n}\left(\frac{x_t - \overline{x}}{s_x}\right)^3$, where s_x is the sample standard deviation. All four of these equations produce slightly different results.

The skewness for all symmetric distributions, such as the normal is 0.

According to von Hippel (2005), many textbooks provide a simple rule stating that a distribution will be right skewed if the mean is right of the median and left skewed if the mean is left of the median. However, he shows that this rule frequently fails.

See *geometric mean, interpolated median, kurtosis, mean, median, mode, standard deviation, trimmed mean.*

skid – See *pallet.*

skill based pay – See *pay for skill.*

SKU – See *Stock Keeping Unit (SKU).*

slack time – The amount of time an activity (task) can be delayed from its early start time without delaying the project (or job) finish date; also called float. ✪

In the project scheduling context, slack time is called **float time** and is defined as the time that a task can be delayed without delaying the overall project completion time. A task with **zero float** is on the critical path and a task that has **positive float** is not on the critical path. In a job shop scheduling context, the slack time is the due date less the sum of the remaining processing time. The minimum slack time rule is a good dispatching rule for both project management and job shops.

For example, a student has a report due in 14 days but believes that it will take only three days to write the report and one day to get copies printed. Therefore, the student has a slack time of $14 - 3 - 1 = 10$ days.

See *critical chain, critical path, Critical Path Method (CPM), dispatching rules, job shop scheduling, Project Evaluation and Review Technique (PERT), project management, project network, safety leadtime.*

slotting – (1) In a warehouse context: Finding a location for an item in a warehouse, distribution center, or retail store; also called put away, inventory slotting, profiling, or warehouse optimization. (2) In a retail context: Finding a location for an item on a store shelf.

In the warehouse context, slotting attempts to find the most efficient location for each item. Factors to consider in making a slotting decision include picking velocity (picks/month), cube usage (cubic velocity), pick face dimensions, package dimensions and weight, picked package size, storage package size, material handling equipment used, layout of the facility, and labor rates. Benefits of good product slotting include:

- **Picking productivity** – Travel time can often account for up to 60% of a picker's daily activity. A good product slotting and pick path strategy can reduce travel time and reduce picking labor time and cost.
- **Efficient replenishment** – Sizing the pick face locations based upon a standard unit of measure (case, pallet) can reduce the labor time and cost required to replenish the location.
- **Work balancing** – Balancing activity across multiple pick zones can reduce congestion in the zones, improve material flow, and reduce the total response time.
- **Load building** – To minimize product damage, heavy products are located at the beginning of the pick path ahead of crushable products. Items can also be located based on case size to facilitate pallet building.
- **Accuracy** – Similar products are separated to minimize the opportunity for picking errors.
- **Ergonomics** – High velocity products are placed in a "golden zone" to reduce bending and reaching activity. Heavy or oversize items are placed on lower levels in the pick zone or placed in a separate zone where material handling equipment can be utilized.
- **Pre-consolidation** – By storing and picking products by family group, it is often possible to reduce downstream sorting and consolidation activity. This is particularly important in a retail environment to facilitate efficient restocking at the stores.

Warehouse operations managers often do a good job of slotting their warehouse initially, but fail to maintain order over time as customer demand changes and products are added and deleted. Therefore, it is important to re-slot the warehouse to maintain efficiency. Some organizations re-slot fast moving items on a daily or weekly basis. Most Warehouse Management Systems (WMS) have slotting functionality.

In a retail context, a **slotting fee** (or **slotting allowance**) is paid by a manufacturer or distributor to a retailer to make room for a product on its store shelves. In the U.S., slotting fees can be very significant.

See *cube utilization, forward pick area, locator system, picking, reserve storage area, slotting fee, task interleaving, trade promotion allowance, warehouse, Warehouse Management System (WMS)*.

slotting fee – Money paid by a manufacturer to a retailer to have a product placed on the retailer's shelves; also called slotting allowance, pay-to-stay, and fixed trade spending.

The slotting fee is charged to make room for a product on store shelves, make room for a product in a warehouse, and enter the product data (including the barcode) into the inventory system. According to Wikipedia, in the U.S., initial slotting fees are approximately $25,000 per item, but may be as high as $250,000.

See *slotting, Warehouse Management System (WMS)*.

slow moving inventory – A product with a low average demand, where low is usually defined to be less than five to nine units per period.

Many products have a low average demand. In fact, for many firms, most products are slow moving, with a demand less than nine units per period. Some slow moving items are high-price (or high-cost) items, such as medical devices, service parts, and capital goods (e.g., jet engines), and often have a high shortage (or stockout) cost. (A distinction between shortage and stockout cost is described in other places in this book.) Clearly, these items need to be carefully managed to find the right balance between having too much and too little inventory. Many other slow moving items are low-price (or low-cost) items and make up a small part of the firm's total revenue (or investment). Most inventory management texts appropriately urge managers to focus on the "important few" and not worry too much about the "trivial many." However, managers still need inventory systems to manage the "trivial many," or they will be overwhelmed by transactions, stockouts, inventory carrying cost, and errors. These items still require significant investment and still have a major impact on customer service. See the *obsolete inventory* entry for a discussion of how to handle inventory that is not moving.

It is often possible to make significant improvements in both service levels and inventory levels for slow moving items by applying the following principles:

- **Use a perpetual inventory system with a one-for-one replenishment policy** – This approach can achieve high service levels with little inventory. This is particularly helpful when inventory is in short supply and must be "allocated" to the multiple stocking locations.

- **Set the target inventory level that finds the optimal balance between the carrying and shortage costs** – If the target is set too low, the system will have too many angry customers and too much shortage cost. If the target is set too high, the system will have too much inventory and too much carrying cost. Given that the order quantity is fixed at one, the target inventory is the only decision parameter for this model.
- **Use a consistent policy across all stocking points and all items** – This will serve customers equitably and manage the balance between customer service and inventory investment.
- **Keep safety stock in the finished goods inventory or central warehouse so the company can "pool" the risk** – The safety stock should be "pooled" in a central location as much as possible so it is available when and where needed.

   See *all-time demand, newsvendor model, obsolete inventory, periodic review system, Poisson distribution, pooling, service level, service parts, stockout.*

SMART goals – An easy-to-remember acronym for a simple goal-setting method; also called SMARTS, SMARTER, and SMARTIE.

   The SMART acronym is a popular and useful goal-setting tool for both organizations and individuals. Although many websites attribute this acronym to Drucker (1954), according to the website www.rapidbi.com/created/WriteSMARTobjectives.html (May 26, 2008), "there is no direct reference to SMART by Drucker … While it is clear that Drucker was the first to write about management by objectives, the SMART acronym is harder to trace."

   Many variants of this popular acronym can be found on the Internet. In fact, only the first two letters seem to be universally accepted. The following list includes what appears to be the most popular variant for SMART goals and is this author's recommended list:

(S) Specific – Goals should be stated in plain, simple, unambiguous, specific language and written down so they are easy to remember, easy to communicate to others, and easy to know when the goal has been accomplished. A goal of losing weight is not specific; a goal of losing 20 pounds by Christmas is specific.

(M) Measurable – Goals should be quantifiable so it is possible to measure progress toward them. The slogan "You cannot manage what you cannot measure" has been popular for many decades. For example, progress toward a weight loss goal is measurable, while progress toward being healthier is not.

(A) Achievable – Goals should be realistic and also under control of the person who defines them. According to goal theory, a goal set too high will be discouraging, and a goal set too low is not motivating. Collins and Porras (1996) suggest that organizations need a "Big Hairy Audacious Goal," or "BHAG," to serve as a clear and compelling vision and catalyst for improvement. It is also imperative that goals be under the control of the organization or individual who defines them. If a goal is outside a person's control, it is just a wish or a dream. For example, a manager may want to increase a firm's profit by 10%, but profit is affected by many actions outside the firm's control (e.g., competitor's pricing).

(R) Results oriented – Goals should be a statement of an outcome and should not be a task or activity. In the words of David Allen (2001), this is the "desired outcome."

(T) Time specific – Goals should have a realistic time limit for accomplishing the outcome. Someone once defined a goal as "a wish with a time limit." It is not enough to set a goal of losing 20 pounds; it is also important to set a time frame (e.g., lose 20 pounds by Christmas).

   Steve Flagg, President of Quality Bicycle Products in Bloomington, Minnesota, wisely asserts that every goal should have a corresponding "purpose statement that precedes it – and that the purpose is just as important as the goal." For example, this author has a goal of exercising three times per week. This goal aligns with my purposes of being healthy, honoring God in my body, loving my wife, and modeling healthy living for my four boys.

   See *mission statement, one-minute manager, personal operations management.*

SME – See *Society of Manufacturing Engineers (SME).*

SME (Subject Matter Expert) – See *Subject Matter Expert (SME).*

SMED – See *Single Minute Exchange of Dies.*

smoothing – See *exponential smoothing.*

sniping – The practice of waiting until the last minute to place a bid in an auction.

   Sniping is a common practice in on-line auctions, such as eBay, and is often an effective strategy for helping bidders avoid price wars and get what they want at a lower final price (Roth and Ockenfels 2002). Some on-line auctions allow the deadlines to be extended to foil the sniping strategy. For example, Amazon auctions have a scheduled end time, but the auction is extended if bids are received near the scheduled end. The rule at Amazon is that the auction cannot end until at least ten minutes have passed without a bid.

See *Dutch auction, e-auction, e-business, reverse auction*.

Society of Manufacturing Engineers (SME) – A professional society dedicated to bringing people and information together to advance manufacturing knowledge.

For more than 75 years, SME has served manufacturing practitioners, companies, and other organizations as their source for information, education, and networking. SME supports manufacturers from all industries and job functions through events and technical and professional development resources.

SME produces several publications, including the practitioner-oriented *Manufacturing Engineering Magazine* and two scholarly journals, the *Journal of Manufacturing Systems (JMS)* and the *Journal of Manufacturing Processes (JMP)*. The *JMS* focuses on applying new manufacturing knowledge to design and integration problems, speeding up systems development, improving operations and containing product and processing costs. The *JMP* presents the essential aspects of fundamental and emerging manufacturing processes, such as material removal, deformation, injection molding, precision engineering, surface treatment, and rapid prototyping. SME's website is www.sme.org.

See *operations management (OM)*.

socio-technical design – See *job design*.

Software as a Service (SaaS) – A software application available on the Internet; also called software on demand and on-demand software; closely related to cloud computing.

With SaaS, customers do not own the software itself but rather pay for the right to use it. Some SaaS applications are free to the user, with revenue derived from alternate sources, such as advertising or upgrade fees. Examples of free SaaS applications include Gmail and Google Docs. Some of the benefits of SaaS over the traditional software license model include:

- **Lower cost** – Saves money by not having to purchase servers or other software to support use. In addition, cash flow for SaaS is better, because it has a monthly fee rather than an up-front cost.
- **Faster implementation** – Customers can deploy SaaS services much faster, because they do not have to install the software on their computers.
- **Greater focus** – Allows customers to focus on their businesses rather than the software implementation.
- **Flexibility and scalability** – Reduced need to predict scale of demand and infrastructure investment up front, because available capacity can always be matched to demand.
- **Reliability** – The SaaS provider often can afford to invest significant resources to ensure the software platform is stable and reliable.

This list of benefits was adapted from http://en.wikipedia.org/wiki/Software_as_a_service (October 1, 2010).

See *Application Service Provider (ASP), cloud computing, implementation, service management*.

sole source – See *single source, sourcing*.

SOP – Standard operating procedures. See *standardized work*.

sourcing – Identifying, qualifying, and negotiating agreements with suppliers of goods and services; also known as purchasing; sometimes called strategic sourcing. ✪

Sourcing is the process that purchasing organizations use to find, evaluate, and select suppliers for direct and indirect materials. The term can also be used for the process of acquiring technology, labor, intellectual property, and capital. **In-sourcing** is the practice of vertical integration so the organization provides its own source of supply. **Outsourcing** is the practice of having another legal entity serve as the source of supply. Although outsourcing is often on another continent, it can be on the same continent. In other words, outsourcing and **offshoring** are not synonyms. **Global sourcing** is the practice of searching the entire world for the best source of supply. **Regional sourcing** (also called **nearshoring**) is the practice of finding local suppliers to assure low replenishment leadtimes and low freight costs. Regional sourcing often also has political benefits, because some countries have local content laws that require a percentage of the product cost to come from local suppliers.

The decision to **sole source**, **single source**, or **multiple source** a **commodity** (a category of items) is an important strategic decision. The *spend analysis* entry discusses these issues in more detail.

See *business process outsourcing, commodity, intellectual property (IP), nearshoring, outsourcing, purchasing, single source, spend analysis, supply chain management.*

spaghetti chart – A diagram that shows the travel paths for one or more products (or people) that travel through a facility.

The numerous colored lines make it look like a plate of spaghetti. This tool helps identify opportunities for reducing the travel and move times in a process.

See *facility layout.*

spare parts – See *service parts.*

Spearman's Rank Correlation – See *correlation.*

SPC – See *Statistical Process Control (SPC).*

special cause variation – Deviations from common values in a process that have an identifiable source and can eventually be eliminated; also known as assignable cause.

Causes of variation that are not inherent in the process itself but originate from out of the ordinary circumstances. Special causes are often indicated by points that fall outside the limits of a control chart.

See *common cause variation, control chart, outlier, quality management, Statistical Process Control (SPC), Statistical Quality Control (SQC), tampering.*

specification – See *specification limits.*

specification limits – The required features and performance characteristics of a product, as defined at different levels of detail.

Specifications are defined in terms of an upper, a lower specification limit, or both. Specification limits may be two-sided, with upper and lower limits, or one-sided, with either an upper or a lower limit. Unlike control limits, specification limits are not dependent on the process in any way. Specification limits are the boundary points that define the acceptable values for an output variable of a particular product characteristic. Specification limits are determined by customers, product designers, and management.

See *control chart, process capability and performance, sigma level, Statistical Process Control (SPC), Statistical Quality Control (SQC).*

speed to market – See *time to market.*

spend analysis – A careful examination and evaluation of where a purchasing organization is currently spending its purchasing dollars with the purpose of finding opportunities to reduce cost or improve value.

Spend analysis answers questions such as:
- How much are we spending in total?
- How much are we spending in each category?
- Who are our suppliers?
- How much is our spend with each supplier?
- How much is our spend in each category with each supplier?
- What parts, materials, and other tools are we getting from each supplier?
- How can we "leverage" our spend to reduce our direct and indirect materials cost?
- How can we reduce our usage?
- Where are we at risk with our spend?

Spend analysis is often motivated by the fact that a $1 reduction in spend is roughly equivalent to a $3 to $5 increase in sales (in some cases). In other words, the contribution to profit of a $1 reduction in purchase cost is about the same as the contribution to profit of increasing sales by $3 to $5. Spend analysis typically achieves savings by identifying opportunities to **leverage the spend**. This means that the organization requires that all business units use the same suppliers, which enables the organization to negotiate a lower price. Other spend analysis tools include reducing demand (e.g., make it harder for workers to make photocopies), substituting cheaper products (e.g., requiring reused toner cartridges), and segmenting suppliers so more important commodities are managed more carefully.

Kraljic (1983) developed a **purchasing portfolio model** (shown below) that can be used to segment items and suppliers, prioritize and mitigate risks, and leverage buying power. Each of the four categories requires a different sourcing strategy. **Non-critical** items require efficient processing, product standardization, and inventory optimization. **Leverage** items allow the buyer to exploit its purchasing power. **Bottleneck** items have high risk but low profit impact and therefore require risk mitigation strategies. **Strategic** items require careful and constant attention and often require strategic partnerships.

Geldermana and Van Weeleb (2003) question the dimensions used in the Kraljic model and note that it is difficult to measure these dimensions. They also suggest that the model should allow for movement between quadrants. Other dimensions that might be used to segment suppliers or items include total spend, number of buyers in the market, number of suppliers in the market, buyer/supplier power, and generic items (commodity) versus customized (engineered) items. The *sourcing* entry addresses similar issues.

Kraljic's purchasing portfolio model

		Low	High
Profit impact	High	Leverage items	Strategic Items
	Low	Non-critical items	Bottleneck Items

Supply risk

Adapted from Karljic (1983)

See *leverage the spend, Maintenance-Repair-Operations (MRO), purchasing, sourcing, supplier, supply chain management.*

sponsor – A project management term for an individual (individuals) who is (are) the main customer and primary supporter for a project.

The project sponsor is the main customer for the project. The project is initiated by the sponsor and is not complete until the sponsor has signed off on it. However, the sponsor is also responsible for holding the project team accountable for staying on schedule, in budget, in scope, and focused on meeting the requirements as defined in the project charter. Lastly, the project sponsor is responsible for ensuring that the project team has the resources (people, money, equipment, space, etc.) and the organizational authority that it needs to succeed.

See *champion, cross-functional team, deliverables, DMAIC, post-project review, project charter, project management, project management triangle, steering committee.*

sprint burndown chart – An agile or scrum software development project management tool that provides a graphical representation of the work remaining in any given sprint.

A sprint burndown chart shows the number of days in the sprint on the x-axis and features (or hours) remaining on the y-axis. The sprint burndown chart is reviewed daily in the scrum meeting to help the team review its progress and to give early warning if corrective actions are needed. The chart is updated daily by the scrum master and is visible to team members at all times.

See *agile software development, prototype, scrum, waterfall scheduling.*

SQC – See *statistical quality control.*

square root law for safety stock – When the replenishment leadtime increases by a factor of f, the safety stock will increase approximately by the factor $\sqrt{f}$.

This relationship is based on the safety stock equation and is often helpful when considering offshoring production. This model can be used to estimate the increase in safety stock due to an increase in the leadtime.

See *inventory management, safety stock.*

square root law for warehouses – A simple mathematical model stating that the total inventory in a system is proportional to the square root of the number of stocking locations.

The practical application of this "law" is that the inventory in stocking locations (such as warehouses) will increase (or decrease) with the square root of the number of stocking locations that serve the market. For example, doubling the number of stocking locations will increase inventory by a factor of the square root of two (i.e., ~ 1.414 or about 41% increase). This law warns managers against the naïve assumption that adding stocking locations will require no additional inventory.

Mathematically, the law can be stated as $I = a\sqrt{n}$, where I is the total inventory, n is the number of stocking locations (typically warehouses), and a is a constant. A more useful version of this model is $I_{new} = I_{old}\sqrt{n_{new}/n_{old}}$, where I_{old} and I_{new} are the old and new inventory levels and n_{old} and n_{new} are the old and new number of stocking locations.

As mentioned above, this law states that if a firm doubles the number of warehouses, it should expect to increase inventory by a factor of $I_{new} / I_{old} = \sqrt{n_{new} / n_{old}} = \sqrt{2/1} \approx 1.414$. In other words, doubling the number of stocking locations should increase inventory by about 41%. Similarly, if the firm cuts the number of stocking locations in half, it should expect to see inventory go down by a factor of $\sqrt{1/2} \approx 0.707$. In other words, cutting the number of stocking locations in half should reduce inventory by about 30%. The table below shows the multiplicative percentage increase or decrease in inventory as the number of stocking points changes.

Multiplicative change in inventory investment with a change in the number of stocking points

		Number of future stocking points, I_{new}							
		1	2	3	4	5	10	15	20
Number of current stocking points, I_{old}	1	100%	141%	173%	200%	224%	316%	387%	447%
	2	71%	100%	122%	141%	158%	224%	274%	316%
	3	58%	82%	100%	115%	129%	183%	224%	258%
	4	50%	71%	87%	100%	112%	158%	194%	224%
	5	45%	63%	77%	89%	100%	141%	173%	200%
	10	32%	45%	55%	63%	71%	100%	122%	141%
	15	26%	37%	45%	52%	58%	82%	100%	115%
	20	22%	32%	39%	45%	50%	71%	87%	100%

Source: Professor Arthur V. Hill

The square root law can be found in the literature as far back as Starr and Miller (1962) and was proven mathematically by Maister (1976) based on a reasonable set of assumptions. Evers (1995) found that the square root law can be applied to both safety stock and cycle stock and therefore can be applied to total inventory. Coyle, Bardi, and Langley (2002) provide empirical support for this model. Zinn, Levi, and Bowersox (1989) found that (1) the square root law is most accurate when market demands are negatively correlated, (2) accuracy increases with the demand uncertainty at each location as measured by the coefficient of variation, and (3) little or no benefit from consolidating stock when demands at stocking points are positively correlated.

See *consolidation, inventory management, supply chain management, warehouse.*

stabilizing the schedule – See *heijunka.*

stage-gate process – A project management and control practice commonly used for New Product Development (NPD) that uses formal reviews at predetermined steps in the project to decide if the project will be allowed to proceed; also called phase review, toll gate, tollgate, or gated process.

Cooper (1993, 2001) developed the stage-gate process to help firms improve their NPD processes. Many have argued that compared to a traditional process, the stage-gate process brings products to market in less time, with higher quality, greater discipline, and better overall performance (Cooper 1993).

A gate is a decision point (milestone or step) where the project status is reviewed and a decision is made to go forward, redirect, hold, or terminate the project. A formal stage-gate process will have a standardized set of deliverables for each gate. This standardization allows the management team to compare the relative value of NPD projects in the new product portfolio and to make trade-off decisions. A gate scorecard can be used to evaluate the deliverables against the standard. For example, demonstrating robust design may be a requirement in an early stage. The scorecard status may be yellow (caution) if the C_{pk} of a critical quality parameter is only 1.

Cooper (2001) outlines the following typical stage-gate phases:

1. **Discovery:** Pre-work designed to discover opportunities and generate ideas. (Gate = Idea screen)
2. **Scoping:** A quick, preliminary investigation of the project. (Gate = Second screen)
3. **Building the business case:** A detailed investigation involving primary research, both technical and marketing, leading to a business case. This business case includes the product definition, project justification, and a project plan.
4. **Development:** The detailed design and development of the product and the production process to make it.
5. **Testing and validation:** Trials in the marketplace, lab, and plant to verify and validate the proposed new product and its marketing and production.
6. **Launch:** Commercialization (beginning of full production, marketing, and selling).

The stages from the Advanced Product Quality Planning (APQP) process of the Automotive Industry Action Group (AIAG) are **Concept approval**, **Program approval**, **Prototype**, **Pilot**, and **Launch**.

A typical stage-gate process is as follows:

1. **Market analysis:** Various product concepts that address a market need are identified.
2. **Commitment:** The technical feasibility of a particular product concept is determined and design requirements are defined.
3. **Development:** All activities necessary to design, document, build, and qualify the product and its associated manufacturing processes are included.
4. **Evaluation:** Final design validation of the product is conducted during this phase. Clinical and field studies are conducted, and regulatory approval to market and distribute the product is also obtained.

Stage-gate processes for new product development

Cooper	AIAG	Typical
Discovery		
Scoping	Concept approval	Market analysis
Building the business case	Program approval	Commitment
Development	Prototype	Development
Testing and validation	Pilot	Evaluation
Launch	Launch	Release

Source: Professor Arthur V. Hill

5. **Release:** The product is commercially distributed in markets where regulatory approval has been obtained. The table above summarizes these three frameworks.

Many lean sigma programs use a similar "gated" process at the end of each of the steps in the DMAIC framework to provide accountability and keep the project on track. However, some experts argue that stage-gates create too much overhead and slow a project down and therefore should only be used for large projects. Some project management experts argue that stage-gates should be based on the nature of the specific project rather than on the DMAIC framework.

See *deliverables, Design for Six Sigma (DFSS), DMAIC, lean sigma, milestone, New Product Development (NPD), phase review, project charter, project management, waterfall scheduling.*

staging – The manufacturing practice of gathering materials and tools in preparation for the initiation of a production or assembly process.

In the manufacturing order context, staging involves picking materials for a production or sales order and gathering them together to identify shortages. This is sometimes called kitting. Staged material is normally handled as a location transfer and not as an issue to the production or sales order. In the machine setup context, staging involves gathering tools and materials while the machine is still running.

See *kitting, setup time reduction methods.*

stakeholder – People, groups of people, and organizations involved in or affected by a decision, change, or activity.

The following is a long list of potential stakeholders for a process improvement project:

- Shareholders
- Senior executives
- Managers
- Administrators
- Process owner(s)
- Doctors/nurses/LPNs
- Project team members
- Operators
- Coworkers
- Previous manager
- Customers/consumers
- Students
- Patients/clients
- Prospective customers
- Network members
- Payers
- Insurers
- Partners
- Suppliers
- Distributors/Sales force
- Other departments
- Support organizations
- Technology providers
- Trade associations
- Unions
- Professional societies
- The press
- Lenders
- Analysts
- Neighbors
- Community
- Future recruits
- Regulators
- Government
- Spouse/children/family
- God[55]

See *agile software development, Business Continuity Management (BCM), product life cycle management, project charter, project management, RACI Matrix, stakeholder analysis.*

stakeholder analysis – A technique for identifying, evaluating, and mitigating political risks that might affect the outcomes of an initiative, such as a process improvement project.

---

[55] *The point here is that organizations should consider ALL of their stakeholders.*

The goal of stakeholder analysis is to win the most effective support possible for the initiative and to minimize potential obstacles to successful implementation. Stakeholder analysis is particularly important in major quality management, process improvement, and Business Process Re-engineering (BPR) programs.

The three steps in stakeholder analysis are:

- **Identify the stakeholders** – Identify people, groups, and institutions that might influence the activity (either positively or negatively). The RACI Matrix is a good tool for helping with this process. See *RACI Matrix*.
- **Evaluate "what is in it for me"** – Anticipate the kind of influence these groups will have on your initiative.
- **Develop communication and involvement strategies** – Decide how each stakeholder group should be involved in the initiative and how the team will communicate with them.

The following example illustrates a formal stakeholder analysis using a new quality control information system as an example. This table can be easily implemented in Excel or Word. The process starts by defining each stakeholder's goals and identifying how the project might help or hinder those goals (the positives and negatives). The involvement strategy seeks to define the right level of involvement for each key stakeholder group and get them involved early in the project. The communication strategy should define the frequency of communication, mode of communication, and audience for each stakeholder group.

Stakeholder analysis example

	Stakeholder			
	Quality	**Manufacturing**	**MIS**	**Manufacturing Engineering**
Goals	Improve product quality and improve reporting.	Improve product quality and reduce cost of poor quality.	Keep the backlog of projects from growing.	Keep the backlog of projects from growing.
Positives	This system could help us quickly find defects and find systemic problems.	This system could help us quickly find defects and find systemic problems.	This project will replace an old system that has been hard to maintain.	The new system will make it easier for us to run reports on the quality data.
Negatives	Our team has no capacity to handle this project right now.	Our team has little capacity for this. We do not have a strong project leader available.	This new system is more complex and will be difficult to integrate with existing systems.	We worry that the new system will not include important features that we need to do our jobs.
Involvement strategy	Someone from our Quality team should be on the project team, but should not lead it.	A Manufacturing person should lead the project because manufacturing is the customer.	Should have a business analyst on the team, but should not lead the project.	Should either have a member on the team or at least have an SME available to the team.
Communication strategy	E-mail weekly report and provide face-to-face monthly report to the quality manager.	E-mail weekly report and provide face-to-face monthly report to the director of manufacturing.	E-mail monthly status report to the director of MIS.	E-mail monthly status report to the manager of manufacturing engineering.

Source: Professor Arthur V. Hill

The following is a general list of potential benefits for employees: remove frustration, remove bottlenecks, reduce bureaucracy, make things simpler, improve morale, improve teamwork, improve communication, accelerate learning, help them serve customers better, and free up time for more important work.

Some experts suggest "co-opting" a potential opponent by inviting them to join the project team as a member or Subject Matter Expert (SME). The idea is to get your potential opponents on your side early in the process and use their energy to move the project forward rather than get in the way. See the *co-opt* entry.

See *Business Process Re-engineering (BPR)*, *change management*, *co-opt*, *force field analysis*, *implementation*, *lean sigma*, *lean thinking*, *project charter*, *project management*, *quality management*, *RACI Matrix*, *stakeholder*, *Total Quality Management (TQM)*.

stamping – (1) A manufacturing process that forms materials. (2) A part made by a stamping process.

Stamping is usually done on **sheet-metal**, but can also be done on other materials. Stamping is usually done with a **press** that applies pressure to form the metal with a **mold** or **die**. For safety purposes, presses often have controls that require the operator to have both hands out of the press. This is a good example of **error proofing**.

See *die cutting, error proofing, manufacturing processes.*

standard cost – A system of estimating product costs based on direct labor, direct materials, and allocated overhead. ✪

The standard costing system in most manufacturing firms defines the standard cost as (standard time for direct labor) x (standard labor rate) + direct materials + overhead. Overhead is typically allocated based on the direct labor cost. More sophisticated firms allocate overhead using Activity Based Costing (ABC) methods.

When firms allocate overhead to products based on direct labor as the only cost driver, they are often allocating the largest component of cost (i.e., overhead) based on the smallest component (i.e., direct labor). Because of product variety and complexity, a constant burden rate (overhead rate) based on direct labor is no longer appropriate for many firms. This approach has several problems, including:

- **Too much focus on direct labor** – Because overhead is allocated on the basis of direct labor, many managers assume that they can reduce overhead by reducing direct labor, which is clearly misguided.
- **Poorly informed outsourcing decisions** – When managers assume that the overhead will go away when direct labor goes away, they sometimes make poorly informed outsourcing decisions and only later discover that the overhead does not disappear.
- **Death spiral overhead costs** – When decisions are made to outsource a product and the overhead does not go away, overhead then has to be reallocated to other products, and the firm enters into a "death spiral" with the same overhead being allocated to fewer and fewer products. (See the *make versus buy decision* entry).
- **Poor understanding of product costs** – Allocation of overhead on direct labor hides the true product costs, especially when direct labor is a small portion of the total cost.

See *absorption costing, Activity Based Costing (ABC), burden rate, make versus buy decision, overhead, setup cost, standard time, variable costing.*

standard deviation – A measure of the dispersion (variability) of a random variable; the square root of the variance. ✪

The *variance* entry has much more information on this subject.

See *coefficient of variation, confidence interval, forecast error metrics, Mean Absolute Deviation (MAD), mean squared error (MSE), range, sample size calculation, sampling, skewness, variance.*

standard hours – See *standard time.*

Standard Operating Procedure (SOP) – See *standardized work.*

standard parts – Components that an organization has decided will be used whenever possible.

Most firms define a set of standard parts to be purchased in commodity categories, such as fasteners (bolts, nuts, clips, etc.), which leads to purchasing economies and also simplifies design and manufacturing. This concept can also be applied to commonly used parts that are designed and manufactured by the firm. The concept can be broadened to include standard containers, standard labels, standard procedures, etc.

See *commodity, commonality, interchangeable parts, pull system, standard products, VAT analysis.*

standard products – A good made repetitively to a fixed product specification.

Many manufacturing firms make standard products and store them in inventory. This make to stock strategy makes sense for many consumer goods products that have fairly predictable demand. In contrast, customized products must be built (made, assembled, or configured) to a customer's specifications.

Note, however, that it is possible to make standard products to customer order when the manufacturing cycle time is shorter than the customer leadtime. This customer interface strategy is particularly helpful for low-demand, high-cost standard products.

See *assembly line, commonality, focused factory, interchangeable parts, make to order (MTO), make to stock (MTS), postponement, product proliferation, respond to order (RTO), standard parts.*

standard time – The planned processing time per part; also called standard hours. ✪

Standard times are used for planning machine and labor load and machine and labor capacity and also for assigning direct labor costs to products as they pass through a process. Standard times are also frequently used as a basis for incentive pay systems and as a basis for allocating manufacturing overhead.

Standard time is calculated as the normal time adjusted for allowances for personal needs, fatigue, and unavoidable delays. See the *normal time* entry for more detail. The allowance should depend on work environment issues, such as temperature, dust, dirt, fumes, noise, and vibration, and can be as high as 15%. Standard times can be set for both setup time and for run time.

Some firms update standard times and costs on an annual basis. Creating standard times is one of the traditional roles for the industrial engineering function.

See *efficiency, industrial engineering, load, normal time, operations performance metrics, performance rating, standard cost, time study, work measurement, work sampling.*

standard work – See *standardized work.*

standardization – See *standardized work.*

standardized loss function – See *safety stock.*

standardized work – The discipline of creating and following a single set of formal, written work instructions for each process; also called standard work. ✪

Frederick Taylor (1911), the father of scientific management, emphasized standardized work and the "one best way" for a job design. Traditionally, organizations in North America have called these work instructions "Standard Operating Procedures" or SOPs. More recently, the Lean Enterprise Institute and other leaders of the lean manufacturing movement have called these Standardized Work Instructions (SWIs). Standardized work is a key element of the Toyota Production System (TPS).

Standardized work is particularly important when a process is performed by different people, in different workcenters, in different locations, or on different shifts. Although it is normally applied to repetitive factory and service work, it can also be applied to less repetitive knowledge work done by professionals and salaried workers. For example, supervisors and managers should also have some standardized work. Doctors should have an SOP for a surgical procedure. Exam rooms should have a standard design so each room has the same layout, equipment, and supplies, which makes it easy for doctors to share several exam rooms.

In lean manufacturing, the term "standard work" emphasizes having standards for the most effective combination of labor, materials, equipment, and methods. For repetitive operations, standard work defines the takt time, work sequence, and standard work in process. Lean firms often use simple text and photos so procedures are clear for workers from a variety of educational, cultural, and language backgrounds. They are located next to the process so operators can see them often and so they are readily available for training purposes.

In some firms, language can be an issue due to a multilingual workforce. In these situations, it is important to provide SOPs in multiple languages. Again, photos and diagrams can be very helpful.

Some firms have implemented SOPs on computer systems. These systems allow for multiple languages and can also provide photos, videos, animations, and games for training. They can also administer tests for internal training and certification programs.

Purpose – The purpose of an SOP is to:		**Benefits** – The benefits of standardized work include:	
•	Document the correct process	•	Less variation in how work is performed
•	Control the organization	•	Improved quality
•	Control work processes	•	Fewer defects
•	Provide training content	•	Reduced cycle time
•	Help implement change	•	Faster training
•	Produce consistent outcomes (reduce variability)	•	Help the organization find new work methods
Requirements – Standard procedures should:			
•	Be clear, complete, and concise.	• Cover emergency situations.	
•	Be realistic.	• Define the process for where to go to get help.	
•	Be written for the user.	• Define the minimum performance standards.	
•	Be revised promptly.	• Define training requirements.	
•	Define the limits of authority.	• Be routinely used for training.	

Suggested format – A suggested format for an SOP follows:		
ADMINISTRATION	CONTENT	• Definitions
• Author	• Purpose	• Responsibilities and
• Approval authority	• Overview	organization
• Title with revision control	• Departments	• Instructions with photos,
• Effective date	• Scope	process maps, steps, etc.
• File name and page numbering		• Regulatory responsibilities
• Approval steps/sign off		Attachments/References

According to the ***Lean Lexicon*** (Marchwinski & Shook 2006), standardized work is based on three elements:
1. Takt time, which is the rate at which products must be made in a process to meet customer demand.
2. The precise work sequence in which an operator performs tasks within takt time.
3. The standard inventory, including units in machines, required to keep the process operating smoothly.

See *5S, Business Process Re-engineering (BPR), division of labor, human resources, ISO 9001:2008, job design, job enlargement, lean thinking, process improvement program, process map, scientific management, Total Productive Maintenance (TPM), work simplification.*

starving – Forcing a process to stop because of lack of input materials. ✪

Starving a **bottleneck process** is bad, because it will reduce the output of the entire system. Starving a **non-bottleneck process** generally has few consequences for the overall output of the system. Starving a non-bottleneck process might signal that the worker should be moved to somewhere else in the process. Given that the bottleneck resource defines the **capacity** for the entire plant, starving a bottleneck resource results in the loss of capacity for the entire plant. Starving a bottleneck resource might signal the need to improve the planning system or increase buffers to avoid the situation going forward. Starving and **blocking** are often discussed in the same context and are important concepts in the **Theory of Constraints (TOC)** literature.

See *blocking, kanban, Theory of Constraints (TOC).*

statement of work (SoW) – See *project charter.*

station time – The "touch time" at each workstation.

See *cycle time.*

Statistical Process Control (SPC) – A set of statistical tools that can be used to monitor the performance of a process. ✪

SPC is usually implemented using graphical methods called control charts to check if the process performance is within the upper and lower control limits. Ideally, a control chart will signal a problem with all special (unusual) causes of variation and ignore normal variation.

People sometimes confuse control limits with product specification limits. Control limits are a function of the natural variability of the process. The control limits are based on the process standard deviation (sigma) and are often set at plus and minus three sigma. Unlike control limits, specification limits are not dependent on the process in any way. Specification limits are the boundary points that define the acceptable values for an output variable of a particular product characteristic. Specification limits are determined by customers, product designers, and management. Specification limits may be two-sided, with upper and lower limits, or one-sided, with either an upper or a lower limit.

Inspection can be performed by variables or by attributes. Inspection by variables is usually done for process control and is performed with an x-bar chart (to control the mean) or an r-chart (to control the range or variance). Inspection by attributes is usually done for lot control (acceptance sampling) and is performed with a p-chart (to control the percent defective) or a c-chart (to control the number of defects).

See *Acceptable Quality Level (AQL), acceptance sampling, attribute, c-chart, common cause variation, control chart, cumulative sum control chart, Deming's 14 points, incoming inspection, inspection, lean sigma, np-chart, operating characteristic curve, p-chart, process capability and performance, process validation, quality assurance, quality management, r-chart, seven tools of quality, special cause variation, specification limits, Statistical Quality Control (SQC), tampering, Total Quality Management (TQM), u-chart, x-bar chart, zero defects.*

Statistical Quality Control (SQC) – A set of statistical tools for measuring, controlling, and improving quality.

> See *Acceptable Quality Level (AQL), acceptance sampling, attribute, c-chart, common cause variation, control chart, cumulative sum control chart, Deming's 14 points, hypergeometric distribution, incoming inspection, inspection, lean sigma, operating characteristic curve, p-chart, process capability and performance, process validation, quality assurance, quality management, r-chart, seven tools of quality, special cause variation, specification limits, Statistical Process Control (SPC), tampering, Total Quality Management (TQM), x-bar chart, zero defects.*

steering committee – A project management term for a group of high-level stakeholders who are responsible for providing overall guidance and strategic direction for a project or program.

> See *project management, sponsor.*

stickiness – The ability of a website to hold the attention of the visitor.

> Stickiness is generally accomplished through intriguing, useful, and/entertaining content.

stock – A synonym for inventory.

> See *part number.*

Stock Keeping Unit (SKU) – See *part number.*

stock position – See *inventory position.*

stockout – A situation in which a customer demand cannot be immediately satisfied from current inventory; often used synonymously with a shortage. ✪

> Stockouts can often be attributed to either incorrect safety stock parameters (e.g., bad numbers in the computer) or poor ordering disciplines (planners not following the numbers in the computer).
>
> The **cost of a stockout** may be nothing if customers are willing to wait or have to wait because they have no other alternatives. However, in many situations, the stockout cost includes the lost margin. In some severe situations, the stockout cost includes the net present value of the lifetime value of the customer or even the total lifetime value of that customer and many others who are influenced by that customer's word of mouth.
>
> Many (if not most) sources use the terms **shortage** and stockout interchangeably and only make a distinction between stockouts with backorders (the customer is willing to wait) and stockouts with lost sales (the customer is not willing to wait). However, the term "stockout" is sometimes used to imply that the sale is lost, whereas the term "shortage" implies that the customer is inconvenienced, but the sale is not lost. If the customer is willing to wait, the demand is said to be "backordered," and we have a shortage, but not a stockout.
>
> Statistical models can be used to infer (impute) the **implied shortage cost** (or implied stockout cost) for a given reorder point, safety stock, or target inventory value. The reorder point (R) that minimizes the sum of the expected carrying and expected shortage cost is the solution to the newsvendor problem for one order cycle, which is $R = F^{-1}(c_{under}/(c_{under} + c_{over}))$, where $F^{-1}(.)$ is the inverse CDF for the demand during leadtime distribution, c_{under} is the underage cost (the cost of setting R one unit too low), and c_{over} is the overage cost (the cost of setting R one unit too high). The underage cost is the shortage cost per unit short, and the overage cost is the cost of carrying one unit for one order cycle (i.e., $c_{over} = icQ/D$), where i is the carrying charge, c is the unit cost, Q is the average order quantity, and D is the expected annual demand. Note that the optimal safety stock is the optimal reorder point less the average demand during leadtime. We can rewrite this equation to determine the shortage cost implied by a given reorder point. In other words, if R is given, the implied shortage cost is $c_s = F(R)icQ/D/(1 - F(R))$, where $F(R)$ is the CDF for the demand during leadtime evaluated at R.

> See *backlog, backorder, goodwill, newsvendor model, opportunity cost, order cycle, safety stock, service level, slow moving inventory.*

stockout cost – See *stockout.*

story board – Large, visual communication of important information and key points.

> Consultants often talk about their "story board" for a PowerPoint presentation. This is a high-level overview of the main points that they want to make in their presentation. Story boards are often taped to the wall in a conference room to help the consulting team envision and improve the flow of ideas in a presentation.

> See *MECE, Minto Pyramid Principle.*

Straight Through Processing (STP) – An initiative used by financial trading firms to eliminate (or at least reduce) the time to process financial transactions.

STP is enabled by computer-based information and communication systems that allow transactions to be transferred in the settlement process without manual intervention. STP represents a major shift from present-day, three-day trading to same-day settlement. One of the benefits of STP is a decrease in settlement risk, because shortening transaction-related processing time increases the probability that a contract or an agreement is settled on time (adapted from www.investopedia.com/terms/s/straightthroughprocessing.asp, December 10, 2007).

See *lockbox*.

Strategic Business Unit (SBU) – A business unit that has either value propositions, core competences, or markets that are different from the other business units in the firm, and therefore must have its own unique strategy. ✪

strategic sourcing – See *sourcing*.

strategy map – A causal map that shows the relationships between the critical elements of the organization's business system. ✪

Kaplan and Norton (2000) proposed strategy maps as a tool for communicating the critical relationships and metrics needed to understand and implement the organization's strategy. According to Larry Bossidy, former Chairman of Honeywell, many companies fail to execute their strategy and therefore fail in the marketplace because they do not clearly communicate the strategy to those responsible for executing it (Bossidy, Charan, & Burck 2002). Many so-called leaders give only a vague description to their "troops" of what they should do and why each task is important. As a result, they ultimately "lead" their firms to failure. With mixed messages and unclear direction from the top, managers will do what they think is in the best interests of the firm, their own departments, and their own careers.

In the information age, businesses must create and manage complex business systems to offer distinctive value. These business systems are defined by highly interdependent relationships between customers, distributors, suppliers, employees, buildings, machines, product technologies, process technologies, information technologies, knowledge, and culture. These relationships must be made clear if the strategy is going to be understood and implemented in these complex business systems.

Strategy maps can show cause and effect relationships for business relationships, such as the following:

- The firm's value proposition, target markets, and business performance
- The firm's value proposition and investments in people, systems, R&D, capacity, and process technology
- Employee recognition programs, employee reward systems, employee motivation, service quality, customer satisfaction, and customer loyalty
- Sales force size, incentives, and sales
- Advertising investment, message, and media selection

Strategy maps can also highlight the key metrics that will be used to motivate and monitor the execution of the strategy. Kaplan and Norton (1996) argue that the strategy map should focus on the few "balanced scorecard" metrics that drive the strategy to success. These metrics should be reported at a high level in the firm. Goldratt (1992) emphasizes that most organizations have only one constraint (bottleneck) that restricts performance and that this constraint should be the focus for the strategy and the metrics.

Kaplan & Norton's four views for a strategy map

Financial
↑
Customer
↑
Internal
↑
Learning and growth

As shown on the right, Kaplan and Norton's strategy maps show the causal relationships going from the bottom up to the top and require four perspectives (views or levels) for the strategy map – financial, customer, internal, and learning and growth. They require that the causal linkages always go in order from learning and growth at the bottom to financial at the top.

The figure below is a simplified example of a strategy map from **Strategy Maps** (Kaplan & Norton 2004). This example shows how the four perspectives cascade up the causal map to create the airline's strategy. The strategic analysis begins at the top with the question, "How do we improve RONA?" The answer in this analysis is to grow the business without adding more aircraft. As the analysis moves down the causal linkages, the key strategic initiative must be ground crew training to improve the ground turnaround time. Spear (2008) asserts that this fast turnaround is the main competitive advantage of Southwest Airlines.

Each link in the strategy map states a "hypothesis" or a belief about the causal relationship. For example, in this strategy map, we see that management believes that "ground crew training" will improve the turnaround time. Now that this link is explicitly communicated as a part of the strategy, it can be openly discussed and even tested.

In the causal mapping work by Scavarda, Bouzdine-Chameeva, Goldstein, Hays, and Hill (2006) and others, strategy maps can be drawn in any direction and do not require Kaplan and Norton's four perspectives. They argue that Kaplan and Norton's strategy mapping process imposes too much structure on the causal mapping process. See the *causal map* entry for a strategy map presented in a causal mapping format. See the *Balanced Scorecard* entry for a complete list of references.

See *balanced scorecard, causal map, DuPont Analysis, hoshin planning, hypothesis, lean sigma, mindmap, mission statement, operations performance metrics, operations strategy, target market, turnaround time, value proposition, Y-tree.*

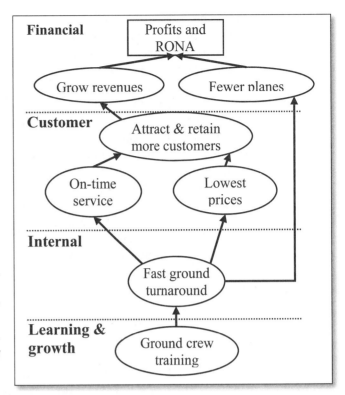

stratification – See *sampling.*

stratified sampling – See *sampling.*

Student's *t* distribution – A continuous probability distribution used when the sample size is small (i.e., less than 30) to test if two population means are different or to create a confidence interval around a population mean; also known as the *t*-distribution, the *T* distribution, and the Student's *t* distribution.

Given a random sample of size n from a normal distribution with mean μ, sample mean $\bar{x}$, and sample standard deviation s, the *t* statistic is the random variable $t = \dfrac{(\bar{x} - \mu)}{s / \sqrt{n}}$, which follows the Student's *t* distribution with $k = n - 1$ degrees of freedom. The density function for the *t* statistic is symmetric around the origin and bell-shaped like the standard normal distribution, but has a wider spread (fatter tails). As the degrees of freedom increase, the tails of the *t* distribution become thinner, and the *t* distribution approaches the normal. Most statistics texts state that when $n > 30$, the normal is a good approximation for the Student's *t* distribution.

The *z* statistic is defined as $z = \dfrac{(\bar{x} - \mu)}{\sigma / \sqrt{n}}$. Both *t* and *z* are approximately standard normal (e.g., $N(0, 1)$) when n is large (i.e., $n > 30$), but *z* is exactly standard normal regardless of the sample size if the population is exactly normal with known standard deviation σ. The *t* statistic is exactly Student's *t* if the population is exactly normal regardless of the sample size.

Parameter: Degrees of freedom, k.

Density and distribution functions: $f(t,k) = \dfrac{\Gamma((k+1)/2)}{\sqrt{\pi k}\ \Gamma(k/2)} \left(1 + t^2/k\right)^{(-k+1)/2}$ with k degrees of freedom,

$k \in I$, $k \geq 1$. $F(t,k) = \dfrac{\Gamma((k+1)/2)}{\sqrt{\pi k}\ \Gamma(k/2)} \displaystyle\int_{x=-\infty}^{t} \left(1 + x^2/k\right)^{-(k+1)/2} dx$ with k degrees of freedom.

Statistics: Range $(-\infty, \infty)$. Mean = 0 for $k > 1$; otherwise undefined. Median = mode = 0. Variance = $k/(k-2)$ for $k > 2$; ∞ for $1 < k \leq 2$; otherwise, undefined.

Graph: The graph on the right compares the normal density function (narrow line) with the Student's t density with $k = 2$ (darker line) and $k = 10$ degrees of freedom (middle line). The Student's t approaches the standard normal as k increases.

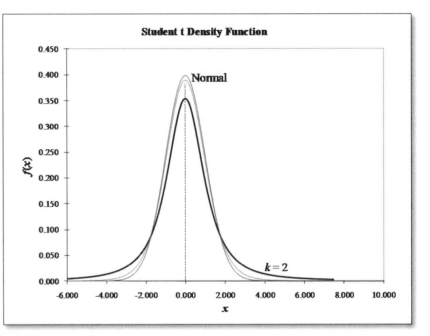

Excel: Caution: The Excel 2003 and 2007 documentation for the Student's t distribution is confusing. TDIST(x, k, *tails*) returns the tail probabilities for a t distributed random variable with k degrees of freedom for one or two tails (*tails* =1 or 2). If *tails* = 1, TDIST(x, k, *tails*) returns the upper tail probability (e.g., $P(t_k \geq x)$ and if *tails* = 2, TDIST(x, k, *tails*) returns $P(|t| > x)$ or equivalently $P(t < -x) + P(t > x)$. If $x < 0$, $F(x) =$ TDIST($-x$, k, 1) and if $x \geq 0$, $F(x) = 1 -$ TDIST(x, k, 1). TDIST is not defined for $x < 0$.

TINV(p, k) is the $100(1 - p)$ percentile of the two-tailed t distribution with k degrees. In other words, if $p < 0.5$, then $-$TINV($2p$, k) $= F^{-1}(p)$ and if $p \geq 0.5$, then TINV($2(1 - p)$, k) $= F^{-1}(p)$. For example, when $(p, k) =$ (0.0364, 10), then $F^{-1}(0.0364) = -$TINV($2 \cdot 0.0354$, 10) $= -2.0056$ and when $(p, k) =$ (0.9636, 10), then $F^{-1}(0.9636) =$ TINV($2(1 - 0.9636)$, 10) $= 2.0056$. The TINV function requires that $p \leq 0.5$.

TTEST(*array1*, *array2*, *tails*, *type*) is used for t-tests. See the *t-test* entry for more information.

Excel does not have a function for the Student's t density function, but $f(t, k)$ can be calculated with the Excel formula EXP(GAMMALN($(k+1)/2$))/SQRT(PI()*k)/EXP(GAMMALN($k/2$))/$(1+(t)\text{^}2/k)$ $\text{^}((k+1)/2)$.

History: Statistician William Sealy Gosset first published the Student's t distribution in an article in ***Biometrika*** in 1908 using the pseudonym "Student." Wikipedia's article on Gosset and many other sources state that Gosset wanted to avoid detection by his employer, the Dublin brewery of Guinness, because Guinness did not allow employees to publish scientific papers due to an earlier paper revealing trade secrets. However, one source (www.umass.edu/wsp/statistics/tales/gosset.html, May 1, 2010) claims that the secrecy was because Guinness did not want competitors to know it was gaining a competitive advantage by employing statisticians.

See *confidence interval*, *gamma function*, *normal distribution*, *probability density function*, *probability distribution*, *t-test*.

subassembly – See *assembly*.

subcontracting – A person or organization that enters into a contract to perform part of or all the obligations of another party's contract.

See *level strategy*, *outsourcing*, *systems engineering*.

Subject Matter Expert (SME) – Someone who is knowledgeable about a particular topic and therefore is designated to serve as a resource for a consulting project or process improvement project team.

SMEs are normally considered advisers to the project team rather than full team members. Consulting firms use the term "SME" for consulting experts who provide deep information on a particular topic. Some consulting firms are now using the term "subject area specialists."

See *project charter*, *project management*.

suboptimization – A situation that occurs when an organization achieves something less than the best possible performance due to (a) misalignment of rewards or (b) lack of coordination between different units.

Suboptimization occurs in organizations when different organizational units seek to optimize their own performance at the expense of what is best for the organization as a whole. For example, the sales organization might exaggerate sales forecasts to ensure that enough inventory is available. However, this practice might result in high inventory carrying cost. Good leaders practice systems thinking, which motivates them to understand the entire system and find global rather than suboptimal solutions.

See *balanced scorecard, Management by Objectives (MBO), systems thinking.*

subtraction principle – Application of the lean thinking to eliminate the waste in a process.

Love (1979) defines the elimination principle for improving a process as removing any unnecessary activities. This is one important application of lean thinking.

See *8 wastes, addition principle, human resources, job design, lean thinking, multiplication principle.*

successive check – See *inspection.*

sunk cost – An important managerial economics principle that once a cost has been incurred, it becomes irrelevant to all future decision making. ✪

For example, a firm has invested $10 million in developing a new product. The firm needs to decide what it should do with respect to the new product. A careful analysis of the situation should consider the future alternatives for the firm without regard to the amount of money already invested. That investment is a sunk cost and is irrelevant to the evaluation of the alternatives. Organizations and individuals should not allow emotions or reputational concerns to confuse their analysis in making sound economic decisions about courses of action.

See *economics, financial performance metrics, marginal cost.*

super bill of material – See *bill of material (BOM).*

supermarket – A lean manufacturing concept of using a buffer inventory on the shop floor to store components for downstream operations.

In the context of lean manufacturing, a supermarket is typically a fixed storage location and is designed to provide highly visual current status information. A withdrawal of a unit from a supermarket will usually signal the need for more production.

See *fixed storage location, lean thinking, pacemaker, periodic review system.*

supplier – An individual or organization that provides materials or services to a customer; also known as a vendor. ✪

Most buyers request materials or services from a supplier through a purchase order, and most suppliers respond to a purchase order with an invoice to request payment. Many suppliers are wholesalers or distributors who purchase and store materials produced by manufacturers. Wholesalers and distributors are often valuable members of a supply chain because they provide **place utility** (by having products close to the buyer) and time utility (by being able to get the product to the buyer quickly) and can reduce transaction cost (by being able to provide a wide variety of products with only one financial transaction). For example Granger, a large supplier (distributor) of MRO products to manufacturers, provides 3M sandpaper and many other factory supplies from a single catalog and from many stocking locations around North America.

See *Accounts Receivable (A/R), invoice, Maintenance-Repair-Operations (MRO), purchase order (PO), purchasing, spend analysis,* supply *chain management, wholesaler.*

supplier managed inventory – See *vendor managed inventory (VMI).*

supplier qualification and certification – Programs designed by purchasing organizations to test if suppliers can meet certain standards.

A supplier is said to be **qualified** by a customer when it has been determined that the supplier is **capable** of producing a part. A supplier is said to be **certified** when it has delivered parts with perfect quality over a specified time period. In many organizations, when a supplier becomes certified, the customer stops inspection. Ideally, the two firms then share in the cost savings. Of course, each purchasing organization will have its own standards for qualification and certification.

See *dock-to-stock, inspection, purchasing, quality at the source, quality management, receiving, supply chain management.*

supplier scorecard – A tool for customers to give evaluative feedback to their suppliers about their performance, particularly with respect to delivery and quality.

A supplier scorecard is a powerful tool for customers to give feedback to their suppliers about their performance and to help them improve over time. In addition, many leading firms, such as Best Buy, also use supplier scorecards as a mechanism for inviting suppliers to give them feedback so they can work together to improve supplier coordination and communication. Each firm has different needs and therefore should have a unique scorecard format. Ideally, supplier scorecards should be as simple as possible, measure only the vital few metrics, and be updated regularly.

Standardizing the supplier scorecard for an entire firm has advantages with respect to systems, communications, and training. Multi-divisional firms need to standardize their scorecards so suppliers that supply to more than one division will see only one supply scorecard – or at least only one supplier scorecard format. However, many firms have found this to be a difficult challenge.

Supplier scorecards have many benefits for both the customer and the customer's supply network, including:

- **Creation benefits** – The process of setting up a supplier scorecard program forces the customer to align competitive priorities and the supply management strategy by deciding which supplier metrics are most important to the business. For example, if a customer competes primarily on product innovation, a responsive supply chain is important and the metrics should focus on new product development collaboration and leadtimes and de-emphasize price (or cost). Similarly, if the customer competes on price, an efficient supply chain is important and the metrics should focus on price (Fisher 1997). It is common for customers to constantly "beat up" suppliers, telling them that they need to improve everything or they will lose business. However, the reality is that many metrics conflict with each other, and a supplier can only successfully focus on improving a few metrics at a time. If too many metrics are chosen, the supplier will spread limited resources too thin and little improvement will be achieved.
- **Communication and prioritization benefits** – An effective supplier scorecard helps customers and suppliers communicate on a higher level. When a scorecard is published, the leadership of the supplier's organization receives a clear message about what is important to the customer.
- **Process improvement program benefits** – An effective supplier scorecard system helps the supplier prioritize process improvement projects in light of the customer's requirements.
- **Rapid correction benefits** – If the measurement period is properly established, a good scorecard program can help point out easily correctable problems. For instance, if the metrics are measured every week, and it is noted that there is a pattern of higher lot rejects every fourth week, it could indicate that problems are arising at the end of each month, because the supplier rushes to get inventory out the door to make monthly shipping goals.
- **Supplier selection benefits** – The scorecard program will also serve as an objective tool for making data-driven supplier selection (sourcing) decisions. It is easy for customers to focus only on the most recent disappointment (e.g., the most recent late shipment or rejected lot) and make judgments based on perception and emotion. Once a scorecard program has been implemented, it becomes easier to analyze the data to reach sound conclusions about which course of action should be taken. The supplier with the highest scorecard rating will likely retain the business and be awarded a larger share of any new business.
- **Commitment benefits** – A properly developed scorecard program can help create a climate of cooperation that can benefit the customer and the supplier.

The typical measurement for make to stock items is the percentage of orders filled immediately from stock. In addition, average days-late information may also be recorded. For make to order and assemble to order items, the metrics relate to on-time delivery. This metric must define the "on-time" standard, which could be defined as the requested delivery date, the original promised delivery date, or a revised promised delivery date. Most firms use the original promised delivery date.

In addition to being delivered on time, a product must also meet the customer's quality requirements. The parts should meet the agreed-to level of quality for construction and tolerances based on the specifications that the parts are ordered to. Quality can either be measured in percentages of lots accepted (first pass yield), defects per million opportunities (DPMO), or other similar measures.

Delivery and quality are the foundation for nearly all supplier scorecard programs, but many firms also use additional metrics such as:

- Customer service	- Planned versus actual leadtime	- Improvement in process capabilities/SPC
- Technical support	- R&D metrics/Product innovation	
- Volume flexibility	- Financial metrics	- Process innovation

- Pricing
- Cost savings ideas
- Risk management

However, many of these metrics are difficult and costly to measure, making it important for the supplier and the customer to define them jointly and agree on the measurement method.

Many companies benefit from a supplier scorecard program. Scorecards have the potential to significantly improve supplier performance without large capital investments. A properly structured program will give the buying organization the necessary tool for making important sourcing decisions. A good supplier scorecard program can also help the purchasing organization prioritize its supplier development/supplier process improvement efforts.

In some cases the customer will see supplier improvement that is due to superficial improvement, such as increased sorting of defective parts. Ideally, a good scorecard program should drive improvements backward through the supply chain so the customer has visibility into the capabilities of the suppliers' processes.

See *balanced scorecard, benchmarking, buyer/planner, customer service, dashboard, incoming inspection, on-time delivery (OTD), operations performance metrics, purchasing, supply chain management, yield.*

supply chain – See *supply chain management.*

Supply Chain Council – A non-profit professional society dedicated to meeting the needs of supply chain management professionals; most famous for its development and use of the SCOR Model.

The Supply Chain Council was founded in 1996 by the consulting firm Pittiglio Rabin Todd & McGrath (PRTM) and AMR Research and initially included 69 voluntary member companies.

The Supply Chain Council now has about 1,000 corporate members worldwide and has established international chapters in North America, Europe, Greater China, Japan, Australia/New Zealand, South East Asia, Brazil and South Africa. Development of additional chapters in India and South America are underway. The Supply Chain Council's membership consists primarily of practitioners representing a broad cross-section of industries, including manufacturers, services, distributors, and retailers.

The Supply Chain Council is closely associated with the SCOR Model. The website for the Supply Chain Council is www.supply-chain.org.

See *operations management (OM), SCOR Model, supply chain management.*

supply chain management – The activities required to manage the flow of materials, information, people, and money from the suppliers' suppliers to the customers' customers. ✪

Supply chain management is the integration of and coordination between a number of traditional business functions, including sourcing, purchasing, operations, transportation/distribution/logistics, marketing/sales, and information systems. It also includes coordination and collaboration with channel partners, which can be suppliers, intermediaries, third party service providers, and customers. In essence, supply chain management integrates supply and demand management within and across companies.

The table below lists the responsibilities, entities, and decisions for each of the primary functions involved in supply chain management. All of these functions must be involved in coordinating with the others for the organization and the supply chain to be successful.

Function	Main responsibility	Main entities	Decisions
Sourcing/ purchasing/ procurement	Finding suppliers and acquiring materials and services.	Suppliers, materials, purchase orders, commodities, technologies	Suppliers, orders, support for new product development
Operations	Making products	Facilities, equipment, workers, materials, products, purchase orders, customer orders, and manufacturing orders	Processes, locations, product/plant assignments, workforce, systems, inventories
Transportation/ logistics/ distribution	Moving and storing products and materials	Carriers, facilities, warehouses, customers, products, transport orders	Modes of transport, carriers, warehouses, inventories, schedules, service levels, contracts
Marketing/sales	Managing the channel to the customer	Customers, channels, channel partners, sales force, customer orders, products	Channel strategy, channel partners, sales force, prices, sales force incentives, forecasting

Information systems	Providing information	Systems, databases, technology suppliers	Systems for the firm (e.g., ERP) and for the supply chain (e-procurement, e-auctions, EDI)

Source: Professor Arthur V. Hill

The Supply Chain View figure on the right was developed from an extensive survey of more than 300 supply chain experts (Scavarda & Hill 2003). The figure emphasizes that supply chain management begins with the fundamental premise that coordination, collaboration, and a sense of co-destiny can be beneficial

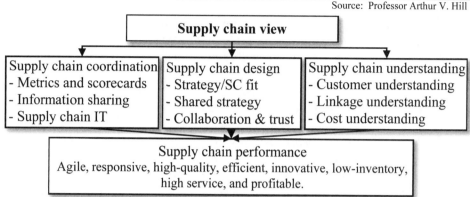

Source: Professor Arthur V. Hill

to all members in a supply chain. In the words of Professor K. K. Sinha[56], "Competition is no longer firm against firm, but supply chain against supply chain." Starting with this supply chain view, the "partners" in the supply chain need to design the supply chain to fit with a common strategy. These activities require collaboration and trust. Based on this strategy, the supply chain "partners" need to coordinate their efforts for both new and existing products. This requires shared metrics, scorecards to communicate these metrics, and information systems to communicate transactional data and the scorecard information. Parallel to the coordination, it is critical that the supply chain "partners" develop a deep understanding of the customers for the supply chain (not just their immediate customers), how they are linked together (information and transportation systems), and the cost structure for the entire supply chain.

The result of good supply chain management should be lower total system cost (lower inventory, higher quality), higher service levels, increased revenues, and increased total supply chain profit. However, the key issue is how the supply chain will share the benefits between the players in the supply chain.

Supply chain management is a major theme of this encyclopedia. The reader can find more information on supply chain management principles by going to the links listed below. The *SIPOC Diagram* and *SCOR Model* entries provide particularly useful frameworks for understanding supply chain management.

See *broker, bullwhip effect, business process outsourcing, buy-back contract, channel conflict, channel integration, channel partner, contract manufacturer, cross-docking, demand chain management, digital supply chain, disintermediation, distribution channel, distributor, dot-com, facility location, forecasting, Institute for Supply Management (ISM), inventory management, inventory position, leverage the spend, logistics, make versus buy decision, maquiladora, materials handling, materials management, offshoring, operations strategy, outsourcing, pipeline inventory, purchasing, risk sharing contract, SCOR Model, SIPOC Diagram, sourcing, spend analysis, square root law for warehouses, supplier, supplier qualification and certification, supplier scorecard, Supply Chain Council, systems thinking, tier 1 supplier, traceability, value chain, vendor managed inventory (VMI), vertical integration, warehouse, wholesaler.*

sustainability – The characteristic of a process that can be indefinitely maintained at a satisfactory level; often equated with green manufacturing, environmental stewardship, and social responsibility. ✪

In the environmental context, sustainability usually refers to the longevity of systems, such as the climate, agriculture, manufacturing, forestry, fisheries, energy, etc. Ideally, these systems will be "sustainable" for a very long time to the benefit of society.

In the supply chain context, sustainability deals with issues, such as reducing, recycling, and properly disposing of waste products, using renewable energy, and reducing energy consumption. Some of the supply chain decisions that affect sustainability include (1) product design (packaging, design for environment, design

---

[56] *Private communication with the author many years ago.*

for disassembly), (2) building design (green roofs, xeriscaping[57], energy efficiency), (3) process design (sewer usage, water consumption, energy efficiency, safety), and (4) transportation (reducing distance traveled, using fuel efficient vehicles, reducing product weight by making liquid products more concentrated).

For example, Bristol-Myers Squibb defined specific goals for 2010 on the following dimensions (source: http://bms.com/static/ehs/vision/data/sustai.html, October 11, 2008):

- Environmental, health, and safety
- Safety performance
- Environmental performance
- Sustainable products
- Supply chain
- Sustainability awards
- Biotechnology
- Community
- Social
- Endangered species
- Land preservation

An executive at General Mills contributed this informal list of bullet points that his company uses in internal training on sustainability (with a few edits by this author):

- Measurement systems – Life cycle analysis of ingredients and materials.
- Tracking systems – Water, gas, electricity.
- External relationships – Paint a picture of the stakeholders, NGOs, governments, shareholders, watchdog groups, for-profit agencies, and rating agencies.
- Public communications – What's in a corporate social responsibility report?
- Agriculture and bio-systems "supply chains" – Where does food come from?
- Sourcing – Where does everything else come from?
- Demographics – World population, consumption of raw materials per capita.
- Emerging economies – Growth of China and India and the impact on the world.
- Recycling – How does it work? Does it work? What can and can't be recycled?
- Politics and taxation of carbon – Cap and trade, world treaties, taxing to manage consumption.
- Organic – Facts and fiction.

See *cap and trade, energy audit, green manufacturing, Hazard Analysis & Critical Point Control (HACCP), hazmat, operations strategy, triple bottom line.*

swim lanes – See *process map.*

switching cost – The customer's cost of switching from one supplier to another. ✪

For example, the switching cost for a medical doctor to change from implanting one type of pacemaker to another is quite significant, because the doctor will have to learn to implant a new type of pacemaker and learn to use a new type of programmer to set the parameters for the pacemaker.

It is often in the supplier's best interest to increase the customer's switching costs so the customer does not defect to the competition the first time the competition offers a slightly lower price. Some suppliers have been successful in increasing switching costs through frequent-purchase reward programs. For example, large airlines offer frequent flyer miles to encourage flyers to be "loyal" to their airlines. Others have increased switching costs by helping customers reduce transaction costs through information systems. For example, a hospital supply firm provided free computer hardware to hospitals to use to order their supplies. This lowered the hospital's transaction cost, but also made it harder for the hospitals to change (switch) to another supplier.

An interesting study by Oberholzer-Gee and Calanog (2007) found that trust increased the perceived switching cost and created barriers to entry. Customers were reluctant to change suppliers when they had a supplier they could trust, even when a competitor appeared to offer superior benefits.

See *core competence, loss leader, outsourcing, search cost, total cost of ownership, transaction cost, Vendor Managed Inventory (VMI).*

SWOT analysis – A popular strategic analysis tool that considers strengths, weaknesses, opportunities, and threats.

SWOT analysis is a tool for auditing an organization and its environment. It is a good place to start a strategic planning process. Strengths and weaknesses are internal factors, whereas opportunities and threats are external factors. Strengths and opportunities are positives, whereas weaknesses and threats are negatives. SWOT analysis is often facilitated using the nominal group technique using Post-it Notes. The

SWOT analysis

	Positives	Negatives
Internal	Strengths	Weaknesses
External	Opportunities	Threats

---

[57] *According to Wikipedia, xeriscaping refers to landscaping and gardening to reduce the need for supplemental irrigation.*

facilitator leads the team through the process of generating many Post-it Notes for each topic and then sorting the Post-it Notes into meaningful groups. After all four topics are analyzed, the discussion should move to defining specific projects that need to be pursued to address the most important issues found in the SWOT analysis.

See *competitive analysis*, *five forces analysis*, *industry analysis*, *operations strategy*.

synchronous manufacturing – The Theory of Constraints' ideal of the entire production process working in harmony to achieve the economic goals of the firm.

When manufacturing is truly synchronized, its emphasis is on total system performance, not on localized measures, such as labor or machine utilization.

See *Theory of Constraints (TOC)*.

system – A collection of interdependent parts that interact over time. ✪

A system is a set of interdependent elements (often including people, machines, tools, technologies, buildings, information, and policies) that are joined together to accomplish a mission. Good examples include factories, supply chains, automobiles, and computers.

See *systems engineering*, *systems thinking*.

systems engineering – An interdisciplinary field and approach that focuses on managing complex engineering design projects.

A system is a collection of entities that interact to produce an objective or result. Large systems are often very complex and require systems engineers to coordinate activities across many engineering disciplines (e.g., mechanical, electrical, aerospace), scientific disciplines (e.g., physics, chemistry), and functional organizations (e.g., new product development, marketing, manufacturing) so the project meets customer needs.

Systems engineering includes both management and technical activities. The management process focuses on program and project management, while the technical process focuses more on tools, such as modeling, optimization, simulation, systems analysis, statistical analysis, reliability analysis, and decision theory. Systems engineers also use a wide range of graphical tools to represent problems.

For example, systems engineers at Lockheed Martin involved in the Joint Strike Fighter project must ensure that the electrical and mechanical systems work together properly and must coordinate work between subcontractors working on each of the subsystems.

The International Council on Systems Engineering (ICOSE) was created to address the need for improvements in systems engineering practices and education. Many schools around the world now offer graduate programs in systems engineering. Many experts believe that practical experience is needed to be an effective systems engineer, which explains why few schools offer systems engineering undergraduate programs.

See *industrial engineering*, *subcontracting*, *system*, *systems thinking*.

systems thinking – A worldview that encourages a holistic understanding of how a collection of related entities interact with each other and the environment over time to fulfill its mission.

Systems thinking is a holistic way of understanding the world. It not only considers the system at a point in time, but also considers how a system changes over time in response to changes in its environment. Contrary to Descartes' reductionist view, systems thinking argues that a system cannot be understood just by studying its parts. Systems thinking acknowledges that a change in one area can adversely affect other areas of the system.

For example, the reductionist approach to improving the braking system in a car would study each component separately (brake pads, brake pedal, brake lights, etc.). In contrast, systems thinking studies all components related to the braking system of the car, including the braking system, the car display, the driver, the road, and the weather, and how these components interact with each other over time.

Application of systems thinking to the supply chain has created what many consider to be a new business discipline with multiple professional societies, journals, and job titles that did not exist until the mid-1980s.

See *process*, *simulation*, *SIPOC Diagram*, *suboptimization*, *supply chain management*, *system*, *systems engineering*.

system reliability – See *reliability*.

T

Taguchi methods – An approach to design of experiments developed by Genichi Taguchi that uses a quadratic loss function; also called robust design.

Dr. Genichi Taguchi developed a practical approach for designing quality into products and processes. His methodology recognized that quality should not be defined as simply within or not within specifications, so he created a simple **quadratic loss function** to measure quality. The two figures below contrast the typical 0-1 loss function used in quality with the Taguchi quadratic loss function.

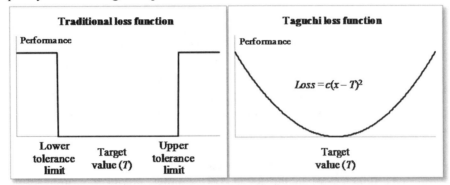

Technicians apply Taguchi methods on the manufacturing floor to improve products and processes. The goal is to reduce the sensitivity of engineering designs to uncontrollable factors or noise by maximizing the signal to noise ratio. This moves design targets toward the middle of the design space so external variation affects the behavior of the design as little as possible. This approach permits large reductions in both part and assembly tolerances, which are major drivers of manufacturing cost.

See *Analysis of Variance (ANOVA)*, *Design of Experiments (DOE)*, *functional build*, *lean sigma*, *robust*, *tolerance*.

takt time – The customer demand rate expressed as a time and used to pace production. ✪

According to a German-English dictionary (http://dict.leo.org), "takt" is the German word for "beat" or "musical time." Several sources define takt as the baton that an orchestra conductor uses to regulate the beat for the orchestra. However, this is not correct. The German word for baton is "taktstock."

The Japanese picked up the German word and use it to mean the beat time or **heart beat** of a factory. Lean production uses takt time to set the production rate to match the market demand rate. Takt time, therefore, is the desired time between completions of a product, synchronized to the customer demand rate and can be calculated as (available production time)/(forecasted demand rate).

Takt time, therefore, is set by the **customer demand rate**, and should be adjusted when the forecasted market demand rate changes. If takt time and the customer demand rate do not match, the firm (and the supply chain) will have either too little or too much inventory.

For example, a factory has a forecasted market demand of 100 units per day, and the factory operates for 10 hours per day. The target production rate should be the same as the market demand rate (100 units per day or 10 units per hour). The takt time for this factory should be (10 hours/day)/(100 units/day) = 0.1 hours per unit, or 6 minutes per unit. The factory should complete 1 unit about every 6 minutes, on average.

Many lean manufacturing consultants do not seem to understand the difference between a rate and a time and use the term "takt time" to mean the target production rate. However, a rate is measured in units per hour and a time is measured in hours (or minutes) per unit. For example, a production rate of 10 units per hour translates into a takt time of 6 minutes per unit.

Takt time is nearly identical to the traditional industrial engineering definition of **cycle time**, which is the target time between completions. The only difference between takt time and this type of cycle time is that takt time is defined by the market demand rate, whereas cycle time is not necessarily defined by the market demand.

Some people confuse takt time and **throughput time**. It is possible to have a throughput time of 6 weeks and have a takt time of 6 seconds. Takt time is the time between completions and can be thought of as time between units "falling off the end of the line." The *cycle time* entry compares cycle time and throughput time.

See *cycle time, heijunka, leadtime, lean thinking, pacemaker, pitch.*

tally sheet – See *checksheet.*

tampering – The practice of adjusting a stable process and therefore increasing process variation. ✪

Tampering is over-reacting to **common cause variation** and therefore always increasing variation.

See *common cause variation, control chart, quality management, special cause variation, Statistical Process Control (SPC), Statistical Quality Control (SQC).*

tardiness – See *service level.*

tare weight – (1) In a shipping/logistics context: The weight of an empty vehicle before the products are loaded; also called unladen weight. (2) In a packaging context: The weight of an empty shipping container or package.

The weight of the goods carried (the net weight) can be determined by subtracting the tare weight from the total weight, which is called the gross weight or laden weight. The tare weight can be useful for estimating the cost of goods carried for taxation and tariff purposes. This is a common practice for tolls related to barge, rail, and road traffic, where the toll varies with the value of the goods. Tare weight is often printed on the sides of railway cars and transport vehicles.

See *gross weight, logistics, net weight, scale count, tariff.*

target cost – The desired final cost for a new product development effort.

Many firms design a product, estimate the actual cost, and then add the margin to set the price. In contrast to this practice, with a target costing strategy, the firm determines the price based on the market strategy and then determines the target cost by subtracting the desired margin. The resulting "target cost" becomes the requirement for the product design team. The four major steps of target costing are:

1. **Determine the price** – The amount customers are willing to pay for a product or service with specified features and functions.
2. **Set the target cost per unit and in total** – The target cost per unit is the market price less the required margin. The total target cost is the per unit target cost multiplied by the expected number of units sold over its life.
3. **Compare the total target cost to the currently feasible total cost to create the cost reduction target** – The currently feasible total cost is the cost to make the product, given current design and process capabilities. The difference between the total target cost and currently feasible cost is the cost reduction target.
4. **Design (or redesign) products and processes to achieve the cost reduction target** – This can be an iterative process until both the product or service and its cost meet marketing and financial objectives.

See *job order costing, target price.*

target market – The group of customers that a business intends to serve.

See *market share, strategy map.*

target inventory – See *order-up-to level.*

target price – The practice of setting a sales price based on what the market will bear rather than on a standard cost.

The target price is the price at which the firm believes a seller will buy a product based on market research. The easiest approach for determining a target price is to study similar products sold by competitors. The target price may be used to calculate the target cost. In an investment context, the target price is the price at which a stockholder is willing to sell his or her stock.

See *Customer Relationship Management (CRM), target cost.*

tariff – A tax on import or export trade.

An **ad valorem tariff** is set as a percentage of the value. A **specific tariff** is not based on the value.

See *facility location, General Agreement on Tariffs and Trade (GATT), tare weight, trade barrier.*

task interleaving – A warehouse management term for combining tasks, such as picking, put away, and cycle counting, on a single trip to reduce deadheading (driving empty) for materials handling equipment.

The main idea of task interleaving is to reduce deadheading for materials handling equipment, such as forklift trucks in a warehouse or distribution center. Task interleaving is often used with put away, picking, and cycle counting tasks. For example, a stock picker might put away a pallet and then pick another pallet and move it to the loading dock. Although task interleaving is used primarily in pallet operations, it can be used with any type of materials handling equipment. Benefits of task interleaving include reduced travel time, increased productivity, less wear on lift trucks, reduced energy usage, and better on-time delivery.

Gilmore (2005) suggests that a Warehouse Management System (WMS) task interleaving system must consider permission, proximity, priority, and the age of the task (time). He also recommends that firms initially implement a WMS system without interleaving so personnel can learn the basics before trying interleaving.

See *picking, slotting, warehouse, Warehouse Management System (WMS)*.

technological forecasting – The process of predicting the future characteristics and timing of technology.

The prediction usually estimates the future capabilities of a technology. The two major methods for technological forecasting include time series and judgmental methods. Time series forecasting methods for technological forecasting fit a mathematical model to historical data to extrapolate some variable of interest into the future. For example, the number of millions of instructions per second (MIPS) for a computer is fairly predictable using time series methods. (However, the underlying technology to achieve that performance will change at discrete points in time.) Judgmental forecasting may also be based on projections of the past, but information sources in such models rely on the subjective judgments of experts.

The growth pattern of a technological capability is similar to the growth of biological life. Technologies go through an invention phase, an introduction and innovation phase, a diffusion and growth phase, and a maturity phase. This is similar to the S-shaped growth of biological life. Technological forecasting helps estimate the timing of these phases. This growth curve forecasting method is particularly useful in determining the upper limit of performance for a specific technology.

See *Delphi forecasting, forecasting, technology road map*.

technology push – A business strategy that develops a high-tech/innovative product with the hope that the market will embrace it; in contrast, a market pull strategy develops a product in response to a market need.

See *operations strategy*.

technology road map – A technique used by many businesses and research organizations to plan the future of a particular process or product technology.

The goal of a technology roadmap is to anticipate externally driven technological innovations by mapping them on a timeline. The technology roadmap can then be linked with the research, product development, marketing, and sourcing. Some of the benefits of technology roadmapping include:

- Support the organization's strategic planning processes with respect to new technologies.
- Plan for the integration of new technologies into current products.
- Identify business opportunities for leveraging new technologies in new products.
- Identify needs for technical knowledge.
- Inform sourcing decisions, resource allocation, and risk management decisions.

One approach for structuring the technology roadmapping process is to use a large matrix on a wall to capture the ideas. The top row should be labeled Past → Now → Plans → Future → Vision. The left column has the rows labeled markets, products, technologies, and resources.

- The **markets row** is used to explore markets, customers, competitors, environment, industry, business trends, threats, objectives, milestones, and strategies.
- The **products row** is used to explore products, services, applications, performance capabilities, features, components, families, processes, systems, platforms, opportunities, requirements, and risks.
- The **technologies row** is used to map new technologies, competencies, and knowledge.
- The **resources row** is used for skills, partnerships, suppliers, facilities, infrastructure, science, and R&D projects.

Post-it Notes are then used to "map" and link each of these dimensions over time.

The Centre for Technology Management at the University of Cambridge has a number of publications on this topic at www.ifm.eng.cam.ac.uk/ctm/publications/tplan. Their standard "T-Plan" process includes four major steps that focus on (1) the market (performance dimensions, business drivers, SWOT, gaps), (2) the product (features, strategy, gaps), (3) technology (solutions, gaps), and (4) roadmapping (linking technology resources to future market requirements). Technology roadmapping software is offered by www.roadmappingtechnology.com. The University of Minnesota Technological Leadership Institute (TLI) (http://tli.umn.edu) makes technology roadmapping a key topic in many of its programs.

See *disruptive technology, New Product Development (NPD), product life cycle management, technological forecasting.*

technology transfer – The process of sharing skills, expertise, knowledge, processes, technologies, scientific research, and intellectual property across different organizations, such as research laboratories, governments, universities, joint ventures, or subsidiaries.

Technology transfer can occur in three ways: (1) giving it away through technical journals, conferences, or free training and technical assistance, (2) commercial transactions, such as licensing patent rights, marketing agreements, co-development activities, exchange of personnel, and joint ventures, and (3) theft through industrial espionage or reverse engineering.

See *intellectual property (IP), knowledge management, reverse engineering.*

telematics – The science of sending, receiving, and storing information via telecommunication devices.

According to Wikipedia, the word "telematics" is now widely associated with the use of Global Positioning System (GPS) technology integrated with computers and mobile communications technology in automotive and trucking navigation systems. This technology is growing in importance in the transportation industry. Some important applications of telematics include the following:

- In-car infotainment
- Navigation and location
- Intelligent vehicle safety
- Fleet management
- Asset monitoring
- Risk management

See *Global Positioning System (GPS), logistics.*

termination date – A calendar date by which a product will no longer be sold or supported.

Many manufacturing and distribution companies use a policy of having a "termination date" for products and components. A product (and its associated unique components) is no longer sold or supported after the termination date. The advantages of having a clearly defined termination date policy include:

- Provides a clear plan for every functional area in the organization that deals with products (manufacturing, purchasing, inventory, service, engineering, and marketing). This facilitates an orderly, coordinated phase-out of the item.
- Communicates to the salesforce and the market that the product will no longer be supported (or at least no longer be sold) after the termination date. This often provides incentive for customers to upgrade.
- Allows manufacturing and inventory planners to bring down the inventories for all unique components needed for the product in a coordinated way.

Best practices for a termination date policy include the following policies: (1) plan ahead many years to warn all stakeholders (this includes marketing, sales, product management, purchasing, and manufacturing), (2) ensure that all functions (and divisions) have "buy-in" to the termination date, and (3) do not surprise customers by terminating a product without proper notice.

See *all-time demand, obsolete inventory, product life cycle management.*

terms – A statement of a seller's payment requirements.

Payment terms generally include discounts for prompt payment, if any, and the maximum time allowed for payment. The shipping terms determine who is responsible for the freight throughout the shipment. Therefore, a shipper will only be concerned about tracking the container to the point where another party takes ownership. This causes problems with container tracking because information may not be shared throughout all links in the supply chain.

See *Accounts Payable (A/P), Cash on Delivery (COD), demurrage, FOB, Incoterms, invoice, waybill.*

theoretical capacity – See *capacity.*

Theory of Constraints (TOC) – A management philosophy developed by Dr. Eliyahu M. Goldratt that focuses on the bottleneck resources to improve overall system performance. ✪

The Theory of Constraints (TOC) recognizes that an organization usually has just one resource that defines its capacity. Goldratt (1992) argues that all systems are constrained by one and only one resource. As Goldratt states, "A chain is only as strong as its weakest link." This is an application of Pareto's Law to process management and process improvement. TOC concepts are consistent with managerial economics that teach that the setup cost for a bottleneck resource is the opportunity cost of the lost gross margin and that the opportunity cost for a non-bottleneck resource is nearly zero.

The "constraint" is the bottleneck, which is any resource that has capacity less than the market demand. Alternatively, the constraint can be defined as the process that has the lowest average processing rate for producing end products. The constraint (the bottleneck) is normally defined in terms of a resource, such as a machine, process, or person. However, the TOC definition of a constraint can also include tools, people, facilities, policies, culture, beliefs, and strategies. For example, this author observed that the binding constraint in a business school in Moscow in 1989 was the mindset of the dean (rector) who could not think beyond the limits of Soviet Communism, even for small issues, such as making photocopies[58].

The Goal (Goldratt 1992) and the movie of the same name, include a character named Herbie who slowed down a troop of Boy Scouts as they hiked though the woods. Herbie is the "bottleneck" whose pace slowed down the troop. The teaching points of the story for the Boy Scouts are (1) they needed to understand that Herbie paced the operation (i.e., the troop could walk no faster than Herbie) and (2) they needed to help Herbie with his load (i.e., the other Scouts took some of Herbie's bedding and food so Herbie could walk faster). In the end, the troop finished the hike on-time because it had better managed Herbie, the bottleneck.

According to TOC, the overall performance of a system can be improved when an organization identifies its constraint (the bottleneck) and manages the bottleneck effectively. TOC promotes the following five-step methodology:

1. **Identify the system constraint** – No improvement is possible unless the constraint or weakest link is found. The constraint can often be discovered by finding the largest queue.

2. **Exploit the system constraints** – Protect the constraint (the bottleneck) so no capacity is wasted. Capacity can be wasted by (1) starving (running out of work to process), (2) blocking (running out of an authorized place to put completed work), (3) performing setups, or (4) working on defective or low-priority parts. Therefore, it is important to allow the bottleneck to pace the production process, not allow the bottleneck to be starved or blocked, focus setup reduction efforts on the bottleneck, increase lotsizes for the bottleneck, and inspect products before the constraint so no bottleneck time is wasted on defective parts.

3. **Subordinate everything else to the system constraint** – Ensure that all other resources (the unconstrained resources) support the system constraint, even if this reduces the efficiency of these resources. For example, the other processes can produce smaller lotsizes so the constrained resource is never starved. The unconstrained resources should never be allowed to overproduce.

4. **Elevate the system constraints** – If this resource is still a constraint, find more capacity. More capacity can be found by working additional hours, using alternate routings, purchasing capital equipment, or subcontracting.

5. **Go back to Step 1** – After this constraint problem is solved, go back to the beginning and start over. This is a continuous process of improvement.

Underlying Goldratt's work is the notion of synchronous manufacturing, which refers to the entire production process working in harmony to achieve the goals of the firm. When manufacturing is synchronized, its emphasis is on total system performance, not on localized measures, such as labor or machine utilization.

The three primary TOC metrics are throughput (T), inventory (I), and operating expenses (OE), often called T, I, and OE. Throughput is defined as sales revenue minus direct materials per time period. Inventory is defined as direct materials at materials cost. Operating expenses include both labor and overhead. Bottleneck management will result in increased throughput, reduced inventory, and the same or better operating expense.

See *absorption costing, bill of resources, blocking, bottleneck, buffer management, CONWIP, critical chain, current reality tree, Drum-Buffer-Rope (DBR), facility layout, future reality tree, gold parts, Herbie, Inventory Dollar Days (IDD), lean thinking, opportunity cost, overhead, pacemaker, Pareto's Law, process improvement program, routing, setup cost, setup time reduction methods, starving, synchronous manufacturing, throughput accounting, Throughput Dollar Days (TDD), transfer batch, utilization, variable costing, VAT analysis*.

Theta Model – A forecasting model developed by Assimakopoulos and Nikolopoulos (2000) that combines a long-term and short-term forecast to create a new forecast; sometimes called the Theta Method.

---

[58] *The Soviet Union was a secretive society, which meant that photocopies were rarely used.*

The M3 Competition runs a "race" every few years to compare time series forecasting methods on hundreds of actual times series (Ord, Hibon, & Makridakis 2000). The winner of the 2000 competition was a relatively new forecasting method called the "Theta Model" developed by Assimakopoulos and Nikolopoulos (2000). This model was difficult to understand until Hyndman and Billah (2001) simplified the mathematics. More recently, Assimakopoulos and Nikolopoulos (2005) wrote their own simplified version of the model. Although the two simplified versions are very similar in intent, they are not mathematically equivalent.

Theta Model forecasts are the average (or some other combination) of a longer-term and a shorter-term forecast. The longer-term forecast can be a linear regression fit to the historical demand, and the shorter-term forecast can be a forecast using simple exponential smoothing. The Theta Model assumes that all seasonality has already been removed from the data using methods, such as the centered moving average. The apparent success of this simple time series forecasting method is that the exponential smoothing component captures the "random walk" part of the time series, and the least squares regression trend line captures the longer-term trend.

See *exponential smoothing, forecasting, linear regression*.

Thiel's *U* – An early Relative Absolute Error (*RAE*) measure of forecast errors developed by Henri Thiel (1966).

Thiel's *U* statistic (or Thiel's inequality coefficient) is a metric that compares forecasts to an upper bound on the naïve forecast from a random walk, which uses the actual value from the previous period as the forecast for this period (Thiel 1966). Thiel proposed two measures for forecast error that Armstrong calls U_1 and U_2. SAP uses still another variant of Thiel's coefficient, labeled U_3 below.

$$U_1 = \frac{\sqrt{\sum_{t=1}^{T} E_t^2}}{\sqrt{\sum_{t=1}^{T} D_t^2} + \sqrt{\sum_{t=1}^{T} F_t^2}} \qquad U_2 = \frac{\sqrt{\sum_{t=1}^{T} E_t^2}}{\sqrt{\sum_{t=1}^{T} D_t^2}} \qquad U_3 = \frac{\sqrt{\sum_{t=1}^{T} E_t^2}}{\sqrt{\sum_{t=1}^{T} (D_t - D_{t-1})^2}}$$

According to Armstrong and Collopy (1992), the U_2 metric has better statistical properties than U_1 or U_3. Although Thiel's *U* metrics are included in many forecasting tools and texts, Armstrong and Collopy do not recommend them because other *RAE* metrics are easier to understand and have better statistical properties.

See *forecast error metrics, Mean Absolute Percent Error (MAPE), Relative Absolute Error (RAE)*.

Third Party Logistics (3PL) provider – A firm that provides outsourced services, such as transportation, logistics, warehousing, distribution, and consolidation to customers but does not take ownership of the product.

Third Party Logistics providers (3PLs) are becoming more popular as companies seek to improve their customer service capabilities without making significant investments in logistics assets, networks, and warehouses. The 3PL may conduct these functions in the client's facility using the client's equipment or may use its own facilities and equipment. The parties in a supply chain relationship include the following:

- **First party** – The supplier
- **Second party** – The customer
- **Third party (3PL)** – A company that offers multiple logistics services to customers, such as transportation, distribution, inbound freight, outbound freight, freight forwarding, warehousing, storage, receiving, cross-docking, customs, order fulfillment, inventory management, and packaging. In the U.S., the legal definition of a 3PL in HR4040 is "a person who solely receives, holds, or otherwise transports a consumer product in the ordinary course of business but who does not take title to the product" (source: www.scdigest.com, 2009).
- **Fourth party (4PL)** – An organization that manages the resources, capabilities, and technologies of multiple service providers (such as 3PLs) to deliver a comprehensive supply chain solution to its clients.

With a 3PL, the supplier firm outsources its logistics to two or more specialist firms (3PLs) and then hires another firm (the 4PL) to coordinate the activities of the 3PLs. 4PLs differ from 3PLs in the following ways (source: www.scdigest.com, January 1, 2009):

- The 4PL organization is often a separate entity established as a joint venture or long-term contract between a primary client and one or more partners.
- The 4PL organization acts as a single interface between the client and multiple logistics service providers.
- All aspects of the client's supply chain are managed by the 4PL organization.

- It is possible for a 3PL to form a 4PL organization within its existing structure.

    See the International Warehouse Logistics Association (www.iwla.com) site for more information.

    See *bullwhip effect, consolidation, customer service, fulfillment, joint venture, logistics, receiving, warehouse.*

throughput accounting – Accounting principles based on the Theory of Constraints developed by Goldratt.

Throughput is the rate at which an organization generates money through sales. Goldratt defines throughput as the difference between sales revenue and unit-level variable costs, such as materials and power. Cost is the most important driver for our operations decisions, yet costs are unreliable due to the arbitrary allocation of overhead, even with Activity Based Costing (ABC). Because the goal of the firm is to make money, operations can contribute to this goal by managing three variables:

- Throughput (T) = Revenue less materials cost less out-of-pocket selling costs (Note that this is a rate and is not the same as the throughput time.)
- Inventory (I) = Direct materials cost and other truly variable costs with no overhead
- Operating expenses (OE) = Overhead and labor cost (the things that turn the "I" into "T")

Throughput accounting is a form of contribution accounting, where all labor and overhead costs are ignored. The only cost that is considered is the direct materials cost. Throughput accounting is applied to the bottleneck (the constraint) using the following key performance measurements: output, setup time (average setup time by product and total setup time per period), downtime (planned and emergency), and yield rate. The bottleneck has the greatest impact on the throughput accounting measures (T, I, and OE), which in turn affect the goal of making money for the firm. Noreen, Smith, and Mackey (1995) is a good reference on this subject.

See *absorption costing, Activity Based Costing (ABC), focused factory, Inventory Dollar Days (IDD), overhead, Theory of Constraints (TOC), Throughput Dollar Days (TDD), variable costing, Work-in-Process (WIP) inventory.*

Throughput Dollar Days (TDD) – A Theory of Constraints (TOC) measure of the reliability of a supply chain defined in terms of the dollar days of late orders.

The entry *Inventory Dollar Days (IDD)* has much more detail on this measure.

See *Inventory Dollar Days (IDD), operations performance metrics, Theory of Constraints (TOC), throughput accounting.*

throughput ratio – See *value added ratio.*

throughput time – See *cycle time.*

tier 1 supplier – A sourcing term for an immediate supplier; a tier 2 supplier is a supplier to a supplier.

See *purchasing, supply chain management.*

time bucket – A time period used in planning and forecasting systems.

The time bucket (period) for most MRP systems is a day. These systems are often called bucketless because they use **date-quantity detail** rather than weekly or monthly time buckets. In contrast, many forecasting systems forecast in monthly or weekly time buckets.

See *Croston's Method, exponential smoothing, finite scheduling, forecasting, Materials Requirements Planning (MRP), production planning.*

time burglar – A personal time management term that refers to anything (including a person) that steals time from someone else; someone who wastes the time of another person.

Time burglars are people who often stop by and ask, "Got a minute?" and then proceed to launch into 20 minutes of low-value discussion. Some situations, such as a friend stopping by to say "hello," are just minor misdemeanors, but disruptions that arrive during a critical work situation could be considered a crime.

The key time management principle for managers is to explain the situation and then offer to schedule another time for a visit. A reasonable script is, "I can see this is going to take some more time to discuss. Let's schedule some time to talk about this further. When is a good time for you?"

The term "time burglar" can also be applied to junk e-mail, unnecessary meetings, too much TV, surfing the Internet, and other time wasting activities. Time burglars are everywhere, so stop them before they strike.

See *personal operations management.*

time fence – A manufacturing planning term used for a time period during which the Master Production Schedule (MPS) cannot be changed; sometimes called a planning time fence.

The time fence is usually defined by a planning period in days (e.g., 21 days) during which the **Master Production Schedule (MPS)** cannot be altered and is said to be **frozen**. The time fence separates the MPS into a **firm order** period followed by a tentative time period. The purpose of a time fence policy is to reduce short-term schedule disruptions for both manufacturing and suppliers and improve on-time delivery for customers by stabilizing the MPS and reducing "system nervousness."

Oracle makes a distinction between planning, demand, and release time fences. More on this topic can be found at http://download.oracle.com/docs/cd/A60725_05/html/comnls/us/mrp/tfover.htm (January 11, 2011).

See *cumulative leadtime, firm planned order, Master Production Schedule (MPS), Materials Requirements Planning (MRP), planned order, planning horizon, premium freight, Sales & Operations Planning (S&OP).*

time in system – The total start to finish time for a customer or customer order; also called customer leadtime.

The time in system is the turnaround time for a customer or customer order. In the queuing context, time in system is the sum of the wait time (the time in queue before service begins) and the service time.

Do not confuse the actual time in system for a single customer, the average time in system across a number of customers, and the planned time in system parameter, which is used for planning purposes.

See *customer leadtime, cycle time, leadtime, Little's Law, queuing theory, turnaround time, wait time.*

time management – See *personal operations management.*

time study – A work measurement practice of collecting data on work time by observation, typically using a stop watch or some other timing device. ✪

The average actual time for a worker in the time study is adjusted by his or her performance rating to determine the normal time for a task. The standard time is then the normal time with an allowance for breaks.

See *normal time, performance rating, scientific management, standard time, work measurement, work sampling.*

time to market – The time it takes to develop a new product from an initial idea (the product concept) to initial market sales; sometimes called speed to market.

In many industries, a short time to market can provide a competitive advantage, because the firm "first to market" with a new product can command a higher margin, capture a larger market share, and establish its brand as the strongest brand in the market. Precise definitions of the starting and ending points vary from one firm to another, and may even vary between products within a single firm. The time to market includes both product design and commercialization. Time to volume is a closely related concept.

See *clockspeed, market share, New Product Development (NPD), product life cycle management, time to volume, time-based competition.*

time to volume – The time from the start of production to the start of large-scale production.

See *New Product Development (NPD), time to market.*

time-based competition – A business strategy to (a) shorten time to market for new product development, (b) shorten manufacturing cycle times to improve quality and reduce cost, and (c) shorten customer leadtimes to stimulate demand. ✪

Stalk (1988) and Stalk and Hout (1990) make strong claims about the profitability of a time-based strategy. The *strategy map* entry presents a causal map that summarizes and extends this competition strategy. The benefits of a time-based competition strategy include: (1) segmenting the demand to target the time-sensitive and price-insensitive customers and increase margins, (2) reducing work-in-process and finished goods inventory, (3) driving out non-value activities (e.g., JIT and lean manufacturing concepts), and (4) bringing products to market faster. These concepts are consistent with the Theory of Constraints and lean thinking.

See *agile manufacturing, flow, operations strategy, Quick Response Manufacturing, resilience, time to market, value added ratio.*

Time Phased Order Point (TPOP) – An extension of the reorder point system that uses the planned future demand to estimate the date when the inventory position will hit the safety stock level; it then backschedules using the planned leadtime from that date to determine a start date for a planned order.

The Time Phased Order Point (TPOP) system is used to determine the order timing in all Materials Requirements Planning (MRP) systems. TPOP uses the gross requirements (the planned demand) to determine the date when the planned inventory position will hit the safety stock level. It then uses the planned leadtime to plan backward in time (backschedule) to determine the start date for the next planned order. The lotsize (order quantity) can be determined with any lotsizing rule, such as lot-for-lot, fixed order quantity, EOQ, day's supply, week's supply, etc. TPOP can be used over the planning horizon to create many planned orders.

See *lotsizing methods, Materials Requirements Planning (MRP), reorder point, safety stock.*

time series forecasting – A forecasting method that identifies patterns in historical data to make forecasts for the future; also called intrinsic forecasting. ✪

A time series is a set of historical values listed in time order (such as a sales history). A time series can be broken (decomposed) into a level (or mean), trend, and seasonal patterns. If the level, trend, and seasonal patterns are removed from a time series, all that remains is what appears to be random error (white noise). Box-Jenkins methods attempt to identify and model the autocorrelation (serial correlation) structure in this error.

A moving average is the simplest time series forecast method, but it is not very accurate because it does not include either trend or seasonal patterns. The Box-Jenkins method is the most sophisticated, but is more complicated than most managers can handle. The exponential smoothing model with trend and seasonal factors is a good compromise for most firms.

Univariate time series methods simply extrapolate a single time series into the future. Multivariate time series methods consider historical data for several related variables to make forecasts.

See *autocorrelation, Box-Jenkins forecasting, Croston's Method, Durbin-Watson statistic, exponential smoothing, forecasting, linear regression, moving average, seasonality, trend.*

time-varying demand lotsizing problem – The problem of finding the set of lotsizes that will "cover" the demand over the time horizon and will minimize the sum of the ordering and carrying costs.

Common approaches for solving this problem include the Wagner-Whitin lotsizing algorithm, the Period Order Quantity (POQ), the Least Total Cost method, the Least Unit Cost method, and the Economic Order Quantity. Only the Wagner-Whitin algorithm is guaranteed to find the optimal solution. All other lotsizing methods are heuristics; however, the cost penalty in using these heuristics is generally small.

See *Economic Order Quantity (EOQ), lotsizing methods, Period Order Quantity (POQ), Wagner-Whitin lotsizing algorithm.*

TOC – See *Theory of Constraints.*

tolerance – An allowable variation from a predefined standard; also called specification limits.

All processes have some randomness, which means that no manufacturing process will ever produce parts that exactly achieve the "nominal" (target) value. Therefore, design engineers define tolerance (or specification) limits that account for this "common cause variation." A variation from the standard is not considered significant unless it exceeds the upper or lower tolerance (specification) limit. Taguchi takes a different approach to this issue and creates a loss function around the nominal value rather than setting limits.

See *common cause variation, Lot Tolerance Percent Defective (LTPD), process capability and performance, Taguchi methods.*

ton-mile – A measure of freight traffic equal to moving one ton of freight one mile. See *logistics.*

tooling – The support devices required to operate a machine.

Tooling usually includes **jigs**, **fixtures**, **cutting tools**, **molds**, and **gauges**. In some manufacturing contexts, the requirements for specialized tools are specified in the bill of materials. Tooling is often stored in a **tool crib**.

See *fixture, Gauge R&R, jig, manufacturing processes, mold.*

total cost of ownership – The total cost that a customer incurs from before the purchase until the final and complete disposal of the product; also known as life cycle cost.

Some of these costs include search costs, purchase (acquisition) cost, purchasing administration, shipping (delivery), expediting, premium freight, transaction cost, inspection, rework, scrap, switching cost, installation cost, training cost, government license fees, royalty fees, Maintenance Repair Operations (service contracts, parts, labor, consumables, repair), information systems costs (support products, upgrades), inventory carrying cost, inventory redistribution/redeployment cost (moving inventory to a new location), insurance, end of life disposal cost, and opportunity costs (downtime, lost productive time, lost sales, lost profits, brand damage)[59].

Life cycle cost is very similar to the total cost of ownership. The only difference is that life cycle cost identifies cost drivers based on the stage in the product life cycle (introduction, growth, maturity, and decline). Both total cost of ownership and life cycle cost can have an even broader scope that includes research and development, design, marketing, production, and logistics costs.

See *financial performance metrics*, *purchasing*, *search cost*, *switching cost*, *transaction cost*.

Total Productive Maintenance (TPM) – A systematic approach to ensure uninterrupted and efficient use of equipment; also called Total Productive Manufacturing. ✪

Total Productive Maintenance (TPM) is a manufacturing-led collaboration between operations and maintenance that combines preventive maintenance concepts with the kaizen philosophy of continuous improvement. With TPM, maintenance takes on its proper meaning to "maintain" rather than just repair. TPM, therefore, focuses on preventive and predictive maintenance rather than only on emergency maintenance. Some leading practices related to TPM include:

- Implement a 5S program with a standardized work philosophy.
- Apply predictive maintenance tools where appropriate.
- Use an information system to create work orders for regularly scheduled preventive maintenance.
- Use an information system to maintain a repair history for each piece of equipment.
- Apply autonomous maintenance, which is the concept of using operators to inspect and clean equipment without heavy reliance on mechanics, engineers, or maintenance people. (This is in contrast to the old thinking which required operators to wait for mechanics to maintain and fix their machines.)
- Clearly define cross-functional duties.
- Train operators to handle equipment related issues.
- Measure performance with Overall Equipment Effectiveness (OEE).

Some indications that a TPM program might be needed include frequent emergency maintenance events, long downtimes, high repair costs, reduced machine speeds, high defects and rework, long changeovers, high startup losses, high Mean Time to Repair (MTTR), and low Mean Time Between Failure (MTBF). Some of the benefits for a well-run TPM program include reduced cycle time, improved operational efficiency, improved OEE, improved quality, and reduced maintenance cost.

See *5S*, *autonomous maintenance*, *bathtub curve*, *downtime*, *maintenance*, *Maintenance-Repair-Operations (MRO)*, *Manufacturing Execution System (MES)*, *Mean Time Between Failure (MTBF)*, *Mean Time to Repair (MTTR)*, *Overall Equipment Effectiveness (OEE)*, *reliability*, *reliability engineering*, *Reliability-Centered Maintenance (RCM)*, *standardized work*, *Weibull distribution*, *work order*.

Total Productive Manufacturing (TPM) – See *Total Productive Maintenance (TPM)*.

Total Quality Management (TQM) – An approach for improving quality that involves all areas of the organization, including sales, engineering, manufacturing, and purchasing, with a focus on employee participation and customer satisfaction. ✪

Total Quality Management (TQM) can involve a wide variety of quality control and improvement tools. TQM pioneers, such as Juran (1986), Deming (1986, 2000), and Crosby (1979) emphasized a combination of managerial principles and statistical tools. This term has been largely supplanted by lean sigma and lean programs and few practitioners or academics use this term today. The *quality management*, *lean sigma*, and *lean* entries provide much more information on this subject.

See *causal map*, *defect*, *Deming's 14 points*, *inspection*, *lean sigma*, *Malcolm Baldrige National Quality Award (MBNQA)*, *PDCA (Plan-Do-Check-Act)*, *quality management*, *quality trilogy*, *stakeholder analysis*, *Statistical Process Control (SPC)*, *Statistical Quality Control (SQC)*, *zero defects*.

touch time – The direct value-added processing time.

See *cycle time*, *run time*, *value added ratio*.

---

[59] *This list was compiled by the author over many years from many sources.*

Toyota Production System (TPS) – An approach to manufacturing developed by Eiji Toyoda and Taiichi Ohno at Toyota Motor Company in Japan; some people use TPS synonymously with lean thinking[60].

See *autonomation, jidoka, Just-in-Time (TPS), lean thinking, muda*.

T-plant – See *VAT analysis*.

TPM – See *Total Productive Maintenance (TPM)*.

TPOP – See *Time Phased Order Point (TPOP)*.

TPS – See *Toyota Production System (TPS)*.

TQM – See *Total Quality Management (TQM)*.

traceability – The capability to track items (or batches of items) through a supply chain; also known as lot traceability, serial number traceability, lot tracking, and chain of custody.

Lot traceability is the ability to track lots (batches of items) forward from raw materials through manufacturing and ultimately to end customers and also backward from end consumers back to the raw materials. Lot traceability is particularly important for food safety in food supply chains.

Serial number traceability is individual "serialized" items and is important in medical device supply chains. Petroff and Hill (1991) provide suggestions for designing lot and serial number traceability systems.

See *Electronic Product Code (EPC), part number, supply chain management*.

tracking signal – An exception report given when the forecast error is consistently positive or negative over time (i.e., the forecast error is biased).

The exception report signals the manager or analyst to intervene in the forecasting process. The intervention might involve manually changing the forecast, the trend, underlying average, and seasonal factors, or changing the parameters for the forecasting model. The intervention also might require canceling orders and managing both customer and supplier expectations.

Tracking signal measurement – The tracking signal is measured as the forecast bias divided by a measure of the average size of the forecast error.

Measures of forecast bias – The simplest measure of the forecast bias is to accumulate the forecast error over time (the cumulative sum) with the recursive equation $R_t = R_{t-1} + E_t$, where R_t is the running sum of the errors and E_t is the forecast error in period t. The running sum of the errors is a measure of the bias and an exception report is generated when R_t gets "large." Another variant is to use the smoothed average error instead of the running sum of the error. The smoothed error is defined as $SE_t = (1-\alpha)SE_{t-1} + \alpha E_t$.

Measures of the average size of the forecast error – One measure of the size of the average forecast error is the Mean Absolute Deviation (*MAD*). The *MAD* is defined as $MAD = (1/T)\sum_{t=1}^{T}|E_t|$, where T is the number of periods of history. A more computationally efficient approach to measure the *MAD* is with the smoothed mean absolute error, which is defined as $SMAD_t = (1-\alpha)SMAD_{t-1} + \alpha|E_t|$, where alpha ($\alpha$) is the smoothing constant ($0 < \alpha < 1$). Still another approach is to replace the smoothed mean absolute deviation ($SMAD_t$) with the square root of the smoothed mean squared error, where the smoothed mean squared error is defined as $SMSE_t = (1-\alpha)SMSE_t + \alpha E_t^2$. In other words, the average size of the forecast error can be measured as $\sqrt{SMSE_t}$. The smoothed *MAD* is the most practical approach for most firms.

In summary, a tracking signal is a measure of the forecast bias relative to the average size of the forecast error and is defined by $TS = bias/size$. Forecast bias can be measured as the running sum of the error (R_t) or the smoothed error (SE_t); the size of the forecast error can be measured with the *MAD*, the smoothed mean absolute error ($SMAD_t$), or the square root of the mean squared error ($SMAD_t$). It is not clear which method is best.

---

[60] *It is important, in this author's view, to separate lean thinking from the Toyota Production System. Lean thinking is a philosophy that can be applied to any organization in any industry and may go well beyond any practices used at Toyota.*

See *cumulative sum control chart, demand filter, exponential smoothing, forecast bias, forecast error metrics, forecasting, Mean Absolute Deviation (MAD), Mean Absolute Percent Error (MAPE), mean squared error (MSE).*

trade barrier – Any governmental regulation or policy, such as a tariff or quota that restricts imports or exports.
See *tariff.*

trade promotion allowance – A discount given to retailers and distributors by a manufacturer to promote products; retailers and distributors sponsor advertising and other promotional activities or pass the discount along to consumers to encourage sales; also known as trade allowance, cooperative advertising allowance, advertising allowance, and ad allowance.

Trade promotions include slotting allowances, performance allowances, case allowances, and account specific promotions. Promotions can include newspaper advertisements, television and radio programs, in-store sampling programs, and slotting fees. Trade promotions are common in the consumer packaged goods (CPG) industry.
See *consumer packaged goods, slotting.*

traffic management – See *Transportation Management System (TMS).*

trailer – A vehicle pulled by another vehicle (typically a truck or tractor) used to transport goods on roads and highways; also called semitrailer, tractor trailer, rig, reefer, flatbed; in England, called articulated lorry.

Trailers are usually enclosed vehicles with a standard length of 45, 48, or 53 feet, internal width of 98 to 99 inches, and internal height of 105 to 110 inches. Refrigerated trailers are known as reefers and have an internal width of 90 to 96 inches and height of 96 to 100 inches. Semi-trailers usually have three axles, with the front axle having two wheels and the back two axles each having a pair of wheels for a total of 10 wheels.
See *Advanced Shipping Notification (ASN), cube utilization, dock, intermodal shipments, less than truck load (LTL), logistics, shipping container, Transportation Management System (TMS).*

transaction cost – The cost of processing one transaction, such as a purchase order.
In a supply chain management context, this is the cost of processing one purchase order.
See *search cost, switching cost, total cost of ownership.*

transactional process improvement – Improving repetitive non-manufacturing activities.

The term "transactional process improvement" is used by many lean sigma consultants to describe efforts to improve non-manufacturing processes in manufacturing firms and also improve processes in service organizations. Examples include back-office operations (e.g., accounting, human resources) and front-office operations (order-entry, customer registration, teller services).

The entities that flow through these processes may be information on customers, patients, lab specimens, etc. and may be stored on paper or in electronic form. The information often has to travel across several departments. Lean sigma programs can often improve transactional processes by reducing non-value-added steps, queue time, cycle time, travel time, defects, and cost while improving customer satisfaction.
See *lean sigma, lean thinking, service management, waterfall scheduling.*

transfer batch – A set of parts that is moved in quantities less than the production batch size.

When a batch of parts is started on a machine, smaller batches can be moved (transferred) to the following machines while the large batch is still being produced. The smaller batch sizes are called **transfer batches**, whereas the larger batch produced on the first machine is called a **production batch**. The practice of allowing some units to move to the next operation before all units have completed the previous operation is called **operation overlapping**. The **Theory of Constraints** literature promotes this concept to reduce total throughput time and total work in process inventory. When possible, transfer batches should be used at the bottleneck to allow for large production batch sizes, without requiring large batch sizes after the bottleneck. It is important to have large batch sizes at the **bottleneck** to avoid wasting valuable bottleneck capacity on setups.
See *bottleneck, lotsizing methods, pacemaker, Theory of Constraints (TOC).*

transfer price – The monetary value assigned to goods, services, or rights traded between units of an organization.

One unit of an organization charges a transfer price to another unit when it provides goods or services. The transfer price is usually based on a standard cost and is not considered a sale (with receivables) or a purchase (with payables). Some international firms use transfer prices (and related product costs) to shift profits from high-tax countries to low-tax countries to minimize taxes.

See *cost of goods sold*, *purchasing*.

transportation – See *logistics*.

Transportation Management System (TMS) – An information system that supports transportation and logistics management; also called fleet management, transportation, and traffic management systems. ✪

Transportation Management Systems (TMSs) are information systems that manage transportation operations of all types, including shippers, ocean, air, bus, rail, taxi, moving companies, transportation rental agencies and all types of activities, including shipment scheduling through inbound, outbound, intermodal, and intra-company shipments. TMSs can track and manage every aspect of a transportation system, including fleet management, vehicle maintenance, fuel costing, routing and mapping, warehousing, communications, EDI, traveler and cargo handling, carrier selection and management, accounting, audit and payment claims, appointment scheduling, and yard management. Most TMSs provide information on rates, bills of lading, load planning, carrier selection, posting and tendering, freight bill auditing and payment, loss and damage claims processing, labor planning and assignment, and documentation management.

Many TMSs also provide GPS navigation and terrestrial communications technologies to enable government authorities and fleet operators to better track, manage, and dispatch vehicles. With these technologies, dispatchers can locate vehicles and respond to emergencies, send a repair crew, and notify passengers of delays.

The main benefits of a TMS include lower freight costs (through better mode selection, route planning, and route consolidation) and better customer service (better shipment tracking, increased management visibility, and better on-time delivery). A TMS can provide improved visibility of containers and products, aid in continuous movements of products, and reduce empty miles.

See *Advanced Shipping Notification (ASN)*, *cross-docking*, *Electronic Data Interchange (EDI)*, *intermodal shipments*, *logistics*, *materials management*, *on-time delivery (OTD)*, *Over/Short/Damaged Report*, *trailer*, *Warehouse Management System (WMS)*, *waybill*.

transportation problem – A mathematical programming problem of finding the optimal number of units to send from location i to location j to minimize the total transportation cost.

The **transportation problem** is usually shown as a table or a matrix. The problem is to determine how many units should be shipped from each "factory" (row) to each "market" (column). Each factory has limited capacity and each market has limited demand.

The **transshipment problem** is an extension of the transportation problem that allows for intermediate nodes between the supply and demand nodes. Transportation and transshipment problems can be extended to handle multiple periods where the product is "shipped" from one period to the next with an associated carrying cost.

The size of these problems can become quite large, but network algorithms can handle large networks efficiently. However, **network algorithms** only allow for a single commodity (product) to be shipped. More general **linear programming** and **integer programming** approaches can be used when the firm has multiple products. Unfortunately, the solution algorithms for these approaches are far less efficient. The transportation and transshipment problems can be solved with special-purpose algorithms, network optimization algorithms, or with general purpose linear programming algorithms. Even though they are both integer programming problems, they can be solved with any general linear programming package and can still be guaranteed to produce integer solutions because the problems are unimodular.

The mathematical statement for the transportation problem with N factories (sources) and M markets (demands) is as follows:

Transportation problem: Minimize $\sum_{i=1}^{N}\sum_{j=1}^{M} c_{ij} x_{ij}$

Subject to $\sum_{i=1}^{N} x_{ij} \geq D_j$, for $j = 1, 2, ..., M$ and $\sum_{j=1}^{M} x_{ij} \leq C_i$, for $i = 1, 2, ..., N$

where c_{ij} is the cost per unit of shipping from factory i to market j, x_{ij} is the number of units shipped from factory i to market j, D_j is the demand in units for market j, and C_i is the capacity (in units) for factory i. The goal is to minimize total transportation cost. The first constraint ensures that all demand is met. The second constraint ensures that production does not exceed capacity.

The transportation model is often formulated with equality constraints. This often requires either a "dummy" plant to handle market demand in excess of capacity or a "dummy" market to handle capacity in excess of market demand. The cost per unit for shipping from the dummy plant is the cost of a lost sale; the cost of shipping to the dummy market is the cost of excess capacity.

See *algorithm, assignment problem, linear programming (LP), logistics, network optimization, operations research (OR), transshipment problem, Traveling Salesperson Problem (TSP)*.

transshipment problem – A mathematical programming term for a generalization of the transportation problem that allows for intermediate points between supply and demand nodes.

The transportation problem finds the optimal quantities to be shipped from a set of supply nodes to a set of demand nodes given the quantities available at each supply node, the quantities demanded at each demand node, and the cost per unit to ship along each arc between the supply and demand nodes. In contrast, the transshipment problem allows transshipment nodes to be between the supply and demand nodes. Any transshipment problem can be converted into an equivalent transportation problem and solved using an algorithm for the transportation problem. Transshipment problems can also be solved by any network optimization model. Both transportation and transshipment problems can handle only one commodity (type of product). Linear and mixed integer linear programs are more general and can handle multiple commodity network optimization problems.

See *network optimization, operations research (OR), transportation problem*.

traveler – See *shop packet*.

Traveling Salesperson Problem (TSP) – The problem of finding the minimum cost (distance or travel time) sequence for a single vehicle to visit a set of cities (nodes, locations), visiting each city exactly once, and returning to the starting city; also spelled travelling salesperson problem; formerly known as the Traveling Salesman Problem.

The Traveling Salesperson Problem (TSP) is one of the most studied problems in **operations research** and many methods are available for solving the problem. The methods can be divided into **optimal** ("exact") methods and **heuristics**. Optimal methods are guaranteed to find the best (lowest cost or lowest travel time) solution, but the computing time can be extremely long and increases exponentially as N increases. On the other hand, many heuristic methods are computationally fast, but may find solutions that are far from optimal. Although optimal methods guarantee the mathematically best solution, heuristics do not.

Extensions of the problem include the **multiple-vehicle TSP** and the **Vehicle Scheduling Problem (VSP)**. The VSP can involve multiple vehicles, time window constraints on visiting each node, capacity constraints on each vehicle, total distance and time constraints for each vehicle, and demand requirements for each node. The **Chinese Postman Problem** is finding the optimal (minimum cost) circuit that covers all the arcs.

Both the TSP and the VSP are important problems in logistics and transportation. Similar combinatorial problems are found in many problem contexts. For example, the problem of finding the optimal sequence of jobs for a machine with sequence-dependent setups can be formulated as a TSP. Some printed circuit board design problems can also be formulated as a TSP.

The mathematical programming formulation for the TSP can be formulated as follows:

The traveling salesperson problem (TSP): Minimize $\sum_{i=1}^{N} \sum_{j=1}^{N} c_{ij} x_{ij}$

Subject to $\sum_{i=1}^{N} x_{ij} = 1$, for $j = 1, 2, ..., N$ and $\sum_{j=1}^{n} x_{ij} = 1$, for $i = 1, 2, ..., N$

$y_i - y_j + (n-1) x_{ij} \leq n - 2$ for all $(i, j), j \notin$ depot; $x_{ij} \in \{0,1\}$ for all (i, j)

The $x_{i,j}$ variables are binary (0,1) variables such that $x_{ij} = 1$ if node i immediately follows node j in the route and $x_{ij} = 0$ otherwise. The c_{ij} parameters are the costs, times, or distances to travel from node i to j. The objective is to minimize the total cost, distance, or time. The first two constraints require all nodes to have one incoming and one outgoing arc. The third constraint prohibits subtours, which are circuits that do not connect to the depot. Alternative formulations for this constraint can be found in the literature. The last constraint requires that the x_{ij} decision variables to be binary (zero-one) variables.

See *algorithm, assignment problem, heuristic, linear programming (LP), logistics, operations research (OR), sequence-dependent setup time, setup cost, transportation problem, Vehicle Scheduling Problem (VSP)*.

trend – The average rate of increase for a variable over time. ✪

In the forecasting context, the trend is the slope of the demand over time. One simple way to estimate this rate is with a simple linear regression using time as the x variable. In exponential smoothing, the trend can be smoothed with its own smoothing constant. The Excel function TREND(*range*) is a useful tool for projecting trends into the future. The *linear regression* entry presents the equations for the least squares trend line.

See *exponential smoothing, forecasting, linear regression, seasonality, time series forecasting*.

trend line – See *linear regression*.

triage – The process of directing (or sorting) customers into different streams based on their needs.

Triage is used to allocate a scarce resource, such as a medical doctor's time to those most deserving of it. The word comes from *trier*, which is old French and means to sort.

In a healthcare context, a triage step can be used to sort injured people into groups based on their need for or likely benefit from immediate medical treatment. In a battlefield context, triage means to select a route or treatment path for the wounded. In a service quality context, adding a triage step means to place a resource (a person, computer, or phone system) at the beginning of the process. This resource "triages" incoming customers and directs them to the right resource and process.

A good triage system protects valuable resources from being wasted on unimportant tasks and assigns customers to the most appropriate service for their needs. For example, a clinic should usually not have a highly paid Ear-Nose-Throat specialist seeing a patient with a minor sore throat. The clinic should have a triage nurse directing patients to the right provider. Patients with minor problems should see RNs or physician assistants; patients with major non-urgent problems should be scheduled to see doctors; patients with major urgent problems should see doctors right away. With a good triage system, a patient will be quickly directed to the proper level for the proper medical help and the system will be able to deliver the maximum benefit to society.

See *service management, service quality*.

triangular distribution – A continuous distribution that is useful when little or no historical data is available.

Parameters: Minimum (a), mode (b), and maximum (c).

Density and distribution functions:

$$f(x) = \begin{cases} 0 & \text{if } x < a \\ \dfrac{2(x-a)}{(c-a)(b-a)} & \text{if } a \leq x \leq b \\ \dfrac{2(c-x)}{(c-a)(c-b)} & \text{if } b < x \leq c \\ 0 & \text{if } c < x \end{cases}$$

$$F(x) = \begin{cases} 0 & \text{if } x < a \\ \dfrac{(x-a)^2}{(c-a)(b-a)} & \text{if } a \leq x \leq b \\ 1 - \dfrac{(c-x)^2}{(c-a)(c-b)} & \text{if } b < x \leq c \\ 1 & \text{if } c < x \end{cases}$$

Statistics: Range $[a, b]$, mean $(a + b + c)/3$, mode b, and variance $(a^2 + b^2 + c^2 - ab - ac - bc)/18$.

Inverse: The following is the inverse of the triangular distribution function with probability of p:

$$F^{-1}(p) = \begin{cases} a & \text{for } p \leq 0 \\ a + \sqrt{p(c-a)(b-a)} & \text{for } 0 < p \leq (b-a)/(c-a) \\ c - \sqrt{(1-p)(c-a)(c-b)} & \text{for } (b-a)/(c-a) < p < 1 \\ c & \text{for } 1 \leq p \end{cases}$$

In other words, when $p = F(x)$ then $x = F^{-1}(p)$. Using the inverse of the triangular distribution is often a practical approach for implementing the newsvendor model when little is known about the demand distribution. When the probability p is set to the critical ratio, the inverse function returns the optimal value.

Graph: The graph below is the triangular density function with parameters $(1, 4, 11)$.

Parameter estimation: An expert (or team) estimates three parameters: minimum (a), mode (b), and maximum (c). When collecting subjective probability estimates, it is a good idea to ask respondents for the maximum and minimum values first so they do not "anchor" (bias) their subjective estimates with their own estimate of the mode. It is imprecise to talk about the "maximum" and the "minimum" for distributions that are not bounded. For example, with a little imagination, the "maximum" demand could be extremely large. In this situation, it would be more precise to ask the expert for the values at the 5th percentile and 95th percentile of the distribution. However, this mathematical fact does not seem to bother most practitioners, who seem to be comfortable using this distribution in a wide variety of situations. The paper entitled "The Triangular Distribution" (Hill 2011c) shows how points (a', b') at the p and $1-p$ points of the CDF can be translated into endpoints (a, b).

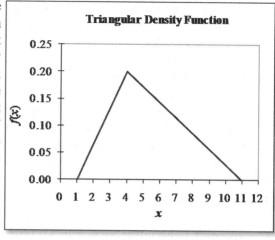

Excel: Excel does not have formulas for the triangular distribution, but they are fairly easy to create in Excel with the above equations.

Excel simulation: The inverse transform method can be used to generate random deviates from the inverse CDF above using $x = a + \sqrt{r(c-a)(b-a)}$ when r is in the interval $0 < r \leq (b-a)/(c-a)$ and $x = c - \sqrt{(1-r)(c-a)(c-b)}$ otherwise. (Note: r is a uniformly distributed random variable in range $(0,1]$). This method will generate x values that will follow the triangular distribution with parameters (a, b, c).

Relationships to other distributions: The sum of two uniformly distributed random variables is triangular.

See *newsvendor model*, *probability density function*, *probability distribution*.

tribal knowledge – Any unwritten information that is not commonly known by others within an organization.

Tribal knowledge is undocumented, informal information closely held by a few individuals. This information is often critical to the organization's products and processes but is lost when these individuals leave the organization. The term is often used in the context of arguments for knowledgement management systems.

See *knowledge management*.

trim – A statistical procedure that eliminates (removes) exceptional values (outliers) from a sample; also known as trimming; in Visual Basic Assistant, the Trim(S) function removes leading and trailing blanks from a text string.

See *mean, outlier, trimmed mean, Winsorizing*.

trimmed mean – A measure of central tendency that eliminates (removes) outliers (exceptional values) from a sample used to compute the mean (average) value.

When data is highly skewed, the trimmed mean may be a better measure of central tendency than the average. The trimmed mean is computed by removing a α percent of values from the bottom and top of a data set that is sorted in rank order. A trimmed mean with $\alpha = 0$ is the simple mean, and a trimmed mean with $\alpha = 50\%$ is the median (assuming that only the middle value remains after the trimming process). The trimmed mean, therefore, can be considered a measure of the central tendency somewhere between the simple average and the median. Whereas trimming removes values in the tails, bounding rules, such as Winsorizing replace values in the tails with a minimum or maximum value.

See *interpolated median, mean, median, outlier, skewness, trim, Winsorizing*.

triple bottom line – An organizational performance evaluation that includes social and environmental performance indicators as well as the typical financial performance indicators.

The term "triple bottom line" was coined by Elkington (1994), who argued that an organization's responsibility is to its entire group of stakeholders rather than just to its shareholders. The stakeholders include everyone who is affected directly or indirectly by the actions of the organization.

The triple bottom line is also referred to as the "Three Ps," which are people (human capital), planet (natural capital), and profits (economic benefit). Wikipedia makes an interesting distinction between the profit for the triple bottom line and the profit that typically shows up on a firm's income statement. The triple bottom line profit is the economic benefit enjoyed by all stakeholders rather than just the shareholders.

See *carbon footprint, green manufacturing, income statement, public-private partnership, sustainability*.

triple exponential smoothing – See *exponential smoothing*.

TRIZ – A methodology for generating creative ideas.

TRIZ is the Russian acronym for the phrase "Theory of Inventive Problem Solving" (Теория Решения Изобретательских Задач), which is a methodology developed by Genrich Altshuller and his colleagues in the former USSR. After reviewing more than 400,000 patents, Altshuller devised 40 inventive principles that distinguished breakthrough products. TRIZ is a methodology that uses these inventive principles for innovative problem solving and design. Furthermore, these principles can be codified and taught, leading to a more predictable process of invention. Although primarily associated with technical innovation, these principles can be applied in a variety of areas, including service operations, business applications, education, and architecture.

The TRIZ list of 40 inventive principles (www.triz-journal.com/archives/1997/07/b/index.html, May 10, 2011) follows:

Principle 1. Segmentation	Principle 21. Skipping
Principle 2. Taking out	Principle 22. Blessing in disguise
Principle 3. Local quality	Principle 23. Feedback
Principle 4. Asymmetry	Principle 24. "Intermediary"
Principle 5. Merging	Principle 25. Self-service
Principle 6. Universality	Principle 26. Copying
Principle 7. "Nested doll"	Principle 27. Cheap short-living objects
Principle 8. Anti-weight	Principle 28. Mechanics substitution
Principle 9. Preliminary anti-action	Principle 29. Pneumatics and hydraulics
Principle 10. Preliminary action	Principle 30. Flexible shells and thin films
Principle 11. Beforehand cushioning	Principle 31. Porous materials
Principle 12. Equipotentiality	Principle 32. Color changes
Principle 13. "The other way round"	Principle 33. Homogeneity
Principle 14. Spheroidality - Curvature	Principle 34. Discarding and recovering
Principle 15. Dynamics	Principle 35. Parameter changes
Principle 16. Partial or excessive actions	Principle 36. Phase transitions
Principle 17. Another dimension	Principle 37. Thermal expansion
Principle 18. Mechanical vibration	Principle 38. Strong oxidants
Principle 19. Periodic action	Principle 39. Inert atmosphere
Principle 20. Continuity of useful action	Principle 40. Composite materials

Source: The TRIZ Journal (www.triz-journal.com).

See *Analytic Hierarchy Process (AHP), ideation, Kepner-Tregoe Model, New Product Development (NPD), Pugh Matrix*.

truck load – Designation for motor carrier shipments exceeding 10,000 pounds.

A motor carrier may haul more than one truck load (TL) shipment in a single vehicle.

See *less than container load (LCL), less than truck load (LTL), logistics*.

true north – A lean term that describes a long-term vision of the ideal.

True north is often identified as the customer's ideal. However, it can (and should) also consider all stakeholders, including the owners, customers, workers, suppliers, and community.

See *lean thinking, mission statement*.

TS 16949 quality standard – A quality standard developed by the American automotive industry.

Beginning in 1994 with the successful launch of QS 9000 by DaimlerChrysler, Ford, and GM, the automotive OEMs recognized the increased value that could be derived from an independent quality system registration scheme and the efficiencies that could be realized in the supply chain by "communizing" system requirements. In 1996, the success of these efforts led to a move toward the development of a globally accepted and harmonized quality management system requirements document. Out of this process, the International Automotive Task Force (IATF) was formed to lead the development effort. The result of the IATF's effort was the ISO/TS 16949 specification, which forms the requirements for automotive production and relevant service part organizations. ISO/TS 16949 used the ISO 9001 Standard as the basis for development and included the requirements from these standards with specific "adders" for the automotive supply chain. The 2002 revision of TS builds off of the ISO9001:2000 document. Adapted from www.ul.com/services/ts16949.html.

See *ISO 9001:2008, quality management*.

TSP – See *Traveling Salesperson Problem (TSP)*.

***t*-test** – A statistical technique that uses the Student's *t*-test statistic to test if the means of two variables (populations) are significantly different from each other based on a sample of data on each variable.

The null hypothesis is that the true means of two variables (two populations) are equal. The alternative hypothesis is either that the means are different (e.g., $\mu_1 \neq \mu_2$), which is a two-tailed test, or that one mean is greater than the other (e.g., $\mu_1 < \mu_2$ or $\mu_1 > \mu_2$), which is a one-tailed test. With n_1 and n_2 observations on variables 1 and 2, and sample means and standard deviations $(\bar{x}_1, s_1)$ and $(\bar{x}_2, s_2)$, the *t*-statistic is $t = \dfrac{\bar{x}_1 - \bar{x}_1}{s_{\bar{x}_1 - \bar{x}_2}}$,

where $s_{\bar{x}_1 - \bar{x}_2} = \sqrt{\dfrac{(n_1 - 1)s_1^2 + (n_2 - 1)s_2^2}{n_1 + n_2 - 2}\left(\dfrac{1}{n_1} + \dfrac{1}{n_2}\right)}$. The term $s_{\bar{x}_1 - \bar{x}_2}$ simplifies to $\sqrt{(s_1^2 + s_2^2)/n}$, when $n = n_1 = n_2$.

If each member in population 1 is related to a member in the other population (e.g., a person measured before and after a treatment effect), the observations will be positively correlated and the more powerful paired *t*-test (or matched pairs test) can be used. The paired *t*-test computes the difference variable $d_i = x_{1i} - x_{2i}$, then computes the sample mean ($\bar{d}$) and standard deviation (s_d), and finally the *t*-statistic $t = \bar{d} / (s_d \sqrt{n})$.

For a two-tailed test, the *t*-test rejects the null hypothesis of equal means in favor of the alternative hypothesis of unequal means when this *t*-statistic is greater than the critical level $t_{\alpha/2, n_1+n_2-2}$, which is the Student's *t* value associated with probability $\alpha/2$ and $n_1 + n_2 - 2$ degrees of freedom. For a one-tailed test, $\alpha/2$ should be replaced by α. For a paired *t*-test, use $n = n_1 = n_2$ degrees of freedom. In Excel, use TINV(α, n_1+n_2-2) for a two-tailed test and TINV(2α, n_1+n_2-2) for a one-tailed test. The counter-intuitive *p*-values (α and 2α) are used because TINV assumes a two-tailed test.

The *t*-test assumes that the variables are normally distributed and have equal variances. If the variances of the two populations are not equal, then Welch's *t*-test should be used.

The *t*-test can be done in one Excel function. The TTEST(A1, A2, TAILS, TYPE) function returns the probability (the p-value) that two samples are from populations that have the equal means. A1 and A2 contain the ranges for sample data from the two variables. TAILS specifies the number of tails for the test (one or two). Two tails should be used if the alternative hypothesis is that the two means are not equal. The TYPE parameter defines the type of *t*-test to use in the Excel TTEST function, where TYPE =1 for a paired *t*-test, TYPE = 2 for a two-sample test with equal variance, and TYPE = 3 for a two-sample test with unequal variances. The table below summarizes the parameters for the Excel functions assuming equal variances.

Number of tails	Test	Level of significance	Degrees of freedom	Excel with TINV	Excel with TTEST
TAILS = 2	TYPE = 1 Paired *t*-test	$1 - \alpha/2$	n	TINV(α, n)	TTEST(A1, A2,2,1)
TAILS = 1	TYPE = 1 Paired *t*-test	$1 - \alpha$	N	TINV(2α, n)	TTEST(A1, A2,1,1)
TAILS = 2	TYPE = 2 Two sample	$1 - \alpha/2$	$n_1 + n_2 - 2$	TINV(α, $n_1 + n_2 - 2$)	TTEST(A1, A2,2,2)
TAILS = 1	TYPE = 2 Two sample	$1 - \alpha$	$n_1 + n_2 - 2$	TINV(2α, $n_1 + n_2 - 2$)	TTEST(A1, A2,1,2)

Source: Professor Arthur V. Hill

See *Analysis of Variance (ANOVA), confidence interval, sampling, Student's t distribution*

Turing test – A face validity test proposed by (and named after) Alfred Turing (1950) in which an expert or expert panel compares the results of two processes, typically a computer program and an expert, and tries to determine which process is the computer process.

If the experts cannot tell the difference, the computer process is judged to have a high degree of expertise. For example, an expert system is presented with a series of medical cases and makes a diagnosis for each one. A medical expert is given the same series of cases and also asked to make a diagnosis for each one. A second expert is then asked to review the diagnoses from the two sources and discern which one is the computer. If the second medical expert cannot tell the difference, the computer system is judged to have face validity.

See *expert system, simulation.*

turnaround time – The actual time required to get results to a customer.

Turnaround time is the actual customer time in system for an oil change, medical exam, and many other types of service. The turnaround time is often the basis for a service guarantee. Turnaround time is synonymous with actual customer leadtime. Do not confuse the average historical turnaround time, the actual turnaround time for one customer, and the planned turnaround time promised to a population of customers. From a queuing theory perspective, turnaround time for a customer is the sum of the customer's wait time and service time.

See *customer leadtime, cycle time, leadtime, strategy map, time in system, wait time.*

turnkey – An information systems term that describes a system designed so it does not require modification or investment when implemented.

Some software vendors claim that their software is "turnkey" software that requires little or no effort to customize for an organization. A joke regarding turnkey systems is that if you leave out the "n" you get "turkey," which describes naïve people who believe that turnkey systems will not require effort to implement.

See *Enterprise Resources Planning (ERP), implementation, Original Equipment Manufacturer (OEM).*

turnover – In the field of operations management, turnover is usually assumed to mean inventory turnover.

However, employee turnover is also an important concept. In most of the world outside North America, the word "turnover" is used to mean revenue or sales.

See *employee turnover, inventory turnover.*

two-bin system – A simple inventory system that has two containers (bins); an empty bin signals the need for a replenishment order.

This popular lean manufacturing concept uses two bins, normally of the same size. When a bin is emptied, it signals the need to send a replenishment order to the supplier to fill up the bin. Meanwhile, the inventory in the other bin is used to satisfy the demand. In many cases, a card is associated with the bin so the card (rather than the bin) can be sent back to the supplier to request replenishment. In some cases, it is a good idea to put a lock on the reserve bin to ensure that the ordering discipline is enforced.

From an inventory perspective, a two-bin system is a **reorder point system**, where the size of the second bin is the reorder point and the combined size of the two bins is **order-up-to** (target) inventory level. In many firms, the empty bins (or cards) are only sent to suppliers once per week, which is a **periodic review order-up-to system** with a minimum order quantity (the size of a bin). The bin size, therefore, should be based on inventory theory where the reorder point is $R = \bar{d}L + z\sqrt{L}\,\sigma_c$ and the target inventory is $T = R + Q$. See the *reorder point* entry for more information on this topic.

This author visited a plant that had implemented a lean system using a two-bin system for managing inventory. When first implemented, the new system ran out of inventory and shut down the plant. The problem was that management had set all bin sizes to "three weeks supply." Evidently, they had failed to check to make sure that the bin sizes were as large or larger than the reorder point discussed above.

See *lean thinking, pull system, reorder point, replenishment order.*

two-minute rule – The time management principle stating that tasks requiring less than two minutes should be done immediately and should not be added to a task list.

It requires about two minutes to record and review a task. Therefore, it is often better to do such tasks and not add them to a list. However, sometimes it is better to make a quick note and stay focused on the task at hand.

See *Getting Things Done (GTD), personal operations management, two-second rule, tyranny of the urgent.*

two-second rule – The personal operations management principle that encourages people to take two seconds to write down a distracting idea so they can quickly regain their focus on their current task.

Hill (2010) observed that people can handle distractions in three ways: (1) ignore the distraction and hope it goes away, (2) pursue the idea and lose focus on the current task, or (3) quickly make a note of the idea and stay focused on the current task. It requires about two seconds to write a note. This "two-second rule" allows people to stay focused but still capture potentially valuable ideas. The two-second rule is similar to a "parking lot" list for a meeting. Do not confuse the two-second rule with the two-minute rule, which is a different personal operations management rule.

See *Getting Things Done (GTD)*, *parking lot*, *personal operations management*, *two-minute rule*, *tyranny of the urgent*.

Type I and II errors – The two types of errors that can be made in hypothesis testing using the scientific method.

A type I error is rejecting a true hypothesis. A type II error is failing to reject a false hypothesis. These concepts are summarized in the table on the right. It is imprecise to say, "We accept the hypothesis," because it might be possible to reject the hypothesis with a larger sample size. It is more precise to say, "We are not able to reject the hypothesis based on the data collected so far."

Type I and type II errors

	Hypothesis is true	Hypothesis is false
Reject hypothesis	Type I error	Correct
Do not reject hypothesis	Correct	Type II error

Some authors define a **Type III error** as working on the wrong problem.

See *consumer's risk*, *producer's risk*.

tyranny of the urgent – A time management concept popularized by Hummel (1967) suggesting that people are often so driven by urgent tasks, that they never get around to the important ones.

See *Getting Things Done (GTD)*, *Personal Operations Management*, *two-minute rule*, *two-second rule*.

U

u-chart – A statistical quality control chart used to monitor the number of defectives in a batch, where the batch size may not be constant.

Unlike the c-chart, the u-chart does not require that the batchsize be constant. Like the c-chart, the u-chart relies on the Poisson distribution.

See *c-chart*, *control chart*, *Poisson distribution*, *Statistical Process Control (SPC)*.

unfair labor practice – A term used in the U.S. to describe actions taken by employers or unions that violate the National Labor Relations Act (NLRA) and administers by the National Labor Relations Board (NLRB).

The NLRA makes it illegal for employers to (1) interfere with two or more employees acting in concert to protect rights provided for in the Act, whether or not a union exists, (2) dominate or interfere with the formation or administration of a labor organization, (3) discriminate against employees for engaging in concerted or union activities or refraining from them, (4) discriminate against an employee for filing charges with the NLRB or taking part in any NLRB proceedings, and (5) refuse to bargain with the union that is the lawful representative of its employees.

Similarly, the NLRA bars unions from (1) restraining or coercing employees in the exercise of their rights or an employer in the choice of its bargaining representative, (2) causing an employer to discriminate against an employee, (3) refusing to bargain with the employer of the employees it represents, (4) engaging in certain types of secondary boycotts, (5) requiring excessive dues, (6) engaging in featherbedding (requiring an employer to pay for unneeded workers), (7) picketing for recognition for more than thirty days without petitioning for an election, (8) entering into "hot cargo" agreements (refusing to handle goods from an anti-union employer), and (9) striking or picketing a health care establishment without giving the required notice.

See *human resources*.

uniform distribution – A probability distribution for modeling both continuous and discrete random variables.

The continuous uniform is for random variables that can take on any real value in the range (a, b). For example, the continuous uniform can be used to model the clock time for a random arrival during a time interval. The discrete uniform is constrained to integer values and is useful when items are selected randomly from a set.

Parameters: Range (a, b). The a parameter is the location parameter and $b − a$ is the scale parameter.

Density and distribution functions: The continuous uniform distribution is defined in the range (a, b) and has density and distribution functions:

Density function $f(x) = \begin{cases} \dfrac{1}{b-a} & \text{for } a \le x \le b \\ 0 & \text{otherwise} \end{cases}$

Distribution function $F(x) = \begin{cases} 0 & \text{for } x < a \\ \dfrac{x-a}{b-a} & \text{for } a \le x \le b \\ 1 & \text{for } b < x \end{cases}$

Statistics: The mean and variance of the continuous uniform are $\mu = (a+b)/2$ and $\sigma^2 = (b-a)^2/12$. The mean and variance for the discrete uniform are $\mu = (a+b)/2$ and $\sigma^2 = ((b-a+1)^2 - 1)/12$. Note that the variances for the continuous and discrete uniform distributions are not the same.

Graph: The graph on the right is the density function for the continuous uniform $(1, 2)$ distribution.

Excel: Excel does not have density or distribution functions for the uniform distribution, but it can be easily implemented using the above equations.

Excel simulation: A continuous uniform random variate in the range (A,B) can be generated in Excel with =A+RAND()*(B-A). A discrete uniform random variable in the range (a, b) can be generated with either RANDBETWEEN(A,B) or A+Int((B-A+1)*RAND()).

See *inverse transform method, probability density function, probability distribution.*

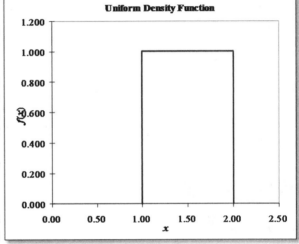

unit fill rate – See *fill rate.*

unit of measure – The standard method for counting an item used for inventory records and order quantities; sometimes abbreviated U/M.

The unit of measure is an attribute of each item (stock keeping unit, part number, material) and is stored in the inventory master. Typical values are box, case, pallet, or each. The commonly used term "each" means that each individual item is one unit. The unit of measure can be ambiguous when a box is inside a box, which is inside another box. Typical abbreviations include case (CA or CS), pallets (PL), pounds (LB), ounces (OZ), linear feet (LF), square feet (SF), and cubic feet (CF). Information systems often need to convert the unit of measure. For example, a firm might purchase an item in pallets, stock it in cases, and sell it in "eaches" (units).

See *aggregate inventory management, part number, production planning.*

Universal Product Code (UPC) – The standard barcode symbol for retail packaging in the U.S.

A UPC is a product identification number that uniquely identifies a product and the manufacturer. It is a series of thick and thin vertical bars (lines) printed on consumer product packages. All UPC identifiers have an associated numeric 12-digit code. The UPC barcode can be scanned at the point-of-sale to enable retailers to record data at checkout and transmit this data to a computer to monitor unit sales, inventory levels, and other factors. Data items can include the SKU, size, color.

The EAN is the international version of the UPC and has 13 rather than 12 digits. EAN stands for European Article Number. When it was introduced, the idea was to expand the UPC across the world with this new code, while still being UPC compliant. To do this, a prefix number was added to the UPC, where the prefix 0 was reserved for existing UPCs. Many firms that import from around the world use both UPCs and EANs in their information systems.

See *barcode, Electronic Product Code (EPC), part number, Point-of-Sale (POS), Radio Frequency Identification (RFID).*

unnecessary waste – See *8 wastes.*

upstream – A manufacturing and supply chain term referring to any process that comes before a given process.

This term makes an analogy between a stream or a river and a manufacturing or supply chain system. Just as water moves downstream, the product flows "downstream." A downstream process is any process that comes after a given process. Therefore, if the painting process comes after the molding process, the painting process is said to be downstream from the molding. Likewise, an "upstream" process is one that comes before. Therefore, the molding process is said to be "upstream" from the painting process.

See *bullwhip effect, Design Structure Matrix (DSM), Drum-Buffer-Rope (DBR), pacemaker, process map, reverse logistics.*

utilization – The percentage of the available work time that a resource is working.

Utilization is the ratio of the actual time worked for a resource to the time available. Utilization is a fundamental concept in operations management, capacity management, and queuing theory. It is also one of the three elements of the Overall Equipment Effectiveness (OEE) metric. In queuing theory, utilization is defined as the ratio of the average arrival rate to the average service rate. See the *queuing theory* entry for more detail.

Operations managers sometimes seek to maximize productivity by maximizing utilization to amortize fixed costs over more units. However, maximizing utilization is often a foolish strategy because high utilization can also mean high inventory, long customer waiting time, and poor customer service. The ideal utilization, therefore, will minimize the sum of the waiting and capacity costs. For example, the ideal utilization for a fire engine is close to zero because the waiting cost is very high. The *capacity* entry discusses these issues further.

In a factory context, most organizations consider setup time to be part of the work time when calculating utilization. However, the Theory of Constraints (TOC) literature defines utilization as the ratio of the run time (excluding setup time) to the time the resource is scheduled to produce.

See *bottleneck, capacity, cellular manufacturing, efficiency, operations performance metrics, Overall Equipment Effectiveness (OEE), productivity, queuing theory, Theory of Constraints (TOC), wait time.*

V

validation – See *process validation.*

validation protocol – See *process validation.*

value added ratio – The ratio of the processing time (direct value-adding time) to the total cycle time (throughput time); also called Manufacturing Cycle Effectiveness (MCE), throughput ratio, and cycle time efficiency.

In a manufacturing context, the total cycle time (throughput time) is the total time in the system, which usually includes the queue time (wait time), run time, post-operation wait time, and move time. The value-adding time is the "touch time" plus time spent in other value-adding operations, such as baking in an oven, curing, drying, etc. In labor-intensive manufacturing operations, the value-adding time is just the "touch time." In a service context, the value added ratio is often defined as the percentage of the time that the customer is receiving actual value-added service divided by the time that the customer is in the system. In this author's experience, most manufacturing plants have a value added ratio far less than 20%.

See *batch-and-queue, cellular manufacturing, cycle time, labor intensive, lean thinking, Overall Equipment Effectiveness (OEE), queuing theory, time-based competition, touch time, wait time.*

Value Added Reseller (VAR) – An organization that adds value to a system and resells it.

For example, a VAR could purchase computer components (e.g., CPU, motherboard, case, and monitor) and graphics software from a number of different suppliers and package them together as a specialized CAD system. Although VARs typically only repackage and sell products, they might also include software or services they have developed themselves. Adapted from www.pcmag.com/ encyclopedia_term, October 25, 2006.

See *Original Equipment Manufacturer (OEM).*

value analysis – See *value engineering.*

value chain – A model developed by Michael Porter that describes the activities in a business that deliver value to a market; this model is used as the basis for a competitive analysis called a value chain analysis. ✪

As shown in the figure below, Porter (1985) suggest business activities can be grouped into primary and support activities[61]. **Primary value chain activities** are those that are directly concerned with creating and delivering a product (e.g., component assembly). **Support value chain activities** are not directly involved in production but may increase effectiveness or efficiency (e.g., human resource management).

Porter's value chain

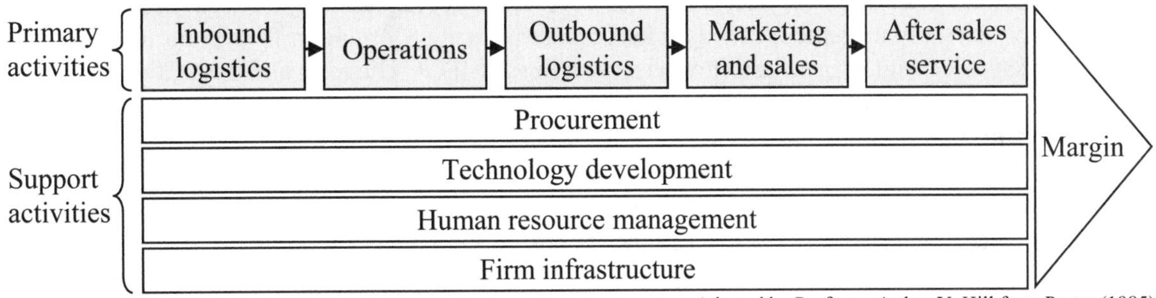

Adapted by Professor Arthur V. Hill from Porter (1985)

A good **profit margin** is the result of well-designed primary and secondary value chain activities. The firm's margin or profit depends on how well the frim's primary activities add value to the market so that the amount that the customer is willing to pay exceeds the cost of the activities in the value chain. It is rare for a business to undertake all primary and support activities for itself. In fact, one of the main benefits of a value chain analysis is to consider which activities should be outsourced to other firms. A competitive advantage can often be achieved by reconfiguring the value chain to provide lower cost or better differentiation.

Primary value chain activities include:

- **Inbound logistics** – All relationships with suppliers, including all activities required to receive, store, and disseminate inputs.
- **Operations** – All activities required to transform inputs into outputs (products and services).
- **Outbound logistics** – All activities required to collect, store, and distribute the output.
- **Marketing and sales** – All activities to inform buyers about products and services, induce buyers to purchase them, and facilitate their purchase.
- **After sales service** – All activities required to keep the product or service working effectively for the buyer after it is sold and delivered.

Support value chain activities include:

- **Procurement** – Acquisition of inputs, or resources, for the firm.
- **Human resource management** – All activities involved in recruiting, hiring, training, developing, compensating, and (if necessary) dismissing personnel.
- **Technological development** – Equipment, hardware, software, procedures, and technical knowledge brought to bear in the firm's transformation of inputs into outputs.
- **Infrastructure** – Serves the company's needs and ties the various parts together. Infrastructure consists of functions or departments, such as accounting, legal, finance, planning, public affairs, government relations, quality assurance, and general management.

Porter suggests that firms can gain competitive advantage through either cost leadership or differentiation. In a **cost leadership** strategy, a firm sets out to become the low-cost producer in its industry. The sources of cost advantage are varied and depend on the structure of the industry. They may include the pursuit of economies of scale, proprietary technology, preferential access to raw materials, and other factors. In a **differentiation** strategy, a firm seeks to be unique in its industry along some dimensions that are widely valued by buyers. It selects one or more attributes that many buyers in an industry perceive as important, and then uniquely positions itself to meet those needs. It is rewarded for its uniqueness with a premium price.

---

[61] *This adapted version of Porter's value chain positions the primary activities at the top and the support activities below.*

Value chain analysis can be broken down into three steps:
- Break down a market/organization into its key activities under each of the major headings in the model.
- Assess the potential for adding value via cost advantage or differentiation, or identify current activities where a business appears to be at a competitive disadvantage.
- Determine strategies built around focusing on activities where competitive advantage can be sustained.

Many authors now use the terms value chain and **supply chain** almost interchangeably. However, most scholars make a distinction between the terms. The value chain takes a business strategy point of view, considers product design and after sales service, and emphasizes outsourcing decisions based on core competencies. In contrast, supply chain management usually takes a materials and information flow point of view and emphasizes suppliers, inventories, and information flow as shown in the SIPOC Diagram and the SCOR model.

See *bullwhip effect, delegation, division of labor, human resources, lean sigma, logistics, SCOR Model, SIPOC Diagram, supply chain management, value stream.*

value engineering – An approach for designing and redesigning products and services to achieve the same functionality at less cost or achieve better functionality at the same cost; also known as value analysis.

Value engineering techniques (1) identify the functions of a product or service, (2) establish a worth for each function, (3) generate alternatives through the use of creative thinking, and (4) select alternatives to reliably fulfill the needed functions to achieve the lowest life cycle cost without sacrificing safety, quality, or environmental attributes of the project. Value engineering is usually conducted by a multi-disciplined team and applies a well-developed methodology. Value engineering is closely related to **product simplification**, which is the process of finding ways to reduce product complexity without sacrificing important functionality. Value engineering is also closely related to **commonality**, which involves using common parts across many products.

See *commonality, Design for Manufacturing (DFM), product life cycle management.*

value proposition – A statement of the benefits offered by a product or service to a market.

The value proposition is a statement of how a bundle of products and services propose to add value to a set of customers and how that value is differentiated from competitors' offerings. In an economic sense, the value proposition is the difference between the life-cycle benefits and the life-cycle cost.

See *service guarantee, strategy map.*

value stream – A lean term used to describe the series of steps (both value-adding and non-value-adding) required to create a product, a product family, or a service.

A value stream includes product and service flows that have similar process steps. A value stream takes a process view focusing on product flows across organizational boundaries. Identifying value streams and creating a value stream map for each one is a good starting point for lean process improvement. This activity can be used to help find and prioritize the non-value-adding steps.

See *functional silo, lean thinking, product family, value chain, value stream manager, value stream map.*

value stream manager – A lean manufacturing term for an individual who has been assigned the responsibility for a value stream; also called value stream leader.

The value stream may be on the product or the business level.

See *lean thinking, value stream, value stream map.*

value stream map – A simple process mapping methodology developed at Toyota Motor Company that highlights waste in a system. ✪

Value stream mapping was popularized in the English-speaking world by the Lean Enterprise Institute in the book ***Learning to See*** (Rother, Shook, Womack, & Jones 2003). Value stream mapping is a visual tool that graphically identifies every process in a product's flow from "door-to-door," giving visibility to both the value-adding steps as well as the non-value-adding steps. The processes that create value are thoroughly detailed for complete process flow of a particular product or product family. The current state is drawn from observation and data gathering of the actual processes. This exercise exposes the waste and redundancy. The future state map is based on lean principles and world-class benchmarks. Value stream analysis activities include:
- Review demand profile (Pareto Chart, histogram)
- Conduct flow analysis (parts process matrix, spaghetti diagram)
- Calculate takt time (peak demand, average demand)

- Create the value stream map (material and information flow diagram using the "learning to see" format, current state and future state gap analysis)
- Identify change loops, kaizen breakthroughs, and the implementation plan.

The diagram below is a simple example of a value stream map created by the author.

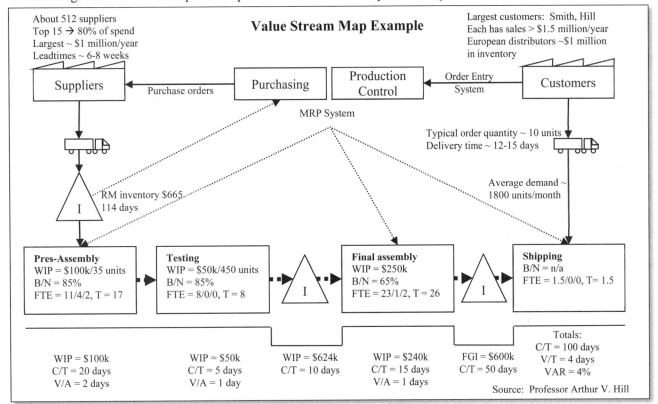

Value Stream Map Example

About 512 suppliers
Top 15 → 80% of spend
Largest ~ $1 million/year
Leadtimes ~ 6-8 weeks

Largest customers: Smith, Hill
Each has sales > $1.5 million/year
European distributors ~$1 million
in inventory

Suppliers ← Purchase orders — Purchasing — Production Control ← Order Entry System — Customers

MRP System

RM inventory $665. 114 days

Typical order quantity ~ 10 units
Delivery time ~ 12-15 days

Average demand ~ 1800 units/month

Pres-Assembly
WIP = $100k/35 units
B/N = 85%
FTE = 11/4/2, T = 17

Testing
WIP = $50k/450 units
B/N = 85%
FTE = 8/0/0, T = 8

Final assembly
WIP = $250k
B/N = 65%
FTE = 23/1/2, T = 26

Shipping
B/N = n/a
FTE = 1.5/0/0, T= 1.5

WIP = $100k
C/T = 20 days
V/A = 2 days

WIP = $50k
C/T = 5 days
V/A = 1 day

WIP = $624k
C/T = 10 days

WIP = $240k
C/T = 15 days
V/A = 1 days

FGI = $600k
C/T = 50 days

Totals:
C/T = 100 days
V/T = 4 days
VAR = 4%

Source: Professor Arthur V. Hill

The data associated with each step can include:

- C/T = Average cycle time.
- V/A = Value-added time or the percentage of total time that is value-added time.
- C/O = Changeover time from one product to another.
- B/N = Bottleneck utilization.
- U/T = The time that the process is available for work or the percentage of the total time that the process is available for work.
- FPY = First pass yield, which is the percentage of the time that the quality standards are met the first time a product goes through the process.
- FTE = Number of full-time equivalent workers required for this process.

The benefits claimed for value stream mapping include:

- Helps users identify and eliminate waste.
- Creates a vision of the future by uncovering wastes and opportunities to create flow.
- Enables broad participation.
- Improves understanding of product cost.
- Helps reduce work in process.
- Helps reduce cycle time.
- Focuses on customer pull signals.

The standard reference on value stream maps is the book *Learning to See Version* by Rother, Shook, Womack, and Jones (2003).

See *A3 Report, causal map, deliverables, lean sigma, lean thinking, process map, value stream, value stream manager.*

values statement – See *mission statement.*

variable costing – An accounting method that defines product cost as the sum of the costs that vary with output and ignores all fixed overhead costs; this usually includes only direct materials and direct labor and possibly the variable portion of manufacturing overhead.

With variable costing, the contribution margin is sales revenue minus variable costs.

See *absorption costing, Activity Based Costing (ABC), overhead, standard cost, Theory of Constraints (TOC), throughput accounting.*

variance – (1) In a statistics context: A measure of the dispersion (variability) of a random variable; the average squared deviation from the mean; the standard deviation squared. (2) In an accounting context: The difference between the budgeted (planned) and actual amount. ✪

The discussion here is only for the statistics definition. Given a set of n observations on a random variable labeled $(x_1, x_2, \ldots, x_n)$, the sample variance is defined as $s^2 = \left(\dfrac{1}{n-1}\right)\sum_{i=1}^{n}(x_i - \overline{x})^2 = \dfrac{1}{n-1}\left(\sum_{i=1}^{n}x_i^2 - \dfrac{1}{n}\left(\sum_{i=1}^{n}x_i\right)^2\right)$.

The first expression is known as the definitional form and the second expression is known as the computational form because it is easier for computing purposes. The computational form requires only "one pass" on the data.

The sample standard deviation is the square root of the sample variance. The population variance and population standard deviation have a denominator of n instead of $n-1$. Most authors use either the symbol $\hat{\sigma}$ (sigma hat) or s for the standard deviation of a sample, whereas the σ (sigma) is used for the standard deviation of the population. The unit of measure for the standard deviation is always the same as the raw data and the mean. The inflection points for the normal distribution are at the mean plus and minus one standard deviation. A rough estimate for the standard deviation of a random variable is the range divided by six. The standard deviation for a normally distributed random variable is theoretically equal to $\sqrt{\pi/2}\,MAD$, which is approximately $1.25MAD$, where the Mean Absolute Deviation $(MAD) = (1/n)\sum_{i=1}^{n}|x_i - \overline{x}|$. This is true asymptotically[62], but will almost never be exactly true for any given sample.

In Excel, the formulas for the sample standard deviation and variance are STDEV(*range*) and VAR(*range*), and for the population standard deviation and variance they are STDEVP(*range*) and VARP(*range*). The Excel formula for the sample covariance is $(n/(n-1))$*COVAR(*x_range, y_range*), and the population covariance is COVAR(*x_range, y_range*).

The variance of the product of a constant a and random variable X is $\mathrm{VAR}(aX) = a^2\mathrm{VAR}(X)$. The variance of the sum of two random variables X and Y is $\mathrm{Var}(X+Y) = \mathrm{Var}(X) + \mathrm{Var}(Y) + 2\mathrm{Cov}(X,Y)$. The variance of the weighted sum of two random variables is $\mathrm{Var}(aX + bY) = a^2\,\mathrm{Var}(X) + b^2\,\mathrm{Var}(Y) + 2ab\mathrm{Cov}(X,Y)$. If Y is the sum of N random variables, then $\mathrm{Var}(Y) = \sum_{i=1}^{N}\mathrm{Var}(X_i) + 2\sum_{i=1}^{N-1}\sum_{j=i+1}^{N}\mathrm{Cov}(X_i,X_j) = \sum_{i=1}^{N}\sum_{j=1}^{N}\mathrm{Cov}(X_i,X_j)$.

See *Analysis of Variance (ANOVA), correlation, covariance, kurtosis, Mean Absolute Deviation (MAD), mean squared error (MSE), standard deviation.*

VAT analysis – A Theory of Constraints classification system used to describe different types of general materials flows and their related bill of material structures.

The shape of each of the letters V, A, and T describes the process flow (Goldratt 1990):

- **V-plant** – A V-plant transforms a few inputs into a wide variety of products in a "one to many" product flow. This type of process should be master scheduled at the raw materials level. The primary problem in V-plants is allocating the material properly to competing products.
- **A-plant** – An A-plant transforms (often assembles) a wide variety of inputs into a small variety of final products in a "many to one" product flow. This type of process should be master scheduled at the finished products level. The primary problem in A-plants is synchronizing the incoming materials so that all materials are available when needed.
- **T-plant** – A T-plant builds standard parts up to a certain point (the crossbar of the "T") and then assembles these into a wide variety of end products. The components for the lower part of the "T" are built to inventory

---

[62] *The difference between the standard deviation and $\sqrt{\pi/2}\,MAD$ will approach zero as the sample size goes to infinity.*

and then "mixed and matched" in a wide variety of ways for a customer order. Examples include appliances ("white goods") and computers that have many standard inputs but can result in a variety of end items. This type of process should be master scheduled at the finished components level. T-plants suffer from both synchronization problems of A-plants (parts are not all available for an assembly) and the stealing problems of V-plants (one assembly steals parts that could have been used in another).

Wikipedia lists the fourth process type as an I-plant, which is a simple linear process, such as an assembly line. The primary work is done in a straight sequence of events. The constraint is the slowest operation.

The terms V-plant, A-plant, and T-plant are probably not the best terms and are not commonly used. In this author's point of view, these terms are a better description of the bill of material than of the plant.

The *Master Production Schedule (MPS)* entry provides much more detail on this subject.

See *bill of material (BOM)*, *Master Production Schedule (MPS)*, *standard parts*, *Theory of Constraints (TOC)*, *white goods*.

VBA – See *Visual Basic for Applications (VBA)*.

Vehicle Scheduling Problem (VSP) – An extension of the Traveling Salesperson Problem (TSP) that can involve multiple vehicles, time window constraints on visiting each node, capacity constraints on each vehicle, total distance and time constraints for each vehicle, and demand requirements for each node.

See the *Traveling Salesperson Problem (TSP)* entry for more detailed information.

See *milk run*, *Traveling Salesperson Problem (TSP)*.

vendor – See *supplier*.

vendor certification – See *supplier qualification and certification*.

vendor managed inventory (VMI) – A supplier-customer relationship where the vendor assumes responsibility for managing the replenishment of stock; also known as supplier-managed inventory (SMI). ✪

In a traditional supplier-customer relationship, a customer evaluates its own inventory position and sends an order to a supplier (vendor) when it has a need for a replenishment order. With VMI, the supplier not only supplies goods, but also provides inventory management services. The supplier-customer agreement usually makes the supplier responsible for maintaining the customer's inventory levels. For VMI to work, the supplier needs to have access to the customer's inventory data. Examples of VMI in practice for many years include:

- Supermarkets and vending machines have used this concept for decades.
- Frito-Lay's route salespeople stock the shelves for their retail customers to keep the product fresh and the paperwork simple. Much fresh produce moves into convenience shops in the same way.
- For more than 20 years, Hopson Oil, a home heating oil supplier, has automatically scheduled deliveries for fuel oil based on consumption forecasts for each customer. In this way, it keeps its order-taking costs down and keeps the process simple for customers.

Rungtusanatham, Rabinovich, Ashenbaum, and Wallin (2007) define **consignment** as supplier-owned inventory at the customer's location and **reverse consignment** as customer-owned inventory at the supplier's location. (See the table below.) They further define "Vendor-Owned Inventory Management" (VOIM) as supplier-owned inventory at the customer location (consignment inventory), but managed by the supplier. The table below calls this "Consignment VMI."

Inventory management alternatives		Location	
		Supplier location	Customer location
Ownership	Supplier owned	Traditional inventory management relationship[63]	Consignment VMI[64]
	Customer owned	Reverse consignment	Traditional VMI

Adapted from Wallin, Rungtusanatham, & Rabinovich (2006), p. 54.

The advantages and disadvantages of VMI over a traditional purchasing relationship are listed below.

---

[63] *Rungtusanatham, Rabinovich, Ashenbaum, and Wallin (2007) call this cell "inventory speculation."*

[64] *Rungtusanatham, Rabinovich, Ashenbaum, and Wallin (2007) call this cell "forward consignment with VMI or VOIM."*

Advantages and disadvantages of VMI compared traditional supplier customer relationships

Advantages of VMI	Disadvantages of VMI
• Maximizes "in-stock" position, which captures more sales for both the vendor and the customer. • Improves data accuracy and speed. • Improves forecast accuracy. • Reduces inventory and inventory carrying cost. • Reduces transportation costs. • Reduces transaction costs. • Reduces coordination cost in the supply chain. • Handles promotions better.	• Increases the vendor's share of the administrative costs (headcount, etc.). • Complicates volume discounts and special pricing. • Complicates the system in the short run. • Increases risks of loss of control and flexibility. • May penalize the manufacturer with a short-term volume reduction if less inventory is required. • Requires that the customer share demand information with the supplier.

Source: Professor Arthur V. Hill

VMI is relatively easy to implement from a technical perspective because the computer hardware and software tools are readily available. However, job functions, processes, and performance measurements all need to change in order to get the most benefit.

Like other customer interface strategies, VMI has strategic implications. The fundamental value proposition is one where the supplier is able to reduce the transaction cost for the customer, but at the expense of increasing the customer's switching cost (the cost to switch from one supplier to another).

See *co-location, consignment inventory, delegation, inventory management, JIT II, outsourcing, purchasing, replenishment order, supply chain management, switching cost.*

Version control – The process of keeping track of changes to software, engineering specifications, product designs, databases, and other information; also known as revision control.

Version control is commonly used in software development, product design, engineering, and architecture, where multiple people may change the same set of files. Changes are usually identified by an alphanumeric code called the **revision number**, **revision level**, or **version number**. For example, the initial design might be labeled revision 1, but when a change is made, the new version is labeled revision 2. Each revision should identify the date and the person who made the change. Ideally, revisions can be compared, restored, and merged. Software version control tools and disciplines are essential for all multi-developer projects.

See *Engineering Change Order (ECO), Product Data Management (PDM), product life cycle management.*

Vertical integration – The process a firm uses to acquire sources of supply (upstream suppliers) or channels of distribution (downstream buyers). ✪

Because it can have a significant impact on a business unit's position in its industry with respect to cost, differentiation, and other strategic issues, the vertical scope of the firm is an important strategic issue. Expansion of activities downstream is referred to as **forward integration** and expansion upstream is **backward integration**. The table below compares the potential advantages and disadvantages of a firm becoming more vertically integrated.

Evaluation of vertical integration

Potential advantages of vertical integration	Potential disadvantages of vertical integration
• Reduces transportation costs if common ownership results in less travel distance. • Improves supply chain coordination. • Provides more opportunities to differentiate by means of increased control over inputs. • Captures upstream or downstream profit margins. • Increases entry barriers to potential competitors. • Helps gain access to downstream distribution channels that otherwise would be inaccessible. • Justifies investment in specialized assets that independent supply chain players might avoid. • Leads to expansion of core competencies.	• Causes capacity imbalance (for example, the firm may need to build excess upstream capacity to ensure downstream supply under all demand conditions). • Causes higher costs due to low efficiencies resulting from lack of supplier competition. • Decreases flexibility due to upstream or downstream investments. However, the flexibility to coordinate vertically-related activities may increase. • Decreases ability to support product variety if significant in-house development is required. • Develops new competencies that may compromise existing competencies. • Increases bureaucratic costs.

Some situational factors favoring vertical integration include:

- Taxes and regulations on market transactions
- Obstacles to the formulation and monitoring of contracts
- Strategic similarity between the vertically related activities
- Sufficiently large production quantities so the firm can benefit from economies of scale
- Reluctance of other firms to make investments specific to the transaction

The following situational factors tend to make vertical integration less attractive:

- The quantity required from a supplier is less than the minimum efficient scale for producing the product.
- The product is a commodity and its production cost decreases significantly as cumulative quantity increases.
- The core competencies between the activities are very different.
- The vertically adjacent activities are in very different types of industries. For example, manufacturing is very different from retailing.
- The addition of the new activity places the firm in competition with another player with which it needs to cooperate. The firm may then be viewed as a competitor rather than as a partner.

Alternatives to vertical integration may provide many of the same benefits without the risks. Some of these alternatives include long-term explicit contracts, franchise agreements, joint ventures, and co-location of facilities (Greaver 1999). Some of the above ideas are adapted from quickmba.com/strategy/vertical-integration.

See *joint venture, make versus buy decision, operations strategy, outsourcing, supply chain management*.

virtual organization – A business model where the selling organization is able to pull together business partners to satisfy a customer order, launch a new product, or supply a product to a market without owning many of the key components of the system.

Virtual organizations have significant flexibility benefits, but given the tenuous nature of their relationships, they may not be sustainable. Many high-technology development firms design products and then find contract manufacturers to build them and distributors to find markets for them.

See *agile manufacturing, mass customization, operations strategy, organizational design*.

virtual teams – Groups that do not meet in person but use technologies such the Internet to communicate.

vision statement – See *mission statement*.

Visual Basic for Applications (VBA) – A programming language built into most Microsoft Office applications.

VBA makes it possible to write user-defined functions and programs in Microsoft Excel. VBA code is sometimes referred to as a "macro." The example on the right shows VBA code for a user-defined function that multiplies the input by two. Winston and Albright (2011) provide excellent instruction on VBA programming and modeling.

```
Function twox(x)
  twox = 2 * x
End Function
```

visual management – See *visual control*.

visual control – A lean manufacturing approach of designing systems that give everyone in a work area immediate information about the current status of a system.

Visual controls are simple, easy-to-see clues that give managers and workers immediate information about the current status of a system. Visual control requires that the **normal** and **abnormal states** be immediately apparent. As Jerome Hamilton of 3M says, "My shop floor speaks to me." Although many computer-based information systems make use of exception reports and "traffic light" reports (with red, yellow, and green fields), most of them do not meet lean standards for truly visual communication of the system status. Examples of visual control include (1) a **shadow board** that clearly and quickly shows, which tools are missing, (2) an **andon light** that clearly shows when a worker is having trouble, and (3) work stoppage in a pull system.

See *5S, andon light, lean thinking, shadow board*.

VMI – See *vendor managed inventory*.

VOC – See *voice of the customer (VOC)*.

voice of the customer (VOC) – Customer opinions, perceptions, desires (both stated and unstated), and requirements. ✪

It is important for organizations to understand both internal and external customers' needs and desires as they change over time. This voice of the customer should inform both new product development and process improvement efforts. **Quality Function Deployment (QFD)** is a tool that can be used to translate the voice of the customer into product features and specifications. The VOC is considered one of the keys to success for process improvement programs and projects.

The voice of the customer can be captured in a variety of ways such as:

- Interviews
- Customer satisfaction surveys
- Market research surveys
- E-surveys
- Comment cards
- Focus groups
- Customer specifications

- Contractual requirements
- Observation
- Warranty and service guarantee data
- Field reports
- Complaint logs
- Customer loyalty (i.e., repeat sales)
- Exploratory marketing (Hamel & Prahalad 1991)

Many of the entries listed below discuss specific VOC tools.

See *Analytic Hierarchy Process (AHP), critical incidents method, Critical to Quality (CTQ), Customer Relationship Management (CRM), ethnographic research, Kano Analysis, lean sigma, New Product Development (NPD), Process Improvement Program, Pugh Matrix, Quality Function Deployment (QFD), quality management, Voice of the Process (VOP).*

Voice of the Process (VOP) – Communication from the system (process) to the process owner.

Process owners receive two important sources of information: the voice of the customer (VOC) and the Voice of the Process (VOP). Whereas the VOC communicates customer desires, requirements, needs, specifications, and expectations, the VOP communicates information about the performance of the process. The VOP can use many quality tools, such as bar charts, Pareto charts, run charts, control charts, cause and effect diagrams, and checksheets. The challenge for the process owner/manager is to use VOP information to better meet the customer needs as defined by the VOC.

See *voice of the customer (VOC).*

voice picking – A speech recognition system that allows warehouse workers to verbally enter data into a system.

Voice picking is a feature available in many warehouse management systems that allows workers' hands to be free while working. Benefits include improved accuracy, productivity, accuracy, and reliability.

See *picking, warehouse, Warehouse Management System (WMS).*

volume flexibility – See *flexibility.*

V-plant – See *VAT analysis.*

VSP (Vehicle Scheduling Problem) – See *Traveling Salesperson Problem (TSP), Vehicle Scheduling Problem (VSP).*

W

Wagner-Whitin lotsizing algorithm – A dynamic programming algorithm for finding the optimal solution for the time-varying demand lotsizing problem.

An implementation of this algorithm (including the pseudocode) can be found in Evans (1985).

See *algorithm, lotsizing methods, time-varying demand lotsizing problem.*

wait time – A random variable indicating the time that a customer (or an order) is delayed before starting in a process; also called waiting time or queue time.

The wait time is the time that a customer or order is delayed before starting in service. The time in system for a particular customer is the wait time (queue time) plus the service time, and the average time in system is the average wait time plus the average service time. The average queue time and the average time in system are important system performance measures. Wait time (queue time) is often the largest portion of the manufacturing cycle time. In the lean manufacturing philosophy, wait time is considered wasteful.

See *cycle time, lean thinking, Little's Law, operations performance metrics, queuing theory, time in system, turnaround time, utilization, value added ratio, Work-in-Process (WIP) inventory.*

waiting line – See *queuing theory.*

warehouse – A building or storage area used to store materials. ✪

Warehouses are used by manufacturers, importers, exporters, wholesalers, distributors, and retailers to store goods in anticipation of demand. They are usually large metal buildings in industrial areas with loading docks to load and unload goods from trucks, railways, airports, or seaports. Nearly all **Warehouse Management Systems (WMS)** allow users to define multiple logical warehouses inside a single building.

Warehouses usually use forklifts to move goods on pallets. When a shipment arrives at a warehouse, it must be received and then put away. When a customer order is received, it must then be picked from shelves, packed, and shipped to the customer.

Having a good inventory system is critical to the success of a warehouse. WMSs can help reduce the cost to receive and put away products and reduce the cost to pick, pack, and ship customer orders. A good WMS also improves record accuracy for on-hand, allocated, and on-order quantities.

A **zone** is an area of a warehouse used for storing one type of product. For example, a hospital inventory might have one zone for forms, another for medical-surgical items, and still another for pharmacy items (drugs). A **rack** is a storage shelf, usually made from metal. An **aisle** is a space for people to walk and for materials handling equipment to move between racks. A **section** or **bay** is usually the space defined by a pair of upright frames and a **shelf** (or **level**) is the level in the section or bay. Finally, a **bin** (or slot) is a specific storage location (or container) used to store multiple units of a single item. Bins are commonly made of metal, corrugated cardboard, or plastic, and may have a cover. Bins may have capacity limits in terms of weight, volume, or units. Bins are referenced by warehouse, zone, rack (or aisle), bay (or section), shelf (level or row), and bin number. Barcoding bins can reduce cost and increase picking accuracy.

Warehouses must have a **locator system** to find items. Items may be stored using a **fixed location system**, a **random location system**, or a **zone location system**. Fixed location systems label the shelves with the item (SKU, material) number and attempt to keep products only in that one storage area. In contrast, random location systems label the shelves with the bin (bay) number and shelf number and then use a computer-based system to keep track of what items are stored in each bin. Zone storage is a combination of the two that uses fixed storage areas for groups of items but uses random storage in each zone.

Warehouses can use a variety of **slotting** rules to guide where an item is stored. Similarly, warehouses can use a variety of **picking** systems to create a **pick list** that guides stock pickers in picking (retrieving) materials from the warehouse to fill orders.

Most warehouses use a **First-In-First-Out (FIFO)** policy for managing physical inventory. However, it is important to note that the accounting system might still use last-in-first-out for costing purposes. Warehouses generally use either **pallet rack** or **carton flow racking**. As the names suggest, pallet racks store **pallets** (or **skids**) and carton flow racking stores cartons. Pallet racks can be either **static** or **flow racks** (gravity rack). Static racks must use LIFO. In contrast, pallet flow racks use gravity so pallets loaded in the rear flow forward on a wheeled track to a picking position. Pallet flow racks, therefore, use FIFO. Carton systems sometimes use wheeled shelves and conveyors to move products and sometimes use gravity flow.

A **public warehouse** is a business that leases space and provides services to customers, usually on a month-to-month basis, and uses its own equipment and labor to provide warehouse services, such as receiving, storage, and shipping. Public warehouses charge based on space and labor usage. In contrast, a **contract warehouse** provides warehouse services for a specified period of time (often yearly) where the owner of the goods pays for the space even if it is not used. Both public and contract warehouses are often used to supplement space requirements of a private warehouse.

A **bonded warehouse** is a facility (or dedicated portion of a facility) where imported goods are stored until custom duties are paid. In the U.S., a bonded warehouse must be approved by the U.S. Treasury Department and under bond/guarantee for observance of revenue laws. A bonded warehouse can be particularly useful when products are received well in advance of sale because the import fees are not usually paid until the products are shipped from the bonded warehouse.

Dry storage is storage of non-refrigerated products, such as canned goods. **Cold storage** is for perishable food and other products that require refrigeration. Cold storage can be either **refrigerated storage** (above freezing) or **frozen storage** (below freezing).

See *ABC classification, aggregate inventory management, Automated Storage & Retrieval System (AS/RS), carousel, cross-docking, cube utilization, discrete order picking, distribution center (DC), Distribution Requirements Planning (DRP), dock, facility location, First-In-First-Out (FIFO), flow rack, forklift truck, forward pick area, fulfillment, locator system, logistics, materials management, numeric-analytic location model, pallet, part number, periodic review system, pick face, pick list, picking, pull system, Radio Frequency Identification (RFID), random storage location, receiving, reserve storage area, safety stock, slotting, square root law for warehouses, supply chain management, task interleaving, Third Party Logistics (3PL) provider, voice picking, Warehouse Management System (WMS), wave picking, zone storage location.*

Warehouse Management System (WMS) – A software application that helps organizations manage the operations of a warehouse or distribution center. ✪

WMSs manage the storage and retrieval of materials in a building and handle the transactions associated with those movements, such as receiving, put away (stocking), cycle counting, picking, consolidating, packing, and shipping. The WMS guides the operator or machine with information about item locations, quantities, units of measure and other relevant information to determine where to stock, where to pick, and in what sequence to perform each operation. Newer warehouse management systems include tools that support more complex tasks, such as inventory management, product allocations, shipment planning, workforce planning/labor management, and productivity analysis. WMSs can be stand-alone systems, modules in an ERP system, or modules in a supply chain execution suite. The benefits of a good WMS include reduced inventory, reduced labor cost, increased storage capacity, improved customer service, and improved inventory accuracy. Traditionally, WMSs have used barcodes or smart codes to capture data; however, more recently, Radio Frequency Technology (RFID) technology has been added to provide real-time information. However, most firms, especially in manufacturing and distribution, still use barcodes to capture data because of their simplicity, universality, and low cost.

See *ABC classification, Advanced Shipping Notification (ASN), Automated Data Collection (ADC), bill of material (BOM), cross-docking, distribution center (DC), Distribution Requirements Planning (DRP), dock-to-stock, fixed storage location, forward pick area, fulfillment, inventory management, locator system, logistics, materials management, Over/Short/Damaged Report, picking, Radio Frequency Identification (RFID), random storage location, real-time, receiving, slotting, slotting fee, task interleaving, Transportation Management System (TMS), voice picking, warehouse, wave picking, zone picking, zone storage location.*

warranty – A guarantee given from the seller to the purchaser stating that a product is free from known defects and that the seller will repair or replace defective parts within a given time limit and under certain conditions.

A warranty and a service guarantee have identical legal obligations for the seller. The difference is that a warranty is for a product (a tangible good) and a service guarantee is for a service (an intangible product). Blischke and Murty (1992) and Murty and Blischke (1992) provide a good summary of the warranty literature.

See *caveat emptor, product design quality, service guarantee, Service Level Agreement (SLA).*

waste – See *8 Wastes*.

waste walk – The lean practice of walking through a place where work is being done to look for wasteful activities; also called a gemba walk.

When conducting a waste walk, it is wise to engage with the gemba, ask the "5 Whys," take notes as you go, and follow-up as necessary.

See *3Gs, 8 Wastes, gemba, lean thinking, management by walking around.*

water spider – A lean manufacturing practice of assigning a skilled worker to re-supply parts to the point of use on the production line; a worker who follows a timed material delivery route; also known as mizusumashi (in Japanese), water strider, water beetle, water-spider, or material delivery route.

The water spider's job is to follow the schedule and maintain the inventory on a production line between a minimum and maximum level. They typically use a cart to deliver materials to workstations in predefined quantities at least every one to two hours on a fixed time schedule. This ensures that the manufacturing line has the right amount of inventory at the right time. Compared to traditional methods, material delivery routes stock line bins more frequently and in smaller quantities, resulting in reduced WIP inventory and reduced waiting time.

The water spider has a routine and knows all processes thoroughly enough to step in if needed. Water spiders sometimes also assist with changeovers, provide tools and materials, and provide other help needed to maintain flow. At Toyota, performing the water spider role is a prerequisite for supervisory positions.

The water spider is named after the whirligig beetle that swims about quickly in the water. The Japanese word for water spider is mizusumashi, which is written as 水すまし in Kanji (source: www.babylon.com/definition/mizusumashi/Japanese, December 28, 2009).

See *lean thinking, point of use.*

waterfall – See *waterfall scheduling.*

waterfall scheduling – (1) A project management approach that does not allow a step to be started until all previous steps are complete. (2) A lean methodology that schedules customers to arrive every few minutes.

Definition (1) – The project management context: In a waterfall process, steps do not overlap. The Gantt Chart for a waterfall process looks like a waterfall, with each step starting after the previous step. The term is often used in a software development context where the design step is not allowed to begin until the requirements step is complete, the coding step is not allowed to begin until the design step is complete, etc. This waterfall scheduling process only works well in situations where the domain is fully specified, well structured, and well understood. However, in the software development context, the term "waterfall process" is often used to criticize old thinking that does not allow for iterative, spiral, lean, and agile development approaches.

Definition (2) – The customer scheduling context: Some lean healthcare consultants use the term "waterfall scheduling" to mean scheduling patients to arrive every few minutes (e.g., 10 or 15 minute intervals) rather than in batches every half-hour. Batch arrivals cause bottlenecks for receptionists and nurses and cause long waits for many patients. Therefore, waterfall scheduling in this context is a positive thing, because it spreads out arrivals and develops a smooth even flow for the service process.

Although both of the above definitions have to do with scheduling, they are used in different contexts. Definition (1) is usually presented as a bad practice, and definition (2) is usually presented as a good practice.

See *agile software development, concurrent engineering, Gantt Chart, New Product Development (NPD), project management, scrum, sprint burndown chart, stage-gate process, transactional process improvement.*

wave picking – A method of creating a pick list where all items for a particular group of orders (e.g., a carrier, destination, or set of work orders) are picked and then later grouped (consolidated) by ship location.

With wave picking, all zones are picked at the same time, and the items are later sorted and consolidated to fill individual orders. The principle is to handle each item efficiently two times, rather than inefficiently once. A wave is a grouping of orders by a specific set of criteria, such as priority level, freight carrier, shipment type, or destination. These orders are released to the different zones in the warehouse as a group. Clearly, the rate for each of the two handling steps, batch picking and container loading (consolidation), must be considerably more than twice as fast as the single step in traditional serial order picking to make wave picking worthwhile.

The two options for wave picking include fixed-wave picking and dynamic-wave picking. With fixed-wave picking, orders are not sent off to be packed until the entire wave's worth of items has been picked. With dynamic-wave picking, each order is sent to the packer as it is completed.

Operations with a high total number of SKUs and moderate to high picks per order may benefit from wave picking. Although wave picking is one of the quickest methods for picking multiple line orders, some distribution centers struggle with order consolidation, sorting, and verifying that the contents are correct.

See *batch picking, distribution center (DC), picking, warehouse, Warehouse Management System (WMS), zone picking.*

waybill – A shipping document created by a carrier identifying the shipper, date of shipment, carrier, number of parcels, weight, receiver, and date received; also called an air waybill, Air Consignment Note.

The waybill confirms receipt of the goods by the carrier. Unlike a bill of lading, which includes much of the same information, a waybill is not a document of title.

See *bill of lading, Cash on Delivery (COD), FOB, terms, Transportation Management System (TMS).*

WBS – See *work breakdown structure.*

weeks supply – See *periods supply.*

Weibull distribution – A continuous probability distribution for modeling lifetimes of objects, time to failure, or time to complete a task that has a long tail; a probability distribution that is commonly used in reliability theory and maintenance for extreme values.

Parameters: Shape parameter $\alpha > 0$ and scale parameter $\beta > 0$. Some sources add a location parameter γ by replacing x with $(x - \gamma)$. (Note: The reliability literature uses shape and scale parameters and β and η.)

Density and distribution functions: The density and distribution functions for the Weibull distribution for $x > 0$ are $f(x) = \alpha \beta^{-\alpha} x^{\alpha-1} \exp(-(x/\beta)^\alpha)$ and $F(x) = 1 - \exp(-(x/\beta)^\alpha)$.

Statistics: Range $[0, \infty)$, mean $\beta\Gamma(1+1/\alpha)$, median $\beta\ln(2)^{1/\alpha}$, mode $\beta((\alpha-1)/\alpha)^{1/\alpha}$ if $\alpha \geq 1$ and 0 otherwise, variance $(\beta^2/\alpha)(2\Gamma(2/\alpha) - (1/\alpha)\Gamma(1/\alpha)^2)$, where $\Gamma()$ is the gamma function.

Graph: The graph on the right shows the Weibull density function with $(\alpha, \beta) = (2, 1)$.

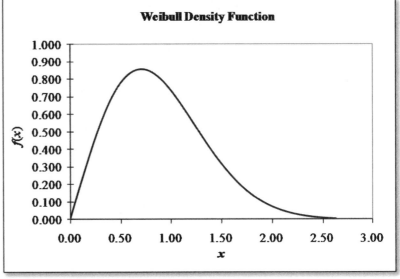

Weibull Density Function

Parameter estimation: Estimating the α and β parameters from a set of observations requires numerical methods for both the MLE and method of moments estimators. See Law and Kelton (2000) for information on the MLE approach.

Excel: In Excel, the Weibull density and distribution functions are WEIBULL(x, α, β, FALSE) and WEIBULL(x, α, β, TRUE). Excel 2003/2007 has no inverse function for the Weibull, but it can be calculated with the Excel formula $x = \beta*(-\ln(1-F(x)))^{\wedge}(1/\alpha)$. Excel 2010 renamed the function WEIBULL.DIST, but it still uses the same arguments.

Excel simulation: In an Excel simulation, Weibull distributed random variates can be generated with the inverse transform method using $x = \beta*(-\ln(\text{RAND}()))^{\wedge}(1/\alpha)$.

Relationships to other distributions: The exponential distribution is a special case of the Weibull when $\alpha = 1$, and the Rayleigh distribution is a special case of the Weibull distribution when $\alpha = 2$. When $\alpha = 3$, the Weibull distribution is similar to the normal distribution.

History: The Weibull distribution was named after Swedish engineer and scientist Ernst Hjalmar Waloddi Weibull (1887-1979) (source: www.wikipedia.org, November 20, 2007.)

See *bathtub curve, beta distribution, exponential distribution, inverse transform method, probability density function, probability distribution, Total Productive Maintenance (TPM).*

weighted average – An average where some values contribute more than others.

A weighted average is commonly used in forecasting where it is important to give more weight to more recent data. Mathematically, a weighted average is $WA = \dfrac{1}{W}\sum_{t=1}^{T} w_t x_t$, where T is the number of values (time periods), t is the period index, w_t is the weight assigned to the value in period t, x_t is the value in period t, and $W = \sum_{t=1}^{T} w_t$. The weights are often required to sum to one, which simplifies the equation to $WA = \sum_{t=1}^{T} w_t x_t$.

See *carrying charge, carrying cost, exponential smoothing, forecast error metrics, moving average, periods supply.*

Weighted MAPE – See *Mean Absolute Percent Error (MAPE).*

what-if analysis – The practice of evaluating the results of a model when input parameters are changed.

What-if sensitivity analysis is often done with mathematical optimization, stochastic simulation, and queuing theory models to help decision makers (1) evaluate different potential scenarios and make risk return trade-offs, (2) refine their intuition about the relationships in the model, and (3) validate that the model fits the real-world.

See *Activity Based Costing (ABC)*, *DuPont Analysis*, *linear programming (LP)*, *queuing theory*, *simulation*.

where-used report – A listing of all materials that are "parents" for a particular material in a bill of material.

See *bill of material (BOM)*, *bill of material implosion*, *Materials Requirements Planning (MRP)*, *pegging*.

white goods – Major electric appliances (machines) that are typically finished in white enamel.

Examples of white goods include refrigerators, freezers, dishwashers, stoves, ovens, washing machines, dryers, and water heaters. White goods are usually classified as consumer durables, but can be sold for either consumer or commercial uses.

See *durable goods*, *platform strategy*, *private label*, *VAT analysis*.

wholesale price – See *wholesaler*.

wholesaler – A distributor that buys goods and resells them to organizations other than final customers; also called a distributor or jobber.

Wholesalers often buy large quantities of goods from manufacturers, store them in warehouses, and sell them to retailers who sell to consumers. The wholesale price is the price wholesalers pay when buying in large quantities. A rack jobber is a wholesaler that provides goods on consignment for rack displays in retail locations. They are given dedicated space in the store in exchange for sharing profits with the retailer.

See *B2B*, *broker*, *distributor*, *supplier*, *supply chain management*.

Winsorizing – A simple bounding procedure that replaces values greater (less) than the maximum (minimum) value allowed with the maximum value.

Data can be Winsorized by setting a maximum and minimum value or by defining the upper and lower percentiles allowed on the cumulative distribution. Whereas Winsorizing replaces values in the tail of the sample, trimming excludes these values.

See *forecast error metrics*, *Mean Absolute Percent Error (MAPE)*, *outlier*, *Relative Absolute Error (RAE)*, *trim*, *trimmed mean*.

WIP – See *Work-in-Process (WIP) inventory*.

WMS – See *Warehouse Management System (WMS)*.

work breakdown structure (WBS) – A project management tool that defines the hierarchy of project activities (tasks) needed to complete the project. ✪

The WBS is a useful way to identify all tasks needed for a **project**, break large tasks into smaller, more manageable tasks, and organize and communicate the list of tasks. The WBS lists all tasks required for the project, starting at the highest level of aggregation and going down to a detailed list of all tasks. It is like a bill of material for the project and can be drawn like the roots of a tree. The WBS does not create the project schedule, communicate precedence relationships between tasks, or define the resources required for each task. The U.S. Air Force encourages suppliers to define a WBS so all tasks require about one week of work.

For example, the top level of the WBS for a wedding might include create invitations, acquire dresses/tuxes, and reserve church. The example below shows a small portion of the WBS for this simple example. This WBS could be broken down into much more detail as needed. The lowest level of the WBS should define all specific tasks needed to complete the project.

It is important to understand that the WBS is not a schedule or sequence of activities. It is simply a hierarchical list of the activities that need to be done to complete the project.

The next step after using the WBS to identify tasks is to identify the precedence constraints between the tasks. That information can then be used to determine the early and late start times and early and late finish times for each task and finally determine the critical path through the network.

Example work breakdown structure for a wedding

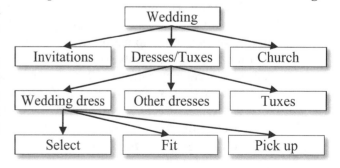

See *Critical Path Method (CPM)*, *Earned Value Management (EVM)*, *mindmap*, *Project Evaluation and Review Technique (PERT)*, *project management*.

work center – See *workcenter*.

work design – See *job design*.

work measurement – The process of estimating the standard time required for a task; also called labor standards, engineered labor standards, labor management systems, and Methods Time Measurement (MTM). ✪

The main reasons for a work measurement system (labor management system) include:

- **Cost accounting** – Standard times are used to assign both labor and overhead cost to products or jobs.
- **Evaluation of alternatives** – Standard times are used to help evaluate new equipment investments or changes in the current equipment configuration.
- **Evaluation and reward systems** – Standard times are often used as a basis of comparison for evaluating and rewarding direct labor, where workers are rewarded when they "beat" the standard times.
- **Scheduling** – Jobs, workers, and machines are often scheduled based on standard times.

The three common ways to measure the time for a task are (1) time study, (2) standard data, and (3) work sampling. A **time study** can be used for almost any existing job with a relatively short duration. **Standard data** only requires that the analyst determine which elemental motions (e.g., pick, drop, etc.) are required for the job. Once these are determined, the analyst simply looks these up in the reference database and adds them up to "assemble" the total time for the task. The data for this type of analysis is often called pre-determined motion and time data. **Work sampling** takes a large number of random "snapshots" (samples) of the process over several weeks and estimates how much time is spent in each "state" based on the percentage of the random samples found in each state. This data is often self-reported and is more appropriate for knowledge work.

See *human resources*, *job design*, *normal time*, *operations performance metrics*, *overhead*, *performance management system*, *performance rating*, *scientific management*, *standard time*, *time study*, *work sampling*.

work order – A request for a job to be done; also called a workorder, job, production order, and work ticket.

In a manufacturing context, a work order is a request to a maintenance organization to perform either preventive or emergency maintenance or a request to a machine shop to make a tool. Work orders should identify the customer, the date the work order was created, and some indication of the urgency of the work.

A work order should not be confused with a manufacturing order.

See *maintenance*, *manufacturing order*, *Total Productive Maintenance (TPM)*.

work sampling – The application of statistical sampling methods to estimate the percentage of time that a worker is spending on each activity (or in each "state"); also called occurrence sampling.

This approach to **work measurement** should only be used for long cycle tasks. For example, a hospital administrator wants to know how much time nurses are sitting at the nursing station per day. The person responsible for collecting the data takes a large number of random "snapshots" (samples) of the process over several weeks. Work sampling assumes that the percentage of the samples in each activity (state) is proportional to the percentage of work time in each activity. From these snapshots, the administrator can estimate how much time nurses spend at the nursing station per day on average.

The advantage of work sampling over other work measurement tools is that the data are gathered over a relatively long time period. In contrast, a time study makes more sense for a task that requires a relatively short amount of time, with the observer recording each repetition of the process.

See *normal time*, *sampling*, *standard time*, *time study*, *work measurement*.

work simplification – The process of reducing the complexity of a process.

Work simplification involves designing the job to have fewer stages, steps, moves, and interdependences, thus making the job easier to learn, perform, and understand. This is closely related to **work standardization**. Although normally applied only to repetitive factory and service work, it can also be applied to less repetitive knowledge work done by professionals and salaried workers. Simplicity is highly valued in lean thinking.

See *Business Process Re-engineering (BPR)*, *error proofing*, *Failure Mode and Effects Analysis (FMEA)*, *human resources*, *job design*, *job enlargement*, *standardized work*.

work standardization – See *standardized work*.

work standards – See *standardized work*.

workcenter – An area where work is performed by people, tools, and machines and usually focuses on one type of process (e.g., drilling) or one set of products (e.g., assembly of a particular type of product).

A workcenter in a factory is usually a group of similar machines or a group of processes used to make a product family. The item **routing** defines the sequence of workcenters required to make a product. When a workcenter has multiple machines or people, the production planning system usually considers them identical in terms of capabilities and capacities.

See *cellular manufacturing, facility layout, routing.*

workflow software – See *groupware.*

workforce agility – The ability of the employees in a firm to adapt to change.

The main benefits of increased workforce agility can include (Hopp and Van Oyen 2001):

- **Improved efficiency** – Better on-time delivery, reduced cycle time, and reduced Work in Process (WIP) because idle time in the production line is decreased.
- **Enhanced flexibility** – Reduced overtime cost, increased productivity, reduced absenteeism and labor turnover because cross-trained workers can absorb some of the work assigned to absent workers.
- **Improved quality** – Increased worker knowledge which enables them to reduce defects.
- **Improved culture** – Improved working environment due to increased job satisfaction, worker motivation, and reduced ergonomic stress.

However, it is possible to have too much agility. Workers cannot be expected to be experts at every job in an organization. Training that is never used is of very limited value to the organization. Some specialization is good from a learning curve and responsibility assignment point of view.

See *absorptive capacity, cross-training, human resources, job design, job rotation, learning curve, learning organization, organizational design, RACI Matrix.*

Work-in-Process (WIP) inventory – Orders or materials that have been started in a production process, but are not yet complete; sometimes called Work-in-Progress inventory and in-process inventory. ✪

Work-in-Process (WIP) includes all orders or materials in queue waiting to be started, in the process of being set up, currently being run, waiting to be moved to the next operation, and being moved. WIP inventory is usually valued as the sum of the direct labor, materials, and overhead for all operations that have been completed. Some factories assign manufacturing overhead to a product when it is started; others assign manufacturing overhead when it is completed. Goldratt recommends not assigning overhead at all.

See *blocking, cellular manufacturing, CONWIP, finished goods inventory, Little's Law, overhead, pipeline inventory, throughput accounting, wait time.*

Work-in-Progress inventory (WIP) – See *Work-in-Process (WIP) inventory.*

X

x-bar chart – A quality control chart that monitors the mean performance of a process. ✪

A sample of *n* parts is collected from a process at regular intervals (either time intervals or production quantity intervals). The mean of the sample is plotted on the **control chart**, and the process is evaluated to see if it is "under control." The name of this chart comes from the sample mean $\bar{x}$, which is read as "x-bar."

See *control chart, Statistical Process Control (SPC), Statistical Quality Control (SQC).*

X-Matrix – See *hoshin planning.*

XML (Extensible Markup Language) – A simple, flexible language used to create webpages.

XML is an extensible version of Hypertext Markup Language (HTML). Another popular way to create webpages is Active Server Pages (ASP). XML is also a robust and flexible alternative to Electronic Data Interchange (EDI).

See *Electronic Data Interchange (EDI), robust.*

Y

yield – (1) In manufacturing: The ratio of units started in a process to completed without defect. (2) In finance: The ratio of return to investment. (3) In service management: The ratio of realized to potential revenue. ✪

See the *yield management* entry for the service management context. See the *Compounded Annual Growth Rate (CAGR)* and *Internal Rate of Return (IRR)* entries for the finance context.

In the manufacturing context, process yield (also called final yield) is used as (1) a **performance measure** (after production) and (2) a **planning factor** (before production) to increase the production start quantity so the final quantity meets the requirements. Process yield planning factors are usually stored in the bill of material. For example, if the requirement is for 100 units and the process yield is 80%, the start quantity should be $100/0.8 = 125$ units so that the final quantity produced is $125 \times 0.8 = 100$ units.

Lean sigma consultants often promote a demanding yield metric called **rolled throughput yield (RTY)**, sometimes also called first pass yield and first time yield. This is the percentage of units completed without needing any rework. The following table compares the traditional process yield with RTY.

Comparison of traditional process yield and rolled throughput yield (RTY)

	Process yield	Rolled throughput yield (RTY)
Definition	Percentage of units started that were completed without defects, including units that were successfully reworked.	Percentage of units that passed through the entire process without needing any rework.
Other names	Yield; final yield.	First pass yield; first time yield.
Uses	Best metric for production planning.	Best metric for performance measurement.
Benefits	True measure of yield.	Exposes the "hidden factory"[65] by making rework more visible.
Calculation	Product of process yields for each step; also the ratio of the final to the starting input.	Product of the RTY for each step in the process.
Criticisms	Does not indicate rework, which is clearly a non-value-adding activity; may not be a very demanding standard.	Rework and repair is often hidden and not recorded; multiple defects occurring on a single unit are not captured.

Source: Professor Arthur V. Hill

The table below provides a simple example of these metrics. Reporting only the overall process yield of 90% hides the extensive rework in this process; however, the RTY of 25.9% makes the rework evident.

Yield metric example

Step	Units in	First pass yield units	Failed on first pass	Rework success	Units out	Process yield	Rolled throughput yield (RTY)
1	100	70	30	20	90	90/100 = 90.0%	70/100 = 70.0%
2	90	60	30	30	90	90/90 = 100.0%	60/90 = 66.7%
3	90	50	40	40	90	90/90 = 100.0%	50/90 = 55.6%
					Overall	90.0% [a]	25.9% [b]

[a] Calculated as 90.0% x 100.0% x 100.0% = 90.0%. Also calculated as (final units)/(start units) = 90/100 = 90.0%.
[b] Calculated as 70.0% x 66.7% x 55.6% = 25.9%.

Source: Professor Arthur V. Hill

Process yield is one of the three dimensions of Overall Equipment Effectiveness, an important performance measure in many firms. Note that yield has little relationship to yield management tools used in services.

See *bill of material (BOM), conformance quality, hidden factory, operations performance metrics, Overall Equipment Effectiveness (OEE), process capability and performance, quality management, scrap, supplier scorecard.*

yield management – A set of metrics and tools for maximizing revenue for organizations that have relatively fixed capacity costs; also called revenue management or perishable asset resource management. ✪

---

[65] *See the hidden factory entry for an explanation of this term.*

The goal – For many capital-intensive businesses, such as airlines, hotels, theaters, stadiums, and utilities, maximizing revenue is equivalent to maximizing profit, because nearly all costs are relatively fixed. The goal is to maximize revenue per unit of resource ($/room night, $/seat mile, etc.). The goal is not to maximize utilization, although that is usually the result.

The control variables – Yield management systems change prices and capacity allocations over time as the date of the event approaches. For example, airlines change their prices thousands of times every day.

The performance metrics – The following yield management terms are used in the airline industry:

Available seat miles (ASM) – A measure of capacity defined as the number of seat miles that are available for purchase on an airline.

Revenue passenger miles (RPM) – The number of available seat miles (ASM) actually sold. This is a measure of an airline's traffic.

Load factor – The RPM divided by the ASM. Alternatively, this can be measured by the percentage of seats that were sold compared to the number of seats that could have been sold.

Yield – How much an airline makes per revenue passenger mile (RPM).

Revenue per available seat mile (RASM) – Sometimes called the "unit revenue," this metric has become the industry standard and is tracked each month because it gives a good overall picture of how an airline is performing.

Cost per available seat mile (CASM) – A widely used metric indicating the cost divided by the available miles that could have been flown (not the miles actually flown), regardless if the seats were occupied.

Stage length – The length of the average flight for a particular airline. As stage length increases, costs per mile tend to go down. Consequently, increases in the stage length of an airline will tend to bode well for the cost side, all other things being equal.

The booking curve – See the *booking curve* entry for more information on this yield management tool.

Other factors – Hotels and airlines place great importance on no-show factors, cancellations/reservation adjustments, and "wash" for groups, all of which help determine the necessary level of "oversell." Businesses with perishable inventory must remember that when the forecasted demand is below capacity, it is better to sell the room at a lower rate than to not sell it at all. In the hotel business, the term "revenue management" is often equated with getting "heads in beds." Additional ways to maximize revenues are to implement length of stay or stay restrictions, overbook effectively, take advantage of up-sell opportunities, and allocate correct inventory to the appropriate channels (discounts in particular). An emerging trend in the hotel business is to move all segments, not just e-channels and rack (standard), to dynamic pricing structures. This will enable the hotels to better control the negotiated/volume accounts, which is one of the larger segments.

See *booking curve, capacity, congestion pricing*.

Y-tree – A tool for creating a strategic linkage between the efforts of individuals and the goals of the organization; also called a goal tree.

The Y-tree begins at the highest level of organizational goals and breaks these down into intermediate goals and objectives, which are finally translated into specific projects. A Y-tree is essentially a strategy map, but goes one step further by connecting the metrics to action plans and projects. Like a strategy map, a Y-tree represents the firm's hypotheses and beliefs about how the highest-level performance variables are connected to intermediate performance measures and how the firm can "move the needle" on these measures with specific projects. All projects should have explicit connections to one or more higher-level goals.

Bossidy, Charan, and Burck (2002) point out that one of the most significant problems with strategic planning is that the strategies too often are not translated into actions. The Y-tree (along with the balanced scorecard and hoshin planning) is a means of accomplishing this difficult task.

At 3M, the highest-level elements of the Y-trees are growth, productivity/cost, and cash. These are often supplemented with two additional high-level strategies, emphasis on the customer and emphasis on corporate values and reputation. The table below is a simple example. Excel is a good tool for a Y-tree.

Super Y metrics	Little y metrics	Critical x metrics	Action plans/projects
Growth	Fill rate	Average leadtime	Queue time reduction project
		Leadtime variation	Machine reliability project
	Product quality	DPMO	Filler line project
Cash	Carrying cost	Lotsize inventory	SMED project
		Safety stock inventory	Forecasting project

Source: Professor Arthur V. Hill

See *balanced scorecard, benchmarking, causal map, DuPont Analysis, financial performance metrics, hoshin planning, issue tree, Management by Objectives (MBO), MECE, mission statement, operations performance metrics, strategy map.*

Z

zero defects – A concept that stresses elimination of all defects; sometimes abbreviated ZD.

Deming introduced the zero defects concept to Japanese manufacturers after World War II. This approach differs from the traditional American approach promoted by American military standards, such as Mil Standard 105D that allowed for a certain percentage of defects, known as an Acceptable Quality Level (AQL).

See *Acceptable Quality Level (AQL), lean sigma, quality management, Statistical Process Control (SPC), Statistical Quality Control (SQC), Total Quality Management (TQM).*

zero inventory – A term used to describe a JIT inventory system.

Professor Robert "Doc" Hall (formerly at Indiana University) popularized this term with a book of the same name (Hall 1983). However, this term seems to have fallen into disuse, partly because lean thinking is so much broader than just reducing inventory.

See *inventory management, lean thinking, one-piece flow.*

zero sum game – A game theory term used to describe a conflict where the sum of payoffs for the players in the game is zero; also known as a constant sum game.

In a zero sum game, one player's payoff can only improve at the expense of the other players. The standard metaphor here is that the players are dividing up the pie, but the size of the pie does not change with the number of players or with any decision made by any player.

See *futures contract, game theory, prisoners' dilemma.*

zone picking – An order picking method where a warehouse is divided into several areas called zones and items are picked from each zone and then passed to the next zone; also known as "pick-and-pass."

Order pickers are assigned to zones and only pick items in their own zones. The items for a customer order are then grouped together later. Sometimes orders are moved from one zone to the next (usually on conveyor systems) as they are picked. Adapted from http://accuracybook.com/glossary.htm, September 7, 2006.

See *Automated Storage & Retrieval System (AS/RS), batch picking, picking, Warehouse Management System (WMS), wave picking.*

zone storage location – A warehouse management practice that defines storage areas (zones) dedicated to particular types of items.

A zone might be created based on temperature requirements, security, typical container size, frequency of picks, etc. Within a zone, the warehouse could use either a fixed or random storage location system.

See *fixed storage location, locator system, random storage location, warehouse, Warehouse Management System (WMS).*

Accounting terms	http://www.a-z-dictionaries.com/glossaries/Accounting_Glossary.html
e-business terms	http://www.bannerview.com/glossary
	http://www.rms.net/gloss_b2b.htm
Economics terms	http://www.economist.com/research/economics
ERP terms	www.4eto.co.uk/ERP-Dictionary-Category.asp
	www.bridgefieldgroup.com/bridgefieldgroup/glos1.htm
	http://help.sap.com/saphelp_glossary/en/index.htm
Financial terms	www.forbes.com/tools/glossary/index.jhtml
	www.duke.edu/~charvey/Classes/wpg/glossary.htm
	http://www.nytimes.com/library/financial/glossary/bfglosa.htm
Forecasting terms	http://armstrong.wharton.upenn.edu/dictionary/defined%20terms.html
General terms	www.en.wikipedia.org/wiki/Main_Page
Human resource terms	http://www.shrm.org/TemplatesTools/Glossaries/HRTerms/Pages/default.aspx
Industrial engineering terms	www.iienet2.org/Details.aspx?id=645
Information technology terms	http://whatis.techtarget.com
	http://www.sharpened.net/glossary
International trade terms	www.itds.treas.gov/glossaryfrm.html
	www-personal.umich.edu/~alandear/glossary/index.html
Inventory terms	www.inventoryops.com/dictionary.htm
	http://accuracybook.com/glossary.htm
Lean terms	www.fredharriman.com/resources/documents/FHcom_Kaizen_Terminology_03.pdf
	www.leanaffiliates.com/glossary/glossary_d.htm
	www.gemba.com/resources.cfm?id=41
	www.gembutsu.com/articles/leanmanufacturingglossary.html
Logistics terms	www.clm1.org/Website/Resources/Terms.asp
	www.scl.gatech.edu/resources/glossary
Maintenance terms	http://www.skf.com/aptitudexchange/glossary.html
Manufacturing terms	www.successfulleanmanufacturing.com/Glossary.htm
	www.glossaryofmanufacturing.com
	www.industryweek.com/manufacturing101/glossary.aspx
Marketing terms	www.marketingpower.com/mg-dictionary.php
Materials handling terms	www.easyrack.org/glossary-terms-t-61.html
Math programming terms	http://glossary.computing.society.informs.org/index.php?page=index_page.html
New product development terms	www.npd-solutions.com/glossary.html
	www.pdma.org/library/glossary.html
organizational behavior terms	http://college.cengage.com/business/moorhead/organizational/6e/students/glossary/index.html
Project management terms	www.maxwideman.com/pmglossary/index.htm
	http://www.projectsmart.co.uk/glossary.html
Purchasing/procurement terms	http://www.mmd.admin.state.mn.us/mn06008.htm
	www.window.state.tx.us/procurement/pub/manual/4-6.pdf
Quality management terms	www.asq.org/glossary/index.html
	www.1stnclass.com/quality_glossary.htm
	www.isixsigma.com/dictionary/glossary.asp
	http://elsmar.com/wiki/index.php/Quality_Assurance_Terms_Glossary
Shipping terms	www.shipping.francoudi.com/main/main.asp?cm=14
Six Sigma terms	www.isixsigma.com/dictionary
Statistics terms	www.cas.lancs.ac.uk/glossary_v1.1/main.html
	http://stat-www.berkeley.edu/~stark/SticiGui/Text/gloss.htm
Supply chain terms	http://cscmp.org/digital/glossary/glossary.asp
	www.logisticsservicelocator.com/resources/glossary03.pdf
Theory of Constraints terms	www.pinnacle-strategies.com/glossary.htm
	www.goldratt.com
Transportation terms	www.eyefortransport.com/glossary/ab.shtml
	www.transportation-dictionary.org
	www.transportation-dictionary.org
Warehousing terms	www.dataid.com/wrhseglossery.htm
	www.inventoryops.com/dictionary.htm

GENERAL REFERENCES

Blackstone, J.H. Jr., editor (2010). *APICS Dictionary – 13th Edition (Revised)*, APICS, Chicago, 165 pages.

Gass, S.I., and C.M. Harris, editors (2000). *Encyclopedia of Operations Research and Management Science - Second Edition*, Springer, New York, 960 pages.

Marchwinski, C., and J. Shook, editors (2008). *Lean Lexicon – 4th Edition*, Lean Enterprise Institute, 125 pages.

Salvendy, G., editor (2001). *Handbook of Industrial Engineering*, Third Edition, Wiley-Interscience, 2796 pages.

Slack, N., and M. Lewis, editors (2006). *Blackwell Encyclopedia of Management – Operations Management*, Second Edition, Blackwell Publishing Limited, 376 pages.

Swamidass, P.M., editor (2000). *Encyclopedia of Production and Manufacturing Management*, Springer, New York, 1048 pages.

CITED REFERENCES

Abramowitz, M., and I.A. Stegun (1964). *Handbook of Mathematical Functions with Formulas, Graphs, and Mathematical Tables*, Dover Publications, New York.

Aggarwal, R., and B. Simkins (2001). "Open-book management – Optimizing human capital," *Business Horizons*, 44 (5), 5-13.

Allen, D. (2001). *Getting Things Done – The Art of Stress-Free Productivity*, Penguin Books, New York.

Anderson, J.C., M. Rungtusanatham, and R.G. Schroeder (1994). "A theory of quality management underlying the Deming management method," *Academy of Management Review*, 19 (3), 472-509.

Armstrong J., editor (2000). *Principles of Forecasting: A Handbook for Researchers and Practitioners*, Kluwer Academic Publishers, Norwell, Massachusetts.

Armstrong, J.S. editor (2001). "The forecasting dictionary," *Principles of Forecasting: A Handbook for Researchers and Practitioners*, Springer, New York.

Armstrong, J.S., and F. Collopy (1992). "Error measures for generalizing about forecasting methods: Empirical comparisons," *International Journal of Forecasting*, 8 (1), 69-80.

Assimakopoulos, V., and K. Nikolopoulos (2000). "The Theta Model: A decomposition approach to forecasting," *International Journal of Forecasting*, 16 (4), 521-530.

Assimakopoulos, V., K. Nikolopoulos (2005). "Fathoming the Theta model," Working paper, National Technical University of Athens.

Axelrod, R. (1984). *The Evolution of Cooperation*, Basic Books, New York.

Barach, P., and S.D. Small (2000). "Reporting and preventing medical mishaps: Lessons from non-medical near miss reporting systems," *British Medical Journal*, 320 (7237), 759–763, found at www.pubmedcentral.nih.gov/articlerender.fcgi?artid=1117768, January 23, 2008.

Barrentine, L.B. (2003). *Concepts for R&R Studies*, Second Edition, ASQ Quality Press, Milwaukee, Wisconsin.

Bartels, A. (2000). "The difference between e-business and e-commerce," *Computerworld*, October 30.

Bartholdi, J.J. (2011). *Warehouse & Distribution Science*, found at www.warehouse-science.com, April 4, 2011.

Bartholdi, J.J., and S.T. Hackman (2008). "Allocating space in a forward pick area of a distribution center for small parts," *IIE Transactions*, 40, 1046-1053

Bass, F. (1969). "A new product growth for model consumer durables," *Management Science*, 15 (5), 215-227.

Berry, L.L., L.P. Carbone, and S.H. Haeckel (2002). "Customer experiences must be managed," *Sloan Management Review*, Spring, 85-89, found at http://wehner.tamu.edu/ mktg/faculty/berry/articles/Managing_the_Total_Customer_Experience.pdf.

Berry, W.L., and V. Rao (1975). "Critical ratio scheduling: An experimental analysis," *Management Science*, 22 (2), 192-201.

Blanchard, K.H., and S. Johnson (1982). *The One Minute Manager*, William Morrow, New York.

Blischke, W.R., and D.N.P. Murty (1992). "Product warranty management – I: A taxonomy of warranty policies," *European Journal of Operational Research*, 62 (2), 127-148.

Blumenfeld, D. (2010). *Operations Research Calculations Handbook*, Taylor and Francis, Boca Raton, Florida.

Bodek, N. (2009). "The ninth waste – saying no," *IndustryWeek.com*, Leadership in Manufacturing, October 9, 2007, found at www.industryweek.com/PrintArticle.aspx?ArticleID=15106.

Boothroyd, G., P. Dewhurst, and W.A. Knight (2010). *Product Design for Manufacture and Assembly*, Third Edition, CRC Press (Taylor & Francis Group), Boca Raton, Florida.

Bossidy, L., R. Charan, and C. Burck (2002). *Execution: The Discipline of Getting Things Done*, Crown Business, New York.

Bowers, D.P. and J.E. West (2011). "Getting on track – The SR standard allows quality professionals to lead organizations in the right direction," *Quality Progress*, May, 25-35.

Box, G.E.P., G.M. Jenkins, G.C. Reinsel, and G. Jenkins (1994). *Time Series Analysis: Forecasting & Control*, Third Edition, Prentice-Hall, Upper Saddle River, New Jersey.

Brandenburger, A.M., and B.J. Nalebuff (1996). *Co-Opetition: A Revolution Mindset That Combines Competition and Cooperation*, Doubleday Business, New York.

Briscoe, B., A. Odlyzko, and B. Tilly (2006). "Metcalfe's Law is wrong," *IEEE Spectrum*, 43 (7), 34-39.

Brown, K., and N. Hyer (2009). *Managing Projects: A Team-Based Approach*, McGraw-Hill/Irwin, New York.

Brown, R.G. (1967). *Decision Rules for Inventory Management*, Holt, Rinehart, and Winston, New York.

Buffa, E.S., G.C. Armour, and T.E. Vollmann (1964). "Allocating facilities with CRAFT," *Harvard Business Review*, 42 (2), 136-158.

Buzan, T., and B. Buzan (1996). *The Mind Map Book: How to Use Radiant Thinking to Maximize Your Brain's Untapped Potential*, Plume.

Cachon, G.P. (2001), "Supply chain coordination with contracts," http://opim.wharton.upenn.edu/~cachon/pdf/cachon_chp_scontract.pdf, March 11, 2011.

Cachon, G.P., and M.A. Lariviere (2001). "Turning the supply chain into a revenue chain," *Harvard Business Review*, 79 (3), 20-21.

Cachon, G.P., and M.A. Lariviere (2005). "Supply chain coordination with revenue sharing contracts," *Management Science*, 51 (1), 30-44.

Canbäck, S., P. Samouel, and D. Price (2006). "Do diseconomies of scale impact firm size and performance? A Theoretical and empirical overview," *Journal of Managerial Economics*, 4, (1), 27-70.

Carbone, L. (2004). *Clued In: How to Create Customer Experiences So They Will Come Back Again and Again*, Pearson Education, Upper Saddle River, New Jersey.

Caroselli, M. (2003). *50 Activities for Promoting Ethics within the Organization*, HRD Press, Amherst, Massachusetts.

Chase, R.B., F.R. Jacobs, and N.J. Aquilano (2006). *Operations Management for Competitive Advantage*, Eleventh Edition, McGraw-Hill, New York.

Cheney, W. and D. Kincaid (1994). *Numerical Mathematics and Computing*. Third Edition, Brooks/Cole Publishing Company, Pacific Grove, California.

Christensen, C.M. (1997). *The Innovator's Dilemma*. Harvard Business School Press, Boston.

Christensen, C.M., and M.E. Raynor (2003). *The Innovator's Solution*. Harvard Business School Press, Boston.

Chua, R.C.H., G.D. Scudder, and A.V. Hill (1993). "Batching policies for a repair shop with limited spares and finite capacity," *European Journal of Operational Research*, 66 (1), 135-147.

Clark, K., and S.C. Wheelwright (1992). "Organizing and leading heavyweight development teams," *California Management Review*, 34 (3), 9-28.

Coens, T., and M. Jenkins (2002). *Abolishing Performance Appraisals: Why They Backfire and What to Do Instead*, Berrett-Koehler Publishers, San Francisco.

Cohen, W.M., and D.A. Levinthal (1990). "Absorptive capacity: A new perspective on learning and innovation," *Administrative Science Quarterly*, 35 (1), 128-152.

Collins, J., and J. Porras (1996). "Building your company's vision," *Harvard Business Review*, 74 (5), 65-77.

Collopy, F., and J.S. Armstrong (2000). "Another error measure for selection of the best forecasting method: The unbiased absolute percent error," Found at www.forecastingprinciples.com/paperpdf/armstrong-unbiasedAPE.pdf, October 7, 2006.

Cooper, R. (1993). *Winning at New Products: Accelerating the Process from Idea to Launch*, Second Edition, Addison-Wesley Publishing, Reading, Massachusetts.

Cooper, R. (2001). *Winning at New Products: Accelerating the Process from Idea to Launch*, Basic Books, New York.

Coyle, J.J., E.J. Bardi, and C.J. Langley (2002). *Management of Business Logistics: A Supply Chain Perspective*, Seventh Edition, South-Western, Boston.

Coyne, K.P., S.J.D. Hall, and P.G. Clifford (1997). "Is your core competence a MIRAGE?," *McKinsey Quarterly*, 1, 40-54.

Crosby, P.B. (1979). *Quality Is Free*. McGraw-Hill, New York.

Croston, J.D. (1972). "Forecasting and stock control for intermittent demands," *Operational Research Quarterly*, 23 (3), 289-303.

Culbert, S.A. (2010). *Get Rid of the Performance Review!: How Companies Can Stop Intimidating, Start Managing – and Focus on What Really Matters*, Business Plus, New York.

Dennis, P. (2002). *Lean Production Simplified: A Plain-Language Guide to the World's Most Powerful Production System*, Productivity Press, New York.

DeMast, J., and A. Trip (2005). "Gauge R&R studies for destructive measurement." *Journal of Quality Technology*, 37 (1), 40-49.

Deming, W.E, (1986). *Out of the Crisis*, First MIT Press Edition, MIT Press, Cambridge, Massachusetts.

Deming, W.E. (2000). *The New Economics for Industry*, First MIT Press Edition, MIT Press, Cambridge, Massachusetts.

Dixon, J.R. (1992). "Measuring manufacturing flexibility: An empirical investigation," *European Journal of Operations Research*, 60 (2), 131-143.

Dixon, M., K. Freeman, and N. Toman (2010). "Stop trying to delight your customers," *Harvard Business Review*, 88 (7/8), 116-122.

Drucker, P.F. (1954). *The Practice of Management*. Harper, New York.

Drucker, P.F. (1959). *Landmarks of Tomorrow*, Heinemann, London.

Drucker, P.F. (1995). "The information executives truly need," *Harvard Business Review*, 73 (1), 54-62.

Dudek, R.A., S.S. Panwalkar, and M.L. Smith (1992). "The lessons of flowshop scheduling research," *Operations Research*, 40 (1), 7–13.

Elkington, J. (1994). "Towards the sustainable corporation: Win-win-win business strategies for sustainable development." *California Management Review*, 36 (2), 90-100.

Elmaghraby, W., M. Goyal, and A. Pilehvar (2010). "The right-of-first-refusal in sequential procurement auctions," Working paper, University of Maryland.

Englund, R.L., R.J. Graham, P.C. Dinsmore (2003). *Creating the Project Office – A Manager's Guide to Leading Organizational Change*, Jossey-Bass (Wiley), San Francisco.

Evans, J.R. (1985). "An efficient implementation of the Wagner-Whitin algorithm for dynamic lot-sizing," *Journal of Operations Management*, 5 (2), 229-235.

Evers, P.T. (1995). "Expanding the square root law: An analysis of both safety and cycle stocks," *Logistics and Transportation Review*, 31 (1), 1-20.

Fagan, M. (2001). "Reviews and inspections," *Software Design and Managmeent Conference Proceedings*, p. 214-225.

Feigenbaum, A.V. (2004). *Total Quality Control*, McGraw-Hill, New York.

Ferdows, K., and A. De Meyer (1990). "Lasting improvements in manufacturing performance: In search of a new theory," *Journal of Operations Management*, 9 (2), 168-184.

Fine, C.H. (1995). *Clockspeed: Winning Industry Control in the Age of Temporary Advantage*, Perseus Books Group, Boulder, Colorado.

Fisher, M. (1997). "What is the right supply chain for your product," *Harvard Business Review*, 1997 (2), 105-116.

Fisher, M., and A. Raman (2010). *The New Science of Retailing*, Harvard Business School Press, Boston.

Friedman, T.L. (2005). *The World Is Flat: A Brief History of the Twenty-first Century*, Farrar, Straus and Giroux, New York.

Galley, M. (2008). *Cause Mapping Workbook*, ThinkReliability, info@thinkreliability.com, Houston, Texas.

Gano, D.L. (2007). *Apollo Root Cause Analysis - Effective Solutions to Everyday Problems Every Time*, Apollonian Publications, Richland, Washington.

Gardner, E.S. (2005). "Exponential smoothing: The state of the art – Part II," Unpublished working paper, Bauer College of Business, University of Houston.

Garvin, D.A. (1987). "Competing on the eight dimensions of quality," *Harvard Business Review*, 65 (6), 101-109.

Geary, S., S.M. Disney, and D.R. Towill (2006). "On bullwhip in supply chains - Historical review, present practice and expected future impact," *International Journal of Production Economics*, 101 (1), 2–18.

Geldermana, C.J., and A.J. Van Weeleb (2003). "Handling measurement issues and strategic directions in Kraljic's purchasing portfolio model," *Journal of Purchasing and Supply Management*, 9, 207-216.

George, M.L. (2003). *Lean Six Sigma for Service: How to Use Lean Speed and Six Sigma Quality to Improve Services and Transactions*, McGraw-Hill, New York.

George, M.L., D. Rowlands, and B. Kastle (2003). *What Is Lean Six Sigma?*, McGraw-Hill, New York.

Gilmore, D. (2005). "Task interleaving in the DC – Reality or myth?," *SupplyChainDigest*, found at www.scdigest.com/assets/FirstThoughts/05-01-27.cfm?cid=371&ctype=content, January 15, 2011.

Goldman, S.L., R.N. Nagel, and K. Preiss (1995). *Agile Competitors and Virtual Organizations*, Van Nostrand Reinhold, New York.

Goldratt, E. M., (1990). *The Haystack Syndrome*, North River Press, Great Barrington, Massachusetts.

Goldratt, E.M., (1994). *It's Not Luck*, North River Press, Great Barrington, Massachusetts.

Goldratt, E.M., and J. Cox (1992). *The Goal: A Process of Ongoing Improvement*, North River Press, Great Barrington, Massachusetts.

Goldratt, E.M., E. Schragenheim, and C.A. Ptak (2000). *Necessary but Not Sufficient*, North River Press, Great Barrington, Massachusetts.

Graham, D., and T. Bachmann (2004). *IDEATION: The Birth and Death of Ideas*, John Wiley & Sons, New York.

Greaver, M.F. (1999). *Strategic Outsourcing: A Structured Approach to Outsourcing Decisions and Initiatives*, AMACOM/American Management Association, New York.

Gunasekaran, A., and E.W.T. Ngai (2005). "Build-to-order supply chain management: A literature review and framework for development," *Journal of Operations Management*, 23 (5), 423-451.

Gupta, D., A.V. Hill, and T. Bouzdine-Chameeva (2006). "A pricing model for clearing end of season retail inventory," *European Journal of Operational Research*, 170 (2), 518-540.

Hadley, G., and T. M. Whitin (1963). *Analysis of Inventory Systems*, Prentice-Hall, Englewood Cliffs, New Jersey.

Hall, R. (1983). *Zero Inventories*, McGraw-Hill, Irwin/APICS Series in Production Management, New York.

Hamel, G., and C.K. Prahalad (1991). "Corporate imagination and expeditionary marketing," *Harvard Business Review*, 71 (4), 81-92.

Hamel, G., and L. Välikangas (2003). "The quest for resilience," *Harvard Business Review*, 81 (9), 52-63.

Hamilton, S. (2003). *Maximizing Your ERP System – A Practical Guide for Managers*, McGraw-Hill, New York.

Hammer, M., and J.A. Champy (1993). *Reengineering the Corporation: A Manifesto for Business Revolution*, Harper Business Books, New York.

Hansen, M.T., N. Nohria, and T. Tierney (1999). "What's your strategy for managing knowledge?," *Harvard Business Review*, 77 (2), 106-116.

Harris, F.W. (1913). "How many parts to make at once," *Factory*, 10 (2), 135-136, 152.

Harris, F. W. (1915). *Operations Cost*, Factory Management Series, Shaw, Chicago.

Harry, M. (1988). *The Nature of Six Sigma Quality*, Motorola University Press, Rolling Meadows, Illinois.

Harry, M., and R. Schroeder (2000). *Six Sigma*, Random House, New York.

Hayes, R.H., and S.C. Wheelwright (1979a). "Link manufacturing process and product life cycles," *Harvard Business Review*, 57 (1), 133-140.

Hayes, R.H., and S.C. Wheelwright (1979b). "The dynamics of process-product life cycles." *Harvard Business Review*, 57 (2), 127-136.

Hayes, R.H., and S.C. Wheelwright (1984). *Restoring Our Competitive Edge: Competing Through Manufacturing*, John Wiley & Sons, New York.

Hays, J.M., and A.V. Hill (1999). "The market share impact of service failures," *Production and Operations Management*, 8 (3), 208-220.

Hays, J.M., and A.V. Hill (2001). "A preliminary investigation of the relationships between employee motivation: Vision, service learning, and perceived service quality," *Journal of Operations Management*, 19 (3), 335-349.

Hays, J.M., T. Bouzdine-Chameeva, S.M. Goldstein, A.V. Hill, and A.J. Scavarda (2007). "Applying the collective causal mapping methodology to operations management curriculum development," *Decision Science Journal of Innovative Education*, 5 (2), 267-287.

Hendreicks, K.B., and V.R. Singhal (2001). "The long-run stock price performance of firms with effective TQM programs," *Management Science*, 47 (3), 359–368.

Heskett, J.L., T.O. Jones, G. Loveman, W.E. Sasser Jr., and L.A. Schlesinger (1994). "Putting the service-profit chain to work," *Harvard Business Review*, 72 (2), 164-170.

Heskett, J.L., W.E. Sasser, and L.A. Schlesinger (1997). *The Service Profit Chain*, Free Press, New York.

Hiatt, J.M. (2006). *ADKAR: A Model for Change in Business, Government and Our Community: How to Implement Successful Change in Our Personal Lives and Professional Careers*, Prosci Research, Loveland, Colorado.

Hill, A.V. (1992). *Field Service Management: An Integrated Approach to Increasing Customer Satisfaction*, Business One Irwin, Homewood, Illinois.

Hill, A.V. (1995). "Service guarantees: The fast track to service quality," *IMD Perspectives*, 2, March, 1-4.

Hill, A.V. (2011a). *Personal Operations Management – Lean Principles for Getting Good Things Done*, Clamshell Beach Press, Eden Prairie, Minnesota.

Hill, A.V. (2011b). "An overview of mapping tools for process improvement," Clamshell Beach Press, Eden Prairie, Minnesota.

Hill, A.V. (2011c). "Causal mapping," Clamshell Beach Press, Eden Prairie, Minnesota.

Hill, A.V. (2011d). "The Triangular Distribution," Clamshell Beach Press, Eden Prairie, Minnesota.

Hill, A.V., V. Giard, and V.A. Mabert (1989). "A decision support system for determining optimal retention stocks for service parts inventories," *IIE Transactions*, 21 (3), 221-229.

Hill, A.V., J.M. Hays, and E. Naveh (2000). "A model for optimal delivery time guarantees," *Journal of Service Research*, 2 (3), 254-264.

Hill, A.V., and I.S. Khosla (1992). "Models for optimal lead time reduction," *Production and Operations Management*, 1 (2), 185-197.

Hill, A.V., and W.J. Sawaya III (2004). "Production planning for medical devices with an uncertain approval date," *IIE Transactions*, 36 (4), 307-317.

Hill, A.V., and C.C. Sum (1993). "A new framework for manufacturing planning and control systems," *Decision Sciences*, 24 (4), 739-760.

Hill, A.V., and T.E. Vollmann (1986). "Reducing vendor delivery uncertainties in a jit environment," *Journal of Operations Management*, 6 (4), 381-392.

Hill, A.V., and W. Zhang (2010). "Six common misuses of the inventory turnover and days-on-hand metrics," *Production & Inventory Management Journal*, 45 (10).

Hopp, W.J., and M.L. Spearman (2004). "To pull or not to pull: What is the question?," *MSOM*, 6 (2), 133–148.

Hopp, W.J. (2006). *Supply Chain Science*, McGraw-Hill, New York.

Hopp, W.J., and M.P. Van Oyen (2001). "Agile workforce evaluation: A framework for cross-training and coordination," *Proceedings 2001 NSF Design and Manufacturing Grantees Conference*, Tampa, Florida.

Hummel, C.E. (1967). *The Tyranny of the Urgent*, Intervarsity Press, Downer's Grove, Illinois.

Humphries, W.S. (1989). *Managing the Software Process*, The SEI Series in Software Engineering, Addison-Wesley Professional, Reading, Massachusetts.

Hyer, N.L., and U. Wemmerlov (2002a). *Reorganizing the Factory: Competing through Cellular Manufacturing*, Productivity Press, New York.

Hyer, N.L., and U. Wemmerlov (2002b). "The office that lean built," *IIE Solutions*, 34 (10), 36-43.

Hyndman, R.J., and B. Billah (2003). "Unmasking the Theta Method," *International Journal of Forecasting*, 19 (2), 287-290.

Hyndman, R.J., and A.B. Koehler (2006). "Another look at measures of forecast accuracy," *International Journal of Forecasting*, 22 (4), 679-688.

Jackson, T.L. (2006). *Hoshin Kanri for the lean enterprise – Developing competitive capabilities and managing profit*, Productivity Press, New York.

Jacobs, R.A., and H.M. Wagner (1989). "Reducing inventory system costs by using robust demand estimators," *Management Science*, 35 (7), 771-787.

Johnson, G. (1998). "Vendor-managed inventory," *APICS Performance Advantage*, June, 30-32.

Juran, J.M. (1986). "The quality trilogy – A universal approach to managing for quality," Paper presented at the ASQC 40th Annual Quality Congress in Anaheim, California.

Kaplan, R.S., and D.P. Norton (1992). "The balanced scorecard – Measures that drive performance," *Harvard Business Review*, January-February, 71-79.

Kaplan, R.S., and D.P. Norton (1996). "Using the balanced scorecard as a strategy management system," *Harvard Business Review*, January-February, 75-85.

Kaplan, R.S., and D.P. Norton (2000). "Having trouble with your strategy? Then map it," *Harvard Business Review*, September-October, 167-176.

Kaplan, R.S., and D.P. Norton (2004). *Strategy Maps: Converting Intangible Assets into Tangible Outcomes*, Harvard Business School Press, Boston.

Kaplan, R.S., and D.P. Norton (2004). "Measuring the strategic readiness of intangible assets," *Harvard Business Review*, 82 (2), 52-63.

Kaplan, R.S., and D.P. Norton (2006). *Alignment: Using the Balanced Scorecard to Create Corporate Synergies*, Harvard Business School Press, Boston.

Kaplan, R.S., and D.P. Norton (2008). *The Execution Premium: Linking Strategy to Operations for Competitive Advantage*, Harvard Business School Press, Boston.

Kim, W.C., and R. Mauborgne (2005). *Blue Ocean Strategy: How to Create Uncontested Market Space and Make Competition Irrelevant*, Harvard Business School Press, Boston.

Knüsel, L. (2005). "On the accuracy of statistical distributions in Microsoft Excel 2003," *Computational Statistics and Data Analysis*, 48, 445-449.

Kotha, S. (1995). "Mass customization: Implementing the emerging paradigm for competitive advantage," *Strategic Management Journal*, 16 (Special Issue), 21-42.

Kraljic, P. (1983). "Purchasing must become supply management," *Harvard Business Review*, 61 (5), 109–117.

Kutner, M.H., J. Neter, C.J. Nachtsheim, and W. Wasserman (2004). *Applied Linear Statistical Models*, Fifth Edition, McGraw Hill/Irwin, Boston.

Law, A.M. (2007). *Simulation Modeling and Analysis*, Fourth Edition, McGraw-Hill, New York.

Law, A.M., and W.D. Kelton (2000). *Simulation Modeling and Analysis*, McGraw-Hill, New York.

Lee, H.L., V. Padmanabhan, and S. Whang (1997). "The bullwhip effect in supply chains," *Sloan Management Review*, Spring, 93-102.

Leschke, J.P. (1997a). "The setup-reduction process: Part 1," *Production and Inventory Management Journal*, 38 (1), 32-37.

Leschke, J.P. (1997b). "The setup-reduction process: Part 2 - Setting reduction priorities," *Production and Inventory Management Journal*, 38 (1), 38-42.

Leschke, J.P., and E.N. Weiss (1997). "The multi-item setup-reduction investment-allocation problem with continuous investment-cost functions," *Management Science*, 43 (6), 890-894.

Levitt, T. (1972). "Production-line approach to service," *Harvard Business Review*, 50 (5), 20-31.

Lewin K. (1943). "Defining the field at a given time," *Psychological Review*, 50, 292-310. Republished in *Resolving Social Conflicts & Field Theory in Social Science*, Washington, D.C., American Psychological Association, 1997.

Liker, J.K. (2004). *The Toyota Way: 14 Management Principles from the World's Greatest Manufacturer*. McGraw-Hill, New York.

Likert, R. (1932). "A technique for the measurement of attitudes," *Archives of Psychology*, 140, 1–55.

Ling, R.C., and W.E. Goddard (1995). *Orchestrating Success: Improve Control of the Business with Sales & Operations Planning*, John Wiley & Sons, New York.

Little, J.D.C. (1961). "A proof of the queuing formula $L = \lambda W$," *Operations Research*, 9, 383-387.

Littlefield, T.K., Jr., and P.H. Randolph (1987). "Reply: An answer to Sasieni's question on PERT times," *Management Science*, 33 (10), 1357-1359.

Love, R.F., J.G. Morris, and G.O. Wesolowsky (1988). *Facilities Location Models & Methods*, North Holland/Elsevier Science Publishing Company, Amsterdam.

Love, S.F. (1979). *Mastery & Management of Time*, Prentice Hall, Englewood Cliffs, New Jersey.

Mckay, A. (2007). *Motivation, Ability and Confidence Building in People*, Butterworth-Heinemann, Oxford.

Macomber, H., and G. Howell (2004). "Two great wastes in organizations – A typology for addressing the concern for the underutilization of human potential," Paper presented at the 12th Annual Meeting of the International Group for Lean Construction in Copenhagen, Denmark.

Mahajan, V., E. Muller, and F. Bass (1995). "Diffusion of new products: Empirical generalizations and managerial uses," *Management Science*, 14 (3): G79-G88.

Maister, D.H. (1976). "Centralization of inventories and the square root law," *International Journal of Physical Distribution*, 6 (3), 124-134.

Maister, D.H. (1985). "The psychology of waiting lines," in *The Service Encounter*, ed. J. Czepiel, M. Solomon, and C. Surprenant, Lexington Books, Lexington, Massachusetts, 113-123.

Malcolm, D.G., C.E. Roseboom, C.E. Clark, & W. Fazar (1959). "Application of a technique for research and development program evaluation," *Operations Research*, 7, 646-649.

Marchwinski, C., and J. Shook (2006). *Lean Lexicon – A Graphical Glossary for Lean Thinkers*, Third Edition, Lean Enterprise Institute, Cambridge, Massachusetts.

Mariotti, J.L. (2008). *The Complexity Crisis*, Adams Media, Avon, Massachusetts.

McKone, K., and E. Weiss (2002). "Guidelines for implementing predictive maintenance," *Production Operations Management*, 11 (2), 109-124.

Metes, G., J. Gundry, and P. Bradish (1997). *Agile Networking: Competing Through the Internet and Intranets*, Prentice-Hall, Upper Saddle River, New Jersey.

Miller, J.G., and T.E. Vollmann (1985). "The hidden factory," *Harvard Business Review*, 63 (5), 142-150.

Minka, T. (2002). "Estimating a gamma distribution," found at http://research.microsoft.com/en-us/um/people/minka/papers/minka-gamma.pdf, September 23, 2010.

Minto, B. (1996). *The Pyramid Principle: Logic in Writing, Thinking, and Problem Solving*, Minto International, Norfolk, Virginia.

Morgan, J.M., and J.K. Liker (2006). *The Toyota Product Development System: Integrating People, Process and Technology*, Productivity Press, New York.

Murty, D.N.P., and W.R. Blischke (1992). "Product warranty management – II: An integrated framework for study," *European Journal of Operational Research* 62 (3), 261-281.

Nahmias, S. (2005). *Production and Operations Analysis*, Fifth Edition, McGraw-Hill/Irwin, New York.

Naveh, E., and A. Marcus (2005). "Achieving competitive advantage through implementing a replicable management standard: Installing and using ISO 9000," *Journal of Operations Management*, 24 (1), 1-26.

NIST (2010). *NIST/SEMATECH e-Handbook of Statistical Methods*, available at www.itl.nist.gov/div898/handbook.

Noreen, E., D. Smith, and J.T. Mackey (1995). *TOC and Its Implications for Management Accounting*, North River Press, Great Barrington, Massachusetts.

Oberholzer-Gee, F., and V. Calanog (2007). "The speed of new ideas: Trust, institutions and the diffusion of new products," Working paper, Wharton School, University of Pennsylvania.

Ohno, T. (1978). *Toyota Production System: Beyond Large Scale Production*, Productivity Press, New York. (English translation copyright 1988 by Productivity Press, ISBN 0-915299-14-3.)

Ord, K., M. Hibon, and S. Makridakis (2000). "The M3-competition," *International Journal of Forecasting*, 16 (4), 433-436.

Pande, P.S., R.P. Neuman, and R.R. Cavanagh (2000). *The Six Sigma Way: How GE, Motorola, and Other Top Companies are Honing Their Performance*, McGraw-Hill, New York.

Parasuraman, A., L.L. Berry, and V.A. Zeithaml (1990). *An Empirical Examination of Relationships in an Extended Service quality Model*, Monograph published by the Marketing Science Institute, Cambridge, Massachusetts.

Parasuraman, A., V.A. Zeithaml, and L.L. Berry (1988). "SERVQUAL: A multi-item sclae for measuring consumer perceptions of service quality," *Journal of Retailing*, 64 (1), 12-40.

Parkinson, C.N. (1958). *Parkinson's Law: The Pursuit of Progress*, John Murray, London.

Peters, T.J., and N. Austin (1985). *A Passion for Excellence*, Random House, New York.

Peters, T.J., and R.H. Waterman (1982). *In Search of Excellence*, Harper & Row, New York.

Petroff, J.N., and A.V. Hill (1991). "A framework for the design of lot tracing systems for the 1990's," *Production and Inventory Management Journal*, 32 (2), 55-61.

Pine, B.J. (1993). *Mass Customization: The New Frontier in Business Competition*, Harvard Business School Press, Boston.

Pine, B.J., and J.H. Gilmore (1998). "Welcome to the experience economy," *Harvard Business Review*, 76 (4), 97-105.

Pine, B.J., and J.H. Gilmore (1999). *The Experience Economy: Work Is Theater and Every Business a Stage*, Harvard Business School Press, Boston.

Pine, B.J., and J.H. Gilmore (2007). *Authenticity: What Consumers Really Want*, Harvard Business School Press, Boston.

Plossl, G.W. (1985). *Production and Inventory Control: Principles and Techniques*, 2nd Edition, Prentice Hall, Englewood Cliffs, NJ.

Porter, A.M. (2000). "The virtual corporation: Where is it?," *Purchasing*, March 23, available at www.purchasing.com.

Porter, M.A., and L. Dixon (1994). *JIT II Revolution in Buying & Selling*, Purchasing Magazine, Cahners Publishing Company, Dallas.

Porter, M.E. (1985). *Competitive Advantage*, Free Press, London.

Press, W.H., B.P. Flannery, S.A. Teukolsky, and W.T. Vetterling (2002). *Numerical Recipes in FORTRAN: The Art of Scientific Computing*, Second Edition, Cambridge University Press, Cambridge, United Kingdom.

Project Management Institute, PMI.org (1996). *PMBOK – Project Management Body of Knowledge*, found at www.tks.buffalo.edu/pm/pmbok1996.pdf, May 26, 2010.

Rasiel, E.M. (1998). *The McKinsey Way – Using the Techniques of the World's Top Strategic Consultants to Help You and Your Business*, McGraw-Hill, New York.

Rasiel, E.M., and P.N. Friga (2001). *The McKinsey Mind: Understanding and Implementing the Problem-Solving Tools and Management Techniques of the World's Top Strategic Consulting Firm*, McGraw-Hill, New York.

Raturi, A.S., and A.V. Hill (1988). "An experimental analysis of capacity-sensitive setup parameters for MRP lotsizing," *Decision Sciences*, 19 (4), 782-800.

Reichheld, F.F. (2003). "The one number you need to grow," *Harvard Business Review*, 81 (12), 46-54.

Ressler, C. & J. Thompson (2010). *Why Work Sucks and How to Fix It: The Results-Only Revolution*, Portfolio Trade, New York.

Roberts, D.M. (1978). *Statistical Auditing*, American Institute of Certified Public Accountants, New York.

Rose, O. (2002). "Some issues of the critical ratio dispatch rule in semiconductor manufacturing," *Proceedings of the 2002 Winter Simulation Conference*.

Roth, A.E., and A. Ockenfels (2002). "Last-minute bidding and the rules for ending second-price auctions: Evidence from eBay and Amazon auctions on the Internet," *American Economic Review*, 92 (4), 1093-1103.

Rother, M., J. Shook, J. Womack, and D. Jones (2003). *Learning to See Version*, Lean Enterprise Institute, Cambridge, Massachusetts.

Rungtusanatham, M., E. Rabinovich, B. Ashenbaum, and C. Wallin (2007). "Vendor-owned inventory management arrangements in retail operations: An agency theory perspective," *Journal of Business Logistics*, 28(1), 111-135.

Saaty, T.L. (2001). *Fundamentals of Decision Making and Priority Theory*, RWS Publications, Pittsburgh.

Sasieni, M.W. (1986). "A note on PERT times," *Management Science*, 32 (12), 1652-1653.

Scavarda, A.J., T. Bouzdine-Chameeva, S.M. Goldstein, J.M. Hays, and A.V. Hill (2006). "A methodology for constructing collective causal maps," *Decision Sciences*, 37 (2), 263-283.

Scavarda, A.J., and A.V. Hill (2003). "The ten commitments of the supply chain management," Presentation at the Production and Operations Management Society (POMS) Annual Meeting, Savannah, Georgia.

Schein, E.H. (1992). *Organizational Culture and Leadership*. Second Edition, Jossey Bass, San Francisco, CA.

Schilling, M.A. (2000). "Toward a general modular systems theory and its application to interfirm product modularity," *Academy of Management Review*, 25 (2), 312-334.

Schlangenstein, M. (2005). "Southwest Airlines profit jumps," *Bloomberg News*, April 15, E05.

Schneiderman, A.M. (1999). "Why balanced scorecards fail!," *Journal of Strategic Performance Measurement*, Special Edition, 6, found at http//www.schneiderman.com.

Schonberger, R.J. (1982). *Japanese Manufacturing Techniques: Nine Hidden Lessons in Simplicity*, Free Press, New York.

Schonberger, R.J. (1986). *World Class Manufacturing – The Lessons of Simplicity Applied*. Free Press, New York.

Schroeder, R.G. (2008). *Operations Management: Contemporary Concepts and Cases*, Fourth Edition, McGraw-Hill/Irwin, Boston.

Schroeder, R.G., and M.J. Pesch (1994). "Focusing the factory: Eight lessons," *Business Horizons*, Sept.-Oct., 76-81.

Schroeder, R.G., S. Meyer Goldstein, and M.J. Rungtusanatham (2011). **Operations Management – Contemporary Concepts and Cases**, Fifth Edition, McGraw-Hill/Irwin, New York.

Schultz, T.R. (1989). *Business Requirements Planning – The Journey of Excellence*, The Forum Ltd.

Senge, P.M. (1990). *The Fifth Discipline*. Century Business, London.

Sethi, A.K., and S.P. Sethi (1990). "Flexibility in manufacturing: A survey," *International Journal of Flexible Manufacturing Systems*, 2 (4), 289–328.

Shewhart, W.A. (1939). *Statistical Method from the Viewpoint of Quality Control*, Dover, New York.

Shingo, S. (1986). *Zero Quality Control: Source Inspection and the Poka-Yoke System*, Productivity Press, New York.

Shapiro, C. and H.R. Varian (1999). *Information Rules: A Strategic Guide to the Network Economy*, Harvard Business Press, Boston, Massachusetts.

Silver, E.A., D.F. Pyke, and R. Peterson (1998). *Inventory Management and Production Planning and Scheduling*, Third Edition, John Wiley & Sons, New York.

Simon, H.A. (1957). *Models of Man: Social and Rational*, John Wiley & Sons, New York.

Skinner, W. (1974). "The focused factory," *Harvard Business Review*, 52 (3), 113-121.

Spear, S. (2008). *Chasing the Rabbit – How Market Leaders Outdistance the Competition and How Great Companies Can Catch Up and Win*, McGraw-Hill, New York. (This book was re-titled *The High-Velocity Edge: How Market Leaders Leverage Operational Excellence to Beat the Competition* in 2010 after the Toyota recall problems of 2009-2010.)

Spear, S., and H.K. Bowen (1999). "Decoding the DNA of the Toyota production system," *Harvard Business Review*, 77 (5), 96-106.

Spearman, M.L., W.J. Hopp, and D.L. Woodruff (1989). "A hierarchical control architecture for CONWIP production systems," *Journal of Manufacturing and Operations Management*, 16 (2), 147-171.

Stalk, G. (1988). "Time: The next source of competitive advantage," *Harvard Business Review*, 66 (4), 41-52.

Stalk, G., and T.M. Hout (1990, 2003). *Competing Against Time: How Time-Based Competition is Reshaping Global Markets*, Free Press, New York.

Starr, M., and D. Miller (1962). *Inventory Control: Theory and Practice*, Prentice Hall, Englewood Cliffs, New Jersey.

Stata, R. (1989). "Organizational learning – The key to management innovation," *Sloan Management Review*, 30 (3), 63-74.

Sterman, J. (1992). "Teaching takes off, flight simulators for management education," *OR/MS Today*, October, 40-44. Also see Professor Sterman's webpage http://jsterman.scripts.mit.edu.

Stern, C.W., and M.S. Deimler (2006). *The Boston Consulting Group on Strategy: Classic Concepts and New Perspectives*, John Wiley & Sons, New York.

Stork, K. (1998). "Why supplier scorecards are critical," *Purchasing*, 125 (5), 31.

Stuart, F.I. (2006). "Designing and executing memorable service experiences: Lights, camera, experiment, integrate, action!" *Business Horizons*, 49 (2), 149-159.

Suri, R. and A. Krishnamurthy (2003). "How to plan and implement POLCA: A material control system for high-variety or custom-engineered products," Technical Report, Center for Quick Response Manufacturing. Found on the Internet at www.meteconline.org/resources/S0600257_POLCA.pdf, April 19, 2011.

Taylor, F.W. (1911). *The Principles of Scientific Management*, Harper Brothers, New York.

Teas, R.K. (1994). "Expectations as a comparison standard in measuring service quality: An assessment of a reassessment," *Journal of Marketing*, 58 (1), 132-139.

Thiel, H. (1966). *Applied Economic Forecasting*. Rand McNally, Chicago.

Tuckman, B.W. (1965). "Developmental sequence in small groups," *Psychological Bulletin*, 63 (6), 384-399, available at http://dennislearningcenter.osu.edu/references/GROUP%20DEV%20ARTICLE.doc.

Tuckman, B.W., and M.C. Jensen (1977). "Stages of small group development revisited," *Group and Organizational Studies*, 2, 419-427.

Turing, A.M. (1950). "Computing machinery and intelligence," *Mind*, 59, 443-460.

Tversky, A., and D. Kahneman (1974). "Judgment under uncertainty: Heuristics and biases," *Science*, 185 (4157), 1124-1130.

Van Dijk, N.M., and E. Van Der Sluis (2007). "To pool or not to pool in call centers," working paper, University of Amsterdam, Faculty of Economics and Business, The Netherlands. Found at http://www1.fee.uva.nl/pp/bin/197fulltext.pdf, April 19, 2011.

Vergin, R.C., and K. Barr (1999). "Building competitiveness in grocery supply through continuous replenishment planning," *Industrial Marketing Management*, 28 (2), 145-153.

Vollmann, T.E., W.L. Berry, D.C. Whybark, and F.R. Jacobs (2004). *Manufacturing Planning and Control Systems for Supply Chain Management*, Fifth Edition, McGraw-Hill, New York.

von Hippel, P.T. (2005). "Mean, median, and skew: correcting a textbook rule," *Journal of Statistics Education*, 13 (2), found at www.amstat.org/publications/jse/v13n2/vonhippel.html, October 25, 2009.

von Neumann, J., and O. Morgenstern (1944). *Theory of Games and Economic Behavior*, John Wiley & Sons, New York.

Walden, D., C. Berger, R. Blauth, D. Boger, C. Bolster, G. Burchill, W. DuMouchel, F. Pouliot, R. Richter, A. Rubinoff, D. Shen, and M. Timko (1993). "Kano's methods of understanding customer-defined quality," *The Center for Quality Management Journal*, 2 (4), 3-36.

Wallace, T.F. (2004). *Sales & Operations Planning: The How-to Handbook*, Second Edition, T.F. Wallace & Company, Cincinnati.

Wallace, T.F., and R.A. Stahl (2003). *Master Scheduling in the 21st Century – For Simplicity, Speed and Success – Up and Down the Supply Chain*, T.F. Wallace & Company, Cincinnati, Ohio.

Wallin, C., M. Rungtusanatham, and E. Rabinovich (2006). "What is the 'right' inventory management approach for purchased items?," *International Journal of Operations & Production Management*, 26(1), 50-68.

Waterman, R.H., T.J. Peters, and J.R. Phillips (1980). "Structure is not organisation," *McKinsey Quarterly*, New York.

Wilson, R.H. (1934). "A scientific routine for stock control," *Harvard Business Review*, 13 (1), 116-128.

Winitzki, S. (2003). "Uniform approximations for transcendental functions," *Proc. ICCSA-2003*, LNCS 2667/2003, 962.

Winkler, R.L, G.M. Roodman, and R.R. Britney (1972). "The determination of partial moments," *Management Science*, 19 (3), 290-296.

Winston, W.L., and S.C. Albright (2011). *Practical Management Science*, Fourth Edition, Duxbury, Pacific Grove, CA.

Winters, P.R. (1960). "Forecasting sales by exponentially smoothed weighted moving averages," *Management Science*, 6 (3), 324-342.

Womack, J.P., and D.T. Jones (2003). *Lean Thinking*, Simon & Schuster, New York.

Womack, J.P., D.T. Jones, D. Roos (1991). *Machine That Changed the World: The Story of Lean Production*, Harper Perennial, New York.

Wu, S.J., S.A. Melnyk, and B.B. Flynn (2010). "Operational capabilities: The secret ingredient," **Decision Sciences**, 41 (4), 721-754.

Zeithaml, V.A., L.L. Berry, and A. Parasuraman (1988). "Communication and control processes in the delivery of service quality," *Journal of Marketing*, 52, 35-48.

Zhang, W., A.V. Hill, R.G. Schroeder, and K. Linderman (2008). "Process improvement program management and organizational performance," *Operations Management Research*, 1 (1), 40-52.

Zhang, W., A.V. Hill, and G.H. Gilbreath (2010). "A research agenda for six sigma research," *Quality Management Journal*, 18 (1), 39-53.

Zinn, W., M. Levy, and D.J. Bowersox, (1989). "Measuring the effect of inventory centralization/ decentralization on aggregate safety stock: The 'square root law' revisited," *Journal of Business Logistics*, 10 (1), 1-14.

Zook, C. (2004). *Beyond the Core: Expand Your Market without Abandoning Your Roots*, Harvard Business School Press, Boston.